Introduction to
COUNSELING

Introduction to COUNSELING

third edition

Gary S. Belkin
Long Island University

Wm. C. Brown Publishers
Dubuque, Iowa

Book Team

Editor *James M. McNeil*
Developmental Editor *Sandra E. Schmidt*
Designer *Carol S. Joslin*
Production Editor *Harry Halloran*

wcb group

Chairman of the Board *Wm. C. Brown*
President and Chief Executive Officer *Mark C. Falb*

wcb

Wm. C. Brown Publishers, College Division

President *G. Franklin Lewis*
Vice President, Editor-in-Chief *George Wm. Bergquist*
Vice President, Director of Production *Beverly Kolz*
National Sales Manager *Bob McLaughlin*
Director of Marketing *Thomas E. Doran*
Marketing Information Systems Manager *Craig S. Marty*
Marketing Manager *Kathy Law Laube*
Executive Editor *John Woods*
Manager of Visuals and Design *Faye M. Schilling*
Manager of Design *Marilyn A. Phelps*
Production Editorial Manager *Colleen A. Yonda*

Cover image: © M. DeCamp/Image Bank

Library of Congress Catalog Card Number: 87–71177

ISBN 0–697–06693–2

Printed in the United States of America by Wm. C. Brown Publishers
2460 Kerper Boulevard, Dubuque, IA 52001

10   9

Contents

PART

2   The Counseling Process   91

Contents   *vii*

PART

4 Counseling Applications   299

Preface

It has been more than fourteen years since I wrote the first edition of *Practical Counseling in the Schools* (Wm. C. Brown Publishers, 1975), the precursor to the three editions of *Introduction to Counseling* (1980, 1984, 1988) which have followed. During this time, my own thinking about counseling and human development, as well as the outlook of the profession as a whole, has undergone considerable changes. As the turbulent political consciousness of the early seventies has evolved into a more staid and pragmatic view of life in the eighties, a spirit of empirical optimism has replaced the hectic and agitated pessimism of the Vietnam/psychedelic era. Some new counseling concerns have emerged, while other, older issues have receded. For example, the popularity of encounter and marathon groups has declined, while family therapy has emerged as an important force in bringing counseling services to the American public. Although many of the problems that we faced earlier still plague us—drug abuse, family violence, adolescent crises—we now place more emphasis on prevention, short-term treatment procedures, and integration of empirical research about counseling effectiveness into day-to-day treatment settings.

This third edition of *Introduction to Counseling* attempts to reflect these changes, while still maintaining the philosophical and theoretical grounding of the earlier editions. New theoretical concepts such as the *Copenhagen interpretation* and *carpenter's gothic* have been included, in the hope of generating research that will ultimately yield practical benefits. The ever-increasing empirical support for the effectiveness of cognitive therapy approaches is reflected in the more extensive coverage given in this edition.

As in the previous edition, the rationale for including this range of material, and for organizing it the way I have, is found in my philosophy of what an introduction to counseling course should accomplish. There are three major objectives. First, all students of counseling should be given a substantial and realistic idea of what the profession of counseling is all about—what skills are required, what type of work the counselor does, and what kind of relationship exists between counseling and the other helping professions. Second, the counselor trainee should be provided with personal motivation to continue his or her study of counseling. The excitement of the endeavor should be made explicit and real. Finally, since counseling is in practice a multifaceted endeavor, the book presents a multidimensional picture of it. This should help the student who is interested in vocational counseling gain an understanding of what that specialty is about, the student who is majoring in nursing get a rough idea of health counseling, and the potential family or group counselor gain insight into those areas.

Of course, 90 percent of this job depends on the abilities of the professor of counseling or the counseling trainer, for it is in the living interaction of the classroom and training setting that the dynamic force of human relationships is most cogently illustrated. Only through the strong example of a competent role model can a trainee begin to *feel, think,* and *act* as a fully effective counselor. But a textbook can help, and throughout this text I have attempted to include as much slice-of-life case material as space permits and as proves relevant to the discussion.

In addition to the more than one hundred new references added since the previous edition, major sections of the book have been completely rewritten, reflecting the perspective of the mid- to late 1980s; a perspective that is notably more secure and confident than earlier decades.

The book has been organized in four parts. Part 1 will present a detailed picture of the counseling field as it exists today. From what roots did it derive, and how have these roots influenced its growth and direction? What are its current assumptions about the person? What are the underlying assumptions concerning the goals and processes of the counseling interaction? What type of training does one need to become a competent counselor? What makes one counselor more effective than another? How does counseling differ from the other helping professions, such as psychotherapy, and why would a client choose one rather than the other?

We will see, as we begin to explore these questions in depth, that the way the counselor conceptualizes counseling affects the way he or she acts in the counseling session.

In Part 2, "The Counseling Process," we will be focusing on the specific moments of the counseling interaction. How does the counselor, through the relationship, communicate appropriate feelings and ideas to the client? How does the process of counseling work toward a specific direction, and how is this direction chosen? What enables a client to grow, to change, to discover a richer life? This discussion will include a sketch of the counselor-at-work, as well as some objective considerations of the types of topics or actions which counselors can select to make their interactions more effective.

In Part 3, "Theories of Counseling," we will turn our attention to the specific theories which currently dominate the field of counseling—the so-called "schools" of counseling, or counseling approaches. We will explore each approach by examining first its origins and then its view of the individual; its underlying theory of personality, of behavior, of what makes the person what he or she is. These sections will explicate the ways in which practitioners of a particular position look at the human condition in general and, particularly, the way counselors regard their individual clients. We will consider the role of the counselor, and examine ways in which the client is expected to contribute to the process. We will see that what is expected from the client varies from one approach to another, and that the counselor's job varies directly with the role of the client. We will also observe that in some schools very little is required of the client, other than that he or she come to sessions. But we also note how other approaches require the client to engage in some risk-taking and to make early commitments to courses of action.

In Part 4, "Counseling Applications," we focus on a variety of target populations (children and adolescents, both in and out of school, older adults, members of minority groups, etc.) with a variety of problems (crisis situations, family conflicts, learning problems, need for rehabilitation, etc.) in several different kinds of settings (elementary and high school, college, community agency, individual, group). We will look specifically at how counseling is actually conducted: to what ends, through which processes, for what kinds of problems. Each chapter will cover in detail one type of counseling application. The theories of counseling presented in Part 3 and the insights about the counseling process delineated in Part 2 will be demonstrated *in practice* in Part 4.

With this framework in mind, let us begin our examination of what can be a most exciting, richly rewarding profession for one who is concerned about others—one who is willing to give, to pursue, and to perfect.

For Larry Earl Bone—A good friend, a warm person, a brilliant mind, whose many contributions to the theory and practice of library collections have helped writers, researchers, and students of counseling throughout the country.

Acknowledgments

I would like to thank the following professors who reviewed INTRODUC-
TION TO COUNSELING and provided many valuable suggestions and comments:

Dr. Daniel Biber, Queen's College, University Park, Illinois
Dr. Joan Deissler, Bethune-Cookman College, Daytona Beach, Florida
Dr. Timothy Dickel, Creighton University, Omaha, Nebraska
Dr. Vance Rhoades, Brewton-Parker College, Mt. Vernon, Georgia
Dr. William Rogge, Governor's State University, University Park, Illinois
Dr. Thomas Russo, University of Wisconsin–River Falls, River Falls,
    Wisconsin
Dr. William Welch, Memphis State University, Memphis, Tennessee.

Introduction to

COUNSELING

Counseling:
The Art and Science
of Helping

As we begin our study of counseling, we are beset by questions and confronted by challenges at the very outset. What is counseling? From what roots did it derive, and how did these roots influence its growth and direction? What are its current assumptions about the person? about goals and processes of the counseling interaction? What type of training does one need to become a competent counselor? On what evidence does the profession defend its efficacy? What makes one counselor more effective than another? How does counseling differ from the other helping professions, such as psychotherapy, and why would a client seek one profession over the other? These are only a few of the fundamental questions we will attempt to answer in this introductory section.

We will see as we begin to explore these questions in depth that they are more than academic in interest. They influence, directly and indirectly, the moment-to-moment interaction of the counseling session. The concept the counselor has of counseling as an activity directly affects activities in the counseling session. The counselor's training, the translation into practice of tomes of empirical research, has a profound influence on how the counselor develops a counseling style and how this style, in turn, affects the client's growth and development. Counseling has developed from many different disciplines, which may be responsible for the multiple purposes and various methods that characterize it today. In this section we will seek definitions that are *operational;* that is, definitions that can be translated directly into practice. As we pursue all of these questions, we will attempt to transform abstract concepts into concrete explanations.

In the following three chapters, we will attempt to sketch a detailed picture of the counseling field as it exists today. In chapter 1, "What Is Counseling?" we will delineate the counseling profession, show how it differs from psychotherapy, and shed some light on the roots of each. We shall see how counseling still embodies many of the roots of education, mental testing, progressive philosophy, and the public health movement from which it is derived. We will also note how the helper views his or her role as counselor, and what effect, if any, this has on the client.

The stage will be set, at the conclusion of this chapter, for further exploration of counseling as an independent discipline, with its own goals, strategies, and frames of reference.

We will outline in chapter 2 some of the basic issues in counseling that are the subject of lively interest today. How relevant today are the classical paradigms of abnormal behavior? Which rely heavily on the "medical model"? And which use diagnostic criteria for differentiating the "normal" from the "abnormal"? What role does a theory of counseling play in counseling practice and how does theory set counseling apart from other helping approaches? What is the legal status of counseling as a profession? What is the practical value of interdisciplinary helping efforts in which expertise from several disciplines is used jointly to help the client? The emphasis here will be on placing counseling in perspective as one of several helping professions, and on showing the diversity of settings in which counseling is used today. The type of training most appropriate for the counselor and the major organizations that represent counselors' professional interests and provide the counselor with resources of professional information and development will also be considered. In this chapter, we should receive a view of the relative status of counseling today and its unique contributions.

Chapter 3, "The World of the Counselor," will, as the title implies, focus more on the helper than on the helping process. We will examine how the counselor's personal problems and conflicts may impede the counselor's work, and may conflict on a variety of levels with the counselor's professional role. We will look at the counselor's defensive behavior and consider its implications in counseling practice. In this chapter we will also look at some of the problems which confront the counselor in the work setting: cultural biases, difficulties in relating to the client, special needs of the minority group client, and the variety of often-conflicting client and agency expectations that may prove confusing.

At the conclusion of Part 1, we should have a clear idea of what counseling really means and what the work of the counselor comprises. This cognitive understanding will enable us to carry our investigation forward and, ultimately, help us to become more successful counselors.

Chapter Aim

To provide a working definition of *counseling* as it exists today, and establish a distinction between counseling, psychotherapy, and other helping professions. To examine the historical roots of the counseling profession, noting how each source contributed to the subsequent development.

CAPSULE 1

The six chief influences on the counseling movement are discussed in some detail: the advent of laboratory psychology; innovative approaches to the treatment of the mentally disturbed, leading up to psychoanalysis; the mental hygiene movement; the testing movement; the humanistic influence; and the vocational guidance movement which prospered at the beginning of this century. Each of these has evolved into a separate facet of the profession of counseling.

The Origins of the Counseling Movement

Attempts to formulate a definition of counseling are challenged by the difficulties in delineating counseling as a distinct helping discipline. Counseling today is a multi-faceted profession by which the so-called ''normal'' person with a wide variety of adjustment problems can be helped.

Counseling—In Search of Identity

There are three positions that have been put forth in attempting to answer the perennial question, Is there a difference between counseling and psychotherapy? First, that the terms are synonymous and there is no functional difference between them. Second, that counseling differs from psychotherapy in relation to the seriousness of the client's problems and the emotional depth of the treatment. Third, that counseling and psychotherapy differ in their theoretical foundations and in their discrepant historical origins. We will examine and evaluate each of these positions.

Counseling and Psychotherapy: Is There a Difference?

7

What Is Counseling?

1

There is now, and always has been, a good deal of confusion and ambiguity regarding the terms *counseling* and *psychotherapy*. The lay public, and to a large extent, the helping professional, cannot say with certainty at which point the purview of the one ends and of the other begins. For the most part, the confusion is born of knowledge and practical experience, not of ignorance. As those familiar with the intimate workings of these specialties know, the terms are used interchangeably, do overlap, and in many instances the same practitioner will think nothing of switching from one term to the other. The result is that over the years, there has arisen a semantic equivalency between counseling and psychotherapy, so that it is altogether appropriate today to speak simultaneously about methods, techniques, or settings for both counseling and psychotherapy.

Moreover, as one engages in the practice of either counseling or psychotherapy, or of both of them, it becomes even more striking how much they have in common in terms of their moment-to-moment interactions; how many parallels of purpose and technique there are between them. It could be argued, and indeed it has been, that to differentiate between them is simply nit-picking. Yet there is a compelling reason to do just this; a reason that becomes emphatic, however, only after the differences between them have become clearly identified. The reason is this: because the human organism is highly complex and specialized, both physically and psychologically, the range of problems and situations which the organism encounters is also complex and specialized. In the psychological realm, for example, problems run the gamut from deeply emotional conflicts to basic decision-making, to interpersonal relationships, to minor conflicts, to learning problems, to vocational problems, and to a score of other types of problems. To deal effectively with this legion of interlocking problems, there evolved over a period of many years specialists of different skills and backgrounds, each equipped to handle expertly one or more categories of problems, yet able to have insight into all of the areas.

These specialists work under a variety of professional titles. They are called psychologists, psychiatrists, psychiatric social workers, counseling psychologists, family counselors, pastoral counselors, psychotherapists, psychoanalysts, learning disabilities specialists, vocational counselors, school counselors, guidance counselors, and so on. Each is equipped to handle a specialized range of problems, yet each is acutely aware of the other specialists' responsibilities, therefore the possibility of referral and consultation is always in the foreground.

In practice, as we shall soon see, it is probably not theory which distinguishes one helper from another, nor is it title or training, nor does the professional designation of the helper determine the quality and value of the help given. Rather, it is a matrix of factors involving, among other variables, the personalities of the client and the helper, the setting, the problems presented and underlying conflicts, the length of time available for treatment, and client motivation.

The purpose of this chapter, therefore, is not simply to resolve a semantic question. While we shall try to provide a basic definition of counseling and establish operational distinctions between counseling and psychotherapy, our goal will be to delineate the profession of counseling as it exists today. To this end, we will examine the historical roots and current assumptions of each field in order to see how these influence counseling and psychotherapy in practice. Let us begin by examining the origins of the counseling movement, noting particularly the forces that are integral in providing a historical, cultural, and contextual perspective for understanding contemporary counseling.

The Origins of the Counseling Movement

The counseling profession derives from six basic sources: laboratory psychology, brought over from Europe; innovative approaches to the treatment of the "insane," leading to the inception of the "talking cure"—psychoanalysis; the mental hygiene movement and the mental testing movement, both originating in the United States; the influence of humanistic psychology; and the vocational guidance movement, which sprang up during the early part of this century. We could also include the influence of sociology, progressive education, and other psychological and sociocultural influences. Let us consider these individually and then together.

Laboratory Psychology

The beginning of modern laboratory psychology is usually traced to 1879 when Wilhelm Wundt set up the first experimental psychology laboratory in Leipzig, Germany. Of course, psychology, like most disciplines, never had an actual moment at which it began, but it did have a very clear evolution, a path of social and intellectual progress that led to increasing recognition, first in the academic profession and then in the public sphere.

The origin of laboratory psychology embodies the history of physiology and the stirring impact of changes that came to philosophy, with the advent of empiricism to continental universities, in the late eighteenth century. When Wundt began his research, he was already familiar with the physiological studies of E. H.

Weber, Johannes Muller (who is sometimes called the "father of experimental psychology"), and Hermann von Helmholtz. These three researchers had discovered a mass of evidence about nervous reflexes, sensation, nerve impulses, and the relationship between physical and mental states.

In this context, the work of Wilhelm Wundt begins to make sense, not so much as a departure from the trend but as a logical continuation of it. He might rightly be considered the first person who ever considered himself *primarily* a psychologist and recognized in his writings that he was inaugurating this field.

Wundt attempted to study the structure of the mind by using the method of *introspection*. This method involved the subject's self-reflection and verbalizing to the experimenter what he or she was experiencing. The use of introspection dates back to the Greek philosophers, especially Plato. This method was sharpened by Plotinus, Augustine, and Descartes, who used introspection for contemplative meditation. But it was the English empiricists who "shifted introspective interests from the area of these higher mental processes to that of sensation" (Watson, 1971, p. 269). It was from that innovation that Wundt's work began.

Wundt took this premise and by directing it at self-observation and making it experimental, extended it so that it became more scientific. In the laboratory, a subject verbalizes his conscious processes aloud. An experimenter then records it and studies how images and sensations and thoughts are connected in consciousness. The problem with this method, of course, is that experiments cannot be replicated and there is too much room for subjectivity. Also, the scope of any investigation, focusing as it does on the structure of mind, is somewhat limited.

In the United States, William James modified Wundt's introspectionist psychology, attempting to discover its *functions,* instead of simply studying the structure of mind. He and his followers became known as the *functionalists.* Although their initial efforts were much like the efforts of the introspectionists, they gradually developed new experimental designs to study perception, attention, responses to stimuli, habit patterns, and so on—with the idea of understanding *why* the mind functions as it does.

While this structuralist-functionalist argument was raging, a new force in laboratory psychology—one that was destined to become the most important element so far as counseling was concerned—began to develop in the United States. It was called *behaviorism.* It appeared in 1912, subjecting the introspectionists, and to some extent the functionalists, to a barrage of critical analysis, from which they would never fully recover.

The behaviorists' major criticism of the introspectionists rests on their emphasis on consciousness, which was an untenable concept for the behaviorists because of its intangibility. "From the time of Wundt on," Watson (1930), the founder of American behaviorism, argues, "consciousness becomes the keynote of psychology. . . . It is a plain assumption just as unprovable, just as unapproachable, as the old concept of the soul. And to the behaviorist the two terms are essentially identical, so far as concerns their metaphysical implications" (p. 14). Instead of building a psychology of consciousness and instead of using introspective techniques, the behaviorists suggested the use of something available for scientific measurement and experimental replication: namely, observable and measurable behavior. With this as its working premise, behavioristic psychology attempted to formulate, through systematic observation and experimentation, the generalizations, laws, and principles that underlie the individual's behavior (Watson, 1919).

The rift between these two early schools of psychology is indicative of the schism that divides the ranks of the mental health professionals today. "Are we," ask practitioners, "to be primarily concerned with feelings, perceptions, associations, and other manifestations of consciousness, or are we to focus our attention on symptoms, actions, learning, and other observable and quantifiable forms of behavior?" Should the counselor be primarily concerned with the client's condition of consciousness—his or her subjectivity—vague as this concept is, or should the counselor deal primarily with the client's behavior, which is observable and empirically modifiable (trainable)? These fundamental questions still challenge us; and it is the responsibility of each counselor entering the profession to decide which premises are right for him or her, which assumptions will act as a guide in practice.

New Approaches to
Treating Emotional
Problems

Despite all of the early efforts to investigate the complexities of the human psyche, there were no psychological attempts to *treat* emotional problems, to "cure" emotional illnesses. In fact, no such discipline arose until the mid-nineteenth century when a number of disparate movements took hold and individually attempted to treat mental and emotional illness in a humane, constructive, scientifically valid manner. Before that, the problem of healing was strictly in the realm of magical healers, of priests or medicine men, who often applied their art in a most bizarre and unscientific fashion. Yet their work ultimately led to the psychological treatment of emotional disorders. As Ehrenwald (1976) dramatically emphasizes,

> If mental healers were to be summoned to the patient's bedside in the order of their appearance in history, the magician or medicine man would be the first one to answer the call. He would be followed by the philosopher-priest . . . who would, in turn, yield his place to the scientifically oriented psychotherapist. There would be a world of difference between their underlying philosophies and the way they minister to their patients' needs. But their goal would be the same: to cure psychological (and sometimes physical) ills essentially by psychological means. (p. 17)

In France in 1793, a young psychiatrist, Dr. Philippe Pinel, was given charge of the notorious Bicêtre asylum. Pinel instituted a program of reform, based on the principle that the job of an asylum was to restore the inmate to *functional mental health*. It was a simple principle, yet one so revolutionary in its time that it met with much opposition from the community and from the national government. But Pinel persisted, at Bicêtre and later at Salpêtrière, and he deserves credit as the first pioneer in the mental health movement.

After Pinel's death, another psychiatric innovator emerged at Salpêtrière. Jean-Martin Charcot was a distinguished neurologist, with a special interest in psychosomatic diseases. He had spent several years diagnosing and treating patients who believed they were suffering from a form of paralysis or epilepsy, but who actually had nothing physically wrong with them. He labeled this disorder *hysteria* and formulated a detailed clinical description of it, distinguishing it from closely related symptomatic disorders. He pioneered the use of hypnosis as a clinical tool in the diagnosis of hysterical disorders, suggesting that hypnosis itself was a form of "artificial" hysteria.

It was a colleague of Charcot, another neurologist named Pierre Janet, who discovered a method to treat this newly diagnosed disorder. Charcot had used hypnosis as a diagnostic tool in working with hysterical patients; Janet took this one step further and began to use hypnosis as a curative agent as well. He discovered through trial and error that persons with hysteria were able under hypnosis to recall memories and feelings from the past. As the hypnotist helped the hysteric remember these buried memories, that person suddenly began to experience a rapid alleviation of the debilitating symptom, a "miraculous" cure. Janet used the term *catharsis* to describe this sudden freeing of the dammed-up memories, and laid down the groundwork upon which a later student would revolutionize the field of treatment. This student was Sigmund Freud.

Freud was deeply impressed by the works of Charcot and Janet. As a needy student he was able to obtain a scholarship in 1885 in order to travel to France to study under Charcot, who was internationally renowned at the time. Studying during the day, reviewing and critically examining at night, Freud returned from his sojourn in France full of new and exciting ideas. He shared these ideas with a colleague, Dr. Josef Breuer, and the two collaborated to use the cathartic-hypnotic treatment in working with hysterical patients. This marked the beginning of what was to emerge a few short years later as the psychoanalytic movement. (This will be discussed further in chapter 7.)

At the same time in the United States, while mental illness was not regarded quite as primitively as in pre-Pinel France, it was still viewed without the slightest sophistication or optimism. No national policy, no prominent physicians, no humanitarian organizations watched out for the interests of the mentally ill. On the contrary, the mentally ill person was at best a pariah—an emotional leper—who had to be separated from society both for his good and for the general welfare. This attitude was pervasive during the same period when the vocational guidance movement was in its flowering stages in the United States.

What was needed was someone to bring the enormity and seriousness of the problem to the attention of a public long motivated by humanitarian and progressive instincts. Such a man, ironically enough, was Clifford Beers, a minor

The Mental Hygiene Movement

clerk in the financial district of New York City. Beers, who suffered from schizophrenia, spent many of his years in mental institutions, outraged by the conditions but helpless to do anything about them. Finally recovering enough to function, he wrote a book about his experiences, *A Mind That Found Itself,* which became an influential bestseller. Even more important, the book, a subtle combination of personal experiences and rhetoric that called for reform, instigated rapid and sweeping changes in the field of mental health care. In the following passage, Beers (1956, orig. 1914) poignantly describes a typical situation at a sanitorium:

> One day a man—seemingly a tramp—approached the main building of the sanitorium and inquired for the owner. He soon found him, talked with him a few minutes, and an hour or so later he was sitting at the bedside of an old and infirm man. This aged patient had recently been committed to the institution by relatives who had labored under the common delusion that the payment of a considerable sum of money each week would insure kindly treatment. When this tramp-attendant first appeared, all his visible worldly possessions were contained in a small bundle which he carried under his arm. So filthy were his person and his clothes that he received a compulsory bath and another suit before being assigned to duty. He then began to earn his four dollars and fifty cents a week by sitting several hours a day in the room with the aged man, sick unto death. . . . The uncouth stranger had never before so much as crossed the threshold of a hospital. His last job had been as a member of a section-gang on a railroad. From the roadbed of a railway to the bedside of a man about to die was indeed a change which might have taxed the adaptability of a more versatile being. (pp. 43–44)

Beers, whose severe psychological problems were ultimately cured, became a social activist and crusader, helping to found the Society for Mental Hygiene. While Freud can be credited with originating the conception of modern mental health treatment, which did so much to change the relationship of the mentally ill to the greater society, it was people like Beers who made possible its implementation.

Once the American public became aware of the need for mental health reform, the innovations of Freud and his contemporaries were quickly imported and put into practice here. From the 1920s onward, psychoanalysis and its derivative approaches (especially Adlerian therapy) began to make an impact on the counseling movement. The laboratory work of Watson, Skinner, and the other behavioral psychologists also began to influence the counseling movement. Combined with the burgeoning vocational guidance movement, something of a specific shape was forming; the winds of change were in the air.

In a short time the impact of Wundt's new science in Europe had begun to make its mark in the United States. Groups of students from all over the United States flocked to his laboratory, eager to learn the new experimental methods being used there. And each brought back to the United States a cornucopia of methodological procedures and intellectual insights which were to be applied in their own special areas of interest and expertise. One of the more famous of these students, who was to have an important impact ultimately on the counseling movement, was a young man named G. Stanley Hall.

Granville Stanley Hall may rightly be said to be the father of American psychology, even though James was the first American psychologist. Although in retrospect, his work is not of an enduring nature, he became an important innovator for others to follow, the leader of the American psychology movement, responsible for giving psychology—and ultimately, counseling, their orientation and direction. He established one of the first psychology departments, organized the American Psychological Association, and was responsible for granting the first doctorates in this new field, thus providing increased recognition for the profession.

In 1883, Hall set up a private laboratory for psychological study at Johns Hopkins University in Baltimore. Within two years, he was given his own laboratory on campus for his work—a notable instance of a major university beginning to support the newly recognized discipline of psychology. During this early period, psychological laboratories were also being formed at Harvard, Pennsylvania, Wisconsin, Columbia, Clark, Cornell, Indiana, Brown, Stanford, Yale, and Chicago Universities. In 1887, Hall left Baltimore to become president of Clark University, where he was also designated Professor of Psychology. There he trained many who were to become leaders of American psychology, including L. M. Terman, soon to become known for his studies of the gifted.

It was at Clark that Hall conducted his famous studies of children and adolescents; these can be considered the first true psychological investigations of human development. Although they are primitive by today's standards, relying as they did mostly on the use of unvalidated questionnaires, they helped to define child and adolescent psychology as significant disciplines. Even more important, these studies indirectly became the source of American psychologists' interest in the quantitative approach to science, which was to have an enduring effect on the American testing movement.

Counselors and counselor educators began to recognize the value of testing, and the testing movement became a significant part of counseling from its very beginning. From the late nineteenth century, when the British scientist Sir Francis Galton attempted to devise a simple measure of intelligence, through Alfred Binet's landmark development of the first IQ tests, through Lewis M. Terman's administration of the test to a large population, up to Edward L. Thorndike's myriad contributions to the American testing movement, the profession of counseling became closely involved with and influenced by the testing and measurement movement. It is easy to understand the glamour of testing with what seem to be quantitatively irrefutable facts. Gould (1981), speaking of the "special status that numbers enjoy," explains why we in the psychological and educational professions have embraced testing so heartily, and often so indiscriminately:

> The mystique of science proclaims that numbers are the ultimate test of objectivity. Surely we can weigh a brain or score an intelligence test without recording our social preferences. If ranks are displayed in hard numbers obtained by rigorous and standardized procedures, then they must reflect reality, even if they confirm what we wanted to believe from the start. (p. 26)

Quantitative tools were developed to help assess the client's needs, to measure his or her abilities, aptitudes, and problems, and to evaluate more accurately the results of the counseling experience. By the 1950s there was no area of counseling which had not been profoundly influenced by the testing movement. Even after reactions against standardized testing during the 1960s and 1970s, counseling still considers assessment and appraisal as central to its effective functioning as a distinct profession.

Together, behavioral laboratory psychology and the use of empirical, quantitative methods (testing and statistics) offered a scientific dimension to counseling. This aspect of counseling, still fundamental today, has both advocates and critics. However, one cannot fail to acknowledge that it has had a profound effect upon the development of contemporary counseling.

The Humanistic Influence

Perhaps the most notable reaction to the quantitative influence in counseling was begun by a young psychologist who had been trained in the psychoanalytic method, but who found it too depersonalizing. Arguing that each patient had to be viewed as a total, distinct, and important individual, not as a proof for some tentative theory of behavior, learning, or psychosexual development, Carl R. Rogers initiated what he called "nondirective psychotherapy" which today bears the eponymous title, Rogerian therapy (see chapter 8). Rogers's ideas have had a more significant impact upon the development of counseling than has any other system of psychotherapy. Rogers's belief in the dignity of the individual and the ultimate worth of the client was compatible not only with the attitudes of professionals in the guidance field but also with the attitudes of many prominent psychotherapists as well. Rogers's influence upon the counseling movement is incalculable, and the tradition he established set the stage for the merging of the terms *counseling* and *psychology* as we know them today.

As the terms were felicitously combined, they revealed new possibilities for further developing the functions embodied within each discipline. Most important, the philosophy of *existentialism,* which postulates that people are free agents, seeking meanings in their lives through their voluntary actions, began to influence the movement. It was not uncommon to hear of existential approaches not only to psychotherapy but to vocational counseling, job training, personnel work, and rehabilitation counseling as well. Existential approaches have also had an impact on such practical areas as student personnel work and vocational counseling.

By the first decade of this century, the revolution began to influence the vocational guidance movement which was springing up throughout the country. This socially progressive educational activity, designed to help individuals find themselves through their work, was originated by Frank Parsons, a Boston educator. Its goals of self-fulfillment made it compatible with the growing counseling movement. Cremin's (1964) description of Parsons's thinking accurately reflects the relationship of vocational guidance to counseling—that is, of helping the individual fulfill his or her capacities:

The Vocational
Guidance Movement

> The key to Parsons's ultimate goal . . . lay in his notion of "the useful and happy life." Parsons, a significant figure in the history of American reform, believed not only that vocational counseling would lead to greater individual fulfilment, but that people suited to their jobs would tend to be active in the creation of a more efficient and humane industrial system. Intelligently practiced, the craft of vocational guidance would serve not only the youngsters who sought counsel, but the cause of social reform as well. (p. 13)

The influences that were brought to bear on the formation of the guidance movement are direct consequences of the events of the time. The closing decade of the nineteenth century pinpoints precisely the birth of the vocational guidance movement. It was a time of change in America, of massive building and rapid technological innovation, of increasing immigration from Europe, and of migration from rural America into the cities. A predominantly homogeneous agrarian society was in the process of being transformed into a primarily heterogeneous urban society as the great swell of European immigrants and American country folk flocked to the great urban centers, filling up the classical melting pot that was to play so great a part in twentieth-century American cultural and social history. The consequences of this demographic displacement were staggering. The cities became kaleidoscopes of ethnic idiosyncracies as each of the assimilating groups gently, but often painfully, began to make their presence felt in their new homeland.

Other changes were also making themselves felt at this time. Barry and Wolf (1963) cite "industrialization, specialization, urbanization, the changing role of women, the growing need for education, rising enrollments, expanding curricula, rising secularism, the desire for useful education, and new educational theories as some of the changes and developments that created or intensified the need for guidance-personnel work" (p. 16). To this list, we must also add other, sometimes subtle, social changes that were beginning to bear profoundly on individual lives as the 1890s arrived. Five years before this decade, the first electric railroad, the prototype for urban mass transportation, had been inaugurated in Baltimore, signaling the massive influence electricity was to play on the course of history. Ironically, in the very year 1890, William Kemmler earned the dubious distinction of becoming the first man in history to be executed by electricity at Sing Sing Prison in Ossining, New York. That same year, Ellis Island replaced the antiquated Castle Garden as the welcoming point for hundreds of thousands of immigrants who flocked to our shores. A strike at the Carnegie Steel Mills in 1892, which resulted in a violent and fatal confrontation between management and labor, emphasized rising antagonism between the classes—a problem that would plague this country for many years. Massive unemployment swept the country, and 20,000 Americans marched on Washington in 1894 to protest the precarious condition of the economy. These were important national events, newsworthy and duly recorded. But meanwhile, unannounced and unknown to most people, seemingly minor isolated events in different parts of the country were the first manifestations of the vocational guidance movement, as it would be known many years later.

The most significant work was Parsons's, but he had influential protegées. In 1895, Parsons began to offer informal vocational counseling to indigent youth in Boston. Emphasizing "choosing a vocation rather than merely looking for a job, he urged young people to acquire a wide knowledge of occupations so as to avoid falling into the first convenient job opening" (Tolbert, 1978, p. 60). At about the same time, George Merrill instituted the first systematic vocational guidance program at the California School of Mechanical Arts in San Francisco. Throughout the country this new movement quickly gained prominence: in Grand Rapids, Jesse B. Davis organized the first large-scale school guidance program; Parsons's seminal work, *Choosing a Vocation,* the first guidance textbook, was published posthumously in 1909. The first doctoral dissertation in guidance was accepted at Columbia University in 1914, one year after the National Vocational Guidance Association (NVGA) was founded; Eli Weaver of Boys' High School in Brooklyn, New York, began to systematically advise his students about their career plans and future education, and he provided summer work opportunities for them; William Wheatly of Middletown, Connecticut, introduced special school courses on vocations and added a unit on vocations to the social studies curriculum. Similar efforts were blossoming throughout the country.

Two useful insights about contemporary counseling can be derived from these events. First, it is clear that counseling as we know it evolved in part from the vocational guidance movement, which was brought about largely by the changing social and demographic forces that played so crucial a role in shaping the United States at the turn of the century. Second, it is evident that underlying all these innovative gestures was a strong commitment to the principles which marked the beginnings of this country, namely, the belief in the individual, the humanitarian spirit, and the inalienable relationship between the individual and society. We see the guidance movement as an inevitable consequence of the American spirit which has so forcefully shaped our national destiny; it was a potent force in shaping contemporary counseling ideology.

Counseling represents the fusion of many influences. It brings together the movement toward a more compassionate treatment of mental problems begun in mid-nineteenth century France, the psychodynamic insights of Freud and psychoanalysis, the scientific scrutiny and methodology of the behavioral approach, the quantitative science of psychometrics, the humanistic perspective of client-centered therapy, the philosophical bases of existentialism, and the practical insights and applications that evolved from the vocational guidance movement. With this has come a recent merging of other concerns indigenous to social work and the helping professions: the treatment and prevention of child abuse; health counseling; family counseling; and the like. We can see, then, that the profession of counseling is not some well-established entity, but rather it is a dynamic movement still in its developing stages.

Counseling—In Search of Identity

Perhaps because it is a new discipline, counseling, in its slow process of gestation and development, has been going through a confusing time of doubt and self-examination, a period of finding itself and defining itself more precisely. While counseling is now a fairly well-established discipline, one which cohered dramatically during the 1970s, confusion still exists about the terms and roles of counselor, counselor educator, counselor psychologist, and clinical psychologist (Whitely, Kagan, Harmon, Fretz & Tanney, 1984). Just what is the relationship today between counseling and psychology, and how does the role of counselor differ from the role of therapist?

More than ten years ago, an entire issue of *The Counseling Psychologist* (Vol 7, No. 2, 1977) attempted to come to grips with the professional identity of counseling as a discipline and of counselors as professionals. In his presidential address to Division 17 (the Division of Counseling Psychology) of the American Psychological Association, Norman Kagan (1977) compared the role of counselors to primary care physicians (general practitioners), who are "broadly skilled and have a holistic approach to the individuals." The role, as he conceptualized it, was preventive as well as therapeutic.

Ten years later, Fitzgerald and Osipow (1986), in trying to determine what counselors and counseling psychologists actually do in their professional time, conducted a national occupational analysis of the counseling profession. They surveyed members of Division 17 to determine their job titles, places of employment, and activities performed. Table 1.1 shows the settings where they were employed. The large majority worked in an academic setting, with a relatively large number having full-time private practices. About 13 percent worked in counseling centers, another common employment setting.

Table 1.1
Primary and Secondary Employment Settings of Counseling Psychologists

Current Position	Primary	Secondary
Academic (APA approved)	21.2	0
Academic (non-APA approved)	26.8	4.3
Counseling center	13.4	23.7
VA hospital	2.8	0
Research facility	0.3	0
Government agency	1.9	1.1
Private industry	0.9	0
Community mental health center	2.8	4.3
Private practice	15.6	43.3
Full-time consultation	2.2	2.2
Other	11.8	21.5

Note: $N = 351$. All figures are adjusted frequencies expressed in percentages.
Source: Fitzgerald & Osipow (1986)

Table 1.2
Approximate Percentage of Time Engaged in Activity

Activity	%	Time Spent			
		Range	25th percentile	50th percentile	75th percentile
Counseling	85	1–99	9	25	59
Research	67	1–75	4	7	14
Supervision	70	1–70	5	9	17
Teaching/training	75	1–94	8	19	35
Administration	68	1–99	5	10	25
Consultation	71	1–85	5	10	25
Writing/editing	65	1–79	4	8	13

Source: Fitzgerald & Osipow (1986)

Table 1.2 shows how they distributed their time. This table reflects the percentage of time in the 25th, 50th, and 75th percentiles. "For example, it can be seen that 85 percent of the sample did some counseling, and the amount of time spent counseling ranged from 1 percent to 99 percent. Of those who counseled, 75 percent spent more than 9 percent of their time that way, one half spent 25 percent or more of their time that way, and one quarter of the sample spent 59 percent or more of their time in this fashion" (p. 537). We see the broad range of duties and activities that constitute the counseling profession today.

Counseling: The Art and Science of Helping

When we speak about the "counseling movement," we are not inquiring about a fixed and static concept that can be precisely defined and explicated. Rather, we are speaking about a growing, evolving, continually changing concept, responsive to a nexus of interlocking pressures and concerns. In the late 1980s, counseling is clearly a movement dedicated to personal and social growth and change, a movement which itself is still in the process of growing, changing, and defining itself.

In attempting to comprehend the contemporary framework of counseling, one of the key issues is understanding the difference between counseling and psychotherapy. This is a confusing question that has been the source of much contention in the professions. Continually asking "Where does counseling end and psychotherapy begin?" counselors have gone busily about their work, with barely enough time to answer.

But this is an important question—one that must be answered. It is a question surrounded by myths and misconceptions, in part perpetuated by an establishment with vested interests. It is to this question that we shall now turn our attention.

What is counseling? What is psychotherapy? Is there a difference between them? How do these processes compare in terms of effectiveness, expediency, and theoretical rationales? Should there be different qualifications for practitioners of each? Are counseling and psychotherapy suitable for the same types of individuals, or is there to be differentiation made according to the problems for which an individual seeks help?

Counseling and Psychotherapy: Is There a Difference?

If we look through the literature in search of definitions, we will find dozens, possibly hundreds, of definitions of counseling and psychotherapy. The reason there are so many different definitions is because there is so much disagreement about what is central to the helping process, and about who should practice counseling and psychotherapy. These disagreements have led to numerous still unresolved problems. Moreover, because psychotherapy is a heavily value-laden concept, with "different images of man, time focuses, concepts of society, assumptions of cause and effect, and orientations toward social change" (Bart, 1974, p. 9), these refractory issues are often central not only to differentiating counseling from psychotherapy, but to conceptualizing the process.

There is no universal agreement about whether counseling and psychotherapy are synonymous or distinct. One predominant point of view is "No, there is no difference, so let us get on with more important issues." Indeed, many prominent thinkers in the field have answered with such finality. Patterson (1973), for example, sets forth this position most cogently, when he states,

If experts in counseling and psychotherapy were asked to list the theories that should be considered under each heading, there would probably be great overlapping in the lists. The difficulty in determining which are theories of counseling and which are theories of psychotherapy is taken as one evidence of the lack of clear or significant differences between them. The position taken by the writer is that *there are no essential differences between counseling and psychotherapy* . . . the definitions of counseling would in most cases be acceptable as definitions of psychotherapy and vice versa. There seems to be agreement that both counseling and psychotherapy are processes involving a special kind of relationship between a person who asks for help with a psychological problem . . . and a person who is trained to provide that help. . . . The nature of the relationship is essentially the same. . . . The process that occurs also does not seem to differ from one side to the other. Nor do there seem to be any distinct techniques or group of techniques that separate counseling and psychotherapy. (pp. xii–xiii)

Patterson goes on to elaborate some of the prevailing counter arguments, but concludes quite firmly that *"there are no essential differences between counseling and psychotherapy"* (p. xiv), a position he maintains throughout.

Kirman (1977), approaching the problem from a different point of view but arriving at much the same conclusion, makes the point that if the client has a problem, and has come to treatment to deal with this problem, it makes no *practical* difference whether we call what we are doing counseling or whether we call it psychotherapy:

When we perceive the helping process from the point of view of the counselee, the differentiation between counseling and psychotherapy becomes meaningless. We take from each helping relationship what it has to offer though we may have hoped for more. We give in each helping relationship what we are able regardless of the definition of role. (p. 22)

This is certainly a pragmatic statement, one that goes right to the heart of the client's perceptual world and attempts to come to grips with a very complex theoretical question as practicably as possible. It also offers strong support to the argument that the terms "counseling" and "psychotherapy" can be used interchangeably.

Despite this well-articulated position, however, there are two strong arguments to the contrary. In fact, the range of literature reflects a remarkable diversity of opinion on this subject, and much of what has been written has important ramifications in the counseling setting. Two other prominent positions are:

1. Counseling differs from psychotherapy by virtue of the seriousness of the client-patient's problems and the emotional "depth" or "intensity" of the treatment.
2. Counseling differs from psychotherapy in its theoretical foundation, in practical concerns, and in its discrepant historical origins.

Let us consider each of these briefly.

This position asserts that counseling and psychotherapy differ in the purview of their concerns or the depth of their approaches. What distinguishes counseling from psychotherapy, this position asserts, is the degree of the client's disturbance; in counseling, the client is an "adequately functioning individual," but in psychotherapy, the patient is "neurotic and pathological."

This type of distinction is popular, and it is difficult to find fault with it. In practice, however, it often fails to delineate. Many cases are not so clearly defined, whether in terms of the personality level, interpersonal functioning, or in the symptoms of the client-patient. It still is not clear precisely where counseling ends and psychotherapy begins, if we view the two terms on a continuum.

Hansen, Stevic, and Warner (1977), reflecting much of the current thinking that views counseling and therapy as a continuum, take care to point out:

> In examining this situation, let us concede that, indeed, there is a continuum between counseling and psychotherapy. While they appear at opposite ends of the continuum, they are neither dichotomous nor mutually exclusive ways of helping people in need. Nevertheless, the counselor and psychotherapist generally operate at different ends of that somewhat mystical continuum. (p. 13)

They go on to explicate a continuum built on a model originally developed by Perry (1955), and they conclude that "counseling is concerned with helping individuals learn new ways of dealing with and adjusting to life situations. It is a process through which people are helped to develop sound decision-making processes either in an individual or group setting. . . . Counseling does not attempt to restructure personality, but rather to develop what already exists" (p. 15).

Juxtaposing this with the generally accepted view of psychotherapy, we can see the similarities and the differences. There would be agreement on one point: *Psychotherapy consists of one person helping another with a psychological problem*. The problem may be symptomatic, that is, it may have disturbing social or interpersonal manifestations, or it may be symptom-free, where only the individual suffering knows he or she is experiencing a problem. The emphasis in therapy may be on changing the patient's cognitive processes and ways of thinking, or on touching emotionally the deepest recesses of the mind. Looking for a broad operational definition of psychotherapy, we would agree with Hoehn-Sarie (1977), who points out that,

> Psychotherapy is . . . a series of cognitive emotional interactions between the patient and therapist. The emotional impact of this interaction forms the basis of the patient-therapist relationship. . . . The actual method of intervention depends on the training and preference of the therapist, the condition of the patient, and the state of therapy. Therapists generally aim to reduce anxiety and to clarify conditions, but often they have to temporarily provoke anxiety and disorganize their patients to modify the relationship and/or to induce a change of maladaptive behavior. (p. 94)

Despite this excellent definition, if we look at Hansen, Stevic, and Warner's conclusions in apposition with Hoehn-Sarie's, we seem to be approaching a consensus that closely parallels what the first position maintains and minimizes the differences between the scope of counseling and that of psychotherapy.

Practical Differences and Historical Influences

There are a number of practical differences between counseling and psychotherapy; these differences are to a large extent the results of the diversity of historical influences and of the underlying theory. We can summarize the major positions regarding these practical differences as follows: counseling is directed toward one set of problems while psychotherapy is directed toward another set; counseling uses one set of methods, while psychotherapy uses another; counseling emphasizes the rational environmental forces, while psychotherapy emphasizes the dynamic inner-dimensions of experience. We have the impression, throughout these different arguments, that the thrust of counseling is directed to helping clients deal with their immediate problems and improve their life situation. And the attitude of the counselor is that of one individual interacting with another, on more-or-less equal footing. This is not always the case in psychotherapy, where "real life situations as presented by the patient are secondary contexts that must be associated with the therapeutic interaction and . . . [where] every communication from the patient must be understood in terms of an adaptive context related to the analytic interaction and especially to the analyst's silences, interventions, and management of the framework" (Langs, 1980, p. 460).

Throughout the literature, counseling also emerges as a procedure with a more comprehensive approach than psychotherapy, in that it is not concerned specifically with the client's problems, but rather with the total client, functioning in an interpersonal world. The historical influences of humanism on counseling are great and affect all areas. In psychotherapy, on the other hand, the problem sometimes takes precedence over the patient's total reality. As Marks (1978) points out, in differentiating therapy from counseling,

> Psychotherapy focuses on *intra*personal conflict which produces pain and discomfort, rather than on resulting *inter*personal conflicts: thus, marital counseling, sex therapy, behavior therapy, and other forms which do not focus on internal issues are excluded from the definition.

There are different theories and axioms about people which influence the perceptions of the psychotherapist and counselor. These are to a large extent based on historical factors. The counselor sees the client, existing in the "here and now," as a responsible, developing individual. This is largely the result of the influences of progressive education, where the early counseling movement flourished, and the Rogerian counseling surge, which helped mark the break between nondirective counseling and psychoanalysis. The psychotherapist, on the other hand, generally views the client as a product of his past, whether that past be viewed in terms of conditioning experiences (influence of behaviorism) or psychosexual stages (influence of Freudianism). The counselor, in viewing the client, is more interested in the *total* person, while the psychotherapist is more interested in certain areas of the personality, particularly areas that are symptomatic of past disturbances of emotional learning. This again reflects counseling's debt to the vocational guidance movement and to testing, and psychotherapy's derivation from the medical disciplines. Admittedly, these distinctions are not valid for all counselors and all psychotherapists, since many occupy middle ground.

There are also theoretical differences which are translated into practice. A theory of psychotherapy generally consists of an underlying theory of personality, a theory of psychopathology, and a body of clinical techniques. Counseling, on the other hand, is built more upon a philosophical foundation; although it may be structured along the lines of scientific reasoning, *it emphasizes the person's innate dignity, one's individuality and uniqueness, one's phenomenological world.* Theories which attempt to explain human actions, feelings, and thoughts, therefore, can be divided between theories of counseling and theories of psychotherapy, according to their pattern of reasoning.

Combining many of these kinds of insights, Bruch (1981) offers what is perhaps the best contemporary definition of psychotherapy, as a situation

> . . . in which 2 people interact and attempt to reach an understanding of each other, with the specific goals of accomplishing something special. . . . The therapist becomes capable of reorganizing a patient's needs through continuous reconstruction and reevaluation of what is going on between him/ herself and the patient. Private self-assessment and reflection aid in becoming aware of the significance and dynamic meaning of the interchange between therapist and patient. (p. 86)

Such a definition demonstrates that despite the theoretical differences we have cited, counseling and psychotherapy are not entirely separate processes, but rather different ways of approaching the same fundamental and highly complex phenomenon: the human being.

Summary

It is appropriate at this point to summarize the topics we have covered in this chapter and to arrive at some conclusions that can guide us through the remainder of our long journey into the field of counseling psychology. First, we surveyed the history of psychological thought, paying attention to how philosophical viewpoints were transformed over centuries into scientific psychologies. We then considered how counseling evolved, its historical roots, and how it has been in search of a professional identity for many years. Finally, we turned to the question of what differentiates counseling from psychotherapy, or if, in fact, they are interchangeable terms. Our findings were:

1. There is a difference in common usage and connotative meaning between the two words, as indicated by the dictionary, by speakers of the language, and by practitioners.

2. There is much disagreement, however, about what this difference is, how it affects practice, and how it can be operationally demonstrated.
3. We also considered the position that counseling differs from psychotherapy by the degree of the problem treated (its severity) and the differences in emphasis in the treatment process. Finally, we saw that these differences are largely a result of their historical origins and basic theories.

Counseling: The Art and Science of Helping

Chapter Aim

To delineate the need for and outline the context of the counseling profession in our society. To elucidate the basic concerns that challenge contemporary counselors, including the fundamental questions they ask themselves as they engage in their work. To show the purpose of counseling theories and discuss their relationship to counseling practice.

2

In the preceding chapter we examined the origins of the counseling movement and provided a tentative working definition. Now, we shall enumerate the eleven basic questions that challenge all counselors, questions which will then be explored more fully in other parts of this book.

The Counseling Way

One of the basic assumptions of most counseling as it is practiced today is that people should be approached on a human or, as Rogers called it, a person-to-person level, rather than as sufferers of some explicit psychopathology. The position of the anti-illness movement is outlined, especially as it is articulated by its major proponents, R. D. Laing and Thomas Szasz, and E. Fuller Torrey.

The Anti-Illness Movement

What purpose does a counseling theory serve in helping the counselor in the actual setting? How are counseling theories developed, and do they exert a powerful influence in the profession? In this section, we look at the need for counseling theories, their practical value as well as their limitations and flaws.

The Need for Counseling Theories

We begin by examining the kind of training a counselor is expected to receive, then looking at the counselor education programs that provide such training. The major organizations representing the counseling field and the main professional journals are enumerated. Finally, we briefly examine the critical question of whether counselors should be licensed, as psychologists are, and consider how the counseling profession can maintain control over its development in light of the pressures exerted by the professional psychology establishment.

Professional Issues

Basic Issues in Counseling

Areas of controversy and debate, particularly those areas in which the controversy has been unruly and the debate perennial, are usually indicative of underlying schisms which threaten the integrity and unity of a discipline. This is not to suggest that a unified discipline should be free of controversy and debate; on the contrary, contention yields a lively interest in the subject and promotes an ongoing growth of attitude and an expansion of proficiencies. Controversy encourages research; research precipitates important breakthroughs; and these in turn lead to improvements in practical applications. But the stubborn recurrence of a particular debate, the persistent unresolved questioning of a single issue, indicates most clearly that fuzziness and confusion underlie a particular aspect of the discipline; and it is the responsibility of the researcher (and practitioner) to attempt to confront this problem.

In counseling there are a number of such areas of persistent controversy, stubborn questions which, despite the surfeit of research and the ingenuity of speculation, just won't go away. These questions, which in the course of time have become issues in counseling, have been approached in three ways: through experimental research, through theoretical argument, and through systematic observation and clinical case studies. While none of these methods is completely satisfactory in itself—each suffers some deficiency—the three methods combined meet the task well.

The experimental method is faulty in not providing a reasonable facsimile of the dynamic counseling situation. No matter how many sophisticated scales we devise to measure empathy, genuineness, and concreteness, no matter how cleverly we test the counselor's efficacy and strategy, the fact remains that the hypothetical conditions of the experiment differ significantly from the unpredictable variables that occur in the counseling setting.

The theoretical approach tends at key times to lose touch with the harsh realities of the counseling situation. We find that ideal, optimistic insights about counseling, for instance, are sometimes not borne out by the experimental evidence. Hardly any intuition has passed gracefully all the key tests of validation, and at times even the most basic axioms of counseling have come under embarrassing challenge by the evidence (see, for example, Gladstein's [1977] "Is Empathy Important in Counseling?").

Observation and recording—the case study approach—is also limited. A single, isolated case is generally selected because it demonstrates something specific, usually success of some type, and we know that not all counseling endeavors work out so favorably.

But together, these three methods, the empirical, the theoretical, and the case study, comprise a formidable triad, each complementing the deficiencies of the others and adding to the substance of the whole. Throughout these chapters, we will use all three methods to explore the basic issues in counseling, and to understand the relationship between different counseling theories and their relevance to counseling practice.

We will begin this chapter by examining some of the premises of counseling, some of the basic issues, and then we will look at the forces (both organizations and journals) that have helped shape counseling into what it has become.

The Counseling Way

Counseling, as has been pointed out, can be differentiated from psychotherapy in a number of ways. One of these is its reliance on philosophy. Counseling usually has an implicit or explicit underlying philosophy, which includes an *ontology*, an *epistemology*, and an *axiology*. Each of these deserves some attention.

The ontological basis of counseling refers to problems of existence—of the real versus the unreal. It deals with such questions as: What is the relationship between the reality of the client and the objective reality of the world? How does the client's existence relate to his "essential" inner qualities? To what higher purposes in life, toward which universals, does man strive?

The epistemological core of counseling, which deals with the question of knowledge and truth, considers such questions as: What is the nature of consciousness and its relationship with the known? How does the client learn new behavior and integrate it into his or her life style? What correspondence is there between what the client "knows" and what is generally accepted to be true?

The axiological premises and bases of counseling, dealing with values, raise such intriguing questions as: How can the counselor conduct herself or himself so that personal values do not unduly influence the client? To what degree do individuals have control over their ethical decisions? What part does conscience play in governing the client's life?

Both the counselor and the client, as they engage in their intensely emotional interaction, consider, either consciously or unconsciously, a myriad of philosophical questions that influence their perceptions, judgments, and actions. Philosophies of counseling, derived from questions in these three areas of philosophy, differ in a number of ways which are of major practical importance. Briefly summarized, they are,

1. How *directive* or *nondirective* should the counselor be in his or her work with the client?
2. What emphasis is placed on the idea of *free will* and what emphasis is placed on the idea of *determinism?* What influence do these concepts have in treatment?
3. How deeply into the personality and the unconcious of the client should the counselor probe?
4. How much of himself or herself should the counselor voluntarily give to the client?
5. To what degree should counselors address themselves to clients' behavior and to what degree should they direct themselves primarily to clients' feelings?
6. How much allegiance is owed to the system or institution by which the counselor is employed? When might this loyalty conflict with the counselor's loyalty and obligation to the client?
7. How do religious or other ethical concerns contribute to the quality and direction of the counseling interaction?
8. What use should the counselor make of his or her own experiences, perceptions, and beliefs in dealing with the client?
9. What feelings of the counselor are appropriate or inappropriate in terms of the anticipated outcomes of the counseling?
10. How should counselors select a theory or counseling "school" to use as the basis for their practice?
11. How should counselors go about resolving conflicts between their intuition and the counseling model they are using?

These and other related questions continue to trouble the counselor and are not readily answered by the broad definition of counseling we offered in the preceding chapter. No, counseling as it is practiced is far more complex. We do find these questions posed within the counseling setting. To assist the counselor in arriving at his or her own answers, we shall have to examine the different conceptions which serve as an integrating force in the counseling profession, holding together the moments of the interaction and blending them into a goal-directed, purposive whole.

Having gone this far in our analysis, we reach a juncture at which a decision must be made. Granted that counseling is a certain class of activity, we must acknowledge that in the category of counseling many different types of activities, rationales, and proposed outcomes are included. Under the heading of counseling we find such divergent theoretical approaches as the psychodynamic, the Rogerian, the behavioral, the existential, the Gestalt, the rational-emotive, and the cognitive. Practitioners of counseling have different approaches to the problems, distinct ways of going about dealing with conflict. The reason for this variety should be clarified at the outset. Our efforts in this direction will be divided into two sections. First, we shall examine the controversy over the concepts of mental health and mental illness; between the normal and the abnormal. This will help us better understand how counselors can accept all of their clients as they are. Moreover, it will highlight a significant distinction between counseling and therapy *in practice*. Whereas psychotherapy is traditionally concerned with ameliorating what are called "abnormal," "pathological," or "maladaptive" disturbances, the broader purview of counseling includes all areas of role functioning and interpersonal adaptation. Secondly, we will examine the role of counseling theory and its effects on counseling practice, to see how the wider compass of counseling is supported by its theoretical rationales.

Let us now begin by focusing on an important influence in contemporary counseling theory and practice, a change in point of view which has far-reaching practical ramifications. We are referring to what is generally called "the anti-illness movement."

The Anti-Illness Movement

Because the counseling approach deals with the *whole* person, synthesizing and unifying the fragmented parts of the individual's totality by means of the counseling relationship, it necessarily rejects the constraints of an orthodox psychopathology. Counseling seeks to integrate into practice the environmental as well as the intrapsychic components of the client's experience. The counseling way, as we use the term, helps us in achieving empathy in understanding the individual's complex organic interaction with the environment; it does this by means of our own "therapeutic" involvement with the individual, free from the burdens of preconceptions, countertransference, and emotional distancing (Peabody & Gelso, 1982).

In recent years there has been a major change affecting the practice of counseling in the United States. At first this change, which is an interrelated alteration in attitude, in technique, and in philosophy, was articulated by a radical few in the ranks of psychiatry and psychology. They argued, in effect, that our perceptions of people in conflict were seriously distorted by our professional biases about the causes of psychological problems. We were wearing blinders, they argued, and these blinders were attached by the strings of science. They rejected the "scientific" viewpoint of mental illness with the same ferocity and indignation that the scientific reformers earlier had rejected the "possession" model and had replaced it with the scientific model. Soon this "anti-illness movement" began to have an impact on the ranks of the counseling profession. As counselors became aware of the diverse needs of our constituency, and as we began to recognize that social, political, and economic factors play a vital part in shaping the individual, we began to question our "scientific" models of mental illness and to reevaluate our derivative models of helping.

One result of the major influence which Freudian thinking had upon the profession of counseling psychology was a tendency among mental health professionals to employ the "medical model" in the treatment of psychological, behavioral, and emotional problems. The medical model assumes that behavioral and emotional problems are surface symptoms of underlying pathological conditions, particularly conditions of a psychological nature. This is analogous to a situation in which a physician might recognize that a fever blister is simply the observable evidence of an underlying physical abnormality. When a patient comes for treatment complaining of a phobic condition and the psychotherapist assumes *de facto* that the cause of this condition lies in the patient's "unresolved Oedipal problems," this professional is employing the psychoanalytic view of the medical model.

The medical model helped shape the field of psychotherapy into what it is today by requiring that the practitioner deal not only with the symptoms—that is, with the observable or verbalized difficulties which the patient presents, but also with what he as the practitioner, the expert, believed to be the latent underlying causes of the problems. Such an approach demanded a new and highly complex terminology to describe these underlying nonmeasurable phenomena. Thus arose over a period of fifty years a nomenclature which was designed to describe the dynamics of patients but which actually reduced the patient's multifaceted existence and wide range of feelings to a set of preconceived categories that satisfied no one but the psychotherapist.

R. D. Laing, a psychiatrist who has achieved acclaim during the past 25 years, has argued against the psychotherapist's reliance on technical language, denouncing this tendency to relate to the patient as if he were an embodiment of these technical words. A technical language, Laing argues, is not necessary for understanding the patient conceptually or for treating him therapeutically. On the contrary, the words of the technical vocabulary are obstacles which stand in the way of understanding the patient in his or her personal reality. This viewpoint has exerted a substantial influence on the counseling profession, especially during the last ten years, when emphasis has been placed on modifying accepted diagnostic systems (such as the psychiatric profession's DSM-III) to account for the real differences between individuals who are grouped under the same diagnostic label (Treece, 1982).

Perhaps the most flagrant misuse of technical language in psychology and psychiatry is found in the process of diagnosing patients. Laing (1967, 1969) cautioned that such diagnostic terms as schizophrenia, psychosis, neurosis, and so on, "split man up verbally," reducing his real existence to overly simplified and somewhat arbitrary categories. The fetish for diagnosis, he argues, makes the patient an object in the therapist's world, which we know is contrary to the counselor's attempt to understand the total person. Probably the strongest argument against the use of diagnostic categories is to cite their high probability of invalidity and unreliability. Stuart (1973), after carefully surveying the literature, concluded that practitioners are unable to agree on particular diagnoses and are unable to predict the course and the success of treatment on the basis of diagnostic categories. Ferrari (1982), examining the diagnostic criteria used for categorizing very disturbed children, points out that generally diagnosis does not function satisfactorily, and that the "lack of criteria makes difficult the interpretation and replication of research." Thus, such diagnosis is both vague and misleading.

In addition to the cited discrepancies between medical and psychological situations, we should also mention that social factors play a vital role in determining psychological diagnostic categories, but they are generally irrelevant to medical diagnosis. Roman and Trice (1974) have discussed at length the influence of social factors in the way we perceive and treat psychological problems, and have pointed out that "psychotherapy does not operate in a social vacuum." Basker, Beran, and Kleinhauz (1982), in studying the cultural implications and social and ethnic bias in the use of diagnostic categories, suggest that diagnosis not only forces us to categorize clients incorrectly, but also to label their behaviors in terms of the diagnosis they have been given, thereby distorting what we are actually seeing. We conclude from the sum of these remarks that the diagnostic tendencies in the mental health profession not only serve little useful purpose but actually may be responsible for a great deal of harm, by misleading the practitioner, by misdirecting the course of the treatment, and by condemning the client as sick, unhealthy, or abnormal.

New Directions   Although years ago it required a certain professional boldness to challenge the concept of mental illness, during the past decade evidence and arguments have been amassed which raise some serious questions about the concept of illness and more especially about the validity of fixed diagnostic categories. Although we still recognize that some individuals are more disturbed than others, that some are well adjusted and some more poorly adjusted, today there is more caution about constructing fixed and inexorable diagnostic categories. Instead, thrust of much recent research has concentrated on what are called *multiaxial* diagnostic approaches, where many different subtle and observable factors about the person's life, behavior, and perceptions are taken into account before formulating a diagnostic category (Schover et al., 1982).

Two practitioners who have contributed a wealth of insight over the years are R. D. Laing and Thomas Szasz, each of whom offers to the counselor many new and invigorating insights. Laing's position is predicated on the assumption that mental illness as we know it is a hypothetical term, describing more a social value than a phenomenological reality. Profoundly concerned with the total person in all his life processes, all his interactions and experiences, all his functional and perceptual encounters as a free agent, Laing exemplifies in every respect the humanistic stance. He argues time and again in his writings that the person who seeks help must be viewed and dealt with not as a sick, unstable, deficient individual, but rather from the standpoint of his or her subjective world, from his or her reference points, from his or her psychological perspective. Moreover, Laing forcefully objects to the stratification typical of the psychotherapeutic relationship, a stratification derived directly from the medical model, which describes an "ill" person seeking the professional assistance of a practitioner who presumably is able to "cure" the illness. With respect to the role of diagnosis in this scheme, he suggests that a diagnostic system should recognize a nexus of interacting factors contributing to what we ultimately perceive as a disturbance. A good diagnostic system must take into account the relationship among constitutional factors, developmental history, and life events (Spiel, 1981).

Another distinguished proponent of the anti-diagnosis viewpoint is Thomas Szasz. His writings, particularly his earlier well-known and influential book *The Myth of Mental Illness* (1961), have argued lucidly and cogently against the position that conceptions of mental illness are objective and dispassionate products of psychopathology. Like Laing, Szasz is also a partisan of the humanistic perspective. He considers mental illness within the context of culture, criticizing its lack of scientific reliability and validity, since the practitioner imposes his own values and his own sociological biases in ascribing an illness to the patient. Szasz (1960) argues:

> Difficulties in human relations can be analyzed, interpreted, and given meaning only within specific social and ethical contexts. Accordingly, the psychiatrist's socioethical orientations will influence his ideas on what is wrong with the patient, on what deserves comment or interpretation, in what directions change might be desirable, and so forth. (p. 115)

Szasz does not dispute that some individuals have more adjustment difficulties than others in fitting into acceptable social patterns of behavior. Rather, he objects to the designation of "mentally ill" for those individuals who either refuse to conform or are unable to acquiesce in the structures and standards of the society in which they live. If we recall the common practice in the Soviet Union today of classifying politically dissident intellectuals as "mentally ill," we can understand in the clearest and most impressive sense what Szasz is referring to.

These terms are often loosely used, and much thought has been directed toward constructing an empirical meaning for them, a meaning which can be tested under different conditions, and can hold up under rigorous scientific scrutiny. Torrey (1974) points out that the very concept of "normality" is related to the medical model, and that this has caused problems for psychiatrists and mental health practitioners:

The "Normal" and the "Abnormal"

> Normality is another aspect of the medical model which has caused problems for psychiatry. The medical profession has always had quite explicit ideas about which persons are considered normal. If a person does not have a disease, then he is normal. . . . Psychiatry, in its attempts to become a subdivision of medicine, has been troubled by this definition of normality. In

trying to define normality as the absence of disease, it has found itself in an awkward position. The reason for this is that there is no accepted definition of mental "disease. . . ." (p. 53)

Problems which may arise from this lack of precision can sometimes be dramatic. Rosenham (1973), in a now classic paper, reports on an experiment in which the very concepts of the normal and abnormal were seriously challenged. Eight experimenters were admitted to psychiatric hospitals as patients, after complaining, as instructed, that they were "hearing voices." Immediately upon admission, the pseudopatients were instructed to act normally, exactly as they do in their everyday lives. Despite their normal behavior, from the time of their admission on, they were not considered sane while in the psychiatric hospital setting. Although in some cases other patients could observe that these pseudopatients were "sane," the staff and the professionals were unable to see this, regardless of how much normal contact took place. The significant conclusion of this study is that *when people are classified as insane, the label sticks with them, no matter how normally they act.* This study supports many of Szasz's and Torrey's observations that mental illness is frequently determined by social perception, that those whom we call *abnormal* or *mentally ill* are merely perceived to be mentally ill, regardless of how normally they act.

Some Counseling Implications   Both Laing and Szasz offer some valuable insights for all of us, insights which can be helpful in understanding our clients in a way that can be especially useful. They are speaking from what is primarily a humanistic point of view. What they are saying is that for one person to "humanistically" or "existentially" relate to another, so as to understand, accept, and respect another, we as counselors should deliberately avoid the temptation to diagnose, to categorize, to regard the other person as mentally ill. It is very easy, and at times very tempting, to describe in technical terms a person with whom we are having difficulties. If I say I can't get along with my boss because she is an obsessive-compulsive, or if I am having trouble with a friend because he is a classical hysteric personality, this conveys nothing. It merely reduces the person's reality into a category; and then we tend to interpret everything the person does in terms of that category.

But if we abandon the medical model as a basis for understanding people, and relinquish the mental illness paradigm, what do we put in their place? What can help us understand the problems of adjustment without reliance on these rigid categories?

One possibility suggests itself in some recent formulations. In place of the medical model, we can rely on the phenomenological approach to replace the paradigms of mental health and illness. Although the phenomenological approach is often associated with existential and humanistic therapies, it has had a profound effect on understanding the range of human relationships, as well as the diverse paths to interpersonal adjustment, mental health, and self-actualization.

Briefly the phenomenological approach attempts to reconstruct the world as it is seen from the point of view of the person we are trying to understand. Free of value judgments, not distorted by perceptual biases, the world of another opens up to us in all of its pristine clarity and internal logic, revealing to us the other person's inner world (Marx, 1981). The phenomenological approach precludes the designation of mental illness by eliminating such broad categories of containment as clinical diagnosis and therapeutic terminology. More important, the phenomenological approach works independently of and in contradiction to the medical model of treatment. Thus, by embracing the phenomenological approach, counselors can free themselves of difficulties implicit in the medical model and inherent in the theory of mental illness.

The phenomenological approach is not endemic to any specific form of therapy; rather, it is a philosophical framework that infuses all the counselor's attitudes toward and understanding of the client. But it goes beyond this in an attempt to understand reality and knowledge in an objective way by pairing together subjectivities to arrive at an objective whole (Jennings, 1986). Specifically, it suggests that to understand the client *for what he is* and *as he is* requires that we strip away all our biases and preconceptions and attempt to grasp the world from the point of view of the client. In this way, phenomenologists suggest, the "is-ness" of the client, his essential sense of being and self-coherence, emerges through the therapeutic process. This makes clear why the phenomepanological approach runs counter to the medical model, which subsumes the client's essential being under the diagnostic rubrics.

Counseling Theory and Counseling Practice

Counseling studies often raise the question of why there are so many different and often conflicting schools of thought, divergent approaches, as well as theories of psychotherapy and counseling that are at odds with each other. At the present time, there are well over one hundred different theories, approaches, and rationales, each competing for its own niche on the counseling-therapy spectrum. If counseling were truly scientific and empirical, students argue, there would be no room for contention over such basic issues as the nature of man, the role of the client, the job of the counselor, effective strategies, and the counselor's appropriate attitude and responses in the treatment setting.

To respond to this paradox, or apparent paradox, it is necessary first to make clear what a theory of counseling is, as well as the relationship between theory and practice. Later in Part 3, we will examine the foundations common to all these theories and the discrepancies which place them in opposition, to determine the true degree of consonance or dissonance which exists among them. Only at that point will we be able to answer adequately this recurring, troublesome question. In this section, we shall explore this first part of the question.

In its fullest sense, a theory has three components or functions: an explanation for associating a number of independent observations; a predictive method (or algorithm) for stating a probability of what will happen *if* and *when* certain specified conditions exist; and finally, a logical (verifiable) connection between presumed causes and observed effects. The key in all three of these is that a theory serves as a bridge in linking up beliefs and actions. A theory of counseling, moreover, predisposes the counselor to certain types of actions; it is therefore related to counseling practice in the sense of providing *a basis for practical judgments*.

Finally, a theory has an explicative function. It explains and clarifies to the counselor phenomena which are not readily apparent or explicit or which do not appear logical. By providing a new dimension to the counselor's awareness, a theory illuminates what is hidden; it brings out into the open certain aspects of the counseling experience which may have been concealed during the interaction. It does this by relating seemingly isolated events or facts to one another, indicating their relative position and relationship within the conceptual scheme (Miller, Belkin & Gray, 1982).

Most theories of counseling were derived from the experiences of a practitioner. Freud, Rogers, Ellis, and Wolpe each developed a comprehensive theory of personality and counseling by observing results of interactions in the clinical setting, then reflecting on a large body of evidence with the goal of trying to find a common concept or element. Each of these investigators refined his theory over the years, as new evidence and new insights impinged upon the fixed categories of the inchoate theory.

Marx (1981) describes two opposing views of theory construction. One he calls the *anarchistic,* which holds in effect that there are no rules at all, that evidence can only be examined after the fact. This might be indicative of the phenomenological position, at least insofar as it attempts to examine the events of a person's life free of the biases that color other theories. The second he calls the *formal* position; this relies on structured categories and fixed linear equations to define behavior. The Freudian point of view might be thus classified. In both cases, he suggests, there is at present a paucity of good modern theories, theories which can furnish full accounts of behavior, partly because of "an anti-scientific trend, and a failure to distinguish between the contexts of discovery and confirmation." He goes on to insist that the faddish theory of today, based on a few independent observations, carries little weight in the world of science. "Theories must be empirically testable," he insists, "and are best if developed gradually and with the kind of diversity that does not require different theoretical approaches."

The Counselor and the Theory

At the present time it is far from clear just what effect counseling theory exerts upon the individual practice of the counselor. Do counselors behave in a certain way because of the theory to which they subscribe or do they identify themselves with a theory because it best describes the way they act?

As a general statement, we can say that the counselors make use of a theory to guide them in the approach they will use with the client. If a counselor subscribes to the tenets of psychoanalysis, he or she may believe that an interpretation of the unconscious would be helpful to the client's growth. If one sees oneself as a behavioral counselor, one might believe that reinforcement is in order. If one holds to the client-centered approach, one might feel reflection or an empathic communication would be appropriate. Whatever the counselor's approach, when he or she makes an intervention to the client based on his or her postulate, the counselor puts theory into practice, testing the validity of the generalized theory *for him* (or her).

If the counseling intervention is successful, that is, if it helps the client move forward toward the goal of the treatment, then the counselor is likely to use it again and again, regardless of what premise it was derived from, regardless of which school supports it. Likewise, if it is unsuccessful, the counselor will abandon it, regardless of how strongly he or she supports the underlying premise, no matter how doctrinaire the counselor has been in this thinking. Because counseling is doing, because it is always a spontaneous, active dynamic, evolving process between two people, there are too many variables, too many *raisons des coeurs* [reasons of the heart] to be contained within the confines of a single theory. Although the validity of a theory is a construct that can be deduced experimentally, the value of a theory emerges only in practice, as the counselor uses it in his or her own counseling practice.

We can say, therefore, that a theory of counseling is no more than a set of postulates proposing a course of action, explicating a pattern of behavior, and indicating a number of predictions, all of which are subject to change during the course of the counseling process.

One problem with any theory, of course, is that it may subtly encourage us to alter our observations and bend evidence to fit the constraints of the theory. Phenomenologists argue that all theories should be abandoned for this reason. While such a position is extreme, there is some cause for concern that the partisan of a theory may be prone to a peculiarly selective peripheral blindness. In perceptual psychology this is known as the theory of cognitive dissonance, that we tend to have difficulty accepting phenomena or situations which contradict our theories of how things *should* be.

This selective perception has been demonstrated in several studies that showed just how strongly our beliefs influence our perceptions, especially in our attributions of cause to external events. Anderson, Lepper, and Ross (1980), in one experimental study, investigated the relationship between theory and evidence. Their question was, How much will people hold on to a theory in light of conflicting evidence? In this experiment, subjects were asked to examine case studies about the relationship between risk-taking and success, with firemen used as the examples. The researchers found that even when the cause-and-effect evidence of the case study unequivocally contradicted the theory, many subjects persisted in accepting the theory, regardless of the strength of the discrediting evidence.

From all this we can draw two conclusions. First, while theories serve a useful purpose in helping counselors and researchers to organize large quantities of independent observations and discrepant events, they can also be misleading, especially if a person allows his or her perception to be subjectively altered by his or her theoretical framework. Second, no single theory can fully account for the myriad phenomena which characterize the range of human experiences we as counselors inevitably are exposed to. Thus, in the reality of the counseling setting, we will probably draw something from one theory and something from another to develop functional, practical guidelines for action.

What the practicing counselor, bombarded by a plethora of theories and assumptions about personality often incompatible with each other, would probably do best to remember is Carl Gustav Jung's (1954) pointed injunction: "Learn your theories as well as you can, but put them aside when you touch the miracle of the living soul."

Professional Issues

The profession of counseling is truly a melting pot of talent. Unlike other professions such as medicine, law, pharmacy, which are relatively homogeneous, counseling includes within its ranks people who have gone through a wide variety of diverse types of training programs; they may or may not be state licensed in one or another of the allied mental health fields (social work, psychology, etc.); and their training, orientation, and professional recognition may be similar or very different from that of others who are also called counselors. Generally, although not exclusively, mental health professionals designated as counselors hold a graduate degree in counseling, in counseling psychology, or in school guidance counseling. At the undergraduate level, counselors may have majored in virtually any subject area, although a large number come from the ranks of education, psychology, and sociology majors.

In this section, we will survey some of the principal professional issues, in the hope of making clear where counselors stand today in the ranks of mental health professionals, who represents them, what their professional recognition is, what disagreements exist regarding their certification and practice standards, and other allied issues.

We will begin by outlining the chief categories of mental health professionals who may call themselves counselors or, even if they do not call themselves counselors, nevertheless practice what is widely regarded as counseling, be it vocational, family, or individual. Then we will discuss the counselor's training, focusing on how counselor trainees are selected, what kinds of skills they are taught, and how their developing competency is assessed along the path to professional expertise. Finally, we will look at the professional organization which represents counselors. In the final pages, we will consider the controversial question of credentialing, of licensing counselors and other mental health professionals.

Who Provides Counseling Services?

It is not unusual for a person entering the mental health profession (or seeking help from a counselor, psychotherapist, or other helping professional) to be confused between the designations *psychologist, psychiatrist, psychotherapist, psychoanalyst, counselor,* and still other related terms. There is actually an overlap between many of these terms, and their specific designation varies from state to state. However, because all of them may engage in the practice of counseling, we should be familiar with their legal and functional similarities and differences. In brief, they can be classified by the following descriptions:

Psychologist A person who holds an advanced degree in psychology from an approved institution of higher education and has passed a state licensing examination. A psychologist need not be oriented toward nor trained in psychotherapy, in fact, psychologists specialize in a range of related studies, including animal behavior, psychological testing, social psychology, clinical psychology, and counseling.

Clinical Psychologist A psychologist who has specialized training in helping people solve psychological problems. This training usually includes working in an institutional as well as a private practice setting.

Counseling Psychologist A psychologist whose training is directed toward helping individuals solve psychological problems, typically of a role area nature: marriage and family problems, job-related problems, school problems, etc.

Counselor A person, usually not a psychologist, trained in helping individuals solve role area problems, such as those mentioned above. The counselor usually works with an agency or school, but may also have a private practice.

Psychotherapist A person trained specifically in the practice of psychotherapy. A psychotherapist may or may not be a psychologist; specific qualifications depend largely upon the institute of psychotherapy which the practitioner attended, since most psychotherapy training does not take place in a university setting.

Psychoanalyst A person trained specifically in the Freudian system of therapy, called psychoanalysis; a psychoanalyst may be a psychologist, a psychiatrist, or neither. What is most distinctive is the intensive professional training and personal analysis required by all reputable psychoanalytic training institutes. Most such institutes require at least three years of training, and many insist that the trainee be licensed as a psychologist or psychiatrist.

Social worker A person who has received an advanced degree in social work and in many states is specifically licensed as a social worker or "psychiatric" social worker. A social worker may be a trained psychotherapist or psychoanalyst, depending upon the individual's professional background.

Psychiatrist A medical doctor who has had advanced training (a residency) in the specialty of psychiatry. A psychiatrist may or may not be trained as a psychotherapist or psychoanalyst. Some psychiatrists specialize in prescribing medication and have not had specific training in psychotherapy.

We see that there are many different job descriptors for providers of counseling services. Although these designations may have critical implications with regard to insurance reimbursement and legal responsibilities, they have little or no influence on the capabilities of the mental health professional with regard to counseling skills, professional competencies, and attitudes toward clients.

The Counselor's Training

Typically, counselors are trained in graduate programs by a highly qualified professional staff with a greater diversity of background and specialization than is ordinarily found in a single academic department. The faculty of a typical counseling department may include school and family counselors, counseling psychologists, clinical counselors and psychologists, psychiatric social workers, psychotherapists, psychometricians, researchers and theorists, philosophers of education, administrators, community psychologists, vocational counselors, and others. This is creditable, inasmuch as counseling is interdisciplinary in substance and scope, and each of these professionals contributes his or her own expertise to the multifaceted training process.

Admission requirements for counselor training programs vary widely, depending to a large extent on whether it is a masters-level or doctoral-level program. In addition to evaluation of past academic performance, a standardized test such as the Graduate Record Examination (GRE) or Miller Analogy Test (MAT) may be mandated. An interview with one or more faculty members is usually required, since the personal qualities of the applicant are regarded as important, if not more important, than ability to perform well on standardized aptitude and achievement tests. In fact, there is now considerable evidence that cognitive attributes are not especially important, at least insofar as developing the critical counseling skills necessary for successful outcomes (Usdan, 1981).

The scope of training can be stated in four general categories, which take into account the range of accepted counseling competencies: (1) mastery of cognitive information relating directly to the counseling process; (2) ability to administer programs and to communicate effectively, both orally and in writing, with other members of the counseling team (consultation), with concerned parents and other interested parties, as well as with the client; (3) self-awareness and the willingness to be introspective, to grow, and when necessary, to change; (4) technical proficiency in the counseling setting, interviewing skills, and the ability to feel comfortable in the role of counselor. Figure 2.1 illustrates how the concept of empathy may be integrated into the training cycle.

During the course of training, which may range from one year to several years, the trainee's professional competencies, ethics, and technical expertise are refined. Thompson (1986) investigated some of the ways counseling trainees change during their training and found increases in their ability to use questions, avoid unnecessary interpretations, and encourage and respond to the client. Cormier and Cormier (1979) suggest that trainees demonstrate growth and proficiency in the three comprehensive areas generally recognized as crucial for

The Training Cycle

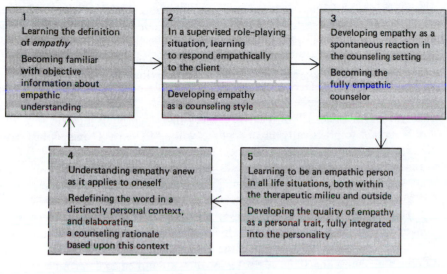

Figure 2.1. Knowing, doing, and feeling. Counselor training involves an integration of knowledge, emotional growth, self-insight, and the learning of facilitative behaviors. This chart shows how the concept of empathy becomes integrated into counseling practice. Empathy will be discussed more fully on pages 68–70.

effective counseling performance: self-development; skill development; and process development. These are all observable and measurable qualities, amenable to the training paradigms typically used during didactic, fieldwork, and internship training. Cormier and Cormier (1979) briefly describe these goals as follows:

Self-development involves professional growth and self-evaluation. . . . The objective of self-development is for [the counselor] to identify some of [his or her] attitudes and behaviors that may facilitate or interfere with a helping relationship. . . . Skill development consists of any experience that helps [the counselor] acquire counseling techniques and develop a counseling-interview style. . . . Process development involves discovering ways to monitor and evaluate [the counselor's] behavior and the client's behavior during the counseling process. The goal of process development is for [the counselor] to make continuous observations of [his or her] behavior and to discriminate its effects during counseling. Evaluation occurs before, during, and after a particular counseling intervention. . . . (p. 2)

One question repeatedly raised among training professionals is whether counseling skills development can be taught by itself to trainees or whether certain identifiable perceptual characteristics are necessary for effective counseling interactions. In other words, can we take any trainee and teach that individual the correct counseling skills, through role-playing, didactic instruction, modeling, etc., or is it necessary to change the trainee's entire way of looking at things, his or her perceptual field? The answer to this question will largely determine how we structure the training program.

Recently a number of prominent and widely employed training models, such as those proposed by Gerard Egan (Egan, 1977), Robert Carkhuff and his associates (Carkhuff, Pierce & Cannon, 1977), Dorothy Molyneaux and Vera Lane (Molyneaux & Lane, 1982), have suggested that counseling interviewing skills can be taught to practically anyone who is willing to learn. Using sophisticated skills training models, these practitioners have applied their paradigms for training teachers, business professionals, nurses, and a wide variety of other individuals who wish to improve their interviewing skills. On the surface, much of this has led to positive and productive outcomes.

However, as Lutwak and Hennessy (1982) correctly point out, there is evidence "that there are substantial individual differences in levels of mastery of these skills" (p. 256). To examine the relationship between perceptual functioning and counseling skills competency, they attempted to determine, in a significant study, the relationship between a counselor trainee's ability to perceive and abstract and that individual's level of empathic understanding.

They begin by identifying four stages of what they call "conceptual systems functioning," which reflect different ways of perceiving and responding to the world (and others):

1. Functioning at a concrete level, where ties to cultural standards and rules are prevalent. There is dependence on external authority, and judgments tend to be both dogmatic and categorical. This stage is characterized by rigid belief systems and an intolerance of ambiguity.
2. Functioning is characterized by a high degree of negativism and a strong resistance to dependency on external authority and control. Beliefs and judgments are still categorical and rigid, but are in opposition to authority.
3. Functioning is at a more complex and abstract level. Relationships are based on mutuality rather than authority, and the use of social skills is the outstanding mode of adjustment. . . .
4. Functioning is the most abstract and integrated mode of perception. Persons at this stage have an open relationship with their environment, receive and evaluate feedback, and are better able to view events simultaneously from several viewpoints. (p. 257)

Lutwak and Hennessy then attempted to find out whether empathic understanding, a critical counseling function, is related to these stages. If so, then the teaching of skills alone might not be sufficient without developing the trainee's perceptual functioning. They found a definite relationship, with trainees who demonstrated functioning at higher conceptual levels better able to show a capacity for empathy. "The one clear finding," they conclude, "is that skills development training alone does not ensure mastery of empathic responding for all individuals. *A counselor's interview behavior is a function of both skill and perceptual framework.*" (Lutwak & Hennessy, 1982, p. 259, italics added).

With this admonition in mind, however, we should point out that there are scores of examples of how specific skills training programs can be used to increase counselor effectiveness in a number of critical areas. The works of Egan, Carkhuff, Molyneaux, and Lane cited above, as well as the interview skills development program explicated by Cormier and Cormier (1979) have all been effective in improving counseling skills. Other paradigms have been shown equally effective in developing specific competencies. Jessee and L'Abate (1981), for example, show how role-playing exercises are excellent methods for increasing the abilities of family therapist trainees. Grotgen (1981) has demonstrated that nonverbal communication skills can be effectively taught in a training program for beginning counselors. He found that such a program could teach beginning counselors how to demonstrate specific nonverbal behaviors *to* their clients, and to recognize the effects of these nonverbal cues coming *from* their clients. Stum (1982) has proposed an excellent consultation skills training program, where a seven-step training model is used to learn effective consultation interview skills.

Professional Organizations and Journals

The organization that most decisively represents the interests of the counseling profession is the American Association for Counseling and Development (AACD), with central headquarters in Alexandria, Virginia. The AACD boasts about 55,000 members, from all fields of counseling. This organization comprises twelve national divisions and three organizational affiliates which, in effect, represent every specialized area of counseling. Presently, the main disseminators of counseling research, news, and professional developments are published by AACD. These are the *Journal of Counseling and Development,* published ten times a year, and the newsletter *Guidepost,* published eighteen times a year. In addition, most of the AACD divisions publish journals dedicated specifically to concerns of that division. An annual AACD convention is held each spring in a different city.

Since abbreviations are used so often in the literature, the following list includes both the abbreviation and full title of the divisions of AACD and organizational affiliates (*). Most of these divisions are self-explanatory. The journal published by each division is also indicated.

ACPA   American College Personnel Association
Journal of College Student Personnel

AMHCA   American Mental Health Counselors Association
AMHCA Journal

ACES   Association for Counselor Education and Supervision
Counselor Education and Supervision

AHEAD	Association for Humanistic Education and Development
	Journal of Humanist Education and Development
ASCA	American School Counselor Association
	School Counselor
ARCA	American Rehabilitation Counseling Association
	Rehabilitation Counseling Bulletin
AMECD	Association for Measurement and Evaluation in Counseling and Development
	Measurement and Evaluation in Counseling and Development
NECA	National Employment Counselors Association
	Journal of Employment Counseling
AMCD	Association for Multicultural Counseling and Development
	Journal of Multicultural Counseling and Development
ARVIC	Association for Religious and Values Issues in Counseling
	Counseling and Values
MECA*	Military Educators and Counselors Association
ASGW	Association for Specialists in Group Work
NCDA	National Career Development Association
POCA*	Public Offender Counselor Association
AADA*	Association for Adult Development and Aging

In addition to AACD, interests of counselors are also represented by The Division of Counseling Psychology of the American Psychological Association. The *Counseling Psychologist,* a prestigious quarterly journal, is published by that division, often organized around specific themes (such as counselor identity, counseling the elderly, etc.).

Professional Ethics

Although questions and issues of ethics invariably pose an intellectual and moral challenge to committed practitioners in most professions, presenting some very difficult and complex problems and questions for which there are often no unequivocally wrong or right answers, they are even more challenging in the counseling and psychotherapy field for two reasons. First, because counselors and therapists not only advise and guide, but also become intimately involved in the existence of their clients, at least in an emotional sense, there are far more opportunities for abuse and exploitation than would be found, for example, in an accountant/client or attorney/client relationship. Whether we call it transference, trust, countertransference, or empathy, there is little question that many clients form powerful attachments to their counselors, and sometimes vice versa.

Second, the expectations, attitudes, and beliefs of clients have changed drastically over the past two decades, so that their very knowledge about counseling raises numerous ethical issues which, though just as important before, formerly were rarely raised. As Cormier and Bernard (1982) have correctly pointed out:

> In recent years there has been a gradual and profoundly important change in the attitudes of clients toward helping professionals. *The client has become a consumer.* As a result, accountability has become an important concept of both counselors and supervisors and ethical issues have evolved into legal issues. Of course, this change is largely for the better. For too long, clients did not discriminate between helpers and assumed that therapeutic failure was their own. In too many cases, this is still true. . . . (p. 486)

In psychology as an academic and research discipline, and in counseling as an applied helping profession, there are many complex ethical problems. These range from day-to-day problems, such as the fairest structure of counseling fees for the poor, to complex theoretical issues regarding the ethics of behavior modification. The question of ethics is so important, and yet beyond the scope of this text. But we will briefly discuss three issues that have raised many ethical questions over the past few years:

Confidentiality—its scope and limits
Sexual contact between counselor and client
The client's rights as consumer

Confidentiality

Most people, when they enter a counseling relationship, require total confidentiality for the free, spontaneous, and uninhibited openness of their expression and feelings. "Confidentiality," as defined by Dulchin and Segal (1982), "involves a relationship of trust in which one person imparts private or secret matters to a second party." In practice this means that the arrangement will not be exploited or abused. "The assumption," they continue, "is that the second party, having grown powerful as a result of such knowledge, discloses the information to others only at the behest or with the consent of the first" (p. 13). Thus, although issues discussed in session might at times be discussed outside, the principle of confidentiality implies that they will be discussed only for the direct benefit of the client.

Legally, the concept of confidentiality is known as privileged communication. Laws regarding privileged communication vary from state to state, with counselors generally enjoying the least legal rights in this area. Thus, even though the concept of confidentiality is theoretically important to counselors as professionals, as Herlihy and Sheely (1987) point out,

> In a broad context, it must be recognized that confidentiality, both as a societal value and as an individual interest, does not and cannot exist in a vacuum. The combination of multiple and sometimes conflicting considerations—privileged communication law, ethical confidentiality, and societal values—leaves practicing counselors with no easy answers.

Table 2.1 shows how different states treat privileged communication by selected helping professions.

Basic Issues in Counseling

49

Table 2.1
Privileged Communication Provisions in Statutes and Regulations of Selected Helping Professions

	AL	AK	AZ	AR	CA	CO	CT	DE	FL	GA	HI	ID	IL	IN	IA	KS	KY	LA	ME	MD	MA	MI	MN	MS	MO
Certified school counselors	No	No	No	No	No	No	Yes[a]	No	No	No	No	Yes	Yes	Yes	Yes	Yes	Yes	Yes	Yes	Yes[a]	No	Yes	Yes	No	No
Licensed professional counselors	Yes	—	Yes	—	—	—	—	—	—	No[b]	—	Yes	—	—	—	—	—	—	—	No	—	—	—	Yes	Yes
Marriage and family therapists	—	—	—	Yes	—	Yes	—	No	—	No[b]	—	Yes	—	—	—	—	—	—	—	No	Yes	—	—	Yes	—
Psychologists	Yes	Yes	Yes	Yes	Yes	Yes	Yes	Yes	Yes	Yes	No	Yes	Yes	Yes	Yes	Yes	Yes	Yes	Yes	Yes	Yes	Yes	Yes	Yes	Yes
Social workers	No	—	—	Yes	Yes	—	—	Yes	No	No[b]	No	Yes	Yes	—	Yes	Yes	Yes	Yes	Yes	Yes	Yes	Yes	—	Yes	—

	MT	NE	NV	NH	NJ	NM	NY	NC	ND	OH	OK	OR	PA	RI	SC	SD	TN	TX	UT	VT	VA	WA	WV	WI	WY
Certified school counselors	Yes	No	Yes	No	No	No	No	Yes	Yes	Yes[b]	Yes	Yes	Yes	No	Yes[a]	Yes	No	No	No	No	No	No	Yes[a]	No	Yes[a]
Licensed professional counselors	Yes	Yes	—	—	—	—	—	Yes	—	Yes[b]	Yes	—	—	—	No[b]	—	No[b]	No	No	—	Yes	Yes	—	Yes	—
Marriage and family therapists	—	No	Yes	—	Yes	—	—	Yes	—	—	—	—	—	—	No[b]	—	No[b]	—	Yes	Yes	—	—	Yes	—	—
Psychologists	Yes	No	Yes	Yes	Yes	Yes	Yes	Yes	Yes	Yes	Yes	Yes	Yes	No	Yes	Yes	Yes	Yes	Yes	Yes	Yes	Yes	Yes	No	Yes
Social workers	Yes	—	—	Yes	—	Yes	Yes	No	No	Yes[b]	Yes	Yes	—	No	No	Yes	Yes	Yes	Yes	Yes	—	—	—	Yes	—

Note. A dash (—) indicates state does not regulate as a separate profession.
[a] Privilege limited to student drug and alcohol problems.
[b] Professions regulated under same state act.

Certainly the issue of sexual contact between helper and client has become the most widely discussed ethical question in counseling and psychotherapy. Not only has it been the subject of over fifty articles in popular magazines and professional journals, but a prime-time television movie and several major talk shows have been devoted exclusively to this topic.

Is the issue really so urgent, or is much of the outcry just a result of its titillating value?

The answer is that the question is of great importance. First of all, it is not as uncommon as we might like to expect. The incidence of sexual contact between licensed psychologists and their clients is about 5.5 percent for male psychologists and about .6 percent for female (Nelson, 1982). Some of the most notable psychotherapists had (or *probably* had) sexual contact with patients (Jung, Ferenczi, Fenichel, Sullivan—to name a few). There is no reason to believe the incidence would be any less among the range of unlicensed people in the helping professions.

Just as important as the incidence of sexual contact is the clear consensus in the profession that such contact is almost always harmful to clients. And there is no evidence that it does any good. The position of the American Psychological Association is that it is unequivocally wrong under any circumstances for a therapist to have sexual contact with a patient.

If you were to purchase a new medication to control your dandruff, only to find out afterward that studies have shown its chances of controlling dandruff were less than 50 percent, you would probably feel cheated. Yet clients enter counseling relationships based on new modalities and paradigms when there is little or no empirical support for their efficacy. This does not mean that such a counseling approach is not valid, it simply means that it has to be accepted on a basis other than empirical evidence.

A few of the questions that are often not answered, or even asked, at the beginning of a new counseling endeavor are:

What are the comparable rates of efficacy between this counselor's methods and other counseling methods?

How long should I expect the process to last?

What are some side effects, known as iatrogenic complications, that should be expected?

Have other methods of treatment proved more effective for the kind of problem I am presenting?

Can I be receiving the same treatment for a lower fee or from a practitioner whom my insurance company will reimburse?

There are valid reasons for not answering these questions. After all, counseling is not the kind of endeavor where we can usually expect in advance such specific answers. But perhaps some middle ground, where the prospective client will have an opportunity before entering counseling, to review some theoretical and practical differences among the major approaches, with the goal of being able to make a more informed decision, would be a fair compromise.

Ethical Guidelines   Presently, both the American Association for Counseling and Development and the American Psychological Association have published detailed ethical guidelines for their members (AACD, 1987; APA, 1977). These documents should certainly be consulted by any practitioner in doubt about specific ethical questions. Although over the years, "codes of ethics adopted by professional societies have been a diverse lot [with many] mere competition-limiting devices . . . devoid of benefit to the public" (Wikler, 1981), the APA and AACD guidelines are fair and beneficial to consumers and to the public.

Licensure and Credentialing   The controversy over licensing and certifying professional counselors has emerged during the past fifteen years as one of the most important issues in the counseling profession, and is considered vital to the survival of counseling as a distinct profession. For many years, counseling lacked the official recognition granted to psychology and social work in the form of state licensure; professional certification; various forms of reimbursement and remuneration from insurance carriers, HMOs, and other third-party disbursers; legal rights to privileged communication and expert testimony; and other socially designated signs of professional recognition and status. From the 1950s onward, the psychology profession, through its representative organization, the American Psychological Association (APA) and the counseling profession, through its representative organization (originally American Personnel and Guidance Association, now American Association for Counseling and Development, AACD), have struggled to define the meaning and limits of the terms psychologist, therapist, and counselor. For most of these years, professional counselors lacked any kind of licensing or certification, unless they worked in the school setting where they enjoyed limited recognition and status, as long as they worked on the scene.

Thanks largely to the efforts of the American Association for Counseling and Development's Commission on Counselor Licensure, and vehement lobbying efforts in many state legislatures during the late 1970s and through the 1980s, the situation has begun to change. As of 1986, eighteen states offered professional counselors official recognition, and movements are underway in half a dozen others that would grant counselors specific rights of practice and establish professional standards of expertise. One way of inferring the recognition granted to a helping profession is to examine the laws of privileged communication granted to the profession in those states where the profession enjoys licensure or certification.

Presently, the licensing and certification situation (see Table 2.1 on privileged communication) is as follows (after Herlihy & Sheely, 1987):

Psychologists Regulated in all fifty states. Enjoy privileged communication in all fifty states, "which may indicate that psychologists as a group have clearly established their professional identities" (p. 479).

Social workers Thirty-three states license or certify social workers, and of these, twenty-six states include some provisions for privileged communications, most of which are comparable to those granted psychologists.

Marriage and family therapists "As of 1985, [only] eleven states regulated marriage and family therapy or counseling as a separate and distinct profession. Statutes in only five of these eleven states (45.5 percent) include a privileged communication provision" (p. 480).

School counselors All fifty states regulate (by certification or licensure) the practice of school counselors. Twenty of these states grant some degree of privileged communication, although generally less than that of psychologists.

Licensed professional counselors "The licensed professional counselor movement had been successful in eighteen states by the summer of 1986. Of the state licensure laws, twelve contain privileged communication provisions and six do not" (see Table 2.1).

The trend toward licensing counselors as a separate profession continues through the late 1980s and into the 1990s. Even in states where counselors are not currently licensed, they can be professionally recognized through credentials and certification offered by the National Board for the Certification of Counselors, the Committee on Rehabilitation, or the National Association of Certified Clinical Mental Health Counselors. These certifying boards, created as part of a movement by AACD to regulate its own profession, have high standards and are independent of any state accrediting agencies. Each sets its own criteria against which applicants can be judged by their peers as qualified to practice in their field.

Summary

In this chapter we outlined five basic issues in counseling. We began by setting forth the eleven questions that challenge all contemporary counselors—questions that will be explored throughout this book. Next, we looked at one of the basic assumptions underlying much of the counseling approach: the anti-illness movement. This view suggests that the client should be approached on a human, phenomenological level rather than as a sick person. Moreover, it suggests that the medical model, so useful in understanding physical disorders, can be irrelevant in counseling and therapy.

We considered the need for counseling theories and explored the relationship between a theory and counseling practice. We then considered some of the practical values of these theories, as well as their limitations.

Finally, we examined three professional issues: counselor training; professional organizations and journals; and the question of credentialing. We noted that there is a growing movement underway to make licensure available to the counseling profession and to correct the long-standing inequity between counselors' professional privileges and those of psychologists, who are licensed.

Chapter Aim

To examine the myriad factors, both personal and professional, which contribute to counseling effectiveness or ineffectiveness. To consider how the counselor's value system and world view affect his or her counseling practice.

One of the major problems in attempting to describe the effective counselor is empirically defining the word *effective* and specifying behaviorally the qualities associated with effectiveness. Having overcome semantic obstacles, we will be able to cite some qualities of a counselor that appear to be associated with effective outcomes. These include empathy, positive regard for another, concreteness of expression, genuineness, warmth, nonjudgmental attitude, sensitivity, openness, respect, self-disclosure, cognitive flexibility, security, trust, courage, and communication skills. We will define and discuss each of these.

The Effective Counselor

The counselor's personal problems, conflicts, and deficiencies may interfere with his or her counseling practice. We begin with the assumption that "counseling is only as effective as the therapist is living effectively," and consider the range of personal problems that may trouble the counselor. Attention is directed toward the problems of meaninglessness, alienation, and the psychological loss of freedom.

The Counselor as a Person

We will discuss five categories of values that influence the way the counselor looks at the world: cognitive values, personal preference values, moral values, self values, and cultural values. The category of cultural values combines elements of the other four into a coherent world view. We then look at the way in which the counselor's world view influences counseling. Two psychological dimensions—locus of control and locus of responsibility—are used to illustrate the interaction between counselors and clients who differ in their world views.

The Counselor's Values

The World of the Counselor

3

In this chapter, we will consider some of the personal and professional qualities that contribute to counselor effectiveness or ineffectiveness, or to both. What do we mean by "personal" and "professional" qualities? Certainly the two are intertwined in practice, so that it is virtually impossible to look at the counselor-as-a-person without considering the counselor's professional life, and vice versa.

While the unity of the counselor's experience is acknowledged at the outset, we maintain that the counselor's existence integrates elements of his or her past with elements of training, that the counselor's life is an expression of what is learned, felt, believed, and what is an essential part of the counselor's personality. Through their work, counselors try to manifest those aspects of themselves that will be most helpful to their clients.

Often working against counselors' efforts are ingrained features of themselves which are not facilitative, for example, unresolved conflicts which trouble them before, during, and after working hours. Although counseling research focuses on the qualities of effectiveness, experience indicates to us that counselors themselves are individuals with their own idiosyncracies.

Our study of the counselor as a total person will be divided into three parts. First, we will focus on general counselor qualities associated with effective counseling outcomes. The empirical problems of identifying these qualities and of defining them operationally, will be considered briefly. We will also ask how each quality contributes specifically to effective counseling interactions. In the second part of the chapter, we will examine the counselor's personal world to observe how some typical counselor problems can interfere with the constructive course of counseling. Finally, we will undertake a candid evaluation of how the counselor's cultural values, including biases, prejudices, the counselor's world view in general, can affect counseling interactions and outcomes. Specifically, we will consider how differences between the counselor's and client's world views can lead to misunderstandings in communication. We should keep in mind throughout our discussion that the counselor's professional qualities are always colored by personal values and perceptions.

The Effective Counselor

Probably no question has received more attention in counseling theory and research than the question, What qualities are indicative of the *potential* and *actual* effectiveness of the counselor? The attention this question has received is justified for several reasons: first, it helps us better understand the nexus of subtle factors which contribute to counseling success; second, it is important to counselor educators who must make crucial decisions in the selection and training of students of counseling; third, it encourages aspiring counselors to find within themselves and strengthen those qualities which have been indicated as predictors of successful counseling; fourth, it helps in developing techniques and strategies which are derivatives of effective counselor qualities; and finally, it assists trainers and researchers in determining the probable outcome of specific counseling interactions, based on tested criteria of counseling effectiveness.

Unfortunately, despite the abundance of research and exposition (or perhaps because of it), this critical question is still surrounded by much confusion, contention, and obscurity, and it is not entirely clear at this point exactly what qualities make one counselor more effective than another. We will examine the semantic problems which make this research difficult and the findings of some contemporary research on this subject, then summarize the consensus of thinking to date.

Language Problems: A Source of Confusion

One of the major obstacles in responding to the question, "What makes a counselor effective?" is the language problem. When we attempt to describe an effective counselor, or more precisely, when we attempt to enumerate those qualities we believe make the counselor effective, we are forced to rely on multidimensional words to condense and epitomize the multifaceted behavioral and emotional matrices we wish to describe. Words such as *genuine, sincere, nonpossessive, honest, warm, empathic, accepting,* are the closest we can come to pinpointing the very human, idiosyncratic, and complex qualities which contribute to counseling success.

But words inevitably fail to define effective counseling, and more importantly, to differentiate effective from ineffective counseling traits. There are too many words with broad, general meanings and not enough specific, descriptive significance to prove of much help in answering our questions. Before we can confidently approach the question of what qualities make an effective counselor, we must confront this problem of language and decide at the outset what we are going to do to make words work for us.

Our problem can be stated simply as follows: if we call X the quality associated with effective counseling, what can we do to determine whether a counselor demonstrates this quality? The question is not easily answered. Let us say X is empathy, and we want to determine if counselor A has empathy for the client. We could, of course, administer an empathy-rating scale and look at the score. But what does this actually tell us? Certainly we would not want to define empathy solely as such-and-such a score on the test. And what is empathy? Can we formulate an objective definition of empathy that will separate empathic counselors from nonempathic counselors? This has been a refractory problem which

Counseling: The Art and Science of Helping

has plagued not only research in empathy but almost all studies on the qualities essential for counseling effectiveness (Barkhaim & Shapiro, 1986).

Another word that gives us trouble is *effective*. We must be able to define accurately and objectively what we intuitively mean by *effective counseling* in order for us to evaluate seriously the component qualities. The term sounds good, but what does it actually mean? Do we mean that counseling effects a change in the client? Do we mean *counseling efficiency,* the ability to accomplish a wide range of objectives over a brief period of time? Do we evaluate effectiveness by the client's impressions and feelings about the treatment, or do we allow the counselor to be the primary judge of its success or failure? Possibly we determine effectiveness by the degree of mitigation of the so-called "presenting symptoms" or "behavioral problems." This issue is far from resolved; during the past few years there has appeared a growing sentiment, matched by a more persistent effort, among counselor educators and researchers to define the term *effectiveness* more accurately and precisely.

A second problem that confronts us at the start of our discussion is what we call the "commonsense bias." This bias implies that some positions are ipso facto logical and sensible; for when we speak of common sense, we assume that some things are obvious even before logical scrutiny, that they are irrefutable or at least presumed to be true until proven otherwise. In reality, however, common sense is always a culturally relative term. What may be common sense to a middle-class counselor may be nonsense or wrong to a person from a different culture (see chapter 18 for a discussion of cultural differences in the counseling setting).

Commonsense is a term that is in fact weak, yet it implies a strong sense of verification. The commonsense bias includes value judgments, culturally-based perceptions, and intuitive beliefs. To humanistic counselors, for example, there is a commonsense position that acceptance, warmth, empathy, and genuineness are positive counseling characteristics. This may or may not be true; there is evidence to support both the affirmative and negative positions, but in any case, it would be best not to prejudge any specific quality or set of qualities until the evidence is assembled and evaluated. The only way to avoid the commonsense bias is to assume that nothing is true until it is proved to be true.

Finally, we face what we call the problem of *generalization.* Is there in fact such a thing as an effective counselor, or are different counselors effective for different reasons to different degrees with different clients? There is evidence to support both positions. While some studies have shown that there are universally important counselor qualities, other studies have indicated that certain traits work well with some clients but not with others. We shall keep in mind, as we explore the literature, that to generalize from a single study to a universal proposition is often an unsound policy.

The Commonsense Bias

The Problem of Generalization

Conclusions   Despite these persistent problems, a good deal has been learned about qualities which contribute to effective counseling outcomes. Certainly we can offer some valid generalizations that would probably meet with hearty agreement by those in the profession and would also endure experimental scrutiny. We know, for example, that the counselor's personal traits play a vital part in the counseling interaction and are determinants of counseling effectiveness. We know, too, that there is no positive correlation between counseling knowledge and counseling effectiveness, and that a counselor's personal self-awareness and personality characteristics are generally more essential than specific skills or techniques (Jevne, 1981). But what does all of this tell us? How can we translate these statements into behavioral equivalents? Again, we are left without a clear answer to our questions.

In this chapter we shall examine some empirical research as well as theoretical models which attempt to clarify the question "What qualities are related to successful counseling outcomes?" As we consider this research we should keep in mind the problems outlined above, but at the same time recognize the importance of considering this question and all of its ramifications. We shall see that although the evidence is not conclusive and is at times confusing, there is enough information to indicate which qualities are most probably related to effective counseling. We shall now turn our attention to the research findings, after which we will synthesize them in the form of statements and attitudes, indicating some general qualities which have been found to indicate effective counseling.

What Makes Counseling Effective: An Overview   Predictably, many of the qualities which we intuitively associate with effective counseling have been identified and borne out in the experimental studies. The value of these studies is that they confirm empirically what our philosophical premises imply are the qualities of an effective counselor. It would seem evident, for example, that an effective counselor would be more emotionally aware, more sensitive, more introspective, and more tolerant of others than an ineffective counselor would be. In an empirical study which compared effective and ineffective counselors, Tinsley and Tinsley (1977), among others, have indeed confirmed these as essential characteristics. We would also assume that the counselor's attitudes exert a crucial influence on his ability to deal effectively with his clients; this has been consistently borne out in the literature.

Many studies have measured and quantified the levels of empathy, genuineness, and respect in the counselor, by using popular rating scales such as the Carkhuff Scales or Hill's Counselor Verbal Response Category System; and there is a general consensus that effective counselors rate higher in these qualities than do ineffective counselors. In one interesting study, Edwards, Boulet, Mahrer, Chagnon, and Mook (1982) analyzed two counseling interviews conducted by Carl Rogers to see how well he provided facilitative conditions, as espoused by his theory, especially during the initial interview. They found that "Rogers manifested moderate levels of empathy, respect, and genuineness throughout both interviews and that his behavior as counselor . . . was stable and consistent across interviews."

While one might expect Rogers exhibited extremely high levels of these three qualities, apparently the counselor's personality and the immediacy of the situation itself affected the level. The authors propose "that Rogers's moderate level may [have been] typical of his approach to counseling. His stability and consistency [were] considered to be in keeping with his theoretical approach to counseling."

The research on counseling effectiveness, we must point out, has not been entirely consistent. Rowe, Murphy, and DeCsipkes (1975), in a thorough review and evaluation of the empirical evidence, found that it was virtually impossible to establish significant relationships between specific counselor characteristics and measures of counselor effectiveness. Continuing the work of the earlier study, Loesch, Crane, and Rucker (1978), confirmed these conclusions. This is why many of the important findings in this area are not considered measures of counselor qualities and counseling outcomes per se, but rather more indirect indices.

One area in which there have been some notable surprises has been that of responses to the question, How well can individuals who are not professional counselors competently perform, after brief training, effective counseling interventions? This is a key question, because it tells us how important personal qualities, as opposed to theory, are in the counseling setting.

In one of the first significant studies in this area, Truax and Lister (1970), in attempting to assess how paraprofessionals should be assigned, set up three conditions for the treatment of cases, which ranged from personality disorders to mental retardation. In the first condition, the experienced counselor worked alone with the patient in the traditional manner; in the second condition, the counselor was assisted by a counselor aide who worked with him under maximum supervisory conditions; in the third condition, the counselor aide functioned autonomously as a counselor, with the experienced counselor present only in a supervisory role. All clients were randomly assigned, in order to assure that each condition included clients with problems of varying degrees of severity. Progress was evaluated by the use of a rating scale which measured the evidence of the rehabilitation in his work endeavors.

When the results were tabulated and analyzed, a most interesting anomaly emerged. To their surprise, the experimenters found that the clients who made the greatest improvement were those who were treated by the untrained counselor aides alone; next in order of improvement were the clients treated by the experienced counselor alone; lowest in improvement were those treated jointly by the experienced counselor and the untrained aide.

To explain these results and their conclusion "that the effectiveness of counseling and psychotherapy, as measured by constructive change in client functioning, is largely independent of the counselor's level of training and theoretical orientation," they suggested that the untrained aides fared better because they were "innately more health engendering than the professional counselors." While they do not fully explicate what is meant by "health engendering," they refer to such counselor qualities as "empathic understanding, nonpossessive warmth, and genuineness." The important point here is that *counselor knowledge and counselor training had no positive effect on counseling outcome*. On the contrary, it seemed to minimize the effects of the counseling. Rather, what did emerge as essential was the attitude and feelings of the practitioner.

Other studies since this early investigation have confirmed, in several different ways, a conclusion that if brief training is provided to individuals whose personalities make them suitable as counselors, they can perform effectively. Messer and Boals (1981), for example, found in working with psychology students trained to work in a university clinic "that the student-conducted therapy was successful and provided a genuine service to the community." They go on to point out that "the positive results are attributed to the careful supervision of each case, the enthusiasm of novice therapists, and the nature of the client sample," variables which parallel those in the earlier Truax and Lister study.

An article which makes this point in an even more dramatic way, tells how college bartenders, who are seen as serving a "gatekeeper role" between mental health professionals and persons in need of help, were trained in a one-day workshop to develop basic counseling skills to help their bar patrons with problem-solving of difficult situations, and with referrals (Bernard, Roach & Resnick, 1981).

One of the most influential contributors to the literature on counselor qualities and effectiveness is Robert Carkhuff, who, with his collaborators, Bernard Berenson and Charles Truax, has published extensively in this area. Truax and Carkhuff (1967) have found a common thread which runs through the divergent theories of counseling and psychotherapy:

> In one way or another, all have emphasized the importance of the therapist's ability to be integrated, mature, genuine, authentic, or congruent in his relationship with the patient. They have all stressed also the importance of the therapist's ability to provide a nonthreatening, trusting, safe or secure atmosphere by his acceptance, nonpossessive warmth, unconditional positive regard, or love. Finally, virtually all theories of psychotherapy emphasize that for the therapist to be helpful he must be accurately empathetic, be 'with' the client, be understanding, or grasp the patient's meaning. (p. 25)

As the research undertaken by Carkhuff and his associates progressed, new dimensions were discovered and counselor rating scales for these additional qualities were developed. The core conditions currently associated with Carkhuff's work are: empathy, respect, warmth, genuineness, self-disclosure, concreteness, confrontation, and an immediacy of relationship.

A related question, one which goes beyond the issue of counselor qualities, is How effective are counseling and psychotherapy in helping individuals resolve their problems and demonstrate growth or better adaption? In the early 1950s, psychologist Hans Eysenck published the first comprehensive and critical study of the efficacy of counseling and psychotherapy. He outlined what would become the concerns for most future studies, and suggested methods for scientifically (as opposed to anecdotally) evaluating therapeutic effectiveness. Although he found little or no effectiveness in psychoanalytic therapy, Eysenck's paper opened up the channels of communication among researchers and made many of the later studies possible.

Almost forty years later, we are still not certain which therapies work best and why, but we have made long strides in demonstrating that for many disorders, counseling, psychotherapy, or behavioral methods do yield measurable positive benefits. For example, Smith, Glass, and Miller (1980), reviewing many of the therapy outcome studies of the past three decades, found that individuals treated with counseling psychotherapy, even briefly, appear to progress significantly better than individuals in control groups who do not receive treatment.

In 1984, Sol Garfield, a prominent researcher in this field, published a paper which reviews, criticizes, and puts together much of the research findings over the past three decades. In it he shows how the sophistication of the more recent studies has yielded some positive findings, especially for behavioral approaches which treat specific symptoms.

While Garfield is largely concerned with methodological problems, he points out in summing up the state of counseling research today: "With the increase in research and research sophistication, we now have some reasonable basis for making tentative appraisals of the effectiveness of psychotherapy or of those psychotherapies that have been evaluated. However, we should not be expected to offer final answers." (Garfield, 1984, p. 42)

One of the most perceptive researchers in this area was Carl Rogers, a man whose persistence and tenacity earned him a well-deserved following and the respect of even his harshest critics. For the past thirty years, Rogers had doggedly attempted to evaluate, in a precise, empirical manner, the qualities of an effective counselor, what he called the "conditions of therapy." His well-known terminology includes *empathy, genuineness,* and *unconditional positive regard* as key words. In a massive research effort, Rogers and his colleagues (Rogers et al., 1967) attempted to test thoroughly his assumption that,

> regardless of what method or technique the therapist uses . . . effective therapy would take place if the therapist fulfilled the following three "conditions"; *a.*) The therapist responds as the real person he actually is in this relationship at the moment. He employs no artificial front . . . *b.*) The therapist senses and expresses the client's felt meaning, catching what the client communicates as it seems to the client. This condition was termed "empathy." *c.*) The therapist experiences a warm and positive acceptance toward the client. (p. 10)

In other words, Rogers was attempting to test out the hypothesis that effective counselor personality factors, what he referred to as "the conditions for therapy," outweighed all other considerations in contributing to therapeutic efficacy in the counseling process. With such findings, we would be able not only

Carl Rogers's
Contribution

to see which qualities are useful but also to understand in what specific way each quality contributes to the client's improvement. Rogers's study sought to resolve this very complex issue once and for all, and in many ways it has succeeded in its goal. Unfortunately, there were several serious problems which limited its application, and these problems should be presented first.

First, the subjects in his study were divided between institutionalized "schizophrenics" and "normals" who were recruited from various community and social organizations. The experiment, therefore, involved a rather specialized population, atypical of those who seek the help of a counselor. Second, as in all studies of therapeutic efficacy, there are many serious questions regarding the validity of the experiment in relation to what it attempts to measure. Finally, despite all of Rogers's positive results, he was compelled by the evidence to conclude that "in many respects the therapy group taken as a whole showed no greater evidence of positive outcome than did the matched and paired control group" (p. 80).

These considerations aside, however, Rogers's research shed light on what qualities are important to the counselor. The crux of his findings is summarized in the following excerpt:

> In spite of the subtlety of the variables being measured, in spite of the crudity of the instruments used in measuring them, there appears to be substantial evidence that *relationships rated high in a sensitively accurate empathic understanding and high in genuineness as perceived by the patient, were associated with favorable personality changes and reductions in various forms of pathology,* particularly in schizophrenic pathology. (p. 86, italics added)

It is clear from these findings that qualities of the counselor, such as empathy, genuineness, and positive regard, play an important role in counseling, but it is still unclear how these qualities work toward attaining whatever we determine to be the "goal" in the treatment.

The question then reduces itself to this: What is it about a person—counselor or otherwise—that contributes to his or her ability to help others, to relate meaningfully with others, to add to the lives of fellow human beings? To approach this very difficult question, we have divided the traditional counselor qualities into three major headings: *knowing oneself, understanding others*, and *relating to others;* we shall look at each of these broad categories to study the relationship among the specific qualities subsumed under each.

Knowing Oneself

Before a counselor can attempt to understand a client, before the counselor is able to reach out and touch another, she or he must have an objective and satisfying understanding of self. Counselors must be able to recognize and accept strengths and limitations, to understand in which areas success is likely to be found and which area is more open to failure. To help the counselor better understand ways of assessing himself or herself with respect to counseling effectiveness, we have listed the three personality characteristics most essential to effective counseling: security, trust, and courage.

The prerequisites to security are self-confidence and self-respect. The types of feeling that these create within individuals are inevitably communicated to all with whom they come in contact. The secure counselor must be free from fear and anxiety, must maintain an objective and flexible view of self. Milliken and Kirchner (1971) found that "the more anxious counselors were less accurate in their ability to recall words spoken and feelings expressed in simulated interviews" (p. 14). Anxiety can only be reduced when one feels good about oneself, when one likes oneself and recognizes the irrational nature of anxiety.

Insecure counselors tend to act more defensively with their clients than do secure counselors. They fear the client's anger and rejection and consequently attempt more to *please* than to *help* the client. Insecure counselors may also take advantage of their clients, manipulating a client into meeting the unhealthy needs of the counselor. Secure counselors, on the other hand, know their own ground and feel comfortable standing on it; they are unshakable and strong, a healthy model for the client.

Security, as a personal quality, also provides counselors with a strategic advantage in the performance of their duties. If counselors know who they are and are comfortable with the knowledge, they are then more likely to allow clients to be themselves. Secure counselors have no need to shape clients in their own images; they are confident enough to allow clients to develop at their own rates and in their own directions.

Trust is a basic quality which develops during the early stages of life. To be able to trust another, in its simplest form, is to be able to give to another, to receive from another, and to depend upon another. To be able to trust and to be trustworthy are different sides of the same coin; people who experience difficulty trusting others are usually themselves untrustworthy.

The counselor who is suspicious, who questions every person's motives, whose cynicism colors all interactions is unlikely to relate to clients in a manner that contributes to growth and adjustment. All too often untrusting counselors attribute feelings and ideas to clients, not because the client has expressed them, but rather because the counselor considers such ideas and feelings common to all people. The distrustful counselor might say, for example, "I am certain that this client doesn't pay the slightest bit of attention to what I say." When asked the reason for feeling this way, it turns out that she or he believes most people do not listen to others, do not trust others.

Trust, unfortunately, is a quality which is difficult to learn. So deeply rooted is it in the personality that the quality of trust must be considered one of the foundations of all subsequent personality development. Counselors who are not trusting would do best to seek for themselves counseling to resolve the problems in this area of their emotional development.

The Courage to Counsel

Counseling demands a special kind of courage. While each of us wants to be liked, to be admired, to be respected, to be loved, counselors must at times put aside many of their own feelings; they must remain ungratified in order for clients to prosper and grow. The committed counselor must be willing to bear the often unjustified brunt of the client's anger, an anger which, although self-inspired, inevitably becomes directed toward the counselor during the course of the treatment. The counselor must be willing to feel a profound and distressing sense of "aloneness" as the client, progressing during the treatment, grows away, becomes autonomous.

The courage required of counselors is much like the courage required of parents. In both cases, stronger persons, powerful forces in another's life, must be emotionally capable of relinquishing their strength and allowing the other to become stronger. The courageous counselor finds that he or she has enough self-confidence, enough self-belief, enough security in his or her job and person, so as not to retreat in the face of adversity, not to waver in the heat of anger.

The true courage of the counselor is found in a willingness to relinquish a part of self without recompense, knowing that inner sources will always bring strength. Counselors are courageous insofar as they are able to confront the challenges before them bravely, with dedication and hope.

Understanding Others

Open-Mindedness

Open-mindedness in the counseling setting may be defined as freedom from fixed preconceptions and an attitude of open receptivity to that which the client is expressing. The open-minded counselor is able to accommodate the client's values, insights, feelings and perceptions that are different from his or her own. Moreover, he or she is able to experience and interact with the client throughout a wide breadth and range of feelings, since a flexible frame of reference does not find itself restricted by preconceived expectations. Open-mindedness, in the sense of accommodation and receptivity combined, produces the second essential quality of the effective counselor: *perceptiveness*.

Open-mindedness also implies the ability to listen, to respond, to interact with the client, free from the constraints of imposing value criteria. Anderson, Lepper, and Ross (1980) found, moreover, that if one is not open-minded, that person will persist in believing incorrect things about a client, even in the face of countervailing evidence. Thus, open-mindedness is necessary for honest communication.

Counseling: The Art and Science of Helping

The open-minded counselor is also *non-judgmental*. This does not mean that he or she has no personal values, or is anomic or amoral; on the contrary, the effective counselor should have a well developed and meaningful sense of values with which he or she feels satisfied. The quality of being non-judgmental "means that the counselor (refrains) from judging the guilt or innocence of the *client;* it does not mean that the counselor may not objectively judge the *attitudes, standards or actions* of the client. The client is hurt when *he* is judged; he is not necessarily hurt if his behavior is evaluated" (Biestek, 1953). As Sue (1979) conceptualizes it in terms of a level of counselor functioning within the total context of the counseling interaction,

> There are three levels of human behavior interaction. First, there is a level of observation (*descriptive*) where a person describes behaviors. For example, a counselor who sees a client avoid eye contact can describe it behaviorally and even quantify it. The second level is an *interpretive* one in which the counselor attempts to add meaning to what he or she observes. For example, the counselor can assume that avoidance of eye contact is due to shyness, unassertiveness, or sneakiness. Motivation is imputed on to the behavior. The third level which is most damaging, is that of *evaluation/judging*. A judgmental act is one where the avoidance of eye contact and whatever motives it implies are presented as bad. It is the imputing of "badness" or "goodness" [to behaviors] which is damaging and tends to cause inability to establish rapport.

The non-judgmental counselor is able to participate effectively in a counseling interaction, in a relationship of therapeutic benefit, in which the client holds a differing set of values, and to accept the client as he or she is, for what he or she is. Acceptance, according to Blocher (1966), means simply, "a belief in the worth of the client," and this belief can only become operative when the counselor is open-minded enough to accept the client without restrictive value judgments.

The importance of openness in the counseling setting, and its manifestation as a counselor personality characteristic, has been discussed by Combs (1976), who makes the point that the secure counselor, through his or her personal openness, helps the client improve in different areas of growth:

> Openness . . . is a function of an attitude, which regards the confrontation of life as not only possible but even enjoyable and rewarding. We have talked much in the theory of counseling about the importance of the counselor's remaining unshockable and demonstrating for his client his own willingness to look at events without fear or hesitation. Mostly we have sought these goals because it made it more possible for the client to look at his problems. But the counselor's demonstration of openness to experience is much more than a technique for the facilitation of talking. It is a most important teaching technique which provides the client with an experience which may add considerably to his strength and stature. (pp. 48–49)

Sensitivity is a prime factor in contributing to counselor effectiveness. While open-mindedness makes possible a comprehensive and accurate view of the client, sensitivity, a cognitive as well as an emotional response to the client as a total individual, makes possible a deeper and more spontaneous response to needs, feelings, conflicts, doubts, and so on. Open-mindedness makes possible what sensitivity actually accomplishes.

It is essential to understand that during the course of a typical counseling interview, the client is continually in a state of flux and change. As a living, responsive organism, the client is reacting at any given moment to the stimulation of the interview, whether that stimulation is in the form of verbal response from the counselor, the counselor's expressions and movements (body language), or internal, reflective thinking going on in the client's own personal, subjective world. Both internal processes (thoughts and associations) and external stimuli (interpersonal responses and cues) affect profoundly the quality and substance of the interaction between the counselor and client. Fortunately, the client does indicate to the counselor, however subtly, that these changes and responses are occurring, by words, body language, and total behavioral pattern, as well as by gestures and by nuances of language. The sensitive counselor is one who is able to discern these miniscule, but nevertheless significant, responses on the part of the client and to assimilate these changes into his or her own perspectives and understanding of the client.

The question arises, How does sensitivity differ from perceptiveness? The distinction between the terms *sensitivity* and *perceptiveness* is small but significant. Whereas perceptiveness is the ability to see and understand the client, sensitivity implies a deeper response on the part of the counselor, an emotional response, an ability to get into the client's skin and feel along with that person. This particular manifestation of sensitivity is usually referred to as *empathy* or *empathic understanding*. Rogers (1975) said of empathy:

> To sense the client's private world as if it were your own, but without ever losing the "as if" quality—this is empathy, and this seems essential to [counseling.] To sense the client's anger, fear, or confusion *as if it were your own,* yet without your anger, fear, or confusion getting bound up in it, is the condition we are endeavoring to describe. When the client's world is this clear to the therapist, and he moves about in it freely, then he can communicate his understanding of what is clearly known to the client and can also voice meanings in the client's experience of which the client is scarcely aware. (p. 77)

Two conditions are critical in this definition: the counselor must be able to experience the client's feelings as the client is experiencing them, in the same way, with the same degree of affect and personal meaning. The counselor must, therefore, put himself or herself emotionally and intellectually in the client's place, *be the client momentarily,* think and feel as the client does. Second, and of equal importance, the counselor must also be able to maintain an individual identity and remain sensitively aware of the differences between himself or herself and the client. This is what Rogers referred to as the "as if" condition, and it is an essential qualifier of empathic understanding. Empathy is a temporary bridge, joining the purposes, perceptions, and feelings of the counselor and client, establishing a unity between them as they face each other during the counseling session; but empathy is not a permanent merging of the two into a single feeling of perception.

Empathy has been hailed as one of the most important, if not *the* most important, of the qualities in the counseling relationship. It must be pointed out, however, that while "there appears to be evidence . . . that therapists agree upon the importance of empathy and understanding" (Patterson, 1973, p. 396), there is, unfortunately, somewhat less evidence to support the idea that empathy is necessarily related to successful outcomes in counseling and psychotherapy. In fact, the bulk of research over the years has not unequivocally supported this assumption, but has instead had the effect of changing the definition of empathy from "an internal state to an external process"—that is, from an inner feeling to an outward expression of that feeling (Hackney, 1978, p. 37).

What this means, in effect, is that counselors and clients don't always agree on perceived levels of empathy, indicating a discrepancy between what is experienced *inside* and what is perceived *outside.* This was confirmed in a study by Barkhaim and Shapiro (1986) who investigated how empathy is experienced and perceived by the counselor and the client at different stages during the counseling process. They wanted to determine if the counselor's feelings inside—his or her empathic response to the client—were sensed by the client in a manner consistent with the way the counselor was experiencing them. They found that these feelings are not always perceived in a mutually consistent way, that counselors and clients did not always rate empathy reliably.

For example, most counselors felt they had a high level of empathy during the initial sessions as they first got to know their clients. But clients did not experience this, and only began to feel their counselors empathic as the sessions progressed. Counseling style also affected how the counselor felt about herself or himself as an empathic person and how the client rated the counselor in terms of empathy. Clients, as a general rule, rated counselors who gave little advice and did a lot of listening as empathic. What this seems to indicate is that although most of us in the profession think of empathy as very important, we are not always very clear about when we are demonstrating it or how the client perceives us.

This is certainly not to discredit the importance of empathy as a *subjective* counselor quality, nor are we trying to refute the idea that empathy is a significant factor in counseling. Rather, we are trying to suggest that at the present time it is uncertain just *how* empathy contributes to counseling and to what degree empathy influences the counseling outcome.

One fact should be pointed out, since it is sometimes a source of confusion to the beginning counselor: empathy is *not* the same as sympathy; it is not a passive feeling of commiserative rapport. Rather, empathic understanding involves the counselor's ability to intellectually and emotionally "grasp" the world of the client, and to communicate that "grasping" to the client. Empathy is an *active* process. Holdstock and Rogers (1977) highlight this important point:

> Empathy is not sympathy. A person who is sympathetic negates himself and by an osmotic process is both absorbed and absorbing. With empathy there is an inner strength which can alienate the giver from the receiver, unless the person being confronted is prepared to stifle initial emotion and "feel" only after chewing the feedback, swallowing it, and then deciding whether to regulate it or not. Thus an intellectualizing process must be put into motion. (p. 139)

Objectivity

To remain objective, in the counseling sense, means to be able to stand back and observe what is happening from a neutral, or nonimposing, frame of reference. In one respect, objectivity seems to imply the very opposite of empathy: when one is objective, one is not involved to an extraordinary degree with another. However, in our discussion of empathy we can see objectivity as the extension of the "as if" quality to the intellectual realm of experience. In another sense, objectivity seems to be very much in accord with our definition of empathy. Insofar as objectivity implies the ability to see a thing as "it is," not distorted by preconceptions, biases, and expectations, it fits into the general category of empathy.

Relating to Others

In the preceding section we discussed the qualities which help the counselor better understand the client. In this section we shall examine those qualities that help the counselor relate and communicate more effectively with the client. Obviously, before a counselor can relate and respond to the client, he or she has to be able to understand the client; this is why all the qualities previously discussed may be looked at as prerequisites for relating to others.

Genuineness

An extremely difficult concept to define, genuineness overlaps in meaning and in implication with such terms as honesty, sincerity, veracity, and candor. Rogers (1957a) said of genuineness:

> It means that within the relationship he is freely and deeply himself, with his actual experience accurately represented by his awareness of himself. It is the opposite of presenting a facade either knowingly or unknowingly. . . . It is not necessary (nor is it possible) that the therapist be a paragon who exhibits this degree of integration, of wholeness, in every aspect

of his life. It is sufficient that he is accurately himself in this hour of this relationship, that in this basic sense he is what he actually is, in this moment of time. (p. 75)

Genuineness in its most basic sense, then, is *acting without using a facade,* functioning openly without hiding behind the veneer of one's role or one's professional status.

To appreciate fully the idea of genuineness, we must be sensitive to the many roles we are expected to play during the course of our daily lives. A role is a social mask—a *persona*—which we wear in the presence of others in order to define and reinforce a situation by establishing clear limits of participation of each character. A counselor wearing a mask is saying in effect to the client, "I am the counselor and you are the client—don't you forget it!" The client, caught in the social strata implied in the counseling situation, agrees to recognize the "superior" role of the counselor and to respond to the counselor as he plays that role. Erving Goffman (1959) describes this process as one of "team cooperation," in which both members of the social team (counselor and client) "cooperate to maintain a given definition of the situation" (p. 238). Such a situation, although common on one level, is directly in conflict with the idea of genuineness we are attempting to put forth. For when a genuine quality of the relationship emerges, the dependence on this type of artifice should diminish. The genuine counselor, in other words, minimizes dependence upon roles and increases giving of self to the client. The genuine counselor is open, honest, and at all times himself or herself.

Such honesty, to oneself and to others, is a remarkable accomplishment in light of the multifaceted role activities through which counselors and clients interact. To help clarify this complex interaction, sociologists (called transactionists) and cognitive psychologists have studied the ways in which we can change our behaviors in different kinds of role situations. Defining a role as a set of behavioral expectations associated with a social position, we note that a minister is expected to behave differently than a hockey player, a counselor differently than a policeman, just as the role of parent is associated with certain behaviors while the role of adolescent is associated with other patterns of conduct. Since each of us holds at the same time several different social positions, we enact different roles simultaneously, each one relevant to one position or another.

This raises questions about how "true to ourself" we really are, how genuine we can actually be, considering that in many or all of our social interactions we are playing a role. How much of this *role-enactment,* as it is called, is our "real" self, we may ask, and how much is for the benefit of others? How do we manage our multiple roles and what effect does it have on our overall adjustment and sense of self?

This idea that our social and occupational roles reveal many different selves has been expanded and developed by Snyder (1980), who points out that quite an array of "selves" emerge in different relationships with people. There may be a dramatic difference, in fact, between one's public self and one's private self, the front and back regions, and even beyond that, between the different private selves we reveal in different situations.

Some people, he goes on to point out, are more concerned with the ways they express themselves through roles than are other people. Such people are able to "monitor" their public self to the extent that they reveal only what they wish to reveal. He calls this control people have over the impressions they make on others, *impression management*.

Snyder (1980) has studied the social and psychological differences between what he calls "high self-monitoring individuals" and "low self-monitoring individuals." HSMs "have developed the ability to monitor carefully their own performances and to skillfully adjust their performances when signals from others tell them they are not having the desired effect" (p. 33). LSMs, on the other hand, "are not so concerned about taking in such information; instead, they tend to express what they feel, rather than model and tailor their behavior to fit the situation" (p. 33). Snyder's research has revealed several salient facts about HSMs.

"High self-monitoring individuals," those who manage their impressions very well, have several notable characteristics. HSMs are outgoing, usually talkative individuals, able to guide conversations to subjects in which they are interested. They tend to direct their social relationships, and to hold the interest of the other person. They are also able to adapt to different social situations, playing a part comfortably in each relationship, and making the other person feel that the HSM is "just like me." They also exhibit good control over their behavior and their emotional expression, and have the ability to express to others at will a wide range of body language and verbal responses. They also exert much effort in trying to figure out others, and are sensitive to what other people are expressing. This is not to imply, he goes on, that they are manipulative; on the contrary, most HSMs have smooth and satisfying social relationships.

This raises some provocative questions in regard to the quality of genuineness. Is the LSM more genuine than the HSM because he or she is not so astute in manipulating a public self? Also, on a broader plane, is genuineness at all possible, since we have so many public selves and roles to monitor?

Nondominance

The nondominant counselor is one who is capable of sitting back and allowing the client to initiate and direct the course of the counseling interview. This may appear synonymous with nondirective counseling; but even in such directive schools as psychoanalysis, dominance is minimized because of the recognition that it is the client, not the counselor, who knows best how to pace the session, what ground to cover, and the like.

Acting in a nondominant manner is often no easy task for the counselor. There is a great temptation to jump up and help the client, to bail him or her out at difficult times, to help when an easy solution to a problem appears in the counselor's perspective. Moreover, remaining nondominant may produce tension and anxiety in the counselor, since he or she has no immediate outlet for the expressions of feelings. But the counselor often helps the client more by listening than by speaking, and listening is possible only if the counselor controls any dominating tendencies. In fact, we might say that in its manifest sense, nondominance appears as the *ability to listen.*

Nondominance as a counselor characteristic should not be confused with dominance as a personality trait. The latter is generally desirable. In fact, "self-confidence, self-esteem, and related dominance variables have been found to be important counselor characteristics" (Ostrand & Creaser, 1978, p. 199). But even the dominant personality has to learn to exhibit nondominance at appropriate times.

Listening is an art unto itself. On one level, we all know how to listen, or at least how to hear. On another level, listening is related to open-mindedness and sensitivity. On still another level, listening is empathizing, moving along with clients as they express their feelings. But at its most basic level, listening is just that: sitting back, paying attention, not interrupting, and not attempting to direct what clients are saying. In this last sense, this very basic sense, listening is related to nondominance.

Although Rogers originally used the term *unconditional positive regard,* the elimination of the first word *unconditional* strengthens the concept and makes it less open to controversy. Rogers himself had been much criticized for the use of the absolute term *unconditional,* since it is probably impossible not to be influenced by certain conditions in our own dealing with others, particularly such an important *other* as the client.

Positive regard is based on the assumption "that growth and change are more likely to occur the more that the counselor is experiencing a warm, positive, acceptant attitude toward what *is* the client" (Rogers, 1962). In explaining the concept, Rogers said,

> It means that he prizes his client, as a person, with somewhat the same quality of feeling that a parent feels for his child, prizing him as a person regardless of his particular behavior at the moment. It means that he cares for his client in a non-possessive way, as a person with potentialities. It involves an open willingness for the client to be whatever feelings are real in him at the moment—hostility or tenderness, rebellion or submissiveness. . . . It means a kind of love for the client as he is. (p. 420)

It is important to note that positive regard is never a pretense or a technique but rather a genuine and sincere feeling of affection for clients, as they are, as they express themselves, with their own feelings, values, and beliefs. Positive regard, even if it is only felt and not communicated intentionally by the counselor,

Listening

Positive Regard

is nevertheless transmitted to the client by the counselor in unspoken communications. Positive regard is an attitude, a health-engendering attitude that inevitably makes the client feel more secure, more worthwhile as a person, more willing to grow and prosper. The manifestations of positive regard, as they appear in the counseling setting, are *acceptance* and *warmth*.

We note, too, that in the case of positive regard, as in the case of sensitivity and nondominance, the counselor's attitude plays a crucial role in communicating to the client the appropriate set of feelings to facilitate development.

Now we turn our attention to the quality most directly conducive to relating effectively to others: communication skills.

Communication Skills 　　Because counseling is essentially a verbal process (with significant nonverbal components), the effective counselor must possess a sensitivity to language which makes possible understanding and communication with the client over a wide range of topics. The counselor who is proficient in language must possess not only a good vocabulary, acceptable speech patterns, and the like, but also be able to direct communications to the levels for which they are intended: to communicate in the language of youth as well as of the aging, in the ghetto language, and in all of the languages and dialects spoken by the clients counseled. For communication, in its real sense, is a cooperative effort by two people to "speak the same language," and this can only be accomplished when the counselor has a fluency in many different subcultural tongues.

One criterion of good communication is the ability to anticipate the effect that words will have on a client, to know in advance, before saying them, the inferences, denotations, and connotations of the words used and the messages transmitted. The science that studies words and their meaning is *semantics,* and an individual who specializes in this study is a *semanticist*. To some degree, all counselors are semanticists, in that they are profoundly concerned with the shades and levels of meaning each word has in their clients' thinking. As a semanticist, the counselor never assumes that a word has the same meaning to a client that it has to him or her. A client might, for example, say, "My father *hates* me." The counselor, aware of the father's true feelings, might be tempted to disagree at once. However, the client may be using the word *hate* in a specialized sense, different from the sense of the word that is familiar to the counselor, and it is necessary for the counselor first to explore with the client the meaning of the word *hate*. Such analyses of language, especially as they deal with the *personal meaning* of words, is a crucial component of effective counseling.

A second criterion of good communication is called "consonance." Every communication is conducted on two levels. The first level, on which the conversational voice speaks its words, is called the "level of content." This is the audible level of communication, the level which the client hears. The other level, the silent one that has no need for words, we shall call the "level of intent." This is the level of meanings and implications, of connotations and inferences, the level that the client *feels*.

Having now surveyed some of the more essential qualities of effective counseling, we will turn our attention to some of the personal, subjective problems in the world of the counselor.

The Counselor as a Person

Although we have discussed what the counselor *should* be doing and what qualities he or she *should* possess, we are well aware that counselors are real people with their own idiosyncratic natures, their own set of particular needs, their own values, problems, conflicts, any of which may at times work to the detriment of the counseling process. While living up to the idealized sketch of the effective counselor is certainly not an impossibility, nor even a rarity, the sketch somewhat oversimplifies the multidimensionality the individual must have to practice counseling, and the description glosses over the levels of diversity within the counselor. It is these levels that make each individual counselor a distinct and complex person, unlike any other counselor.

In this section we will examine how the counselor's problems, perceptions, feelings, and values exert a continuing influence upon the counseling process. Particular attention will be directed toward ways in which the counselor's subjectivity, insofar as it is a distortion, can be kept to a minimum. Moreover, in keeping with our premise that counseling is a way of life, we will suggest ways in which counselors may more effectively conduct their own lives, both for their personal benefit and to meet their professional obligations.

The Counselor's Problems

It would be ideal if, when the counselor enters the counseling setting, all of his or her personal problems and adjustment difficulties could miraculously disappear, or at least, be put aside so that they would not interfere with the counseling. It would be ideal; but unfortunately it is not the case. On the contrary, the counselor brings into the counseling situation all his or her personal problems and difficulties; and these problems, despite all efforts to the contrary, exert a powerful influence during counseling activities. Mature counselors can control these factors so that they do not exert a disruptive force on their work, but to do so they must first be intimately aware of the types of their problems and the types of interference these problems are likely to cause.

Counselors have, in effect, the same types of problems as everyone has. There are family problems, financial problems, interpersonal relationship problems, sexual problems, health problems, problems in self-esteem and confidence, social problems, and the like. While circumstances beyond the counselor's control may dictate the extent to which these challenges interfere in daily living and professional practice, it is the counselor's responsibility to govern his or her own life, to shape his or her destiny in an intelligent, effective, and productive manner. If they are to serve clients well, counselors must have their own lives in order, for their work with clients will reflect in many ways the condition of their lives, particularly in regard to stability, purpose, constancy and direction. Counseling, as I have been suggesting throughout this book, is a reflection of the counselors themselves.

Meaninglessness   The problem of meaninglessness is a serious problem for the counselor. Meaninglessness cuts the counselor off from the world, restricts emotional interchanges with others, and prevents her or him from experiencing life to the fullest. Meaninglessness is a serious obstacle in the counselor's striving for effectiveness in counseling exchanges with the client. It is the responsibility of every counselor to search for meanings in his or her own life.

Viktor Frankl, a Viennese psychiatrist who was imprisoned in Dachau and Auschwitz during World War II, found that the degree of meaningfulness in a prisoner's life very much influenced the probability of the prisoner surviving the catastrophic experience. In his well-known book *Man's Search for Meaning* (1962), Frankl discusses the importance of each person's developing a sense of meaning in life and how this sense of meaning keeps one alive, gives one a purpose for living, and generally tends to minimize the neurotic component of one's existence. It is only as the individual comes to understand and strive toward ultimate ideal purposes and goals—toward significant meanings—that life becomes full and rich, that one's existence becomes important and special.

Alienation   Rollo May (1967*b*) discusses alienation in terms of the modern individual's loss of significance in the world. There are a number of factors that contribute to this loss of significance, ranging from rapid technological change to the danger of thermonuclear war, but whatever the cause, "when the individual loses his significance, there occurs a sense of apathy, which is an expression of his state of diminished consciousness." This apathy may be appropriately called "alienation."

In its purest sense, alienation means being cut off from the world around us, isolated spiritually from our environment. The existential psychiatrist R.D. Laing describes it as a condition "of being asleep, of being unconscious, of being out of one's mind," and then goes on to suggest it "is the condition of the normal man" (Laing, 1967, p. 28).

What form does alienation assume? Many forms, including a deep sense of isolation and loneliness, a separation from others, and a loss of a coherent sense of self. Erich Fromm (1955), one of the more prominent thinkers in this area, presents a psychologically vivid picture of the alienated individual:

> By alienation is meant a mode of experience in which the person experiences himself as an alien. He has become, one might say, estranged from himself. He does not experience himself as the center of his world, as the creator of his own acts—but his acts and their consequences have become his masters, whom he obeys, or whom he may even worship. The alienated person is out of touch with any other person. He, like the others, is experienced as things are experienced; with the sense and with common sense, but at the same time without being related to oneself and to the world outside productively. (p. 111)

Fromm attributes this condition of alienation to a variety of social, economic, political, and psychological causes. But regardless of the cause, he feels strongly that many individuals in our society are alienated below a healthy level.

Counselor burnout, a phenomenon that incorporates elements of both mean- **Burnout** inglessness and alienation, has come under considerable scrutiny in recent years. Burnout is characterized by loss of feelings for one's work, despair of ever improving the situation, and general malaise about the poor quality of one's life, all largely blamed on the strains caused by work (Falck & Kilcoyne, 1985; Fimian, 1986). The counselor experiencing burnout may also feel unable to cope with personal tasks and may experience sporadic pervasive physical exhaustion (Fimian, 1987). While no specific personality types have been associated with burnout, it appears to affect many teachers and counselors, as well as school administrators, who were conscientious and committed at the beginning of their careers (Mattingly, 1986). An existential examination of one's job role in relation to one's life view can serve as an important first step in acknowledging and assessing feelings of burnout. Such an analysis will typically shed light on how the underlying sense of meaninglessness fuels the alienating feelings in the interpersonal context of the job situation.

A critical component of our personal growth and professional development Loss of Freedom is to discover our individual freedom. In the sense it is used here, "freedom" has a special meaning of "feeling free inside," much in the way that it is used by Csikszentmihalyi and Graef (1979):

> While the word *freedom* has many connotations, it has a personal meaning that most people recognize and share. Feeling free is an experience: a sense of being in control of one's actions, of not being determined by outside forces. It is an experience that seems to be increasingly threatened by the stresses of modern life, by the demands of impersonal bureaucracies, by the pressures of work, by our own aspirations to savor life and our talents to the fullest, and even, occasionally, by the claims made on us by those we love. (p. 84)

This type of *psychological* freedom is to some extent influenced by the social conditions of freedom and bondage, but is not entirely dependent upon these circumstances. The personal discovery of one's freedom is just as significant as the social environment in which we attempt to exercise our freedom.

One critical objective of almost all counseling endeavors is to help the client discover individual freedom. In the sense it is used here, *freedom* is a term with a myriad of psychological and sociological meanings. One indispensable aspect of becoming a free person is finding internal, psychological freedom. "Freedom," argues Rollo May (1967a) "is a special characteristic of the individual who has come to terms with his instinctual urges." He goes on to point out:

> One cannot be free, of course, while his consciousness is locked in warfare with tendencies from his unconsciousness. That is why the aim of psychotherapeutic treatment is often summed up as setting the individual free— free from special inhibitions and repressions, free from childhood fixations, from training formulae, and so on. Counselors likewise aim to help the person become free. People need to be freed; one feels great pity for the great majority of people that they should be enslaved by unnecessary fears. One sees them going through life carrying great psychological burdens which keep them from freedom even more really than the prisoner's iron ball and chain. It is a truism that most people develop to only a third or less of their personality possibilities. The counselor will aim to set people free, so that they can develop into their own unique, autonomous selves and realize some of the rich, untapped potentialities in their personalities. (p. 192)

This type of *internal* freedom, to which May refers, is inevitably bound up, in principle and in effect, with external conditions of freedom and bondage. That is why the counselor must strive, in all counseling efforts, to produce a healthy, prosperous congruence between himself or herself, the individual client, and the society in which they both live.

In conjunction with each other, alienation, meaninglessness, and loss of freedom are the three variables that most directly threaten the counselor's professional efficacy and personal life-style. While none of these is directly a condition of the time, each one is present in our age and each must be confronted within the context of the conditions of our age, which govern our values, assumptions, and approaches to counseling. Counselors whose commitment to counseling permeates all their activities will recognize at every juncture of human interaction the impact of these variables on their feelings and on the feelings of others. Such counselors will understand their human limitations and strive to overcome them, to transcend them in order to become more effective, more therapeutic, more facilitative counselors.

The Counselor's Values

Although you may not think about your values until you have to make a decision, almost all your behavior is influenced, directly or indirectly, by your value system. We can define values as "convictions or beliefs which prescribe or determine acceptable or preferable behavior in relation to needs or goals" (Strickland, 1978, p. 428). The two key words here are *needs* and *goals*. For values not only tell us what is acceptable and what is not acceptable, but also reflect what our needs are, the way we go about satisfying these needs, the way we set up goals, and how we perceive these goals.

"A person's values," suggests Ajzen (1973), "may be defined as his or her basic ideas and beliefs about what is right or good and what is wrong or bad" (p. 77). We all have such a set of beliefs, which permeate decision-making, ability to appreciate the things around us, our consciences, and our perception of others. To the extent that the counselor's values are an integral part of his or her personality, and, therefore, a part of the counselor's professional role, they are of interest to us in examining how they contribute to the counseling process.

There are, of course, many different types of values. One type, which we may call "cognitive values," asserts that one thing, *A,* is better or worse than another, *B,* citing objective and scientific evidence as the reason. For example, a counselor may believe that behavioral counseling is more effective in working with stutterers than is Rogerian counseling. Citing studies to prove this point, the counselor would deny that it is a personal value, arguing strongly that it is a conclusion based on fact rather than on subjectivity or preference. In the broad sense, however, any belief, no matter how strongly based in fact, is a value. But the more the individual believes that a particular value is a cognitive value, the less likely she or he is to change that value. While other values are often susceptible to change, cognitive values carry with them a sense of certainty which is maintained with a stubbornness that borders on the uncompromising. Consider, for instance, how Copernicus or Galileo fared when they, by citing objective evidence, attempted to contradict the cognitive values of the societies in which they lived.

Second, we have values that are clearly not objective, but rather are indicative of a personal preference. I prefer the Dutch masters to the Impressionists. This is not to say that one is judged to be better than the other, but merely that one gives me more pleasure than the other. These we may call "preference values." Individuals holding preference values recognize that they are values and not facts, thus they are more likely to tolerate in others values which are different from their own. Because preference values, unlike cognitive values, do not define the world around us, they are in less danger of being challenged. A counselor might say, "I prefer face-to-face counseling over group counseling, but I don't believe that one is necessarily better than the other," thus acknowledging it is a preference value rather than a cognitive value.

Third, we have moral values. These are values based on higher principles of conduct. Moral values are taught to us when we are very young, and although we are able to modify what we have learned, many of the moral "isms" instilled within us hold throughout our lives. Moral values, like cognitive values, are strong values. We tend to believe that our moral values are the right values, and we judge others by them. The counselor who believes that lying is wrong is likely to judge clients who lie according to the prescripts of this value. In other words, while we tolerate diversity in values of preference, we tend to be more restrictive and less adaptive in matters of truth and morality.

Fourth, we have self-values. These values represent our feelings of self-esteem and self-importance. Although some sociologists argue that this value is culturally determined, a more popular position is that one's self-esteem is more dependent upon early upbringing, particularly upon the relationship with one's parents. In either case, one's feelings about oneself deeply influence choices, perceptions, and judgments.

Finally, we have cultural values. These overlap the other four categories, but they differ in that they are shared social values rather than individual values. Cultural values pose a particularly challenging problem to the counselor. Because they are values of consensus, shared by all those with whom the counselor interacts, they may not be recognized as values and be considered absolutes or truths instead. A counselor who believes that when a client is ill he or she should see a physician, a cultural value judgment, may not be able to understand the values of a Christian Scientist who does not concur in this conclusion. Because cultural values are so subtle, they often elude our rational ability to evaluate and react objectively.

While other categories of values could be set forth, these five cover the ground sufficiently. The counselor has values in each of these categories, and these values together help constitute the counselor's world view and influence his or her counseling activities in manifold ways. As Pedersen, Holwill, and Shapiro (1978) point out, "Counselors who are most different from their clients in terms of culture . . . are likely to have more difficulty communicating empathy, respect, congruence, and general assistance than counselors who share or understand their clients' cultural point of view." (p. 233)

Carpenter's Gothic

What we can see from the previous observations about the counselor as a person is that the effective counselor has to be a well constructed, well balanced, fully functional mature adult, capable of integrating into himself or herself a myriad of values, problems, and existential conflicts. This is easier said than done. For many individuals, the outside appearance, what they show to the world, takes precedence over what is happening inside, and they strive throughout life to create an illusory self that will placate the public, get positive responses, and conceal an underlying lack of depth or introspection. Such a person hides behind appearance. But only when an individual allows his or her outer self to be a true reflection of a functional inner self can he or she serve others who are seeking interpersonal help and emotional growth.

Gaddis makes this point brilliantly in his book *Carpenter's Gothic* (1985), where he uses an architecturally anomalous house as a psychological metaphor for the way people behave, feel, and deal with their feelings. Gaddis illustrates the carpenter's Gothic metaphor with an old house in Rockland County that is designed to look historically accurate outside without any consideration or thought for the practicality and function of the interior design. The builders tried to model it after Gothic architecture, but didn't have the materials and skill to work through the full design. Because the inside rooms have to conform to the outside specifications, some rooms are too narrow to be practical; ceilings suddenly slope so unmercifully that one can't stand up; and windows are placed at such impractical points that they offer neither light nor view. Gaddis shows throughout this book,

Counseling: The Art and Science of Helping

as he does in his earlier work, *The Recognitions* (1953), that illusions often constitute what we present to the world and that our inner selves are often forced to conform to the demands of an experiential reality in which we do not feel entirely comfortable, do not feel entirely ourselves. Many of us, in other words, live in a world where we don't fully feel we belong.

With this in mind, let us turn our attention to some of the ways in which the counselor's world view exerts an influence on the counseling process.

World Views and Counseling

By Derald Wing Sue. This section originally appeared in *Personnel and Guidance Journal*, April 1978, pp. 458-462. Copyright 1978 American Personnel and Guidance Association. Reprinted with permission.

Counselors who hold world views different from their clients' views and who are unaware of the bases for these differences are most likely to impute negative traits to their clients. In most cases, culturally different clients such as Asian-Americans, blacks, Chicanos, and native Americans have a greater probability of holding different perspectives. In a previous article (Sue, in press *a*), I defined a world view as the way in which people perceive their relationship to nature, institutions, other people, and things. World view constitutes our psychological orientation in life and can determine how we think, behave, make decisions, and define events. Our cultural upbringing and life experiences frequently determine or influence our world views. For minorities in the United States, however, a strong determinant of world views is very much related to racism and the subordinate position assigned minorities in society (Hall, Cross & Freedle, 1972; Jackson, 1975; Sue, 1975).

In this article, I would like to discuss how culture and racial-specific factors may interact in such a way as to produce people with differing world views. The implications that world views have for counselors will then be explored. I will draw heavily on previous works in which a conceptual model for the development of world views was proposed. Two psychological dimensions, locus of control and locus of responsibility, have been identified as important in understanding people with different viewpoints.

Locus of Control

The concept of locus of control is seen as a corollary to the social-learning theory developed by Rotter (1954). According to Rotter, an individual's history of reinforcement can determine two psychological orientations in life. Internal-control (IC) people believe that reinforcements are contingent on their own actions. External-control (EC) people, however, believe that reinforcements are not entirely contingent on their own actions; thus, what happens to EC people is perceived as the result of luck, chance, fate, or powerful others. High internality has been associated with greater job efficiency, higher need achievement, greater school success, greater attempts at mastering the environment, greater expressions of satisfaction with life, lower anxiety, greater social-action involvement, and greater willingness to accept responsibility for personal actions (Lefcourt, 1966; Rotter, 1966, 1975). These attributes are highly valued by Western society and constitute the core characteristics of mental health.

Many studies investigating the relationships among ethnicity, socioeconomic level, sex, and locus of control conclude that ethnic-group members (Hsieh, Shybut & Lotsof, 1969; Levenson, 1974; Strickland, 1973; Tulkin, 1968; Wolfgang, 1973), lower-class people (Battle & Rotter, 1963; Crandall, Katkovsky & Crandall, 1965; Garcia & Levenson, 1975; Lefcourt, 1966; Strickland, 1971), and women (Sanger & Alker, 1972) tend to be more external. If we were to use the internal-external (I-E) dimension as a criterion of mental health, most of the minorities, poor, and women would be regarded as unhealthy and as possessing less desirable traits. Thus, a counselor who encounters a minority client with a high external orientation (It's no use trying; there's nothing I can do about it; and, you shouldn't rock the boat) may interpret the client as being inherently apathetic, procrastinating, lazy, depressed, or anxious about trying. The problem with an unqualified application of the I-E dimension is that it fails to take into consideration different cultural and social experiences of the individual. This failure may lead to highly inappropriate and destructive applications in counseling.

Some investigators (Crandall, Katkovsky & Crandall, 1965; Hersch & Scheibe, 1967) argue that the locus-of-control continuum must make clearer distinctions on the external end. For example, externality related to impersonal forces (chance and luck) is different from that ascribed to cultural forces and to powerful others. Chance and luck operate equally across situations for everyone. The forces, however, that determine locus of control from a cultural perspective may be viewed by the particular ethnic group as acceptable and benevolent. In this case, externality is viewed positively. Two ethnic groups may be used as examples to illustrate this point.

Hsieh, Shybut, and Lotsof (1969) found that Chinese, American-born Chinese, and Anglo-Americans varied in the degree of internal control they felt. The first group scored lowest in internality, followed by the Chinese-Americans, and finally by Anglo-Americans. These investigators felt that the individual-centered culture in the United States emphasizes the uniqueness, independence, and self-reliance of each individual. The culture places a high premium on self-reliance, individualism, and status achieved through personal efforts. In contrast, the situation-centered Chinese culture places importance on the group (an individual is not defined apart from the family), tradition, social-role expectations, and harmony with the universe. Thus, the cultural orientation of the more traditional Chinese tends to elevate the external scores. Note, however, that the external orientation of the Chinese is highly valued and accepted.

Likewise, we might expect Native Americans to score higher on the external end of the I-E continuum on the basis of their own cultural values. A number of authors (Bryde, 1971; Trimble, 1976) have pointed to Native American concepts of noninterference and harmony with nature that may tend to classify Native Americans as high externals. Anglos are said to be concerned with attempts to control the physical world and to assert mastery over it. To Native Americans, accepting the world (harmony) rather than changing it is a highly valued lifestyle.

The fact that Rotter's I-E distinction is not a unidimensional trait is also mentioned in other studies (Gurin et al., 1969; Mirels, 1970), which indicate the presence of a political influence (powerful others). For example, a major focus in the literature dealing with locus of control is expectancy that a person's behavior cannot determine the outcomes or reinforcements that he or she seeks. It is entirely possible that lower-class individuals and minorities are not given an equal opportunity to obtain the material rewards in Western culture. Because of racism, many of these individuals may be realistically seeing a discrepancy between their ability and attainment.

In this case, externality may be seen as a malevolent force to be distinguished from the benevolent cultural ones just discussed. On the basis of their study, Gurin et al. (1969) concluded that while high-external people are less effectively motivated, perform poorly in achievement situations, and evidence greater psychological problems, these behaviors do not necessarily hold for minorities and low-income persons. Focusing on external forces may be motivationally healthy if it results from assessing personal chances for success against systematic and real external obstacles rather than unpredictable fate. Several factors of importance were identified by Gurin et al. (1969).

The first factor, *control ideology,* is a measure of general belief about the role of external forces in determining success and failure in the larger society. This factor represents a cultural belief in the Protestant ethic; success is the result of hard work, effort, skill, and ability. The second factor, *personal control,* reflects a person's belief as to his or her own sense of personal efficacy or competence. While the former represents an ideological belief, the latter is more related to actual control. Gurin et al. (1969) cited data that indicate that blacks are as internal as whites on the control ideology but if a personal referent (personal control) is used, blacks are much more external. These data indicate that blacks may have adopted the general cultural beliefs about internal control but find that these beliefs cannot always be applied to their own life situations (racism and discrimination). It is interesting to note that whites endorse control-ideology statements at the same rate as personal-control ones. Thus, the disparity between the two forms of control does not seem to be operative for white Americans. Another interesting finding was that personal control as opposed to ideological control was more related to motivational and performance indicators. A student high on personal control (internality) had great self-confidence, high test scores, and high grades. Those who were high on the ideological measure were not noticeably different from their externally oriented counterparts.

The I-E continuum is a useful one for counselors to use only if they make clear distinctions as to the meaning of the EC dimension. High externality may be the result of chance or luck, cultural dictates that are viewed as benevolent, and a political force (racism or discrimination) that represents malevolent but realistic obstacles. In each case, it is a mistake to assume that the former is operative for a culturally different client. To do so would be to deny the potential influence of cultural values and the effects of prejudice and discrimination. The problem becomes even more complex when we realize that cultural and discriminatory forces may both be operative; that is, Native American cultural values that dictate an external orientation may be compounded by their historical experience of prejudice and discrimination in the United States. The same may be true for other ethnic groups as well.

Locus of Responsibility

A third factor, besides personal control and control ideology, is an *individual system blame dimension*. I have taken the liberty of referring to this dimension as locus of responsibility or the degree of emphasis placed on the system or person. High internal-locus-of-responsibility (IR) people believe that success and failure may be attributed to a person's skills or personal inadequacies. High external-locus-of-responsibility (ER) people believe that the sociocultural environment is much more potent than the individual. What happens to a person is more a function of the environmental conditions than personal attributes.

In discussing the causal attribution of social problems, Caplan and Nelson (1973) state that Western society tends to hold individuals responsible for their problems. Such an approach has the effect of labeling those segments of the population (racial and ethnic minorities) that differ in thought and behavior from the larger society as deviant. Defining the problem as residing in the person enables society to ignore situationally relevant factors and to protect and preserve social institutions and belief systems. Caplan and Nelson (1973) said:

> What is done about a problem depends on how it is defined. The way a social problem is defined determines the attempts at remediation—problem definition determines the change strategy, the selection of a social action delivery system, and the criteria for evaluation. Problem definitions are based on assumptions about the causes of the problem and where they lie. If the causes of delinquency, for example, are defined in person-centered terms (e.g., inability to delay gratification, or incomplete sexual identity), then it would be logical to initiate person-change treatment techniques and intervention strategies to deal with the problem. Such treatment would take the form of counseling or other person-change efforts to "reach" the delinquent, thereby using his potential for self-control to make his behavior more conventional. If, on the other hand, explanations are situation centered, for example, if delinquency were interpreted as the substitution of extralegal paths for already preempted, conventionally approved pathways for achieving socially valued goals, then efforts toward corrective treatment would logically have a system-change orientation. Efforts would be launched to create suitable opportunities for success and achievement along conventional lines; thus, existing physical, social, or economic arrangements, not individual psyches, would be the targets for change. (pp. 200–201)

Avis and Stewart (1976) pointed out that counseling has traditionally placed the burden of responsibility on the individual. A person who experiences difficulties is likely to be blamed for his or her present state. Because counseling is

Figure 3.1. Graphic representation of world views.

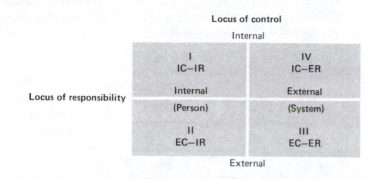

person centered, the onus of responsibility for change in counseling also resides with the person. While this philosophy may be appropriate for many clients, it may work to the detriment of minorities who have experienced severe discrimination. For example, a black male client who has been unable to find a job because of prejudice and discrimination may blame himself (What's wrong with me? Why can't I get a job? Am I that worthless?). Thus, an internal response becomes reinforced by counseling when, in actuality, an external response may be more realistic and appropriate (Institutional racism prevented my getting the job).

In previous writings, I described in some detail how these two factors, locus of control and locus of responsibility, are probably independent of one another. They can interact in such a way as to form four quadrants when plotted on a graph. Each quadrant represents a different world view (see Figure 3.1).

Four Kinds of World Views

The IC-IR world view is the exemplification of American culture. The IC-IR people believe they are the masters of their fate and responsible for what happens to them. Stewart, Danielian, and Festes (1969) and Stewart (1971) described in detail the United States patterns of cultural assumptions and values. They constitute the building blocks of the IC-IR world view and typically guide our thinking about mental health services. This philosophy incorporates a belief that activism (doing as opposed to being) is the dominant means of problem solving and decision-making; a belief that individual rights are more important than group responsibilities and goals; a belief that self-achievement and competition are motivationally healthy; a belief that man is separate from the world and that the world can be controlled, exploited, and developed; and a belief that people can solve their own problems.

The IC-IR World View

Minority individuals who fall into this category are likely to have very little control over how others define them. They accept the dominant society's definitions and blame themselves or their own people for their plight. Jackson (1975)

The EC-IR World View

described a stage of passive acceptance experienced by many blacks who are victims of cultural racism. These individuals accept and conform to white social, cultural, and institutional standards, believe that race problems are the result of laziness and personal inadequacies of the person, and derive a sense of self-worth only from white society. A sense of racial self-hatred (being ashamed of their own race and culture) develops, which may lead to marginality. First coined by Stonequist (1935), the term *marginal man* was used to describe individuals who exist on the margins of two different cultural traditions but have not fully accommodated themselves to either. The particular dynamics of how this occurs were pointed out by Jones (1972), who described how white society has fostered a belief in the superiority of its own culture and a belief in the inferiority of minority life-styles.

In the past, mental health professionals have assumed that marginality and self-hatred were internal conflicts of the person, almost as if these problems arise from the individual. In challenging the traditional notion of marginality, Freire (1970) stated that:

> Marginality is not by choice, marginal man has been expelled from and kept outside of the social system and is therefore the object of violence. In fact, however, the social structure as a whole does not "expel," nor is marginal man a "being outside of." Marginal men are "beings for another." Therefore the solution to their problem is not to become "beings inside of," but men freeing themselves; for, in reality, they are not marginal to the structure, but oppressed men within it. (pp. 10–11)

It is evident that marginal persons are oppressed, have little choice, and are powerless in the face of the dominant-subordinate relationship between the middle-class WASP culture and their own minority culture. If this relationship were eliminated, the phenomenon of marginality would disappear. For if two cultures exist on the basis of total equality (an ideal for biculturalism), the conflicts of marginality do not occur in the person.

The EC-ER World View   Minorities who hold an EC-ER world view see that their current plight (poverty, poor housing, unemployment, and poor education) is the result of an oppressive social system (ER) but feel powerless to do anything about it (EC). Sue (in press *a*) described two reactions that may occur. First, under constant and intense racism, a phenomenon that Seligman (1975) called learned helplessness can occur. The basic assumption in the theory of learned helplessness is that organisms exposed to prolonged lack of control in their lives develop expectations of helplessness in later situations. Unfortunately, this expectation occurs even in situations that are now controllable. The individual has given up and may exhibit passivity, apathy, and depression.

A second mode of adjustment is that of the placater or appeaser. This is a person who has not given up but sees the forces of prejudice and discrimination as too powerful to fight directly. Suffer in silence, don't rock the boat, and survival at all costs, are the covert scripts. Direct expressions of anger and attempts to confront people and institutions about discriminatory practices are seen as invitations for massive retaliation. Thus, it is best to keep a low profile and to follow the rules. Life is fixed, and there is relatively little a person can do to change it. Smith (1977) discussed this mode of adjustment that many blacks used during slavery.

The major orientation of IC-ER people is a belief in their ability to achieve personal goals if given a chance. Minorities in this sector perceive realistically that barriers in the forms of prejudice and discrimination often prevent them from achieving their goals. A number of studies (Caplan, 1970; Caplan & Paige, 1968; Forward & Williams, 1970; Turner & Wilson, 1976) lend credence to the belief that this world view is correlated with racial pride, racial identity, and militancy among third-world groups. For example, many of these studies conclude that riot participants of the 1960s were those with high aspirations for their lives, strong beliefs in their own ability to achieve these goals, and perceptions that environmental forces (discrimination) rather than personal inadequacies were causes for their current situation. Fogelson (1970) presented data in support of the thesis that the ghetto riots were the result of just grievances within a racist society. IC-ER individuals believe that a person-blame approach relieves white institutions of blame. Such a conceptualization means that psychotherapy, social work, mental hospitalization, or imprisonment should be used against protesters. Demands for system change are declared illegitimate because they are the products of sick or confused minds. Maintenance of the status quo rather than needed social change (social therapy) is reaffirmed. Since IC-ER people are most likely to engage in collective action to deal with discrimination and to engage in greater civil-rights activities (Gurin et al., 1969), this latter point is especially important. Figure 3.1 illustrates the four world views just discussed.

The IC-ER World View

Now, what does all this have to do with counseling? What implications does it have for us? Space does not permit me to go into detail, but let me briefly outline several important implications.

Counseling Implications

1. It is obvious to me that counseling and psychotherapy in the United States fall into the IC-IR world view. Clients are seen as able to initiate change and are held responsible for their current plight. The popularity of self-help approaches is illustrative of this world view. A counselor operating within this framework will probably be person centered and likely to focus attention on the individual. While such a world view is not necessarily incorrect or bad, it may be inappropriately applied to clients who do not share this perception. When counselors are culturally blind and impose their world views on clients without regard for the legitimacy of other views, they are engaging in a form of cultural oppression. Diaz-Guerrero (1977)

made an excellent point when he challenged the universality of the philosophical-political forces behind the three major systems in psychology in the United States: psychoanalysis, behaviorism, and humanistic psychology. He criticized the systems' focus on the self, because in many societies, the family, state, or society is the psychosocial unit, not the individual.

Therefore, what is needed is for counselors to become culturally aware, to understand the basis of their world views, and to understand and accept the possible legitimacy of others. Only when counselor-education programs begin to incorporate cross-cultural concepts in their training (not from a white perspective, but from the perspective of each culture) will counseling possibly lose its oppressive orientation.

2. Another implication that I see from this conceptual model is its use as an aid to understanding possible psychological dynamics of a culturally different client. For example, an EC-IR client who experiences self-hatred and marginality may be a victim of the dominant-subordinate relationship fostered in American society. The problem is not inherent or internal, and counseling may be aimed at a reeducative process to get that client to become aware of the wider social-political forces at the basis of his or her plight.

An EC-ER person, whether or not he or she has given up or is placating, must be taught new coping skills to deal with people and institutions. Experiences of success are critically important for clients in this sector.

IC-ER clients are especially difficult for counselors to deal with, because challenges to counseling as an act of oppression are most likely to arise. A counselor who is not in touch with the wider social-political issues will quickly lose credibility and effectiveness. In addition, IC-ER clients are externally oriented, and demands for the counselor to take external action on behalf of the client will be strong (setting up a job interview, helping the client fill out forms, etc.). While most of us have been taught not to intervene externally to help the client, all of us must look seriously at the value base of this dictate.

3. Finally, I am intrigued by observations and by some empirical studies which seem to suggest that each world view may dictate certain counseling skills or approaches more appropriate in this instance. For example, it is my contention that a client with an IC-ER world view is most receptive to counseling skills that are action oriented (give advice, suggestions, and directions) as opposed to the more inactive (reflection of feelings, paraphrasing, and summarizing) ones. One of the reasons why there is such a high percentage of premature terminations among minority clients may be that counselors do not share their world view and use counseling approaches inappropriate to

their life-styles. I think future research might profitably identify which skills seem most appropriate to a world view. We already have microcounseling systems that may need only minor modifications to initiate our research venture.

In closing, I would like to echo Ivey's (1977) statement concerning the culturally effective counselor. This is a person able to share the world views of his or her client and to generate the widest repertoire of microcounseling skills appropriate to the life-style of the individual client. In essence, the counselor must become a functional integrator, a person who integrates positive aspects of each world view without losing a sense of his or her own integrity.

Summary

In this chapter, we looked at the world of the counselor, including his or her personal characteristics and professional qualities, along with the counselor's value systems and how they influence counseling practice.

We began by defining the concept of counseling "effectiveness" and specifying some of the counselor qualities that are generally associated with effective outcomes. Carl Rogers's contribution to this area of study was discussed. Specific attention was then directed toward defining and explicating these key qualities of the effective counselor: open-mindedness, perceptiveness, a non-judgmental attitude, sensitivity, empathy, objectivity, genuineness, nondominance, listening ability, positive regard, effective communication skills (semantics), and the self-knowledge and self-respect that produces security, trust and courage.

Next, we turned to the counselor's personal problems and considered how they may impede counseling progress. We began with the assumption originally stated by Berenson and Carkhuff that "counseling is only as effective as the therapist is living effectively" and discussed how the counselor's personal problems, such as meaninglessness, alienation, and loss of freedom, can place limits on his or her effective living. We explored some of the implications of this in terms of the counselor's existence as a person as well as a professional helper.

Finally, we looked at the counselor's value system. We discussed five categories of values that profoundly influence the way the counselor views the world. These are cognitive values, personal preference values, moral values, self values, and cultural values, which fuse together elements of the others. We used an excerpt from "World Views and Counseling" by Derald Wing Sue, to explore the counselor's world view, which is very much a product of his or her culture and upbringing, in terms of the psychological constructs called *locus of control* and *locus of responsibility*. Dr. Sue concluded that an effective counselor is "a person who integrates positive aspects of each world view without losing a sense of his or her own integrity."

The Counseling Process

In the first part of this book we surveyed, in a general way, the profession of counseling, examining its origins in different disciplines, exploring how counseling exists as a distinct mode of helping, and considering what kind of work the counselor typically does and what types of problems the contemporary counselor faces. In this part, we will examine in depth some facets of the counseling process, focusing more directly on the actual moments of the counseling interaction. How does the counselor communicate appropriate feelings and ideas to the client? How does the process of counseling work in a specific direction, and how is this direction chosen? What stimulates a client to grow, to change, to discover a richer life? This discussion will include a sketch of the counselor-at-work, as well as some objective considerations of the types of actions counselors can use to make their interactions with clients most effective.

First, we will examine the basis of the counseling relationship. How does the professional role of counselor fit in with the counselor as a person? How do counselor and client establish, explicitly or implicitly, a working agreement between them? What types of perceptions and values do the counselor and client share during this time, and how do these shared values influence the structure and direction of the counseling process? In what personality variables is the basis of the counseling relationship to be found? Case material will be used throughout to illustrate the expression of theoretical ideas in practice.

We will explore components of the counseling interview in chapter 5. What can be done to assure the most effective initial interview? How do counselors translate theory into practice in the counseling setting? How does the counselor select the techniques to be used? How does the counselor go about implementing these techniques and objectively evaluating the results?

We will, throughout Part 2, examine the counseling process in terms of the *structure* and *content* of the transaction. If counseling is truly a helping relationship, what efforts of the counselor and of the client can work productively toward facilitating that relationship?

In chapter 6, we examine ways of making growth and change easier. We begin by considering some client expectations and how these affect the development of counseling goals. Some of the accepted ways of responding to the client, particularly to the client's questions, are considered. Finally, we will discuss some ways in which counseling goals can be consistent with the aim of helping the client grow.

Chapter Aim

To illustrate the importance of the counseling relationship in determining the success or failure of the counseling process, and to offer specific guidelines for making the counseling relationship most effective.

In the counseling setting, the counselor assumes a particular role, which may be congruent or incongruent with his or her personality. Goffman's concepts of "back" and "front" regions are used to illustrate the social meaning of *role* as it pertains to counseling.

Counselor Role and the Counseling Relationship

Several guidelines for maintaining a facilitative relationship, which is communicated to the client, are presented. We point out that, in general, the constructive expression of feelings becomes the foundation for any such relationship. The counselor should be willing to listen to all of the client's feelings and to communicate to the client the message, I am here to help you. Counselors should be nonjudgmental, especially at the beginning, and should encourage the client to assume responsibility for the treatment. Finally, the counselor should be able to express freely the feelings and ideas which will help the client grow.

Some Guidelines

Case material is used to illustrate how the interplay of forces underlying the counseling relationship contributes to the quality of treatment. Different models of counseling relationships—horizontal, diagonal, and vertical—are discussed.

The Counseling Relationship

Borrowed from modern physics, this viewpoint suggests that our interpretation of reality—and reality itself—depends largely upon the way we look at the world and measure it. Applied to the counseling relationship, it insinuates that counselors and clients change through their relationship, each becoming something he or she would not become were it not for the existence of the relationship. The interpretation also shapes our view of therapeutic growth as an ongoing process that involves more probability than certainty.

The "Copenhagen Interpretation"

The Counseling
Relationship

4

Practitioners generally agree that the counseling relationship is the critical variable in all counseling efforts. Without a "facilitative" relationship, there can be little or no success in counseling. We can define a facilitative relationship as one that offers a nexus of emotional elements necessary for growth and change. This involves certain specific personality qualities (empathy, genuineness, etc.) which we discussed earlier. It also involves certain kinds of communications within the relationship—called facilitative responses—that make free expression of feelings easier to articulate.

In the previous chapter we explored some of the personal and professional qualities of the counselor which contribute to or detract from the counseling relationship. In the following chapter, we will consider some of the client's characteristics (expectations, motivation, perceptual barriers, defenses, etc.) which affect the counseling relationship and hence, the counseling process. In this chapter, however, to establish a point of orientation from which we can proceed, we shall focus attention exclusively on the behavioral and dynamic components of the counseling relationship itself, paying special attention to how these elements affect the counseling process.

We shall begin by asking, How can the counselor translate the effective qualities enumerated in the preceding chapter into good counseling practice? Then, we will look at some practical counseling guidelines counselors can use, integrating their own personal feelings as part of the relationship. While we would maintain that the counselor's feelings have priority over his or her actions, we want to point out that there are some important principles underlying what the counselor does, and that the counselor should be aware exactly how his or her actions affect the client.

We have pointed out that it is necessary to differentiate between the counselor as a "professional," acting a certain role, and the counselor as a "real person," spontaneously expressing through behaviors his or her inner self; the two are al-

**Counselor Role
and the Counseling
Relationship**

ways entwined. In fact, the counseling relationship provides a context in which the counselor's personality and professional role reveal their congruence or incongruence.

To help clarify this concept, we should explicate the concept of *role,* which has been exhaustively studied in the discipline of sociology. One of the first social scientists to deal with this subject was Ralph Linton, who established the groundwork from which role theory developed. Linton (1936) suggested that individuals within a social group exhibited a narrow range of behavior, which was defined and reinforced by the group. The *role,* as he viewed it, is a cooperative effort between the individual and society. It represents a compromise between the "self" of the individual and the expectations society has for her or for him, including the cues and reinforcement it offers.

This concept can be translated, in terms of this discussion, into the relationship between the counselor as a person and the counselor playing a professional role. How much of his or her real self, we may ask, infuses the counselor's professional poise and posture? Erving Goffman (1959) points out that all professionals—counselors, ministers, teachers, and others—react in different ways to different social situations, changing, at the drop of a hat, their dress, their speech pattern and vocabulary, their level of formality and intimacy, their gestures and body language, and a variety of other social and interpersonal signs and signals. Personal selves remain the same, to be sure; but the image which is shown to others changes according to the social setting.

Goffman (1959) speaks of a "social establishment" as "any place surrounded by fixed barriers to perception in which a particular kind of activity regularly takes place" (p. 238). The counseling situation is just such an establishment, with the counselor deliberately expressing his or her image of the counselor's role, and the client setting forth his or her image of the role of the client. Other workers in the professional setting, school personnel, social workers, hospital staff, and so on, work together to maintain the image of the counselor—this mask (persona)—both for their own benefit and for the benefit of the system they serve. Even though their individual feelings about the counselor may be different, they nevertheless conscientiously perform the expected role functions:

> Within the walls of a social establishment, we find a team of performers who cooperate to present to an audience a given definition of the situation. This will include the conception of "own team" and of audience, and of assumptions concerning the ethos which is to be maintained by roles of politeness and decorum. We often find a division into back region where the performance of a routine is prepared and front region where the performance is presented. (p. 238)

We can extend this dichotomy between "back region" and "front region" to the counseling situation. The counselor's personal world is the *back region* where the professional performance is prepared. This back region also includes the counselor's fantasies, wishes, fears, problems, defenses, anxieties, conflicts, values, and the like. The *front region* is in the office, where the counselor carries out the counseling duties and makes a professional impact. The relationship between the counselor-as-a-person and the counselor-as-a-professional can be restated as the degree of consonance or dissonance between the counselor's back region and front region. Earlier, we explored the qualities which ideally should be at work in the front region. We also examined some facets of the back region, considering how the personal problems of the counselor (such as alienation, meaninglessness, etc.) play a part in defining his or her professional role, limiting who the counselor is, and determining what the counselor is incapable of doing. Now, we will see in more detail how the interaction between these regions affects the counseling relationship.

Successful counseling begins with the counselor's understanding of and empathic response to the client, and progresses further by the client's reactions to the counselor. As the counselor shows a willingness to listen to the client, to experience along with the client, and to give a part of herself or himself to the client, the client finds new avenues of growth, which include exploring his or her feelings about the counselor. The establishment of a facilitative relationship is a mutual process in which client and counselor give to each other—spontaneously, genuinely, within the context of the counseling setting.

Some Guidelines

One thing is certain: the qualities of the counselor constitute a dynamic component of the therapeutic process—a component that must be reckoned with. Torrey (1972) cites an interesting example of how counseling would appear if it were devoid of the human relationships:

Therapist   Hello. Please tell me your name.

Client   Torrey.

Therapist   It's nice to meet you, Torrey. I would like to discuss your problem with you. Please tell me first whether you are male or female.

Client   Male.

Therapist   How old are you?

Client   Thirty-two.

Therapist   Are you married?

Client   Yes.

Therapist   Now, how can I help you?

Client   I don't know.

Therapist   Tell me something about your wife.

Client   She is a fine wife. We have a good marriage.

Therapist   I understand. Now tell me something about your parents.

Client   My father is dead. My mother has been sick.

Therapist   Tell me more about her.

Client   She is getting better now.

Therapist   Does your wife tend to be like your mother?

Client   No, not at all.

Therapist   I understand. Now let me ask you something else about your mother. Was she very strict in raising you?

Client   No, she was lenient. I made all my own decisions.

Therapist   Does it bother you that you made all your own decisions?

Client   No, I like to.

Therapist   Why do you like to?

Client   Because then I have created my own existential meaning.

Therapist   I understand. Please tell me more about someone close to you.

Client   Why are you so insensitive?

Therapist   I am doing my best under these conditions.

Client   You are just a crazy machine.

Therapist   You seem interested in me personally.

Client   Who do you think you are?

Therapist   Please think of me as a doctor trying to discuss your feelings about people close to you. Call me anything you wish. (pp. 29–31)

As I am sure you have guessed by now, the "therapist" in this dialogue is a computer especially programmed to function as a psychotherapist. Torrey uses this as an example of artfully executed therapeutic techniques devoid of the richness of human contact. It demonstrates most dramatically the human component of the multidimensional therapeutic process.

The counselor's behaviors and activities in the counseling setting are planned expressions, or transformations, of the counselor's feelings. This does not necessarily detract from their genuineness; rather, the counselor attempts to present "true" feelings in terms that will be most constructive to the client. *The constructive expression of feelings becomes the foundation for a facilitative relationship.* For example, if the client is expressing hostility toward the counselor, and the client is not aware of these feelings, the counselor can point this out to the client in a way that is nonthreatening and accepting. This conveys to the client, in effect, "You may feel hostile toward me, but I can accept these feelings from you." If we are to sum up the principal actions which the counselor performs to help establish this facilitative relationship between herself or himself and the client, they can be stated in five guidelines:

1. The counselor must be willing to listen to *anything* and *everything* the client has to say. The beginning of a constructive counseling relationship requires the counselor to listen without censure or perceptual defense. Clients sometimes test out how carefully or nonjudgmentally the counselor has been listening.

Example (The client tests the counselor to see if something he or she mentioned the preceding session is still remembered . . . or, if the counselor is going to pretend it was never said.)

Client   Maybe I could go into some of this in a future session. It really is something I should talk about, but it doesn't seem pressing now.

Counselor   I thought you mentioned last week that this would be your last session.

Client   (*Laughs*)   Oh, you remembered that. . . .

2. The counselor must communicate to the client, from the very beginning, the message, I am here to *help* you. Counselors sometimes try too hard to communicate, "I want you to like me," but this is not always the right message. The theme of being helpful is more appropriate.

Example (The counselor shows a need to be liked.)

Counselor   (*At the end of a session*)   I hope I've been helpful. I think you're really moving now. (*Apologetically*) It's a shame this session has to end, but I have another client waiting.

3. Although expressions of positive feelings are helpful, they should be restrained, especially in the early phases of counseling. Avoid giving the client *any* judgments—even positive ones.

Example (The counselor tells the client at the first session too many nice things. The client feels now that she or he has to live up to a certain standard . . . cannot fully be herself or himself.)

Counselor   Well, from what you've been telling me, you are a dedicated person . . . that is, really dedicated to helping others. That's an admirable quality, and I think I am going to enjoy working with you. *I* will find it rewarding. . . .

Client   (*Uncomfortably*)   Oh, I'm not all that good.

4. Clients progress best when they have to bear some (or most) of the responsibility for the treatment. This attitude is weakened if the counselor takes the role of trying to always reassure the client. It then appears to the client that the burden of successful treatment is on the counselor's shoulders.

Example (The neophyte counselor reassures the client too much too soon. He or she is anxious about the client not having enough confidence in the treatment and tries to assure him or her that the counseling will work, and that it will work quickly.)

Client   How long do you think it is going to take before I can find the right job? I hope another eight months isn't going to go by.

Counselor   Oh, you have nothing to worry about. We'll work out this problem, and we'll do it quickly. You'll be surprised at how quickly we can work it out.

5. The counselor should freely and unceremoniously express those feelings and ideas that can help the client grow. When the client sees the counselor talking openly, this communicates the message that the counselor is really interested in her or him as a person.

Example (The counselor relates a feeling he or she once had that is helpful to the client in dealing with a problem.)

Client   I don't know if you can understand what I'm saying. You're not handicapped—you can walk—and I'm not sure you really see what I'm trying to tell you.

Counselor   No, I'm not handicapped, but I can remember one point in my life when I was handicapped.

Client   You were?

Counselor   Yes, when I was in high school, I broke both my legs playing football. I had to use crutches for a year. I remember how I wasn't able to participate with the other kids, wasn't able to go out on dates or to play ball again. I remember some of those feelings as if it were yesterday. . . .

The Counseling Relationship   We have considered five guidelines to help the counselor establish a facilitative relationship between herself or himself and the client. We are now ready to turn our attention to the dynamics of the counseling session. But before we do, let us take a brief look at one phase of a counseling session to better understand how the interplay of forces underlying this very complex and intense relationship contributes to the quality of the treatment. The following excerpt is from a session between Ellen, an eighth-grade student, and the school counselor, Mrs. Block. This is the third meeting between them, and a key point of the experience. Long pauses are indicated by ellipses.

A Counseling Session   **Counselor (1)**   I believe we were talking last time about how you felt when you were in the hospital.

Ellen (1)   Oh, the hospital, that's right. It seems like a long time ago now, even though it was just last term. I don't remember how I got into that—talking about that, I mean. Do you remember?

Counselor (2)   Yes. You were saying that you haven't been as depressed lately as you were when you were in the hospital, but that you were beginning to feel more depressed now than you have been before.

Ellen (2) That's right. I was talking about the depression. Yes. Now I remember. Well, in the hospital I just kept talking about even if I got well, how I wouldn't be any better off than when I went in. I mean, here I was in all that pain and the best I could expect was to come out just as well as I was before I went in. The doctors weren't sure that my leg would heal all right, so I was always scared that maybe I would be a cripple. That, and all the people who came to visit me—I mean they meant well, but. . . .

Counselor (3) They meant well, but they weren't able to make you feel any better, is that it?

Ellen (3) Well . . . I guess that's it. You know, it's funny, but they kept telling me how I was lucky I wasn't injured worse in the accident. The car was totaled you know, and one of the people in the other car was in critical condition. They kept saying to me "Thank God, it wasn't worse. It could have been worse, you know. You should consider yourself lucky." I guess they were trying to be nice, to cheer me up. But I didn't feel lucky, even though I know things could have been worse. I guess we're never happy with what we have. (*Laughs*)

Counselor (4) What struck you as funny?

Ellen (4) That expression. It sounded just like what my mother always says. It's her expression, We're never happy with what we have.

Counselor (5) Does your mother still tell you that?

Ellen (5) I guess so. But I don't tell her about the way I feel anymore. I mean she just makes me feel bad about feeling bad. Does that make sense to you?

Counselor (6) You mean that if you feel depressed now, you are told that you shouldn't be depressed?

Ellen (6) That's it. Like I don't really have anything to be depressed about. I have a nice family, plenty of clothes, good friends, nothing to complain about. . . . Don't you think I'm kind of ungrateful for complaining so much? I mean what do I have to be depressed about?

Counselor (7) Maybe there are reasons to feel depressed that you just don't know about.

Ellen (7) Reasons that I don't know about? Like what?

Counselor (8) I don't know. But I'm sure that if you feel depressed, there is a good reason for it. We have to find the reason, and that's often not easy.

Ellen (8) But what can it be? I've always had everything that I've wanted. My parents are good to me—I have no real complaints. What possible reason could there be for my feeling depressed?

Counselor (9) (*Sits quietly and waits.*)

Ellen (9) Can you help me find the reason, if there is one? I tell you, I'd really like to know. I think I'd feel better just knowing the reason that I'm depressed. Not that I really think there is a reason.

Counselor (10)   What do you think then? Do you really believe that you're an ungrateful person because you feel depressed?

Ellen (10)   I don't know about "ungrateful." Maybe I'm just stupid not to appreciate the things I have. Maybe my mother's right that we're never happy with what we have.

Counselor (11)   Isn't it possible to feel happy about some things and depressed about others?

Ellen (11)   Sure, it's possible. But I know the things I feel happy about. How come I don't know the things that are depressing me? When I was in the hospital with my leg broken, I knew what I was depressed about. But it healed fine, and I'm not sick anymore. Why should I feel depressed? It's crazy.

Counselor (12)   (*Sits quietly and waits.*)

Ellen (12)   I see you're not going to be able to help me. . . .

Counselor (13)   This seems to be a mystery that neither of us can easily solve. We may both have to put some concentrated effort into this.

Ellen (13)   (*Sits silently and appears to be thinking.*)

Counselor (14)   (*Sits silently and waits.*)

Ellen (14)   You know, I find that I feel most depressed on weekends. During the week, I guess I'm too busy with schoolwork to feel depressed. But on the weekends I have a lot of time to think, and sometimes, I don't know why or when, I just start getting what you'd call "the blues."

Counselor (15)   Tell me what you do when you get these blues.

Ellen (15)   Oh, sometimes I go up to my room and listen to music or watch TV. Sometimes I'll go over to my friend Theresa's house, or if the weather is nice go down to the playground. Why? What's the difference what I do then? Is that some kind of psychological thing?

Counselor (16)   It's not a psychological thing. It's something about you, and I want to learn about you. After all, if we're going to work on this problem together, we should both know something about you. Right now, you know more about you than I do. After all, you've known yourself much longer than I've known you. You have a head start.

Ellen (16)   (*Laughs*)   You're really funny sometimes, Mrs. Block. I wish I had a sense of humor like yours. How did you learn to become a psychologist? Do you have to go to a special college for that or is it the same college that the teachers go to?

We'll leave this counseling session between Ellen and Mrs. Block for the time being, but return to it later in this section. Several things should be noted at this point. First, the client appears to feel comfortable speaking to the counselor and relates well to her throughout the interview. The complaint presented, depression, is a typical one which counselors encounter frequently in their practices. Although specific points about dealing with depression will be covered in Part 5 of this text (see chapter 14, "Crisis Intervention Counseling"), it should be mentioned at this time that it is always desirable, in working with the depressed client, to allow the client to fully experience the depression as a rightful feeling, that is, one that has a reason, a cause, even though this cause or reason may be beyond the client's awareness at the moment.

Second, we should note that the counselor allowed the client to direct the course of the interview, although the counselor did ask germane questions designed to help the student speak and to assist her in articulating her problem. Third, we see that several times during the discussion (Counselor 3, 6, 7, 11) the counselor subtly offered an interpretive communication to clarify something that the client had said previously. But what is most important is this: the counselor carefully established with the client a team approach in which they would deal with the problem together. It was no longer just the client's problem, but now a joint problem of the client and the counselor, a problem that they would work on together.

The counseling relationship itself, as opposed to any specific techniques of counseling or counseling strategies, played an important part in this encounter. The counseling relationship may be defined as the cumulative sum of feelings and perceptions held by each member of the counseling team, and the total effect of these feelings and perceptions along with the structure and quality of the interactions between them. It is, in short, the client's and counselor's feelings about each other. Much research in counseling has been directed toward this relationship; and we should consider some of the observations before returning to Ellen and Mrs. Block.

Wiggins (1972) discusses the counseling relationship in terms of the "life space of [clients]." The counselor, he suggests, should work to make the counseling office a part of the client's life space. To do this it is not necessary for the counselor to adopt the styles and manners of youth, but rather to make the counseling services relevant and appropriate to the needs of the clients. For example, a middle-class, middle-aged counselor did this by extending to her students understanding and acceptance. The students, in turn, found her office a comfortable, welcome place for private as well as group discussions. Another school counselor chose to become part of the life space of students by spending most of his working day out of the office. This counselor made sure to visit at least half the teachers and all the students in their classes during the day. In both of these cases, the counselor extended the counseling services. In order for the counselor to do this, of course, it is necessary for him or her to understand where the client's life space is, both physically and psychologically.

From these examples emerges a picture of the counselor as one who establishes a relevant, meaningful, productive relationship. The counseling relationship, as illustrated here, extends to all areas of interaction between counselor and clients.

Although this discussion has told us something about the structure of the counseling relationship, it tells little about the qualitative dimension of the relationship. A number of studies have investigated this subject. Carkhuff and Berenson (1969) have discussed counselor commitment as an important variable in the relationship. This commitment to the client, they argue, begins with a commitment to his or her own personal emergence, which in turn "frees him or her to make personal commitments to others." The argument is quite logical and well defined, and it does much to integrate the counselor's self-perceptions and feelings with his perceptions and feelings about the client. The nature of the commitment is expressed in four propositions:

1. The counselor is committed to living and relating independent of society's goals.
2. The counselor is committed to his own well-being and fulfillment.
3. The counselor is actively committed to his own personal experience in a lifelong learning process.
4. The counselor is fully aware of the implications of not being committed to constructive potency in his world.

A number of essential points are touched upon in these four propositions. First, we note that the committed counselor thinks highly of herself or himself and is able to formulate goals independent of social structures and to "devote [his] full energies to what is best for the individual involved, whether it be [himself] or the counselee." Such a counselor will certainly prove instrumental in making the society in which he or she lives better for all. Second, we note that this counselor cares about herself or himself, and we know that only the individual who is able to care about his or her self is ultimately able to care about others. Third, the committed counselor recognizes the value of growth; he or she "is aware that only with [his] own personal experience can he be truly creative and truly constructive." Finally, the counselor is courageous in the very special sense of honestly confronting the good as well as the bad, the pleasant as well as the unpleasant possibilities of existence. He or she "openly confronts the complete meaning of death, the hell of impotency, of having lived without personal meaning, feeling, reason, or human concern, without touching the life of yourself or another." Such a counselor will certainly be able to transfer this commitment to the client within the context of the counseling relationship.

Carkhuff and Berenson go on to examine the structure of the commitment as it applies to the client:

5. The counselor views his clients as he views himself.
6. The counselor will do anything for the client that he would do for himself under the same conditions.

    A sharing of the commitment between himself and the client—a mutual respect and rapport—becomes the foundation of the counseling relationship. As we know intuitively, a relationship which is built on mutual trust generates mutual trust.

7. The counselor is committed to personal and intimate involvement in a fully-sharing relationship.

What is meant by *personal* and *intimate?* They mean a unity of purpose, a pervasive empathy and warmth, a giving up of roles and pretenses, a healthy, productive identification. The next two propositions prove this.

8. The counselor is fully aware that if the client fails as a person, the counselor must share part of the pain.
9. No boundaries will limit the counselor's commitment to the client.

Finally, as we look at the concluding propositions we see the harmony and the inner beauty of the counseling relationship in clear focus. Between the counselor and the client a new world is built. It is a world where neither is alone, but where each shares joyfully and painfully in the other's life. It is a world of expanding possibilities, where each person gains strength from the other and gains energy by giving to the other. It is an exciting, limitless world.

10. The commitment of the counselor extends to full movement into the life of the client.
11. The counselor's commitment extends to the expansion of his own boundaries.
12. The commitment of the counselor extends to nourishing constructive forces and fighting destructive forces. (pp. 13-14)

As we speak of the counseling relationship, we must be sensitive to the limits of language in expressing the complexity of interaction between counselor and client. It is only by experiencing the counseling relationship—by participating in it—that we can fully appreciate the powerful dynamics that charge it with life energy. Our brief discussion only touches the surface; to get beneath the skin, we have to be there.

If we now turn our attention once more to the counseling session between Ellen and Mrs. Block, it should be clearer how these important elements of the counseling relationship form an interplay of forces that contribute to the productivity of the session. We will note, as we continue to reproduce the transcript, that the relationship between counselor and client is essentially what Drasgow and Walker (1960) call a *horizontal* relationship, with no intentional hierarchical stratification separating the two. At times, however, the relationship becomes more *diagonal,* especially when the client seeks some professional advice from the counselor. We should also note how Mrs. Block acts as what Thoresen (1969) would call an "applied behavioral scientist." She investigates the symptoms and causes of the client's situation logically and scientifically, but maintains at the same time a humanistic, personal, dynamic relationship with the client. Finally, we will note the manifestations of the counselor's commitment to the client. Mrs. Block is genuinely concerned with Ellen's problem and concerned for Ellen; and her concern "extends to full movement into the life of the client."

Ellen and Mrs. Block

As we look into the conclusion of this counseling session, then, we should note how these qualities of the counseling relationship begin to make an impact.

Counselor (17)   I was a teacher at one time, Ellen. I went back to school to learn to be a school psychologist.

Ellen (17)   Oh, I was just wondering. Do you mind that I asked you? I know sometimes counselors don't want to answer questions.

Counselor (18)   I don't mind at all. I'll try to answer any other questions you would like me to answer, also.

Ellen (18)   Just the big question of why I feel so rotten.

Counselor (19)   (*Sits quietly and waits.*)

Ellen (19)   I guess that is a question I'll have to find the answer to myself. You know, it's funny, but even though I'm really busy with school and things, sometimes I'm bored. I mean . . . well, it's like nothing is really interesting to me. I don't know if you know what I mean? Do you ever feel that way? I guess *bored* is the right word.

Counselor (20)   I've had that feeling at times. Why don't you tell me what it was like when you had it?

Ellen (20)   Well, when I was in the hospital I had it—a little anyway. Here I was each day, just hoping to get better, wishing that it wouldn't hurt so much . . . physically hurt, I mean. I don't know—it wasn't like I had something to think about that I really wanted to happen. I remember when I was a kid how I used to look forward to Christmas. For days, maybe weeks, I would count how long it was until I'd get my presents. All year I would think I'd like this or that—I'd have to wait for Christmas to get it. Not that my parents didn't buy me things. It's just that Christmas was sort of special, and I knew that everybody got things on Christmas and that I could have almost anything I wanted, even if I had misbehaved a little during the year. Does this sound stupid? But I loved Christmas and it's just that . . . it's just that there are no Christmases any more. Not for me, anyhow.

Counselor (21)   (*Sits quietly and waits.*)

Ellen (21)   What do you think about all this? Is it crazy?

Counselor (22)   I think that we all need a Christmas to look forward to. We all need something to hope for—something that is important to us—something that we really want and care about.

Ellen (22)   (*A broad smile lighting up her face, nods in agreement.*) It's not that things are really terrible; it's just that I don't have anything important to look forward to. . . .

Counselor (23)   Well, it looks, then, like there is a reason for your feeling depressed after all. Perhaps if we could find some things that you could look forward to—some important things in your life—these feelings of depression would begin to change. How do you feel about that?

Ellen (23)   I think so. It makes sense, anyway. But what things?

Counselor (24)   Well, that's something that we'll have to talk about some more. Do you think you could come back here next Thursday at this hour? You have a study period then, don't you?

Ellen (24)   Yes, I'll be able to come then. Are you sure it's no trouble? I mean I know how busy you are.

Counselor (25)   (*Smiles gently.*)   It will be my pleasure to work with you on this.

We note the progress that was made during this brief session. An existential explanation of this encounter would suggest that Ellen's feelings of depression were caused by a lack of active commitments in her life. The counselor helped her come to this conclusion; but it was a conclusion that Ellen herself reached without the direct intervention of the counselor. The quality and substance of the counseling relationship—the richness and warmth that it provided to the client— enabled the client to deal effectively with a feeling that had eluded her for some time. By finding an understanding, empathic, nonimposing interlocutor, the client was able to initiate and maintain a dialogue that allowed her to release her feelings and come to grips with her problems.

In Mrs. Block we find a skillful blending of the scientific-objective and the humanistic-subjective qualities which the counselor brings to the relationship. At no time was she detached and impersonal. In such interactions as (17) and (20), she offered a part of herself—information and personal feelings—to the client. Yet, like a scientist, she explored the hidden meanings and concealed dimensions of the client's communications. In later sessions, Mrs. Block, at Ellen's request, met with Ellen's parents and advised them of ways to help Ellen find and sustain nurtured meanings in her life. She spoke to one of Ellen's teachers, too, and Mrs. Block freely and fully entered the life space of this student.

The counseling process is characterized primarily, if not solely, by the helping relationship that exists between the counselor and the client. This helping relationship, in which the counselor uses his or her self—his or her feelings and perceptions—to help the client grow and prosper, has been the subject of much study and research. It is generally agreed that the counselor is an "instrumental self" (Combs, 1982) in the counseling relationship; that is, the feelings and personality of the counselor—the counselor as a person—become the basis of much of the client's growth, development, and change. In this section, we will show that a long-accepted principle from particle physics can shed light on how the moment-to-moment interaction between counselor and client becomes a reciprocal basis for change within each of them.

The "Copenhagen Interpretation"

One revolutionary twentieth-century development in scientific thought is known as the "Copenhagen Interpretation." This position, articulated by some of the world's greatest scientists in the period between world wars, and now universally recognized and accepted by the scientific community, has had a profound impact on every area of philosophy, science, and technology, but has been largely neglected in the field of counseling and psychotherapy. At the present writing, no major discussions of the Copenhagen Interpretation are included in any of the introductory textbooks on counseling and therapy, and it receives scant mention in all but a few specialized treatises. Yet, the theory holds much relevance to understanding the dynamics and practical implications of the counseling relationship from a perspective not otherwise available.

Although some attempts have been made to apply the Copenhagen Interpretation to specific psychological and sociological problems over the years (Zukaw, 1982), for the most part, it has been neglected by counseling practitioners and theorists. But the Copenhagen Interpretation can aid our understanding of how people change—especially the subjectivity and paradox that govern the relationship between clients and their counselors, and the often elusive nature of the counseling process itself.

The essence of the "new" physics on which the Copenhagen Interpretation is based—that all reality is "observer-created" and does not exist independently of our observation and participation in it—has a number of striking parallels in contemporary theories and practices of counseling and psychotherapy. More importantly, the Copenhagen Interpretation helps clarify why so many competing theories of counseling and views of the counseling relationship can exist side-by-side, working equally effectively for so many different individuals experiencing a wide range of personal problems.

Background

By the early 1920s, the leading physicists of the world found themselves confronted with a barrage of empirical incongruities that threatened the logic of an ordered and predictable physical universe which had been accepted without challenge since the time of Newton. Formerly, each new formula or physical discovery had made more and more sense of the universe, or at least of the concept of the universe that we understood and accepted. There had been consistency in the new findings, with each supporting the others in a logical way. But then, as a result of some bizarre scientific discoveries, the axioms of nature that had held together the many formulae used to explain the physical world were beginning to crumble. For example, the certainty that the long-accepted Newtonian laws of mechanical motion explained all physical movement and the axiom that all scientific findings were objective and empirical (free of the subjectivity of the observer) had both been disproven by the 1920s.

This revolution in physics began in 1900 when Max Planck made a discovery that would change forever our complacent trust in an ordered universe. Planck was investigating the phenomenon of black body radiation (energy emitted by heat without light sources) when he noted that the emission of energy from objects was discontinuous; that is, the energy was emitted in little packets, or *quanta*, rather than in a stream as would be expected. Each of these little packets, moreover, contained the same amount of energy. There was no explanation of why this was so.

Then, in 1913, the Danish physicist Niels Bohr offered an explanation that made this observation comprehensible (and for which he won the Nobel Prize). He found that there are "shells" of specific distances around the nucleus of an electron and that the number of electrons each shell can hold may be calculated. Electrons can travel from one shell to another, giving off energy. Since the amount of this energy is so small, it appears as a stream, rather than as the discontinuous little bursts that actually comprise it.

One of Bohr's students, a brilliant young German named Werner Heisenberg, studied the results of Planck's and Bohr's discoveries and made a discovery of his own that would upset our entire concept of nature. Heisenberg proved (through a mathematical technique called matrix algebra) that when we study subatomic particles, it is impossible to know at the same time both the position and the momentum of a moving particle. In other words, if we know where a particle is, we don't know where it is heading; if we know where it is heading, we don't know where it is. This is called *indeterminacy*.

Moreover, Heisenberg postulated that as we try harder and harder to find out where a particle is and where it is going—as our observations become more focused and acute—we change the very thing we are observing! We, the observer, become part of the process we are observing, so that we can never actually know what the process would have been like had we not chosen to observe it. This is called *uncertainty*. In short, the Heisenberg principle of uncertainty states that there is no real "path" of an electron; that an electron is never in one real place at a given time. Rather, where it is and what it is depends on how we measure it.

Does this mean that there are no such things as subatomic particles—the very basis of reality? It would seem that way, except for one explanation developed by physicists Louis de Broglie and Erwin Schrodinger that helped resolve the paradox.

The suggestion was made that matter travels in waves of probability. These waves can be specifically defined and drawn, say, on paper. But they are not waves that describe the actual path of an electron in reality—rather, they are indications of where an electron will most probably or least probably be found at a given time.

Even at this point, the analogy with the human life span, with psychosocial development and even physical growth, is striking. A person, like a subatomic particle, moves through life in a fairly predictable direction over time. We know from the works of Freud, Erikson, Piaget, Kohlberg, and many other theoreticians the probabilistic course of development, expressed through typical stages. But these stages are like the Schrodinger waves—never accurate indices of where a person is or has been, but rather indications of a general probability. They introduce indeterminism into our view of the person.

Furthermore, the problems which bring clients into a counseling setting are rarely expressed as linear formulae; on the contrary, they are usually non-explicable contradictions to the client's perceived existence and beliefs. The person unable to make a choice doesn't understand why he can't make a choice and why he is so upset by not choosing; the melancholic student, unable to study, socialize, or enjoy life, doesn't know why she is in this situation or what it means. Be it depression or a marital problem, the presenting symptom is almost always something discrepant with the articulation of the client's life plan, which was never devised to include this problem. A person's life is much like a probability wave that, even taking into account all aspects of free choice, genetic endowment, social and economic circumstances, etc., still yields to the laws of indeterminacy and uncertainty.

The Paradox of Reality

A formulation which attempted to unite the discrepant findings in physics came out of the 5th Solvay Congress held in Belgium in 1927. "The Copenhagen Interpretation marks the emergence of the new physics as a consistent way of viewing the world" (Zukaw, p. 62). The major implication is that reality does not correspond to rational thought. Rather, our participation in observing reality helps define the reality we are observing. As Wolf (1981) explains it,

> there is no reality until that reality is perceived. Our perceptions of reality will, consequently, appear somewhat contradictory, dualistic, and paradoxical. . . . The instantaneous experience of the reality of *Now* will not appear paradoxical at all. It is only when we observers attempt to construct a history of our perceptions that reality seems paradoxical.

The reason for this paradoxical appearance of reality—at least, atomic reality observed by physicists—is that no clear dividing line exists between ourselves and the reality we observe to exist outside ourselves. Instead, *reality depends upon our choices of what and how we choose to observe. These choices, in turn, depend upon our minds or, more specifically, the content of our thoughts. And our thoughts, in turn, depend upon our expectations, our desire for continuity* (Wolfe, p. 128, italics added).

This is the essence of the Copenhagen Interpretation and its relevance to counseling and psychotherapy in particular. Everything that goes on in life, including everything that transpires between client and counselor, is shaped and colored by an inevitable subjectivity that cannot be avoided.

Counseling Implications

Many of the psychological models that have been put forth to clarify the structure and function of the counseling relationship begin to make more sense in light of the Copenhagen Interpretation. For example, the widely accepted belief that counselor qualities predominate over technique makes perfect sense in an observer-created universe. In such a universe, the quality of the relationship coasts along a probabilistic wave of feelings, shaping and defining itself through the empathic communication of these feelings. Counselor commitment can then be conceptualized as the intensity of the interaction, and client response as its measured position of change.

Moreover, when we consider the "life space" of clients and counselors, we have to recognize that they intermix in the quantum sense of indeterminacy. No one is ever the same after being emotionally or intellectually "touched" by another; and the change is always reciprocal, so that not only are the two individuals different, but the relationship is different as well. This recognition may, in time, help explain the very nature of the counseling process and why talking is helpful in resolving emotional and role area problems.

We can sum up the counseling implications of the Copenhagen Interpretation (along with the indeterminacy principle and uncertainty) in these four statements:

1. A client in counseling or a patient in psychotherapy is different from the person he or she was before treatment in that the "reality" of the world of the person-in-treatment depends (in part, at least) upon the observations and reconstructions by the counselor or therapist.

2. A client's explication of his life and problems alters the life and problems as they were before the explication. The act of reconstructing and articulating parts of one's existence changes the very nature of that existence. In other words, the subjective reconstruction of one's subjective past leads to a second-tier subjectivity, rather than to the objectivity one might hope for.

3. The processes of therapeutic growth exhibit both indeterminacy and uncertainty. As a client changes, his needs for growth are never the same as they were before, and consequently, growth goals ("cure" so to speak) for any client can only be determined probabilistically (rather than mechanically).

4. Counselors of different schools would appear no more different to a particular client than counselors of the same school. The effects, likewise, would be indeterminate and uncertain. Because the actual experience of counselor and client is in fact the wave of probabilistic subjectivity of the moment, it is only what is happening at the time that matters.

You might make note as you study the main theories in the rest of this book how the Copenhagen Interpretation can help shed new light on the actual processes of the different kinds of counseling perspectives. Specifically, note how the Copenhagen Interpretation may help you reconcile theoretical as well as many practical differences among these schools of therapy.

Summary

In this chapter, we examined some fundamental aspects of the counseling relationship. We began by considering the role of counselor and exploring the congruence or incongruence between the counselor's "front region" and "back region." We then furnished several guidelines for a productive counseling relationship, which included the ability to listen to all of the client's feelings and to communicate to the client the message, I am here to *help* you. We also pointed out how these guidelines took into account many of the characteristics of the effective counselor discussed in the preceding chapter.

We examined part of a counseling session to see how the interplay of forces underlying the relationship contributed to the quality of treatment. Several important points were noted, including how a counseling relationship may be "horizontal," "diagonal," or "vertical," referring to the relative status positions of counselor and counselee.

Finally we examined the "Copenhagen Interpretation," a foundation principle of modern physics that has extensive implications for better understanding the counseling relationship. This interpretation of natural physical phenomena proposes that there is no objective reality until that reality is perceived and measured by an observer. When applied to the counseling relationship, the Copenhagen Interpretation suggests that the facilitative partnership between the client and counselor helps define the life situation, growth goals, and historical pasts of both individuals as they interact with one another.

Chapter Aim

To focus on the interaction between counselor and client during the counseling interview, citing, with illustrations, some of the specific techniques that are employed. To outline some principles for conducting the initial counseling interview.

The Initial Interview

The initial counseling interview is often critical to the ultimate success or failure of the entire course of the counseling process. We point out the necessity of the counselor dealing with the client's initial expectations, as well as with the client's fears. We suggest that the purpose of the interview is to set the stage for further meetings by helping the client clarify his or her future expectations and set tentative goals. Establishing rapport is a central goal of the first meeting.

Varieties of Counseling Techniques

The relationship between the counselor and the technique is far more complex than it appears on the surface; it is an interaction of personality traits, cognitive beliefs, and the setting of variables. Eclecticism allows the counselor to integrate techniques from different counseling and therapy orientations. Seven of the main counseling techniques are discussed, with examples given of each: clarification, reflection, probing, silence, interpretation, empathic response, and investigating alternatives. A segment of a counseling interview conducted by Carl Rogers is used to see some techniques as they are actually applied.

The Helping Dimension

There is more to conducting a counseling interview than simply using techniques. The affective concept of "experiencing" (which is felt, rather than thought or verbalized) lends a human dimension to the counseling process.

Conducting the
Counseling Interview

5

In this chapter we will focus on the face-to-face interaction between the counselor and client engaged in individual counseling. Our discussion in chapter 2 of the relationship between counseling theory and counseling practice revealed that much of what the counselor actually does may be the result of the counselor's personality and underlying philosophy, rather than a result of the theory to which the counselor subscribes. In Part 3 we will look at some of the theories of counseling in detail and enumerate a variety of different recommended techniques from which the counselor can draw. Now we shall explore some of the general techniques available to the counselor, to see how these are evolved, how they are implemented, and what results they produce. First we should consider what we mean by a *counseling technique*.

The question we must first answer is, Is a technique an explanation of what the counselor is doing, or is it, as has often been suggested, designed to assist the counselor prior to action? In its most basic sense, a technique may be conceptualized as a preferred strategy of the counselor. It is a form of behavior or response that communicates something to the client.

A technique may or may not be associated with a specific theory of counseling. To be sure, each theory has its own repertoire of techniques, integrated into the total theoretical approach, and its own list of implicitly prohibited techniques. Yet most of the behaviors exhibited by counselors in the setting neither meet the explicit requirements of the theoretical technique nor are common to merely one particular counseling orientation. On the contrary, most counseling interactions are universal, regardless of theoretical considerations. To arrive at the criteria for a successful counseling technique, let us, therefore, consider the technique in practice, rather than in theory.

To be effective, a counseling technique must be flexible, organized, and practical. Flexibility is necessary because of the far-ranging possibilities of client problems, client expectations, and client needs with which the counselor will be confronted. A technique that is too prescriptive and dogmatic will severely limit the counselor in the interaction with the client and restrict the possibilities of growth within the counseling situation.

In addition, a technique must be organized around a fundamental principle of treatment and directed toward the ultimate goal of the treatment. By organized, we mean specifically that the technique is addressed to the facet of the client that is prominent in the treatment milieu. If the client-centered attitude is dominant with the counselor, he or she should then use techniques that will meet the conditioned expectations of the client who has now been exposed to this attitude and approach. If a psychoanalytic approach is dominant, the counselor would then use techniques that are compatible with the client's expectations. This assures that the technique itself will contribute to the total process, becoming an integral part of the goal by becoming an assimilated force in the counseling relationship.

The technique should also be practical. I use this word both in its meaning of *realistic* and *pragmatic* to convey the dual responsibility of an effective counseling technique. On the one hand, the technique must not call on the counselor to offer more than she or he is capable of offering, to say or do what is not truly believed. On the other hand, the technique should work, should achieve a specific end, and should help affect a therapeutic change in the client.

With these ideas in mind, we will explore the relationship between the counselor and his or her counseling techniques. But first, let us look in some detail at the initial counseling interview to consider ways that the counseling process can get off to a better start.

The Initial Interview

Initiating the counseling process is critical to the ultimate success or failure of the entire course of the counseling. The very continuity and integrity of the counseling experience attests to the importance of the beginning phase. When we consider the initial interview, therefore, we should keep in mind that our discussion transcends the narrow time limitations of this single session and extends throughout the course of the counseling experience. Moreover, we will note that the operational definition of the term *interview* tells us a great deal about what should happen at the first interview.

First, we raise the question, What is an interview and how does it differ from other encounters between two people, such as ordinary conversation? Kadushin (1972) states that an interview differs from conversation in that it has a central purpose that is agreed to by the participants: "the interaction is designed to achieve a consciously selected purpose. The purpose may [even] be to establish a purpose for the interview" (p. 8). Gorden (1975) also makes the point that an interview always has a central purpose and this is what distinguishes it from conversation. Schubert (1971) expands these ideas, citing the concepts of "mutuality and purposeful talking" as central to the structure of an interview. He raises the following basic questions that help us define an interview and determine its structure:

Who does the talking? How is the purpose determined? How is mutuality achieved? The rather unsatisfactory answer to these questions is that "it depends"—it depends on a complex constellation of factors that have to do with the nature of the problem or task at hand, the person who feels some concern about it, the auspices under which help is being offered, the psychological, cultural, and social attributes of the person involved in the interview, and the physical setting in which the interview takes place. (p. 1)

This emphasizes the point that the counselor makes an ordinary encounter an interview by his or her actions and by the setting in which the encounter takes place.

The moment the client enters the counselor's office for the first time, a number of things should be going through the counselor's mind. Under what circumstances was this appointment arranged? Was it voluntary or was it made under some type of compulsion: required by a teacher, by the court, by the parents of the client, and so forth? How does the client appear as he or she walks through the door? Does body language reveal anything to the counselor? Does his or her face indicate any particular attitude? What might his or her expectations be at this moment? The counselor recognizes that because this is the client's first appointment he or she is most likely nervous, unsure of what to expect, and probably in the throes of some type of conflict.

Eisenberg and Delaney (1977) cite as the goals of the first interview "stimulating, open, honest, and full communication about the concerns needing to be discussed and the factors and background related to those concerns; working toward progressively deeper levels of understanding, respect, and trust between helpee and helper; providing the helpee with the view that something useful can be gained from the helping sessions; identifying a problem or concern for subsequent attention and work; and establishing the "gestalt" that counseling is a process where both parties must work hard to understand the client and his or her concerns" (p. 99). This set of goals is theoretically ideal, but at times difficult to implement. There are many factors, some of which are seemingly extraneous, that work against open communication during the initial interview. These have to be dealt with before the goals of counseling can move forward.

Vontress (1973) points out, for example, some of the cultural barriers between counselor and client that may impede progress at the beginning. These include racial and socioeconomic class differences. Sue (1977), carrying this point even further, suggests that the counselor's white, middle-class bias may confuse his or her "role behaviors" during the first interview and "predispose us to assume that a client's initial expectations and requests are not indicative of real needs" (p. 221). Factors beyond the counselor's control may also influence what transpires. Cash, Begley, McCowen, and Weise (1975) have found that clients perceive physically attractive counselors more positively in many dimensions than they do physically unattractive counselors. Stone and Morden (1976) found that the physical distance between counselor and client affects the client's ability to produce verbal material (they suggest 5 feet as the optimum distance). Newton and Caple (1974) found that clients who came into counseling with a personal problem perceived the same counselor differently than those who came for help with a vocational-educational problem, indicating that clients' needs influences their perceptions. All of these things need be taken into account during the initial counseling interview.

To meet the multifaceted and interacting demands of the initial interview, the beginning counselor might do well to have a tentative, but very flexible, routine worked out so as to feel comfortable conducting the interview. One must in effect find a practical compromise between total spontaneity and preparedness. On the one hand, a general protocol might be useful to help the counselor in a forward direction and to assure him or her that essential areas of discussion are not omitted. On the other hand, it is not always expedient to have a plan of specific questions, because this can sometimes have the effect of diverting the client from where he or she wants to head slowly. In fact, the best way to obtain information and at the same time establish the foundation for a successful relationship during the initial interview is to use questions as a starting point, then to be sensitive and alert to factual clues and responses, on the bases of which appropriate new questions can then be asked (Cox, Rutter & Holbrook, 1981).

In other words, the counselor should have an overall structure from which he or she may freely deviate as the need arises. Counselors should have a repertoire of possible responses available to meet the specific needs of the client during the initial interview: they should have a *tentative* structure planned. But most important, and this is what must be kept in mind, in the first interview the decision about what kind of questions to ask or what kind of approach to take is less important than the need to establish a working relationship; and this can only happen by virtue of the counselor's emotional response to the client, not by preplanned questions or techniques (Margulies & Havens, 1981).

We can state then that although the counselor may walk into the initial interview with some tentative ideas of what will be covered and some plans for the direction in which the interview will move, the counselor's sensitivity and response to the "here and now" communications by the client takes precedence over this plan. Thus, the structure of an initial counseling interview combines the objective and the subjective, the theoretical and personal, reflecting in the finest sense of the word the counselor's grasp of the immediate situation.

The goals or objectives of the initial interview, though varying slightly from one counseling approach to another, generally find agreement throughout the counseling profession. Specifically, Molyneaux and Lane (1982) suggest the following "interviewer objectives [as] appropriate for the opening portion of an interview":

Making the respondent comfortable and at ease;

Obtaining preliminary perceptions that may influence the conduct of the interview;

Alerting the respondent to any time limitations or procedural restrictions of which he or she may not be aware;

Establishing a working relationship with the respondent;

Creating an atmosphere that will facilitate the type of interview you wish to conduct.

To this structure we should add the essential element of establishing the terms of the future counseling sessions, the rules, guidelines, and formal expectations, what we call a "counseling contract." A contract in counseling differs from the use of the word in its legal context. A counseling contract is an unwritten but usually explicit agreement between the counselor and the client about what the treatment should do, how many sessions are expected, what general rules and guidelines will be followed, etc. It is not intended to fix rigidly the course of the counseling, but rather to assure both the counselor and the client that an understanding exists between them and that any deviations from this understanding should be mutually agreed upon by both parties. Some counselors, particularly behavioral counselors, use the contract to establish the particular goals of the treatment, while other counselors use the contract to explore the range of ideas to be examined during the course of treatment. Ezell and Patience (1972) have suggested that the use of the contract is itself a counseling technique.

Helping the counselee talk is often the most difficult part of the initial interview. The silent client, who sits and stares blankly at the counselor (or the client who is silent out of fear), is a challenge to most counselors. There are a number of gentle, appropriate ways of helping the client speak. These include asking questions, suggesting subjects which the client may wish to speak about, asking him whether he is comfortable, and so on. A general guideline is that the counselor should only make such statements as are intended to act as a catalyst for the client in his or her efforts to communicate. Rarely does the situation occur in which the counselor makes the client feel comfortable and the client is still unable to speak.

Remaining alert to the client's feelings and providing for his needs is the first distinctively therapeutic phase of the counseling process. The counselor wants to get a *sense of the client*, an appreciation of the client's unconscious reservoir of feelings. Typically, the client will demonstrate certain needs during the session. He or she may request information, vocational advice, or assistance in working out a personal problem. The client may explain that he "just needs someone to talk to," or wants sympathy for some predicament about which he or she has been unable to find someone to speak to. This individual may be seeking punishment and chastisement for something he or she has done which is considered "bad" or "evil." While the client may not directly comment on such needs, he usually offers a number of subtle indications of what he is presenting or will be looking for during the course of the counseling treatment.

Termination

The skillful termination of the counseling interview (and counseling process) has also been the subject of much research and discussion. We know that the conclusion of the initial interview is important both in bringing the client back again (when required) and in shaping this individual's judgment about the entire session. Moreover, the skillful termination of the counseling interview helps the client feel more positive about the experience as well as increasing the likelihood of his or her returning if the need arises.

The counselor should recognize that as the close of an interview nears, confusion, anxiety, or other forms of distress may occur. No matter how smoothly the session was progressing before, as the end appears, the emotional climate may become inordinately charged. Often, a client feels that critical topics were not discussed, central issues left uncovered, and stubborn problems left unresolved. Although these assumptions are probably correct, they are not necessarily the cause of the uncomfortable feelings. After all, there is always another day on which to come back to these questions and problems. Rather, what may be the root of the uncomfortable feeling is an end-session anxiety so familiar to many clients and counselors. This may be in part because of a feeling of lack of fulfilment, a sensation of the incompleteness of task, which the client or counselor experiences. Molyneaux and Lane (1982), among others who recognize this phenomenon as important when the conclusion of the interview approaches, point out:

> The last few minutes of an interview are special. The interview must be brought to a close; more than that—it should be brought to a satisfying close. Both interview participants have the need for completion of task. The gestalt psychologists have made us aware of the human need for closure—perception of an item as an organized whole. An unsolved problem or an uncompleted task can be considered an incomplete gestalt. As such, it can cause tension and frustration in an individual—a tension that can be relieved or discharged only when the incompleteness is somehow resolved, and the situation can be perceived as an organized whole. In an interview, this feeling of satisfying closure can be achieved if the purpose of the interview is accomplished. (Molyneaux & Lane, 1982, p. 143)

The termination can be made easier by ending the session with the appropriate question or remark. Any of the following statements by the counselor (in context) may serve as an adequate closing of the interview:

> "Well, I think we have a number of things to discuss in our next session."
> "So, our next appointment is Thursday at noon. Perhaps then we can better understand *why* this problem between you and your boss persists."
> "I believe today we gained some insight into why you get up in the middle of every night. Perhaps at the next session we can explore this further."
> "I would like to explore this further with you."

Each of these statements conveys to the client a distinct sense of continuity.

The termination of the counseling process poses challenges as difficult as, or more difficult than, the termination of the interview. Lack of closure may be a problem here as well. Termination may be viewed as temporary, since there is always the possibility that the client will return at some later point. Eisenberg and Delaney (1977) state that the goals of the termination session are to "(1) reinforce the client's behavior changes in the direction of the goal as stated by the client; (2) make sure the client has no other pressing concerns; and (3) help the client realize that he may seek the counselor's aid at any time in the future, as the 'door is always open' " (p. 199). There are several ways of doing this.

First, the counselor should encourage the client to discuss openly his or her feelings about termination (these probably are ambivalent). On the one hand, the client may be pleased about the progress made; but on the other hand, the client may feel a sense of loss at the prospect of not seeing the counselor again. The counselor may reassure to the client that he or she can return to visit whenever the need is felt. It is only through individual experiences, however, that the counselor acquires a sense of how to terminate an interview, or the counseling process, in the manner which is most in accord with the counselor's own, personal style.

The relationship between the counselor and his or her techniques changes as the counselor becomes more experienced, more confident in his or her abilities, more mature as a person, more comfortable in the counseling situation, and more aware of the client as a person. At first the counselor is likely to hold onto techniques as a person who cannot swim would hold onto a life preserver: they not only provide the ability to stay afloat, but they continually support her or him and conserve efforts. As the counselor gains experience and confidence, however, he or she gradually becomes less dependent upon techniques and more reliant upon a personal counseling intuition. The counselor may continue to use the same techniques with the same frequency as before, but the techniques are now at the service of the counselor. Soon the counselor begins to modify techniques to suit his or her own characteristics; the counselor amplifies the bland, objective, impersonal techniques with a personal touch.

Varieties of Counseling Techniques

It is at this point that counselors often become troubled by conflicts which arise between their theoretical orientation (and the techniques dictated by that theory) and the feelings they are experiencing in the immediacy of the counseling setting. A client-centered counselor, for example, may be unable to feel positive regard for a certain client. In spite of what the counselor believes should be done in a specific situation, the feelings experienced are communicated to the client above and beyond the application of the technique being employed. At this point in the interview, the "style" of the counselor becomes more prominent than the technique. A counseling style integrates the counselor's feelings and techniques and has a dramatic impact on the client's ability to communicate (Hawes, 1972).

This compatibility evolves slowly and requires flexibility and openness on the part of the counselor. The counselor must be willing to observe herself or himself in the counseling situation, to learn where capabilities and weaknesses lie, where she or he has much to offer the client and where little to offer, where personal needs might conflict with the client's needs, and where his or her personality might inadvertently distort perceptions of the client. Although evidence does not indicate either that feelings have priority over techniques, or that techniques are more important than the counselor's feelings, it appears from the research that techniques and feelings are interrelated, that each is to some extent functionally dependent upon the other. For this reason most counselors, knowingly or unknowingly, draw from many different schools of counseling to discover the techniques that work for them. Counselors who draw upon different schools of thought in their choice of techniques are said to be eclectic.

Specific Techniques

As a rule, the technique is named after the type of response the counselor offers to the client. Some of the techniques below are assoicated with only one or two schools of therapy, while others are used extensively by all of the schools. For example, interpretation is less used by humanists than by psychoanalysts. Eight of the most common (and most useful) counselor techniques (responses) are offered below, with a brief illustration of each:

Clarification

This is intended to illuminate or explicate, either for the counselor or for the client, the meaning of one of the client's communications. In addition to achieving cognitive understanding of information, it may help the client to understand ambiguities or confusions in his thinking.

Client   I can't get along with Mr. Jones or Buzzy, so I don't go to class.

Counselor   In what ways does going to class require you to interact with Buzzy or with Mr. Jones?

Client   Well, since Buzzy sits in front of me . . . you know, its pretty hard to avoid him . . . especially since he's always starting up with me. And since Mr. Jones always takes his side, I always get caught in the middle.

Reflection

"Reflection consists of bringing to the surface and expressing in words those feelings and attitudes that lie behind the interviewee's words." (Benjamin, 1974, p. 117). It is not so much a restating in words what the client has expressed as it is an empathic mirroring of the feelings behind the words. The counselor never expresses his or her judgment in a reflective statement, but rather captures the emotional perspective of the client, reflecting his or her perceptions of a situation. Because it is a communication of feeling rather than words, it is difficult to illustrate its impact in transcript form.

Client   I've been feeling badly lately . . . like I've done something bad.

Counselor   Like you've done something bad? (*said empathically*)

Client   Yes. Like I deserve to be punished.

Counselor   You feel that you should be punished. (*said empathically*)

Confrontation

Not every counselor uses confrontation. It is much more acceptable to cognitive counselors (Rational-emotive and Reality) than to Rogerian. Confrontation is often a perturbing technique, and requires the client be able to deal with the feelings and realities revealed through the technique. Confrontation "means a responsible unmasking of the discrepancies, distortions, games, and smoke screens the client uses to hide both from self-understanding and from constructive behavioral change. It also involves challenging the undeveloped, the underdeveloped, the unused, and the misused potentialities, skills, and resources of the client, with a view to examining and understanding these resources and putting them to use in action problems. Confrontation is an invitation by the helper to the client to explore his defenses—those that keep him from understanding and those that keep him from action (Egan, 1977, p. 158).

Client   I would be studying for my boards now if I thought there was the slightest chance in the world I could pass them.

Counselor   Really?

Client   Of course. Do you think I like this worrying, day after day?

Counselor   Well, could it be that maybe all the worrying is in a way preferable to studying because this way you are building up a case for your anticipated failure? "Since I'm too anxious to study I can't pass the test." It's better than feeling dumb, isn't it?

The counselor, through the use of questions, attempts to encourage the client **Probing** to expressions of greater depth and to a personal awareness of deeper understanding and self-insight. The probing questions should never be overwhelming to the client.

Client   I find that I just can't study, even if I know that I'm going to fail the test.

Counselor   What happens when it gets down to study time?

Client   I get blocked. I can't concentrate.

Counselor   And your feelings at such a time are. . . ?

Client   I feel like I'm going to fail.

Although it is sometimes not recognized as a skillful, facilitative response, **Silence** silence is one of the most helpful expressions that the counselor can offer to the client. It is particularly useful when the client is engaged in self-analysis, which can be helpful to achieve the ultimate success of the counseling process.

Client   Why do you think I'm so upset about this test? Intellectually, I know I can pass it, but emotionally. . . .

Counselor   (silence)

Client   Why do I feel this tenseness whenever I have to take a test?

Counselor   (silence)

The counselor explains to the client a hidden meaning behind his statements **Interpretation** or actions. "Although interpretations have diverse form and content and are often difficult to distinguish from other interventions, they may be broadly conceptualized to include all interventions that present discrepant information to the client. The discrepancy may be semantic, as with interventions that label or re-frame client material, or it may be propositional, connecting events in the client's experience that were not previously connected in the same way. The discrepancy may range from small, in the form of simple paraphrases, to large, as in inter-ventions that question perceptions or beliefs the client had taken for granted. . . . (Claiborn, 1982, p. 452).

Client   I'm sorry that I'm laughing at you—don't take it personally. I can't help it, but I find you very funny looking. Whenever I think of you, I laugh.

Counselor   Perhaps it is really feelings of anger that you are experiencing.

Interpretation is one of the most widely used and yet controversial techniques in counseling. Many practitioners disagree concerning its efficacy and content. Some argue that interpretation attributes too much credence to the counselor's per-ceptions; others, that it is based on fallacious assumptions, such as the priority of the unconscious. Claiborn (1982) proposes three models for understanding the possible relationship between interpretation and change. These models help us better understand how interpretation can be used differently by partisans of dis-tinct perspectives.

The Relationship Model   The interpretation itself is not important except insofar as it becomes a part of the client/therapist relationship. This is conveyed by the attitude in which the interpretation is given, not by the content of it.

The Discrepancy Model   Basic to this view is the assertion that the interpretation shows the client a cognitive discrepancy between his view and the therapist's and as a result of this discrepancy he begins to change. "According to the discrepancy model, interpretations effect change in the assumptive world by presenting the client with discrepant communication that influences the client in the direction of the interpretation content. Changes in the assumptive world may mediate changes in the client's thoughts, feelings, and overt behavior" (p. 446).

The Content Model   This model says the effect of an interpretation depends upon its content. "If the content model is to receive an adequate test, the content of interpretation must be discrepant from client beliefs on dimensions directly relevant to the problem. . . ."

Empathic Response   The counselor shows that he or she accepts the client and understands emo-tionally what the client is attempting to communicate. It is essential that the counselor be able to differentiate between sympathy and empathy. The former is an expression of commiseration, while the latter is an acknowledgement that the counselor too, has these same feelings. As *000* (Reviewer #12, 1982, personal communication) points out:

> The word 'empathy' usually means a capability or action of putting oneself in the client's perceptual or attitudinal framework and communicating an understanding of the client with regard to both feeling and content. It is the counselor's communication both verbally and nonverbally of the understanding of the client's message. The client's message includes both stated and unstated meanings. Empathic understanding is the counselor's expression of both these aspects.

As an example, *00* suggests the following counselor response for this client question:

Client   I feel like such a stupid idiot . . . such a failure. Everyone has a date for the party except me. No one has asked me . . . and I know nobody is going to.

Counselor   Since most other persons have dates for the party and you haven't been asked, you are feeling rejected and left out. I can understand this hurts you deeply.

Like interpretation, counselor self-disclosure is viewed differently as a counselor characteristic by partisans of different viewpoints. While "humanistic/existential theorists claim that counselor disclosures provide a critical relationship building function and are necessary for developing a climate of authenticity, genuineness, and integrity thought to be essential for effective counseling," Dowd and Boroto (1982) point out that "social learning theorists support the use of counselor disclosure for modeling appropriate counseling behavior to the client and as a social reinforcer." But, they go on, "opponents of counselor disclosure view the role of the counselor as that of a mirror, and thus counselor disclosures are seen as interfering with the development of the transference. . . ." [p. 8]. **Self-Disclosure**

Client   I don't see how I will ever get over this hurt. . . . I don't see myself ever back to normal.

Counselor   (after a silence). I know how you feel this minute. I lost my parents too. At that time, I didn't think I would ever make it through. (a brief silence) It does take time.

This has two purposes: to assist the client in making choices and to help the individual understand the reasons underlying whatever choices he or she is disposed to. This technique is particularly helpful in terms of the client's reality orientation. **Investigating Alternatives**

Client   Since I wasn't able to get into any college, I guess I'm going to be a failure.

Counselor   I wonder what other possibilities you might consider?

Client   Well, I guess I could pursue carpentry. I do love working with wood.

Counselor   Tell me what you know about getting a job in that field?

Client   I guess I could ask my uncle Al. He's in the union, you know.

These represent only a few of the many counseling techniques. They have been selected because they are the most general in scope and the most widely used. Another that should be mentioned is the open-ended question which allows the client flexibility of response because of the question's lack of structure. This type of question—What can you tell me about yourself? for instance—is particularly helpful during the first interview.

Rhoades (1987) has identified some basic rules that might help the beginning counselor synthesize intellectually and apply in practice effective counseling principles:

1. Converse with a purpose.
2. Don't be in a hurry.
3. Avoid asking questions that can be answered with a simple "yes" or "no."
4. Don't put words in your client's mouth.
5. Be selective when you talk.
6. End the interview, firmly but gently, on time.
7. Listen carefully.
8. Don't complete the client's sentences.
9. Keep the client on the subject and begin gently to get the client to interpret his/her problem.
10. Don't sugarcoat bad news.
11. Be selective when you give information.
12. When you approve or disapprove of what the client is saying, don't be overindulgent or overcritical.

These are particularly helpful do's and dont's that a counselor can keep in mind until sound counseling practices are fully integrated on an emotional level within the personality.

Let us now examine a fragment of an actual counseling interview conducted by Carl Rogers. In this section from the famous "Case of Mary Jane Tilden," Rogers was helping a client discover her negative attitude toward self and learn how it is interfering with her social efforts. Counselor techniques and client responses are indicated (by Carl Rogers) in the margin.[1]

1. This passage is from "The Case of Mary Jane Tilden" by Carl R. Rogers. In *Casebook of Non-Directive Counseling*, ed. by William U. Snyder. (Boston: Houghton Mifflin, 1947), pp. 128–203.

Counselor Well—how do you want to use the time today?

Client Well—I don't quite know. (*Long pause*) I was just wondering. I was reading a book the other day. It was called, uh—*Your Life as a Woman*—and the subtitle was "How to make the most of it." In this book it showed different types of people and their work, and it didn't go into the causes of it or anything—but—uh—it showed how that person is not living a full life, and it sort of shows why—I mean, uh—it shows why there are different responses to people and it defines for you the reasons why people didn't like them—I mean, uh—it went into how, uh—they thought too much of themselves when they were in a group. They didn't give anything and it explains very carefully that the person was just lazy—and didn't make the effort to do those things. Well, I thought this book was very good, and it said that the person who doesn't grasp those things isn't necessarily crazy, he just hasn't made the effort to do those things, and it's a constant effort to improve—to change. Well, when I read it, it gave me a sort of clear insight into the thing. . . . But still—I didn't know where to start. When I read it I realized that people do go through those things—I don't even know why I brought that up—it just seemed to be sort of a good start.

Answer

Insight

Problem

Counselor M-hm. You felt that you gained something from reading that book that indicated that not getting along with a group wasn't necessarily abnormal, but that it might be a constant effort to keep building an association with a group. Is that it? But it still leaves you feeling "Where do I start?" Is that right?

Simple acceptance

Clarification of feeling

Client   That's right. (*Long pause*) Well, in the first place, if I *were* to take a job right now, I don't think that it would be fair to the employer, I mean, I really don't think it would be—when I'm in a rut like this. The point is, am I just raising that as a defense mechanism for not getting out? Or am I really thinking that it just wouldn't be fair? That's an important question to me.

Agreement

Problem— Negative attitude toward self

Insight— Ambivalent attitude toward self

Counselor   You feel that it wouldn't be fair, and at the same time there rises in your mind a question, are you just putting that up to keep from undertaking what would be a hard thing to do?

Clarification of feeling

Client   That's right. (*Pause. Laughs.*) You shake your head. Is that all?

Agreement

Counselor   You feel perhaps I should know the answers, then.

Clarification of feeling

Client   That's right. Is it fair to an employer to go out and take a job that you feel, well, it may help you but it may not do very much for him? (*Pause*) Is it justifiable?

Agreement

Asking for information

Counselor   You feel you might really be cheating the employer by doing that?

Clarification of feeling

Client   That's right. I've said that before. I know we've covered that once before. Uh-huh. (*Long pause. Laughs.*) Well, what's the answer? Am I supposed to get the answers?

Agreement

Asking for information— Negative attitude toward counselor

Counselor   You are wondering that, too, aren't you, whether maybe the answer is in you?

Clarification of feeling

Client   In other words, I'd have to make a radical change before I—I'm supposed to change in attitude, and change in everything.

Insight

Counselor   You realize that it would mean a pretty radical shift if—uh—if you tried some of those things.

Clarification of feeling

Client   That's right. (*Long pause*) I suppose it would be better for me, I mean, I probably wouldn't like it at first, but then maybe it would help me, wouldn't it? It would sort of force me to do the things I don't want to do, I guess—

Agreement

Insight—ambivalent attitude

Counselor You think that maybe it would be a tough proposition, but maybe it would really have a lot in it for you.	**Clarification of feeling**
Client Yes, it would probably force me to do something. (*Pause*) But then where do you go from there? What's next?	**Agreement, insight, asking for information**
Counselor You realize that, even if you did that, there'd still be plenty of unanswered questions and plenty of difficulty still ahead.	**Clarification of feeling**

....

Counselor That is, you're wondering if you picked some goal like a job or something that you could definitely work on, would that really change any of your basic thinking or would it just be a temporary distraction, kind of?	**Clarification of feeling**
Client That's right. In other words, if I ever stopped thinking about—the things that are bothering me—somehow or other I still don't think that just by not thinking about those things for a month or two months and trying to think about other things—still I don't feel as though it would have changed me much, basically.	**Agreement** **Insight** **Problem—negative attitude toward self**

If counseling were only technique, of course, there would actually be very little need for counselors. It would simply be a mechanistic process. In reality, there is much more to the counseling experience than the counselor's use of techniques: there is the human dimension of the interaction, and this dimension comes through, without exception, in every counseling interview. This is beyond explanation and can only be experienced in person, in the "here and now" of the interaction. We call it the "helping dimension."

There are two significant variables in the counseling process: the counselor and the client. To learn about the process and to discuss it intelligently, we break down these two variables into subvariables, such as age, sex, race, background, motivation, personality, and so forth. Motivation is discussed at the beginning of chapter 6, and race and cultural orientation will be discussed later.

The Helping Dimension

One variable not yet mentioned is what Gendlin (1961) calls "experiencing." He describes it this way:

(1) Experiencing is *felt,* rather than thought, known, or verbalized. (2) Experiencing occurs in the *immediate* present. It is not generalized attributes of a person such as traits, complexes, or dispositions. Rather, experiencing is what a person feels here and now, in this moment. Experiencing is the changing flow of feeling which makes it possible for every individual to feel something any given moment. (p. 234)

Gendlin sees this variable as significant because it affects the client's ability to change and grow. In fact, the quality of experiencing is central to every counseling interview, and the congruence between the client's experiencing and the counselor's is an important contributor to a successful outcome.

We can now focus more closely on the key facet of the entire counseling process: the helping dimension. Rogers (1961) listed the questions that circumscribe this dimension; and we should look at these questions in light of the Rogerian case material presented earlier:

Can I *be* in some way which will be perceived by the other person as trustworthy, as dependable or consistent in some deep sense? . . . Can I be expressive enough as a person that what I am will be communicated unambiguously? . . . Can I let myself experience positive attitudes toward this other person? . . . Can I be strong enough as a person to be separate from the other? . . . Am I secure enough within myself to permit his separateness? . . . Can I let myself enter fully into the world of his feelings and personal meanings and see these as he does? . . . Can I receive him as he is? (p. 50–54)

The answers to these questions and several others like them led Rogers to the "process conception" of client-centered counseling that is discussed in chapter 8. This conception examines the various movements of the client toward growth as she or he experiences the facilitative communications of the counselor.

Summary

In this chapter we looked at the counseling interview in some detail, and outlined a few of the main techniques used. We began by focusing on the initial counseling interview, and considered ways in which that interview could be used constructively. We also examined some of the difficulties the counselor faces in working out a termination procedure, either for the initial interview or for the entire counseling process. In both cases we noted how the opportunity for future contact between client and counselor should be maintained through closing statements. Next we set forth the idea of integrating the counselor's personality with the technique, and looked at seven of the commonly used techniques of eclectic counseling: clarification, reflection, probing, silence, interpretation, empathic response, and investigating alternatives. Case material by Carl Rogers was used to illustrate the fluidity of the counseling process. Finally, we discussed the helping dimension, which is the most essential quality of all successful counseling endeavors.

Chapter Aim

To show some of the ways the goals of counseling are formulated through the counselor-client interaction; to explore what the counselor can do to facilitate the client's growth and to help the client change those behaviors she or he wishes to change.

The reasons clients enter the counseling situation differ widely, and often a client may have difficulty saying why he or she is there. In general, client motivation is a significant factor in the counseling outcome. The prognosis is much better for a client who comes voluntarily than for someone who is forced into counseling.

Client Expectations

Much of the client's growth and progress is a result of how the counselor responds to what he or she communicates. Appropriate responding requires empathic understanding, but it also includes a cognitive dimension in which the counselor mentally anticipates the best response to make to this client. This decision is much influenced by the counselor's value system; and we emphasize freedom as being a predominant value, which proliferates into other values. Answering the client's questions is an essential phase of responding. The cardinal rule is: only answer questions when you are clear about why the client is asking the question, what the client means by the question, and what your answer will mean to the client. Questions and answers between counselor and client can be a helpful way of building up the relationship, of achieving insight and self-understanding.

Responding to the Client

We begin with the assumption that for change to have real meaning, it must be meaningful to the client. One necessary aspect of growth and change is the lessening of defensiveness. We differentiate between coping and defensiveness, and look at the following major defense mechanisms to find out how they impede realistic, mature functioning: repression, projection, reaction formation, intellectualization, denial, isolation, rationalization, displacement, regression, introjection, and identification.

Factors and Directions of Client Change

Practical Considerations   We examine some case material to see how a client was helped by the sensitivity and skillful interventions of the counselor. In these case studies, we learn how the client was able to gain insight through her questions to and discussions with the counselor.

Facilitating Growth
and Change

6

We have now examined in some depth some of the interactions that take place during the counseling session. We have seen ways in which the counseling relationship expresses itself through interaction, and have considered some constructive ways in which the counselor can relate to the client in a therapeutic way through the use of techniques and facilitative responses. Now we shall look more deeply at the goals of counseling, paying particular attention to how the client and counselor formulate counseling goals for growth and change, how expectations of counseling affect the process, and how a variety of forces interact to become a part of the counseling relationship. By the conclusion of this chapter, you should have acquired a "feel" for how the counseling process, with its myriad complexities and diversities, facilitates growth and change.

Client Expectations

When the client enters the counselor's office, he or she is there for a reason, although the reason may be as obscure or elusive to the client as it is to the counselor. Moreover, not only is the client there for a reason, but he or she has entered the office accompanied by certain beliefs, presuppositions, feelings, and expectations which immediately color the situation and the client's responses to it. It is the counselor's first responsibility in the counseling session to find out why the client is there and to discuss his or her expectations of and goals for the sessions. This will have the very positive effect of eliminating (or at least minimizing) misunderstandings and clarifying the raison d'être of the treatment.

What are some of the typical reasons that individuals enter counseling? They are, of course, as varied as the individuals, but we can list a few of the more common reasons. Some clients enter because they are compelled to by vocational or school personnel, legal authorities, parents, or other powers-that-be. Some enter for particular guidance or advice, information or professional insight into alternatives which confront them. Some enter because of inner pain: the torment of anxiety or depression, the nagging hurt of guilt, the hollow emptiness of insecurity and self-despisement. Still others enter counseling because they themselves believe that their behavior must be changed, that new ways of living have to be discovered, alternative life-styles explored. A few enter to maximize their potentialities in life, to become more in touch with themselves and others, and even, to one day become counselors themselves.

Although we can state these reasons with clarity, the client often has difficulty expressing the reason that has brought him or her to counseling. The counselor, through patient questioning, even more patient silence, and communication of respect for the client, enables the client to express his or her reason for being. The counselor is well aware that not only does this reason influence and help shape the course of the counseling process; it also reveals something about the client and his or her life hopes as well.

This *motivational* reason, translated into practice, becomes what White (1973) calls the "guiding idea" of the counseling process:

> When two people meet in an office, one of whom defines himself as a counseling psychologist, the other in need of expert help with problems of living, the ensuing conversation takes place under the influence of a guiding idea. In its most general form, this guiding idea is that the client can lead his life better and that the counselor can help him do so. If the client comes with a highly specific complaint, such as being afraid to cross streets, the guiding idea is so obvious as to escape notice. . . . But the difficulties of living that clients put before their counselors are not often so sharply circumscribed. Sometimes they are broadly encompassing, as when a client announces that he does not know who he is. Whatever procedure the counselor adopts, he can hardly be of service if he has no guiding ideas of his own on the subject of how to live. (p. 3)

The guiding idea, as White presents it, is a combination of the client's expectations of counseling and the counselor's own view of counseling—and of living, in general.

One reason a client comes to counseling, a reason that usually augurs an unfavorable prognosis, is that he has been forced to come and would rather not be there. Strictly speaking, this person should not be considered a client. He becomes a client only after indicating a motivation to be there—a need for counseling. "Counseling," Lewis (1970) argues, "cannot take place with a client who has no counseling need. . . . The person who enters the counselor's office with no reason of his own for being there is not at the moment a client. He may become one eventually, but his motivation must first be aroused" (p. 2).

Boy (1974) compares the unmotivated with the motivated client:

> Clients who voluntarily enter counseling are in a better position to profit from the relationship. Since it is their idea to engage in counseling, voluntary clients are less resistant, more willing to move toward behavioral change, more honest in appraising their behavior, more willing to expend their psychic energy needed to change their behavior, and more trusting of the counseling relationship. (p. 166)

Ritchie (1986) points out some techniques and strategies for working with the involuntary client, a frequent situation in penal and residential treatment facilities. He emphasizes the need for structure at the beginning and suggests using the initial interview for explaining the counseling process, and trying to help the client see what he or she may possibly gain from it. After pointing out some specific techniques for resolving resistance, he suggests:

> When the involuntary client does admit to having a problem and expresses a desire to work on it, setting both long-term and intermediate goals may help minimize resistance by reducing the change process into small steps. Clients who lack the skills to change may be helped through behavioral techniques such as modeling, rehearsal, and role play. When clients rehearse new behaviors in the safety of the counseling setting, they may make a commitment to try the new behaviors outside of counseling. In dealing with the client's attempts to change, the counselor should be instructive and supportive and should show appreciation of the difficulties involved in trying to change part of one's life-style. (p. 518)

Client motivation, even where it is clouded by some ambivalence, is desirable for two reasons. First, it provides the client with the required inner support and encouragement for the initial decision to enter counseling; it says, in effect, "This was the right decision." Second, motivation offers reassurance and strengthens commitment when movement and change are not progressing as smoothly as one hopes; it says, "Stick with it, even when the going gets tough." Both of these elements are essential for successful counseling outcomes. "People often begin therapy wanting to change painful person behavior," Peterson and Melcher (1981) point out, but as much as they may try, as much effort as they put into it, the unwanted behavior persists, with the unfortunate result that "even though a wealth of energy has been spent, no desired change occurs" (p. 101). It is at this point that client motivation is indispensable to successful continuance.

In short, for counseling to be successful, both counselor and client need an extraordinary amount of patience, persistence, and confidence. They have to believe in the process and recognize the likelihood of a successful outcome, even at the dimmest moments. Heilbrun (1982) call this quality of counseling readiness "psychological-mindedness" and it indicates a willingness to look at matters from a psychological point of view, which offers favorable prospects for a successful outcome. It is clear from these comments that if the client is not initially motivated, no meaningful counseling can take place; therefore the counselor's first responsibility is either to motivate the client or to terminate the pseudocounseling relationship, a move which the unmotivated client will surely respect.

Exploring the motivated client's expectations of counseling is essential before the change process can begin. What do you expect from your visits here? What would you like to talk about while you're here? How long do you plan to see me? What do you hope to gain from counseling? These and other questions touch upon the central problem of *client expectation*. It is imperative that when the client's expectations are unrealistic, the counselor helps her or him develop realistic expectations that can be met during the counseling experience. Such an act is in itself therapeutic, since realistic expectations are a part of healthy living.

In establishing the goals of the counseling process, the counselor should place the major burden on the client, for it is only the client who knows what he or she wants. As we noted, however, certain psychotherapeutic approaches have inherent goals (*integration* in psychoanalysis, *self-actualization* in humanistic psychotherapy, *authenticity* in existentialism, etc.); the counselor should be careful to maintain a flexible attitude which will allow the individual client to articulate his or her own goals, even if these do not conform entirely to the goals of the theory to which the counselor subscribes. One of the great contributions of the counseling profession is the willingness, even encouragement, to allow the client to define the goals for the counseling process.

Setting Goals   It is generally agreed that the setting of goals at or near the beginning of the counseling process is essential to the ultimate success of the endeavor (Ryle, 1979). Practitioners of almost all counseling positions agree that the setting of goals is a significant factor in giving the counseling process some direction; but the emphasis placed on this stage, and the discrepant ways they suggest going about it, differ markedly from one point of view to another. Moreover, the specific ways, overt and covert, intentional and unintentional, in which counselors go about helping their clients to formulate, articulate, and assess their personal goals are extremely complex; this can be alternately explained by means of a number of cognitive, social-psychological, and information-processing theories (Senour, 1982).

For example, the psychoanalytic approach, at one extreme, suggests that all tentative goals are encumbered initially by resistances and that resolving these resistances is necessary before realistic goals can be set (Kirman, 1977). Thus, the psychoanalytic counselor will help the client formulate goals by assisting him or her to resolve resistances and to be less defensive. The behavioral approach, at the other extreme, maintains that the setting of goals is predominantly controlled by the rational, logical dimension of the client's thinking; it is a basis, in fact, for the counseling contract. Thus, the behavioral counselor will approach the task on an entirely logical, practical level, with little interest in the underlying dynamics and no interest in the so-called resistances. Between these extremes are many various ways of establishing goals.

A useful middle ground which can be applied by practitioners of almost all perspectives, is set forth by Cormier and Cormier (1979). They point out that the process of defining and establishing goals in counseling can generally be divided into the following stages, each of which can be described operationally:

1. *Defining the Goal Behavior* The behavior of an outcome goal describes what the client . . . is to *do* as a result of the counseling. This part of an outcome goal defines the specific behavior the client is

to perform. Some examples of a behavior include reducing one's weight, asking for help from a teacher, verbal sharing of positive feelings about oneself, or thinking about oneself in positive ways (p. 183).

2. *Determining the conditions under which the goal behavior is to occur* [This] specifies the condition—that is, the *situation* or *circumstances* where the behavior will occur. . . . The condition suggests a particular person with whom the Client may perform the desired behaviors, or a particular *setting* (p. 184).

3. *Establishing the Level or Extent of the Goal Behavior* This part describes *how much* the client is to do or complete in order to reach the desired goal. The level of outcome goal serves as a barometer that measures the extent to which the client will be able to perform the desired behavior (p. 184).

4. *Identifying and Sequencing Subgoals* The change represented by counseling goals can be achieved best if the process is gradual. Any change program should be organized into an 'orderly learning sequence' that guides the client through small steps toward the ultimate desired behaviors (p. 187).

5. *Obtaining an Oral or Written Client Commitment for Working toward the Goal* After the goals have been selected and defined, the counselor will begin selecting counseling strategies to meet the client's goals. At this point, the counselor should elicit some commitment from the client to do the work necessary for goal attainment (p. 189).

Of course, these stages are not always as clear-cut as might appear. For one thing, clients are often not sure of what kind of problem has brought them to treatment. A person may just not be feeling right, may have been asked to come to sessions by a spouse, parent, or teacher, or may be confused about what is actually bothering him or her.

While psychiatrists and psychologists have often relied on diagnostic categories to classify their clients' problems, this has proven ineffective or inconclusive for a variety of reasons (see discussion of diagnosis in chapter 2). During the past thirty years, counselors have come to view clients' problems more in terms of manifest, or practical implications, and have developed counseling strategies accordingly. Many organizational frameworks have been proposed. In what is possibly the most comprehensive and simple to use, Celotta and Telasi-Golubcow (1982) have developed a taxonomy for classifying clients' problems into five basic levels. Some problems may overlap, but the levels help us better understand how to approach problems. The five kinds of problems are defined as follows:

General Expectation Problems "Problems of this type are perceptual in nature. They exist when the environment is seen to be threatening and when the self is seen to be a passive victim of the hostile environment." **Level 1**

Level 2   *General Cognition Problems* "This type of problem . . . is said to exist when the client is making broad maladaptive statements about self or others on either an unconscious or conscious level. General cognition problems affect a broad spectrum of roles and activities. . . . These problems can be formed at any time after language comprehension develops."

Level 3   *Specific Cognition Problems* "Like the preceding type of problem this too is cognitive in nature, but it deals with ideas, attitudes, or beliefs that seem to affect the problem at hand. Unlike the preceding problem, this one does not have negative consequences for many of the important areas of a client's life. . . . These cognitions are usually derived from the culture at large, specific religious groups, or the family group."

Level 4   *Information Problems* Problems of this type exist when the client has inadequate information or facts. . . . This type of problem is readily dealt with in an 'educative' manner by supplying the necessary information through discussion, lecture or file-viewing, books, and so on."

Level 5   *Behavior Problems* These are "characterized by a behavioral lack or excess of some type. The client shows no resistance to following a logical solution and to practicing new behaviors. The client is able to profit from practice with new behaviors or contingencies and is then able to adapt optimally."

While certain modifications to this taxonomy may be made, depending on the counselor's orientation, this is basically an inclusive framework that can better help the counselor understand the client's problems. After correctly perceiving and understanding the client, responding to the client is made all the easier.

Responding to the Client

Much of the emotional learning—and hence, growth—that takes place in counseling is the result of the way the counselor responds to the client. The counselor's responses, when taken as a totality, comprise the core of the counseling process. According to Rhoades (1987), the counseling process functions simultaneously on three dimensions. The *personal* dimension consists of messages that clients send to the counselor regarding themselves. In the *contextual* dimension, the context of the message becomes more important than its content. The *relational* dimension is governed by the messages the client sends regarding his or her feelings about the counselor. Together, these dimensional levels help make clear what counselor *responding* is and why it is at the heart of the counseling process. In their taxonomy of the affective domain, in which they outline the hierarchical stages of emotional learning, Krathwohl, Bloone, and Masia (1964) cite *responding* as the second level of affective development, immediately following *receiving* (awareness) and preceding *valuing*. The precondition for any kind of responding, they point out, is that the individual be aware of the world around her or him: that she or he be willing to and capable of "receiving" the world, of attending to it. Immediately after this receiving of the world—and of others in the world—the individual is able to respond to it—and to others!—and from there is able to develop values about things. This sequencing is relevant to our discussion of the counselor's responding to the client, for the counselor must first be open to receive what the client is communicating before he or she can respond to the client. Another way of saying this is that sensitivity is a precondition for empathy, which itself is a precondition for effective communication. This will become more meaningful as we look at Krathwohl's breakdown of what the level of responding comprises. This level is divided into three stages: acquiescence in responding; willingness to respond; and satisfaction in response. A brief description of each stage should clarify what responding entails.

Acquiescence means passive agreement, and indeed this level involves a compliant individual—one who responds passively to the stimuli around. At this level, the individual "makes the response, but he has not fully accepted the necessity for doing so" (p. 179). This would be characteristic of a counselor who is only half listening to what the client has to say, who is picking up the words but not the feelings behind the words. Such a counselor is, in effect, saying to the client, "I am willing to hear your words, but not to feel what you are feeling."

Next, the emotionally developed individual develops what Krathwohl (Krathwohl et al., 1964) calls a "willingness to respond," at which point he or she feels a commitment to a certain response. It is at this point that the counselor not only hears what the client is saying but also feels compelled to react to what the client is communicating. The counselor at this level is saying to the client, "I not only hear your words, but they are having an effect on me . . . causing me to act a certain way, to feel a certain way."

Finally, at the third level, *satisfaction in response,* the individual derives "a feeling of satisfaction, an emotional response, generally of pleasure, zest, or enjoyment" from the response. The difference between this stage and the two that precede it can be illustrated in the difference between reading a book because it is required and reading a book for pleasure. Not only is the qualitative experience different but the quantitative experience (of learning, of what is gained) also differs because of the increased motivation that characterizes the second level. A counselor at this satisfaction level responds to the client because he or she is really involved with the client, is experiencing along with the client.

Thus, appropriate responding requires empathic understanding. But this is only the beginning. How can we assure that our response is facilitative for the client: *that we are responding to what the client is communicating in such a way that the client will be helped?* It is not enough to simply respond according to our feelings. One may have good intentions, but lack the knowledge needed to make a facilitative response. Every response should have a purpose, and this purpose should extend beyond the demands of the moment. Schmidt (1976) makes the point that "If we are truly going to make a difference, we must not only listen to feelings or reinforce specific verbal statements and behaviors, we also must develop strategies that will give our clients new skills that they can use away from the counseling relationship" (p. 71). He goes on to discuss an approach he calls "cognitive restructuring," which is becoming an increasingly important guideline in helping counselors decide how to respond to clients. "Cognitive restructuring," he points out, "is any therapeutic technique that employs the change of 'self-thoughts' in order to alter emotional reactions and behaviors toward more favorable outcomes." He offers some examples of how this works in the counseling setting:

> In general, what happens in the treatment goes something like the following: A self-defeating thought, for example, "It is terrible to make mistakes" is challenged by a counterthought, "Everybody makes mistakes." This counterthought is positively reinforced in that the ensuing emotion and behavior are pleasant and more productive. Furthermore, these counterthoughts can be positively reinforced more intentionally by asking clients to engage in reinforcing thoughts or activities immediately following each counterthought. For example, after using the counter, "Everybody makes mistakes," a client can fantasize a pleasant scene for thirty seconds. In a similar manner, negative self-thoughts can be punished by instructing clients to engage in unpleasant fantasies following such thoughts. (p. 72)

As we see from this description, *cognitive restructuring* as a technique, as a form of responding to the client, embodies the principles we are suggesting as necessary for all categories of responses to the client. In cognitive restructuring, the taxonomic stages of affective functioning are recapitulated: first, the counselor becomes aware of what the client needs; second, he or she feels compelled to respond to these needs, and, finally, the counselor feels a pleasure in helping the client get over the obstacle. Although other methods differ from cognitive restructuring in substance, they embody the same principles in different forms.

To see how this works, let us consider two aspects of counselor response: the counselor's values and answering clients' questions.

Valuing

Recall that we mentioned that the level next to responding in the taxonomy is *valuing*. In the taxonomy, valuing is used in its common meaning, referring to the attribution of worth to a thing, a behavior, a goal or purpose, and so forth. Valuing is manifestly a process that influences the forming of goals in the counseling setting. The question of what the counselor values, then, has a substantial influence on how the counselor helps the client formulate the goals of counseling.

We will discuss later how being nonjudgmental is a quality associated with effective counseling. Even so, it is necessary that the counselor be committed to some values in order to maintain a sense of meaning in life. The core question we are concerned with is this: to which types of values, to which logical biases, should the counselor commit himself or herself? The answer to this crucial question becomes quite evident when we look at the literature and consider the issues at hand. The primary value to which the counselor must be committed is *freedom*, the value from which all other values are derived. Peterson (1970), in his thorough study of counseling and values, calls freedom the "valuational basis for counseling." Viewing the ultimate task of the school counselor as "helping the individual to become the free person that he potentially is" (as we have been suggesting throughout this book), Peterson goes on to speak of the counselor's own valuation of freedom:

> The essential quality of freedom is that it allows man room to be himself, to be creative, to make choices and be responsible for them. Freedom allows man to choose higher values if he desires. It allows him to follow his own quest for truth, to develop his own philosophy of life. Freedom is a matter of degree. We must talk in terms of *more* or *less* rather than of *presence* or *absence*. Freedom involves man in his individual functioning, in his functioning with others, and in his search for meaning. It has many facets, and man is confronted by choices involving them. Freedom can be at least part of a base from which one can examine and evaluate practice. (p. 182)

As a value influencing how the counselor works, freedom is an ideal which propels the individual to certain types of actions. Freedom guides the individual in the direction in which to move; it always entices the individual. "Rather than command, dictate, or affirm, freedom as an ideal attracts. It pulls man, for it offers enhanced possibility for fulfillment. It is always out of reach in an absolute sense but at the same time is within reach to a relative degree" (p. 186).

It is easier to speak about freedom as a concept than to experience it as a condition. Many of us, unfortunately, are unable to experience freedom because of constraints within us as well as forces from the outside. One factor that might influence the degree of freedom an individual can experience is his or her upbringing. There are also forces exerted upon us by the system: the fact, for example, that a counselor may be required to maintain a professional facade in the agency setting may alter his or her choices as well as the opportunity to choose meaningfully and responsibly.

A systematic analysis of the typical counseling interaction will undoubtedly reveal that one of the major forms of communication between counselor and client is the question. The question is a viable and productive medium of communication because it requires an answer and therefore promotes the interactive nature of the relationship between the counselor and client. Often questions asked by the counselor are dealt with in the area of techniques. In this section, we will examine some of the ways in which the counselor might answer questions posed by the client.

Answering Clients' Questions

First, we must ask, What kinds of questions does the typical client pose to the counselor? There are four basic types: information questions, questions of value, direction questions, and personal questions. Let us examine each individually.

Information questions may be either objective or subjective. What colleges offer degrees in forestry? is an objective question. So are the questions, Where can I find an abortion clinic in this city? What kind of work do you think I am best suited for? and What were the results of the test I took last month? When such a question is asked, certainly all the counselor has to do is give an answer. This will satisfy the client and provide types of information that may help with his or her plans. But what if the counselor does not know the answer, what should be done then? Might the client not lose confidence because she or he doesn't know?

The solution to this problem is simple. The counselor must acknowledge that she or he does not have the answer. For it is only when the counselor is truthful with the client (as well as with herself or himself) that the client can develop the respect that is prerequisite for a successful counseling relationship. "If the client asks a question regarding facts," Darley (1950) points out, "and you don't have the facts, it is better to say 'I don't know' rather than to run with a lot of vague generalities or in some other way try to cover up your own ignorance. The client is likely to have more confidence in the interviewer who does not hesitate to admit his ignorance. It would be desirable for the counselor to get these facts later, and to tell the client where to get them."

Felker (1972) takes a different tack. She feels that in many cases when approached with questions the counselor cannot answer, he or she must "turn the table back to the obstinate inquirer." She gives a number of examples:

The first response you could try is bold-faced and direct. It consists of the counter question, "What do you think the answer is?" A second alternative response builds in a bit of reinforcement for the questioner, and while he basks in the compliment he may decide not to persist in seeking an answer. It goes something like this: "I can see that you devoted a good deal of thought to this issue, and since you seem to be a very critical thinker, let me get your views first." The third approach is one I recommend when you want to bolster your own ego or position. . . . You say something like this: "I've spent a good deal of time thinking about that very question, let me see if your opinions are similar to mine." (p. 684)

Felker's manipulative methods may be adequate for dealing with a hostile questioner who is out to prove how ignorant you are. We include them here, not to advocate their unlimited use with sincere clients, but because these methods may be useful with certain types of clients whose needs are not for information, but rather for challenge and confrontation. Moreover, this type of response is often used inadvertently or unintentionally by counselors who do not feel comfortable when they don't know the right answer. There is no shame in not knowing, but there is shame in using tricks to cover up one's ignorance, unless the intentions or the questioner are objective and provocative.

Benjamin (1969) probably sums up the middle position best when he says, ". . . we ought to supply the information requested when it is feasible and appropriate to do so, but we should always be open to the possibility that there is something behind and beyond the question which is worth getting at" (p. 75). What this means in practice is that we take each question as it appears—receiving and *then* responding—and subjugate the general rule to the specific instance.

Subjective information questions refer to personal information about the client. Why am I feeling this way? or, Is there something wrong with me? are typical questions requiring information that is subjective, interpretive, or down-right speculative. These are not, in the technical sense, questions for information, but merely assume the form of such questions. "Questions are often disguises for more penetrating and deep concerns," suggest Dimick and Huff (1970). "It is the job of the counselor to assess the nature of the questions—to 'hear' what is meant. . . . When a legitimate request for information is 'heard', then the counselor responds with whatever data resources he may have. When some other request is 'heard', he responds to that need."

Clients often ask for value judgments from the counselor. Particularly in areas where their own value orientation is fuzzy, the client may seek a resolution of a moral dilemma by eliciting from the counselor an evaluative response. But because the counselor may be perceived as an authority figure—or at least an *authoritative* figure—his or her value judgments will be weighed more heavily by the client than they should be. Therefore, the appropriate response in such a situation is to help the client arrive at his or her own moral decisions, rather than imposing moral or value decisions.

When a client seeks information regarding the direction he or she should take (what choice to make, what approach to use, etc.), there is always a strong temptation on the counselor's part to tell him or her, particularly if the counselor feels that she or he knows the best answer to the client's problems. This should generally be avoided, however, inasmuch as the client will gain strength if allowed to make his or her own judgments. Certainly, one of the most valuable goals of counseling is to enable clients to make better decisions, and part of this process may require that the counselor become an active agent in the decision-making process. But to answer a client's decision-oriented question with a specific, close-ended answer diminishes significantly the possibility that the client will grow enough to make decisions.

To do this, the counselor should respond to the client's directional questions with questions of his or her own, questions that are designed to help the client arrive at solutions. For example,

Client   Which college do you think I should apply to? Harvard, where I don't have much of a chance of getting accepted, or State, where I can probably get a scholarship?

Counselor   Well, how would you feel about going to Harvard and how would you feel about going to State?

Or,

Client   I'm not sure if I should enroll in that special weight-watchers' program or not. What do you think?

Counselor   What are your feelings about that program?

Note how the counselor, through questioning, is helping the client make his or her own decisions; decisions that are very important for the client's future growth, development, and above all, independence as a person. Giving the client the appropriate response helps the client learn how to answer key decision-making questions.

Personal questions asked the counselor by the client—"How old are you?" or "Are you married?"—are often a source of confusion to the beginning counselor. There is no absolute rule here, and much depends on the kind of question asked. Very personal questions require a different kind of evaluation than seemingly more innocuous questions such as, "Where did you go to graduate school?" In both cases, however, there is usually more to the question than appears on the surface, and it is the counselor's job to find out what lurks underneath.

Each counselor has to decide for himself or herself how much personal information he or she is willing to give out. A good rule of thumb is that before answering any personal questions the counselor should have a good idea of why the client is asking them, and what the question really means. This deeper level is not always clear at the outset. As Sue (1979) points out,

There are many subjective emotional components to even a question such as "How old are you?" The client might actually be asking "Are you competent and qualified, or do you have enough experience to work with me?" Also, questions that are subjective or which ask for personal self-disclosure on the part of the counselor are very sticky. For example, in cross-cultural counseling a question often asked of white counselors from a culturally different client might be "How do you feel about interracial relationships?" The question, while it might appear innocuous, is a very loaded one.

Often clients ask personal questions not so much because they desire information but because they feel that if they are willing to share their personal selves with the counselor, the counselor should be willing to share his or her personal self with the client. This may be a fair request, at least on the surface, and yet the policy of withholding most personal information seems to have some practical advantages.

In conclusion, then, the counselor should answer questions for information if the answers are helpful to the client, give some personal information, and acquaint the client with resources he or she can use for further answers to questions. The counselor should avoid answering moral or value judgment questions or directional questions, and encourage the client to arrive at his or her own answers to these questions.

What Makes Counselors Angry

Fremont and Anderson (1986) explore the interesting question of "What client behaviors make counselors angry?" Recognizing that it is not always possible for even the most committed counselor to feel free of anger at all times, they try to find out just what clients do to provoke anger in their counselors. This information can better help counselors understand and possibly accept the kinds of behaviors that would likely interfere with their empathic, nonjudgmental efforts to do effective counseling. Fremont and Anderson found five main categories of events that made counselors angry: (a) client resistance to counseling, (b) client impositions on the counselor, (c) client verbal attacks on the counselor, (d) counseling being overly involved in client dynamics, and (e) other factors.

Resistances to counseling may take different forms, from the client not showing up for treatment to the client rebuffing the counselor's attention and interest, refusing to follow necessary advice, and being unwilling to discuss his or her problems or feelings. Resistance may take the form of overt hostility or more subtle communication of frustrating feelings. For example, one client induced anger in her counselor when she failed to understand the simple instructions the counselor was giving her about how to fill out a health insurance application for reimbursement of counseling costs. A simple, seemingly objective matter became an issue of anger for the counselor as time and again he had to repeat information he felt a child could have understood without effort.

Impositions on the counselor, including phone calls at home, dropping by unexpectedly, and making unreasonable demands for additional appointments, can also make counselors angry. Many clients do this at times of stress, when their need for nurture and succor becomes especially strong because of their personal problems, feelings of deprivation, or irrational automatic thinking (cognitive distortions). In such situations, the counselor may not only feel put upon in terms of time, but may begin to experience emotional drain as well. As with the anger generated by client resistance, this type of anger is not always apparent, since a subtle rather than overt stimulus is provoking it.

Verbal attacks are a more overt provocation for angry responses. Such attacks on the counselor may range from the very general to very specific. While counselors are taught that they should accept all the client's feelings nonjudgmentally, this sometimes works better in theory than in practice, especially when a very angry client with the perceptions and language necessary to strike a deadly verbal blow, lets go with full force at the unwary counselor. Upon reflection, the counselor will often realize that the client's cutting words were an expression of inner frustration, not of real anger. But the immediate visceral response is one of upset, rage, and indignation that someone the counselor is so committed to helping is responding in such an ungrateful way.

The counselor, Fremont and Anderson suggest, may also be drawn into the client's pathology, or dynamics. This can be done in several ways, from a client seeing several counselors simultaneously and pitting them against each other to the client making suicide threats for which he or she blames the counselor. The key element in all of these, according to the authors "is the client's conscious or unconscious manipulation of the counselor's emotional responses" (p. 68).

Some other reasons cited include the client's misuse of information gained in therapy or violation of the value system, integrity, or confidentiality of treatment.

An Overview of an Organic or Developmental Model of Helping and Interpersonal Relating

From: Gerard Egan, *The Skilled Helper* (Brooks/ Cole Pub. Co.) 1977. Reprinted by permission.

Pre-helping or Pre-communication Phase: Attending

The model has a pre-helping phase and three stages:

Helper's Goal: Attending   To attend to the other, both physically and psychologically; to give himself entirely to "being with" the other; to work with the other.

Stage I: Responding/ Self-exploration

Helper's Goal: Responding   To respond to the client and what he has to say with respect and empathy; to establish rapport, an effective collaborative working relationship with the client; to facilitate the client's self-exploration.

Client's Goal: Self-exploration   To explore his experiences, behavior, and feelings relevant to the problematic in his life; to explore the ways in which he is living ineffectively.

Stage II: Integrative Understanding/ Dynamic Self-understanding

Helper's Goal: Integrative understanding   The helper begins to piece together the data produced by the client in the self-exploration phase. He sees and helps the other identify behavioral themes or patterns. He helps the other see the "larger picture." He teaches the client the skill of going about this integrative process himself.

Client's Goal: Dynamic self-understanding   Developing self-understanding that sees the need for change, for action; learning from the helper the skill of putting together the larger picture for himself; identifying resources, especially unused resources.

Stage III: Facilitating Action/ Acting

Helper's Goal: Facilitating action   Collaborating with the client in working out specific action programs; helping the client to act on his new understanding of himself; exploring with the client a wide variety of means for engaging in constructive behavioral change; giving support and direction to action programs.

Client's Goal: Acting   Living more effectively; learning the skills needed to live more effectively and handle the social-emotional dimensions of life; changing self-destructive and other-destructive patterns of living; developing new resources.

A key element of effective psychological functioning, one which profoundly affects all aspects of our lives and is integral to the success of the counseling process, is the ability to make decisions effectively. Each of us must make decisions on a regular basis, and this may involve a variety of factors, external and internal, controllable and uncontrollable. Decisions range in complexity from relatively minor to major determinations which affect the rest of one's life. Many of the problems for which individuals seek help in counseling, regardless of which of the five levels of the taxonomy the problem falls under, are in the final analysis, problems in decision-making.

Decisions, Values, and Conflicts

All our decisions reflect values. Although you may not think about your values until you have to make a decision, almost all your behavior is influenced, directly or indirectly, by your value system. We can define values as "convictions or beliefs which prescribe or determine acceptable or preferable behavior in relation to needs or goals" (Strickland, 1978, p. 428). The two key words here are *needs* and *goals*. For values not only tell us what is acceptable and what is not acceptable, but also reflect what our needs are, how we go about satisfying these needs, and the way we set up goals and perceive these goals. When there is a logical or practical discrepancy between the need, value, and goal, we call it a *conflict*. Let us consider these relationships briefly to see in context how a client's values may be a central underlying factor in the decision-making process.

Decisions and Values

An individual's needs and values are related, since to a large extent an individual's values are defined by, and in some ways help satisfy, his or her needs. For example, if something is very important to us as a need, we value it highly. The person dying of thirst in a desert will value a glass of water quite differently than would a patron in an expensive restaurant who lets the glass of water stand untouched and looks over the wine list. If John loves Mary, he values her differently than would Larry who loves Pam.

Humanistic counselors have proposed several theories to explain (and to organize) the myriad human needs. Carl Rogers said that there are two universal needs: the need for *positive regard* and the need for *self-regard*. The need for positive regard develops as awareness of the self emerges, early in life. This need leads the individual to desire acceptance and love from the important people in his or her life. They may accept him or her conditionally ("I will love you only if you do this or that . . .") or they may accept the person unconditionally ("I will love you no matter what . . .") as he or she is, offering what Rogers called *unconditional positive regard*. The person needs positive regard not only from others but from himself or herself as well.

Theories of Human Needs

The need for self-regard develops out of self-experiences associated with the satisfaction or frustration of the need for positive regard. If a person experiences only unconditional positive regard, his or her self-regard will also be unconditional. Such a state represents genuine psychological adjustment and full functioning.

Many people, unfortunately, do not achieve such ideal adjustment. Inevitably, a child's need to retain parental love conflicts with his or her individual needs. When this occurs, according to Rogers, the child begins to avoid or deny altogether the experiences that he or she has learned are not worthy of positive regard, such as trying to live up to parental expectations. This can then affect the kind of people the child becomes involved with later in life.

Abraham Maslow suggests that human beings have different kinds of needs which are ordered in a hierarchy, with certain basic needs which must be satisfied before other, higher level needs can emerge. At the bottom of the hierarchy are the basic physiological drives that must be gratified in order for the person to survive. When these needs are met, and they usually are, the need for safety and security emerges. Once we feel safe and secure in our surroundings, we try to satisfy the need for love and belonging, for affectionate relations with people, for being with our own group, our home, our family. The need for esteem comes next, the need for a stable, firm, positive evaluation of ourselves, a need for self-respect, achievement, adequacy, and mastery. Then, at the top of the list is self-actualization, the highest goal of all. This represents the need to be all that we can be, to be true to our nature, to accept ourselves as we are. When all our lower needs are met, we can satisfy our aesthetic needs—for justice, goodness, beauty, order, unity. These needs are called *metaneeds,* and when they are met, Maslow says, we rejoice in the experience of living; we have made the most of our abilities and have become all we are capable of being.

Sicinski (1978) has proposed a four-level hierarchy of needs which, although simpler than Maslow's, is more closely related to value development and decision-making. On the first level are the fundamental needs, much like Maslow's basic needs. Next come these needs which, if not satisfied, interfere with the individual's ability to perform some social function. For example, an individual may not be able to appreciate cultural activities because the aesthetic needs were never properly satisfied. Third are those needs which, when not satisfied, interfere with general social functioning, deficiencies (wants or needs) which make the person socially maladjusted. For instance, a person whose need for affiliation, for friendship, was never satisfied may not be able to make friends later in life. Finally, there are those needs which, when not satisfied, interfere with individual emotional development and growth, even though a person may be functioning appropriately socially. These are the most severe, and would describe individuals who are very disturbed and socially dysfunctional. Systems of values are developed, according to Sicinski's theory, to help a person orient him or herself to satisfying these different levels of needs.

Often, when individuals come for counseling many of their need-satisfying abilities are impaired. It is not unusual for a client to know exactly what he or she wants, but to lack the emotional, intellectual, familial, or social resources to obtain it. Defensiveness, either as a perceptual blockage or as a disingenuous way of interacting with others, militates against one's need-satisfying efforts. So too does a lack of assertiveness. Many individuals know *what* they want and *how* to get it, but they lack the ability to assert their needs to others. Together, lack of assertiveness and a high level of defensiveness are twin sources of frustration to individuals who are trying to make critical decisions that affect their needs. Massong, Dickson, Ritzler, and Layne (1982) point out that assertive and nonassertive individuals use different types of defense mechanisms; assertive people using more intellectualization, rationalization, and isolation of affect. Nonassertive individuals use more primitive and socially ineffective defenses, by turning against objects and themselves. These investigators found in a study that assertive individuals demonstrate higher levels of intellectual achievement than their nonassertive counterparts.

Because we hold values and believe in them, and because in the course of living we are confronted with myriad occasions for decisions, conflicts are bound to arise between what we *want* to do, what we feel we *should* do, and what we *can* do. Some conflicts may take of the form of just not knowing what to do, being halted at a critical point in decision-making. Other conflicts may be the result of frustration at not being able to do what we want to or feel we should.

Resolving Conflicts: A Social Learning Perspective

Social-learning psychologists have evolved a typology of conflict which can help counselors understand better the processes of conflict resolution. We can say generally that conflict occurs whenever we are faced with a choice that involves the pairing of two or more competing motives or goals. The four main kinds of conflict situations are called: (1) approach-approach; (2) avoidance-avoidance; (3) approach-avoidance; and (4) double approach-avoidance. (Dollard & Miller, 1951)

Types of Conflict

An *approach-approach* conflict occurs when an individual must make a choice between two positive goals, both equally attractive. For example, as he enters his second year, Peter has a choice of taking Honors English or Tactical Warfare, two courses given at the same hour, both of which he would love to take. This is a relatively easy kind of conflict to deal with; since both the alternatives are positive ones, no matter what the decision, the person ends with something he or she wants. Usually, this type of conflict is resolved when one alternative becomes more positive than the other. In this case, Peter realizes that the Tactical Warfare course, though more work, would give him advanced standing next year. Therefore he decides to take that over the English.

An *avoidance-avoidance* conflict involves making a choice between two unpleasant alternatives. While Peter is making his decision in Annapolis, Mark, who hates and fears science, is faced with the unpleasant choice of selecting a required science course, which he will need for graduation. It is a choice between chemistry or biology, and he dreads both equally. Typical behavior in this type of conflict situation is characterized by vacillation, that is, the individual approaches first one goal, then the other. The nearer one comes to each alternative, the stronger the avoidance response. So, as Mark tentatively decides on chemistry he looks over the textbook and says to himself, "I could never learn this stuff." If the strength of one of the avoidance responses is increased, the person withdraws from the situation he or she dislikes most, and overcomes the conflict. For example, if the school announces that the chemistry course will be more difficult than the biology, this makes it easier to solve the problem: i.e., to choose biology. But if both alternatives remain equally unpleasant, the individual may attempt either literally to run away from the situation, or figuratively, by avoiding the conflict, by daydreaming or sleep, to refuse to deal with it. This type of situation is resolved when one alternative becomes more positive than the other. Mark finally decided to take chemistry when the school instituted a policy of providing tutors for the graduating chemistry students, since so many were having problems in this course.

An *approach-avoidance* conflict involves a single goal that has both positive and negative characteristics; it attracts and repels at the same time. This is a considerably more difficult conflict situation to resolve than the other two types, and it tends to induce a high level of anxiety. Shari would like to see a therapist or counselor privately to discuss the problems she is having with Ted (approach), but fears that she will be stigmatized by her new friends for not being able to deal with the situation on her own (avoidance). In the psychological laboratory, where a paradigm of this type of conflict has been set up, rats have been trained to run an alley for a food reward; then, as they approach the food, they are given an electric shock. Studying the results of these experiments, and generalizing them to human behavior, researchers have concluded that

> When goals are at once satisfying and threatening . . . people's behavior vacillates at a point near, but not too near the goal; at a distance the tendency to approach predominates; near the goal the tendency to avoid is greater. The result is a stable or self-maintaining conflict that tends to keep the organism at the point where the two tendencies cross. (Berelson & Steiner, 1969, p. 272)

This helps explain why some people such as Shari may never be able to resolve their conflicts and can literally go for years vacillating between "I should go for counseling; I shouldn't; I should; I shouldn't." Each time she has a fight with Ted the "I should" becomes stronger. But when she thinks of actually making an appointment, the "I shouldn't" predominates. This is the classical stalemate of the approach-avoidance conflict.

Often two goals, not just one, have both positive and negative components. Mr. Vickers, for example, is approaching the age at which he will be eligible for retirement, after twenty-five years of service as a dispatcher with the Transportation Authority. He would like to retire and looks forward to the prospect of having his days free for golf and fishing, but knows full well that he'll have to struggle to live on his retirement pension. Yet if he stays on, although he will have enough income to live at his present level, he fears that the continued stress of the job is going to give him an ulcer. What should he do?

This is known as a *double approach-avoidance conflict*. In life, most conflicts fall into this category, since most of our choices have both positive and negative features. Unfortunately, there is never a completely satisfactory solution to this conflict, because each alternative has disadvantages that we would like to avoid. Thus, when we finally make a decision in the hope of resolving this type of conflict, we are still likely to feel some regret afterwards.

We see from this social learning typology that there are different kinds of conflicts with different types of obstacles involved in their resolution. Each of them poses different problems to the individual seeking to make a decision. From this perspective, a key element in coping successfully with problems is to find ways of maximally resolving these conflicts, of achieving our goal and avoiding frustration.

It is generally agreed that successful counseling endeavors involve more than merely resolving conflicts. Rather, this is a positive process, characterized by growth. "Growth," Cardinal Newman once said, "is the only evidence of life." There are so many potential areas of growth in human life that it is impossible to list them all. But as clusters, they include the humanistic goals of self-actualization, assimilation, and integration; the behavioral goals of appropriate responses to situations; the psychodynamic goal of nondefensive and psychically balanced behavior; the cognitive goals of rational thinking and decision-making.

Some of the principles of facilitating growth and change outlined in this and in the preceding two chapters can best be illustrated if we look over some case material. This transcription is from an individual counseling session between Dr. Cirillo (DR) and Mrs. Jackson (MJ). The meeting was conducted in an urban social agency setting. Mrs. Jackson and her three boys, aged 14 (Alonzo), 11 (Willi), and 9 (Stan) have been in family counseling with Dr. Cirillo, and now Mrs. Jackson has entered individual counseling with Dr. Cirillo, as well. This is her second session of individual counseling. There are several phenomena we should observe in the interaction. First, note how the counselor allows the emotional tone and the objective content of the session to be determined by the client. He allows the client to "lead the way," and he follows her lead with his response. She is the determiner of change; he the catalyst.

Second, we should note how skillfully he parries questions when necessary, avoiding some of the obvious pitfalls. You will see too that he answers questions directly when this is helpful to the client, and when he feels that he understands the intent behind the question. Finally, note how Dr. Cirillo combines all the qualities of counselor sensitivity and counselor effectiveness with the perspicacity of a keen mind, and how he helps the client "discover" parts of herself as she works to resolve the entrenched family conflict. Deletions are indicated by ellipses.

MJ   (*Out of breath, panting*) I'm sorry I'm late, Doctor, but my car wouldn't start on the way over here, and then the lady who comes to take care of Stan didn't come over. Guess I'm lucky that I got over here at all.

Practical
Considerations

DR (*Gesturing to the chair*) Why don't you have a seat?

MJ Thank you. Say, I don't remember if I asked you last time about that note.

DR Note?

MJ The one for the school. I think that the principal said he needed it. I promised Alonzo's teacher that I'd bring it in with me when I go up to see her, and she said that was good and that I didn't have to have Alonzo bring it with him to school.

DR No, I don't believe we discussed this.

MJ I just need a note that Alonzo is coming to see you so that the principal can know. He said a note from you would be enough, and that he could get the information.

DR I am a bit confused about this. What do you want me to say in the note? Does Alonzo know about the note?

MJ Oh, just to say that Alonzo is seeing you and that . . . (*she hesitates*) . . . that he needs extra work for school. Tell the principal that he needs a tutor for school.

DR I see. You want a note that Alonzo is seeing me for counseling and that he needs a tutor for school. Is that it?

MJ Oh yes, that would be good. And if you write it, I'll take it with me, and give it to Alonzo's teacher when I see her. She said she would take it to the principal for me.

DR Well, I'm a little confused. I don't believe we discussed anything about tutoring. Why does the principal want this note?

MJ Oh, I see, . . . the note. You see, Mrs. Flynn (the social worker assigned to the Jackson family) said she could get me the money for the tutor if the principal gives her a letter. So when I asked him he said that I needed to get a note from you first.

DR I see. If I write the note, then you will receive extra money in your check. The note has to say that Alonzo needs extra tutoring.

MJ That's it. Then they pay sixteen dollars extra for the tutor. See, if you write the note, then we can get the money.

DR Oh, I'm beginning to understand now. The note will help you get sixteen dollars extra every two weeks.

MJ That's it.

DR How will you use that money? The extra sixteen dollars.

MJ You see, I'll buy things for the family. We need more money for food. Why I hardly have enough to even buy a meat dinner on Sundays. We also need clothes. Willi needs a new winter coat, and Stan has to have his shoes fixed.

DR So the money will not actually be used for tutoring, then?

MJ Oh, you see, I could spend the money on that too. Sure, that's a good idea.

DR Have you mentioned this to Alonzo? I don't recall our discussing it when we were all together.

MJ Oh, yeah, I'm going to tell Alonzo. Soon as I get the note I'm going to tell him.

DR So in other words, you will tell him *after* you have the note. Not before.

MJ Oh, I could tell him if you wanted me to. I don't know what's the difference.

DR Well, we should consider the possibility that Alonzo may resent having his name used in a note when he doesn't directly benefit from it. And when he hasn't given us permission to use his name. Maybe we should discuss it with him when we are all together. I believe that will be this Thursday.

MJ Oh, good. That's a good idea.

....

MJ So, if I go to work, then I have to leave the kids all night. There just isn't any day job I could take, and I don't think that they can be on their own all night. I told you what happened to my aunt's children when she left them alone, and I don't want that to happen to mine.

DR That certainly makes sense. I get the impression that you feel you are protecting your children by staying with them. Is my impression correct?

MJ Yes. I think that I am keeping them out of trouble. And I know that I am.

DR How does that make you feel as a mother?

MJ (*Pauses, thinking*) I don't know what you mean.

DR Well, what I want to know is how you feel being so devoted a mother. After all, you have mentioned a few times that many of your friends, and even your aunt, don't pay nearly as much attention to their children as you do. How do you feel being so devoted to your children?

MR Why, I feel real good. Why shouldn't I?

DR No reason. I just wanted to know. How do the children make you feel? Do they appreciate what you do for them?

MJ (*Hesitantly*) I guess so. You know how kids are. They're too busy trying to have a good time that they don't know what you're doing for them. So long as it gets done. I don't know.

DR (*Not pressing the point, but reinforcing the client*) I think that you show many fine qualities as a mother, Mrs. Jackson. Probably even more than you realize.

There are two aspects which should be pointed out at this time. In the first segment, note how the counselor probed Mrs. Jackson's reason for the request for the principal's note until he found out the "real" purpose behind her request: her stipend would be increased as a result of writing the note. He sensed that this might be subtly unfair to Alonzo. It should be mentioned that in the family meetings Alonzo often expressed the feeling that his mother took advantage of him, that she made him do chores for the neighbors and then kept the money he earned. Mrs. Jackson's rationale was that it wasn't good for a young boy to have too much money. Dr. Cirillo felt that he might be getting involved in this conflict before there was an opportunity to fully explore it, and he therefore suggested that it be saved for the family session. His response to the request (to the question) was made only after fully considering all of its implications. He could have easily agreed at once to write the note, but that may have caused many hard feelings later on.

In the second segment, we see an example of how the counselor "retreated" from his probing when he realized that he was treading on ground which the client was not yet emotionally ready to explore. He began to allude to a subtle theme that he had noticed during the family sessions: that Mrs. Jackson felt her children did not appreciate her or what she was doing for them. Dr. Cirillo believed that this unexpressed feeling was at least in part responsible for her taking advantage of them economically. He got the sense, as he approached this subject, however, that the client was not ready to talk about it, and he let her gently lead him away from it, onto safer ground.

MJ So the problem, doctor, is that if I don't go to work I'm just not going to have enough money to take care of my children. And, you know what. . . .

DR What?

MJ That Mrs. Flynn don't believe me. She thinks we have enough to live on. I told her, "Why don't you just try living on my check." That's what I told her!

DR So Mrs. Flynn gives you the feeling that you should be "making do" with what you've got. She can't understand how difficult it is for you.

MJ You bet she can't. What do you think I should do? How am I going to get enough money to take care of my family. I don't like to talk about this in front of the kids. I think it gets them upset.

DR So you try to protect them from the problems you are having. You don't want them to worry with you. (*Long pause, during which the counselor reflects to himself, experiencing the client's feelings*) You want to carry your problems all by yourself.

MJ It won't do no good for them to worry. Won't do no good at all.

DR But maybe it will help them understand what *you're* going through. I notice that you try to protect them. They're big boys now—especially Alonzo—and maybe it wouldn't hurt for them to know what you're going through for them.

MJ   They sure don't know now.

DR   How do you think they would react if they knew all the difficulties you have to face? How would they feel?

MJ   I don't know. I guess they would be mad at me.

DR   Mad?

MJ   For not being a better mother, you know. For not giving them a good home.

DR   So by not telling them your problems, you feel they will think you are a better mother.

MJ   I guess so.

In this segment, the counselor, by responding facilitatively to the client's communications helps the client gain an insight into how she feels. Later on in the treatment, Mrs. Jackson realizes that her feelings about sharing her problems with the boys are ambivalent. On the one hand, she tries to protect them by refusing to share her problems with them. On the other hand, she resents having to carry the burden alone. Her recognition of this will take time, but today she has made an important first step.

Finally, let us look at the close of this session. As Mrs. Jackson stands up to leave, a short exchange takes place between her and Dr. Cirillo. This brief exchange illustrates how the counselor's appropriate responses make growth for the client a realistic possibility.

MJ   Look, Doc. I'll talk to Alonzo before Thursday. I'll explain to him all about the note.

DR   That will be fine, Mrs. Jackson. Also, you might keep in mind that you are asking me to lie in the note.

MJ   Lie? How?

DR   You want me to say that Alonzo needs tutoring. We haven't even discussed that. I don't know that he needs tutoring.

MJ   You know, I never thought of it that way. I really don't want you to lie, so I don't know why I asked that. We never did talk about it, did we?

DR   No, we haven't. Does he need tutoring?

MJ   (*Laughs*) To tell you the truth, Doc, I don't know. I'm going to talk to that boy when I get home and if he does need tutoring, I'm going to see that he gets it. If he don't, then we can forget about the note.

In this chapter, we considered ways of facilitating client growth and change: the essential core of the counseling process. First, we examined how client expectations affect the counseling process; specifically, how the client's motivation is an important variable in making the counseling goals possible. We pointed out that in formulating the goals of counseling, the burden should be placed on the client to decide what he or she wants and expects from the counseling interaction.

Summary

We then considered how the counselor responds to the client. We began by considering *responding* as a level of the taxonomy of affective development, and examining its implications as part of the affective counseling interaction. We pointed out the technique of *cognitive restructuring,* which embodies many of the principles of facilitative response to the client. We also looked at *valuing,* the second level, and asked the question, How does the counselor's process of valuing influence the formulation of counseling goals?

We turned our attention next to answering client's questions. Different viewpoints on this matter were presented, and some case examples were examined. We noted that it is essential that the counselor, before responding to a question, should understand the full implication of what the client is asking. We then considered effective types of responses.

The client's ability to adjust to difficult situations is, of course, integral to healthy functioning. We considered some of the factors that influence client change and the direction of that change. Finally, we looked at some case material to see how these principles of counselor response translate into action. We saw how a mother of three boys learned to express some of her ambivalent feelings in the counseling setting. The counselor used a synthesis of techniques and his own views in responding to the client's requests and in helping the client gain insight.

Theories of Counseling

PART

3

In Part 1 of this book, we examined the parameters of the counseling discipline and considered some basic questions that challenge the counselor today. We began by delineating the concerns of the counseling profession, as they exist both in theory and in practice. This led us to consider the world of the counselor as it is influenced by theory, shaped by settings, and colored by other practical considerations. Then in Part 2 we explored in considerable detail the counseling process—the multi-levelled interaction of the counseling setting.

Now, it is time to turn our attention to the specific theories which currently dominate the field of counseling, the well-known "schools" of counseling, or counseling approaches.

It is more than coincidental that the terms *theories* and *schools* are used interchangeably to describe counseling approaches. This common usage of these two words reflects a subtle relationship between the parts and the whole. For, in fact, each counseling approach is built on an underlying theory, a view of the individual; and each has practitioners, partisans of the theory, who *apply* the theory in clinical settings and teach it to others, hence the alternate term, *school*. We shall, in this part of the book, present an overview of each approach by examining first its origins and then its view of the individual, its underlying theory of personality, of behavior, of what makes the person what he or she is. These sections will explicate the ways in which practitioners of a particular position look at the human condition in general as well as the ways they look at the individual client in particular.

Next, we will consider the role of the counselor and examine ways in which the client is expected to contribute to the counseling process. We will see that what is expected from the client varies from one approach to another, and that the counselor's job varies directly with the role of the client. We will also observe that in some schools of counseling very little is required of the client except that he or she come to sessions. But we also note how other approaches require the client to engage in some risk taking and early commitments to courses of action.

We will then examine techniques and goals. Here we come to the crux of the counseling process. What specifically does the counselor do (and for what reasons) in order to help the client overcome the difficulties he or she came into counseling to work out? It is at this stage that we get a clear idea of the underlying theoretical rationale of the counseling process that we explored in previous parts of the book. Finally, we will briefly evaluate each position and examine its applications in different settings.

In organizing the many theories of counseling into a workable scheme, I have relied on the paradigm developed by David H. Frey (see especially Frey, 1972; Raming & Frey, 1974), who has done significant work in constructing a taxonomy of counseling approaches. I have modified the paradigm somewhat, to make it more relevant for the beginning student eager to see a clear rationale behind the diverse approaches. Namely, I have divided the approaches into four categories: psycho-dynamic; humanistic; rational; and behavioral. This division, while debatable on levels of theory, clearly emphasizes the similarity of goals and techniques under each rubric.

In studying each of these schools of counseling, the counselor should be asking, "What parts of each approach are relevant to *my* needs, aptitudes, and interests? What parts are compatible with *my* personality?" Not every counselor is equipped to undertake the emotional dissection required by the psychodynamic approaches, just as not every counselor can maintain the scientific objectivity necessary for the behavioral approaches. Most counselors fall somewhere in between, and in their practices they are probably more eclectic than they would like to admit. But, as the counselor comes to recognize what he or she can draw from each position, each will be better able to extract from his or her own emotional and intellectual reservoir. This will inevitably serve as the counselor's first step in efforts to establish and perfect his or her own counseling techniques, held together by a personal theory of counseling.

Chapter Aim

To outline the basic concepts of psychoanalysis, such as the unconscious, the theory of psychosexual stages, transference, and resistance, indicating wherever appropriate, how the historical development of psychoanalysis influenced subsequent psychotherapies and counseling approaches.

Background

Psychoanalysis was developed by Sigmund Freud, whose research in the use of hypnotism in treating hysteria led him to the fundamental method of psychoanalysis: free association. Studying the free associations and dreams of his patients and himself, Freud then developed a comprehensive psychology of the unconscious mind, comprising the concepts of ego, id, and superego. Neo-Freudians, such as Adler, Jung, and Horney, as well as the modern psychoanalytic movement led by Dr. Hyman Spotnitz, are also briefly discussed.

The View of the Person

Psychoanalysts view people as creatures of instinct who learn to sublimate their primitive urges into socially acceptable activities. The individual's personality develops through the psychosexual stages—oral, anal, phallic, the Oedipal conflict, and latency—until the healthy person reaches what Freud calls genital primacy. The unconscious mind is a powerful determinant of all our behaviors; and psychopathological disturbances are directly attributable to unconscious conflicts.

Role of the Psychodynamic Counselor

Although classical psychoanalysis is not directly applicable to counseling, some of the dynamic concepts are. Recognition of transference, countertransference, and resistance can be of value in the counseling setting. Modern psychoanalysis, on the other hand, offers direct ways of helping clients grow without relying on interpretation or long-term treatment.

Techniques and Goals

The principal technique in psychoanalysis is to lead the client to helpful interpretations. The goal of psychoanalysis is to reduce the client's anxieties and to help her or him reach a stage of integration where the ego can organize drives and discharge intrapsychic tensions.

Evaluation and Applications

Although psychoanalytic approach has not enjoyed wide application in the counseling setting (as compared to the psychotherapy setting), it has influenced many counselors in either their development and practice, or both.

Theories of Counseling

Psychodynamic Approaches

7

As we have seen in Part 1, psychoanalysis has played an important part in the evolution of all Western psychotherapies and, indirectly, in the development of the counseling movement in the United States. While its partisans and critics are sometimes intemperate in their bold assertions and blanket denunciations, a dispassionate assessment of psychoanalysis reveals some significant strengths as well as some glaring weaknesses. Many of the weaknesses of the Freudian legacy, interestingly enough, have encouraged bold new therapeutic approaches that began as reactions to classical psychoanalysis. Many of the acknowledged strengths of psychoanalysis have been incorporated into these new therapies, making them derivative approaches, often referred to as neo-Freudian or psychodynamic approaches. In this chapter we shall look at psychoanalysis from both a historical and theoretical perspective. At the conclusion of our examination, we shall evaluate the application of different psychoanalytic principles to short-term and long-term counseling, in a variety of settings.

Background

Psychoanalysis evolved during the 1880s from the research conducted by Sigmund Freud and Josef Breuer in their treatment of hysteria. When Freud returned from Paris, where he had been studying hypnosis with Charcot (see p. 13), a colleague, Dr. Joseph Breuer, reported to him a fascinating case that had preoccupied his attention for some time. He had been treating a young woman named Bertha Pappenheim who had been suffering from a variety of ailments that together were diagnosed as hysteria. Breuer was personally intrigued by Bertha, and had been spending an inordinate amount of time sitting by her bedside, patiently listening to her speak freely about whatever came to mind. She, in turn, felt enormous affection for the empathic doctor and began to relate to him thoughts and feelings that she had probably never expressed before; perhaps she had not even acknowledged them herself.

Breuer discovered that as Bertha began to remember things that had happened to her in the distant past, often under the influence of a mild trance he induced, her symptoms began to disappear. He began to use hypnosis to help her talk freely, and as she talked, the symptoms lessened. But while the symptoms lessened, the patient and doctor became more attached to each other, although neither would acknowledge the feelings. This attachment led in time to the termination of the treatment. Breuer's wife, unsympathetic to her husband's above-and-beyond-the-call-of-duty devotion, insisted on his terminating the treatment. Breuer, satisfied that his patient was sufficiently improved, agreed, and promised to take his wife on a much belated vacation. He made his plans, confident that he was leaving his patient healthy and cured. Within a matter of days, however, to his shock and chagrin, Bertha had a relapse. Breuer did not recognize that this hysterical relapse was directly related to his plans for leaving her. Nor did he realize that the powerful feelings they had for each other were as integral a part of the treatment as were her memories. When these feelings were ignored, it was not possible for the treatment to be successful. It took his younger colleague, Freud, to realize the significance of this and to put it all together.

Using this case as a starting point, Freud and Breuer discovered that the physical symptoms of hysteria could be alleviated as the patient, under hypnosis, recalled and verbalized unpleasant forgotten memories, thereby releasing psychic energy bottled up inside the body. They published the case as "The Case of Anna O," now considered the first case of psychoanalysis. Freud *inferred* the rudiments of a psychoanalytic method from what Breuer had related to him. "Though Freud knew nothing about the treatment of hysteria by hypnosis, he was fascinated. He asked questions, and together they discussed the implications of such a cure. He believed Breuer had made a revolutionary discovery in treating hysteria and should inform the medical world" (Freeman, 1972, p. 187). The sudden freeing of the repressed material was called a *catharsis* (purging), and this type of treatment was called a cathartic treatment.

Freud gradually abandoned the use of hypnosis. In its place, he encouraged the patient into a state of mental relaxation in which the patient was able to produce spontaneous verbalization, without regard to proprieties and tact. Through analysis and interpretation, these verbalizations led to the repressed memories. This technique came to be known as the method of *free association*.

The discovery of the free association method marked the beginning of *talking* as a therapeutic strategy. For the first time in history, mental disorders producing physical symptoms were being treated medically and scientifically by no other means than the direct use of the patient's verbalization. The articulation of feelings into language in a controlled, analytic setting was replacing the use of hypnosis, exorcisms, and water treatments that sometimes resulted in drownings, which characterized the treatment of mental illness in earlier periods. The patient talked and got well—how remarkable this must have seemed to those who heard of it! Despite all of the subsequent rebellions and reactions to psychoanalysis over the years, this simple principle of a "talking cure," as Freud called it, was to remain the guiding principle for most subsequent psychotherapies.

Over the next few years, by studying the free associations of his patients, Freud discovered the significant influence of childhood sexuality upon the development of personality and the importance of dreams as a way of understanding the sexual feelings that are repressed in the unconscious. Freud referred to dreams as "the royal road to the unconscious," because they revealed in symbolic and disguised form the person's deepest wishes.

Psychoanalysis emerged as a major social force during the 1920s. In addition to its popularity as a form of treatment for emotional disorders, its influence was clearly felt in literature and the arts. By this time, a number of Freud's closest colleagues—most notably, Alfred Adler and Carl Gustav Jung—had broken away from the fold and were developing their own original theories. Adler emphasized the individual's struggle for power—a fight against feelings of inferiority, style of life, and relationship to the society in which he or she lives. Rejecting Freud's notion of the primacy of the sexual instinct as a basis for all human motivation, Adler suggested that the person instinctively strives for superiority to compensate for feelings of inferiority (the terms inferiority complex and superiority complex are from Adler's writings). Moreover, Adler considered social striving equivalent in intensity, importance, and pervasiveness to Freud's ubiquitous sexual instincts.

De-emphasizing the Freudian psychosexual stages, Adler (1958) developed in their place a comprehensive scheme of people and their actions, dominated by alternative social and psychological motivations, feelings, intuitions, and strivings. Adler and his followers call his approach "individual psychology," and although it may have been originally inspired by Freudian psychoanalysis, it is not in the truest sense psychoanalytic. Adler was the first of the psychoanalysts to show a direct interest in child guidance. In 1920, he established child guidance clinics in Vienna in which difficult as well as normal children were offered counseling in joint sessions with their teachers and parents.

Another disciple of Freud's who subsequently broke ranks with him to found his own approach—called "analytical psychology"—was Carl Gustav Jung. Jung, like Adler, believed that Freud placed too much emphasis on sexuality. While he is in agreement with many of Adler's points, he differs from Adler on many crucial practical and theoretical issues. Although Adler and Jung expressed a similar disinclination to the Freudian schema, they took off in different directions, each pursuing the specific area of psychology that he knew best and which to him explained most clearly the complexities of the human psyche (Whitmont & Kaufman, 1973).

Jung contributed a number of specific ideas for which he earned fame. He introduced the concepts of *introversion* and *extroversion*, which are still widely used terms today. He rejected Freud's assumption of a single unconscious, arguing instead that we have two unconsciouses: a *personal* unconscious and a *transpersonal* or *collective* unconscious. The personal unconscious closely resembles Freud's version, consisting of everything that has been repressed during one's development. The collective unconscious, Jung's unique contribution to the theory of psychoanalysis, consists of *archetypes:* innate predispositions derived from the cumulative experiences of the race.

Karen Horney is another important figure in neo-Freudian psychoanalysis. Horney became disillusioned with the narrowness of some of Freud's ideas. In her writings (1937, 1950, 1959), she stresses the social and environmental factors that influence the personality development of the individual. Her theory of neurosis is a vividly detailed theory of intrapsychic conflicts, with different systems of the psyche at war with each other. Cantor (1967) points out that while Freud emphasized the early sexual fixation, Horney spoke of the current conflicts between systems of the psyche. Consequently, her treatment strategies differ in many ways from those of Freud. Horney sees as the primary task of the analyst eliciting constructive forces in the patient's life and helping the patient mobilize these forces to resolve his or her problems and conflicts. Although early childhood experiences are significant in both systems, they play less of a role in Horneyan therapy than in Freudian.

During the 1950s and 1960s, a number of practicing psychoanalysts forthrightly conceded some of the weaknesses of classical (Freudian) psychoanalysis as a form of treatment. From the 1940s to the present, the thrust of new psychoanalytic developments has been in the treatment of seriously disturbed patients, particularly schizophrenics. Freud disqualified from psychoanalysis a large portion of the population whom he deemed "analytically unfit" because they were isolated from interpersonal relations by what he termed the "stone wall of narcissism." These patients, many of whom had serious problems, did not respond to the interpretative method advocated by Freud. Moreover, a large percentage of neurotic patients could not fully be treated because their underlying narcissism—a concomitant of most of their problems in life—would not respond to the traditional psychoanalytic methods.

To overcome these serious deficiencies, Hyman Spotnitz (1963, 1968, 1976), an innovative psychoanalytic psychiatrist, introduced a variety of new psychodynamic treatment techniques that did not require that the patient be emotionally or intellectually capable of understanding interpretations. As Spotnitz's following grew during the late 1960s, his influence began to be felt throughout the country. The Manhattan Center for Advanced Psychoanalytic Studies (MCAPS) was founded in 1973 in New York City by the leading practitioners of modern psychoanalysis, including Benjamin D. Margolis (a founder, along with Theodore Reik, of the prestigious National Psychological Association for Psychoanalysis), Phyllis W. Meadow (the first dean of MCAPS), and William J. Kirman, a pioneer in the area of emotional education. By 1976, there were affiliated centers for the study of Spotnitz's new approach to psychoanalysis in Boston, Philadelphia, Tampa, and other places throughout the United States.

Under the rubric of *modern psychoanalysis,* Spotnitz and his colleagues have developed treatment techniques for dealing with the narcissistic patient—particularly with schizophrenics. Because these techniques avoid the rigidity of the classical Freudian methods, they have found wide application in areas traditionally closed off to psychoanalysis. During the past two decades, modern psychoanalysis, and particularly modern psychoanalytic counseling, has made an impact in the classroom setting (Kirman, 1977), in the social work area (Strean, 1974), and in the family treatment setting (Love, 1972; Bloch, 1978), among other related disciplines.

Freud viewed people as inherently instinctual creatures, driven by their strivings for infantile gratification. Throughout life, the individual is strongly motivated to seek out satisfaction of his or her primitive instinctual drives, sex, and aggression, often beclouding in the process his or her perceptual and emotional awareness of self and others. We distort the reality of the world around us by utilizing defense mechanisms (see pp. 179–84), which protect the ego by allowing us to block out and subjectively redefine that which we cannot accept. While this protects the ego, it alters the world and our relationships in the world significantly, so that what we see, think, and feel consciously is only a fraction of the wide range of possibilities that are within us.

What makes us different from lower animals is our ability to transform brute lust into such socially productive forces as art, politics, medicine, humanitarian projects, and the like. Our social capabilities are psychological transformations of our instinctual drives, and the unequivocal sexual and aggressive nature of the infant at birth is ultimately responsible for all our great deeds and actions. Freud's classic study of Leonardo da Vinci is an example of his thinking in this matter, for here he demonstrates how a great genius, artist, and inventor is motivated by his incestuous maternal fantasies. The psychoanalytic view of the individual is underlined by the belief that the primitive fires of fury that burn within us become the fuels to move civilization from one stage to the next. This process, by which persons rechannel their instincts into socially constructive actions that benefit humankind, Freud called *sublimation*.

The View of the Person

The Freudian theory of personality is a deterministic one, which proposes that by the time the child is five years old the basic foundation of personality is already well-established and experiences of the later years are relatively unimportant in effecting changes on the deeper, dynamic level of the mind. Freud divides the early years of development into five stages, each of which has its own characteristics and problems. Each of the first three stages is named after the part of the body that is most sexually stimulating to the child during that stage— the primary erogenous zone. These are the *oral, anal,* and *phallic* stages.

The Psychosexual Stages of Development

The oral stage is the first psychosexual stage, extending from birth to about the middle of the second year of life. It is a critical period during which the child's awareness of reality (the ego) begins to develop. During this period, the mouth is the primary erogenous zone, thus giving the stage its name. The skin serves as another erogenous zone, and the child demonstrates tactile eroticism in its pleasurable responses to touch.

The Oral Stage

The main source of gratification during this period is incorporation, or eating—the taking in of nourishment, through the processes of swallowing and spitting out. When the teeth develop, pleasure is also obtained through biting. If, while passing through this stage, the child does not receive enough oral gratification, or if the child receives too much gratification (that is, if the mother is overstimulating), he or she may become fixated at the oral level, maintaining in later years emotional characteristics that are more appropriate to the infant. For example, emotional disorders such as psychosis, severe depression, obesity, and addiction—as well as loss of reality orientation—are associated with fixation at the oral stage. Because the oral child is completely dependent on the mother for nourishment and security, deprivations may result in lifelong feelings of inadequacy, overdependency, and worthlessness.

The Anal Stage

At approximately eighteen months of age, there is a shift of erotic activity from the mouth to the anus, marking the beginning of the anal stage. During this period, children receive erotic pleasures from the act of defecation, and they express their will, their *individuality* through the retention or explusion of feces. Society in general, and parents in particular, reinforce the child's interest in anal behavior in many ways. At this age, much attention is focused on toilet training and the child learns that she or he can exert control over parents through the manipulation of this natural bodily function. If the parent is overly strict in toilet training, the child may hold back feces and become constipated. This might show itself later in such adult traits as hoarding, stinginess, excessive neatness, or obstinacy.

The Phallic Stage

At about the beginning of the third year, the genital area itself becomes the primary erogenous zone. During this stage, genital masturbation is not uncommon, nor is an intense interest in the genitals of the opposite sex. The stage is notable for the introduction of two controversial concepts, castration anxiety and penis envy, both of which have become the subject of heated debate in recent years.

According to Freud, when the boy first becomes sensitive to the differences between the male and female genitalia, he cannot accommodate the fact that women do not have penises and therefore fantasizes that women must have lost the penises they once had. He develops, from this false premise, an anxiety about the loss of his own penis, and may express this fear in the forms of play, dreams, or some other symbolic communication. When the girl, at the same age, recognizes the difference in the male and female genitalia, she attributes this absence of a penis to some loss from the past; that is, that she once had a penis and that it has been taken away from her. As she attempts to compensate for this loss and to get the penis back, she develops *penis envy,* which too can take many social forms, in home and at school.

While this aspect of Freud's theory is central to much of his thinking, it has been roundly rejected in recent years by psychologists, feminists, and many social scientists. At the present time, there is certainly inconclusive proof to support or refute this position, but it still stands as a central concept in the Freudian schema.

This period derives its name from the famous Greek legend of Oedipus, the king of Thebes, who unwittingly killed his father and married his mother, unaware of who either was. When he discovered what he had done, he blinded himself in an agony of remorse. Freud suggests that during this Oedipal conflict the child falls in love with the parent of the opposite sex and develops feelings of rivalry and hostility toward the parent of the same sex, who is the "rival parent." The boy wants to possess his mother, although he does not have full-formed ideas of sexuality. He views the father as the prime competitor and wishes to remove him. The girl, likewise, desires her father and wishes to remove the mother.

The healthy resolution of the Oedipal conflict requires the boy to identify with the father and the girl to identify with the mother. Through this identification, the child takes on characteristics of adults of the same sex, and this contributes not only to emotional development but to social development as well. Irene Josselyn (1948), an interpreter of the classical psychoanalytic position and noted for her practical applications of Freud's more technical ideas, explains that the resolution of the boy's conflict is "to identify with the father and incorporate the father's goals and standards into his own pattern of behavior." For the girl "to advance toward healthy emotional maturation, she must find gratification and security in the feminine role. To do this she identifies with her mother" (p. 58). In both cases, we see that *identification* is the key word.

The successful resolution of the Oedipus complex leads into the latency period: a time when the sexual strivings remain dormant and the child concentrates primarily on socialization. It is during this period that the child enters the elementary school and the important processes of school socialization begin. It is also during this period that the teacher will have an opportunity to observe directly the strengths and weaknesses of the child's earlier development.

Although the Freudian position is controversial and not directly supported by empirical evidence, many of its insights have proven useful in understanding and dealing with children and adult clients (Anna Freud, 1935). While a totally Freudian perspective may be an exaggeration of the child's complex functional reality, no doubt many children's interests, inclinations, fantasies, and pathologies are amenable to a Freudian explanation. Moreover, one of the truly important contributions of this approach is to emphasize the vital, dynamic influence of childhood sexuality, often obscured in the myths and presuppositions of childhood innocence that permeate our cultural outlook. Freud may have been extreme in one direction, but many of his insights have nevertheless served his opponents well by counterbalancing their opposite positions.

Freud's view of the person is deeply influenced by his notion of the unconscious. Our personality and our actions, argues Freud, are in a large part determined by the thoughts and feelings contained in the unconscious. These thoughts and feelings are not directly accessible to consciousness, cannot be readily recalled, and are consequently outside the individual's field of awareness, observation, and self-reflection. In *The Psychopathology of Everyday Life* (1901), he demonstrates how the repressed content of the unconscious inadvertently slips through in our words and deeds, resulting in what is commonly called the "Freudian slip." The belief that most activities are governed by the unconscious indicates that the individual may have a limited responsibility for his or her actions. It is not so much that Freud views persons as victims of circumstances but rather as victims of their own past.

Psychopathology   According to Freud, each person is fixated to varying degrees at different stages of development, and the result of these fixations determines to a large part adult conduct and abilities to react in situations. Persons who are stingy and stubborn are not that way because they choose to be or because they have evaluated all of the options, but rather because during the anal stage of development, certain difficulties arose that were never adequately resolved. An overly timid woman, who has difficulties dealing with people around her, according to Freud, might be suffering from repressed Oedipal fixations of which she is unaware. The implications of this type of reasoning are clear: *We are enslaved to our past to the degree that our past repeats itself in our present situations.*

Role of the Psychodynamic Counselor   Psychoanalysis has at times been much criticized, even by some of its strongest adherents (Rank, 1945) for its rather restricted view of the client and his or her place in treatment. According to Phipps (1959), the psychoanalytic client must accept the validity of the psychoanalytic theory in order to improve. Rogers's (1942) criticisms of the psychoanalytic view of the client focus on the notion that the client is viewed as ill, or somehow disturbed—a point of view to which he objects strenuously. Torrey (1972), too, feels that at the onset of the treatment, the client is put into a weakened position in which he is highly suggestible to the analyst's interpretations. There is much truth to these criticisms, particularly insofar as the basis of psychoanalytic treatment is that the patient is initially disoriented and not entirely in touch with reality and that the analyst will ultimately help him or her see the truth. However, we must keep in mind that more humanistic and client-oriented concerns have over the years made themselves felt in even the most classical psychoanalytic approaches.

Psychoanalytic clients are expected to bring all their thoughts and feelings into the analytic counseling session and to verbalize them through the use of free association. It is expected that clients, no matter how eager they are for treatment, will resist the analysis because of their unconscious fears. This resistance can take many forms, including missing appointments, refusing to speak, telling jokes, falling asleep, and so on. The purpose of resistance is to avoid anxiety by protecting the ego from feelings it cannot accept.

Most important of the resistances therapeutically is the *transference* resistance. Transference can be defined as transferring onto the person of the counselor feelings that were once attached to emotionally significant figures early in life. Originally, Freud considered transference an obstacle to treatment; but eventually he realized that it was the phenomenon of transference that made the treatment and the cure possible. As the client transfers feelings onto the counselor, he or she is able to reexperience emotionally the early life conflicts from which the present difficulties arise. Through this transference neurosis, as it is called, the counselor is able to learn directly of the client's childhood.

For example, consider the case of a young male client who has developed a transference relationship with his counselor. He begins to experience the counselor as rejecting and ungratifying in the same way he unconsciously experienced his parents many years earlier. If he communicates these transference feelings to the counselor, as he should, and if the counselor is perceptive enough to see them, as he or she hopefully is, the counselor will then have an understanding of the client's early childhood that could not be provided by the client himself, since he is not consciously aware of these feelings. Clients often reveal many of their unconscious wishes, fears, distortions, and conflicts through the transference relationship. Whenever counselors feel they are being perceived *as if* they were someone other than who they really are, it is reasonably certain that transference is at work.

Although the client is expected to resist the treatment, she or he is also expected to be cooperative. This simply means that she or he will avoid *acting-out;* that is, discharging repressed feelings by gratifying them outside the analytic session rather than verbalizing them within. In order to have a successful psychoanalytic experience, the client is asked to avoid making any major decisions without first discussing them fully with the analyst. Freud's injunction against marrying, divorcing, having children, changing jobs, or anything else during the course of the treatment was designed to prevent acting-out, which he viewed as a dangerous detriment to therapy. While such enjoinders do insure a certain integrity in the course of treatment, they place an emotionally stressful burden on the client and may foster an attitude of dependency upon the analyst that is difficult to break even after the analysis is completed. Pattison (1970), however, cites another point of view, that after the treatment is completed, "the past relationship with the therapist show[s] a gradual shift from a therapeutic relationship to a human sharing relationship . . . [the] patient was able to use the psychotherapeutic relationship as a paradigm for forming, extending, and using relationships with others after psychotherapy" (p. 213). It may well be that the client's dependency during the treatment is a necessary first step for subsequent independence after the treatment is completed.

An important part of the counselor's role in the psychodynamic counseling framework involves helping the client overcome the "neurotic" use of defense mechanisms. As we understand these mechanisms and the role they play in impeding successful maturation, we see how important their resolution is. Let us look briefly at a few of the defensive mechanisms and how they affect functioning.

The Defense
Mechanisms

Repression The most common defense mechanism is repression. In its most basic form, repression simply means forgetting. Whatever was once part of consciousness but no longer is has been repressed. We repress both feelings and situations, thoughts and occasions, using as our guiding principle the reduction of anxiety. Whatever causes us pain or provokes anxiety becomes a likely candidate for repression and is then no longer accessible to our conscious mind. "Being repressed," said Freud (1924), "means being unable to pass out of the unconscious system."

Repression may cause innumerable difficulties in the counseling situation, and these can be viewed as resistances. When a client forgets an appointment, forgets until after the session to tell the counselor something he or she had on his or her mind, or even forgets the counselor's name, the psychodynamic counselor can fairly well assume that the client is repressing some material. To dismiss such instances casually—"Oh, it just slipped my mind"—shows an unwillingness to examine more dynamic motives for deeper causes. Then again, whenever a client makes what is commonly called a Freudian slip of the tongue (*parapraxis*), we can also be assured that repression is at work. For Freud pointed out in his important work, *Psychopathology of Everyday Life,* that all such slips are signs of unconscious repressed material trying to break through to consciousness.

Projection Projection, another common defense mechanism, is the process of attributing to another person or to an object in the outside world, feelings that emanate from within. A person who feels that no one likes him, for example, may be projecting internal feelings of hostility onto all of the people around her or him. Projection protects the ego by confusing self and other, and by attributing to the other the unacceptable feelings of the self. Projection, even more than repression, presents a serious problem in the counseling situation by offering the possibility that what the client is experiencing in others (such as the counselor) are actually qualities that he or she does not like about himself or herself. For instance, paranoid individuals tend to project their hostility onto others, imagining a conspiracy of forces against them, or against someone else.

Reaction Formation Reaction formation is a defense mechanism that is often difficult to recognize. Simply stated, this mechanism involves acting in a way that is in total contradiction to the way one unconsciously feels. While the individual is acting in this way, however, he or she is not aware of unconscious feelings and is, therefore, unable to recognize the mechanism at work. Let us say, for example, that a woman is experiencing some unrecognized hostility toward a friend but that her ideas about friendship preclude such feelings from her subjective inventory. If you like your friends, you will never feel angry at them, the unrealistic expectation goes. One way of handling this unconsciously is to react to this anger. She may, for instance, feel compelled to buy her friend an expensive present, one well beyond her means: a present given not for love, but rather for self-protection. The giving of the present is a direct reaction to the unrecognized feelings of hostililty. It would be far better if this client were to recognize her angry feelings and deal with them directly, thus working them out so that they might be productively integrated into the multidimensional relationship, which is what a true friendship relationship should be.

Intellectualization

Intellectualization is a defense mechanism that is often considered an occupational hazard to people in counseling and psychotherapy. It makes itself felt when a person understands something intellectually, but not emotionally. Manifestations of intellectualization include describing a person in technical, non-emotional language; relating to others through planned, impersonal techniques, rather than through spontaneity and genuine feelings; perceiving people professionally in terms of their symptoms and ignoring their personal complexity; understanding a friend's problems in systematic, logical, theoretically-oriented perspective, rather than from the other's own frame of reference. Intellectualization is avoiding the reality of another person and seeing him or her as an object instead. We intellectualize when we attempt to grasp our own feelings and other's feelings conceptually rather than emotionally. Unfortunately, because counselors and psychotherapists have been trained to understand diagnostic and symptomatic categories, they are more prone than others to misuse these categories to separate themselves from the client.

Denial

The mechanism of denial is sometimes confused with repression and reaction formation because of the similarities among the three. Denial, in its most general form, is when the conscious mind denies feelings from within or situations from without that prove threatening to the ego. True, denial often involves repressive and reacting components; but, more importantly, denial involves blocking out a portion of the world, denying it, rather than reacting to it or forgetting it. A husband, for example, may fail to recognize that his wife is experiencing hostile feelings toward him, thereby blocking out of his perceptual world an important part of their relationship. Parents are sometimes prone to deny their children's angry feelings toward them. Sexual feelings are a class of feelings that are often subject to denial.

Isolation

Isolation, like intellectualization, involves the severing of the affective from the cognitive realm, the cutting off of feelings from intellectual understanding. With isolation, however, the major emphasis is on perceiving the world as an affectless, emotionless world in which the perceiver feels uninvolved in what is happening, not, as with intellectualization, placing the world within intellectual constructs. As a person "distances" herself or himself from another, refusing to confront and experience the other's feelings, he or she utilizes the defense mechanism of isolation.

Rationalization

When a person uses rationalization, he or she develops a pseudo-explanation for actions or attributes false, more favorable motives to explain behavior. Commonly referred to as sour grapes, rationalization is typified by the famous Aesop fable of the fox who tried repeatedly without success to get at a bunch of grapes. Failing time and again, the fox finally gave up his attempts, rationalizing that the grapes looked sour anyway. The client who rationalizes his or her problems defends himself or herself from real feelings by creating a false situation of motives and causality.

Displacement

Displacement involves the shifting (or replacement) of an object of a feeling or drive. A man employed in a personnel department, for example, may take out some of the aggression he feels toward his supervisor by displacing it onto clients who are safer objects for his wrath. In general, displacement involves displacing to a *safe* object feelings unconsciously held toward a more *dangerous* or *threatening* object. Since there is an imbalance of power in many interpersonal relationships, the use of displacement can make the person in the lesser-power position a victim of the other. We see this all the time when one person says to the other, "Why are you always picking on me for things I didn't do?"

Regression

Regression means "returning," particularly returning to an earlier stage of emotional or intellectual development. When a person becomes overpowered by feelings he or she can no longer handle, one way of dealing with the situation is to return to an earlier level of development in which one was able either to avoid confronting such feelings or to feel comfortable with them. The counselor may find at times that the client is exhibiting behavior that is less mature than his or her normal behavior and indicative of feelings at some earlier point in development. In such instances, it can safely be assumed that the client is regressing to some earlier point in development in order to deal with the difficulties he or she is consciously or unconsciously experiencing in life.

Introjection and Identification

Introjection and identification, two mechanisms that are often confused with each other, are common occurrences in the counseling situation. Introjection occurs when an individual's personality incorporates part of another person. For example, the client may introject a part of the counselor—take on some of the counselor's values and beliefs—which can be therapeutically productive.

Freud initially used introjection to explain the learning of values by the child. A child introjects—takes inside—its parents' system of values, and they become a part of the child. But an adult may introject, too, for entirely different reasons. Introjection may be used as a method of gaining strength from another, of actually incorporating a part of another's will within oneself. This can be healthy or unhealthy, depending upon why and what we introject. We see clear pathological examples in the followers of the Reverend Jim Jones, who committed mass suicide in Guiana because they had taken on his values so that what he told them to do was more important than life itself.

Introjection may also be a part of the process of getting love from another: the romantic concept of lovers uniting as one is interpreted in psychodynamic language as introjecting with each other. In either case, whether the motivation be strength or love, the individual introjects from another when he or she feels, but cannot fully acknowledge, the powerful feelings drawing him or her and the other together.

Identification is the process whereby an individual confuses his or her identity with the identity of someone else. Rycroft (1968) points out that in identification the person may either extend identity into someone else, borrow identity from someone else, or fuse his or her identity with someone else's. Three common modes of identification in the counseling situation are identification with the *aggressor,* identification with the *victim*, and *narcissistic* identification. In the first case, the client, exposed to an aggressive and threatening person who makes her or him feel endangered, begins to act and feel as aggressively as the threatening person. She or he does this, albeit unconsciously, as protection from the presumed dangers of the other person.

We may also identify with a victim. We do this when we see ourself being hurt as the other person describes his or her own hurt. A close friend may, for example, be describing mistreatment she or he has been exposed to by a parent. Recalling our own mistreatment during childhood, we begin to feel mistreated along with our friend. This differs from empathy, because we are not experiencing the world from the friend's point of view but rather from a point of view that, while it parallels our friend's, is actually our own. This is closer to the mechanism of projection, therefore, than to the quality of empathy.

Narcissistic identification describes the process by which one acts out fantasies and experiences vicariously through another's life. Sometimes called over-identification or over-involvement, this defense occurs whenever an individual begins to confuse his or her own identity with the identity of the other person. A severely disturbed individual, for example, may live more in a fantasy life, obsessively admiring heroes on TV and in books, than in his or her own life.

While all of us make use at times of these various defense mechanisms, they do present difficulties for us (especially when used in extreme) in living realistically, in relating to others, in making appropriate decisions, in facilitating self-growth and self-understanding. Defense mechanisms distort perception and block off part of the world. Theoretically, the better adjusted an individual is, the less need he or she will have for defense mechanisms. But even the best adjusted person will at times have no recourse but to use them. An important part of facilitating the growth of the client is to help him or her rely less on defensive behaviors and more on reality-oriented coping.

We will now look briefly at four examples of the use of defense mechanisms, extracted from real case material, to see how these mechanisms function in real practice. As we look at these cases, keep in mind instances in your own life where similar patterns of what psychodynamic counselors would call defensive behavior, thought, and feelings occurred, and try to analyze the forces that prompted these mechanisms to work for you.

Case One Mr. Cunningham forgets an important business appointment, is chided by his boss, and then goes home and yells at his wife about what a lousy dinner she made for him.

Defenses Repression and displacement.

Case Two   Georgia believes that Betty doesn't like her, although this is not so. In fact, Betty has no feelings at all about Georgia; doesn't even notice her. Which is probably what burns Georgia, since Betty is pretty, bright, and the most popular girl in her class. Georgia says to her friends, "That Betty thinks she's hot stuff, and I wouldn't go to her lousy party even if she asked me."

Defenses   Projection and rationalization.

Case Three   Quentin acts overly nice to Mrs. Agoradis, his boss, without ever realizing the sad truth that he doesn't really like her . . . but has to work for her anyway.

Defenses   Reaction formation.

Case Four   Bobby believes things are going really well with Debbie, the girl he is dating and thinking about getting engaged to. He is shocked when he receives a letter that she has met someone else whom she has been seeing and thinks it would be better for both of them if they didn't see each other any more. Bobby had no idea she was seeing anyone else! He can't believe it! Thinking about it, he becomes very morose and inactive, crying and looking at Debbie's picture, knowing he will never have her again.

Defenses   Denial and regression.

The Adlerian Counselor

Many contemporary psychoanalytically-oriented counselors would find themselves in strong disagreement with Freud's theory of personality and version of psychoanalytic counseling. Partisans of the Adlerian position, called Individual Psychology, have defined and explored a comprehensive method of counseling and a detailed personality theory to explain human behavior and to help in the treatment of problems. The method, although psychoanalytic, has an entirely different emphasis than Freud's procedure. "In contrast to Freud," Leibin (1981) points out, "Adler considers man as a social being. Although Freud also mentions social ties and a 'social drive,' he only puts the question. Adler considers social interest *the basis of human existence.*" He goes on to suggest that,

> Adler's Individual Psychology is more positive than Freud's psychoanalysis. It affirms man's spontaneous activity. Adler views man as the product of his own creation. This opens the way to the understanding of the active side of the subject who creates his own being in the world. (p. 3)

Adler's emphasis on man's social qualities infuses every aspect of his theory, from the formation of personality to the specific ways of treating clients in the clinical setting. Of central importance is the organizing principle of social interest, which strikes the chords of dissonance between him and Freud.

Adler's theory of personality, in contrast to Freud's, emphasizes the individual's social nature and the influence of the social environment on development. Adler views human behavior as motivated primarily not by unconscious sexual drives, but by a matrix of innate social striving which he calls *social interest*. He believes "social interest to be the primary personality trait and to be the criterion for adjustment and mental health" (Schneider & Reuterfors, 1981). Throughout his writings, Adler suggests that the healthy individual is able to act in a way that is socially productive and, at the same time, individually fulfilling. To Adler, adjustment and sound psychological functioning represent a combination of deep personal feelings, cognitive assumptions, and social behavior.

Kaplan (1986) has outlined the behaviors, feelings, and cognitions associated with social interest. These are summarized briefly below, but his excellent article should be consulted by those who want a richer understanding of the Adlerian viewpoint. It makes practical the possibility of translating to clients how their thinking, feeling, and behaving relates to social interest.

Helping behavior Willingness to use one's abilities, knowledge, or talents in order to aid others.

Sharing behavior Willingness to provide others with some of one's own possessions.

Participating behavior Joining in such group activities as social clubs, political organizations, etc.

Respectful behavior Recognizing and being sensitive to others' human rights, knowledge, and experiences.

Cooperative behavior Willingness to work or play with others in order to reach mutual benefits and/or goals.

Compromising (flexible) behavior Ability to "give and take," in the hope of reaching mutually acceptable solutions to conflicts or problems.

Empathic behavior Shows others that their thoughts and feelings are understood and appreciated.

Encouraging behavior Helps motivate others.

Reforming behavior Tries to improve social conditions for the common good. This includes taking the initiative to expose problems, and then devoting time and investing effort toward ending or ameliorating the problems (usually by meeting with people, educating people, and influencing people).

Belonging Feeling that one belongs to a group or several groups and that one has a secure place in a social organization.

Feeling "at home" Feeling at ease and comfortable when interacting with others.

Communality Feeling similarity to and communion with other people.

Faith in others Social interest in all people, especially recognizing their good traits.

"Courage to be imperfect" Feeling that making mistakes is a natural part of being human and that one does not always have to be best, first, or most famous.

Being human Feeling a part of all humanity, especially in an existential sense.

Optimism Feeling that the world can be made a better place to live, not only for us but for all fellow humans.

Five Cognitions Associated with Social Interest

1. "As a human being, my rights and obligations in society are equal to the rights and obligations of others."
2. "My personal goals can be attained in ways consistent with the welfare of the community."
3. "The prosperity and survival of society are dependent on the willingness and ability of its citizens to learn to live together in harmony."
4. "I believe in trying to respond to others as I would like them to respond to me."
5. "The ultimate measure of my character will be to what extent I promoted the welfare of the community."

Style of Life

Central to understanding Adler's psychotherapeutic orientation is the concept of life-style (or style of life). The term refers to the organized patterns, themes, behaviors, and orientations that are organically expressed through an individual's life activities. Each person, according to Adler, has a unique life-style that enables him or her to compensate for inferiority feelings and strive toward superiority.

Style of life can be roughly equated to a central theme that runs through the individual's personality. For some individuals, the style of life is centered around aggressive, manipulative, and exploitive experiences in which they take advantage of others. This becomes the person's characteristic style of striving for superiority. For another person, the style of life may be centered around intellectual and social achievement—working toward attaining superiority through the application of intellectual and social skills. Still another person's style of life may be centered around acquiring large sums of money or other possessions. An Adlerian counselor, in trying to pinpoint a client's style of life, might categorize the person as striving after difficult or impossible attainments or as striving after realistic goals and being satisfied when he or she attains them. These behaviors and attitudes are all characteristic patterns of existence that transcend any individual behavior or action and form recurrent patterns.

In each case, the overriding preoccupation of the personality reflects the person's striving for superiority and at the same time his or her feelings of inferiority. Style of life is formed very early in childhood, usually by the age of four or five, and is determined largely by one's experiences within the family. Adler points out that the position a child occupies in the family strongly influences his or her personality development. This idea, in fact, has become one of the more accepted parts of Adlerian theory and has been borne out by much experimental evidence (Nystul, 1981).

In its broadest sense, then, one's life-style is an expression of oneself and the way one sees oneself, and at the same time, a way of encouraging others to respond in a manner consistent with this perception.

At the beginning of treatment, a life-style assessment is usually undertaken in the form of a questionnaire and interview. This allows the therapist and patient to jointly examine the interacting forces that contributed to the development of the life-style and to consider their implications. It also serves as a framework for shaping many of the goals of therapy.

The concepts most often associated with Adler are the "inferiority complex" and "striving for superiority." Every child is born helpless, dependent on others, and therefore, overwhelmed by feelings of inferiority that he or she must struggle to overcome for the rest of his or her life. We do this, Adler suggests, by striving for superiority. This process, which includes a striving for social power, recognition, and internal perfection, becomes a major motivation in a person's life. In the healthy individual, the striving for superiority is in accord with the needs of society, and the person acquires such traits as courage, independence, and wholesome ambition. On the other hand, maladjustment and unhealthy development are seen when a person grows up with feelings of inadequacy and powerlessness, which Adler calls the inferiority complex.

The Inferiority Complex

The process by which a person overcomes his or her innate feelings of inferiority is called compensation, and it plays a crucial role in personality development. Compensation often encourages a person to excel in an area where he or she was most deficient as a child. For example, an individual who is constitutionally weak may compensate by developing the body, such as by studying karate. A child who stutters may grow up to become an actor or singer. A classic case of compensation was exemplified by Theodore Roosevelt, a sickly youngster who worked hard to overcome his physical weaknesses and as an adult, became the fearless leader of the Rough Riders in the Spanish-American War. Another example of compensation is the case of former Supreme Court Justice William O. Douglas, who was known for his love of sports and outdoor life. He actively participated in camping, long-distance hiking, and dangerous mountain climbing, until he was well into his late sixties. As a child, Douglas had suffered from polio, and had spent his adolescent years building up and strengthening his crippled legs.

Compensation

Compensation and social interest are related in actual living. For the healthy person, compensation serves as a way of achieving socially desirable goals:

> Social interest expresses itself as a healthy compensation for the feelings of inferiority which all people experience. When inferiority feelings are not too intense, an individual is capable of adaptive and normal compensation through the expression of social interest. However, if the feelings of inferiority be-

come very strong, neurotic compensations impair the development and expression of an individual's innate potential for healthy social concern and cooperation. Development of cooperation and avoidance of excessive competition and rivalry thus promote growth of the individual and society. (Schneider & Reuterfors, 1981, p. 102)

From the perspective of the Adlerian counselor, therefore, it is important to understand how the client's inferiority feelings affect different areas of interpersonal functioning, such as marital and family relationships and work or school interactions.

Ordinal Position
(Birth Order)

A child's position within the family is also central in understanding the nexus of forces that shape us into what we ultimately become. Birth order, or ordinal position, means more than simply the numerical order of birth: it refers, rather, to the psychological position of the child in the family constellation. For example, two siblings whose births are separated by many years may both be raised as oldest children. Shulman and Mosak (1982) point out the main features of Adler's concept:

Adler's classic description of the effects of birth order contains the following features: (1) Children of the same family are not born into the same environment. The second child is born into a different psychological situation than the first. (2) It is not the actual order of birth but the psychological situation which is important. If the eldest is feeble-minded, the second may assume the role of a first-born. (3) Marked difference in age between siblings tends to reduce competition between them. (4) Birth order is not an absolute determinant, only an influence. The reaction of the parents to the child is at least as important. (Shulman & Mosak, 1982, p. 114)

Other Concepts

In many ways, Adler's philosophy (or psychology, or world view—whatever one chooses to call it) fuses together principles of existentialism, humanism, psychoanalysis, and cognitive psychology. A central force in each person's life is striving for significance, particularly striving to overcome early feelings of inferiority that originated in the family. This generalized striving is concretized in life-style and in the specific life tasks one views as instrumental in promoting growth. Adler's view of *tasks* brings him into the behavioral and cognitive camps, especially insofar as he recognizes the importance of changing certain behaviors in order to change people's thinking and feelings about themselves. He believes that establishing specific and measurable tasks allows the client to make specific and measurable changes in a limited amount of time. This is accomplished with a variety of techniques, including "spitting in the soup," in which the client comes to realize negative implications by perceiving the task as part of a larger game.

Clearly, Adler's influence extends well beyond his own therapeutic domain into behavioral, cognitive, gestalt, and rational approaches. Many of the insights he discovered and techniques he promoted are now widely used in other therapeutic modalities.

Adler's concept of "private logic" includes a person's logical assumptions and their logical processes of reasoning. If either is wildly distorted or out of sync with the rest of the world, therapeutic intervention is required to correct it. There are several advantages to using the patient's private logic in therapy (Mozdzierz, Murphy & Greenblatt, 1986): Private Logic

> An advantage of understanding a person's private logic is that it avoids the building of resistance while simultaneously facilitating understanding and cooperation. For example, the paranoid person has had the life-long experiences of not being able to trust others. If the therapist is naive and not respectful of this orientation with the paranoid client, he or she may find him- or herself trying to defend the confidentiality of clinical records. On the other hand, if a paranoid person inquires about the confidentiality of the record, the therapist could respond: "I'd like to be able to tell you that these records are secure after they leave my office, but I don't know who might get their hands on them after they leave. We have to be as careful as possible about this sort of thing." This establishes the basis for a common understanding and also avoids the resistance that could ensue as a result of the patient seeing things one way . . . and the therapist seeing things another way.

Using the patient's private logic also helps establish rapport between the therapist and client. It makes the patient feel that the therapist understands and accepts his or her thinking.

At the time they were first published, Adler's ideas did not receive nearly as much attention as Freud's theory had been given earlier. Only in recent years, when other psychologists began to use some of the same concepts, have we come to realize how far ahead of his time Adler was. His interest in the effects of birth order on personality development preceded by more than a quarter of a century the many recent studies on this subject. Also, his recurring emphasis on social factors was an important precursor to other dynamic personality theories, which has added immeasurably to the growing acceptance of psychoanalysis in the counseling profession. Most significant, perhaps, is the fact that Adler's theories have had a wide impact on education, resulting in a comprehensive theory of what Adlerians call Individual Education, in which "children operate . . . in terms of their perceptions of how to achieve success, superiority, competency" Evaluation of Adler's Theory

(Whittington, 1981, p. 247). The application of Adler's theory to the school setting has been felt strongly in the area of school counseling, where it vies with the humanistic approaches as the most accepted and widely practiced modality.

The Modern Psychoanalytic Counselor

In discussing the role of the psychoanalytic counselor, we see that a notable discrepancy exists between the classical conception of the psychoanalyst and the modern, more expansive descriptions of the analyst. The major question that the psychoanalytic counselor faces today is, How active is he or she expected to be during the sessions? How much of himself or herself should be given to the client? What feelings can be shown? To what degree can he or she respond objectively to the client, and to what degree is he or she supposed to respond primarily to the unconscious communications of the client?

Typically—or stereotypically, as the case may be—the psychoanalyst is viewed as extremely passive and detached, offering little of herself or himself and repeatedly responding with the famous "Um-hum." This image is not entirely accurate, however. True, the classical psychoanalyst, as defined in Freud's writings, is one who maintains an attitude of objective neutrality, of "evenly suspended attention" (Freud, 1912), who refrains from responding positively or negatively to any of the client's expressions, and studies with detachment the meaning of the client's associations, communications, and dreams. But even Freud himself was not a strict classical analyst, according to his own teachings. He was "intuitively" active with his patients, sometimes gossiping, arranging marriages, offering friendly advice, and even having analytic sessions while strolling along the boulevard (Roazen, 1975). Still, he always told his analytic trainees, "Do as I preach, not as I do."

But even during Freud's own time, this passive image of the analyst began to change. Sandor Ferenczi (Eng. trans., 1950), one of his most influential colleagues, proposed what he called "active psychotherapy," in which the analyst became a responsive contributing member of the treatment team. Other innovators, such as Otto Rank, began to expand the original doctrine to make it more relevant for a wider client population. The work of these two men served as a theoretical beginning for a future generation of psychoanalysts who recognized the therapeutic significance of the analyst's active participation in the treatment.

Spotnitz, leading the modern psychoanalytic movement, made substantial inroads. Arguing that the modern psychoanalyst uses his or her own counter-transference feelings, which have been induced by the client, to inject verbally back into the client, at an appropriate time, the "toxic" and harmful feelings he or she is experiencing, Spotnitz (1963) introduced the therapeutic *toxoid response:*

> This process was conceptualized as one of immunizing a patient against toxic effects. . . . Mutual contagion emerged as a basic factor: the analyst has to experience the patient's feelings in order to "return" them to him; the patient, through experiencing them from the analyst, is helped to discharge the feelings in language. (pp. 87–88)

Spotnitz's work has become so influential that, despite its general lack of renown outside the profession, it can rightfully be considered the modern heir to the Freudian legacy and the most important of the neo-Freudian therapies. While the theory is somewhat beyond the scope of this book, we can summarize its contributions in four basic principles that, at the same time, will show its relevance for counseling; a relevance that has often been neglected in discussing psychoanalysis:

1. Each person comes to the counseling setting with unmet maturational needs: deep emotional needs that arose at a specific period of life and that were not adequately met then. As a result, the patient does not know how to go about satisfying these needs now.

2. Resistances to solving one's problems can be divided into two categories: Oedipal and pre-verbal. The former are rooted in the Oedipal period of development, while the latter, more difficult, more stubborn resistances are from the period of life before we learned to speak.

3. The psychoanalytic counselor relies on his objective counter-transference feelings to understand the feelings that the client is unconsciously communicating. "The objective countertransference refers to those feelings that the counselor experiences toward the client which are a function of the client's ego. These *induced feelings* were felt toward the client by other significant people in his past . . . or, they may reflect feelings the client has for himself." (Kirman, 1977, p. 75)

4. The main job of the counselor is to help the client learn how to meet his or her maturational needs. This does not necessarily involve the classical technique of interpretation. Dr. Spotnitz describes the role of the analyst as a "maturational agent, helping people . . . resolve whatever obstacles to personality maturation they have experienced." (Spotnitz, 1976, p. 16)

Although these modern psychoanalytic techniques were originally developed to be used with severely disturbed clients, recent efforts to apply these principles to typical neurotic clients indicate a significant trend in the psychoanalytic profession; a trend that may have great implications for the counseling profession in future years.

In any case, the most important therapeutic task of the modern analytic counselor is still to help the client resolve resistances that disrupt treatment and prevent his or her living maturely. In classical psychoanalysis, this is accomplished by *interpreting* to the client his or her unconscious. Modern psychoanalysis, however, differs from the classical approach by concentrating on those deeply imbedded resistances that do not respond to interpretation. The modern analytic counselor uses reflective and mirroring techniques, in addition to interpretation, in order to *help the client resolve resistances*—to enable the client to experience them emotionally—instead of explaining them to him or her.

Whenever an analytic counselor works with a client over a period of time, it is inevitable that the counselor will develop some feelings about the client. These are called *countertransference* feelings. According to the modern analysts, whether or not these feelings are positive or negative is not as important as whether or not they are realistic, objective responses to the way the client is feeling about the analyst. Whenever the counselor's feelings are objective, they are productive in the treatment. When, on the other hand, they are subjective, neurotic distortions by the analyst, they are counterproductive to the goals of the treatment. Thus, if the client is inducing positive feelings in the counselor and the counselor, in turn, feels positive toward the client, this is said to be an objective countertransference. If the client is expressing a great deal of invisible hostility, and the counselor begins to pick up these negative feelings from the client, this is also objective countertransference. In both cases, the counselor's feelings, as long as they are objective responses to the client's feelings, serve as an indicator of what the client is feeling unconsciously. Thus, the countertransference serves the same purpose for the counselor as the X-ray machine serves for the physician: to reveal those parts of the client that are hidden from view.

Theodore Reik (1948), a disciple of Freud, describes the concept of "listening with the third ear." The counselor does this by associating along with the client, experiencing his or her own relevant feelings as the client speaks. The counselor, naturally, is not daydreaming while the client is speaking, but rather is allowing the client's words to stimulate in him or her feelings and ideas that are relevant to the communications that the client is offering. This is a further use of countertransference, whereby the counselor relies on his or her own feelings to understand and empathize with the feelings of the client.

We can best clarify the role of the psychoanalytic counselor by stating five cardinal rules that would probably be acceptable to most psychoanalytic practitioners, regardless of their specific orientation. These rules are:

1. Never offer personal information about yourself unless there is a specific and compelling therapeutic reason for doing so.
2. Analyze resistances as they appear. Do not try to quash or minimize a resistance; confront it head-on, interpreting or reflecting as may be necessary.
3. Learn about the client, not only by listening to what she or he is saying, but by examining your own feelings about the client, which are responses to her or his communication.
4. Give priority to freeing the client's unconscious by making her or him feel comfortable. Avoid interjections and interpretations that are solely designed to reduce anxiety, and emphasize those communications that are compatible with the long-range goals of the treatment.

5. Consider all comments, requests, and other communications from the client within the total context of the treatment, rather than as isolated instances. This not only helps the counselor understand the implications of specific material in the client's mind but helps unify and structure the treatment in a progressively curative manner.

The predominant technique of classical psychoanalysis is interpretation. The analytic counselor uses interpretations in order to help the client understand his unconscious mechanisms. Ideally, the counselor, rather than directly interpreting to the client, guides the client to his own interpretations, since the client is more likely to accept the conclusions that he has arrived at himself rather than those the counselor has forced him to recognize. Using his or her own countertransference feeling as a map, the psychoanalytic counselor can guide the patient through the recesses of his or her unconscious conflicts until the gleams of self-realization begin to appear (Marcus, 1980). Thus, we can describe the predominant method of classical psychoanalytic counseling as *leading the client to correct interpretations*.

The goal of these interpretations in not only self-insight, but also what Freud called ego integration; the ability of the parts of the psyche to function together harmoniously. In fact, the classical analyst does not strive primarily to help the patient with each problem as it arises, but rather views the problems presented by the patient in terms of the total context and goals of the treatment. The long-range goal—of symptomatic or characterological resolution—takes priority over short-term resolution of life problems. As Langs (1980) points out,

> The ultimate goal of psychoanalysis is the insightful adaptation and resolution of the patient's symptoms or characterological disturbances. Real-life situations as presented by the patient are secondary contexts that must be attached to the therapeutic interaction and the stimuli generated by the analyst's intervention. Every communication from the patient must be understood in terms of an adaptive context related to the analytic interaction and especially to the analyst's silences, interventions, and management of the framework. (p. 460)

Modern psychoanalytic counselors, as we have mentioned, rely less on interpretations. In their place, they use *paradigms*. A paradigm, derived from the Greek word for "model," is "a showing by example" (Nelson et al., 1968). It is a technique of teaching the patient something emotionally; a technique used in lieu of interpretation. The authors go on to explain.

> By "example" we do not mean that the therapist presents his feelings, his belief of his behavior as a model for the patient to emulate. We mean that the therapist initiates, induces or prolongs modes of interaction with the patient which promote the latter's self-understanding without manifest recourse to interpretation in the explanatory sense. (p. 45)

Psychodynamic Approaches

Paradigms offer an advantage to the counselor in that they do not require the client to "confront" his or her unconscious difficulties in order to resolve them. Where a classical analyst may tell a client that his or her stubbornness is a result of overly strict toilet training, a paradigmatic counselor would deal with the client's stubbornness by allowing him or her to be constructively stubborn, thereby compensating for the parents' severity at an earlier point in life.

Strean (1968) offers an interesting clinical example of how a paradigm may be used successfully to treat an adolescent who is compelled to make up bizarre fantasies: whenever the patient made up a fantasy, the analyst made up an even more bizzare fantasy, in effect demonstrating to the client that the analyst's "craziness" was equal to the client's own. Finally, after a year and a half, the client expressed his or her real hostility to the analyst.

The Reluctant Retiree: A Case Example

When Mr. Collingsworth came to see Dr. Stevens, the company counselor, his complaint was that he was having difficulties with his co-workers. He described some of the problems he was having and they sounded typical enough: fighting about who was doing too much or too little work on the assembly line; arguing over who made a minor mistake in one recent assembly; confusion about scheduling and vacation. It was only after Dr. Stevens explored the matter a little deeper that she noted something quite strange: Mr. Collingsworth had had a perfect record at the plant for twenty-nine years: no fights, no complaints, good attendance, no disciplinary proceedings. But now, during the past eight months, he had suddenly become what might be called a "troublemaker." What was especially surprising about this sudden change in behavior was that at the end of this year, he was scheduled to voluntarily retire on full pension.

Dr. Stevens thought that there might be some relationship between the impending retirement and Mr. Collingsworth's change in behavior and attitude and she explored this with him. He denied adamantly any relationship, insisting that changes in plant conditions and the quality of the men he was working with had caused the changes in his behavior. But Dr. Stevens, whose orientation was psychoanalytic, sought out the unconscious reasons that might be influencing his behavior.

During one session, the following exchange took place, and Dr. Stevens took this as an important sign:

M.C. If these people (his co-workers and the foreman) were any good, they'd listen to me. After all, I'm the one with experience. I'm the one who knows what's going on around here.

D.S. And what are they going to do when you leave? How will they get by without your experience?

M.C. You think I give a damn? I'll tell you something. I learned *a long time ago* not to worry about people when you're gone. If they don't listen to you when you're there, they're just not worth the effort. You should try to help them when you can and then just forget about them. I don't expect that *your* mind is gonna be on me when I leave. You're just doing your job now. That's what you're getting paid for. That's all.

D.S. You said you learned this lesson, "a long time ago." When was that? Can you remember?

M.C. (*Thinks for a moment*) Well, one thing comes to mind. My brother. (*He pauses and becomes pensive and reticent.*)

D.S. (*After waiting a few minutes*) An older or younger brother?

M.C. Neither. A twin. I had a twin brother, not identical though. It's a long story, but I was going out with this girl—this was maybe thirty-five years ago—and then she left me and got engaged to him. To my brother, Jed. He died, of TB it was, and that was the end of that. I met someone else and married a few years later.

D.S. And what was the lesson that you learned "a long time ago?"

M.C. (*Thinks deeply*) I guess the lesson I learned was that no one cares about you.

Several sessions later the subject of the dead twin was returned to. At the time of its introduction, Dr. Stevens realized that there was probably an important unconscious connection between this and what was happening at the plant now. She inferred this not because she knew anything specific, but rather because the client had *free associated* to the dead twin in the context of his discussion. When it came up again, a key point emerged:

M.C. You know, when my brother died, I guess I felt guilty as hell. I mean, I cried for a week. I really loved him even though he did take the girl from me. She really wasn't important. But maybe . . . (*He pauses with a pained look.*)

D.S. Maybe?

M.C. Maybe I wanted him dead. I don't know . . . this seems crazy. What does it have to do with what is going on now? I don't even know why I'm talking about it.

As Dr. Stevens and Mr. Collingsworth discussed it, the connection became clear: even though he was voluntarily retiring from the job, he unconsciously saw this as the company abandoning him, casting him aside as he had been cast aside many years ago. This brought back the unresolved feelings about his brother's death, and he was working out this conflict with his co-workers and supervisor. He was expressing his rage to them, saying in effect, "HOW DARE YOU TAKE THIS JOB AWAY FROM ME. IT IS MINE! I DESERVE IT!"

Once he was able to get in touch with this conflict, to express his long-repressed feelings about his brother's death, he no longer had the need to act out on the job. Dr. Stevens helped him to learn to accept his unconscious feelings . . . to make them conscious.

The differences between classical and modern psychoanalysis can be summed up as follows: classical psychoanalysis believes that as clients come to understand their problems, they will be able to overcome them; modern psychoanalysis offers the position that to grow, the client must learn about his or her unmet maturational needs, and must discover with the analyst how to go about meeting these needs. The job of the analyst is to resolve the client's resistances to meeting these needs.

The goal of psychoanalysis is to reduce the client's anxieties and to enable her or him to reach a stage of *integration*. At this stage, the ego is able to organize and unite the drives of the personality, enabling the individual to think, behave, and feel in a constructive and satisfying way: in short, to sublimate. This is generally considered the highest level of psychological development.

Evaluation and Applications

Psychoanalysis has often been minimized as a technique applicable to the counseling setting. Its critics argue that it places too much emphasis on sexuality and early childhood experiences; that as a treatment it requires too much time and an impractical frequency of sessions; that it does not deal directly with the problem; that it brings to the surface more repressed material than is necessary; and that it only works for certain kinds of clients. While many of these criticisms are justified and essentially valid, psychoanalysis does, in fact, have much to offer the counselor in a variety of settings.

Variations of the basic psychoanalytic technique allow a broader application. Many of the fundamental principles of psychoanalysis can be translated into counseling applications in different settings. For instance, the resolution of unconscious resistances may be an essential part of vocational counseling when the client unknowingly works against his or her own conscious efforts to find the appropriate job, or when neurotic conflicts make the client unemployable:

> Richard has been out of work for a year. He complains to his employment counselor that there are no jobs for him—that he is "overqualified" for most of the jobs he is being sent to. The employment counselor, who has sent Richard on many leads, doesn't believe this. She thinks that it is Richard who believes he is overqualified. As they discuss it, she recognizes his sense of grandiosity, and assumes that he probably communicates this to the personnel people who have interviewed him. She explores this as a resistance, and by using psychoanalytic techniques helps him understand that it "may be necessary to take a job far below his real abilities." She goes on to join his resistance, telling him that no one understands how really qualified he is, and that he can't expect people to recognize his true abilities.

Psychoanalytic techniques have been applied in family counseling and in group counseling settings. While many contemporary family counselors reject the psychoanalytic model, they are nevertheless deeply influenced by its basic insights into family dynamics and transference. Likewise, many of group counseling and group therapy principles are derivatives of or reactions to modern or classical psychoanalytic insights.

Summary

In this chapter, we examined the basic psychodynamic approaches, including Adlerian counseling and modern psychoanalysis. We gave a brief historical background of Freudian analysis, originating with Breuer's fortuitous treatment of "Anna O." The basic concepts of psychoanalytic theory were defined: the unconscious; ego—id—superego; resistance; transference; countertransference; psychosexual stages of development, including the oral, anal, phallic, Oedipal conflict, and latency. The role of the modern analytic counselor was viewed as a maturational agent who helps the client resolve resistances to mature functioning. Five basic rules of modern psychoanalytic technique were discussed.

Chapter Aim

To outline the main humanistic approaches to counseling—including existential, client-centered, and Gestalt—indicating the similarities and the differences between them. To sketch the humanistic view of the person implicit in these approaches, and a pervasive influence in all areas of counseling.

Background

The development of humanistic counseling, the "third force," is examined as a reaction against the first two forces that made an impact in counseling and therapy: psychoanalysis and behavioral psychology. The history of existentialism, which is the philosophical precursor of humanistic psychology, is briefly outlined.

The Existential Position

The basic categories through which the existentialist views the individual and the principles through which the existential counselor tries to help the client are outlined. These principles include: "existence precedes essence"; authenticity; choice and commitment; individual freedom; phenomenological perception; and the search for meaning.

Client-Centered Counseling

The history and impact of the client-centered approach are discussed. We note how the Rogerian view of the person reflects the foundation principles of all humanistic psychology. The individual is viewed as essentially good and capable of sustaining growth, if given the right emotional climate and circumstances. Rogers argued that the counselor's attitudes, feelings, and personal qualities are more important than any specific techniques he or she uses. The counseling process is conceptualized as a series of stages, leading to self-actualization.

Gestalt Therapy and Counseling

The development of Gestalt therapy, and its tremendous popularity as a short-term approach, are evaluated. The emphasis on the individual's "wholeness" is explained in terms of the figure-ground paradigm. Some of the Gestalt techniques that facilitate "experiencing" are outlined, along with Perls's own theory of neurosis as being composed of different layers.

Evaluation and Applications   We evaluate the successes and failures of each of these approaches, especially as they are regarded in the counseling profession.

Humanistic Approaches

In this chapter, we are going to look at the major humanistic approaches, with special emphasis on client-centered counseling, existential counseling, and Gestalt therapy. We shall see that humanistic counseling does not consist of a single systematic theory or body of techniques, but rather it describes and emphasizes a set of underlying attitudes that govern all of the counselor's interactions with the client. This attitude generates, in the counseling setting, facilitative strategies. We shall begin with a general overview of humanism as the "third force" in counseling, and then proceed to consider the specific approaches in some detail.

Humanistic psychotherapy evolved, both in Europe and in the United States, as a reaction to the determinism of psychoanalysis and to the mechanism of the behavioral psychologies. Its major proponents in the United States are the late Carl Rogers, Eugene Gendlin, Rollo May, Eric Fromm, Victor Frankl, Frederick Perls, Abraham Maslow, and Gordon Allport. In Europe, existentialists such as Ludwig Binswanger and Medard Boss translated the philosophy of existentialism into a practical psychology. There are substantial differences in origin and purpose between the European existential movement and the American self-actualization psychologies; but each acknowledges the influence of the other, and they are generally compatible. As we examine the origins of humanistic counseling, we will see that so many of its fundamental concepts are reactions to the theories and practices of psychoanalysis and behavior modification therapy.

When we examine Freudianism and behaviorism, the first two major forces in psychology and counseling, we observe that both emphasize the mechanistic, cause-and-effect model of human activity, each implying in its own way that human thought and behavior are predictable consequences of identifiable training processes. May (1967*b*) offers a good humanistic critique of Freudian determinism and its inherent difficulties:

Background

The danger of the Freudian system of analysis arises when it is carried over into a deterministic interpretation of personality as a whole. The system can become simply a scheme of cause and effect: blocked instinctual urge equals repression equals psychic complex equals neurosis . . . the danger lies in the influence of Freudian theory in setting up a mechanistic, deterministic view of personality in the minds of the partially informed public. (p. 48)

Sprinthall (1971) offers a similar type of critique about behavioral counseling. "Reinforcement theory," he argues, ". . . does not hold all the answers as to how people learn. How we learn about the world around us, or how we learn about ourselves, resists singular or monolithic theories." The two major forces in counseling psychology, therefore, seem to fall prey to the same fallacy: of assuming that the individual is reducible to a series of logical, causative, deterministic propositions. The humanistic psychologists reject this *"a + b = c"* formulation, arguing that the human being is far too complex a creature to be so easily reduced to equations.

The major spokesmen for the humanistic, or third force positions are the late Carl Rogers, Abraham Maslow, and Gordon Allport. Since we will cover Rogers in depth in the following section, we will focus our discussion now on the ideas of Maslow and Allport.

Maslow begins with the assumption that psychology should start by studying the normal healthy personality rather than the pathological, unadapted personality. "If one is preoccupied with the insane, the neurotic, the psychopath, the criminal, the delinquent, the feebleminded," Maslow (1954) argues, "one's hopes for the human species become perforce more and more modest, more and more 'realistic,' more and more scaled down: one expects less and less from people. . . ." To break away from the traditional constraints of the first two forces (psychoanalysis and behavioral psychology), he abandoned in part the scientific facade of detachment and total objectivity, and used in its place a subjective, personal perspective. As Goble (1970) points out,

Maslow was convinced that we can learn a great deal more about human nature through consideration of the subjective as well as objective. . . . Maslow felt that a comprehensive theory of behavior must include the internal or intrinsic determinants of behavior as well as extrinsic or external and environmental determinants. Freud had concentrated on the first, the Behaviorists on the second. Both points of view needed to be combined. An objective study of human behavior was not enough; for complete understanding of the subjective must be considered as well. We must consider people's feelings, desires, hopes, and aspirations in order to understand behavior. (p. 184)

This attitude (and methodology), which characterizes all the attempts at formulating a humanistic psychology, becomes the basic assumption of the humanists' position. In some respects it parallels an approach that developed in Europe as the reaction to Freudianism that we now call existential psychology.

Existential psychology and existential counseling derive from the philosophy of existentialism, which was promulgated by Soren Kierkegaard, a nineteenth-century Danish theologian and philosopher. Although Kierkegaard did not call his philosophy *existentialism* (the word was applied to his work some years after his death), he laid down the basic framework upon which all later existentialist thinking was built, namely, that each person carves his or her own destiny and that one's *essence,* one's inner being, is the product of one's actions. Kierkegaard, however, shaped his philosophy in the context of theology. It was not until seventy years after his death that existentialism took hold as a distinct philosophical movement, with the publication of major works by Martin Heidegger and Jean Paul Sartre, the German and French existential leaders.

The merging of existentialism, psychotherapy, and counseling was inevitable. Throughout its history, counseling has always been deeply influenced by the social, cultural, and intellectual trends of the time. All that was required was for practitioners to translate the principles of existential philosophy to psychotherapy and counseling. The first to do so was a Swiss psychiatrist named Ludwig Binswanger.

Binswanger realized the enormous possibilities in applying existentialist principles to his psychiatric practice. He explored in his day-to-day practice how existential concepts could be used to understand and treat the client, elaborating a complex system of classifications and techniques based on explicit analyses of being.

Victor Frankl (1967), an Austrian born psychiatrist, developed *logotherapy,* a specialized form of Binswanger's existential analysis. Frankl, who was incarcerated in a German concentration camp for several years, studied the psychology of people under severe stress and hardship, concluding that many of the insights about these extreme cases could be applied to neurotic and psychotic clients he later encountered in his practice. Specifically, in addition to an analysis of being, Frankl was concerned with an analysis of meaning in the client's life. Unlike the Freudian contention of the organism's will to pleasure or the Adlerian contention of the will to power, Frankl sees the will to meaning as the underlying drive of man's authentic existence.

Rollo May, probably the most famous existentialist in the United States, may be the person most responsible for the popularity of humanistic-existential counseling today. May articulated some of the more practical applications of existential thought. In his writings, he emphasizes each person's individuality and the need for counselors to separate themselves from preconceived diagnostic categories in attempting to understand and help their clients.

The Existential Position

The convenient catch phrase that expresses the basic tenet underlying all the philosophies and theologies found under the rubric of existentialism is *existence precedes essence.* In its most simple form, this means that what a person does with his or her life—the way one lives it—determines what and who one is. We are not born to be anything in particular, argues the existentialist, but we become what we are through our actions and our commitments to those actions. We make choices between alternatives, exercising our free will and judgment, and then accept complete responsibility for the choices we have made. In this way, we govern our own lives, shape our destinies, and develop our essential nature.

Heidegger introduced the concept of *authenticity,* in which a person, seriously engaged in projects that are meaningful to his or her life, exhibits deep concern for the projects, commitment to the goals, and responsibility for the results. This notion pretty well sums up the feelings of all existentialists regarding the importance of meaningful activities in one's life. We cannot simply live our life as if it were a part in a play, prearranged and inevitable. Rather, we must actively participate in making our life something special, that which we desire. Paul Tillich, the existential theologian, calls this vigor of character "the courage to be."

Perception, to the existentialist, is studied through the discipline of *phenomenology,* the branch of existentialism concerned with perception by consciousness of phenomena in the world "out there." Edmund Husserl (1859-1938), who was Heidegger's teacher, developed the system of phenomenology. In terms of counseling, the phenomenological approach suggests a way of perceiving, of understanding the client. It is the method of existential psychotherapy, just as it is the method of existential philosophy. "The phenomenological approach," argues Arbuckle (1965), "seeks to understand the behavior of the individual *from his own point of view.* It attempts to observe people not as they seem to outsiders, but as they seem to themselves" (Combs & Snygg, 1959, p. 11). The phenomenological method helps existential counselors understand the world, and their places and their clients' places in the world.

The existential concept that influences all aspects of existential counseling is the notion of *choice and commitment,* which functions as a single action. The individual, as a free agent, is constantly choosing between possibilities of action. We alone are responsible for our choices and for the consequences of these choices. Since whatever choices we make help determine our existence, and hence *who* we are, choosing is an essential part of being. The validity of our choices is not determined by how successful the choices were in attaining the ends (as they would be in pragmatism), but in how willing the individual is to accept the consequences of the choices as one's own—as a part of oneself.

Concern about others is an important part of existentialist thought. The fact that we live with others, work with others, have feelings about others, and share our values with others does not mean that we maintain an authentic mode of existence with others. This depends more on our ability to see others as distinct entities from ourselves, our ability to meet others on their terms and yet maintain our own sense of integrity and wholeness, our desire to share with others because of the validity of their being to us. Charity is a poor substitute for communion.

The existentialist's view of the person can be summed up in five basic tenets, which underlie the philosophy:

1. Existence precedes essence: what we do determines who we are.
2. We are free to choose and are responsible for the consequences of our choices—our existence.
3. One's life is always lived with a *view-toward-death*. Our authenticity derives from our ability to be aware of this, and to courageously confront our existence.
4. Our existence is never completely separate from the existence of others and the world, and the existence of the world is never completely separate from our existence.
5. Perception is more valid when we try to understand another person from his or her subjective point of view.

The client in the humanistic-existential setting is always seen as a total person; the end product of his or her choices, not as a passive product of circumstances. The humanistic-existential counselor believes that clients are responsible for their actions, capable of changing themselves, the shapers of their destinies. Cohn (1984) points out some of the key characteristics of the existential therapy approach:

Role of the Existential Counselor

> The realization that existence is a process helps avoid the temptation to view the person as a collection of "mechanisms" that can be overhauled or dismantled when faulty. The existential approach also avoids a preoccupation with the past and the neglect of present phenomena and future possibilities. People are considered free to choose, within the limits of their present conditions, and have the responsibility for this choice. The possibility of therapeutic change is closely tied to this idea of choice. (p. 311)

The existential counselor has three basic tasks in the counseling relationship: to help clients discover valid meanings in their existence; to help them develop the freedom to govern their own destiny; and to help them deal more effectively in their encounters with others. In many ways, the function of the existential counselor is to provide the right attitude that will enable the client to accomplish these things. Dreyfus (1971) states it most explicitly:

> Existential counseling . . . is not a system of techniques but an underlying attitude toward counseling. . . . The method employed by the existentially oriented counselor is . . . concerned with the immediate, existing world of the client at the moment. He is concerned with the raw data offered by the client. Hence the approach is ahistorical in the sense that the counselor does

not attempt to actively delve into the client's past. The past is important only insofar as the client introduces it into the present. . . . The point of departure during the counseling hour is the conflict which brought the client to the counselor, not that which led up to the conflict. (p. 416)

The existential counselor can only be successful to the extent that he or she is able to understand the client in terms of the client's philosophy. In practice, this means examining many of the client's feelings as philosophical ideas. Anxiety and guilt, two of the most important concepts in treatment, are viewed phenomenologically when they appear in the counseling relationship.

Existential Techniques and Goals

Kemp (1971) points out that in existential counseling, "*technique follows understanding* . . . the existential counselor's primary goal is to understand the counselee as a person, a being, and as a being-in-the-world. This does not mean that he has low respect for technique, but rather the technique takes its legitimate place in a new perspective." (p. 18)

When techniques are employed, however, existential counselors differ markedly in the kind of techniques they use. Many of them, trained in the classical Freudian approach, rely heavily on free association and interpretation, while others, whose background is in the client-centered approach, deal more with active verbal interactions with the client. In either case, it is likely that the existential counselor, more perhaps than any other type of counselor, will rely most on whatever techniques are most compatible with his or her personality. In existential counseling, the "being" of the counselor is always a dynamic force in the counseling interaction, with the consequence that far greater emphasis is placed on the meaningfulness of the relationship than on the particular application of techniques.

It would be wrong, however, to give the impression that existentialists have some type of aversion to techniques. Frankl (1967), for example, discusses an important technique which he calls "paradoxical intention." The counselor uses paradoxical intention when he tells the client to wish for something, attempt to do something, or think intensely about something—when *the something* represents the client's worst fears. Frankl gives the example of a phobic patient who had a fear of sweating and was encouraged by the therapist to show people whom he met how much he was able to sweat. "A week later he returned to report that whenever he met anyone who triggered his anxiety, he said to himself, 'I only sweated a liter before, but now I'm going to pour out at least ten liters!' . . . After suffering from this phobia for four years, he was quickly able, after only one session, to free himself of it for good by this new procedure" (p. 146). It is not immediately clear, however, if this type of dynamic technique is a basis for Frankl's existential approach, or incidental to it.

One example of applied existential technique, more clearly related to the existential (or as the author calls it "experiential") psychology than Frankl's paradoxical intention, is Eugene Gendlin's *focusing* approach (Gendlin, 1981). This practical method derives from the accidental finding that the difference between successful and unsuccessful therapeutic outcomes is not so much a result of what the therapists do, but rather of what the successful patients do, especially in the way they focus a special kind of attention on how they feel about a specific problems within themselves. Gendlin believes that this inner activity is teachable, when by means of a number of focusing exercises, individuals are encouraged to discover and change the deepest feelings within themselves by discovering what he calls their felt sense:

> [Focusing] is a process in which you make contact with a special kind of internal bodily awareness. I call this sense of awareness a *felt sense*. A felt sense is not an emotion, and focusing is not a process in which you "face" painful emotions nor one in which you sink down into them and risk drowning. Conversely, it is not an intellectual or analytical process either. When you learn how to focus, you will discover the body finding its own way provides its own answers to many of your problems. (p. 11)

One's "felt sense" is actually discovered through awareness of one's body. By focusing on a different aspect of one's experience, an individual can learn to interpret and react to inner feelings which were previously beyond the realm of awareness and change. What happens, according to Gendlin, is that from discovering this felt sense, "new and changed feelings and aspects of experience emerge . . . and the problem changes" (Gendlin, 1982). Perhaps the most significant and innovative aspect of this technique is that it can be conducted outside the therapeutic setting—at home—by using the focusing guide written by Gendlin.

B. Helping a Felt Sense Form   It is possible for a person to focus a little between one communication and the next. Having made a point, and being understood, the person can focus before saying the next thing.

Most people don't do that. They run on from point to point, only talking.

How can you help people stop, and get the felt sense of what they have just said?

This is the second focusing movement. Finding the felt sense is like saying to oneself, "That, right there, *that's* what's confused," and *then feeling it there*.

The focuser must keep quiet, not only outwardly but also inside, so that a felt sense can form. It takes as long as a minute.

Some people talk all the time, either out loud or at themselves inside. Then nothing directly felt can form, and everything stays a painful mass of confusion and tightness.

When a felt sense forms, the focuser feels relief. It's as if all the bad feeling goes into one spot, right there, and the rest of the body feels freer.

Once a felt sense forms, people can relate to it. They can wonder what's *in* it, can feel around it and into it.

An Existential "Focusing" Exercise

By Eugene T. Gendlin. This section originally appeared in *Focusing.* New York: Bantam Books, 1981. Reprinted by permission.

When to help people let a felt sense form. When people have said all that they can say clearly, and from there on it is confusing, or a tight unresolved mess, and they don't know how to go on.

When there is a certain spot that you sense could be gone into further.

When people talk round and round a subject and never go down into their feelings of it. They may start to say things that are obviously personal and meaningful, but then go on to something else. They tell you nothing meaningful, but seem to want to. In this very common situation, you can interrupt the focuser and gently point out the way into deeper levels of feeling.

Focuser   "I've been doing nothing but taking care of Karen since she's back from the hospital. I haven't been with me at all. And when I do get time now, I just want to run out and do another chore."

Listener   "You haven't been able to be with yourself for so long, and even when you can now, you don't."

Focuser   "She needs this and she needs that and no matter what I do for her it isn't enough. All her family are like that. It makes me angry. Her father was like that, too, when he was sick which went on for years. They're always negative and grumpy and down on each other."

Listener   "It makes you angry the way she is, the way they are."

Focuser   "Yes. I'm angry. Damn right. It's a poor climate. Living in a poor climate. Always gray. Always down on something. The other day, when I. . . ."

Listener (interrupts:)   "Wait. Be a minute with your angry feeling. Just feel it for a minute. See what more is in it. Don't think anything. . . ."

The goal of existential counseling, if we may speak of a singular goal, is to help the client find and develop meanings in life. This is generally accomplished in two stages. First, the client must be shown his or her condition as *free agent*, capable of choosing both that which is right for her or him and that which is not. Some clients believe that they can only make choices that repeat the early choices that their parents taught them. After clients realize the myriad possibilities they are capable of exploring, they must begin to understand how the consequences of these different choices have profound ramifications in their existence.

The existential counselor, unlike the psychoanalytic or behavioral counselor, does not view anxiety as a dangerous or neurotic condition. Rather, anxiety is seen as a fundamental condition of existence. The job of the counselor is to help the client accept anxiety as part of his or her fundamental being. In this respect, the existential counselor is working with the client to help her or him come to grips with the crux of existence, his or her "essential self."

Client-centered therapy is America's first distinctively indigenous school of counseling. It was conceived and nurtured by the work of a single man, Carl R. Rogers, and consequently it is sometimes referred to as Rogerian counseling, or Rogerian therapy. Socially and intellectually, Rogers emerged from a background of liberal education and progressive social beliefs. Steeped in liberal Protestant theology, the progressive educational ideas of Dewey and Kilpatrick, and Franklin D. Roosevelt's new social policy, Rogers's character was not at all suited to the strict Freudian tenets to which his training in clinical psychology exposed him. Disturbed by the belief that Freudian psychotherapy did not focus on the inner world of the client, but rather placed the client in a category of preconceived diagnosis, Rogers reacted against its narrowness, injecting into his counseling practice his own liberal, humanistic values, adapted to the therapeutic milieu.

Perhaps even more powerful than the intellectual influences which were brought to bear on Rogers's thinking are the personal influences: the intrasubjective world in which he matured, the emotional context of his family setting. These kinds of personal insights are usually difficult to establish for public personalities, but psychotherapists have always been generous and relatively uninhibited in revealing their own psychological background (Freud's *Interpretation of Dreams* is rich in information about himself). Rogers was no exception, and throughout his writings we get a clear sense of the man and the myriad forces that shaped his personal growth and development. Consider this passage about his lonely and often painful youth:

> I knew my parents loved me, but it would never have occurred to me to share with them any of my personal or private thoughts or feelings because I knew these would have been judged and found wanting. . . . I could sum up these boyhood years by saying that anything I would today regard as a close and communicative interpersonal relationship with another was completely lacking during that period. My attitude toward others outside the home was characterized by the distance and the aloofness which I had taken over from my parents. I attended the same elementary school for seven years. From this point on, until I finished graduate work, I never attended any school for longer than two years, a fact which undoubtedly had its effects on me. Beginning with high school, I believe my hunger for companionship came a little more into my awareness. But any satisfaction of that hunger was blocked first by the already mentioned attitudes of my parents, and second by circumstances. (Rogers, 1973a, pp. 3–4)

We can see from this honest and sensitive portrayal how the qualities of care and love and understanding that are central to the client-centered philosophy were probably inspired, at least in part, by Rogers's emotional deprivations during his formative years. However, to fully understand the forces that combined to shape the ideas of a man as complex and compassionate as Rogers, we must take great care to balance the personal with the intellectual influences and therapeutic approaches to which he had been exposed in his training.

What contributed most powerfully to Rogers's thinking, in a negative way at least, was his dissatisfaction with the psychoanalytic approach to therapy. His early thinking, particularly, is a pronounced reaction to the Freudian position. First, Rogers (1951) objected to the use of the word *patient* because of its connotations of debility. In its place, he substituted the word *client* to convey "one who comes actively and voluntarily to gain help on a problem, but without any notion of surrendering his own responsibility for the situation" (p. 79). Next, he reacted against the directiveness of Freudian therapy. Recognizing that the initiative for change in therapy must come from the client, Rogers began to conceptualize his client-centered point of view, referring to it at the time as *nondirective* counseling. Finally, where Rogers totally parted company with the psychoanalytic approach was at the point at which he rejected the principle of the unconscious, attempting to have in its place what we now call a *phenomenological* view of the client: that is, accepting the client's feelings and world view as they are presented, rather than looking for hidden meanings underneath. This important step enabled Rogers to take a new, uncolored view of the client and, consequently, to evolve his new form of treatment.

Rogers was a prolific author, one whose basic philosophy was constantly evolved into a variety of practical applications. If there was one compelling quality of his work, it was his continual willingness to evaluate and revise his thinking. From the very beginnings at Ohio in the 1940s, Rogers was actively engaged in research to test out the hypotheses he had intuitively arrived at in his practice. Where evidence indicated that a change of position was appropriate, he never hesitated to revise his views, bringing them in accord with the evidence. His theories have also evolved from the strictly clinical to the more expansively sociocultural and educational spheres of our lives.

From his earliest works, *The Clinical Treatment of the Problem Child* (1939) and *Nondirective Counseling and Psychotherapy* (1942), through his important middle period in the 1950s and early 1960s when *Becoming a Person* and *Client-Centered Therapy* brought his cohesive viewpoint to the attention of the entire profession, Rogers consistently attempted to redefine, reevaluate, and reapply his views. During the 1950s, Rogers and his colleagues persisted in pursuing their research, attempting to isolate those factors which contributed most substantially to therapeutic efficacy. Several influential studies and position papers (Rogers & Dymond, 1954; Rogers, 1957a, 1959b, 1967) emerged from this research. Rogers then began to explore the possibilities of client-centered counseling as an approach in dealing with psychotic patients, with mixed results, which were published in 1967 under the title, *The Therapeutic Relationship and Its Impact*.

In 1964 he moved to California, where he formed the Center for Studies of the Person at La Jolla and continued his work with groups. The works he published during the late 1960s and 1970s on encounter groups and on marriage translate client-centered principles into practical, helpful concepts for living. His more recent works, *Carl Rogers on Personal Power* (1977) and *A Way of Being* (1981) have evidently kept up with the times. The former is the most expansive attempt to bring to bear on social and organizational problems the insights which have characterized Rogers's work for the past forty years. As Nash and Griffin (1977) point out. "[This work] is an impassioned reaffirmation of his person-centered philosophy set with a political context [and] also a vigorous new effort to apply the principles and procedures of humanistic psychology to administration, family counseling, intercultural groupings, education, and leadership workshops." Even more personal in tone, *A Way of Being* shows that the client-centered approach is not just a belief, but also a way of conducting one's life. Carl Rogers died in February, 1987.

While client-centered therapy seems to have lost some of its influence in recent years (to the newer therapies, such as cognitive therapy and multimodal approaches), it is still one of the most popular forms of therapy in the counseling profession and has gained wide acceptance in group work and in the schools.

The client-centered counselor perceives the individual as essentially good in nature, inherently capable of fulfilling his or her destiny and living life in a peaceful, productive, and creative way. The forces that interact to impede this type of natural growth are not intrinsic to an individual's personality; but rather they represent an amalgam of interacting social and psychological forces that militate against the realization of one's potentialities. In the Rogerian philosophy, people are seen as having the capacity to deal with their own conflicts, but are limited in doing so insofar as they lack knowledge about themselves.

Client-Centered View of the Person

Rogers developed his view of the person within the context of the counseling situation. One of Rogers's (1957*b*) clearest and most direct statements on the subject is found in his response to those writers who have discussed his "view of man":

My views of man's most basic characteristics . . . include certain observations as to what man is not, as well as some description of who he is.

I do *not* discover man to be well characterized in his basic nature by such terms as fundamentally hostile, antisocial, destructive, evil.

I do *not* discover man to be in his basic nature, completely without a nature, a *tabula rasa* on which anything may be written, nor malleable putty which can be shaped into any form.

I do *not* discover man to be an essentially perfect being, sadly warped and corrupted by society.

In my experience I have discovered man to have characteristics which seem inherent in his species, and the terms which have at different times seemed to me descriptive of these characteristics are such terms as positive, forward-moving, constructive, realistic, trustworthy. (p. 199)

We might also add that the philosophy of Rogers (1965) has an "existential flavor—man choosing himself, man the architect of himself" (p. 4). We see from these comments that Rogers's view is an integral part of his counseling ideology.

Moreover, like Dewey, by whom he was greatly influenced, Rogers looked at the person in continual interaction with the environment. The environment, argued Rogers, is not an objective reality, mutually perceived by all the people in the world, but a subjective, personal reality, dependent upon the individual's feelings, perceptions, and abilities. This reality as it is perceived, is called the "phenomenological field." As a person's experiences and feelings change, so, too, does his or her environment, which is a product of these feelings and experiences. Thus, one's interaction with the environment is based on both the individual and the perceived environment change, as they are related to each other.

The individual's sense of self emerges from this interaction with his or her phenomenological field. Rogers (1951) defined the self as "an organized, fluid but consistent conceptual pattern of perceptions of characteristics and relationships of the 'I' or 'me,' together with values attached to these concepts . . . which emerge as a result of evaluational interactions with others" (p. 498). Because the self is the center of the individual's experiences with the environment, the individual's perceptions of and interactions with the environment change as his or her sense of self changes. This constitutes the basic movement of the client-centered counseling process.

The ways in which the individual adapts to situations is always consistent with his or her self-concept. One's actions are reflections of one's perceptions. Rogers's general rule was that the experiences the individual undergoes are: (1) organized into the self-structure, (2) ignored because they are inconsistent with the sense of self, (3) perceived distortedly because they are not harmonious with self-perceptions. Consequently, the individual is said to be well adjusted when she or he is able to assimilate on a symbolic level all experiences into a consistent relationship with the concept of self. In contrast to Freud's deterministic viewpoint, Rogers saw people as creatures of expanding destinies, capable of dealing with their own problems, of constructively reorganizing their perceptions, and of learning to understand others differently.

The Client   The client is expected to learn to deal with conflicts, to order and direct the forces of his or her life, to come to grips with problems, and to "overbalance the regressive and self-destructive forces" (Rogers, 1951, p. 122) which are the source of difficulties. Most succinctly stated, the client's job is to cure himself or herself through a constructive relationship with the counselor, from whom he or she is able to gain support, encouragement, and understanding.

The premise underlying this conception is that clients, in order to grow, must exercise options for choice; they must exercise their conscious and intentional abilities to choose. As Rogers (1969) explained:

In the therapeutic relationship some of the most compelling subjective experiences are those in which the client feels within himself the power of naked choice. He is *free*—to become himself or to hide behind a facade; to move forward or to retrogress; to behave in ways which are destructive of self and others, or in ways which are enhancing; quite literally free to live or die, in both the physiological and psychological meaning of those terms. . . . We could say that in the optimum of therapy the person rightfully experiences the most complete and absolute freedom. He wills or chooses to follow the course of action which is the most economical vector in relation to all the internal and external stimuli, because it is that behavior which will be most deeply satisfying. (p. 294)

What clients are actually engaged in as they undergo counseling is a process of self-exploration, which leads to the eventual understanding of and coming to grips with one's essential freedom. The client's task within the counseling context is to explore his or her feelings and behavior, to discover, with a sense of wonder, new aspects of self, and to blend these new aspects into the image of self that holds together the range of his or her perceptions.

The client may not, however, be immediately capable of this difficult task. Because of previous experiences with a counselor or therapist, or because of erroneous preconceptions about counseling, the client may regard the counseling experience as "one where he will be labeled, looked upon as abnormal, hurt, treated with little respect [or] look upon the counselor as an extension of the authority which has referred him for help" (Rogers, 1951, p. 66). He or she may feel threatened by the counseling setting, self-conscious, ashamed. In such a case, it is the counselor's job to communicate to the client the nonjudgmental, warm, and accepting reality of the situation. This type of communication will help clients begin to help themselves.

The primary job of the client-centered counselor is to develop a facilitative relationship with the client. This is accomplished not by formal techniques and procedures, but rather by the counselor's total attitude toward the client and toward the counseling interaction.

The Client-Centered Counselor

The client-centered counselor must enter the subjective personal world of the client and experience along with him or her manifold feelings and perceptions. As Rogers described it, the counselor's task is to assume "the internal frame of reference of the client, to perceive the world as the client sees it, to perceive the client himself as he is seen by himself, to lay aside all perceptions from the external frame of reference while doing so, and to communicate something of the empathic understanding to the client" (Rogers, 1951, p. 29). By doing so, the counselor helps the client overcome his or her frightening and negative feelings about the counseling situation, engenders a feeling of trust and rapport with the client, and helps the client begin to reorganize and restructure his or her own subjective world wherever it is *incongruent* (defined as *the discrepancy between the individual's experience and his or her distorted perception of the experience*).

Rogers emphasized above all else the need for open communication, for *dialogue,* as the prerequisite for all counseling (and, for all interpersonal relationships). He called his concern with communication the "one overriding theme in my professional life. . . . From my very earliest years it has, for some reason, been a passionate concern of mine. I have been pained when I have seen others communicating past one other" (Rogers, 1974, p. 121). Rogers suggested that the counselor establishes communication not so much through what he or she does, but rather through what he or she is. It is the personal qualities of the counselor that make him effective or ineffective.

Three of the most important qualities that Rogers considered essential for the client-centered counselor are *genuineness, empathy,* and *unconditional positive regard.* This trinity of traits has become the signature of the Rogerian counselor, and the bulk of Rogers's research during the 1950s and 1960s was designed to operationally define and evaluate these conditions and to test their validity as counseling variables. The significance attached to these qualities is based on the principle that,

> constructive personality growth and change comes about only when the client perceives and experiences a certain psychological climate in the relationship. The conditions which constitute this climate do not consist of knowledge, intellectual training, orientation in some school of thought, or techniques. They are feelings or attitudes which must be experienced by the counselor and perceived by the client. (Rogers, 1962, p. 422)

Genuineness simply means that the counselor be herself or himself in the relationship, avoiding presenting a facade or acting with contrivance because she or he is the therapist. The counselor must be able to accept all of his or her own feelings, even those that may be inappropriate to the relationship. "Genuineness," Rogers (1957a) said,

> means that within the relationship he (the counselor) is freely and deeply himself, with his actual experience accurately represented by his awareness of himself. It is the opposite of presenting a facade, either knowingly or unknowingly. . . . It should be clear that this includes being himself even in ways which are not regarded as ideal for psychotherapy. His experience may be "I am afraid of this client" or "My attention is so focused on my own problems that I can scarcely listen to him." If the therapist is not denying these feelings to awareness, but is able freely to be them (as well as being his other feelings), then the condition (of genuineness) is met. (p. 97)

Empathy, a condition that has probably been investigated more thoroughly than any other, constitutes the central focus of the counselor's perception of the client. Rogers's (1962) description of empathy demonstrates its importance dramatically:

The second essential condition in the relationship . . . is that the counselor is experiencing an accurate empathic understanding of his client's private world, and is able to communicate some of the significant fragments of that understanding. To sense the client's inner world of private, personal meanings as if it were your own, but without ever losing the "as if" quality. . . . To sense his confusion or his timidity or his anger or his feeling of being treated unfairly as if it were your own . . . this is the condition I am endeavoring to describe. (p. 419)

"Over the years," Rogers (1975) pointed out in a paper reaffirming the importance of empathy ". . . the research evidence keeps piling up, and it points strongly to the conclusion that a high degree of empathy in a relationship is possibly the *most* potent and certainly one of the most potent factors in bringing about change and learning" (p. 3).

Unconditional positive regard occurs when the counselor accepts the client and all of his or her experiences, without judgment, without evaluation, and without any conditions. This has been criticized as a condition of client-centered counseling because it is nearly impossible to accept so totally another person. But as Rogers explained, this is the optimum level of acceptance to be strived for.

In short, we can say that the client-centered counselor acts as an *empathic ear and an invisible guiding hand*. Client-centered counselors, through their listening, empathize along with their clients' feelings and experiences. Their communications to the client act as a catalyst for growth and are not intended to impose changes upon the client's life. They help their clients guide themselves to better understanding by their nondirective and unobtrusive attitudes. The counselor is there, as Rogers said, primarily to motivate and support clients in their personal quests for answers to their difficulties.

Although the counselor's attitude and personality are of prime importance in client-centered counseling (and Rogers *does* deemphasize the use of psychotherapeutic stratagems) there are several *techniques* that are prominently used. Lister (1965) mentions "reflection of feeling, listening, and clarification" as the main client-centered techniques. Most important of these is *reflection,* in which the counselor reflects emotionally what the client verbalizes. While this seems simple enough, it serves two important purposes: first, it enables the client to see how another (a very important other) is perceiving what he or she is saying; second, it helps clients feel that the counselor is accepting them, with whatever they say and for whatever they are.

Rogers (1958) examined the process of counseling in terms of the stages of development by which personality change takes place. He concluded that, in successful counseling, the client moves from fixity to changeableness; from rigid structures to flow; from stasis to process. He pinpointed seven crucial stages of the change process (Rogers, 1958). At the first stage, internal communication is blocked; there is no communication of self or personal meanings, no recognition

The Stages of Counseling

of problems, no individual desire to change. At this stage, the client is closed, "and communicative relationships are construed as dangerous . . . there is no desire to change."

When the client feels himself to be fully accepted as she or he is (and for what she or he is), the second stage follows naturally. The second stage is characterized by a number of factors, both positive and negative:

> Expression begins to flow in regard to nonself topics . . . problems are perceived as external to self . . . there is no sense of personal responsibility in problems . . . feelings are described as unowned, or sometimes as past objects . . . feelings may be exhibited, but are not recognized as such or owned . . . experiencing is bound by the structure of the past . . . personal constructs are rigid, and unrecognized as being constructs, but are thought of as facts . . . differentiation of personal meanings and feelings are very limited . . . contradictions may be expressed, but with little recognition of them as contradictions. (p. 144)

The third and fourth stages involve further loosening of symbolic expressions in regard to feelings, constructs, and self. These stages constitute an important moving forward in the process. In the fifth stage, feelings are expressed freely as being in the present and are very close to being experienced:

> They "bubble up," "seep through," in spite of the fear and distrust which the client feels at experiencing them with fullness and immediacy . . . there is a beginning tendency to realize that experiencing a feeling involves a direct referent . . . there is an increasing ownership of self feelings, and a desire to be these, to be the "real me." (p. 145)

The sixth stage continues this process of growth, self-discovery and a self-acceptance, congruence, and responsibility. This is a crucial stage: the client has become very close to an organic being that is always in the process of growth; he or she is in touch with the flow of feelings; his or her construction of experiences is free flowing and repeatedly being tested against referents and evidence within and without; experience is differentiated and thus internal communication is exact.

The client often enters the seventh and last stage without need of the counselor's help. She or he is now a continually changing person, experiencing with freshness and immediacy each new situation, responding with real and accepted feelings, and showing "a growing and continuing sense of acceptant ownership of these changing feelings, a basic trust in his own process" (p. 147).

This seven-stage conceptualization represents Rogers's clearest, most explicit description of the stages of personal growth, although these stages are implicit throughout his writings.

The main goal of client-centered counseling is *congruence,* the concordance between the client's perceptions of experiences and the reality of those experiences. In one respect, congruence is the ability to accept reality. This requires a critical reorientation of the sense of self in interaction with the environment. The client must come to understand herself or himself and care about herself or himself in a different way than when counseling began.

Goals of Client-Centered Counseling

Rogers (1959a) described specifically some of the changes he expected successful counseling to produce:

The person comes to see himself differently.

He accepts himself and his feelings more fully.

He becomes more self-confident and more self-directing.

He becomes more the person he would like to be.

He becomes more flexible, less rigid, in his perceptions.

He adopts more realistic goals for himself.

He behaves in a more mature fashion.

He changes his maladjustive behaviors, even such a long established one as chronic alcoholism.

He becomes more acceptant of others.

He becomes more open to the evidence, both to what is going on outside of himself, and to what is going on inside himself.

He changes his basic personality characteristics in constructive ways. (p. 232)

We see from this description the relationship between the stages of counseling and the desired goals. Rogers's criteria for successful counseling reflected his deep concern for the self-actualization processes of the individual client, and this highlighted his general idea of what a healthy life should be like.

At the time of this interview, I had been seeing Mr. Brown on a twice a week basis (with the exception of some vacation periods) for a period of eleven months. Unlike many of the clients in this research the relationship had, almost from the first, seemed to have some meaning to him. He had grounds privileges, so he was able to come to his appointments, and he was almost always on time, and rather rarely forgot them. The relationship between us was good. I liked him and I feel sure that he liked me. Rather early in our interviews he muttered to his ward physician that he had finally found someone who understood him. He was never articulate, and the silences were often prolonged, although when he was expressing bitterness and anger he could talk a bit more freely. He had, previous to this interview, worked through a number of his problems, the most important being his facing of the fact that he was entirely rejected by his stepmother, relatives, and, worst of all, by his father. During a few interviews preceding these two he had been even more silent than usual, and I had no clue to the meaning of this silence. As will be evident from the transcript, his silences in these two

Client-Centered Counseling: A Session with Carl Rogers

Reprinted from, The Therapeutic Relationship and Its Impact, University of Wisconsin Press. Selection from: "A Silent Young Man."

interviews were monumental. I believe that a word count would show that he uttered little more than fifty words in the first of these interviews! (In the tape recording mentioned above, each of the silences has been reduced to fifteen seconds, no matter what its actual length.)

In the two interviews presented here I was endeavoring to understand all that I possibly could of his feelings. I had little hesitancy in doing a good deal of empathic guessing, for I had learned that though he might not respond in any discernible way when I was right in my inferences, he would usually let me know by a negative shake of his head if I was wrong. Mostly, however, I was simply trying to be my feelings in relationship to him, and in these particular interviews my feelings I think were largely those of interest, gentleness, compassion, desire to understand, desire to share something of myself, eagerness to stand with him in his despairing experiences.

To me any further introduction would be superfluous. I hope and believe that the interaction of the two hours speaks for itself of many convictions, operationally expressed, about psychotherapy.

The Interviews

Tuesday

Therapist   I see there are some cigarettes here in the drawer. Hm? Yeah, it is hot out.
[*Silence of 25 seconds*]

Therapist   Do you look kind of angry this morning, or is that my imagination?
[*Client shakes his head slightly.*] Not angry, huh?
[*Silence of 1 minute, 26 seconds*]

Therapist   Feel like letting me in on whatever is going on?
[*Silence of 12 minutes, 52 seconds*]

Therapist   [*softly*] I kind of feel like saying that "If it would be of any help at all I'd like to come in." On the other hand if it's something you'd rather—if you just feel more like being within yourself, feeling whatever you're feeling within yourself, why that's O.K. too—I guess another thing I'm saying, really, in saying that is, "I do care. I'm not just sitting here like a stick."
[*Silence of 1 minute, 11 seconds.*]

Therapist   And I guess your silence is saying to me that either you don't want to or can't come out right now and that's O.K. So I won't pester you but I just want you to know, I'm here.
[*Silence of 17 minutes, 41 seconds*]

Therapist   I see I'm going to have to stop in a few minutes.[1]
[*Silence of 20 seconds*]

1. Long experience had shown me that it was very difficult for Jim to leave. Hence I had gradually adopted the practice of letting him know, ten or twelve minutes before the conclusion of the hour, that "our time is nearly up." This enabled us to work through the leaving process without my feeling hurried.

Therapist   It's hard for me to know how you've been feeling, but it looks as though part of the time maybe you'd rather I didn't know how you were feeling. Anyway it looks as though part of the time it just feels very good to let down and—relax the tension. But as I say I don't really know—how you feel. It's just the way it looks to me. Have things been pretty bad lately?

[*Silence of 45 seconds*]

Therapist   Maybe this morning you just wish I'd shut up—and maybe I should, but I just keep feeling I'd like to—I don't know, be in touch with you in some way.

[*Silence of 2 minutes, 21 seconds*] [*Jim yawns.*]

Therapist   Sounds discouraged or tired.

[*Silence of 41 seconds*]

Client   No. Just lousy.

Therapist   Everything's lousy, huh? You feel lousy?

[*Silence of 39 seconds*]

Therapist   Want to come in Friday at 12 at the usual time?

Client   [*Yawns and mutters something unintelligible.*]

[*Silence of 48 seconds*]

Therapist   Just kind of feel sunk way down deep in these lousy, lousy feelings, hm?—Is that something like it?

Client   No.

Therapist   No?

[*Silence of 20 seconds*]

Client   No. I just ain't no good to nobody, never was, and never will be.

Therapist   Feeling that now, hm? That you're just no good to yourself, no good to anybody. Never will be any good to anybody. Just that you're completely worthless, huh?—Those really are lousy feelings. Just feel that you're no good at *all,* hm?

Client   Yeah. [*muttering in low, discouraged voice*] That's what this guy I went to town with just the other day told me.

Therapist   This guy that you went to town with really told you that you were no good? Is that what you're saying? Did I get that right?

Client   M-hm.

Therapist   I guess the meaning of that if I get it right is that here's somebody that—meant something to you and what does he think of you? Why, he's told you that he thinks you're no good at all. And that just really knocks the props out from under you. [*Jim weeps quietly.*] It just brings the tears.

[*Silence of 20 seconds*]

Client   [*rather defiantly*] I don't care though.

Therapist   You tell yourself you don't care at all, but somehow I guess some part of you cares because some part of you weeps over it.

[*Silence of 19 seconds*]

Therapist   I guess some part of you just feels, "Here I am hit with another blow, as if I hadn't had enough blows like this during my life when I feel that people don't like me. Here's someone I've begun to feel attached to and now *he* doesn't like me. And I'll say I don't care. I won't let it make any difference to me—but just the same the tears run down my cheeks."

Client   [*muttering*] I guess I always knew it.

Therapist   Hm?

Client   I guess I always knew it.

Therapist   If I'm getting that right, it is that what makes it hurt worst of all is that when he tells you you're no good, well shucks, that's what you've always felt about yourself. Is that—the meaning of what you're saying? [*Jim nods slightly, indicating agreement.*] M-hm. So you feel as though he's just confirming what—you've already known. He's confirming what you've already felt in some way.
[*Silence of 23 seconds*]

Therapist   So that between his saying so and your perhaps feeling it underneath, you just feel about as no good as anybody could feel.
[*Silence of 2 minutes, 1 second*]

Therapist   [*thoughtfully*] As I sort of let it soak in and try to feel what you must be feeling—it comes up sorta this way in me and I don't know—but as though here was someone you'd made a contact with, someone you'd really done things for and done things with. Somebody that had some meaning to you. Now, wow! He slaps you in the face by telling you you're just no good. And this really cuts *so* deep, you can hardly stand it.
[*Silence of 30 seconds*]

Therapist   I've got to call it quits for today, Jim.
[*Silence of 1 minute, 18 seconds*]

Therapist   It really hurts, doesn't it? [*This is in response to his quiet tears.*]
[*Silence of 26 seconds*]

Therapist   I guess if the feelings came out you'd just weep and weep and weep.
[*Silence of 1 minute, 3 seconds*]

Therapist   Help yourself to some Kleenex if you'd like—can you go now?
[*Silence of 23 seconds*]

Therapist   I guess you really hate to, but I've got to see somebody else.
[*Silence of 20 seconds*]

Therapist   It's really bad, isn't it?
[*Silence of 22 seconds*]

Therapist   Let me ask you one question and say one thing. Do you still have that piece of paper with my phone numbers on it and instructions, and so on? [*Jim nods.*] O.K. And if things get bad, so that you feel real down, you have them call me. 'Cause that's what I'm here for, to try to be of some help when you need it. If you need it, you have them call me.[2]

Client   I think I'm beyond help.

Therapist   Huh? Feel as though you're beyond help. I know. You feel just completely hopeless about yourself. I can understand that. I don't feel hopeless, but I can realize that you do.[3] Just feel as though nobody can help *you* and you're really beyond help.
[*Silence of 2 minutes, 1 second*]

Therapist   I guess you just feel so, so down that—it's awful.
[*Silence of 2 minutes*]

Therapist   I guess there's one other thing too. I, I'm going to be busy here this afternoon 'til four o'clock and maybe a little after. But if you should want to see me again this afternoon, you can drop around about four o'clock. O.K.?—otherwise, I'll see you Friday noon. Unless I get a call from you. If you—if you're kind of concerned for fear anybody would see that you've been weeping a little, you can go out and sit for a while where you waited for me. Do just as you wish on that. Or go down and sit in the waiting room there and read magazines—I guess you'll really have to go.

Client   Don't want to go back to work.

Therapist   You don't want to go back to work, hm?

This is the end of the interview. Later in the day the therapist saw Mr. Brown on the hospital grounds. He seemed much more cheerful and said that he thought he could get a ride into town that afternoon.

The next time the therapist saw Mr. Brown was three days later, on Friday.

No concept of helping has received a more rapid popularity in a short period of time, both in the press and in the profession, than did Gestalt therapy during the 1960s and 1970s. Dynamic, dramatic, intensive, and absorbing, the Gestalt therapy movement has already exerted a powerful influence upon therapeutic counseling, encounter group therapy, marathon groups, family counseling, school counseling, counseling of delinquents and prisoners, and drug counseling. Institutes, such as Esalen at Big Sur, California, that emphasize the Gestalt approach have received national attention and have attracted as workshop leaders such diverse and impressive figures as Abraham Maslow, Buckminster Fuller, and B.F.

Gestalt Counseling

2. Two words of explanation are needed here. He seemed so depressed that I was concerned that he might be feeling suicidal. I wanted to be available to him if he felt desperate. Since no patient was allowed to phone without permission, I had given him a note that would permit a staff member or Jim himself to phone me at any time he wished to contact me, and with both my office and home phone numbers.

3. This is an example of the greater willingness I have developed to express my own feelings of the moment, at the same time accepting the client's rights to possess *his* feelings, no matter how different from mine.

Skinner (Murphy, 1967). Unfortunately, the Gestalt approach seems to have inspired a glittery show business atmosphere at times, although this is certainly more a reflection of unscrupulous promoters and exploiters than of the therapy and its serious, ethical practitioners. An advertisement in a New York weekly recently advertised a "weekend of skiing and Gestalt therapy" at a mountain resort hotel!? Another newspaper ad promoted a "singles Gestalt encounter" as an ideal opportunity to meet one's future mate. Such blatant exploitation is the inevitable liability of an approach that achieves so much popularity in so short a period of time.

Here we shall examine some of the premises and applications of the legitimate Gestalt approach. The emphasis will be on the serious, counseling-oriented applications of Gestalt therapy, rather than on the social and entertainment uses mentioned above. At the conclusion of the chapter, we shall evaluate the relevance and utility of Gestalt counseling in a variety of settings.

Background

Gestalt counseling derives from the school of the same name in the psychology of perception that originated in Europe in the years prior to World War I. The Gestalt movement in psychology instituted a new kind of examination; one that began with the view of the perceptual field as a whole, differentiating it into figure and background, and then examining the relative properties of each of these and their interrelationship with each other. The German word *gestalt,* which is roughly equivalent to the English word *pattern,* expresses the basic meaning of the movement; namely, that all perceptions are dependent upon a number of distinct stimuli that are organized by consciousness into a perceptual whole, a total pattern.

Unfortunately, Gestalt psychology remained essentially an academic theory of perception, limited in its ability to account for the activity of the human organism *as a whole.* "The academic Gestalt psychologist," Wallen (1970) points out, "never attempted to employ the various principles of Gestalt formation . . . to organic perceptions, to the perceptions of one's own feelings, emotions, and bodily sensations" (p. 8). It is in this area that Frederick (Fritz) Perls made his contributions that subsequently blossomed into the birth of Gestalt therapy and Gestalt counseling.

Perls received his medical degree from Friedrich Wilhelm University in Berlin in 1921 and continued his training in psychoanalysis at the Psychoanalytic Institute of Berlin, Frankfort, and Vienna. Forced to flee Germany in 1933, he settled in Amsterdam where he worked in private practice until the specter of Nazism drove him to South Africa in 1935. In 1947, he published *Ego, Hunger, and Aggression,* the first statement of the principles of Gestalt psychology applied to personality development. In 1946, he moved to the United States and set up a private practice. Between 1964 and 1969, he conducted training workshops in Gestalt therapy in the Esalen Institute in California. His publications include *Gestalt Therapy: Excitement and Growth in the Human Personality* (1969, with Ralph Hefferline and Paul Goodman) and *Gestalt Therapy Verbatim* (1969).

Perls developed a systematic therapeutic approach, utilizing the large body of literature in Gestalt psychology, which could be used in psychoanalysis, in experimental psychology, and in the practical insights and experiences of a working therapist (Knapp, 1986).

The Gestalt counselor considers the individual's perceptions (and this means perceptions of oneself, one's feelings, one's relationships, etc.) in terms of the *figure-ground* dichotomy. Gestalt counselors believe that a healthy personality exists when a person's experiences form a meaningful whole, when there is a smooth transition between those sets of experiences that are immediately in the focus of awareness (what they call the *figure*) and those that are in the background (which they call the *ground*). "The basic premise of Gestalt psychology," Perls (1973) writes, "is that human nature is organized into patterns or wholes, that it is experienced by the individual in these terms, and that it can only be understood as a function of the patterns of wholes of which it is made." Proper functioning is dependent upon one's abilities to continually shift the figure-ground relationship.

The key word in understanding the Gestalt conception of psychological health and proper functioning is *growth*. Harman (1975) points out that "from the Gestalt therapy point of view, growth occurs when a person is willing to make contact with people, objects, and situations in the environment" (p. 363). Supporting this position, Carmer and Rouzer (1974) suggest that the "Gestalt conception of healthy functioning is derived from certain premises about the nature of living organisms and their relationship to the surrounding environment" (p. 20). These premises are that the individual must be able to differentiate between the more prominent and less prominent stimuli in the environment at any given time, and be flexible in his or her interaction with the environment. "The organism/environment interaction," Carmer and Rouzer continue, "is regulated according to the principle of homeostasis. From a relative stage of equilibrium, needs arise which must be met to restore the balance" (p. 21). The healthy individual is able to meet these needs by accommodating his or her perceptions accordingly.

The Gestalt theory of psychopathology, as expounded by Perls (1966), is a far cry from the Freudian or existential theories. In language and content, Perls offers a dramatic, metaphorical description of neurosis as consisting of five layers. He writes, for example, that,

> The first layer we encounter is what I call the Eric Berne layer, or the Sigmund Freud layer, or the phony layer, where we play games, play roles. It is identical with Helene Deutsch's description of the "as if" person. We behave *as if* we were big shots, *as if* we are nincompoops, *as if* we are pupils. . . . It is always the "as if" attitudes that require that we live up to a fantasy that we or others have created, whether it comes out as a course or as an ideal. . . . It's an attempt to get away from oneself. The result is that

the neurotic person has given up living for his self in a way that would actualize himself. He wants to live instead for a concept. . . . We don't want to be ourselves; we don't want to be what we are. We want to be something else, and the existential basis of this being something else is the experience of dissatisfaction. (p. 20)

Perls (1966) calls this the *implosive layer* of the neurosis. It is the task of therapy to help the patient pass through this layer to the explosion, in which the neurotic energy is released.

Although the Gestalt view of the person tends to be humanistic, there are a number of explicit values underlying the philosophy. Naranjo (1970) has listed nine important "moral injunctions" implicit in Gestalt therapy. They are:

1. Live now. Be concerned with the present rather than with the past or future.
2. Live here. Deal with what is present rather than with what is absent.
3. Stop imagining. Experience the real.
4. Stop unnecessary thinking. Rather, taste and see.
5. Express rather than manipulate, explain, justify, or judge.
6. Give in to unpleasantness and pain just as to pleasure. Do not restrict your awareness.
7. Accept no *should* or *ought* other than your own. Adore no graven image.
8. Take full responsibility for your actions, feelings, and thoughts.
9. Surrender to being as you are. (pp. 49–50)

In many ways, these nine principles are existential, and it would be difficult to distinguish them from the basic tenets of existentialism, even though the language in which they are expressed may at points differ. The Gestalt view of the person, like the existential position, looks at the individual in continuous interaction with others and with his or her environment, striving for authentic engagements and commitments, actualizing as he or she lives life meaningfully, fulfilling his or her potential.

Role of the Gestalt Counselor

The Gestalt counselor believes that the client ultimately changes through his or her own activities. "The task of the counselor," Ponzo (1976) suggests, "is to operate in a way that increases both the client's and counselor's awareness of the situation and communicates a caring, honest, and competent atmosphere" (p. 415). The counselor, in this respect, serves as a "catalyst" or "helper" (Raming & Frey, 1974).

The Gestalt client is asked to *experience* rather than simply to intellectualize. Whereas in some forms of counseling it is sufficient for clients to verbalize their feelings, in the Gestalt approach it is imperative that clients be willing to expose themselves to a direct experiential reliving of their feelings. This is true in the Gestalt method of interpreting dreams, in confronting resistances, in coming to grips with the repressed past. Rosen (1972) cites an example of how this approach works:

> As an example of direct experiencing, not talking about, a patient who says that he has trouble expressing his hostility may be asked to say something hostile to each member in a group, or to the therapist in an individual session. He and the therapist and others, if present, can directly experience his difficulty in doing this, and can also experience with appropriate focusing on patient's voice, posture, response of others, etc. what are the factors involved in this difficulty. Finally, he may be urged to try again using his newly gained awareness. He may observe, when asked "What are your hands saying when they clasp one another?" that they are holding one another for reassurance. When asked to say what he feels when he holds them apart he may experience his fear more intensely. He may be directed to try saying to someone "I'm afraid and also furious at you for. . . ." If the timing is good and he feels safe he may then have a different experience in expressing his anger, perhaps more clearly and forcefully than ever before in his life. (p. 96)

We see from this example how the client who comes for Gestalt counseling must be willing to experience heightened and difficult moments directly. There is no beating around the bush in Gestalt counseling, no sugarcoating with words and euphemisms the true depths of one's feelings, no manipulating or "fooling" the counselor.

The Gestalt counselor's real job is restoring a personality to its *gestalt,* its organized whole. One method of doing this is to help the client better understand the relationship between himself or herself and his or her environment. The Gestalt counselor may use several types of exercises, also called "experiments," "games," and "gimmicks," to help the client redefine and integrate himself or herself within the environment. The Gestalt counselor may also use principles from the Gestalt psychology of perception insofar as he or she helps the patient understand the *patterns* of his or her life. Within the framework of Gestalt therapy, studying one's own patterns of behavior and perception allow the client to reevaluate and change maladaptive behaviors (Tyson & Range, 1987).

The Gestalt counselor avoids as much as possible intervening directly in expressions of the client's will. But by his or her gentle guidance and dynamic influence, the Gestalt counselor assists the client in making appropriate and well-thought-out choices. He or she is an active presence in the interpersonal encounter. Levin and Shepherd (1974) point out that "an alive, active, exciting, creative therapist . . . views the present . . . interaction as the basis for change and experience. The therapist is his [the client's] companion and guide, in part his safety valve and contact with reality" (p. 29). This dynamic interpretation of the client's perceptions of and relationship with the counselor clearly differentiates the Gestalt approach from other humanistic approaches, which are similar on other levels.

The Gestalt counselor is interested in finding out as much as possible about the client's life. While the client may remain unaware of the underlying and embedded conflicts that are the source of his or her problem,

> some dissociation or other is bound to become manifest in the first interview. Some anxiety, some talking around the subject will provide the opportunity to show him (the client) the existence of unrealized conflicts. (Perls, 1948, p. 564)

As the counselor discovers these conflicts, he or she attempts to help the client resolve them by enabling her or him to identify with all vital functions—to accept herself or himself as a total, functioning organism, a whole entity. The counselor does this by emphasizing (and at times insisting on) the "here and now"—the immediacy of the counseling situation.

One method of accomplishing this is to "provoke" the client into coming to grips with his or her feelings. Provocation, therefore, is a legitimate, integral part of the Gestalt repertoire of techniques. The Gestalt counselor plays provocative games with the client; games that are intended to force the client to confront and acknowledge the feelings that he or she has been so arduously trying to avoid. One of the main purposes of the Gestalt games is to help the client become more aware. "Awareness," Harman (1974) points out, "means being in touch with, being aware of, what one is doing, planning and feeling" (p. 259).

Mintz (1971) offers a veritable catalog of interesting Gestalt games that she uses in her marathon groups. In one of the games, "Feedback," each group member selects three people whom he or she likes and three about whom she or he feels critical. These feelings are relayed to the group members, and feedback then ensues. In another game, "Hand Dialogue," two group members, acting as partners, improvise dances with their hands. This game is designed to lessen the rigidity between them. In "Name Game," two interlocutors carry on a conversation using only their two names and no other words. In the "Yes-No Game," they do likewise, using only the words *yes* and *no*. As we can see from these examples, some of the Gestalt games are rather unconventional and quite dramatic. But as Perls explained earlier, it is the counselor's job to help the client mobilize his or her resources, and this at times may require that the client experience unpleasurable feelings of absurdity and unrelatedness.

The goal of Gestalt counseling, like the goal of psychodynamic counseling, is the integration of the personality.

> The treatment is finished when the patient has achieved the basic requirements: to change in outlook, a technique of adequate self-expression and assimilation, and the ability to extend awareness to the verbal level. He has then reached that state of integration which facilitates its own development, and he can now be safely left to himself. (Perls, 1948, p. 585)

This is all to be accomplished, however, without the need for intensive probing into the psychological past of the client.

Theories of Counseling

Beverly I guess I'm supposed to say something. I don't have any interesting dreams. Mine are sort of patent.

Fritz Are you aware that you're defensive? . . . I didn't ask you in only to bring dreams.

B You asked for them last night and I was afraid that would disqualify me. If I could manufacture a few. . . .

F Now you have a very interesting posture. The left leg supports the right leg, the right leg supports the right hand, the right hand supports the left hand.

B Yeah. It gives me something to hang onto. And with a lot of people out there you kind of get some stage fright. There are so many of them.

F You have stage fright and there are people outside. In other words you're on stage.

B Yeah, I suppose I feel that way.

F Well, what about getting in touch with your audience. . . .

B Well they look very good. They have wonderful faces.

F Tell this to them.

B You have very warm faces, very interested, very interest*ing*. . . with— with a lot of warmth.

F So then shuttle back to your stage fright. What do you experience now?

B I don't have any more stage fright. But my husband doesn't look at me.

F So go back to your husband.

B You're the only one that looks self-conscious. Nobody else looks self-conscious at me. (laughter) You sort of feel like you're up here, don't you? Or sort of like your youngster's up here? . . . No?

X (from audience, yells) Answer!

Husband She's the one who's up there and she's trying to place me up there.

F (to husband) Yah. You've got to answer. (to Beverly) You have to know what I feel.

B Well he doesn't usually answer. Did you want him out of character? (much laughter)

F So, you are a clobberer.

B You need an ashtray.

F "I need an ashtray." (Fritz holds up his ashtray) She knows what *I* need. (laughter)

B Oh, no—you have one. (laughter)

F Now I get stage fright. (laughter) I always have difficulties in dealing with "Jewish mothers." (laughter)

B Don't you like "Jewish mothers"?

F Oh, I love them. Especially their matzo-ball soup. (laughter)

B I'm not a gastronomical Jewish mother, just a Jewish mother. (chuckles) I don't like gefilte fish either. I guess I'm a pretty obvious Jewish mother. Well that's not bad to be. That's all right. Matter of fact, that's good to be.

F What are your hands doing?

B Well, my thumbnails are pulling at each other.

F What are they doing to each other?

B Just playing. I do this often. See, I don't smoke, so what else are you gonna do with your hands? It doesn't look good to suck your thumbs.

F That's also the Jewish mother. She has reasons for everything. (laughter)

B (jokingly) And if I don't have one I'll make one up. (chuckles) The ordered universe. What's wrong with being a Jewish mother?

F Did I say there's something wrong with a Jewish mother? I only say *I* have difficulties in dealing with them.

There is a famous story of a man who was such an excellent swordsman that he could hit even a raindrop, and when it was raining he used his sword instead of an umbrella. (laughter) Now there are also intellectual and behavioristic swordsmen, who in answer to every question, statement, or whatever, hit it back. So whatever you do, immediately you are castrated or knocked out with some kind of reply—playing stupid or poor-me or whatever the games are. She's perfect.

B I never realized that.

F You see? Again the sword. Playing stupid. I want once more to restate what I said earlier. Maturation is the transcendence from environmental support to self-support. The neurotic, instead of mobilizing his own resources, puts all his energy into manipulating the environment for support. And what you do is again and again manipulate me, you manipulate your husband, you manipulate everybody to come to the rescue of the "damsel in distress."

B How did I manipulate you?

F You see, again. This question, for instance. This is very important for maturation—change your questions to statements. Every question is a hook, and I would say that the majority of your questions are inventions to torture yourself and torture others. But if you change the question to a statement, you open up a lot of your background. This is one of the best means to develop a good intelligence. So change your question to a statement.

B Well, th—that implies that, ah, there's a fault to me. Didn't you intend it so? . . .

F Put Fritz in that chair and ask him that question.

B Don't you like Jewish mothers? Did you have one that you didn't like?

Well, I like them. They're just a very difficult lot to deal with.

Well, what makes them so difficult?

Well, they're very dogmatic and very opinionated and inflexible and the box that they construct for themselves to grow in is a little narrower than many. They're less easy to therapize.

Does everybody have to be subject to your therapy?

No. (laughter)

(to Fritz) Did you ever switch chairs like this with yourself?

F (laughing) Oh yes—*Oh!* Even *I* get sucked in! (laughter)

B You said you had problems with Jewish mothers. (laughter)

Husband Do you understand now why I didn't answer? (laughter and applause)

F That's right, because you see how a Jewish mother doesn't say "You shouldn't smoke so much." She says, "You need an ashtray. (laughter) Okeh. Thank you.

Evaluation of Humanistic Approaches

The Client-Centered Approach

Despite the popularity of client-centered counseling, and despite the large number of studies which have demonstrated its efficacy, there are certain limitations and criticisms which should be addressed. In part, the popularity of this approach may be attributed to the optimistic attitude of the underlying philosophy, to the simplicity of its techniques, and to a number of other factors. In any case, it is quite clear that at the present time and probably for some time to come, many counselors will be using the client-centered approach in their practices.

There are some inherent difficulties in the client-centered approach. Most notably, it requires an attitude by the counselor which many counselors are unable to maintain, although there is persuasive evidence that Rogerian skills can be learned in classroom training and that they can increase one's potential for effective counseling (Goddard, 1980). Still, while it is theoretically desirable to speak of unconditional positive regard, total acceptance, warmth, and empathy, in the real world of counseling these fine feelings are sometimes farthest from the counselor's mind.

On the other hand, client-centered counseling can be practiced successfully with a minimum of academic training. Because it relies more on the feelings and personality of the counselor than on his technical know-how, it offers many possibilities to the counselor who has not had an opportunity to study intensively the more directive and technique-oriented therapeutic approaches (Kohler, 1981). Confronted by the complex and sometimes overwhelming forces that disrupt many clients' lives, it is sometimes more expedient as well as more facilitative to offer the client appropriate feelings and genuine concern rather than to attempt to treat the unconscious, repressed factors underlying his problem.

Speaking of Rogers's total contribution, which is reflected throughout his writings, Farson (1974) points out what was probably his greatest accomplishment.

> In effect he managed to *demystify* the practice of therapy. He showed how it really works, and he did this so convincingly and helpfully that thousands were encouraged to try to develop such relationships with their own clients, patients, students, employees, customers, or inmates. His demystification of therapy not only made extensions into other fields possible, but it encouraged many other workers to further uncover the mystifying practices of psychotherapists. (p. 198)

Such a statement eloquently reflects Rogers's contribution not only to counseling and psychotherapy, but to the quality of life in general.

In recent years, the client-centered approach has found its way into a large number of settings, often combined with other techniques to offer an eclectic multimodal approach to treating individual problems and interpersonal conflicts. Client-centered counseling has been combined with behavior modification in parent training groups (Bondroff, 1981), used widely in schools (Rogers, 1981) and in rehabilitation settings with many positive results (Kohler, 1981).

Evaluation of Existential Counseling

Existentialism, although not a widely practiced treatment approach, has grown over the years. A number of attempts have been made to integrate many of the concepts of the earlier existentialism with other, more contemporary approaches. Butcher (1984), for example, has shown that many of the key issues of existentialism—death, freedom, isolation, and meaninglessness—can be viewed as cognitive variables. This suggests the possibility that cognitive approaches can be combined with existential insights to facilitate client growth.

The humanistic existential therapies have proven valuable in many clinical settings. Many practitioners have combined aspects of existentialism with other clinical approaches in order to harvest the philosophy in a practical way. Haldane and McClusky (1982), among others, have applied existentialism to family therapy. They show its value in understanding family dysfunction and conflict among family members from a new perspective, which focuses on alienation and meaninglessness, as well as on the overt symptoms and behavioral distortions.

Dienelt (1984) sees in existential counseling a tremendous potential in working with youth, who are often suffering crises that are clearly existential in nature. A "spiritual distress" experienced by many young people, he suggests, can be ameliorated (or at least clarified) through existential understandings and appropriate interventions. Schmolling (1984) attempted to use existential therapy to treat a schizophrenic patient who had been hospitalized for twenty years. Although no treatment success can be claimed, he points out how many of the thinking processes of the schizophrenic can be understood through existential concepts. In short, existentialism's greatest value has been through its broadening of other therapeutic approaches.

Gestalt therapy offers counselors a number of ideas and techniques which may prove applicable to their work in a variety of settings, from the school to the clinic to the community mental health organization (Buchan & Hale, 1981). The emphasis on the "here and now" is especially attractive to the counselor whose limitations of time may demand direct intervention into the immediacy of the client's situation. The Gestalt therapist's concern with the *wholeness* of his client expresses an intuitive belief which is already held by many counselors on a personal level. Furthermore, the Gestalt emphasis on body language proves a fruitful resource to the counselor, who has a rich opportunity to study the body language of clients even during a short period of time.

During the past ten years over a thousand professional papers have been published, suggesting uses for the Gestalt approach, evaluating clinical, school, or organizational applications, or considering its theoretical validity. For example, Hatcher and Himmelstein have edited a comprehensive handbook outlining scores of Gestalt treatment programs that have worked successfully in these different settings. Tyson and Range (1987), in a valuable contribution to the field, point out that Gestalt self-dialogues can be used to treat mild depression in a relatively short time, apparently with long lasting results. In an innovative experiment, Kastner and Neumann (1986) have combined Gestalt approaches with traditional psychoanalytic approaches in the group setting, finding the combination more effective than either used singly. Lawe and Smith (1986) have cited success using Gestalt counseling with family problems.

Many clinical and experimental studies support the value of Gestalt counseling in treating marital, family, sexual, and gender-role disturbances and conflicts. Jessee and Guerney (1981) found, for example, that Gestalt techniques were helpful in relationship enhancement treatments with married couples. Couples exposed to Gestalt counseling were better able to learn how to handle their problems and communicate with each other, exhibiting a sense of trust and a willingness to change. Gestalt approaches have also been used to treat marital sexual problems, particularly orgasmic difficulties. In one interesting twist, Beane (1981) used Gestalt techniques in working with gay men who were "coming out," and were experiencing consequential conflicts about their gender-identity. The Gestalt approach, according to the author, helped the clients to attain a "positive gay identity," to find resources and support which would help them through their difficult times.

All in all then, by the 1980s, Gestalt techniques have been widely adopted and applied in all areas of clinical counseling, in elementary, high school and college counseling, in industrial and career-decision counseling, in all types of groups, in the ministry, and in many other settings.

Summary

In this chapter we examined some of the chief features of the humanistic counseling approaches, including existential, client-centered, and Gestalt, indicating the similarities and differences between them. The development of humanistic counseling, the "third force," was examined as a reaction against the first two forces which made an impact on counseling: psychoanalysis and behavioral psychology. Each humanistic approach was then discussed individually.

The basic categories through which the existentialist views the individual and the principles through which the existential counselor tries to help the client were outlined. These include "existence precedes essence"; authenticity; choice and commitment; individual freedom; phenomenological perception; and the search for meaning.

The history and impact of the client-centered approach was then discussed. We noted how the Rogerian view suggests that the individual is essentially good and capable of sustaining growth, if given the right emotional climate and circumstances. Rogers argued that the counselor's attitudes, feelings, and personal qualities are more important than any specific techniques he or she uses.

The Gestalt approach emphasizes the individual's "wholeness" in terms of the figure-ground paradigm. Some of the Gestalt techniques that facilitate experiencing were outlined, along with Perls's own theory of neurosis as comprising different layers.

Chapter Aim

To outline the theory and techniques of rational-emotive counseling, reality counseling, and transactional analysis, indicating the similarities and the differences among them. To show how the "rational" view of the person implies that therapeutic change takes place when the client can think through his or her problems in terms of the concepts (e.g., "illogical thoughts," "reality," or "ego states") offered by the particular approach.

Developed by Albert Ellis, the rational-emotive therapy approach emphasizes that emotion and reason are entwined in the human psyche. In the process of growing up, we learn from our parents and others to think certain things about the feelings that we have. When our thinking is illogical it can lead to nonfacilitative behavior and psychological problems. The rational-emotive therapist or counselor is directive, and uses authoritarian, and sometimes provocative, techniques to help the client see the irrationality of his or her thoughts.

Rational-Emotive Therapy

Cognitive therapy, one of the most dominant counseling approaches of the 1980s, has proven tremendously successful for treating a wide range of problems, from phobias to learning disabilities. Largely American in origin, pragmatic in scope, and short-term in treatment expectation, it has offered to the counseling public a therapeutic remedy that is acceptable and appropriate for a wide variety of settings and practitioners. We will look at some of the specific techniques used by the cognitive counselor to change clients' thinking processes which, in turn, help them change their behaviors.

Cognitive Therapy

Reality therapy, developed by William Glasser, emphasizes the development of individual responsibility and personal moral values, as the individual goes through life trying to satisfy two basic needs: the need to love and be loved, and the need to feel worthwhile. The reality therapist or counselor uses didactic as well as dynamic techniques to help the client learn values and responsibility. This approach is highly directive, but it also recognizes the important dynamic components of the relationship.

Reality Therapy

Transactional Analysis   Although it has its root in psychodynamic therapy, transactional analysis, as developed by Eric Berne, stresses the person's ability to rationally recognize underlying components of his or her interactions and to make emotional and behavioral changes based on this recognition. Using the concepts of "ego states" and "life script," the transactional analyst helps the client directively by analyzing interactions with others as these interactions recapitulate past experiences.

Cognitive Approaches

Four indigenous American schools of treatment that together have made a powerful impact on the counseling profession are (1) reality therapy, (2) cognitive therapy, (3) transactional analysis (TA), and (4) rational-emotive therapy (RET). Although there are substantial differences among these four approaches, they all rely on the individual's mobilization of logical faculties to overcome his or her emotional difficulties. Moreover, all of them, with their emphasis on the cognitive dimensions of emotional conflicts, integrate a variety of dynamic and behavioral constructs into counseling practice by helping the client rethink assumptions and restructure cognitions. Thus we call them "cognitive" approaches.

This synthesis of techniques has allowed partisans of both the psychodynamic and behavioral poles to find practical ways of integrating some seemingly contradictory (or at least, exclusionary) constructs in the counseling setting. A number of practitioners call themselves "cognitive" counselors, using that rubric to include TA, reality therapy, cognitive (behavior) therapy, or RET. In this chapter we shall examine the basic positions of each.

The person most often associated with rational-emotive therapy is Dr. Albert Ellis, its founder and leading exponent. Ellis was originally trained in the traditional classic psychoanalytic method, which he practiced during the late 1940s and early 1950s. Like Carl Rogers, Ellis (1973b) became disillusioned with the confines of the psychoanalytic approach when he realized that "no matter how much insight client[s] gained, nor how well they seemed to understand the events of their early childhood and to be able to connect them with their present emotional disturbances, they rarely lost their presenting symptoms . . . and when they did, they still retained tendencies to create new troubling symptoms" (p. 168). Exploring this problem, he discovered that the sources of his clients' emotional difficulties and psychological misperceptions were not simply a result of what had happened in the past but were also a reflection of an active, ongoing process in their lives.

Rational-Emotive Therapy

In working out his theoretical position, Ellis undertook a number of experimental strategies with his clients. He discovered, in his own words,

> that people are not exclusively the products of social learning (as the theories of the psychoanalysts and the behavior psychologist emphasize) but that their so-called pathological symptoms are the result of *bio*social learning. That is to say, *because they are human* . . . they tend to have several strong, irrational, empirically unvalidatible ideas; and as long as they hold on to these ideas . . . they will tend to be what we commonly call "neurotic," "disturbed," or "mentally ill." (Ellis, 1973*b*, p. 169)

During the middle 1950s, Ellis began to abandon the psychoanalytic approach and concentrate his enormous energies on his newly discovered rational-emotive psychotherapy. In 1959, he organized the Institute for Rational Living, a non-profit scientific and educational organization in New York City. Nine years later a state-chartered training institute, The Institute for Advanced Study in Rational Psychotherapy, was founded to train rational-emotive therapists. During the decade that followed, thousands of RET therapists were trained for work in the clinical, agency, and school settings.

Ellis has always been a prolific writer, and has written many valuable books and articles outlining or defending his position. His seminal works in which his principal ideas are outlined include: *Reason and Emotion in Psychotherapy* (1962), *The Art and Science of Love* (1969*a*), *Growth Through Reason* (1971), *A Guide to Rational Living*, coauthored with Robert A. Harper (1961), and *Rational-Emotive Therapy: A Handbook of Theory and Practice* (with R. Grieger, 1977). In the past decade, he has applied his store of rich clinical observations to a host of practical problems in such books as *How to Master Your Fear of Flying* (1972), *Sex and the Liberated Man* (1976), *Overcoming Procrastination* (1977), and *The Intelligent Woman's Guide to Dating and Mating* (1980).

Ellis sums up his present philosophy toward life and toward others this way (Ellis, 1982):

> I now see that I have given up any addiction to MUSTurbation many years ago—to thinking that I must do well; that others must treat me considerately or fairly; and that the world must provide me with the things I want easily and quickly. I now almost always think that it would be better or nicer if I did well, others treated me fairly, or the world proved easy and pleasant. But it doesn't have to turn out those ways—and that makes quite a difference!

View of the Person

The rational-emotive view of personality is dominated by the principle that emotion and reason—thinking and feeling—are intricately and inextricably entwined in the psyche. "A human is primarily a responding or creative individual," Ellis (1973*b*) points out. "He not only perceives external and internal stimuli but he concomitantly thinks or conceptualizes about them" (p. 32). Ellis goes on to suggest that as the person thinks about things, he or she distorts and generalizes according to preconceptions and misguided ideas: "Humans, in other words, are *highly suggestible, impressionable, vulnerable, and gullible*" (p. 34, italics added). This strong statement becomes, in effect, the RET theoretical basis for the connection between the individual's feelings and ideas. More explicitly, Ellis (1958) explains the relationship between the cognitive and affective domains this way:

> Thinking and emoting are closely interrelated and at times differ mainly in that thinking is more tranquil, less somatically involved . . . and a less activity-directed mode of discrimination than is emotion . . . among adult humans raised in a social culture, thinking and emoting are so closely inter-related that they usually accompany each other, act in a circular cause-and-effect relationship, and in certain . . . respects are essentially the *same thing*, so that one's thinking *becomes* One's thought . . . since man is a uniquely sign-, symbol-, and language-creating animal, both thinking and emoting tend to take the form of self-talk or internalized sentences; and that for all practical purposes, the sentences that human beings keep telling themselves *are* or *become* their thoughts and emotions. (p. 36)

In the process of growing up, he suggests, the child is taught to think and feel certain things about himself and others. Those things that are associated with the idea of, This is good! argues Ellis (1958), become positive human emotions, such as love or joy, while those associated with the idea, This is bad! become negative emotion, with painful, angry or depressive feelings. Psycho-pathological behavior, he goes on to point out, is illogical and irrational, associating, This is bad! with things which really are not. He offers, as an example, the etiology of a phobia in which an individual experiences an early life disturbance upon discovering that he has strong death wishes against his father. Because he thinks such wishes are bad, he feels that he should be blamed and punished for having these feelings. As a result of this incongruity, he develops a neurotic phobia against dogs (because dogs remind him unconsciously of his father, who loves to hunt). "Later on," Ellis (1958) continues,

> this individual may grow to love or be indifferent to his father, or his father may die and be no more of a problem to him. His fear of dogs, however, may remain: not because, as some theorists would insist, they still remind him of his old death wishes against his father, but because now he hates himself so violently for *having* the original neurotic symptom—for behaving, in his mind, so stupidly and illogically in relation to dogs—that every time he thinks of dogs his self-hatred and fear of failure so severely upset him that he cannot reason clearly and cannot combat his illogical fear. (p. 39)

The rational-emotive view of the person emphasizes that we are born with the potential to be rational and logical but become illogical and influenced inordinately by "crooked thinking" because of distortions during childhood and the contemporary repetitions of these distortions. "The central theme of RET," Ellis (1962) explains, "is that man is a uniquely rational as well as uniquely irrational animal; that his emotional or psychological disturbances are largely a result of his thinking illogically or irrationally; and that he can rid himself of most of his mental or emotional unhappiness, ineffectuality, and disturbance if he learns to maximize his rational and minimize his irrational thinking" (p. 36).

The Role of the Counselor

In many counseling approaches, the client conducts a monologue, presenting to the counselor his or her past history, current problems, perceptions, feelings, and so on. In rational-emotive therapy, on the other hand, the client is responsible for engaging in an ongoing *dialogue* with the therapist; a dialogue that is dynamic, reactive, introspective, and, at times, painful and provocative. Clients in rational-emotive therapy function much as the learner does in the educational setting, and their ability to improve is contingent upon their motivation and cooperation in the learner's role. They must be willing, specifically, to recognize and deal with those feelings or beliefs that they once considered logical and natural and that now they are discovering are illogical and unhealthy. This is often no easy matter. "No matter what a person's past history may be," Ellis and Harper (1961) explain,

> or how his parents, teachers, and other early associates may have helped him to become emotionally disturbed, he only remains disturbed because he *still* believes some of the unrealistic and illogical thoughts which he originally imbibed. To become undisturbed, therefore, it is only necessary that he sees what his present irrational and self-indoctrinations are and that he energetically and consistently work at deindoctrinating and reindoctrinating himself in these connections. His understanding of how he *first* became neurotic may be of some help, but it is most unlikely that it will be truly curative. (pp. 50–51)

The rational-emotive client, therefore, must live in and deal with the present rather than the past.

The rational-emotive counselor is unequivocally directive and intentionally attempts to "lead" the client to a "healthier" perspective. In keeping with his or her view that "not only are all psychotherapies more or less authoritative but they are also to some degree authoritarian" (p. 70), Ellis (1962) unabashedly favors the counselor's providing a high degree of direction to the client:

> The therapist, because of his training and experience, is invariably some kind of authority in his field; and by virtue of the fact that he is presumably less disturbed than his patient, and is often older and/or wiser, he is something of an authority—or parental—figure. Even if *he* does not look upon himself

in this manner, the members of his clientele almost invariably do. And whether he likes it or not, a considerable portion of his effectiveness with patients results from his being or appearing to be something of an authority figure to them. (pp. 364–365)

The counselor, according to Ellis (1962), devotes his or her efforts toward distinguishing what he or she sees as the difference between understanding and a deeper level of involvement on his or her part. "That the therapist should normally understand his patient's world and *see* the patient's behavior from his patient's *own* frame of reference," he points out, "is highly desirable."

That the therapist should literally *feel* his patient's disturbances or *believe* in his irrationalities is, in my opinion, usually harmful rather than helpful to the patient. Indeed, it is precisely the therapist's ability to comprehend the patient's immature behavior *without* getting involved in or believing in it that enables him to induce the patient to stop believing in or feeling that this behavior is necessary. (p. 115)

We note the sharp contradiction between Ellis's conception of the role of the counselor and Carl Rogers's conception of it. To Rogers, the effective counselor empathically reflects the client's feelings, and accepts these feelings as real, whatever they may be. The client-centered counselor does not seek either truth or falsity in feelings. To Ellis, on the other hand, the counselor works directly and authoritatively as a "lead" figure for the client, helping the client to understand and resolve the illogicalities in thinking that have led to emotional difficulties. Thus, the RET counselor does not indiscriminately accept any and all feelings; he or she deals with them as paralogical systems.

Ellis sees no reason why the counselor should not be able to inject his or her own values into the counseling encounter when such experience dictates that this course is advisable. After all, he argues, the counselor's values are presumably healthy values, and there is no logical reason why the client should not be exposed to healthy values—or at least values that are healthier than his or her own. Like Glasser, whose ideas we will examine later in this chapter, Ellis believes that the counselor's values are a legitimate therapeutic tool. His key remarks on the value of directiveness in rational-emotive therapy are found in his passage from *Reason and Emotion in Psychotherapy* (1962):

Patients [learn] to reperceive or rethink their life events and philosophies and thereby to change their unrealistic and illogical thought, emotion, and behavior. . . . The more emotional and less persuasive methods of psychotherapy are, when employed with most disturbed persons, relatively ineffectual and wasteful. On the other hand, the more direct, persuasive, suggestive, active, and logical techniques of therapy are more effective at undermining and extirpating the basic causes (as distinct from outward symptoms) of the emotional difficulties of most—though by no means necessarily all—individuals who come for psychological help. (pp. 36–37)

Rational-emotive counseling consists largely of what we might call "teaching techniques," but teaching techniques that synthesize the cognitive and emotional facets of the client's existence. The content of the RET experience, Ellis and Harper (1961) point out,

> largely consists of *teaching* the patient effective self-analysis: How, specifically, to observe his own feelings and actions, how to evaluate them objectively instead of moralistically and grandiosely, and how to change them, by consistent effort and practice, so that he may achieve the things he most wants to do in this brief span of human existence while, simultaneously, not interfering seriously with the preferences of others. Self-analysis, in this sense of the term, is not merely an important but actually a requisite aspect of successful psychotherapy.

We see, then, that the ultimate goal of rational-emotive teaching is that clients become capable of introspectively analyzing and correcting their distortions of the world.

"All the techniques in rational-emotive therapy," Ellis (1973a) argues, "are designed to do more than change behavior and help the client feel better. They are also used to change basic philosophies and to give him or her specific means of restructuring these philosophies again and again, until he or she rarely reverts to personally sabotaging and other-hating views and actions" (p. 62). He views the rational-emotive approach as "scientific," and many of his statements about the importance of techniques conjure up images of the behavioral counselor systematically working to alleviate symptoms. But, unlike the behavioral counselor, who is more mechanistic, Ellis considers the necessity of determining the right proportion of behaviors, feelings and cognitive ideas as a major factor in finding the appropriate prescription for emotional conflicts.

Ellis (1973b) divides the course of counseling into three basic modes, each comprising a set of techniques: *cognitive, emotive,* and *behavioristic.* "Cognitive therapy," he explains,

> attempts to show the individual that he is an arrant demander and that he'd better give up his perfectionism if he wants to lead a happier, less anxiety-ridden existence. It teaches him how to find his *should, oughts,* and *must;* how to separate his rational . . . from his irrational beliefs; how to use the logico-empirical method of science in relation to himself and his own problems; and how to accept reality, even when it is pretty grim. (p. 182)

This is the level of rational-emotive counseling that is most indicative of its emphasis on the importance of logic and reason in human thought. The second level, which focuses on the emotive aspects of thinking and behavior, integrates this cognitive emphasis with aspects of the more dynamic approaches. "Emotive-evocative therapy," Ellis goes on to explain,

Theories of Counseling

employs various means of dramatizing truths and falsehoods so that he [the client] can clearly distinguish between the two. . . . The therapist may employ *role-playing,* to bring forth to the client exactly what his false ideas are and how they affect his relations with others; *modeling,* to show the client how to develop different values; *humor,* to reduce some of the client's disturbance—creating ideas to absurdity; *unconditional acceptance* of the client, to demonstrate to him that he is acceptable, even with his unfortunate present traits; . . . *exhortation,* to persuade him to give up some of his crazy thinking and replace it with more efficient notions. (p. 183)

I continue actively teaching and depropagandizing Martha. Not only do I deal with the irrational philosophies that she brings up, but I prophylactically mention and attack others as well. I keep trying to expose to her a few basic groundless ideas—such as the ideas that she must be loved and must perform well—and to show her that her symptoms, such as her self-sacrificing and her lack of self-confidence, are the natural results of these silly ideas.

A Session with Albert Ellis: Case Example

By Albert Ellis. This section originally appeared in *Growth Through Reason,* Wilshire Book Co., 1975. Reprinted by permission.

C[111]   I have tremendous self-doubts about every part of my existence.

T[112]   Yes, you must, because you have so much of a belief that you must please others. If you have so much of this belief, you cannot have confidence in you. It's virtually impossible, for how can you do two opposite things at once—have confidence that you are a valuable person to yourself, no matter what others think, and believe that you are not valuable to you unless others approve of you? Confidence in yourself is really a high-class term for not giving that much of a damn what other people think of you. That's all it is. But you do care terribly about what other people think of you—about what your parents, especially, think. But also, probably, about what many other people think. Because if you were a poor daughter, what would the neighbors think? What would your friends think? You're really petrified!

C[113]   It's not the neighbors and friends. The thing that ties me up mostly is my parents.

T[114]   Yes, they're the primary ones. What would *they* think of you if you acted mainly in your own behalf? So what, if they think you're a louse? Let's even suppose that they disinherit you, excommunicate you from the family—

C[115]   Then I should think, "If they care that little about me, why should I care about them?"

T[116]   That's right. That would be tough! But it would just prove that they were benighted. It just would follow from their philosophy, which they're entitled to hold—however miserable it has made them. It would prove that they are fascistically trying to force you to believe this philosophy; and because they're failing, they excommunicate you. They're entitled to do so, of course; but you're entitled to say, "Who needs them?" Suppose, for example, you lived down south for awhile, that lots of people didn't like you because you weren't against Negroes, and that they called you a nigger-lover. What are you going to do—get terribly upset about them?

C[117]   No, that wouldn't bother me, because that never entered my life. I mean the fact that they hate Negroes. There are people who hate Negroes who never entered my life. Because I went to school with Negroes. Nobody ever told me that they were bad. If somebody ever said, "You're bad because you don't hate Negroes," that wouldn't bother me because that's not something—

T[118]   All right. But why should it bother you if somebody says you're bad because you don't put your parents' interests before your own?

C[119]   I guess because I've been indoctrinated with this idea.

T[120]   You believe *it*. It's exactly like hard-shelled Baptism. In fact, it has some of the aspects of orthodox religion; for this kind of religion says that the family comes first and the individual second; and that you're supposed to have children and not use birth control, and so on. That's what many orthodox religions, like Catholicism and orthodox Judaism, teach. Everthing for the church, the family—and somewhere, away underneath, the individual is buried.

C[121]   But the individual—whatever contributions he has to make, whatever his capabilities are—can be lost that way; and I don't want to be lost.

T[122]   Not only can he be, he must be lost that way.

C[123]   I don't want to be self-effacing!

T[124]   Right! Then why do you have to be? Who said you must be? The answer is: your parents. Who the hell are they? Poor, sick, benighted individuals. They're not educated; they're not sophisticated. They're probably bright enough, but they're disturbed. Your father, as we said before, has probably been seriously upset all his life, in an undramatic manner. More recently, he became dramatically ill. But it doesn't come on like that. *(Snaps his fingers)* You can see the signs clearly over the years. And your mother has probably been fairly disturbed, too, though probably not as much as he. But that's the way it is: you were raised in a pretty crazy family. Does that mean you have to kowtow to their beliefs for the rest of your life?

C[125]   No; I want to get away from it. I want to be myself. I don't want to be—

T[126]   What's preventing you from being yourself? Nothing can prevent you right now, if you really want to be. You just would do better, every time the feelings of being weak arise, to trace them to the indoctrinations of your parents and of your society and your acceptance of these indoctrinations. And you'd better counter them—because you're suggesting to yourself, a hundred times a day now, those same creeds.

You've taken them over, internalized them. And that's really fortunate. Because it's now become *your* belief—you can get rid of it. Not immediately—but you can. Just like you got rid of your religious views.

C127 And I also want to find out—I suppose it's all basically the same thing—why I have been promiscuous, why I lie—

T128 For love. You think you're such a worm that the only way to get worth, value, is to be loved, approved, accepted. And you're promiscuous to gain love, because it's an easy way: you can gain acceptance easily that way. You lie because you're ashamed. You feel that they wouldn't accept you if you told the truth. These are very common results; anybody who desperately needs to be loved—as you think you do with your crummy philosophy, will be promiscuous, will lie, will do other things which are silly, rather than do the things she really wants to do and rather than gain her own self-approval.

C129 That's what I don't have; I don't have any.

T130 You never tried to get it! You're working your butt off to get other people's approval. Your parents' first, but other people's second. That's why the promiscuity; that's why the lying. And you're doing no work whatever at getting your own self-acceptance, because they only way you get self-respect is by not giving that much of a damn what other people think. There is no other way to get it; that's what self-acceptance really means: to thine *own* self be true!

In my response, T130, I epitomize one of the main differences between RET and most other "dynamic" systems of psychological treatment. Whereas a psychoanalytically-oriented therapist would probably have tried to show Martha that her promiscuity and lying stemmed from her early childhood experiences, I, as a rational-emotive therapist, believe nothing of the sort. I assume, instead, that her childhood lying, for example, was mainly caused by her own innate tendencies toward crooked thinking—which in turn led her to react inefficiently to the noxious stimuli her parents may have imposed on her. What is important, therefore, is her own reactivity and not her parents' actions. I also believe, on theoretical grounds, that the reason for Martha's present promiscuity and lying is probably her current need to be inordinately loved; and she freely seems to admit (as she also previously did in C19) that my educated guess about this is true.

If I proved to be wrong in this guess, I would not be perturbed but would look for another hypothesis—for example, her promiscuity might be a form of self-punishment, because she thought she was unworthy on some other count. As a rational-emotive therapist, I am willing to take a chance on being wrong with my first hypothesis because, if I am right, I will usually save my client a good deal of time. Moreover, by taking a wrong tack, I may well help myself and the client get to the right tack. If, however, I try the psychoanalytic, history-taking path, in order to arrive at the "real" reasons for my client's behavior (1) I may never find what these "real" reasons are (for they may not exist, or years of probing may never turn them up); (2) I may still come up with the wrong reasons; and

(3) I may sidetrack the client so seriously that she may never discover what her basic disturbance-creating philosophy is and therefore never do anything about changing it. For a variety of reasons, then, I take a very direct approach with Martha.

This is the level of the treatment that is most overtly dramatic and is generally associated with the showy side of the rational-emotive approach. It is essential for the counselor to remember, however, that this is only one phase of the treatment, not the entire course of treatment, as some lay people and a number of critics would lead us to believe.

Behavior therapy methods are employed "to help the client change his dysfunctional symptoms and to become habituated to more effective ways of performing, and to help him radically change his *cognitions* about himself, about others, and about the world" (Ellis, 1973*b*, p. 183). These behavioristic methods may include giving clients homework assignments, encouraging them to take risks, or having them intentionally fail at some effort in order to learn to cope with the feelings of failure. Some of these techniques resemble respondent conditioning techniques, and others look remarkably similar to Frankl's technique of paradoxical intention, in which the client is told to wish for the very thing he or she most fears.

The RET counselor uses what Ellis calls the "*A-B-C* theory of personality" as the underlying basis and rationale for his or her technique. *A* stands for the activating event; *B* is the belief system; and *C* stands for the emotional and behavioral consequences. It is the job of the therapist, Ellis argues, to show the client the *A-B-Cs* of his or her disturbances: "RET is . . . based on and consistently uses the principles of empirical validation and logical analysis. . . . It shows the individual that whenever he upsets himself at point *C* (the emotional consequence), it is not . . . because of what is happening to him at point *A* (the activating event). Rather it is because of his own irrational and unvalidating suppositions at point *B* (his belief system). More precisely, when a person feels depressed at point *C*, it is not because he has been rejected by someone or has lost a job at point *A*, but because he is convincing himself, at point *B*, of both a rational and an irrational hypothesis" (Ellis, 1971, p. 6).

The *A-B-C* hypothesis, Ellis suggests emphatically, "is central to the whole field of RET and cognitive-behavior therapy and has an enormous amount of research that solidly supports it" (Ellis, 1977, p. 3). Probably no area of personality has been explored in more detail, and Ellis concludes unequivocally, from an exhaustive review of the research, that "innumerable studies and reviews of research have appeared that support the view that, in general, human emotion and behavior include cognitive mediation and for the most part have important cognitive origins" (p. 4). It is on this premise that much of the RET corpus of counseling techniques rests.

We see from these remarks that the rational-emotive approach comprises a variety of different types of techniques, all clustered around the central goal— to correct the client's illogical beliefs and irrational feelings. The goals of the counseling are therefore specifiable in terms of the ideas and thoughts that are to be corrected. Ellis (1958) offers a tentative list of twelve common illogical beliefs that often require correction during the treatment. It must be mentioned, however, that a complete list would be as limitless as the number of clients who seek counseling.

Evaluation of RET

In recent years, the rational-emotive counseling approach has come to enjoy wide acceptance in many different settings. Although critics have not hesitated to speak their minds and vent their objections, Ellis has consistently rejoined attacks with a hearty spirit and a veritable cornucopia of empirical evidence (i.e., Ellis, 1976a, 1977, 1980). The RET approach has been criticized particularly for its willingness to accept very literally whatever the patient says, ignoring almost completely psychoanalytic, cultural, and social learning limitations on interpersonal communication.

Bernard (1981), for example, argues that RET is too dogmatic, especially in its assessment of a client's problem and in the interpretation of the client's private thoughts. Citing a matrix of dynamic, psycholinguistic, and behavioral factors which interfere with the ability of a person to report thoughts accurately to a therapist, Bernard suggests "therapeutic instructions should be expressed in a form that is compatible with and can be incorporated within the client's idiosyncratic intrapersonal communication system and cognitive structure" (p. 125). Still, Ellis maintains firmly in his recent writings that the effects of RET are pervasive and deep enough in the patient's life to make long-lasting and significant changes (Ellis, 1980). The wide application of RET, promulgated by Ellis and others, seems to attest to this.

By the 1980s, RET had been extensively adopted in the clinical, school, social work, group, industrial, family counseling, and health settings. Saltzberg (1979) suggests that because the greatest strength of RET resides in its emphasis on learning self-helping emotions which trigger productive behaviors while, at the same time, eliminating self-defeating feelings which auger failure, it can be applied rather flexibly to many settings. Ellis himself has done much to promote the application of rational-emotive techniques for teaching and for dealing with educational problems. Ball and Henning (1981) find RET, with its emphasis on the dichotomy of logical/illogical thinking, especially suitable for premarital counseling, where the diminution of irrational premarital expectations can serve toward producing a stronger marriage relationship ultimately.

Cognitive Therapy

While we tend to think of cognitive therapy as a relatively new development, its main idea goes back to the Stoics, "who considered man's conceptions (or misconceptions) of events rather than the events themselves as the key to his emotional upsets" (Beck, 1976, p. 3). Cognitive therapy begins with that age-old assumption, but adds to it many of the empirical findings of cognitive science and an arsenal of clinical techniques that are adapted from several different rational and psychodynamic forms of therapy. Because the early studies of its efficacy were so encouraging, it has gained wide credence during the past fifteen years, and subsequent studies have confirmed it as an effective treatment modality.

Background

The development of cognitive psychotherapy has taken place in the context of an entire revolution in the study of human thinking and behavior, sometimes called the *cognitive revolution*. This new science, cognitive science, brings together researches in physiology (especially neurophysiology and neuroendocrine chemistry), philosophy and linguistics, computer science, medicine and pharmacology, and different areas of psychology. As Hunt (1982) points out, more research in human cognition has probably been conducted during the past twenty years than throughout the entire previous history of scientific study. Mahoney (1985, p. 13) also sees the revived interest in cognition as a central element in human change, "a bonafide revolution in science" with important practical application in helping people resolve their problems.

Cognitive therapy, as a modality, brings together the findings of cognitive science with many of the clinical applications that have proven effective in rational-emotive therapy, reality therapy, and (to a smaller extent) psychoanalysis, especially the scientific research on unconscious processes. Combining all these elements, Aaron Beck, more than any other single person, developed an organized therapeutic modality called cognitive therapy, which after fifteen years of thorough testing, has established its clinical worthiness.

Cognitive therapy has gained such wide credibility in the profession primarily because of its success in changing clients' automatic thoughts—those irrational and maladaptive thoughts that produce undesirable or maladaptive responses. But it does more than this: it actually changes the broad assumptions underlying the specific thoughts. "One of the major goals of cognitive therapy," Young and Beck (1982, p. 200) argue, "especially in the later stages of treatment, is to help patients identify and challenge those maladaptive assumptions that affect their ability to avoid future depressions." These changes of assumptions are what ultimately enable clients in cognitive treatment to lead better, fuller, more productive lives.

View of the Person

The basic assumption in cognitive therapy is that "the individual's primary problem has to do with his construction of reality" (Beck, 1985, p. 328). Individuals in growing up develop distorted views of connections between themselves and the environment, and these distortions extend to the way they feel about themselves and the way they take in and process the outside world. In order to function appropriately, one should perceive the world and one's relationship with it in a manner that is consistent with the responses one is likely to get to one's actions.

A cognitive disturbance, such as depression, has three components of distortion: (1) view of self; (2) view of experiences; and (3) view of the future. In the case of depression, the view of self "centers around the [client's] view of self as inadequate, unworthy, deficient, and/or defecting in mental, moral, or physical character" (Rush and Giles, 1982, p. 150). The view of experiences in life is also distorted, leading to a depressive interpretation of the world: "Experiences are constructed as evidence for defeat and loss. This evidence is then taken as support for notions of personal rejection, deprivation, and increased dependence" (Rush and Giles). Finally, the view of the future is also colored by a negativity that manifests as feelings of hopelessness, a belief that things will never get better, never change. With other disturbances, such as phobia or obsessional neuroses, the specific components may differ, but in any case, part of the counseling process is to determine what distortions are causing the client to exhibit the maladaptive behaviors.

The Cognitive Triad

"The remedy," Beck goes on to assert, "lies in modifying the cognitive set. This psychological modification then produces biochemical changes which in turn can influence cognitions further." This connection between psychological states and physiological responses is central in supporting the cognitivists' views on how changes in thinking can affect the entire personal behavior structure.

The cognitive counselor may have arrived at his or her position after a background in psychodynamic, behavioral, humanistic, or another counseling modality. He or she will typically integrate techniques and philosophies from these other perspectives into the cognitive counseling process. It is central to understand, however, that the view and philosophy of the cognitive counselor are as central to the actual counseling process as the feelings and openness of the client-centered practitioner. As Beck et al. point out (p. 61),

Role of the Counselor

> The therapist should keep several specific principles in mind during treatment. The depressed patient's personal world view, his negative ideas and beliefs, seem reasonable and plausible to him even though they appear far-fetched to the therapist. He seriously believes and is quite consistent in his beliefs that he is deprived, defective, useless, unlovable, etc. In fact, this internal consistency is often maintained in the face of repeated and dramatic external evidence contradictory to these beliefs.

Young and Beck (1982) make the point that in cognitive therapy the counselor and client collaborate on the treatment plan and work together as partners throughout the treatment.

Collaboration

> This collaborative approach has at least three goals. First, collaboration helps insure that the patient and the therapist have compatible goals at each point in the course of treatment. Thus, they will not be working at cross-purposes. Second, the process minimizes the patient resistance that often arises when

the therapist is viewed as a competitor or an aggressor, or is seen as trying to control or dominate the patient. Third, the alliance helps prevent misunderstandings between patient and therapist. Such misunderstandings can lead the therapist to go down blind alleys or can lead the patient to misinterpret what the therapist has been trying to convey.

Therapy Process

Clarke and Greenberg (1986, p. 11) point out the main differences between cognitive and affective therapies:

Cognitively oriented therapists attend primarily to how clients think about their problems. Interventions are aimed at changing thoughts, cognitive structures, and ways of processing information, often to promote more effective problem solving. Affective therapists, on the other hand, pay more attention to the feeling domain. Their interventions focus on emotional experience and are thought to lead clients to the wisdom of the organism, which is regarded as having a rationality that integrates all the affective and cognitive information available to the organism.

Beck (1979, p. 20) points out that "the cognitive therapist induces the patient to apply the same problem-solving techniques he has used throughout his life to correct fallacious thinking." What this basically means is that by a variety of techniques, the therapist re-educates the patient. These techniques include a thorough assessment (possibly using Beck's Depression Inventory), encouraging the patient to articulate treatment goals, homework and reading assignments, rapport, and an exchange of views that teaches the patient better problem-solving skills.

Another important point to remember is that according to the cognitive theory, changes in thinking, in the construction of reality, produce real physical—neuroendocrinological—changes in the client which make him feel less depressed, anxious, and anhedonic. Beck (1985, p. 329) explains it this way:

The psychological intervention by the therapist was processed by the patient's information-processing apparatus. This processing involves changes in the brain, reflected in a biochemical modification and simultaneously modification in the cognitive set. If we took a "psychological biopsy" after the cognitive-neurochemical modification, we would obtain cognitions such as, "He really believes he can help me" and "I didn't believe I could write this letter—but I did." If we took a neurochemical biopsy at that point in time, we would find an intricate pattern of neurons firing and chemical changes at the synapses. (p. 329)

Theories of Counseling

The cognitive counselor has an armamentarium of specific techniques which, taken together, enable rapid penetration of the problem and relatively quick resolution. These techniques are designed to help the patient clarify his or her automatic illogical thoughts, re-evaluate those thoughts, and modify the assumptions underlying them. Some of these techniques overlap with techniques used in the humanistic, behavioral, or psychodynamic approaches, while some are unique to the cognitive perspective.

Young and Beck (1982, pp. 192–211) identify some of the specific techniques used in cognitive therapy which differentiate it from other therapies. Many of these are exercised in persuasive logic, whereby the counselor, using his or her logical abilities, helps the client achieve a new clarity in thinking. These are summarized briefly below:

Techniques

Clients are typically unaware of the "automatic thoughts" that link external events to their perceptions of these events. "Ideally, the therapist and patient work together as collaborators to discover the specific thoughts that preceded such emotions as anger, sadness, and anxiety" (p. 192).

Eliciting Automatic Thoughts

One of the ways the counselor or therapist can help the client see what his or her automatic thoughts are is through inductive questioning, which focuses specifically on the connection. This encourages the client to introspectively analyze his or her emotional reactions to external stimuli.

Inductive Questioning

The client can also be encouraged to picture in his or her mind situations that prove distressing. "If the images are realistic and clear, patients are often able to identify automatic thoughts they were having at the time" (p. 193).

Imagery

Role playing is especially effective when dealing with interpersonal problems. The counselor can play the role of the "other person" involved in the problem, exploring with the client how he or she is reacting to this person and what, if any, cognitive distortions are interfering with effective functioning.

Role Playing

Using a special form, called the "Daily Record of Dysfunctional Thoughts" (see figure 9.1), the client learns how to pinpoint his or her automatic thoughts, which he or she may not be consciously (cognitively) aware of.

Daily Record of Dysfunctional Thoughts

The client should learn the specific meaning of an event—*for him or her*—that precedes an emotional response. "For example, one patient began to cry whenever he had an argument with his girlfriend. It was not possible to identify a specific automatic thought. However, after the therapist asked a series of questions to probe the meaning of the event, it became obvious that the patient has always associated any type of argument or fight with the end of the relationship. *It was this meaning, embedded in his view of the event, that preceded his crying*" (p. 196, italics added).

Ascertaining the Meaning of an Event

Figure 9.1. Daily record of dysfunctional thoughts.

Date	Situation Describe: 1. Actual event leading to unpleasant emotion, or 2. Stream of thoughts, daydream, or recollection, leading to unpleasant emotion.	Emotion(s) 1. Specify sad/anxious/angry, etc. 2. Rate degree of emotion, 1–100.	Automatic Thought(s) 1. Write automatic thought(s) that preceded emotion(s). 2. Rate belief in automatic thought(s), 0–100%.	Rational Response 1. Write rational response to automatic thought(s). 2. Rate belief in rational response, 0–100%.	Outcome 1. Rerate belief in automatic thought(s), 0–100%. 2. Specify and rate subsequent emotions, 0–100.

Explanation: When you experience an unpleasant emotion, note the situation that seemed to stimulate the emotion. (If the emotion occurred while you were thinking, daydreaming, etc., please note this.) Then note the automatic thought associated with the emotion. Record the degree to which you believe this thought: 0% = not at all; 100% = completely. In rating degree of emotion: 1 = a trace; 100 = the most intense possible.

Testing Automatic Thoughts

In this procedure, the client is asked to suspend his abiding belief in the automatic thought, to question its validity as a construct, and to be sensitive to its influence as a cognition. The automatic thought is treated as a hypothesis, and tested by the counselor and client for its truthfulness, practicability, and conformity to the interpersonal reality in which the client lives. For example, a client might realize that he functions in life with the automatic thought, "When I am criticized by my teachers, superiors, or authority figures, it means I have done something wrong or inadequate and should feel ashamed." But testing this out, he can come to realize that these people may be wrong—that he may actually be right—or that even if he is wrong, we all have a right to be wrong, which in no way implies a deficit in our thinking or our abilities.

Examining Available Evidence

In collaboration, the counselor and client examine the evidence supporting or refuting the automatic thoughts. Special attention is directed to the consequences of living under the rule of automatic thoughts.

Again, using the scientific method, the counselor and client work in conjunction to set up real-life experiments to test out whether the automatic thoughts are workable or not.

Setting Up an Experiment

By using his or her own experience, the counselor can ask the client a series of questions that pose a logical dilemma when examined in conjunction with the acceptance of the illogical automatic thoughts.

Inductive Questioning

Many of the negative terms clients use to describe themselves have a personal meaning to them that is not consistent with the logical meaning of the word. For example, a client who describes herself as "evil" may mean something entirely different from the accepted meaning of the term ("evil," for example, because she didn't listen to everything her mother told her!). "This procedure can help patients recognize the arbitrary nature of their self-appraisals and bring them more in line with common sense definitions of these negative terms" (p. 198).

Operationalizing a Negative Construct

In conjunction with the counselor, the client finds new solutions to the problems that have been giving him difficulty. The client can be guided to new responses, new behaviors, that are more adaptive and satisfying than the previous ones. This is most likely to occur when the client has abandoned his or her illogical thoughts.

Generating Alternatives

Here, the counselor helps the client focus on the underlying assumptions behind his or her automatic thoughts. These maladaptive assumptions are in effect the basic axioms of living, which infuse all different areas of the client's perceiving, thinking, and responding. "In order to identify these maladaptive assumptions, the therapist can listen closely for themes that seem to cut across several different situations or problem areas. The therapist can then list several related automatic thoughts that the patient has already expressed on different occasions, and asks the patient to *abstract the general 'rule' that connects the automatic thoughts*" (p. 200).

Identifying Maladaptive Assumptions

This process involves several strategies for examining, challenging, and modifying underlying assumptions which are illogical or maladaptive. The counselor should guide the client to a new understanding, in which the client can logically defend and support underlying assumptions which are consistent with his or her way of living and logical with the assumptions of the counselor and with others around him or her.

Analyzing the Validity of Maladaptive Assumptions

Considerable evidence supports the effectiveness of the cognitive approach, especially for the treatment of depression and phobias (Beck, 1985). A number of serious efforts have also been made to work with schizophrenics, but at this time there is not enough support to show whether cognitive therapy is an effective modality in that area.

Evaluation

Cognitive Approaches   253

Reality Therapy   Reality therapy, which was originally developed and made famous as an approach for working with delinquent girls who had been institutionalized, has enjoyed a wide following during the past two decades. It has been applied to virtually every counseling setting, with varying degrees of success. It is now considered one of the staples of counseling approaches, with advocates and practitioners at every end of the spectrum. It has been widely and successfully applied not only in the school setting, where it has achieved immense popularity, but in the correctional setting, in mental hospitals, in vocational rehabilitation and psychiatric clinics, in halfway houses, and in other clinical and social service settings (Bassin, Bratter & Rachin, 1976). In these sections, we shall examine the theoretical underpinnings of reality therapy and comment on its direct application to counseling problems in a variety of different settings.

Background   Reality therapy, like client-centered therapy, is largely the product of a single man, Dr. William Glasser. Glasser, like Rogers, was trained in the psychoanalytic approach, with which he became discouraged late in his training. He objected primarily to the concepts of neurosis and mental illness, arguing instead that the patient is weak, not ill, and that if his or her abilities were strengthened, he or she would be a more fit member of society. At the time, Glasser's teacher, Dr. G. L. Harrington, was having his own doubts about the merits of psychoanalysis as a curative science. Harrington believed that there was no significant proof that psychoanalysis had any curative powers, and he sought a more effective type of psychotherapy. His doubts inspired Glasser to develop what emerged as reality therapy.

Again like Rogers, Glasser arrived at his treatment through experimentation and trial and error. In the first place, he found that in treating clients it was not necessary to explore their past histories in any detail. What counted most was what was happening at the present time, not what had transpired in the past. Second, he also rejected the Freudian notion of transference, arguing that the client perceived the counselor as another human being, a real person, and not as some imagined figure of the past. Thirdly, he rejected the very important Freudian idea that to be mentally healthy, one had to have insight into one's unconscious mind. In discussing the origins of reality therapy, Glasser (1982) points out,

> A major problem for me was that when I did the things I was taught to do, such as encourage people to talk about their parents, feelings, upsets and a lot of what had happened to them in the past, the basic thing I was involved in was helping them avoid taking responsibility for what they were doing now. They might have temporarily felt better when they found out that they were upset because their mother didn't nurture them properly or their father was absent too often [but] it became apparent to me that this wasn't the way to go, that what we ought to be talking about was what they were doing now in their life, and what they could do about what they were doing. . . . That seemed to me to be the key thing. (p. 460)

In 1962 Glasser joined the staff of a school for wayward adolescent girls at Ventura, California. Three years later he published *Reality Therapy: A New Approach to Psychiatry,* which outlined the details of his counseling and offered rich examples of its use at the Ventura school. He has extended many of his original ideas in *Schools Without Failure* (1969), which applies the principles of reality therapy to the school setting, and *The Identity Society* (1972). More recently, his book *Positive Addiction* (1976) shows how individuals can take control of many aspects of their lives, thereby reducing stress, anxiety and frustration. He has lectured widely in recent years on the application of reality principles to education and social change.

The reality counselor, like the behaviorist, views the individual largely in terms of his or her behavior. But rather than examining behavior in terms of the stimulus-response model as the behaviorist does, or looking at the individual's behavior phenomenologically as the client-centered counselor does, the reality therapist considers behavior against an objective standard of measurement, which he or she calls "reality." This reality may be a practical reality or a moral reality. In either case, the reality counselor sees the individual as functioning in consonance or dissonance with that reality.

View of the Person

"When a man acts in such a way that he gives and receives love, and feels worthwhile to himself and others, his behavior is right and moral," argues Glasser (1965, p. 57). Throughout his thinking, the criterion of "right" plays an important role in determining the appropriateness of behavior. He uses such terms as *satisfactory, improved, good,* and *moral* to describe behavior, and his view of mental health is directly related to how well one's behavior meets these standards of measurement. The reality counselor's view of the person is continually shadowed by the normative points of these higher goals.

Glasser sees as the main motivation in people's behavior their attempts to fulfill their needs. He suggests that there are two basic psychological needs: the *need to love and be loved,* and the *need for "achievement of self-worth,* the feeling that you are worthwhile as a person both to yourself and to others" (Glasser, 1971). In a later paper (Glasser & Zunin, 1973), he reduces this to one basic need: the need for identity. It is

the need to feel that we are somehow separate and distinct from every other living being on the face of this earth; that no matter where we go we will not find another person who thinks, looks, acts, and talks exactly as we do. This need is universal and transcends all cultures. Its significance is evidenced, for example, in religious teachings of both primitive and civilized societies. (p. 292)

When individuals are frustrated in satisfying these needs, they may lose touch with the objective reality, stray from the imposing confines of the real world, and lose their ability to perceive things as they are. "In their unsuccessful effort to fulfill their needs," Glasser (1965) argues, "no matter what behavior they choose, all patients have a common characteristic: they all deny the reality of the world around them."

It is in our strivings to satisfy these basic needs, argues Glasser, that the patterns of our behavior are determined. A person's sense of responsibility for himself or herself helps that individual change and modify behavior, to arrive ultimately at more acceptable and satisfactory standards that, in turn, enable him or her to gratify needs more successfully. Glasser (1965) says,

> To be worthwhile we must maintain a satisfactory standard of behavior. To do so we must learn to correct ourselves when we do wrong and to credit ourselves when we do right. If we do not evaluate our behavior, or having evaluated it, we do not act to improve our conduct where it is below our standards, we will not fulfill our need to be worthwhile and we will suffer. (p. 10)

Thus, the reality counselor attaches direct values to behavior, measuring in counseling a person's success or failure against these values and how well the values have been met. Responsibility serves as a foundation concept: a value in itself, against which all other values are measured. It is not so much that the individual is taught to be responsible, but rather that responsibility becomes the means utilized for the therapeutic end. As Rachin (1974) points out,

> Reality therapy differs from conventional therapy in that it labels behavior as either responsible or irresponsible (not the person as mentally ill) and it emphasizes dealing with his behavior in the present (not the person's psychological history). Responsibility is considered the basic concept of reality therapy and is defined as the ability to meet one's needs without depriving others of the ability to meet theirs. Realistic behavior presumably occurs when an individual considers and compares the immediate and remote consequences of his actions. (p. 46)

The view of the individual, then, can be summarized as follows: the healthy person is a responsible being in the process of satisfying his or her basic life needs (to love and be loved; to feel worthwhile), which together give the individual a sense of experiential unity, of personal identity, of purpose in life.

Role of the Counselor

The primary task of the client in reality counseling is to learn to make appropriate choices, to develop a sense of responsibility, to be able to interact constructively with others, and to understand and accept the reality of his or her existence. Although this appears on the surface to be identical to the role of the client in existential counseling, it differs in two important aspects: the client in reality counseling, unlike the existential client, is not in the process of creating his or her own existence and own destiny through choices; rather, the client is conforming to the counselor's notions of reality; secondly, the reality client's sense of responsibility is defined as "the ability to fulfill one's needs, and to do so in a way that does not deprive others of the ability to fulfill their needs" (Glasser, 1965, p. 13).

Clients come to treatment to fill a void in their lives. "Almost [filled with] emptiness . . . they look to the psychiatrist to supply in a measure what they lack, and in proper psychiatric treatment he does this. When the patient finally begins to establish a real feeling of identity, the empty feeling leaves and the person begins to become alive and vital" (Glasser, 1961, p. 26). Glasser views this emptiness as a lack of genuine involvement with others and attributes many of the major psychological problems to this source.

Glasser (1965) says the following about the role of the counselor in reality counseling:

> The therapist has a difficult task, for he must quickly build a firm emotional relationship with a patient who has failed to establish such relationships in the past. He is aided by recognizing that the patient is desperate for involvement and suffering because he is not able to fulfill his needs. . . . The ability of the therapist to get involved is the major skill of doing Reality Therapy. . . . One way to attempt an understanding of how involvement occurs is to describe the qualities necessary to be a therapist. . . . The therapist must be a very responsive person—tough, interested, human, sensitive. He must be able to fulfill his own needs and must be willing to discuss some of his own struggles so that the patient can see that acting responsibly is possible though sometimes difficult. . . . The therapist must always be strong, never expedient. He must withstand the patient's request for sympathy, for an excess of sedatives, for justification of his actions no matter how the patient pleads or threatens. Never condoning an irresponsible action on the patient's part, he must be willing to watch the patient suffer, if that helps him toward responsibility. . . . Finally, the therapist must be able to become emotionally involved with each patient. (pp. 21–23)

The counselor, in other words, establishes a relationship with the client in which he or she is able to exert a critical awareness for the client's benefit. The counselor guides the client, directively and dynamically, to a condition of congruence with objective reality; but unlike the client-centered counselor, the reality counselor is unabashedly judgmental and advisory at every juncture. He or she uses his or her own experiences and feelings, when these are appropriate and relevant, to help the client.

The basic technique of reality counseling is a teaching technique, specifically, to teach the client the meaning of reality and to show her or him how to act responsibly within the context of that reality. Prior to this teaching, the counselor must first gain the necessary involvement with the client, for "unless the

Techniques and Goals of Reality Counseling

requisite involvement exists between the responsible therapist and the irresponsible patient, there can be no therapy" (Glasser, 1965, p. 21). After the reality counselor gains the necessary involvement, he or she begins to point out to the patient the unrealistic aspects of his or her irresponsible behavior. "If the patient wishes to argue that his concept of reality is correct," Glasser (1965) points out, "we must be willing to discuss his opinions, but we must not fail to emphasize that our main interest is his behavior rather than his attitude." Glasser's statements on techniques and goals are clear:

> Along with the emphasis on behavior and as a continuing part of the involvement, the therapist freely gives praise when the patient acts responsibly and shows disapproval when he does not. . . . The skill of therapy is to put the responsibility upon the patient and, after involvement is established, to ask him why he remains in therapy if he is not dissatisfied with his behavior. . . . As therapy proceeds, the therapist must teach the patient that therapy is not primarily directed toward making him happy . . . the therapist must guide the patient toward understanding that no one can make another person happy for long unless he becomes responsible. . . . As part of becoming involved the therapist must become interested in and discuss all aspects of the patient's present life. . . . We are interested in him as a person with a wide potential, not just as a patient with problems. . . . We must open up his life, talk about new horizons, expand his range of interests, make him aware of life beyond his difficulties. Anything two people might discuss is a grist for therapy.
>
> The patient develops an increased sense of self-worth in the process of parrying his convictions and values with a trusted, respected person. The therapist relates the discussions to what the patient is doing now, confronting him with the reality of what he does as compared to what he says.
>
> The therapist now directly, but skillfully, interweaves the discussion of the patient's strong points. Discussing those areas in which he acts responsibly, we show how they can be expanded. . . . To do Reality Therapy the therapist must not only be able to help the patient accept the real world, but he must further help him fulfill his needs in the real world so that he will have no inclination in the future to deny its existence. (pp. 7, 28–32)

Glasser (1982) conceptualizes reality therapy in seven steps, which, taken together, involve all the energies of an individual's ingenuity and creativity. To see that the client progresses this way is the chief responsibility of the reality counselor. These steps, we should note, are cooperative endeavors between the counselor and the client:

1. Make friends or get involved, or get along, create a relationship or gain rapport.
2. De-emphasize the patient's history and find out what are you doing *now*.

3. Help the patient learn to make an evaluation of his behavior. Help the patient find out if what he is saying is really *helping* him.
4. Once you have evaluated the behavior, then you can begin to explore alternative behaviors—behaviors that may prove more helpful.
5. Get a commitment to a plan of change.
6. Maintain an attitude of: No excuses if you don't do it. By now the patient is committed to the change and must learn to be responsible in carrying it out.
7. Be tough without punishment. Teach people to do things without being punished if they don't; it creates a more positive motivation.

If we summarize the basic techniques and goals of reality counseling, we note some striking similarities to behavioral counseling, to the psychodynamic approaches, and especially to rational-emotive counseling. While it can certainly be argued that the overlap is greater than the differences, in the clinical setting the subtle shades of emphasis make reality counseling a truly unique modality.

Since the publication of Glasser's first book in 1965, reality therapy has gained many adherents in the counseling ranks. Silverberg (1984) has successfully used reality therapy in running men's groups. He found that this approach is especially useful in helping men make decisions that affect their lives and improve their overall functioning and performance at work, in their personal lives, and in their relationships with women.

A spate of research projects has shown the value of reality therapy in a number of diverse settings. Vogt (1985) has pointed out how reality therapy can be used in a convalescent home, where patients are taught to take increasing levels of responsibility for meeting their own needs and developing appropriate skills and behaviors to increase their functioning. Cohen and Sordo (1984) have used a modified version of reality therapy to work with adult offenders in a variety of offender settings. They conclude that this is an effective modality with prisoners, and point out how the essential concepts of responsibility and personal worth are relevant to the offender population. Evans (1984) has demonstrated how reality therapy can be used to train physicians to manage their alcoholic patients more effectively. Ford (1983) has cited several examples of how reality therapy can be effective in helping families come to grips with their problems, and many other studies show reality therapy is a powerful family treatment modality.

Evaluation of Reality Counseling

Transactional analysis (TA) has the distinction of being the only counseling approach that had its two seminal books on the national best-seller list for longer than a year. These two landmark works, Eric Berne's *Games People Play* and Thomas A. Harris's *I'm OK—You're OK* are but two of the several books on TA that have achieved wide public recognition and popularity, bringing to millions the basic ideas of TA, and making TA, in the process, one of the most popular

Transactional Analysis

therapeutic modalities. As of this writing, there are half a dozen institutes of transactional analysis, a professional organization devoted solely to its study and propagation, and over two hundred book titles relating directly or indirectly to it. While TA has achieved professional recognition as an important modality of individual counseling, by far its greatest impact has been in the areas of group counseling, in organizational psychology, and in the educational and school counseling settings.

Background

The individual primarily responsible for developing transactional analysis was Eric Berne, a medical doctor by training. Berne, like Rogers, Glasser, and Ellis, began in the Freudian tradition. He was born in Montreal, Canada, in 1910, and attended medical school at McGill University. Soon after graduation he settled in New York City, where he studied psychoanalysis. He attended the New York Psychoanalytic Institute, a traditional Freudian stronghold emphasizing classical methods geared for the medical doctor. During World War II, Berne joined the Army Medical Corps, where he practiced medical psychiatry at several hospitals, and finally settled at the Mental Hygiene Clinic of the Veterans Administration Hospital in San Francisco.

It was at this point that Berne began to develop some of the basic principles of TA. Recognizing many of the limitations of the classical method in which he was trained, Berne sought a more "rational" approach, less dependent on the unconscious. Many of his ideas evolved from his experiences in conducting group therapy during the war and afterwards. Berne's ideas were explained in his early professional publications, such as his first technical paper on TA, "Ego States in Psychotherapy," published in 1957, several years before his approach would achieve public recognition. His important books include *Transactional Analysis in Psychotherapy* (1961) and *The Structure and Dynamics of Organizations and Groups* (1963) and his most popular works, *Games People Play* (1964) and *What Do You Say After You Say Hello?* (1972).

Eric Berne died in 1970 in Carmel, California, where he was practicing transactional psychiatry.

View of the Person

In exploring the foundations concepts of TA, we should look at it first as a way of understanding the person, and second as a way of helping people overcome their problems. These two viewpoints converge in the underlying theory.

Central to TA are the concepts of *transaction* and *ego states*. A transaction is the most basic unit of social interaction. A transaction occurs whenever one person acts as a stimulus for another, and the other responds to the first. What makes TA unique in its analysis of human transactions is that people are not viewed as uniform bodies. Rather, each person is viewed in terms of his or her *ego states,* "which are coherent systems of thought and feeling manifested by corresponding patterns of behavior" (Berne, 1972, p. 11). As we analyze transactions, then, we are actually diagramming the communications between two people's ego states.

Each of us has three ego states, which together, constitute our personality. These states are designated Parent (P), Adult (A), and Child (C). While the three terms are sometimes used metaphorically, there is at least some empirical evidence that they are in fact distinct and identifiable phenomena—that is, that they are real—with a significant level of agreement among objective raters (Falkowski, Ben-Tovim & Bland, 1980).

The Parent is "a huge collection of recordings in the brain of unquestioned or imposed external events perceived by a person in his early years" (Harris, 1969, p. 40). The Parent ego state is filled with values, injunctions, shoulds and oughts, goods and bads. "In this state," Berne (1972) suggests, the individual "feels, thinks, acts, talks and responds just as one of his parents did when he was little." This ego state is active, for example, in raising one's children. Even when we are not actually exhibiting this ego state in our transactions, it influences our behavior as the "Parental influence, performing the functions of a conscience" (pp. 11–12). The Parent is roughly equivalent to Freud's "superego."

The Adult state (A) is the most rational, reality-oriented ego state. It is "principally concerned with transforming stimuli into pieces of information, and processing and filing that information on the basis of previous experience" (Berne, 1972, p. 93). Unlike the Parent, the Adult reacts to the situation as it is actually experienced, rather than to the way it was programmed in the past. Berne uses the metaphor of the adult state as a computer, processing information without introducing distortion or neurotic bias. This state is roughly equivalent to Freud's concept of a fully developed or mature ego.

The Child state is conceptualized as the little boy or girl within us, "who feels, thinks, acts, talks, and responds just the way he or she did when he or she was a child of a certain age." Berne (1972) goes on to make an important distinction:

> The Child is not regarded as "childish" or "immature," which are Parental words, but as childlike, meaning like a child of a certain age, and the important factor here is the age, which may be anywhere between two and five years in ordinary circumstances. It is important for the individual to understand his Child, not only because it is going to be with him all his life, but also because it is the most valuable part of his personality. (p. 12)

This concept of ego states, which helps explain how transactional analysts view personality, will play an integral part in the counseling process and in the development of counseling goals.

Analyzing our relationships with others is a central part of transactional analysis. When do we function well with others and when do we function poorly? Unlike Freudian theory, which relies on its psychopathology (built on its underlying personality theory) to help explain the strength and weaknesses of inter-

The Four Life Positions

personal relationships, the contribution of TA is most dramatically represented in its concept of the *four life positions* that replace an explicit psychopathology. They are designated (Harris, 1969):

> I'M NOT OK – YOU'RE OK
> I'M NOT OK – YOU'RE NOT OK
> I'M OK – YOU'RE NOT OK, and
> I'M OK – YOU'RE OK

These "positions" are shorthand ways of describing of the way we feel in our relations with others. They describe four types of human transactions, and at the same time show developmentally how such transactions evolved. They can also be represented schematically,

> $(-, +)$
> $(-, -)$
> $(+, -)$
> $(+, +)$

The bottom position, "I'm OK, You're OK" $(+, +)$ is the healthy one—the goal of therapy. All of them, however, help us analyze how we interact (and did interact!) with the people that are (and were) most important to us.

These positions are developmental. They are associated with growth. The infant's earliest response to the world is "I'm not OK—You're OK," $(-, +)$. This means that the infant feels inadequate, incompetent, or in Adlerian terms, inferior. But it also means that the infant recognizes the world outside as more competent, as superior, as able to provide an emotional nurturance, which transactional analysts call *stroking,* even if it is not fully satisfying. As Harris (1969) describes this infantile view of the world,

> In the first position the person feels at the mercy of others. He feels a great need for stroking, or recognition, which is the psychological version of the early physical stroking. In this position there is hope because there is a source of stroking—You're OK—even if the stroking is not constant. The Adult [in this position] has something to work on: What must I do to gain their strokes, or their approval? (p. 68)

As the infant attempts to become more autonomous, he or she may evolve into the second position, "I'm not OK—You're not OK" $(-, -)$. The cause of this is the increasing independence from and lack of stroking by the parents. This is a most difficult life position, one characterized by feelings of hopelessness. Were the person to remain in this position, as unfortunately many do, life would be almost impossible. "A person in this position gives up. There is no hope" (Harris, 1969, p. 70). Unfortunately, where no opportunities for growth and warmth exist, the child may become stuck in the third position.

The next position is also pathological. "A child who is brutalized long enough by the parents he initially felt were OK will switch positions to the third, or criminal, position: I'm OK—You're not OK." This type of person suffered from not receiving enough stroking early in life, from not developing the trusting relationship with loved ones that is so necessary to feel OK about oneself. As a result, he or she develops a feeling of distrust for all around and survives only by acceding to this position, which in effect saves him or her. Harris (1969) explains,

> For this child the I'M OK—YOU'RE NOT OK position is a life-saving decision. The tragedy, for himself and for society, is that he goes through life refusing to look inward. He is unable to be objective about his own complicity in what happens to him. It is always "their fault." It's "all them.". . . The ultimate expression of this position is homicide, *felt* by the killer to be justifiable (in the same way that he felt justified in taking the position in the first place). (p. 73)

Finally, we come to the position of hopefulness, of health: "I'm OK—You're OK" (+,+). This differs from the other three positions in an important way. While they are all unconscious, arising at the early period of life as a result of child-parent interactions, this position is conscious, rational, verbal. "The first three positions," Harris (1970) maintains "are based on feelings. The fourth is based on thought, faith, and the wager of action." (p. 74)

This fourth position is expressed behaviorally through our ability to have successful interpersonal relationships, to feel good about ourselves, to feel we deserve the best, and to be capable of getting the best for ourselves. It is roughly equivalent to Freud's ideal of full psychosexual development and sublimation. In the following section, we will look more closely at how this life position can be developed through the TA therapy process.

"The basic interest of transactional analysis," Eric Berne (1972) suggests, "is the study of ego states" (p. 11). Most of the theory and techniques of TA counseling revolve around this process, which is called *structural analysis*. The methods of TA were developed in order to facilitate the analysis of ego states. The process is diagrammatic and presumably precise.

The TA Counseling Process

The transactional analyst believes the therapeutic process should help the client get in touch with his or her feelings. Claude Steiner (1984), one of the leading theoreticians in TA, has conceptualized this goal as an important concept, called *emotional literacy,* which he defines as the ability to experience all of one's emotions with appropriate intensities and to be able to understand what is causing the feelings. The TA process, consisting, as we shall see, of the analysis of ego states and specific exercises to increase emotional literacy, is guided by this principle. The process of analysis is simple. For convenience, a diagrammatic representation of the three ego states is shown in Figure 9.2.

Figure 9.2. The ego states: Parent (P), Adult (A), and Child (C)

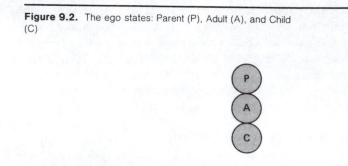

Figure 9.3. Complementary transactions are represented by parallel lines. The top line represents the stimulus communication and the bottom line the response. For example, in (a), Parent to Parent, a husband tells his wife he will take her out to her favorite restaurant for dinner and she responds that he treats her very well—he is a good husband. In (b), Adult to Adult, Jack asks Jerry who won the ball game, and Jerry answers that the Pirates won, 3 to 1. In (c), Child to Child, Paula tells Joy she wants to cut school and Joy says, "That's a great idea. Let's hang out at the park today."

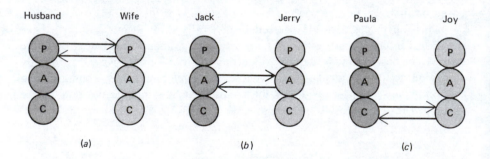

Transactions between two people may be complementary or crossed. They are complementary when the lines representing the transaction are parallel, as in Figure 9.3. This type of interaction indicates that a person is responding from the level from which he or she is being addressed. But a transaction may also be crossed; that is, the person responds on a level other than that on which he or she is addressed. If Bob's Adult addresses Gene's Child ("I'll be happy to loan you this book when I'm done with it"), and Gene responds through his Child ("Oh sure, you always have to read everything first so you're up one on me"), it would look like Figure 9.4. On the other hand, if Sue's Parent addresses Lydia's Child

Figure 9.4. A crossed transaction occurs when the stimulus communication and the response are not parallel. Here we see a crossed transaction between Bob and Gene.

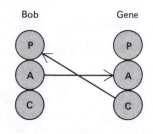

Figure 9.5. In this crossed transaction, Sue's Parent addresses Lydia's Child, and Lydia's Adult then responds to Sue's Adult.

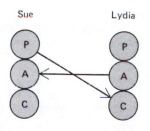

("You always think you can get away with things, but just wait . . . everyone gets what they deserve in the end"), and Lydia's Adult responds in turn to Sue's Adult ("My observation is that people don't always get what they deserve"), it would look like Figure 9.5.

Altogether, there are 72 possible types of crossed interaction, but Berne and others agree that there are actually only four of real significance. Berne (1972) classifies these as types: "Type I (AA-CP), the transference reaction; and Type II (AA-PC), the counter-transference reaction; Type III (CP-AA), the 'exasperating response,' where someone who wants sympathy gets facts instead, and Type IV (PC-AA), 'impudence,' where someone who expects compliance gets what he considers a 'smart aleck' response instead, in the form of a factual statement" (p. 17). The preceding illustration is a Type IV interaction.

The TA counseling process begins by examining all the transactions and determining what level they are on. Are they complementary or crossed? Does the person have a particular pattern that permeates his or her interactions with others? From this, a great deal of information can be attained and used to help the client reach more mature functioning; i.e., more adult-adult interactions.

Strokes, Games, and Scripts

Three important TA concepts in understanding the counseling interaction are *strokes, games,* and *scripts.*

On its most superficial level, a stroke is a unit of recognition, such as saying Hello to someone. But more significantly, on its deeper level, stroking is the process demonstrated by the mother caring for her infant. Stroking is a sign of concern, of caring for another.

Throughout our lives, we are stroked by others through their recognition and treatment of us. If we are not sufficiently stroked, we suffer from one of the not-OK positions discussed above.

The concept of games helps us better understand stroking. As the structural analysis is being conducted, the transactional analyst tries to figure out what kind of games the client is playing. The concept of games is of prime importance, for it reveals how people are communicating and what they are trying to get out of their relationships. Goldhaber and Goldhaber (1976) explain the transactional concept of game this way:

> A game is a complementary, ulterior transaction leading to a payoff. The complementary transaction enables the game and its communication to continue until completion. The ulterior transaction enables the game players to hide their real meanings. And the payoff enables the players to justify their reasons for playing. (pp. 137–138)

In short, then, a game is a way of cooperatively interacting on a superficial level for the purpose of concealing the real meaning of the interaction on a deeper level.

If the game is a way of understanding the short-term interaction, a more long-ranging analysis is done through explicating the script, or *lifescript.* "A script," according to Berne (1972), "is an ongoing program, developed in early childhood under parental influence, which directs the individual's behavior in the most important aspects of his life" (p. 418). Scripts contain many cultural and familial elements—as if each script were written by many coauthors, each putting in his or her individual say. For instance, a script may contain many cultural characteristics ("Democracy is good, so I am to be a democratic person in my dealings with others") which combine with personal characteristics, learned from the parents ("I am a good boy").

People play out their scripts through the many different games they play. There is always a central theme to the person's script, and this theme reveals the nexus of a person's life choices and problems. The transactional analyst then addresses herself or himself to these problems, trying to help the patient rewrite the script, making it better for his or her life.

Goals

If we look for the specific goals of transactional analysis as a counseling approach, we find them expressed through the concepts we have just described.

First, the transactional analyst analyzes the structural interactions. Diagrams may be made of how the person is relating to others through the P-A-C paradigm.

Second, these structural analyses are interpreted in terms of the client's unique life script. This may include such things as the need for stroking. Games are pointed out as they are played, and their implication in the person's life script is explored. Transactional analysts have given commonly played games their own names (such as RAPO) to quickly identify a series of transactions.

Finally, the client, through his or her script analysis, is taught how to function on the mature adult level. This involves making the client more aware of how he or she is functioning, followed by cognitive-affective restructuring through the changing of certain essential elements in the script.

We see, then, that as we look at TA in these conceptual terms, it is clearly a cognitive-dynamic counseling approach in that it holds to the axiom that a certain level of rational functioning (expressed by the interaction AA-AA) is the epitome of psychological health and the goal of the counseling.

Transactional analysis offers several advantages as a counseling application. **Evaluation of TA** It is conducive to short-term treatment, works well in a large variety of settings, can easily be adapted to group counseling, and provides opportunities even in brief-term treatment for developing effective problem-solving skills along with insight and personality change (Jensen, Baker & Koepp, 1980). Most useful, from a practical point of view, is the fact that even counselors who do not view themselves primarily as practitioners of transactional analysis can integrate many aspects of it into their practices. Mellecker (1976) points out that TA offers all counselors, regardless of orientation, "rewarding techniques for graphing characterizations of [their] counselees which can serve as baselines for charting progress as it occurs" (p. 197).

During the 1970s and 1980s, as counselors-in-training at the many university counseling departments where partisans of TA dominated entered the ranks of professional counselors, more and more articles began to appear in the professional journals suggesting new ways of interpreting common problems and showing innovative applications of TA in a variety of settings.

Since the 1970s, more than one hundred studies have demonstrated the value of TA for different clinical applications and settings. Every few years, one case or another is published that hints at new problems treatable by TA. Bonds-White (1984), for example, has shown that TA is particularly applicable in treating the passive-aggressive personality. She argues that such individuals are locked into patterns of helplessness and frustration, and suggests a four-stage treatment plan consisting of (1) relationship building, (2) contract setting, (3) permission giving, and (4) redecision.

Rumney and Steckel (1985) have used TA in treating anorexia nervosa. Using a "reparenting" approach and working with diagrams of the client's ego states, they help her center on her fears of growing up and starting a new career. James (1984) has applied TA concepts to grandparenting, showing how grandparents can be emotional facilitators for the entire family.

Summary   In this chapter we examined three indigenous American counseling approaches: rational-emotive therapy, cognitive therapy, reality therapy, and transactional analysis. While they differ substantially from each other, each emphasizes the cognitive, or rational, dimensions of emotional conflicts as central to our understanding of their causes and treatment. Each also argues that logical approaches to treating maladaptive behavior is empirically superior to psychodynamic approaches.

Rational-emotive therapy (RET), developed by Albert Ellis, is based on the assumption that healthy functioning can be guided by and consistent with reasonable, logical principles of thought. As we grow up we get into trouble by being taught illogical ideas, which distort our thinking, impair our logic, and impede our functioning. The rational-emotive counselor attempts directively to *correct* the counselee's misconceptions by pointing out their illogicalities and by jolting the client emotionally into new recognitions. The techniques in RET are designed to change the client's basic philosophy of life—to offer the client new, more constructive ways of living.

Cognitive counseling has gained wide acceptance because of its emphasis on changing a client's unproductive thoughts by combining a variety of behavioral, rational, and psychodynamic techniques. The cognitive counselor "collaborates" with the client to form a therapeutic alliance that enables the client's underlying belief system to change. Techniques discussed include: changing automatic thoughts; inductive questioning; imagery; role playing, keeping a daily record; and discovering the meaning of events.

Reality therapy, developed by William Glasser, asserts that individuals are guided by two pervasive psychological motives which help explain all their behaviors: the need to love and be loved, and the need to feel worthwhile. Problems arise in life as one is unable to satisfy these basic needs in a way that is reality oriented. To the reality counselor, an appropriate, socially-acceptable standard of behavior is integral to feeling positive about oneself. The reality counselor acts as a teacher, helping the client learn values that are helpful to living and pointing out to the client his or her errors of judgment that are leading to the difficulties.

Transactional analysis, developed by Eric Berne, is a derivative of the psychodynamic approaches. It is a rational approach insofar as it offers a schematic ego structure in which to explain behavior. It posits three ego states—Parent, Adult, and Child—and the interactions between people are diagrammed according to these states. The TA counselor analyzes these transactions with the goal of helping the client reach more adult states of interaction. The concepts of strokes, games, and scripts are used to understand some of the complexities of the counseling process and human growth.

Chapter Aim

To present the major paradigms of behavioral counseling, including classical conditioning, operant conditioning, systematic desensitization, implosion therapy, and modeling. To provide an outline of steps for setting up a behavior modification program.

10

The behavior modification approaches derive from behavioral psychology, developed by John B. Watson and Edward L. Thorndike in the early years of this century. Behaviorism emphasized using observable, measurable behavior as the basis of psychology and introduced the stimulus-response relationship in interpreting behavior patterns. Thorndike developed a "connectionist psychology" of learning based on a principle he called the "law of effect." Using many of the principles developed by Watson and Thorndike, B. F. Skinner then formulated the principles of operant conditioning.

Background

The behavioral counselor views the individual as a product of his or her conditioning. The two main types of conditioning are classical (respondent) and operant (instrumental). Classical conditioning involves the pairing of an unconditioned with a conditioned stimulus, so that the response associated with the unconditioned becomes associated with the conditioned. Operant conditioning requires that the subject respond to a stimulus, and that the response be reinforced. Behavioral counselors, it is pointed out, do not necessarily hold a mechanistic view of the person, and Skinner particularly has argued against the restrictive view of the client as an "empty organism."

View of the Person

The behavioral counselor's principal task is to design a program through which specified target behaviors will be modified. This involves working out a contract with the client, outlining the client's responsibility, and assessing at different stages the effect of the program.

Role of the Behavioral Counselor

Techniques and Goals

The salient techniques of behavioral counseling (in addition to classical and operant conditioning) are presented. Systematic desensitization involves the client imagining, vicariously, anxiety-evoking stimuli in a hierarchical order, while the counselor presents relaxing, anxiety-inhibiting stimuli at the same time. Implosive counseling requires the subject to vividly fantasize anxiety-evoking images until they are neutralized. Extinction involves breaking an established response pattern by not reinforcing it. Specific types of operant conditioning models (reinforcement approaches) are then discussed. Three other techniques—shaping, modeling, and time-out—are covered briefly.

Evaluation and Applications

Although behavior modification has been criticized for not recognizing the "human dimension" of the client, it has been shown to be effective in treating a wide variety of symptomatic problems.

Behavioral
Approaches

10

The behavioral approaches to counseling differ substantially from the other counseling approaches we have examined. For unlike the other approaches we have looked at, behavioral counseling does not utilize as the fundamental principle the axiom that the client improves by talking; nor does it emphasize the importance of the counseling relationship. Instead, behavioral counseling comprises a body of related approaches held together by the common belief that *emotional, learning, and adjustment difficulties can be treated through a variety of prescriptive, mechanical, usually nondynamic, techniques and procedures.* While the other modalities we have looked at could be called either "internalistic," focusing as they do on the inner person, or "rational," focusing on objective parameters of logic and reality, the behavioral approaches could be called "external determinism," focusing on the environmental factors that shape the individual's behaviors (Mahoney, 1977). In this chapter we shall explore the origins of behavioral counseling and survey its present applications in a wide variety of settings.

The various (and sometimes conflicting) approaches which make up behavioral counseling were each introduced by an important and innovative seminal thinker who was disturbed by the status quo. While the philosophical and psychological premises of the behavioral approach can be traced to the empirical philosopher John Locke, the psychological foundation of the behavioral approach—the groundwork that led to the subsequent systematic exposition of the theory—was set down at the beginning of this century in the United States. Two important figures who should be acknowledged are John B. Watson and Edward L. Thorndike.

Much of contemporary behavioral counseling derives from the system of psychology called "behaviorism," which was expounded by an American psychologist, John B. Watson, in 1913. Watson was attempting to develop what he called an "objective psychology," one that would deal only with the observable behavior

Background

of the organism and avoid probing into what he considered to be the subjectivity of mental activity, which he felt deprived psychology of its scientific basis. He considered objective observation of the organism the only valid method of psychological investigation.

Watson (1913) begins by arguing that the dominant psychology of his time (Wundt's introspectionism) was too bound up with philosophy and religion; that it was lacking the scientific integrity necessary to make it an effective and practical study. He goes on to suggest that for psychology to become truly scientific it must rely solely on observable behavior as its subject matter, and it must "attempt to formulate, through systematic observation and experimentation, the generalizations, laws, and principles which underly man's behavior" (Watson, 1924).

"As a science," he continues, "psychology puts before herself the task of unravelling the complex factors involved in the development of human behavior from infancy to old age, and of finding the laws for the regulation of behavior." To help formulate these laws, he explicates the concepts of *stimulus* and *response* and the law that from any given stimulus we can deduce a predictable response. This idea—that each stimulus is linked up to a response—has become the basic rule of behavioral psychology and behavioral counseling.

Watson applied the principles of experimental psychology to human behavior problems. In 1920, Watson and his associate Rosalind Rayner reported a clinical example of a phobia being induced by methods of conditioning. They took an eleven-month-old boy, Albert, and taught him to be fearful of white rats. They did this by emitting a loud, frightening noise whenever Albert reached out to touch the rat, which he was not initially frightened of. After a few of these trials, the boy developed a fear whenever he saw the rat, even if the noise was no longer emitted. Ultimately, he acquired a phobia for all furry objects, apparently generalizing the fear of the rat to these other objects as well.

What is most important about this experiment is that if such a fear can be instilled through conditioning, then it can also be removed by conditioning. In fact this is exactly what happened. Four years later, Mary Cover Jones used these same principles in reverse to cure the phobia of a three-year-old boy, thus providing the first clinical example of behavioral principles applied to the treatment situation.

A decade earlier, Edward L. Thorndike had conducted a series of notable experiments in psychology which influenced Watson's thinking and the course of behaviorism. In one famous study, he put a hungry cat into a cage that was constructed in such a way that the cat could trigger a mechanism to allow him access to food that was immediately outside the grating of the cage. At first the cat tried to force his way out of the cage in order to get at the food. He struggled in vain, continually repelled by the inflexibility of the steel grating. Finally, by accident he triggered the mechanism that allowed him to leave the cage and obtain the food. After a brief interval, he was placed back in the cage and the situation was repeated. Thorndike observed that the cat gradually learned the relationship between triggering the mechanism, leaving the cage, and obtaining the food. After many such repetitions, the cat could immediately trigger his release after he was placed in the cage.

Thorndike called the principle that was at work here the "law of effect." Simply, this law states that an act that is reinforced positively will tend to be repeated, and an act that is reinforced negatively will tend to be avoided. Thorndike developed and refined this law into his comprehensive *connectionist psychology,* which stated that the individual makes connections between external and internal events and that these connections lead to goal-directed behavior.

One of Thorndike's major contributions to behaviorism is found in his concept of punishment. While he conceded that behavior is shaped by both reward and punishment, it is the former that produces a far more satisfying and productive result. "The strengthening of a connection by satisfying consequences seems," Thorndike (1949) said "to be more universal, inevitable, and direct than the weakening of a connection by annoying consequences" (p. 37). Punishment for its own sake, he went on, is of little value. It is only when the punishment is coupled with something positive that it becomes a viable learning tool. This is a view that is generally still held in high regard by behavioral counselors.

Although the research of Thorndike and Watson became the groundwork for behavioral psychology, other "neobehaviorists" expanded the research and applications of behavioral principles. Clark L. Hull and E. C. Tolman developed highly sophisticated theories of learning based on the behavioral model. But it wasn't until the landmark laboratory work of B. F. Skinner that behavioral psychology—and particularly behavior modification—became as influential as it ultimately did.

Skinner was born in Susquehanna, Pennsylvania, in 1904. He came from a middle-class family, and from his earliest years Skinner was an avid reader. He had his heart set on becoming a poet and writer when he set off for Hamilton College in upstate New York. He showed considerable writing talent, but after undergraduate school, as his plans to write professionally were frustrated, his interest turned increasingly to psychology. In 1928, after living a Bohemian life in New York's Greenwich Village, Skinner was accepted at the Harvard Graduate School of Psychology. Thus began the career that would influence the course of American psychology for almost half a century.

During the 1930s, Skinner set forth some of the assumptions that would influence his thinking for the next fifty years. He strongly rejected the psychoanalytic notion that behavior problems were the result of unconscious conflicts, arguing instead that drive and motivation are not intrinsic to the person but the result of outside stimulation and training. Skinner also expounded the basic idea of *operant conditioning,* a method through which the subject is conditioned by changing the consequences of his behavior. As positive behavior is rewarded and negative behavior punished, argued Skinner, the subject learns to behave more positively. Skinner conducted a series of animal experiments, usually with rats as subjects, and he is well known for his invention of the Skinner box, which is actually a training maze. His novel, *Walden Two*, attempts to portray a utopian social system, based on his principles of learning and conditioning. In 1976, he published his autobiography, *Particulars of My Life*.

View of the Person

To the behavioral counselor, the individual is a product of conditioning. The behaviorist speaks of the S-R paradigm as the basic pattern of all human learning. Each person reacts in a predictable way to any given stimulus, depending on his or her training. "Behavioral counselors . . . are not concerned with inner states but rather with how the integrated organism behaves. Change to the behaviorist means change in *behavior*. . . . Understanding the nature of the problem is not enough; clients must arrange with the counselor step-by-step processes to change responses or to develop new responses" (Ewing, 1977, p. 336). Behavioral counselors, of course, realize that observable behavior itself does not adequately explain the *totality* of human nature, so they have set forth a number of concepts to explain the legion of processes through which learning and behavioral change take place.

The key word underlying their view of the person is *conditioning*. Although there are several types of conditioning, two basic classes are usually discussed: *classical* (respondent) conditioning and *operant* (instrumental) conditioning (see Figure 10.1). Classical conditioning always involves the pairing of stimuli. One of the paired stimuli elicits a response that either has already been learned or one that doesn't have to be learned. For instance, if you are given a shock and you jump up, this is a response that never had to be learned; it is autonomic. But, you may also receive a stimulus, such as a four-letter word, which causes you to wince. This response was learned many years ago, but is now natural and much like the autonomic response of jumping to a shock. In either case, this stimulus elicits a natural immediate response. We call this stimulus the *unconditioned* stimulus, commonly abbreviated UCS. The response it elicits is called the *unconditioned* response, or UCR. The term *unconditioned* is used since the stimulus and response are natural and require no training.

But as we stated, in classical conditioning there are always two stimuli *paired* together. The other stimulus can be neutral and elicit either no specific response or one that is different than the UCR. This is called the conditioned stimulus, commonly abbreviated CS. Levis (1970) clearly explains the classical conditioning paradigm and how it differs from operant conditioning:

Descriptively, the classical conditioning paradigm differs from the instrumental procedure in that the sequence of events presented is *independent* of the subject's behavior. This sequence consists of an unconditioned stimulus (UCS), a stimulus known to evoke a regular and measurable response (UCR), and the conditioned stimulus (CS), a stimulus which at the outset of the experiment does not evoke the UCR. The usual order of the sequence is to present the CS followed closely in time by the UCS. The regular and mea-

Figure 10.1. Classical (respondent) and operant (instrumental) conditioning.

Classical conditioning

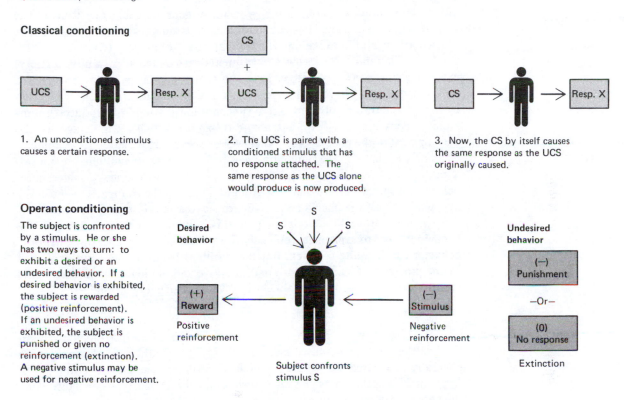

1. An unconditioned stimulus causes a certain response.

2. The UCS is paired with a conditioned stimulus that has no response attached. The same response as the UCS alone would produce is now produced.

3. Now, the CS by itself causes the same response as the UCS originally caused.

Operant conditioning

The subject is confronted by a stimulus. He or she has two ways to turn: to exhibit a desired or an undesired behavior. If a desired behavior is exhibited, the subject is rewarded (positive reinforcement). If an undesired behavior is exhibited, the subject is punished or given no reinforcement (extinction). A negative stimulus may be used for negative reinforcement.

surable response elicited by the UCS is called the unconditioned response (UCR). If conditioning occurs, the CS presentation will elicit a conditioned response (CR) which resembles the UCR and which occurs prior to or in the absence of UCS presentations. (p. 15)

This is the type of conditioning illustrated in Pavlov's famous experiment with the dog. As you may recall, Pavlov discovered, while studying digestion in animals, that if a bell rang immediately before a dog was fed, after a time the ringing of the bell itself would cause the dog to salivate. The pairing of the ringing bell (conditioned stimulus) and the feeding (unconditioned stimulus) caused the dog to respond to the bell by salivating.

Likewise, a number of the basic learning experiences of the average individual can be explained through the classical conditioning paradigm. Most important of these experiences, from the counselor's point of view, are the maladaptive or neurotic learning experiences. Eysenck and Rachman (1965) have suggested a three-stage explanation of the development of abnormal behavior.

Behavioral Approaches   277

The first stage involves a series of traumatic events that produce autonomic reactions in the individual. These autonomic reactions are considered as unconditioned responses, which in turn may result in neurotic behavior patterns. The second stage utilizes the classical conditioning paradigm directly. This stage is particularly useful in explaining the generalization of anxiety to unhealthy proportions. The final stage involves instrumental avoidance of painful or anxiety-provoking situations. Let us consider, as an example, a boy who has developed a fear of dogs. It may have begun with a traumatic incident in which he was bitten by a dog. The trauma of being bitten (unconditioned stimulus) produced an immediate body reaction (pain-autonomic response), which set the stage for the development of the phobia. Now, whenever he sees a dog (conditioned stimulus), he associates this with the traumatic event and runs away (conditioned response). Running away from dogs and avoiding them (operant avoidance) produces a relief of his original anxiety that was brought about by the traumatic event in the first place. Thus, the phobia and avoidance serve as a *reinforcing stimulus*.

As we see from this description (and this is only one of many paradigms the behaviorists use to explain neurotic behavior), the mechanics of learning neurotic behavior can be quite complex. But the resultant behavior is always explained by the processes of learning that are descriptive and predictable and that, in the classical conditioning models, always involve the pairing of stimuli.

Operant Conditioning

The second major class of conditioning is operant or instrumental conditioning; the terms can be used interchangeably. This is the type of conditioning generally associated with the work of B. F. Skinner. The term *operant* comes from combining the words *operate* and *environment*. In this type of conditioning, the person's actions produce a consequence that either increases or decreases the probability of the behavior recurring. Skinner (1974) uses the term *reinforcement* to describe this process.

> The standard distinction between operant and reflex behavior is that one is voluntary and the other involuntary. Operant behavior is felt to be under the control of the behaving person and has traditionally been attributed to an act of will. Reflex behavior, on the other hand, is not under comparable control. (p. 44)

Consider, for example, what happens in a simple Skinner box. In this contraption, an animal is taught to push a lever and is rewarded with food (*positive reinforcement*). This pattern of behavior eventually becomes learned. The learning principle behind operant conditioning is that new learning occurs as a result of positive reinforcement, and old patterns are abandoned as a result of the lack of reinforcement, or because of punishment.

It would be unfair to imply that the entire behavioral view of the person is dominated solely by these mechanistic learning theories. True, the concepts of reinforcement and stimulus-pairing play a key role in the explanation of how human behavior is learned; but the behaviorists also recognize that other factors play a vital role as well. Carter and Stuart (1970), in responding to a highly critical assessment of the behavioral approach, argue that "the common accusation that behaviorists explain all behavior in terms of learning history is inaccurate. Behaviorists [also] recognize as well the impact of physiology and contemporary events" (p. 44).

Speaking in an interview, Skinner (1976) made clear how his position goes beyond the constraints of S-R psychology:

Let me emphasize first that I do not consider myself an S-R psychologist. As it stands, I'm not sure that response is a very useful concept. Behavior is very fluid: it isn't made up of lots of little responses packed together. The stimulating environment is important among the variables of which behavior is a function, but it is by no means the only one. It is a mistake to suppose that there are internal stimuli and to try to formulate everything as S-R psychology. . . . I think, however, that the problem goes deeper than that. If the "O" represents the organism, then the question arises, How important is the O? I guess I'm even more opposed to postulating the influence of O than I am to the strict S-R formulation. As I see it, psychology is concerned with establishing relations between the behavior of an organism and the forces acting upon it. Now the organism must be there . . . I don't really believe in an "empty organism." (p. 85)

We can see that the criticism of the "empty organism," the argument that the "totality" of the client as a person is not considered which is often lodged against behaviorists such as Skinner, is unjust when we look directly at his own writings. The behavioral counselor, as much as anyone else, recognizes the human side of the client, but approaches the problems besetting the client from a scientific, empirical standpoint.

The Role of the Counselor

Before we can appreciate the role of the behavioral counselor, we must understand the responsibilities of the client (which differ from the client's expected role in other approaches) and the full meaning of the term *behavior modification*. Let us consider each of these individually.

The Client

The primary task of the client in behavioral counseling is to learn new responses to old situations. The client may be asked to do a number of things. For example, he or she may be asked to provide the counselor with a list of the stimulus situations that provoke the greatest anxiety. In order to be conditioned to respond in a healthy and appropriate way to anxiety-evoking stimuli, it may at times be necessary for the client to expose himself or herself directly to those stimuli, no matter how painful the anticipation of exposure may be. A client who has difficulty asserting himself or herself may be taught to do so in the counseling setting and then rewarded for his or her successful attempts (positive reinforcement).

The role of the behavioral counselor is confined primarily to dealing with the client's *observable* behavior. Unlike the psychodynamic and humanistic counselors we have discussed, the behavioral counselor makes little attempt to probe and explore the "inner reaches" of the psyche. On the contrary, she or he avoids such excursions, considering them irrelevant to the task at hand. Michael and Meyerson (1962) emphasize the point that to the behavioral counselor, "Conceptual formulations such as ego-strength, inferiority feelings, or self-concept are not behavior but simply ways of organizing and interpreting observable behavior by referring it to an inner determiner" (p. 395).

Although the behavioral counselor is limited to dealing with observable behavior, it is agreed that much of this observable behavior will touch upon the realm of feelings. But the counselor's manner of approaching feelings, and changing them, requires direct interventions in the behavior itself. These interventions are known as *behavior modification approaches*.

The Modification of Behavior

Behavior modification can be broadly defined as any procedure or set of procedures designed to change an individual's behavior through the use of any of the conditioning or modeling paradigms. This definition suggests that the *goal* of any behavior modification program is to change behavior. Does this mean that the individual has to act differently after the program than he or she did before? Yes and no. We would expect that if the problem that the individual entered the program with is a behavioral problem, then the specific behavior will be changed by the end of the program. On the other hand, if we are trying to teach children to be less aggressive, not only would we expect their behaviors to change, but we would also expect their attitudes, beliefs, and feelings to change as well. In such a situation, we would be speaking about more than behavior itself; we would be speaking about feelings, perceptions, cognitions.

Most simply, behavior modification is a way of "influencing" a person. The sphere of influence may extend only to behavior or far beyond behavior, into other realms. The single factor that holds behavior modification together is the belief that the present environment is a greater force on the person than are past experiences (Skinner, 1975). The scientific manipulation of variables in the environment becomes the art of behavioral psychology. "Most behavior modification procedures are based on the general principle that people are influenced by the consequences of their behavior. Behavior modification assumes that the current environment is more relevant in affecting an individual's behavior than most early life experiences, enduring intra-psychic conflicts, or personality structure. Insofar as possible, *the behaviorally oriented mental health worker limits the conceptualization of the problem to observable behavior and its environmental context*" (Stolz, Wienckowski, & Brown, 1975, p. 1028).

The determining concept in thinking about any kind of behavior modification program is that it is a *planned* intervention, with a specific goal stated at the outset. The fact that we happen to do something, and as a result of our action the person's behavior changes, does not make our intervention necessarily behavior modification. On the contrary, lacking in such a case is the most essential element of behavior modification: the *planned goal* of the intervention.

John D. Krumboltz (1965), a leading proponent of the behavioral counseling approach, makes two important points regarding the role of the behavioral counselor. First, he suggests that "the central purpose of counseling is to help each client resolve those problems for which he requests help" (p. 383). This involves the setting up of a contract and the statement of goals. Second, he suggests that when operant conditioning is in use, the counselor's ability to time the reinforcements maximally can be the critical variable between success and failure. Krumboltz (1966b) also emphasizes the important principles that "we learn to do those things which produce certain kinds of desirable conditions . . . [and] the attention and approval of a counselor might have reinforcing effects for a client, especially if the client feels that the counselor understands his problem and can do something to help" (Introduction).

Techniques and Goals

Behavioral counseling is clearly the most technique-oriented of all the counseling approaches we have studied. Because the quality of the counseling relationship is de-emphasized, and because the main priority is the resolution of the client's symptoms, the behavioral counselor relies heavily on a repertoire of empirical techniques to deal with each specific problem. It should also be mentioned that although in other systems the counselor's technique may be considered a part of the counselor's personality or emotional disposition (see chapter 2 for a full discussion of theory and technique), in behavioral counseling the employment of a technique is independent of the counselor's feelings, beliefs, and personality. Behavioral techniques are prescriptive operational procedures designed to achieve certain specifiable ends.

The behavioral techniques are all derived from models in learning theory, with the assumption that emotional growth requires new learning patterns. As we examine each of these techniques, therefore, we will note that there is at work a learning principle applied to a psychological-behavior problem.

Respondent Conditioning Techniques

Techniques using respondent conditioning always involve the pairing of stimuli, as described earlier in this chapter. In the counseling setting, the counselor's job is to decide which stimuli to pair in order to effect the desired changes. This may require innovative apparatus, or it may be direct and simple. In a landmark experiment, Mowrer and Mowrer (1938) treated a case of enuresis (bedwetting) using classical conditioning methods. Willis and Giles (1976) summarize the procedure used:

> Treatment was based on Pavlovian or classical conditioning principles. The goal was to associate waking up with a full bladder. To accomplish this association, a special mattress pad was developed which basically consisted of two pieces of bronze screening separated by a piece of absorbent cloth. When wet, however, the pad became a good conductor and closed a circuit that included a battery and an electric doorbell.

The bell served as an unconditioned stimulus for awakening. When the pad was placed on the child's bed, the ringing of the bell coincided with the beginning of bed wetting and with a relatively full bladder.

The child was instructed to get up when the bell rang and go to the bathroom. In theory, a full bladder, which occurs at the same time as the ringing bell, would become a conditioned stimulus for awakening.

The apparatus was used nightly until seven successive dry nights occurred. Then the child was given one or more cups of water more than normal just before going to bed. When seven more consecutive dry nights occurred, use of the apparatus was discontinued. (p. 27)

We see from this example how the basic classical conditioning model, unaltered, can be used to change an unhealthy symptom. In practice, however, there are more sophisticated applications of the classical conditioning paradigm. One of the most widely used is systematic desensitization.

Operant Conditioning Techniques

Operant conditioning, in its various forms, is probably the single most popular behavior modification paradigm. Whereas in classical conditioning it is the *pairing* of stimuli that elicits new responses from the subject, in operant conditioning it is the *reinforcement* that follows the subject's responses that determines the new behaviors that are to be formed. Some of the client's responses (behaviors) are reinforced; that is, they are strengthened. Others are not. It is the combination of these that changes behavior.

Reinforcement Programs

In psychological context, a reinforcer is anything that increases the probability of a response. Sometimes called a reinforcing stimulus, the reinforcer is some kind of reward that either strengthens a response or increases its frequency of occurrence. "A reinforcing stimulus," Lindsley (1971) points out, "is the powerful thing which builds behavior." He goes on to suggest that we can think of reinforcers in terms of *accelerating* or *decelerating* responses. In this way, we see directly their relationship to behaviors.

Operant conditioning programs always involve instrumental learning. "The essential feature of the instrumental learning paradigm," McLaughlin (1971) points out, "is that the response is instrumental in the achievement of a goal. If a hungry organism is offered a choice of equally attractive responses, only one of which leads to food, the tendency will inevitably be to make the response that leads to food once the consequences of each response are known" (p. 52). The subject operates on the environment (hence, operant conditioning), and his or her choices result in certain predictable consequences. This is the fundamental principle underlying all operant conditioning reinforcement programs.

The ultimate success or failure of any operant conditioning program is determined by the kind of reinforcers used, the planned intervals of reinforcement, and the consistency of reinforcement. Let us consider each of these important areas.

Since a reinforcer must serve to strengthen behavior, it is imperative that we select a reinforcer that will have precisely this effect on the subject. Let's say that we want John and Ellen to do certain tasks that we do not feel they will be willing to do. To encourage them, we offer John a ticket to the Rams game and we offer Ellen a ticket to the ballet as rewards for performing the tasks. This may be well and good if John likes football and if Ellen likes ballet, but it just so happens that John is an avid ballet aficionado and Ellen a passionate football fan. We see that we have chosen inappropriate reinforcers for each of them; that we were incorrectly influenced by sex-role stereotypes; and that therefore the likelihood of either performing the task is greatly diminished. The point is this: *it is important that we select the correct reinforcer for any individual—the reinforcer that will be most appropriate for him or her.*

We used in this example a ticket for an event. We could have also chosen a candy bar, a dinner at a French restaurant, money, or any other concrete thing that directly gives pleasure. These are called "primary reinforcers." In many cases, however, we do not use a reinforcer that is so direct, but rather, we use something like praise, a smile, an encouraging remark. These are called "secondary reinforcers." They have value insofar as they have been associated in the past with primary reinforcers, and they retain this value for many years. If you recall that your parents gave you candy when they said you were good, then being told you are good will have a positive effect even if no candy is given many years later. In both cases, it is necessary that we select the correct reinforcer for the individual. With primary reinforcers, it is easier to determine exactly what the individual likes: John could have been asked if he preferred a ballgame or a ballet, as could have Ellen. With secondary reinforcers, however, it is sometimes more difficult to determine the appropriate reinforcement of an individual. As Krumboltz and Thoresen (1969) point out, "Words of praise or approval cannot be used with the assurance that they will always be effective reinforcers" (p. 26). It is necessary, they go on to suggest, that the counselor test out reinforcers, since the selection of reinforcers is of critical importance in effectively strengthening or weakening certain behaviors. One of the most direct ways of doing this is by asking the client what will best serve as a reward or punishment.

Positive Reinforcement

Positive reinforcement is probably the most widely used and the most successful of all the behavior modification techniques. This approach simply involves providing a reward for a positive behavior. The reward (positive reinforcer) can be anything ranging from a token that can be used to purchase goods, to a star in one's book, to a verbal compliment, to a smile. The principle underlying positive reinforcement is that *the tendency to repeat a response to a given stimulus will be strengthened as the response is rewarded.*

The counselor who wishes to use positive reinforcement is confronted at the outset by a number of questions. Which behaviors should be rewarded? What type of reward should be used and how frequently should it be dispensed? Should the positive reinforcement be combined with another technique, such as extinction, punishment, or modeling? What is probably most important for the counselor to remember is that positive reinforcement is used all the time, even if we are not aware that we are using it. So long as we respond with a variety of responses, we are reinforcing some behaviors more than others.

Negative Reinforcement and Punishment

The terms *negative reinforcement* and *punishment* are often used interchangeably. However, they are not the same. It is necessary to understand the distinction because they are used in different ways, for different purposes. Greer and Dorow (1976) describe negative reinforcement as "the process whereby the removal of an ongoing event acts to increase a behavior" (p. 66). They give the example of "the seat belt warning buzzer [an unpleasant stimulus] which continues to sound until the seat belt is buckled [the desired behavior]." In general, a negative reinforcer is any unpleasant stimulus presented to a person to encourage a desirable behavior that is designed to escape or to avoid the unpleasant stimulus.

Punishment, on the other hand, is used *after* a behavior has occurred. Whereas negative reinforcement involves the *removal* of a negative stimulus, punishment involves the presentation of it. If the parent scolds the child who is caught stealing from the cookie jar, this is a form of punishment. Skinner (1974) offers a clear differentiation between the functional roles of punishment and negative reinforcement:

> Punishment is designed to remove behavior from a repertoire, whereas negative reinforcement generates behavior. Punishing contingencies are just the reverse of reinforcing. When a person spanks a child or threatens to spank him because he has misbehaved, he is presenting a negative reinforcer rather than removing one, and when a government fines an offender or puts him in prison, it is removing a positive reinforcer . . . rather than presenting a negative one. (p. 69)

In many cases, negative reinforcement and punishment are used in tandem to increase the probability of eliminating undesirable behaviors. Most studies have shown that positive reinforcement, combined with punishment, is more effective than punishment alone.

Extinction

"When a learned response is repeated without reinforcement the strength of the tendency to perform that response undergoes a progressive decrease" (Dollard & Miller, 1950). This is the simplest definition of extinction. Let us say that a teacher has been giving a star to each student who hands in a neat homework assignment. When the teacher's supply of stars runs out, he or she forgets to buy a new box. After a period of time, according to the theory of extinction, the students will be less likely to hand in neat assignments because the reinforcement they had been receiving is no longer there. "The rate of extinction," Bandura (1969) points out,

> is governed by a number of factors, among them the irregularity with which the behavior was reinforced in the past, the amount of effort required to perform it, the level of deprivation present during extinction, the ease with which changes in conditions of reinforcement can be discerned, and the availability of alternative modes of response. Because of the diversity of the controlling variables, a number of different theoretical conceptualizations of extinction have been proposed. (p. 355)

The theory of extinction becomes much more complicated than the simple definition just given. Calvin, Clifford, Clifford, and Harvey (1956) have shown, for example, that the time interval between extinction trials influences the rate of extinction. Bandura (1969, pp. 356–423) cites over a hundred different studies of different factors that influence the rate of extinction.

Benoit and Mayer (1974) have discussed the uses of extinction as a classroom behavior modification technique. They point out the critical questions that the counselor must answer before deciding whether extinction is the appropriate technique: Are the reinforcers of the behavior that is to be extinguished known? Can these reinforcers be withheld? Have alternative behaviors been identified? Can an increase in the negative behavior be tolerated? Benoit and Mayer also point out the important difference between simply ignoring a behavior and having it extinguished. Extinction requires that the reinforcement for a particular behavior be withheld. It may well be, they suggest, that the reinforcement for a specific behavior is not always apparent on the surface. For example, the client may deriving pleasure from some fantasy associated with the behavior rather than with any overt response.

Answering the kinds of questions just suggested will help the counselor decide if he or she can use extinction, or whether it will be necessary to find an alternative technique such as desensitization or operant conditioning.

It is especially important to note that in using extinction, the negative behavior is likely to get worse before it gets better. Consider, for example, the situation in which a counselor calls the child-client's mother into the office every time the child has a temper tantrum. This, of course, would reinforce the child's inappropriate behavior by showing that such behavior brings a reward, the presence of the mother. The counselor decides to use extinction; to eliminate the reinforcement. At first, the child's rate and intensity of tantrums increases, as the child tries to provoke the counselor into acting-out and calling in the mother. The counselor must be able to withstand this pressure if the extinction is to be successful. On a more subtle level, if the counselor shows disgust for the child's behavior, this in itself may be enough reinforcement for the child to continue the behavior. In such a situation, the child may develop a different reinforcer for the same behavior, and if the counselor is not aware of it, he or she cannot extinguish it. This is why it is so important in using extinction to decide at the outset which reinforcers actually can be withheld and which cannot.

Systematic
Desensitization

Systematic desensitization is a form of classical conditioning in which anxiety-evoking situations are paired with inhibitory responses. Wolpe (1961) describes the process this way:

> The desensitization method consists of presenting to the imagination of the deeply-relaxed patient the feeblest item in a list of anxiety-evoking stimuli—repeatedly, until no more anxiety is evoked. The next item in the list is presented, and so on, until eventually, even the strongest of the anxiety-evoking stimuli fails to evoke any stir of anxiety in the patient. (p. 191)

The technique of systematic desensitization is based upon the learning principle of *reciprocal inhibition,* which was developed by Wolpe (1958). Reciprocal inhibition means that if a relaxing response is paired with an anxiety-producing stimulus, a new bond develops between the two so that the anxiety-provoking stimulus no longer provokes anxiety. Bugg (1972) explains the theory this way:

> The essential principle of reciprocal inhibition is that an organism cannot make two contradictory responses at the same time. Behavior therapy assumes that anxiety responses are learned (conditioned) behaviors and may be extinguished by reconditioning. If the response that is contradictory to anxiety results in a more pleasant state or more productive behavior for the subject, the new response to anxiety-evoking stimuli will gradually replace the anxiety response. (p. 823)

For example, let us say that a client has a fear of flying on a plane. If every time the client thinks of flying in a plane, she or he is relaxed more and made to feel comfortable by the therapist, ultimately the stimulus (of flying on a plane) will fail to elicit the anxiety it once did.

The systematic desensitization approach "is essentially characterized by a treatment package which includes relaxation training, construction of hierarchies of anxiety-eliciting stimuli via imagery with relaxation" (Unikel, 1973, p. 4). The client discusses the components of his or her fear with the counselor, in order to construct a list of anxiety-evoking stimuli in order of intensity (e.g. driving to the airport, waiting in the lounge, boarding the plane, taking off, being in the air, etc.). The stimuli are dealt with, one at a time, until the one that is the most anxiety provoking is no longer capable of generating anxiety. This approach comprises, in other words, cumulative, sequential processes of desensitization. Rachman (1967b) aptly describes the technique of desensitization:

> The patient is relaxed and then requested to imagine the anxiety-producing stimuli in a very mild and attenuated form. When the image is obtained vividly, a small amount of anxiety is usually elicited. The therapist then relaxes the patient again and instructs him to stop imagining the scene and to continue relaxing. The full sequence is: *relax, imagine, relax, stop imagining, relax* [italics added]. . . . This process is then repeated with the same stimulus or with a stimulus which is slightly more disturbing. The patient is again relaxed and the next stimulus is then presented and dissipated. With each evocation and subsequent dampening of the anxiety response, conditioned inhibition is built up. . . . Eventually the patient is able to imagine even the previously most anxiety-provoking stimulus with tranquility, and this tranquility generalizes to the real-life situation. (p. 95)

Garvey and Hegrenes (1966) offer an example of how a school psychologist used systematic desensitization to treat a child suffering from school phobia, a disorder that responds well to this technique. The client, a ten-year-old boy, was unable to get into the car that was to take him to school in the morning. The desensitization consisted of twelve stages. During the first stage, the psychologist sat with the boy in the car that was parked in front of the school. When the boy finally felt comfortable in this situation, the next step was applied, and so on until the final step was taken. Following the first stage, the steps were:

2. Getting out of the car and approaching the curb
3. Going to the sidewalk
4. Going to the bottom of the school steps
5. Going to the top of the steps
6. Going to the door
7. Entering the school
8. Approaching the classroom a certain distance each day down the hall
9. Entering the classroom
10. Being present in the classroom with the teacher
11. Being present in the classroom with the teacher and one or two classmates
12. Being present in the classroom with a full class

We note in this example how systematic desensitization slowly builds up, step-by-step, to the highest anxiety-producing situation. This necessitated, according to the authors, twenty treatments, involving a total of ten to twelve hours of the therapist's time. Of course, the time and success will vary directly with the kind of problem, the cooperation of the client, and the design of the program.

Multimodal Behavior Therapy

Table 10.1

Modality	Problem	Proposed Treatment
Behavior	Poor eye contact	Rehearsal techniques
Affect	Unable to express anger	Role playing
Sensation	Tension in jaw/neck	Differential relaxation
Imagery	Distressing scenes of sister's funeral	Desensitization
Cognition	Irrational self-talk	Deliberate rational disputation and self-correction
Interpersonal Relationships	Childlike dependency	Specific self-sufficiency assignments
Drugs/Diet	Periodic depression	Possible use of antidepressants

(Adapted from Lazarus, 1976, pp. 17, 22)

One of the criticisms leveled at the behavior therapies over the years is that they address themselves specifically to the symptom or pathology rather than to the more complex interactive and psychological difficulties the client is experiencing. In recognition of this, Arnold Lazarus developed a new form of treatment called multimodal behavior therapy in the 1970s. Lazarus, recognizing that most problems are interactive throughout different areas of a person's functioning, attempted to identify specific areas where treatment interventions should take place and to develop effective strategies for implementing these interventions. While this is a behavioral approach, it goes beyond the limits of most behavioral approaches and focuses on the total person in all areas of functioning.

The areas that have been identified, some possible problems, and treatment interventions are shown in Table 10.1.

As you can see from the table, by identifying problems in different modalities of a person's functioning, it is possible to gain a broader view of how well or how poorly the person is doing in life. Moreover, by combining a number of different treatment paradigms, the therapist is better able to "attack" each problem area than if he or she were constrained by a single treatment model.

When a client comes to treatment, he or she is evaluated in each of these areas of functioning. The assessment procedure is comprehensive, beginning with an initial interview where present complaints, past history, and symptom-influencing factors are outlined. "The initial phase of multimodal assessment is not too different from that of most broad-spectrum clinicians. Rapport is established, and an attempt is made to develop a productive liaison" (Lazarus, 1976a, p. 26). But while this is going on, the counselor systematically attempts to collect information which will allow him or her to evaluate the client in each of the modalities. This information becomes the basis of the treatment plan.

Following assessment, a plan is devised for using treatment interventions. The multimodal approach is quite eclectic, drawing from the behavioral, cognitive, and Gestalt repertoires. These may include individual or group/family treatment, and even medication where necessary. "A multimodal orientation," says Lazarus (1976, pp. 3–4), "presupposes no identification with any specific school of psychological thought. Nor is it a separate school in itself. Its practitioners are pragmatists who endorse scientific empiricism and logical positivism without succumbing to unnecessary reductionistic reasoning." In short, they attempt to use the most effective technique or combination of techniques for the specific problem or problems.

For example, in the treatment of anorexia, medication and hypnosis may be used, along with operant conditioning and modeling, not only to alleviate the symptom, but to help the patient restructure his or her life as well. In treating a single client with colitis and incapacitating anxiety, Briddell and Leiblum use nine different techniques, ranging from rational-emotive thinking exercises to relaxation training.

Where multimodal behavior therapy differs from most other forms is in its emphasis on improving the quality of life—both emotional life and interpersonal functioning—for the "whole person," rather than focusing on a single symptom, or problem. Lazarus (1976, p. 5) points out,

> The model employed [multimodal behavior therapy] may be viewed as "actualization," "growth," or "educational" rather than as one based upon disease analogies, medicine or pathology. Everyone can benefit from a change in behavior that eliminates unwanted or surplus reactions while stepping up the frequency, duration, and intensity of useful, creative, fulfilling responses. Similarly, the control or absence of unpleasant emotions coupled with an increase in positive feelings is a most worthy goal. . . . (p. 5)

Various studies over the past decade have confirmed that multimodal behavior therapy is an effective treatment approach in clinical, school, and institutional settings.

It has been recognized, by both partisans and critics of behavior modification, that if any of these learning approaches are to prove of real practical value, the changes effected by the intervention must persist after the behavioral modification which lessens an undesirable behavior. Having that behavior reappear in the same or in different form after the program has ended would be of very dubious value.

For this reason, investigators during the 1970s and 1980s focused a great deal of attention on what we call *behavioral self-control programs*. These are behavioral change models, which may incorporate any combination of the learning paradigms discussed above, but where primary emphasis is placed on the subject learning to monitor and control his or her own behavior, both during the course of the program and after termination. Theory and research during the 1970s

Behavioral Self-Control Programs

generally supported the idea that self-reinforcement may prove to be a valuable new modality, with learning implications that are separate and distinct from external reinforcement programs (Bandura, 1976).

While some behavioral psychologists argue that changes tend to persist after behavior programs end because of "stimulus generalization" or "intrinsic reward," this has not been fully proven. A counter argument is that if a person learns during the program to control his or her behavior, the person is more likely to be able to do so afterward.

In fact, it has become a subject of intense debate in the professional literature and in behavioral change clinics whether programs based on external-reinforcement are as effective, less effective, or more effective than programs that emphasize self-reinforcement. Studies have shown at different time instances of all three effects; the best we can say at the present is that the evidence is far from convincing (Martin, 1980). Still, the growing popularity of programs where subjects learn specific ways to monitor and control their own behavior, during and after the formal program, indicates that practitioners are finding such models useful.

Basic Terminology

The key terms are sometimes used interchangeably, so that our definitions will of necessity be somewhat overlapping. We can describe a behavioral program in which the measurement of behaviors and/or the dispensing of reinforcements are controlled by a person other than the subject, for example, by a teacher, psychologist, or school counselor, as an *external-reinforcement* program. All illustration of this is a token reinforcement program, where appropriate behavior is rewarded with tokens by some outside person who is the dispensing agent.

A program in which the subject himself dispenses the reinforcers (based, of course, on predetermined rules and contingencies), is called a *self-reinforcement* program. A broader term, *self-control* refers to a range of programs using different types of reinforcement and modeling paradigms. These programs are designed to teach the individual to implement specific learning strategies to control his or her behavior under a variety of conditions. Thus, under the heading behavioral self-control, we find programs through which individuals learn to change their internal thinking (cognitions) about things in order to feel less stress, or less anxiety, or in order to overcome a phobia. We also find eating control programs by means of which an individual learns specific ways to manage his or her eating behaviors by developing contingencies that work to lessen the impulsiveness.

Implementation

Models abound in the professional literature, each offering its own application of learning theory to individual self-control; but what most have in common is that they teach the subject ways of measuring and controlling behaviors. With a few differences these programs parallel external-reinforcement programs. Some of the principal types will be considered in the following section under the heading "Cognitive Behavior Modification."

Neilans and Israel (1981) suggest a four-component model for a self-regulation behavioral change program. This is typical of how these programs work, and their model has been used successfully in decreasing the disruptive behavior of school-age children directly in the classroom environment. Their stages are: self-monitoring, self-goal-setting, self-evaluation, and self-reinforcement. Each stage can be operationally defined as follows:

Self-monitoring Observing one's own behavior and charting or recording in an organized way relevant behaviors.

Self-Goal setting Setting a specific goal or goals, thereby establishing criteria for subsequent performance evaluation.

Self-evaluation Making a comparison between the individual's performance (as monitored and recorded) and the performance criterion (the goal).

Self-reinforcement Distributing (or withholding, if necessary) appropriate rewards after evaluating one's performance with respect to the goal.

Stages of Behavioral Self-Regulation

After T. H. Neilans and A. C. Israel, 1981.

By breaking the stages into simpler components, each aspect of the total problem can be regulated separately. For example, a multiphobic person may work separately on each feared object or event, recording phobic responses, setting goals, evaluating and reinforcing appropriate responses.

One advantage of a self-control program over external-control is that it gives a person the feeling that he or she can control actions and events which affect his or her life. This is a concept psychologists call *self-efficacy*. As one learns to control one's own behaviors, it becomes more likely that one will feel this sense of competency than if one were merely a subject in a behavioral program administered by another. As Bandura (1982) points out, the more self-efficacy a person feels in general, the more he or she is able to accomplish and the better he or she feels about self. To the extent that self-control programs help a person feel self-efficacy, they serve the purpose of helping one's adjustment by making one feel more competent in living, while at the same time reducing undesirable behaviors.

Evaluation

Behavioral self-control programs have been widely used in a number of settings for different types of problems. They have proven especially effective in stress innoculation, an approach designed to lessen the amount of unnecessary and unproductive stress an individual experiences. Self-instructional training programs, using audiocassettes, training booklets, and some direct contact with the trainer, are widely used today. Such programs typically combine elements of cognitive change behavior modification with self-administered reinforcement and desensitization; they have proven effective in treating a range of stress-related disorders (Deffenbacher & Hahnloser, 1981). Self-control training has been used to reduce very specific symptomatic disorders, such as compulsive nailbiting behavior (Frankel & Merbaum, 1982).

Other Behavioral Counseling Techniques

Shaping

Shaping is a technique sometimes used by behavioral counselors. It involves reinforcing behavior that approximates the desired goal. "In shaping," Patterson (1973) points out, "the experimenter at first reinforces behavior that is only similar to the behavior that is ultimately desired but does not exist at the present." Through gradual changes in the pattern of reinforcement, the desired behavior is finally reached. In a sophisticated operant conditioning program, where the desired behaviors require the coordination of a number of complex responses, shaping would probably be useful in building up response repertoires.

Modeling

Modeling is another valuable technique used by behavioral counselors. With this technique, a person models himself or herself after another's behavior or actions. It may not be necessary for the client to perform in any particular way in order to learn from modeling; merely observing the model's behavior is often sufficient. "When a person observes a model's behavior," Bandura (1969) suggests, "but otherwise performs no overt responses, he can acquire the modeled responses while they are occurring only in cognitive, representational forms." This constitutes a form of sensory conditioning.

In its most obvious form, modeling is learning by example. If the example is a positive one, then positive behavior will be the likely outcome; if, on the other hand, the example is a negative one, then undesirable behavior will be the outcome. Thus, the child who models himself or herself after the best behaved child in the class (perhaps because of the teacher's attitude toward this "good" child) will try to behave well, while another child who uses the class troublemaker as a model (perhaps because the teacher also gives this troublemaker special attention) will tend toward similar disruptive behavior.

Time-out (TO)

Time-out is a simple procedure in which the individual is removed from the area where the inappropriate behavior is reinforced. It is similar to extinction in that in both situations the behavior is changed because of a lack of consistent reinforcement, but differs in one basic way: "The chief difference between extinction and time-out," Benoit and Mayer (1976) point out, "is that in extinction, reinforcement for a particular behavior is withheld, while in time-out the client is denied access to all sources of reinforcement through either transferring him or her to a nonreinforcing situation or removing the source of reinforcement from the present situation" (p. 208).

Patterson, Cobb, and Ray (1973) have written about a multifaceted behavior modification program in which parents of aggressive boys were trained to be behavior therapists. One of the chief techniques they used was time-out. "Most of the studies," they point out, ". . . indicated that the effect of repeated applications of TO was to produce rapid decreases in rate of coercive social behaviors in children" (p. 178). In this experiment, time-out was used as an alternative to the parents' previously unhealthy method of dealing with the child's aggressiveness; namely, beating the child. "The parent learned to observe, to apply TO, and to reinforce prosocial behaviors as alternatives to beating the child" (p. 178). Time-out allowed the parent an opportunity to "cool off," as well as allowing the child the opportunity to find alternative, more productive behaviors. In this sense, time-out serves a dual purpose.

Cognitive Behavior Modification (CBM)

A useful variant of the behavior modification approaches we looked at before is an approach called cognitive behavior modification (CBM). While the behavioral techniques discussed earlier focus almost entirely on behaviors that can be observed and measured, "the critical assumption of [these] cognitively-based techniques is that altering various thought and problem-solving processes will alter behavior (Kazdin, 1982, p. 77). Thus, cognitive behavior modification therapy works by changing one's maladaptive thinking in order to change one's maladaptive behaviors. Instead of putting primary emphasis on observable behavior, cognitive behavior counselor "rely chiefly on speech as the instrument of change" (Ledwidge, 1978). They believe that changing one's thinking processes is an integral part of changing one's behavior.

Much of the research and clinical work has centered around reducing anxiety and stress levels by teaching individuals to control their bodily reactions by controlling their thinking. Donald Meichenbaum's (1977) landmark work in this area clearly suggests, for example, that levels of stress can be lessened and levels of self-control increased if the subject learned to think in more logical, less stress-producing ways. Since thinking is the mediating process between sensation and response, Meichenbaum argues: if we learn to change our thinking, our cognitions, we gain greater control over our physical responses, our behaviors. In this way, we can in effect "innoculate" ourselves against high levels of unnecessary stress (Deffenbacher & Hahnloser, 1981). Moreover, because we can easily measure and quantify an individual's levels of stress and self-control we are also able to assess immediately how well or how poorly the subject's rethinking, or cognitive restructuring, is working.

Cognitive Restructuring

There are many different approaches to cognitive behavior therapy, known under many different names. Schmidt (1976) discusses an approach called *cognitive restructuring,* which is becoming an increasingly popular form of CBM. "Cognitive restructuring," he tells us, "is any therapeutic technique that employs the change of 'self-thoughts' in order to alter emotional reactions and behaviors toward more favorable outcomes." He offers some examples of how this works in the clinical setting:

In general, what happens in the treatment goes something like the following: a self-defeating thought, for example, "It is terrible to make mistakes" is challenged by a counterthought, "Everybody makes mistakes." This counterthought is positively reinforced in that the ensuing emotion and behavior are pleasant and more productive. Furthermore, these counterthoughts can be positively reinforced more intentionally by asking clients to engage in reinforcing thoughts or activities immediately following each counter-thought. For example, after using the counter, "Everybody makes mistakes," a client can fantasize a pleasant scene for thirty seconds. In a similar manner, negative self-thoughts can be punished by instructing clients to engage in unpleasant fantasies following such thoughts. (p. 72)

As we see from this description, the technique of cognitive restructuring embodies the behavioral principles of reinforcement and conditioning, but does so with the patient's thinking (and perceptions) as goals, rather than behavior. Mahoney and Kazdin (1979) point out, quite correctly, that it is hard to discriminate in practice between noncognitively oriented behavior therapists and true partisans of the cognitive approach, since there is much overlap between the two. Although other CBM methods differ from cognitive restructuring in substance, they embody many of the same principles used differently. This is why they are sometimes categorized with RET, as opposed to behavioral counseling.

While RET has many assumptions and some techniques in common with CBM, the two are not identical. Much confusion has arisen because of a tendency to equate the two approaches, or to see RET as a type of CBM. Ellis (1980), in trying to clarify this, suggests the principal differences between the two approaches are that unlike CBM, rational-emotive therapy "has a pronounced philosophic emphasis, includes a humanistic-existential outlook, strives for pervasive and long-lasting rather than symptomatic change . . . [and] discourages problem solving that is not accompanied by changes in clients' basic belief system" (p. 325). He considers his approach more of an integral part of the person's total interaction with the environment, while CBM is more a specific treatment approach for eliminating unproductive behaviors and disturbing symptoms.

Evaluation of CBM   Although there is some controversy over its ultimate effectiveness, there is considerable evidence at this point that CBM is a highly useful modality in treating a range of problems, but particularly helpful with phobias, stress-related disorders, and depression. Beck (1976), for example, has demonstrated its efficacy in serious depressive and emotional disorders which years ago many practitioners found unresponsive to behavioral interventions. Still, as Kazdin (1982) has pointed out, we have to resist the temptation to see CBM as a panacea, and try to remain objective in the waves of enthusiasm and excitement that have swept the field. If we look at the specific experimental results of CBM with such a dispassionate eye, he suggests, research will ultimately pinpoint which CBM techniques and theories are most worthy of our serious consideration.

Goals   While most of the counseling approaches we have discussed are oriented around theoretical goals (*integration* in psychoanalysis; *self-actualization* in client-centered counseling; the "will to meaning" in existential counseling), the goal of behavioral counseling depends entirely on the type of problem for which the client has sought treatment. Krumboltz (1966*a*) argues that "it is the counselor's job to help the client translate his problem into a behavioral goal that the client wants to attain and that the counselor believes will contribute to the welfare of his client" (p. 154). In behavioral counseling, the aim is directed always to the presenting problem, and the removal of that problem is the goal of the counseling process.

In general, the goal of most behavioral counseling—particularly with the method of desensitization—is the elimination of neurotic anxiety, or its manifest symptoms. The behavioral counselor believes that this anxiety acts as an inhibiting factor against healthy, adaptive behavior.

Bandura (1969) has stated this goal of behavioral counseling quite succinctly: "The patient has a repertoire of previously learned positive habits available to him, but these adaptive patterns are inhibited or blocked by competing responses motivated by anxiety or guilt. *The goal of therapy, then, is to reduce the severity of the internal inhibitory controls, thus allowing the healthy patterns of behavior to emerge"* (p. 112, italics added).

Evaluation and Applications

Ironically, what has often been cited as the greatest fault of behavioral therapy proves to be its greatest advantage in the counseling setting; namely, it deals directly with the symptom. Most of the difficulties that the counselor is confronted with take the form of behavioral problems. Individuals do not generally seek counseling for long-term self-insight, but rather because they are troubled by a specific, symptomatic problem. These are problems in role areas of functioning, in the client's relationship with others, in successfully carrying out his or her work, and so on. Or, they are problems involving inordinate degrees of anxiety (neurotic anxiety) which interferes with the client's living. In this respect, behavioral counseling, with its emphasis on the symptom itself, offers a practical bonus to the counselor.

Considerable research over the past twenty-five years has shown different forms of behavioral therapy and behavior modification effective in the treatment of alcoholism, juvenile delinquency, drug addiction, and anxiety as well as in child therapy and many other conditions (O'Leary, 1984). It has been used successfully in hospital and prison settings, in rehabilitation counseling, in special education, and in treating school phobia (Trueman, 1984). The cognitive approaches particularly have proven to be potent methods in lessening anxiety, reducing depression, and curing phobias (Kendall, 1984). On the whole, research supports the effectiveness of behavior modification more than any other group of approaches.

Summary

In this chapter we examined some of the major models of behavioral counseling, including classical conditioning, operant conditioning, systematic desensitization, multimodal therapy, and modeling. Behavior modification, we indicated, developed from the behavioral psychology of John B. Watson in the early years of this century. Behaviorism emphasized using observable, measurable behavior as the basis of psychology, and introduced the stimulus-response relationship in interpreting behavior patterns. Using many of the early principles, B. F. Skinner then formulated the basic principles of operant conditioning, and Joseph Wolpe introduced the process of systematic desensitization.

The behavioral counselor views the individual as a product of his or her conditioning. The two main types of conditioning are classical (respondent) and operant (instrumental). Classical conditioning involves the pairing of an unconditioned with a conditioned stimulus, so that the response associated with the unconditioned stimulus becomes associated with the conditioned. Operant conditioning requires that the subject respond to a stimulus and that the response then be reinforced. Behavioral counselors, it was pointed out, do not necessarily hold a mechanistic view of the person, and Skinner, particularly, has argued against the restrictive view of the client as an "empty organism."

The behavioral counselor's principal task is to design a program through which specified target behaviors will be modified. The techniques (in addition to classical and operant conditioning) used to this end include systematic desensitization (which involves the client imagining anxiety-evoking stimuli vicariously, in a hierarchical order, at the same time the counselor presents relaxing, anxiety-inhibiting stimuli); and extinction (breaking an established response pattern by not reinforcing it). Specific types of operant conditioning models (reinforcement approaches) were also discussed. We also looked at multimodal behavior therapy, which transcends the limitations inherent in many behavioral therapies by addressing the totality of interpersonal, intrapsychic, cognitive, and behavioral difficulties the client is experiencing. This form of therapy brings together a variety of techniques to attack problems simultaneously in all these different areas. Three other techniques—shaping, modeling, and time-out—were discussed briefly.

Counseling
Applications

In this part of the book, we will apply many of the insights and ideas discussed in the preceding three parts. We will focus on a variety of target populations (children, adolescents, older adults, members of minority groups, etc.) with a number of different types of problems (crisis situations, family conflicts, need for rehabilitation, etc.) in several different kinds of settings (school, community agency, private, group). We will look specifically at how counseling is actually conducted, to what ends, through which processes, for what kinds of problems. Each chapter will cover in detail one type of counseling application. The theories of counseling presented in Part 3 and the insights about the counseling process delineated in Part 2 will be demonstrated in practice in Part 4.

In chapter 11, we examine counseling over the life span, explicating developmental counseling applications specifically relevant to the childhood years, to the adolescent period, and to adulthood. We will present a brief view of play therapy, an important child counseling approach, along with a case study. We will then consider some of the typical problems with which the adolescent counselor has to deal—problems such as confusion about sex, drug and alcohol abuse, and truancy. The new and growing field of counseling the older adult will also be given attention. This chapter will serve as a general overview of the types of needs, problems, and treatment approaches associated with specific developmental epochs.

In chapter 12, we turn our attention to some basic positions on *family counseling,* focusing on to how the counselor can serve as a facilitator of family growth. The general goal of teaching the family to solve its own problems is discussed, along with some of the theories of the reasons for family conflict.

Then, in chapter 13, we briefly consider *group counseling,* a widely applied modality which is used in the treatment of almost every kind of problem and has been applied successfully in almost every kind of counseling setting.

We examine a specialized area, *crisis intervention counseling,* in chapter 14. We will establish some practical guidelines for intervening in a crisis situation, and examine five specific types of crisis conditions that often precipitate requests for counseling: grief crisis, anxiety crisis, suicidal crisis, family crisis, and rape crisis. For each of these we will attempt to formulate some concrete guidelines to help the counselor deal with what is at best a very difficult situation.

Chapter 15, "Health Counseling," will introduce a new and increasingly useful area of counseling concern. While at the present time, health matters are generally not viewed as a central part of most counseling efforts, we see a trend developing towards recognizing physical health as an integral part of all psychological counseling efforts. We need not go back more than two thousand years to Plato's comment "a sound mind and a sound body" to sense the feeling that the interactive relationship between mind and body demands that counselors pay more attention to the health of the body than they have been doing. We will also observe, in this chapter, how people suffering from physical debilities need specialized types of counseling. From these observations, we will educe several important applications of the general principles of health counseling.

Rehabilitation and community counseling are combined in chapter 16. Here, we offer a comprehensive definition of rehabilitation and outline the major problems of rehabilitation and the settings in which the rehab counselor typically works. Because so much of rehabilitation is inseparable from an understanding of the special needs of the disabled client, these needs will be given special attention.

How do counselors extend the range of counseling services within the community in which they live or work? How do they deliver services to the largest number of people? How can they prepare community members to receive counseling? These are a few of the questions we will answer in chapter 16. We will also look at some recent efforts to make counseling more available and consider the implications of wider availability for the individual counselor. We will then attempt to answer the question, How must the counselor alter his or her style or professional value system to deal with the new client population?

Next, in chapter 17, "Counseling in the Schools," we will consider the multiple roles of the school counselor, how he or she is perceived by teachers, students, administrators and by the counseling profession. We will also devote special attention to the needs of exceptional students in the schools, and consider ways in which the counselor can effectively work with parents and other school personnel.

In chapter 18, "Vocational and Educational Counseling," we will examine a compellingly practical area, and direct our attention to the contemporary world of work. We shall consider how career counseling can help many individuals who are either conflicted or misinformed about their work or training possibilities.

Finally, in chapter 19, "Cross-Cultural Counseling" we will look at some of the specific problems involved when the counselor and client come from different backgrounds, have membership in different ethnic, religious, or socio-economic groups. This will serve as a broad research overview, from which more detailed research can be placed in perspective.

Together, these eight chapters will demonstrate that counselors perform valuable services to a wide range of clients in a diversity of settings.

Chapter Aim

To outline the main psychosocial characteristics of the developmental epochs (childhood, adolescence, and adulthood), using Erik Erikson's categories as starting points, and to consider specific counseling applications and goals appropriate for each, regardless of the counselor's orientation.

The use of play in child counseling can be adapted according to the theoretical orientation of the counselor. We look at psychoanalytic and client-centered play therapy, comparing and contrasting them. A case study of a ten-year-old girl who was experiencing severe difficulties in school is presented. We see how the use of an eclectic counseling approach, where play and drawing were combined with verbal discussion, helped her to express her feelings and to develop more mature behaviors.

Child Counseling: Play Approaches

Adolescence and puberty are discussed in terms of Erikson's stage of "identity vs. role confusion," and the psychological conflicts and developmental challenges of each period are briefly outlined. Several types of problems common to this period are discussed. First, adolescent adjustments in the area of sexual functioning are considered. Some constructive measures through which the counselor can help the adolescent meet these challenges of sexual development are considered.

Next, drug and alcohol abuse are defined in operational terms. The scope of the problem is briefly outlined, and several counseling interventions are then discussed.

Counseling the Adolescent

Erikson divides adulthood into three periods: *intimacy vs. isolation; generativity vs. stagnation;* and, *ego integrity vs. despair.* Each of these describes the challenges the individual faces at critical points in adult development. We look at the social trends and specific developmental challenges associated with this period, including sexual adjustments, residence choices, social stereotyping, along with personal and career decisions.

Counseling the Adult

Counseling Over the
Life Span

11

The November 1976 issue of the *Personnel and Guidance Journal,* entitled "Counseling Over the Life Span," signified that at long last this developmental emphasis in counseling had come into its own. Although the special issue concentrated on counseling the adult, particularly the adult in transition, it set forth the tone of what would provide a major perspective in counseling for years to come. In its most basic sense, the underlying concept of counseling over the life span is that of recognizing the importance of developmental epochs in shaping the person, and in the counselor's understanding of the individual client.

A decade later, with thousands of research studies and dozens of models now available on life span psychology, Levinson (1986) suggests a paradigm that can help the counselor better understand developmental characteristics of the life span; one which differentiates between what he calls the *life course* and the *life cycle.* The life course, he argues "refers to the concrete character of a life in its evolution from beginning to end" (p. 3).

> The word *course* indicates sequence, temporal flow, the need to study a life as it unfolds over the years. To study the course of a life, one must take account of stability and change, continuity and discontinuity, orderly progression as well as stasis and chaotic fluctuation. (p. 3)

He then conceptualizes *life cycle,* which suggests there is an underlying order in the human life course:

> The imagery of "cycle" suggests that there is an underlying order in the human life course; although each individual life is unique, everyone goes through the same basic sequence. The course of a life is not a simple, continuous process. There are qualitatively different phases or seasons. (p. 4)

He conceives of the life cycle in terms of a sequence of *eras,* each of which has its own developmental characteristics. The eras and their developmental stages will be outlined in this chapter.

We will divide our discussion into the three developmental periods that are conventionally used as marking points: childhood, adolescence, and adulthood. These are rather arbitrary and culturally laden markers, of course. We could just as easily have two or twenty markers. But the threefold distinction is convenient for our purpose, which is to introduce the topics. As our organizing framework, we will use Erikson's ages of man, which set forth the developmental tasks of each period.

We will begin with child counseling, focusing on counseling procedures, particularly play therapy. To really understand the child it is necessary to understand child psychology, especially the relationship between cognitive and personality development, but this is far beyond the scope of this book. We will look at a case study to illustrate some of the main points of our discussion.

Next, we will spend some time understanding a few of the complexities of the adolescent period, during which so many critical counseling interactions take place. Probably there has been more written on adolescent counseling as a distinct developmental period than on any other single period.

Finally, we will discuss counseling the adult, an exciting new area of research; one with perhaps the greatest potential. We will note especially how the adult client can learn to make valuable use of his or her leisure time.

Erik Erikson's "Eight Ages of Man" describes the stages of psychosocial development, presented in his major work, *Childhood and Society* (1963). These stages integrate the social and psychological perspectives of the growing person. They help us better understand how the individual client perceives and responds, in relation to his or her age. We will, therefore, use the stages as a basic framework in this chapter.

Child Counseling

The first four stages relate directly to the childhood years, and they will help us understand some of the problems that may bring children to counseling. The first two stages occur before the child will see a counselor, but the child client may be in stages three or four at the time of counseling.

Basic Trust vs. Basic Mistrust

In the earliest part of development, the infant, through its relationship with the mother, develops feelings of basic trust or basic mistrust, depending upon the care given. "Mothers," Erikson (1963) points out, "create a sense of trust in their children by that kind of administration which in its quality combines sensitive care of the baby's individual needs and a firm sense of personal trustworthiness" (p. 49).

The emergence of the child as an autonomous creature, capable of choosing from options within the environment, is crucial for the child's individual survival and psychological maturation. While the child may require some external control and parental restraint during these early years, the child must at the same time be allowed outlets to grow as an independent, autonomous creature. "For if denied the gradual and well-guided experience of autonomy of free choice," Erikson (1963) argues, ". . . the child will turn against himself all his urge to discriminate and to manipulate" (p. 252). Shame and doubt ("doubt is the brother of shame") are consequences of stifling the child's striving for autonomy, and can be avoided when the parents allow the child the appropriate outlets to develop autonomously.

During the stage of initiative vs. guilt which extends from about the time the child is three years of age to the end of the kindergarten year, the child extends the autonomy of the second stage into initiative; the willingness to contemplate and execute new actions on his own. This brings about the emergence of an individual identity, derived from but also differentiated from the parents' identities.

With this new direction toward *initiative,* many changes come into the child's life. The child transforms his or her infantile sexual behavior and feelings, growing from a "pregenital attachment to his parents, to the slow process of becoming a parent, a carrier of tradition" (p. 256). The boy's identification with the father or the girl's identification with the mother, both characteristics of this stage, become the basis for later sexual identification, and during the stage this identification itself motivates the child to activities that help differentiate its identity. When the child is thwarted in its efforts toward initiating behaviors, he or she may experience *guilt* from the reactions of the parents.

The stage of industry vs. inferiority covers the elementary school years. The child now has greater intellectual and social resources than he or she had during the earlier stages, and puts these into use. This is a period of interest in hobbies, a period in which the child is more willing and capable of solving complex tasks, and in which there is greater perseverance and sense of accomplishment from construction. But, it is also a time when, if the child is thwarted in his or her industrious pursuits, a feeling of inferiority and incompetence is likely to result. Erikson views this as a decisive social stage, since it is the child's first real opportunity to interact with peers in complex social relationships.

Because child clients in these early developmental stages require a specialized type of intervention, play approaches are widely used in the child counseling setting. Let us consider the basic ideas of play therapy and counseling approaches, and then examine briefly a case example.

Child Counseling: Play Approaches

This section is written by Janet Finell. Reprinted by permission.

Play is to the young child what words are to the adult. Play provides a means through which thoughts and feelings can be communicated, and distressing conflicts resolved. Through play, the child's attention can be captured and maintained as he or she enacts inner fears and wishes in the safety and acceptance of the counseling relationship.

The use of play in child counseling can be adapted according to the theoretical orientation of the counselor. The two main play approaches have traditionally been the psychodynamic and the client-centered. The former was developed through the works of Anna Freud and Melanie Klein: the latter is most closely identified with the writings of Virginia Axline. There are some similarities and some discrepancies between these two orientations.

Anna Freud (1964) stressed some essential differences that exist in the treatment of children compared to adults, and these would hold true regardless of the counseling approach used. Children do not come to treatment voluntarily. They may be unaware that they have a problem. Their real need for and dependency on their parents minimizes the possibility of their expressing many of their hostile feelings about their parents. Finally, the control which the parents continue to exercise over the child's life can threaten gains achieved through treatment. Therefore, in order for counseling with children to be successful, the counselor must work to capture the child's interest, and to motivate him or her for the work ahead. Moreover, without parental cooperation, success is highly unlikely.

So much for the similarities between approaches. What are the main differences?

Child psychoanalysts have adapted the basic psychoanalytic techniques to the treatment of children. The use of free association, analysis of the transference, resistance, dream analysis, and the unconscious are still the basic ingredients of child psychoanalysis [author's note: see chapter 7 for a discussion of these]. The major adaptations of these techniques to the treatment of children involve the use of play as an additional means of communication for the child whose lack of verbal and conceptual sophistication makes impossible the singular reliance on words that is characteristic of the treatment of adults.

In contrast to the psychoanalytic approaches, client-centered child counselors focus on the phenomenological relationship between the client and counselor. According to this school of thought, the counselor, above all, should provide a permissive environment in which the child is free to dramatize his conflicts and difficulties. The child is never told that he or she is in treatment for a particular problem, and no attempt is made to direct, control or structure his or her play activities. The child is in total command of the situation, and is responsible for his own behavior. Unless his behavior becomes destructive, no limitations are placed upon him. It is believed that an inner drive towards health and maturity provides the motivating force that makes the counseling play encounter a meaningful one.

Client-centered child counselors believe that play is the child's most natural means of self-expression. The provision of simple toys such as dolls, trucks, cars, as well as paints, drawing materials and clay are sufficient tools for the young child to enact the vivid and anxiety-evoking events of his or her inner life. The privacy of the counseling office, the counselor's interest in the child and his problems, and the promise of confidentiality all contribute to a sense of trust and security in the child.

Therefore, play activities in the counseling office are the means through which the child communicates to the counselor. His freedom to play in any way that he wishes, in an atmosphere of respect and understanding, are believed to foster his self-esteem. In the classic study, *Dibs in Search of Self,* Virginia Axline (1967) provides a detailed description of the manner in which a disturbed youngster's play opened up a world that had formerly been closed by controlling parents.

The case presented here provides an example of play counseling in the school setting. The approach is eclectic, reflecting some aspects of the psychodynamic orientation and some aspects of the client-centered philosophy. What is most important to note is how the counseling process is adapted to the special needs and capabilities of a ten-year-old.

Debbie, aged ten, was referred for counseling by her teacher because of violent behavior that was characterized by attacks against her peers. Although she was undersized for her age, she often tyrannized her classmates by hitting them, stealing their possessions, and hurling insults at them. Academically, although she was in fourth grade and had already been left back one year, Debbie could not read a first-grade reader, and had not mastered any of the basic academic skills. She was extremely hyperactive, and could rarely concentrate on anything for longer than a few minutes. She made inordinate demands on the teacher for attention, and flew into a rage when she couldn't get her way.

The counselor referred Debbie to the school psychologist for testing, and after obtaining permission from her guardian, an aunt, a battery of intelligence and personality tests were performed. The results showed that Debbie was of low normal intelligence, and suffered from intense feelings of anger and rejection.

In consultation with Debbie's aunt, Mrs. S, it was learned that when Debbie was seven years of age, her mother had died as a result of an overdose of drugs. Debbie and her two older siblings had discovered her dead body one morning. They thought their mother was sleeping and shook her to try to awaken her. When she didn't move, they became terrified and rushed to their aunt's and uncle's home, where they were taken in and cared for. Shortly after their mother's death, their father died also.

Mrs. S was quite communicative about the children's past, and offered a considerable amount of information to the counselor. She was quite concerned about the three children, whom she now considered as her own. She knew about

Debbie: A Case Example

Debbie's disruptive behavior and academic failure, but in spite of her pleas and interest in the child, which she considered to be greater than the interest provided by Debbie's natural mother, the child's behavior and work were unchanged.

Debbie was delighted at the prospect of coming to counseling, and responded to the counselor in a very positive manner. She expressed the desire to come for sessions as frequently as possible. Therefore, sessions were scheduled on a twice-a-week basis, and an appointed time was arranged. In the counseling office, Debbie took the lead without prompting, explored the materials, and appeared comfortable with the counselor. Despite her "dull normal" tested IQ, she was quite articulate, and could communicate her needs very clearly.

Debbie made active use of the play materials. She would often play "house," and tended to act as a stern and punitive mother to the dolls and stuffed animals. After she had been coming to counseling for a few months, she began to insist that the toys be left exactly where she had placed them. Although she was told by the counselor that she was free to do anything she wanted to with the toys during her time, no promise could be made that they would be exactly where she had placed them when she returned. Debbie's reasonable ego accepted these limitations, and although she was annoyed when, in subsequent sessions, the toys were not where she had left them, she gradually accepted the fact that the counselor saw other children too.

Debbie was not so reasonable, however, when her sessions came to an end, and it was time to return to her classroom. Her difficulty in accepting limits, and her inordinate need for the counselor's attention reached its height, when after four months of counseling she flew into rages at these times. She kicked the counselor and screamed, "I hate you. I'm not coming here anymore." She would run away, hide, hang onto stairway railings, and had to be carried bodily back to her classroom. Her behavior disturbed nearby classes, and the situation became critical when the principal warned that if the counselor could not control Debbie, her sessions would have to be ended.

The play materials proved to be the means through which Debbie was able to communicate to the counselor what she was feeling at these times. The counselor made the following request of Debbie: "Show me what you are feeling when it's time for you to leave." Debbie responded by wrapping a doll in newspaper, and placed it deep within the counselor's closet. She demanded that no other child be allowed to touch the doll. The counselor understood that Debbie wished to be with her constantly. Separation was painful for this child who had experienced the loss of her parents when she was quite young. If Debbie felt certain that a doll was hidden away in the counselor's closet, she would feel that she herself was symbolically with the counselor even when she had to leave her. Moreover, the demand that no other child be allowed to touch the doll indicated that Debbie regarded the counselor's other clients as rivals for her love.

Debbie's request was granted—the doll would remain in the closet, but Debbie would have to leave at the scheduled time without a tantrum. The counselor reflected Debbie's anguish at separating:

> "You get very angry at me when it's time for you to leave. Perhaps you feel that I don't care about you, or that I won't be here for your next visit. But you know that when it's your turn to be here, I always see you. I have never disappointed you."

Thus, the counselor assured Debbie that the relationship was a warm and stable one. Unlike Debbie's mother, the counselor would not suddenly disappear. Debbie could count on her to be there.

In these months of counseling, Debbie had shown that she could be not only charming and winning, but manipulative and excessively demanding as well. Therefore, the setting of limits was an important part of Debbie's treatment.

In her second year of counseling, Debbie played with the toys in a manner that was quite similar to her earlier game of "house." She frequently set up a mock classroom in which the dolls and stuffed animals were made to represent children. They were given writing materials, and were tested on their knowledge of reading, math and spelling. The dolls and animals generally made mistakes, failed exams, and were threatened by Debbie with being left back. She screamed at them, told them they were bad and stupid, and sometimes hurled objects at them. The counselor was a silent observer of this play. However, before long Debbie insisted that the counselor too must play act that she was one of the children in the "class." Like the others, she had to make mistakes and was insulted and ridiculed for her stupidity. As the "teacher," Debbie was in her glory. She was experiencing the opportunity to master in an active manner what she had experienced passively almost continuously throughout her schooling: failure and humiliation.

This play continued repetitively for a number of months. During this time, the counselor learned that Debbie was now beginning to participate in classroom activities. Her previous stubborn refusal to attempt to read or write had now yielded to persistent attempts on her part to catch up to her classmates. The remedial reading teacher reported that, for the first time, Debbie consented to read aloud in front of other children. She was beginning to overcome her shame at being such a poor reader, and to behave in a manner that opened the way to academic improvement. Thus, through her play, Debbie had managed to overcome, to a considerable extent, the shame and anger that she had experienced in the classroom situation. It is quite possible too, that the mean and punitive teacher symbolized the mother who through her death had abandoned Debbie. Debbie's teacher game may have given her the opportunity to work out some of these feelings as well.

Unfortunately, Debbie's progress was interrupted when, quite suddenly, her uncle died of a heart attack. As surrogate father, Debbie's uncle had been very loving and involved with the children. He and the aunt together provided a sense of security that Debbie had apparently not experienced in her early years. His sudden death left Debbie with feelings that she could not handle. She retreated from all academic efforts, and spent her days in her classroom with her head resting on her desk. In counseling, she was lethargic. She complained of fatigue. It was difficult for her to climb steps, and she had an intense desire to sleep. It appeared that Debbie was depressed, and was retreating into a world where nothing could hurt her anymore. In doing so, however, she was cutting herself off from involvement with her love objects. Such a retreat from the real world can be cataclysmic at any age. For this psychologically delicate and vulnerable child, her retreat from reality was frightening to observe.

During this time, the counselor sat quietly with Debbie, and accepted her retreat. She was not forced to come out of her shell. The hours were quiet ones in which little activity occurred. Debbie knew, however, that the counselor understood how bad, and how frightened she felt. The counselor's facial expression, her acceptance of Debbie's withdrawal, and her sympathetic presence were available throughout this difficult period.

After a few months, Debbie's depression appeared to ease. She began to draw pictures. About a house she had drawn, she said:

> "This is a lonely house. I'm going to put a man and woman there to make it a happy house."

Debbie then ripped up the picture into tiny bits. She was apparently trying to deny how lonely and empty she felt inside.

Debbie drew faces, with empty staring eyes, and expressionless mouths. They all looked very much alike. Her comments about some of her pictures were as follows:

> Face of a woman: "There ain't a lot of woman, just one. This woman is a nice woman."
>
> Face of a man: "The man. This man is a lonely man so you know what I'm gonna do? I'm going to put the man and the woman together so she can be happy."
>
> Her comments about a picture of herself were: "She's sad, skinny. No one likes to play with her. She doesn't have a family."

Thus, the theme of loneliness and sadness pervaded Debbie's pictures, and her comments about them. As she drew these pictures, Debbie expressed certain infantile longings as well as fears of the future. She wished she could be a baby again; everything was nice when she was a baby. She wished she had a mother and father. She remembered her mother's death. It frightened her. She was afraid her aunt would die too. She didn't know how her aunt would have enough money to support them.

The recollection of her past suffering, and her expressions of anxiety about the future apparently unburdened Debbie from some of the anguish that she had been suffering from inwardly. She regained some of her high energy level, and seemed to come out of the depression. An extremely difficult crisis in her life had been mastered.

The final problem in Debbie's long-term counseling revolved around termination. The approach of her graduation to junior high school meant that Debbie and the counselor would be separated. How would this child, whose relationship with the counselor had been so intense, and so gratifying, deal with the separation? Would she experience it as another abandonment, and become depressed?

In order to avoid termination being experienced as a sudden shock, the implications of Debbie's graduation were taken up by the counselor many months before it was due to occur. Debbie was frightened at the prospect of her sessions coming to an end. At the same time, she was excited about the thought of going to a new school, and being more "grown-up."

By June, it was obvious that the months of discussion regarding termination had prepared Debbie for the separation. Her behavior had become more mature. Although she was still behind in her school work, she had improved considerably. Her social adjustment was good: she rarely fought and had had no temper tantrums for over a year. A follow-up revealed that Debbie's adjustment to junior high school had gone smoothly; she appeared to be holding her own. Occasional visits to the counselor were joyful occasions for both Debbie and the counselor; Debbie seemed self-confident and happy.

Discussion

The case of Debbie demonstrates the importance of a warm, stable and supportive relationship in the life of a child who had experienced a number of traumatic losses. Play and drawings were combined with verbal discussion in the counseling approach described above. Minimal use was made of interpretation, and the child took the lead in most of the therapeutic encounters. Mature behavior came to replace immature behavior, and Debbie was eventually able to function without the counselor's support.

Counseling the Adolescent

Adolescence is traditionally divided into three parts: puberty (early adolescence); middle adolescence; and late adolescence, the transitional period to adulthood. While there is continuity and contiguity between these periods, each has characteristic stresses and problems of its own.

Puberty is the period of life that links childhood and adolescence. While it occurs simultaneously with the early period of adolescence, and the two terms are used interchangeably with some degree of freedom, puberty describes more the physical period of development, while adolescence is used more to describe a psychological period (Udry and Cliquet, 1982).

A number of factors have been identified as important forces during puberty (Adams, 1976). Social constraints, which check and stifle the burgeoning forces of sexuality, may become objects of rebellion. In the school, where the pubescent spends a large portion of time, teachers and other personnel may be viewed as oppressors, encouraging, by their mere presence, rebellion and rage. McCary (1973) also points out that "this is a period of 'sexual awakening' that is met with ambivalent reactions by both sexes" (p. 31).

Hamburg (1974), in an analysis of the stresses of puberty, pinpoints three key challenges as central to the pubescent's growth: (1) the challenges posed by the biological changes of puberty; (2) the challenges posed by entry into a new social system, the junior high school; and (3) the challenges derived from the sudden entry into a new role status (as a member of the "adolescent sub-culture") (pp. 105–106).

Views of Adolescence

Erikson (1963) outlines the basic developmental challenge of the adolescent period as the individual's search for self-identity. It is through this search that the adolescent comes to see himself or herself as a unique individual, different from all other people. Failure to establish identity during these years leads to what Erikson calls "role confusion," and this may be responsible for many of the conflicts of adolescence. Often, the term *identity crisis* is used to describe the adolescent in transition, who is unable to feel secure with an identity.

One view of adolescence, developed during the 1950s and early 1960s, approaches this period as a time of painful growing in which the individual is beset by numerous conflicts, doubts, and difficulties in adjustment. The contemporary view, on the other hand, de-emphasizes the "storm and stress" conception of adolescence, and emphasizes the stabilizing, goal-directed aspects of adolescent development. One of the more significant manifestations of this is the development of intimate paired relationships, the precursors to marriage and family life in adulthood.

The Development of Intimate Relationships

Developing intimacy and adult-like social relationships are central tasks of adolescence. In general, two characteristics of all social relationships are that (1) each person in the relationship takes the other into account in enacting important elements of many of their behaviors and (2) each party in the relationship can predict the behavior of the other with a fairly high degree of accuracy. Together, what this says is that a social relationship is an organized way of interacting between the participants (Houser & Berkman, 1984).

We are especially interested in the "paired" consensual relationships (dating) that develop during adolescence. Consensual relations include all kinds of social relationships, from casual friendship to deep friendship to intimate, passionate love and romance. These can be viewed on a continuum of social relationships, from the casual, almost nonexistent, to the very intense. Levinger (1982) offers a model of the continuum that illustrates the increasingly intense levels of pair relationships that lead to intimacy. He explains each level this way:

Level 0 Another individual exists only potentially.

Level 1 A person is oriented toward either an actual or imagined other, who is viewed from some distance and without benefit of interaction.

Level 2 Person's and Other's lives touch each other in interaction that has outcomes for each of them.

Level 3 This level is a continuum of Person-Other mutuality . . . The relationship may vary from the shallowest to the deepest degrees of interdependence. (p. 5)

Levels 2 and 3, which often lead to the choice of a lover with whom we decide to cohabit or marry, begin to develop during adolescence. These *intimate relationships,* while they are emotionally powerful, also have a strong cultural component. They did not always exist in the form they do today. In fact, as Gadlin (1984) points out,

> Intimate relationships, as we understand them today, emerged during the early decades of the nineteenth century. Those years mark a rapidly accelerating pace of modernization in America. The transformation of intimate relationships can best be understood within the context provided by the rapid urbanization and industrial development that characterize that period. It is the epoch in which the world of work is severed from the world of the home. For the individual, this separation of the public from the private leads to a great expansion of personal consciousness. Contemporary forms of interpersonal intimacy emerge with this self-conscious bourgeois individual whose life is torn between the separated worlds of work and home. Individualism and intimacy are the Siamese twins of modernization. (Gadlin, 1984, p. 34)

In other words, the feelings of intimacy and love that adolescents experience are part of our modern experience as humans in the contemporary Western world. Still, they are not always clearly defined aspects of our experience. Just what constitutes intimacy in contemporary life is a subject of lively speculation. Rubenstein and Shaver (1982) point out the main defining features of intimacy: "openness, honesty, mutual self-disclosure; caring, warmth, protecting, helping; being devoted to each other, mutually attentive, mutually committed; surrendering control, dropping defenses; becoming emotionally attached, feeling distressed when separation occurs." They go on to point out that *sexual intimacy* also includes "physical openness, physical caring, mutual bodily exploration, and physical attachment" (p. 21). We see in this definition not only different levels of intimacy, but a distinction between sexual and nonsexual intimacy.

Physical attractiveness is an important quality for most of us, but especially significant during the adolescent years. The way we perceive others in terms of their attractiveness deeply affects the way others behave toward us, the way they perceive us, and the way they feel about us. This bias toward the beautiful appears to be part of our socialization very early in life. More positive expectations are expressed of beautiful babies than of unattractive babies. In one study, for example, adults were asked to look at pictures of infants under a year, each of whom was rated for physical attractiveness. The researchers found that both white

Physical Attractiveness and Its Social Meaning

and non-white adults associated attractive children with good qualities, demonstrating that even as we perceive and evaluate infants, a "beauty-is-good" stereotype governs our expectations and thinking (Stephan & Langlois, 1984).

Of course, we don't need scientific studies to convince us of this—we have probably seen or experienced it hundreds of times in our everyday living—but research does help us understand the subtle ways that our physical appearance affects our social standing. Evidence generally indicates that physical attractiveness offers an adolescent a special social status, higher than he or she would otherwise have, whereas physical unattractiveness is a stigma that actually lowers one's social status. Popularity among peers, as well as teachers and adults, is often based on attractiveness. Some other manifestations of this attribute may be enlightening.

Research has shown, for example, that physical attractiveness is related to almost every facet of how we are treated by others, including individuals and social institutions (Rand & Hall, 1983). This appears to be true across racial lines, with blacks, whites, and Latinos associating desirable personality characteristics with individuals they perceive as attractive (Cash and Duncan, 1984). In one study, people who were unattractive were more likely to be perceived by clinicians as mentally disturbed than were people who were physically attractive and acting the exact same way (Jones, Hansson & Phillips, 1978). In another study, it was found that in simulated court cases, attractive defendants fared far better with the jury than did unattractive defendants (Stephen & Tully, 1977), and in the case of mock civil suits, they were awarded higher sums than their unattractive counterparts. Other studies have shown that a person's status is affected by the attractiveness of the company he or she keeps: college women were rated more positively by their peers when they were seen with an attractive male partner than with an unattractive one (Strane & Watts, 1977).

So, we see the social advantages of being physically attractive, or if that is not possible, of being seen with someone who is. This helps us understand why we prefer physically attractive partners in our intimate relationships over physically unattractive ones. It also helps us see why being physically unattractive is a significant disadvantage during the adolescent years.

The Signs of Adolescent Love

We all recognize that being-in-love can cause even the most stable, predictable, logical person to act strangely. Love has its own internal "language"—its own way of inspiring us, of motivating us, of changing the predictable course of our behavior. Literature is full of examples of lovers whose behavior ranged from the bizarre to the fantastic, all because of the intense feelings of love they experienced. And, from our own experiences, we probably realize the effect that being-in-love has upon us personally.

Contemporary commentators have gone well beyond making simple philosophical distinctions, but still primary is the difference between passionate or *romantic* love and such other forms as friendship, filial and sororal love (for brothers and sisters), and parental love. We recognize still, in other words, that a key element in defining love is whether or not passion is a part of it. Both passionate and nonromantic love, however, can be fulfilling and important healthful aspects of living. As Fine (1985) concludes after looking in depth at the psychology of love, "The human being reaches the greatest degree of happiness when he or she can love, enjoy sex, have pleasure, feel yet be guided by reason, be part of a family, have a role in a social order, communicate with his or her fellows, work, has a creative outlet and is free from psychiatric symptomatology. The effectiveness of love can be evaluated by the degree to which a person's life reaches this analytic idea" (p. 304).

Much has been written on the different signs of being in love. Love affects us in multiple ways. We know that it can, and usually does, have a physical effect as well as a psychological one, and that it pervades many areas of our thinking and functioning. Some of the more common measurable signs, according to Pope (1980), are:

A preoccupation with another person. A deeply felt desire to be with the loved one. A feeling of incompleteness without him or her. Thinking of the loved one often, whether together or apart. Separation frequently provokes feelings of genuine despair or else tantalizing anticipation of reuniting. (p. 4)

When some people fall in love, they lose their appetites, while others become absolutely gluttonous, eating as never before. Specific physical changes in heartbeat, blood pressure, pulse, respiration, and sweating have also been recorded in the presence of the loved one or while thinking about that person. Liebowitz (1983), in fact, has written extensively on the "chemistry of love," citing what he believes are specific physiological and biochemical changes that occur as a person experiences the joys of a love relationship or the pains of rejection from such a relationship. He concludes that both the capacity and experience of romantic love are based in human biological design, and that in life situations, biology combines and intermixes with the social and psychological forces in our world:

Romantic love is a basic human potential or capacity, something that we have been wired for for eons but only free to pursue on a broad scale in recent generations. Love involves a complex set of biological processes that we are only beginning to understand, but which appear to involve distinct attraction and attachment mechanisms. The allure of romance is, in part, due to the power with which these processes, once set in motion, can affect us. (Liebowitz, 1983, p. 8)

Researchers have consistently attempted to understand how the biological, psychological, and sociological work together in human emotional activities such as love relationships. Stanley Schachter has proposed a two-factor theory of emotion, which Walster and Berscheid think may be helpful in explaining passionate love and its effects upon us. It is also helpful in understanding why we think of a certain state as being-in-love.

This theory says that whenever we experience an emotion, two factors determine our reaction: our physiological arousal and the way we label the emotional state. For example, if you are given a drug secretly in a cigarette and it makes you feel slightly dizzy and unable to think clearly, this is a marked physical change. If somebody then says, "I just slipped some wonderful marijuana into your cigarette and you are experiencing a high," you may interpret your physical feelings as pleasant and high. But if someone says instead, "I think you just smoked some contaminated tobacco," the very same physical feelings may be interpreted just the opposite, as "Help me, I'm sick."

What does this theory have to do with love? Walster and Berscheid (1971) suggest that the same two components are necessary for a passionate experience: *arousal* and *interpretation*. They suggest, for example, that negative experiences are effective in inducing love because they intensify one's physiological arousal: that is, they cause such reactions as rapid breathing, heart palpitations, nervous tremors, and flushing. Jealousy, anxiety, guilt, loneliness, hatred, sexual stimulation, and confusion all increase one's physiological arousal and thus intensify one's emotional experience. If, because of particular circumstances, the person attributes his or her agitated state to passionate love, he or she will then experience love.

In other words, any factor that increases one's level of physiological arousal or one's tendency to label one's arousal as love would intensify the amount of passion one experiences. This idea received some support in a study in which experimenters told male subjects they would receive painful electric shocks, thus arousing fear. Subsequently, those subjects were more attracted to a young girl to whom they were introduced than were men in the control condition who had not been told to expect shocks and were therefore not excited or aroused by fear (Brehm et al., 1974). The experimenters concluded that fear, though irrelevant to the emotion of liking, facilitated the attraction that could ultimately lead to love.

Sex and the Adolescent
During the adolescent years, as the young person begins to establish his or her own identity outside the nuclear family, dramatic new social roles are explored. These roles are increasingly, though not exclusively, defined by the peer group. Although the family continues to exert some influence, the unique sway it formerly held over the younger child's life and life values gives way as the peer group becomes the primary source of information (and misinformation), attitudes, and models in all areas of sexual behavior (Walters & Walters, 1983).

There is an important reason for this. The adolescent's search for identity, for the "Who I am," which is the major developmental task of adolescence, is complicated by the fact that the adult world does not place much value on what he or she is doing. It is in the peer group that the adolescent finds those who share many of the same circumstances and problems. Thus it is quite reasonable for the adolescent to seek confirmation and approval there.

Many activities are directly related to the adolescent and young adult's new sexual awareness and interests. By far, most people have their first homo- or heterosexual experiences (not necessarily intercourse or even genital sex) during their adolescent years. These experiences constitute an important part of adolescent socialization.

Adolescents are typically confronted with complex sexual choices, and they are not always sure how to react. Questions generated by such choices include: Should I have sex with someone I don't really care about, but whom I think can satisfy my physical needs? How am I supposed to feel when I discover the boy or girl I am dating has been sleeping with someone else—even though he or she insists it had no real meaning but was just an opportunistic encounter? How will others judge me if I decide not to have sexual relations in high school—or, if I choose to have sex with many partners?

In the late 1940s, Professor Alfred C. Kinsey (a zoologist by training!) and his associates published a landmark volume called *Sexual Behavior in the Human Male*. Five years later, it was followed by *Sexual Behavior in the Human Female*. Together, these two works, based on more than 18,000 personal interviews, provided the first comprehensive survey of sexual attitudes, standards, and behaviors in the United States. In effect, they brought sex out of the closet and made public what the public was thinking and doing in the privacy of their bedrooms.

Attitudes and Behaviors

Even though these studies are now more than forty years old, they are still useful in providing a baseline against which we can measure changes in sexual attitudes and behaviors as indicated in more recent surveys. They serve as a marker against which we can measure the changes in contemporary sexual behaviors.

Kinsey's data revealed two important points about nonmarital (including premarital) sexual behavior. First, there were significant differences between boys' and girls' expectations and standards of acceptable behavior. For instance, although boys expected to marry girls who were virgins, they did not expect to remain virgins themselves. This reflects what we call the "double standard," about which we will say more later. Second, Kinsey found some notable social class differences which indicated that the so-called "middle-class morality" was not always applicable to members of the lower socioeconomic class.

Over the next thirty-five years, several other large-scale surveys were conducted, and comparison of them with Kinsey's data allows us to measure social changes with a fair degree of accuracy. One example of research on adolescent sexual behavior was published in 1973 and is called *Adolescent Sexuality in Contemporary America* (Sorenson, 1973). This detailed and comprehensive study sampled the sexual attitudes of hundreds of 13- to 19-year-olds who represented a cross-sample of the country's adolescent population in terms of race, family income, geographical location, etc. Thus, even though the sample is much smaller than Kinsey's, it is a more statistically controlled representation, and probably more accurate. Respondents were given a series of statements and asked to choose "Agree," "Disagree," or "Not Sure." The resulting data indicated that, in general, young people were more willing to experiment sexually, to have sexual relations before marriage, and to more openly discuss sex with peers and with parents than were adolescents thirty years earlier. Most young people said they would be willing to have sexual intercourse with partners with whom they shared a serious loving relationship, but would avoid the casual sexual encounter commonly (although apparently erroneously) thought to be part of the typical teenage experience. To these young people, the intensity and seriousness of love appeared more important than its duration, with the key ingredient being the ability to relate to another person on a deep and loving level. Love is seen as truly fulfilling and as justifying the relationship.

These findings are reaffirmed in a more recent analysis that offers a picture of contemporary adolescent sexual behaviors. Zelnik and Shah (1983), surveying demographic and research studies through 1979, point out,

> In 1979, 50 percent of women aged 15–19 and 70 percent of men aged 17–21 living in metropolitan areas of the United States reported that they have ever had sexual intercourse. The average age at which young women had their first sexual experiences was 16.2, compared with 15.7 among the men; women tended to have their first intercourse with a partner nearly three years older than themselves, whereas men had their first intercourse with a partner less than one year older. . . . Young womens' first coitus generally occurred with someone toward whom the respondent felt a commitment; more than six in ten young women said they had been going steady or engaged to their first sexual partner. (p. 64)

Zelnik and Shah (1983) conclude from their survey that "premarital adolescent sex has been relatively common and generally considered acceptable for men, but the increasing magnitude and acceptance of premarital adolescent sex for women is a far more recent phenomenon" (p. 69). Still, women approach their first sexual encounters through the context of a committed relationship more commonly than men do.

Many adolescents are in conflict with their parents about sexual attitudes. Apparently, parents do not change as quickly as the times do. Many young people feel their parents have given them too little information about sex (Furstenberg et al., 1984). As adolescents grow older, into late adolescence, their opinions differ even more from their parents'. This may cause a conflict as parents seek to become a source of sexual information and their adolescent children reject them in that role. As Obstfeld and Meyers (1984) point out, recent studies show that adolescents prefer "to learn about sex from friends and indicate a decreasing desire to learn about sex from parents [while] the majority of parents questioned preferred sex education to be at least partially home-based." This discrepancy of opinion between parents and adolescents, according to the authors, suggests that parents may not be effective providers of sexual information.

In a review of the research about adolescents' sexual knowledge and practices, Gochros (1982) points out that society has been slow in accommodating many of the changes that have taken place during the last decade. Adults still have difficulty accepting the adolescent's sophisticated awareness of sexuality and increased sexual practices, and adult society is failing to provide "safe, responsible, nonexploitive means for its expression" (p. 37).

The evidence from these surveys, conducted over a period of almost forty years, is that a new sexual *awareness* or outlook has evolved, differentiating young people of the current generation from those of the 1940s and 1950s. This contemporary sexual outlook evolved during the tumultuous social changes in the 1960s and became stabilized and integrated socially during the 1970s. In the present decade, all of its ramifications appear to have remained intact, though at a quieter and less public level.

Most studies indicate significant changes in premarital sexual behavior as well as in attitude, with some clear differences noted between men and women. In one survey, data from questionnaires completed by undergraduate women at a southern university over a ten-year period, from 1965 to 1975, was compared. It was found that "the premarital sexual revolution which was reported to have begun during the late 1960s has actually accelerated during the 1970s" (King, Balswick & Robinson, 1977). Specifically, their data suggests that women, even more than men, have changed their attitudes and behavior in regard to premarital intercourse. Davis and Harris (1982), reviewing the major surveys, conclude that: "Adolescent sexual activity in the United States has increased in recent years, with a steady rise in the number of teenagers who are sexually active and a downward trend in the age at which sexual intercourse is experienced for the first time" (p. 236).

But still, evidence is consistent that even in the 1980s, men and women from adolescence through college age do hold differing opinions about premarital sex, with the man's attitudes slightly more receptive to the possibility than the woman's (Medora & Woodward, 1982). Even where there is similarity in the percentage of men and women favoring premarital sexuality, women still tend to be more interested in one-partner rather than multiple-partner relationships.

What can we conclude from this data? The most prudent conclusion is that the so-called sexual revolution of the 1960s has left many significant and important changes in adolescent (and young adult) sexual behaviors and attitudes in the 1980s (Philliber & Tatum, 1982). This is especially true as it relates to sexual activity outside the marital relationship. These changes demonstrate the existence of gender differences in attitudes and behaviors between adolescent males and females.

Alcohol and Drug Abuse

One of the more refractory problems facing the counselor today is the widespread misuse of drugs and alcohol by adolescents. Much has been written about this problem, much research has been conducted, and large sums of money have been spent by the government to combat drug and alcohol abuse, yet the problem stubbornly persists. In this section, we shall examine some causes and symptoms of drug and alcohol abuse, noting particularly what the school and adolescent counselor can do preventively and therapeutically, both in the school and outside, to alleviate the problem.

What Is Drug "Abuse"?

Although there may be nothing intrinsically dangerous or destructive about a certain drug, it can be abused in a number of ways. Overuse of drugs, using them at an inappropriate time, taking a drug when it is not required, or forming a psychological addiction are all forms of drug abuse. If the drug in itself is not specifically dangerous, the problem arises as a result of the uses to which the drug is put. Alcohol, for example, is imbibed moderately at counseling conventions with no discernible harm to anyone. But when a seventh grade boy comes to school drunk each day or when the parents of a high school girl cannot give her appropriate supervision because of their dependence upon alcohol, drug abuse exists. Marijuana, a drug with no proven danger to the occasional user, produces pleasant, relaxed feelings and heightened sensual awareness. When a high school youth, however, becomes unable to study because of excessive marijuana use or when a student loses his or her ability to function except when using it, we are dealing with a serious drug problem.

Some drugs, on the other hand, are inherently dangerous and may always be considered instances of drug abuse unless taken under the supervision of a physician. Heroin, a synthetic derivative of morphine, is a highly addictive substance with no legitimate medical uses. Crack, a derivative of cocaine, gained a deadly prominence during the mid-1980s. The hallucinogenic (psychedelic) drugs—LSD, DMT, mescaline, and psilocybin—give the user the illusion of expanded consciousness, of greater awareness and sensitivity; in fact, however, these drugs produce gross distortions of reality, hallucinations, and erratic behavior and thinking. Barbiturates and other depressant drugs produce a feeling of relaxation and blissfulness that enables the user to forget all the problems that must be faced in life. Such drugs are highly addictive and may result in fatality upon withdrawal. Cases of suicide under the influence of barbiturates are not uncommon. Amphetamines are stimulant drugs that result in great feelings of optimism as well as mania. They are used by adolescents as sleep inhibitors, appetite suppressants, and for relief of depression. Prolonged use of amphetamines may result in hallucinations, psychosis, and violent behavior.

Perhaps the single most accurate criterion of what determines drug abuse is the attitude the individual has toward the drugs. If drug experiences serve as an occasional social meeting ground, this is a far different situation from one in which the drug has become a panacea the young person cannot live without. If the addictive or nonaddictive substance becomes the central focus of the adolescent's existence—his or her *raison d'être*—the individual is clearly exhibiting signs of drug abuse.

Beginning in the mid-70s and continuing through the present, alcohol has been the single most abused drug in adolescent culture. It is estimated that more than three million teenagers today are alcoholics, most of them enrolled in schools. No one knows exactly why this is, but it may represent an ironic adolescent rebellion against the prevailing adult acceptance of marijuana.

The manifest symptoms of alcohol abuse among teenagers are as evident or more evident than the symptoms of drug abuse, which at times may be obscure. The adolescent problem drinker is likely to have a high absentee rate, appear intoxicated in class, and fall behind in schoolwork. It is not uncommon to find a flask of alcohol concealed on the person of the student, and the student may even imbibe during the class itself, so strong is the drive and so weak the control. The counselor, rather than responding punitively, should recognize the serious medical-psychological nature of this problem and encourage the student to seek help.

No one fully understands why drugs are used and what underlies the compulsion to fall into drug abuse. Several theories currently prominent or under investigation are shown in Table 11.1:

Causes and Treatment of Abuse

Table 11.1
Theories of Drug Use and Abuse

Disease-Addiction Theory	Perceives drug use as an aberrant phenomenon afflicting otherwise healthy people. The exposure and use of the drug, with its addictive potential is the reason for the abuse. This disease model is central to medical treatment of drug abuse.
Gateway Theory	Emphasizes the orderly progression from one drug to another as young people get more involved in drug use. Also called stepping-stone theory.
Social Theories	Specify how features of the social structure that are external to an individual produce observable patterns of drug-using behavior.
Psychological Theories	Examine the individual's personality and psychopathology to explain drug abuse as a maladaptive behavior.
Political Theory	Believes that each individual has the right to use drugs as he or she sees fit, and that society should have a hands-off policy.
Psycho-Social Theories	Suggest that an individual's personality, environment, and behavior are interrelated and organized so as to develop a dynamic state designated as *problem-behavior proneness.*
Life-Style Theories	Point out that groups of adolescent drug users share unique and identifiable characteristics. Drugs are linked to other activities and play an important part in defining a group, both to its members and to outsiders.
Peer Cluster Theory	Suggests that small, identifiable peer clusters determine where, when, and how drugs will be used.

(Adapted from Oetting and Beauvais, 1986)

Oetting and Beauvais (1986) have suggested that *peer cluster theory* helps explain the prevalence of drug abuse among the adolescent population in the schools:

> The potency of peer influence is not new; peer influence, however, is a broad and general term. Peer cluster theory differs—its proponents contend that small, identifiable peer clusters determine where, when, and how drugs are used and that these clusters specifically help shape attitudes and beliefs about drugs. Although there is still much to learn about peer clusters, the theory is very useful for understanding adolescent drug use. It focuses the counselor on those key groups that actually maintain and encourage drug involvement. Peer clusters theory also emphasizes the importance of the psychosocial characteristics that underlie drug use and that set the stage for these peer clusters to work. (p. 19)

What the Counselor Can Do

The counselor who deals with this problem of abuse might begin by exploring honestly his or her own feelings about drug use, alcohol use, and the adolescent drug culture in general. An empathic understanding of why many adolescents have the need to abuse drugs may follow such reflection; but most of all, objective information should be separated from values and cultural stereotypes. In general, as Peele (1986, p. 24) points out,

> The mission of those concerned with adolescent drug abuse is to create a cultural climate that encourages children to value and to achieve independence, adventure, intimacy, consciousness, activity, fun, self-reliance, health, problem-solving capacities, and a commitment to the community. There is no better antidote for drug abuse than adolescents' beliefs that the world is a positive place, that they can accomplish what they want and that they can gain satisfaction from life. Enabling children to develop this outlook is certainly no small order; however, all efforts to simplify the task are doomed to fail. . . . (Peele, 1986, p. 24)

A counselor should also understand that a person undergoing severe stresses in adolescence is more likely than a mature person to rely on drugs for escape, for fantasy, and for peer group approval and recognition. The escape values of these drugs lie in their potential for allowing one to forget one's problems and to seek refuge temporarily from the real world; and who needs this more than the conflict-torn, changing, disequilibrated adolescent? A fantasy world is set up, a world where the individual is freed of all responsibilities, where nothing is important, and where there is no way to get hurt by others.

The counselor should work closely with school personnel, providing objective information as well as psychological counseling. Films and other presentations designed to lessen alcohol abuse among adolescents are available from the National Council on Alcoholism, Washington, D.C. Local school boards have also acquired resources for preventive education in this area. But most importantly, as in the case of drug abuse, the counselor's own awareness and sensitivity are critical factors in all preventive efforts.

What can the adolescent counselor do to help the adolescent client develop the skills and competencies needed to achieve a sense of identity and to mature into a healthy adult? How do some of the developmental aspects of this period affect counseling applications? Specific counseling approaches for reaching adolescents are plentiful. Many studies have demonstrated the efficacy of the school as a setting for improving young people's intellectual, social, and emotional development simultaneously. There are several other key points that have consistently been emphasized in most of the studies that have investigated adolescent counseling in the school, agency, or private counseling settings:

Some Practical Counseling Suggestions

1. Adolescents respond best when there is support from (or, at the least, when there is minimum opposition from) their peers. For this reason, the likelihood of a program's success is increased when the program comprises a peer approach (such as group counseling or cooperative school projects).
2. Equal to the peer group is the influence of the family. In most situations, then, family should be included. Since many of the difficulties experienced by the adolescent involve the family setting as either a cause or contributing factor, the most direct approach to effective treatment suggests the active participation of family members.
3. Adolescents typically respond well to informational programs, as long as their emotional needs have been taken into account. Because the adolescent is capable of "formal operational thought," the provision of information and the exchange of ideas can be conducted on a relatively high level.
4. The group is an effective medium for reaching the adolescent. Generally, positive changes occur in the group context because adolescent clients are "given an opportunity to release their tensions and to examine their behavior with the help of their peers" (Goodman, 1976, p. 520).
5. The counselor can play a unique role in bridging the communication gap between troubled adolescents and their parents. Kifer, Lewis, Green and Phillips (1974) have described an innovative approach for training predelinquent adolescents and their parents to negotiate conflict situations. The results indicate that with appropriate training, the adolescent and the parents can learn ways to communicate that will avoid conflict. Woods (1974) too has argued that parents' groups are important contributors to growth in the treatment of their adolescent children.

Counseling the Adult

There are several unique developmental challenges associated with the adult years. While childhood is a period of foundation learning (both emotionally and cognitively) and adolescence is an experimental, transitional period in which new social behaviors are explored and new perceptions integrated into a coherent image of self, adulthood, by far the longest period, comprises many vastly different stages of development. During these years the individual takes on major new roles and develops new responsibilities. He or she may marry and have children, creating what the sociologists call a "nuclear family of procreation"—or raise a family alone. Moving from the role of child, one becomes the head of the household. The challenges of the world of work are dominant. A career, or job, or vocational (or *non*vocational) life-style is established during these years. Growth and development in interpersonal relationships, along with a new social recognition, emerge. You have arrived, made it!

Because the adult's life expectancy has increased greatly, and along with longer life, the promise of healthy physical functioning, the vocational options available to the adult have changed dramatically. As Rebelsky (1975) points out,

> This longer life brings with it new potentials and problems. For example, a forty-year-old professor, teaching for ten years, could learn an entire new field at age forty and devote more time to the new field than he gave to the first one. Women who have opted to stay home until their children are grown are now able to be ready for entire new careers at an age when, at the turn of the century, mothers were dead or still having babies. (p. xix)

Career options are, therefore, a vital element in the new challenges of this period.

Then, of course, there are the challenges of working together to make a marriage work, of raising a family, of dealing with the economic realities of life. Some of these difficulties are discussed in the following chapter, "Family Counseling."

Finally, there occur what to many prove the two most difficult problems of adulthood: poor health and retirement. It is a time of awareness of the ever approaching prospect of one's own death; of seeing one's contemporaries die; of losing those whom we love. But even before that time the person who has worked for so many years to build a career, and with it a sense of self-esteem and self-worth, now faces possibilities of retirement and loss of all these roles. Moreover, during the adult years aging is viewed as much more detrimental than it is earlier in life. The child or adolescent lies about his or her age by making himself or herself a little older; it is just the opposite with the adult.

If this sounds staggering and overwhelming, fraught with difficulties, it is! But many of these can be ameliorated by counseling interventions which are especially designed to meet the special needs of the adult client.

Several outstanding social, economic, and demographic factors have brought about major changes in the lives of middle-age and older adults in our contemporary American society. Many of these changes have direct implications for the counselor working with the adult client in the clinical, agency, occupational, or college setting. In the following pages, we will review briefly how changes in age distribution of the U.S. population, in the average age at which children leave home, and in the sex-role adjustments of mature men and women are all affecting multiple areas of role functioning and interpersonal adjustment which are often amenable to counseling interventions. Let us consider some of these factors.

First, we know that "the fraction of the population aged sixty and over rose from less than four percent in 1830 to fifteen percent in 1976" (Clark & Spengler, 1978, p. 8). Middle-aged persons, between forty-five and sixty-five, now constitute about twenty percent of the population, that is between these two age groups, we are speaking about thirty-five percent of all Americans. Moreover, about forty percent of the American workforce are women, many of them from this group of forty-five to sixty-five.

There have also been dramatic changes in the timing of the family cycle over the past few decades. Neugarten (1977) points out that children leave home at an earlier age, and that the life span has lengthened because of the advances in medicine and the growing availability of health care. These changes have led to an extended postparental interval in which the husband and wife are the only members remaining in the household. A survey of one hundred normal women aged forty-three to fifty-three from working-class and middle-class backgrounds revealed that this stage, rather than being a stressful time for women, as the researchers had expected, is associated with a higher level of satisfaction than is found among other women. Evidently, Neugarten says, caring for children at home is more taxing and stressful than having children who are married and launched on their own lives. Another surprising finding of the survey was that overall, these women held relatively favorable views of the menopause and did not regard it as a major loss of feminine identity, no matter how severe their physical symptoms had been. Middle-aged women, then, are assuming a new social role, more active and quite different than the one they had been enacting for generations.

In another study of men and women aged forty to seventy, Neugarten found that in middle age there is an emphasis on stock-taking and introspection. There is movement from "outer-world to inner-world orientation." Another characteristic of middle age appears to be a difference in the way in which time is perceived. People at this age look to changes in their physical condition, career, and family rather than to their chronological age for their "primary cues in clocking themselves." Many of the subjects in Neugarten's survey could not give their exact age when asked but had to stop and think, often saying, "Let's see, 51? No, 52. Yes, 52 is right" (p. 39). And, we know from our own experiences that it is not unusual for someone in this age group to say, "I remember, that was about a year before Linda graduated," or "Let's see, that must have been around the time Paul got married."

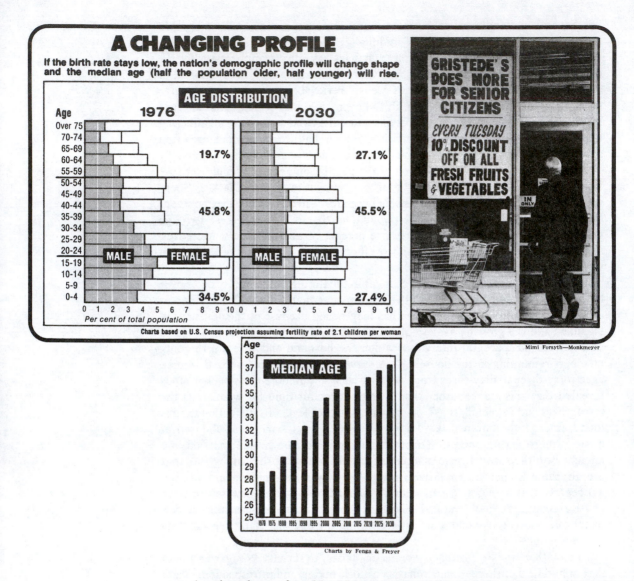

A CHANGING PROFILE

If the birth rate stays low, the nation's demographic profile will change shape and the median age (half the population older, half younger) will rise.

AGE DISTRIBUTION

1976 — 2030

Age	1976	2030
Over 75		
70-74		
65-69	19.7%	27.1%
60-64		
55-59		
50-54		
45-49		
40-44	45.8%	45.5%
35-39		
30-34		
25-29		
20-24	MALE FEMALE	MALE FEMALE
15-19		
10-14		
5-9		
0-4	34.5%	27.4%

Per cent of total population

Charts based on U.S. Census projection assuming fertility rate of 2.1 children per woman

MEDIAN AGE

Age 25 to 38 — years 1970 1975 1980 1985 1990 1995 2000 2005 2010 2015 2020 2025 2030

Charts by Fenga & Freyer

GRISTEDE'S DOES MORE FOR SENIOR CITIZENS
EVERY TUESDAY 10% DISCOUNT OFF ON ALL FRESH FRUITS & VEGETABLES

Mimi Forsyth—Monkmeyer

Another change found by Neugarten among the middle aged is the personalization of death. Death in middle age "becomes a real possibility for the self . . . no longer the . . . extraordinary occurrence that it appears in youth" (p. 39).

With these in mind, we will examine some of the general stages and challenges of the adult years, as they have been conceptualized theoretically, and then focus on some of the specific kinds of problems and conflicts in which a counselor may intervene.

Erikson designates three stages as particular to the adult years. Each stage in his paradigm, as you may recall, is named after the developmental challenge associated with the period it describes. We will see later that many of the real-life problems and conflicts adults experience are related to these developmental challenges.

Stage 6 is called *Intimacy vs. Isolation.* Following immediately the adolescent period, in which a sense of identity is acquired, "the young adult . . . is eager and willing to fuse his identity with that of others. He is ready for intimacy, that is, the capacity to commit himself to concrete affiliations and partnerships and to develop the ethical strength to abide by such commitments, even though they may call for significant sacrifices and compromises" (p. 184). The individual who is not able to achieve intimacy during this period, who finds himself or herself cut off from others, suffers from "a deep sense of isolation and consequent self-absorption."

Stage 7, *Generativity vs. Stagnation,* refers to the conflict between the drive to provide for future generations, directly or indirectly, versus the tendency to become over-absorbed in self, unable to foster growth. In its broader sense, according to Erikson, generativity means not only bringing children into the world, but it also refers to the varied forms of creativity.

Finally, we have the final stage, *Ego Integrity vs. Despair.* "Only in him who in some way has taken care of things and people and has adapted himself to the triumphs and disappointments adherent to being, the originator of others or the generator of products and ideas—only in him may gradually ripen the fruit of these seven stages. I know no better word for it than ego integrity." With these words, Erikson sums up what is perhaps the highest point of human development, and at the same time, they help us see how the development of a successful individual is not only compatible with but also contributes to the perpetuation of the species: specifically, by contributing new ideas and advancements to human civilization.

Although it is helpful to have such convenient stages in which to fit our perceptions of adulthood, they do not tell us enough. What are some of the practical kinds of problems and challenges of this period? Specifically, what kinds of adult problems are most likely to reveal themselves in the counseling setting? Kimmel (1976) has suggested three common crisis points in adult life that are likely to bring an adult into the counselor's office. We should consider each briefly since they are so typical of adult problems.

The first one Kimmel calls, "Where Did We Go Wrong?" This is a conflict of late parenthood, where parents "are tempted to look to their children's success and accomplishment—or lack of it—for validation of their own success as parents and, to an extent, for validation of their sense of generativity" (p. 104). This type of crisis can occur whenever parents discover that their grown children did not turn out the way they wanted them to be. Often, of course, it represents a failure of the parents to get what they wanted from their own lives; that is, it is a displacement onto their children.

"I Hate Putting Mother in There!" is the second crisis. Nowadays, it is not at all uncommon for grown children to place their aging parents either in a "retirement home," a "hotel," or a "nursing home," or whatever euphemism is used. "Many adults," Kimmel points out, "face the difficult choices of having the parents move into their home, trying to find support services for their parents in the community, or placing them in a nursing home." This is a common psychological conflict that the counselor can help the person deal with.

Finally, one of the most poignant conflicts is—"How Can I Go On?" The loss of a loved one, especially a spouse, results in a grief crisis. We shall discuss this in chapter 15.

In concluding his sensitive article, Professor Kimmel lists the four areas of adult counseling and of counseling the elderly that deserve more attention:

1. *Work:* the need to provide counseling services for adults of all ages for seeking out and beginning new careers; and the need for preretirement and retirement counseling.
2. *Leisure:* the need to develop leisure counseling to teach persons of all ages how to best employ leisure and how to integrate leisure into their work and other roles in a life span counseling/education framework.
3. *Aging:* the need to offer a full range of counseling services to middle-aged and aging persons, explicitly including sex therapy, marital counseling, and psychotherapy that is free of the stereotypes of ageism.
4. *Heterogeneity of society:* the need to develop a range of counseling services for the growing variety of lifestyles. . . . (p. 105)

Career and leisure counseling will be discussed in greater detail in chapter 19. At this point, let us consider some of the specific ways in which large numbers of adults in our contemporary society are confronted by myriad social and psychological challenges. We will note also how counselors can help their clients resolve, or at least mitigate, many of these problems.

Adult Counseling Applications

Many of the general problems, conflicts, and situations discussed throughout this book are relevant for the adult counselor. But there are also specific areas of adjustment that affect the adult and older population more greatly than their younger counterparts.

Sexual Adjustments

We mentioned earlier that there are many complex sexual adjustments that have to be made during the periods of middlescence and later adulthood. Some specific sexual and role adjustments of marriage will be discussed in detail in chapter 12, "Family Counseling." At this point, we should note a special area of adult sexual adjustment.

For many years the sexual expectations of married couples in the middle age group were consistent with the myth of less sexual activity, and therefore they were, at least superficially, not troubled by the decline in their marital sexual activity. But things have changed in just the opposite direction now, and couples may find themselves confused about their new roles and the "new norms" of middle-age sexuality. As Cleveland (1976) points out,

> During the past few years there has been a growing trend which is essentially a reversal of the traditional norms defining aging as a-sexual. . . . Post-parental couples are urged to develop a "second honeymoon" marriage. They are encouraged to read marital enrichment manuals, to learn new sexual arousal techniques which will make their sex lives as exciting as they had been in the early years of marriage. Rather than defining aging as a-sexual, the new norms imply a continuation of sexual behavior throughout life. (p. 235)

Cleveland goes on to suggest that to some extent these new norms may be just as unrealistic as the old ones, and they may place just as many social pressures upon couples to conform to values they do not personally feel comfortable with.

The important point is that sexuality in the mature marriage can still contribute to its satisfactions or to its difficulties, but it cannot and should not be taken for granted. It requires as much thought and attention as do other aspects of the marital role that are changing over the life cycle. As the counselor helps the marriage counseling clients understand this reality better, they become more capable of communicating with each other their needs, expectations, and satisfactions.

One of the major problems facing the older person or the widow(er) is where to reside. Too often the apartment or home in which the family was raised is no longer appropriate to the needs of the older person or couple. This is especially true in large cities and their suburbs, where maintaining a house or renting an apartment is too great a financial burden for the older person, especially a retiree living on a pension. Even when the house is owned, the cost of heating it and the job of taking care of it may require more effort and cost than the older person is able or willing to expend.

There is sometimes the option of moving in with grown children and their families, but this can cause conflicts and result in a generally uncomfortable living situation. Where once the older person enjoyed the role of parent and authority (or head) of the nuclear family, he or she is now a "guest" in the child's home. This requires quite a bit of adjustment.

Retirement homes in special communities are another option, for those who can afford it. Here, while there are opportunities to socialize with one's peers, there is invariably a tendency to lose touch with the "outside," that is, the multigenerational world. At the very point when interactions with young people could

Residence Choices

stimulate their own drive and change their perceptions and expectations of life, the retirement community cuts off the youthful world, along with its potential for important late-life socialization.

A recent concept called "congregate housing" has been receiving some positive attention. Congregate housing works something like a college dormitory, where elderly people share the common facilities, but have their own one-bedroom or efficiency apartment. The advantage of congregate housing is that it does not institutionalize the person, as would an old age home, nor does it require the time, energy, and responsibilities that living on one's own in a retirement community would. It also facilitates companionship and provides many opportunities.

Going beyond these general decisions and crises, we must look separately at the challenges for the middle-age or older man as opposed to the middle-age or older woman. For, as we will see, there are important social and psychological differences between them, and these affect our counseling profoundly.

Differences between the Sexes

Because of their sex-stereotyped socialization, there are considerable differences in career expectations, challenges and adjustments between men and women in middle-age or maturity. Typically, it is the man's career, its successes, failures, rewards, and stresses, which exerts the most profound effect on the family. Some of the ways the family may be affected by the provider's career include: the need for mobility (where the family as a unit may be forced to uproot and move to a new city or state so that the man can rise in his profession); the requirement of maintaining certain social relationships advantageous to occupational advancement (entertaining the boss and his wife); demonstrating certain social attitudes and beliefs to which one may not really ascribe (belonging to the "right" church or club). The man's career can also contribute to a family mid-life crisis, especially where he feels he has not succeeded at accomplishing what he set out to do when he first entered his profession. Such a man may look now, after many years of relative disinterest, to finding new satisfactions in the family. But it is often a family that has learned to get along without him. As Berger and Wright (1978) point out, the career dissatisfied man, "having failed to conquer and dominate the work world now turns inward to seek solace, satisfaction, and meaning from his marriage and family. Chronologically, this usually occurs when the children have left or are in the process of leaving and the wife, having spent years looking inward to the family and marriage, is now beginning to look outside the home for her satisfaction" (p. 51). Thus, their expectations at this period are different, and while the man is looking inside for fulfillment, the woman is seeking new fulfillments outside.

While the woman's career has not traditionally been as important a factor in affecting the family, this is changing somewhat. Now, many older women, having raised their children, are eager to get into (or get back into) the job market. Still, "even today when childbearing and family responsibilities are less significant components of women's lives, it is true and probably will continue to be true that many women will withdraw from participation in the occupational structure for periods due to family responsibilities" (Richardson, 1979, p. 35). This can cause many frustrations when a woman finds there is no place for her in the job market, that she has no contacts, that her skills are no longer needed. She may resent the younger women who are working, or she may mobilize her resources and try to develop the skills and contacts necessary for job survival. The problems women face in the world of work will be discussed in more detail in chapter 19, "Career Counseling."

A part of the problem faced by the older woman is that she is very much a victim of stereotypes that categorize her in a way that is not only false, but is also fundamentally damaging. "The older woman in our society," Payne and Whittington (1976) point out, "is socially devalued and subject to a number of harmful, negative stereotypes that picture her as sexless, uninvolved except for church work, and alone." In their investigation of some of the more common stereotypes, they found some supportive but much contradictory evidence when they actually examined the available research data on women from late forties to late sixties. The following summary is from Payne and Whittington (1976):

The Mature Woman

Stereotype	Research Evidence
Older women are usually either widowed or have never been married.	While most older women are widowed (53%), a relatively large number (38%) are married and only about 9 percent have never married or are divorced.
The older woman is both sexually inactive and sexually uninterested.	Research clearly demonstrates that there is no reason the older woman cannot and should not be sexually active, although the extent of her activity is determined by the availability of a partner and by the partner's sexual capacity.
The older woman is depicted as a pleasantly plump granny, who spends her time in a rocking chair knitting or sewing.	Although many older women do have difficulty constructively using their leisure time, this is beginning to change. Women have been socialized to enjoy limited types of activities and this may persist into old age. Some leisure activities older women rank highly are: church and volunteer work, gardening, cooking, playing with children, television viewing and radio listening. Also, "most older women still prefer the activity they enjoyed most five years ago and expect little change in preference during the next five years."
Women are more religious than men at every stage of the life cycle and particularly so in old age.	The stereotype is generally supported, at least insofar as religion is typically the most meaningful value in these women's lives. But church attendance begins to decline with advancing age, perhaps because of the physical difficulties of getting to church.

The Mature Man   Important research on the middle-aged man's psychosocial development has been conducted in recent years by Levinson and his colleagues at Yale University (Levinson et al. 1977). They have developed a comprehensive view of male development, from the end of adolescence to the middle forties, and Levinson himself has presented these ideas and others in a worthwhile book called *The Seasons of a Man's Life* (Levinson, 1978).

After studying forty men representing four occupational groups—blue- and while-collar workers in industry, business executives, academic biologists, and novelists—for a total of from ten to twenty hours over two years, the researchers constructed a five-stage theory of adult male development in the age span of about twenty to forty. These stages explain how the male's socialization has prepared him to continue developing in a fairly predictable pattern.

The first stage, leaving the family (LF), is a transition period between adolescence and entry into the adult world, covering roughly the ages sixteen or eighteen to twenty or twenty-four. It is a transitional stage because the person is usually half in and half out of the family. He is making an effort to separate from the family and to develop a new home base, but still maintains many deep attachments to his nuclear family of orientation. This stage usually begins at the end of high school and ends when the family balance shifts and some independence is attained; when a young man has in fact separated from the nuclear family of orientation, and has begun to make a place for himself in the adult world.

The second stage, getting into the adult world (GIAW), begins when the center of gravity shifts to the person's new home base. It starts in the early twenties and extends until about age twenty-seven or twenty-nine. It is a time of "exploration and provisional commitment to adult roles, memberships, responsibilities and relationships." According to the investigators, the overall developmental task of the GIAW period is to "explore the available possibilities of the adult world, to arrive at an initial definition of oneself as an adult and to fashion an initial life structure which provides a viable link between the valued self and the wider adult world" (p. 51).

The third stage is settling down (SD). This period ordinarily begins in the early thirties. The man now makes deeper personal commitments, gives more of himself to his work, his family, and to a set of highly-valued interests. It is during this stage that he makes and pursues long-range plans and goals. This period extends until the late thirties or early forties, when various internal and external changes bring on new developments.

The fourth period is called becoming one's own man (BOOM), and it occurs in the middle to late thirties. The investigators see this as the high point of early adulthood. A key element is that no matter what he has actually accomplished to date, the individual feels that he is not sufficiently his own man. He feels overly dependent on the people who have authority over him or who exert great influence on him, such as his superiors at work, or someone, teacher, adviser, or protector, who has played the role of mentor to him up until this point. The final renunciation of mentors usually occurs between the ages of thirty-five to thirty-nine. This is the period in which a man tries very hard for a crucial promotion or other form of *public* recognition (writing a best seller or being recognized as a scientist, or becoming a full professor).

The fifth period is called the midlife transition (MLT). In this period, which may or may not involve considerable turmoil, the person asks himself whether what he has gained up to that point is really what he wants. To the investigators, it is "a matter of the goodness of fit between the life structure and the self" (p. 57). A man may achieve his goals but find his success hollow. He has a midlife crisis if he questions his life structure and decides to modify or change it drastically. During this period, there is a sense of physical decline and a recognition of one's mortality, a sense of aging, which means being old rather than young, and of the polarity of aging, by which is meant the emergence and integration of the more feminine aspects of the self.

The MLT reaches its peak sometime in the early forties, following which there is an important period of restabilization, in which a new life structure begins to take shape. This stage, which is the outcome of the midlife transition, is currently being studied by this research team, who view it as a period with great developmental possibilities as well as a period of potential threat to the individual as well as the family. Some well-known men, such as Gandhi, Freud, and Jung made great personal and professional strides during their forties, whereas others such as Dylan Thomas, Ernest Hemingway and F. Scott Fitzgerald, could not manage the crisis and destroyed themselves in it. Though the Yale team has provided a useful addition to our understanding of mature men, it should be clear that its generalizations need not be unconditionally accepted without recognizing that it is a single study using a small selected sample. Nevertheless, this study does provide some interesting insights into the development of mature men.

The Elderly Person

The psychologist Carl Gustav Jung recognized that in all cultures throughout history there has been what he called an "archetype" of the "wise old man," an unconscious image of wisdom attached to age. While this may or may not be so anymore, clearly our culture expresses directly and indirectly certain attitudes about old people, and these not only influence how they are treated and their status and role in the social hierarchy, but also to a very great extent, how they feel about themselves.

A number of studies have been done over the years to find out "How are old people perceived by the young and by themselves?" and "Are there differences in social perception between class and educational levels?" Several formal questionnaires have even been developed and used and we generally believe now that there is a direct relationship between educational attainment and attitudes toward old people, with respondents who have higher levels of education generally showing more positive attitudes (Thorson, Hancock & Whatley, 1974), while race and social status have not been found to be significant in how old people are perceived by others (Thorson, 1975).

The "Empty Nest" Syndrome

After the long period of family life in which rearing a child (or children) was of primary importance, the sudden absence of children in the home can be difficult to adjust to. Just as early in marriage there is an adjustment to the new role of parenthood, so too later in life is there an equal adjustment to not being in this role anymore.

The difficulties of adjustment may be eased somewhat if the parents can assume the role of grandparents. When their children begin having children, it offers the parents opportunities to provide (usually unrequested) advice on child-rearing, and to tell many nostalgic stories of how they raised their child, who is now the mother or father of the new baby. But it also gives them a feeling of purpose and continuity, not only to observe the perpetuation of the family line, but also to experience once again the pleasures of holding an infant and of teaching a young child. There is a social prestige to be enjoyed as well, as they interact with their peers, trading stories about their grandchildren and looking at the latest photos.

Summary

In this chapter, we presented a life span overview of applied counseling. Using Erik Erikson's ages of man, we outlined some of the principal psychosocial characteristics of the developmental epochs, and considered their relevance for counseling practice.

As is traditional, we divided the life span into three parts: childhood, adolescence, and adulthood. For the childhood period, we demonstrated the value of play counseling approaches, and offered a case study. We pointed out that play approaches are flexible and fit into almost any kind of counseling orientation. The case study of Debbie illustrated how many of the psychosocial tasks of this period can be explored through play.

For the adolescent period, we used Erikson's age of "identity vs. role confusion" as our paradigm. Proceeding from this, we considered some of the typical problems with which the adolescent counselor must deal: sexual adjustment and drug and alcohol abuse. In each instance we asked, How can the counselor help the adolescent deal with these developmental challenges?

In examining the adult years, we began with Erikson's final three stages and then explored some of the prevailing social trends and typical adult crises. We noted how the mature man and woman face different, but equally compelling, challenges during these periods.

Chapter Aim

To delineate family counseling as a specific counseling modality, to survey the forms of the contemporary American family and outline the basic framework of family counseling approaches, indicating some directions of study worth pursuing.

CAPSULE

What Is Family Counseling?

We develop a broad, operational definition of family counseling, including both marriage counseling and joint parent-child counseling. Some of the differences between individual and family counseling are discussed.

A Look at the Contemporary American Family

A survey of the four main family forms predominant in the United States today: nuclear family; extended family, including modified extended family; the single-parent family; and, the "reconstituted" family, which describes a second family composed of members of two earlier, now dissolved, families.

Criteria of Healthy Family Functioning

We consider some of the research and theory which help explain what makes a family healthy and what enables its members to interact productively with each other. We identify several criteria that identify a healthy, fully-functioning family.

Issues in Family Counseling

The setting for family counseling is established in part by the counselor's attitude: i.e., conveying the feeling of being there to help the entire family function better together, as a unit. The goals of counseling differ from family to family, but generally there is emphasis on constructive functioning and improved intra-family communication. The concept of "socio-emotional intactness" helps us view the family as an emotionally functional unit within a social context.

Theories of Family Counseling

Although the basic theories of counseling presented in Part 3 are applicable in the family setting, there are some specialized theories based on the structure of the family rather than on a specific school of psychotherapy. We look at four paradigms which help explain how a family changes: the insight/working through paradigm; the conditioning/reinforcement paradigm; the modeling paradigm; and, the paradox paradigm.

Techniques of Family Counseling

Some specific techniques applicable for family counseling are discussed. "Contracting" involves setting up the rules, guidelines, and goals of treatment. "Timing" of interventions refers to their appropriateness: eight criteria of appropriate interventions are explicated. Behavioral techniques are also widely used for helping families in conflict.

Family Counseling Applications

We look at some of the main applications of family counseling in contemporary practice. Marriage counseling involves helping the partners learn to adapt to compatible role situations and to communicate openly. Counseling separated or divorced persons, and their children, requires recognition of the phenomenon called post-divorce reaction. Family violence counseling involves working with an entire family where one or more members is physically abusive or the victim of abuse.

Family Counseling

Family counseling is probably the single most rapidly growing field in professional counseling today. There are a number of reasons for this prominence, including a new public awareness of the values of counseling in general, a wider availability of services, and a reduction in any stigma connected with being in counseling or therapy. The field is so replete with its own comprehensive literature of theory and treatment that it would be presumptuous for us to attempt to explore it in any depth in so brief a chapter. Nevertheless, we will use this chapter to outline some of the main points of family counseling, drawing upon case material to highlight practical strategies of dealing with the family constellation. Our goal will not be to help the reader become an accomplished family counselor, but rather to point out the basic framework of the field, and to indicate some directions of study worth pursuing.

Although there are a number of ways of defining family counseling, we will use a broad operational definition that includes marriage counseling, parent-child counseling, and counseling more than one family member in a joint session. The important point is to be able to functionally differentiate family counseling from individual counseling and not to confuse one with the other. Such a confusion would impair the status of family counseling as a unique modality of treatment. Family counseling is *not* simply counseling several individuals from the same family. Rather, it involves looking at and dealing with each individual—both in terms of surface functioning and psychological depth—within the family context.

Robinson (1975) suggests that differences between individual and family counseling extend to three areas that affect our counseling approach: personality development and the study of personality; symptom formation; and counseling strategies and techniques. In each of these areas, he suggests, the individual plays an interactive role with the other family members. "In family therapy," he argues, "the dominant forces in personality development are thought to be located

What Is Family Counseling?

externally, in the organized behavioral characteristics of the family. . . . Family therapy also views symptoms as connected with conflict, but that conflict is viewed as originating outside of the individual. The conflict is located in the transactional interface between the natural developmental strivings of an emerging individual and the distorted relational objectives of a dysfunctional family system" (p. 1046). We see from this that the basic underlying conceptions of the individual's psychology are intimately related to family interactions. Indeed, this is a hallmark of family counseling: it has broken away from individual psychotherapy because its seminal thinkers found the individual approaches they studied insufficient for dealing with many complex human problems (Allen, 1975).

Ackerman's (1958) historical comment is typical of the way in which family counseling derived from weaknesses inherent in the individual therapy approach.

> We have somehow kept ourselves so busy, so preoccupied with studying and treating the suffering of individuals, that we have, in effect, blinded ourselves to the significance of the concurrent struggles of the family for mental health, and to the way in which the ongoing content of family experience affects the emotional struggles of its adult members. I do not mean to imply that the treatment of the individual patient, the alleviation of the very real sufferings of a single human being, is unimportant or unnecessary. To the contrary. But I do question the effectiveness of any such treatment that does not take into consideration the sum total of this individual, which must of necessity include his environment, and his interactions with it.

In practice, family counseling involves the joint participation of several family members. It is used descriptively for all settings in which family members are working together to solve common problems. However, most writers also emphasize the conceptualization of personality or psychopathology from a family systems point of view. As Feldman (1976) points out,

> Family therapy has generally come to mean conjoint family therapy, in which two or more members of a family meet (either by themselves or with a group of other families) with one or more therapists. Family therapy with a marital couple (marital therapy) is sometimes distinguished from family therapy with two or more generations. [In the present report,] family therapy will be defined as any form of therapy with one or more members of a family which is guided by a family systems conceptualization of psychopathology. No attempt will be made to differentiate between the goals of family therapy with groups of families, single families, multigenerational families, marital couples and individuals. (p. 103)

We are using this definition because it is most inclusive, and allows us greater leeway in examining the subject. Also, it illustrates how the family systems conceptualization of psychopathology influences all family counseling efforts.

Before attempting to understand the dynamics and processes of family interaction, and how these translate into productive or maladaptive outcomes, we should survey, however briefly, the current status of American families. This will show us the array of family forms and point to patterns of socially-related family difficulties the contemporary American family counselor is likely to encounter.

We can define a family, in its broadest sense, as a group of individuals related to each other by a recognized legal process which establishes a consenting relationship (such as marriage and adoption), by blood ties (natural parent/biological child, siblings), or by both (for example, mother-son-stepfather family or step-siblings). Throughout the cultures of the world, and throughout history there have been numerous and diverse family forms; but we will limit ourselves in this chapter to those few typical patterns which are prevalent in our culture, and especially those four forms whose members are likely to be candidates for family counseling.

Although our concept of what a family typically consists of may be guided by our own past or present family experiences, the reality of our diverse culture reveals that there are many different, viable family forms, each with its own strengths and weaknesses, economic, social, and psychological. The United States has long passed those halcyon times when the uniform, saccharine, and quite false image of "Father Knows Best" family life prevailed in any serious discussions of family sociology and psychology. While there are some forms of family living we will not consider here (nonconsanguine homosexual family bonds, for example), we will briefly survey the four most common forms.

The traditional family form in our culture is called the *nuclear family*. A nuclear family consists of parents and children who live together. Some individuals if asked about their nuclear family may be confused: they are children in one family but parents in another. This is because there are actually two types of nuclear families, depending on whose position it is being viewed from, the child's or the parents'.

The *nuclear family of orientation* is the nuclear family as seen through the eyes of children. It is the home in which the child receives his or her first and most continuous orientation to life, hence its name. It consists of the child, the parents, and all siblings. It is the primary agent of socialization through infancy and childhood as well as an extremely important one throughout the person's life.

The *nuclear family of procreation* is the same nuclear family from the parents' perspective. Inasmuch as the children and parents in a family look at their roles from different vantage points, the family unit is perceived simultaneously in different ways. Moreover the nuclear family of procreation is created voluntarily, through marriage, rather than by birth, a circumstance the child certainly cannot control.

Uzoka (1979) argues that in our contemporary American society the nuclear family system, at least insofar as it has been viewed traditionally through this classical dichotomy of orientation and procreation, is "essentially a myth"

(p. 1095). He suggests, rather, that the more typical family today consists of a small nuclear unit and an extended network of kin, who may be geographically close or distant but are still functionally a part of the family. A couple who were raised and who met in Tennessee, but who married and now live and work in New York is strongly attached, emotionally and socially, to their "extended" family down south, almost as if they still lived there. They may phone regularly and visit several times a year. Many of us, therefore, are functioning members of both types of nuclear families throughout a large portion of our lives.

The Extended Family   We use the term *extended family* to describe this network of nuclear families bound together by several connected parent-child relationships. Traditionally, especially in small-town settings, members of the extended family might have all lived under one roof, or at least on the same general tract of commonly owned land. Such a community often contained two or three generations of married sons and their families as well as all unmarried dependent children. Married daughters typically joined the extended family of their husband. Nowadays, this arrangement has generally disappeared, but we still find many instances where newly married couples live in an apartment in their parents' house, or where they live next door or nearby. This is especially true among certain newly-arrived ethnic groups, such as the Koreans in New York City, who have managed to establish a large and profitable business network based on their extended family network ties. Note, however, that while this arrangement provides certain practical comforts, it may also cause problems in terms of family adjustment. The extended family form tends to close itself off from change, to force values upon and demand conformity from its members. Maladaptive behavior patterns, especially, thrive in such a milieu.

In our contemporary society, where the automobile, airplane, and telephone can assure frequent contact between people who are geographically separated, this form is called a *modified extended family.* Although members of this unit live apart, their lives are intimately interwoven in a network of rights and obligations that clearly separate them from strangers, casual acquaintances, and even close friends. The essence of the extended family is in the powerful bond between parent and child, and between siblings. In practice, these particular bonds make the extended family immortal: it continues generation after generation and, like the society as a whole, survives its individual members. The extended family also helps maintain cultural continuity, with the likelihood that ethnic, religious, or social customs will be maintained, generation after generation (Stein, 1978). In fact, part of the fascination with genealogy, with tracing our family history as Alex Haley did in *Roots,* is that it shows us the extended family we were often not aware of, as well as its values and beliefs. Even in the realm of law, the concept of extended family has gained significant recognition, although less precise than that of nuclear family (Robertshaw & Curtin, 1977).

Studies often prove inadequate in answering questions about the child from the single-parent family, because the absence of a parent is only one of the many different factors affecting the child, and "absence of parent" per se tells us little about the family condition. Recognizing this problem, Nass and Nass (1976) pinpoint seven "variables which contribute to the differences in the children of split and intact families," and these might carefully be considered by the counselor in assessing the child's situation:

1. the age at which the child is deprived of the parent;
2. the sex of the single parent who rears the child;
3. the family attitudes and social values of the parent in charge of the household;
4. the economic consequences of the divided household;
5. the circumstances which deprive a child of either parent (i.e., death, divorce, separation, illegitimacy, military leave, etc.);
6. the race and cultural norms of any particular one-parent household; and,
7. the sibling composition of a one-parent family.

Most of these variables are equally relevant in assessing the typical child from the intact family, an observation which may imply that the same factors that influence all children's behaviors influence the child from the single-parent family.

Which parent, the mother or father, is viewed as primarily responsible for the care of the child is another relevant factor in considering single-parent family structure. It was once taken for granted that the mother would care for the child while the father would go off to work; but today this arrangement is being reassessed, and may be changed. No longer is the former pattern universal, as more and more career mothers return to the workplace while a separated or divorced father helps with the care of his children.

However, the change is not quite as significant as we expected. In the early 1970s, sociologists and psychologists routinely predicted massive shifts in child-care roles, with forecasts ranging to as high as seventy percent for the number of fathers that would be primary or equal caretakers for their children. But this has not happened. Moreland and Schwabel (1981), in a survey of the American situation as of 1980, found that "fathers' actual contributions to their children's care is [still] very small" (p. 45). Though there is some evidence of an increase in the father's involvement, psychologists now recognize that the process will be slow and will have to be simultaneously accompanied by many social changes. Bernard (1981) points out that before we can really have equal parenting by men, or even truly shared parenting on a fifty/fifty basis, there are a number of serious and stubborn social obstacles still to be overcome; many of these involve gender-role stereotyping, but some of them derive from compatibility preferences or financial realities. What is most essential is that the child not be made to feel responsible for preventing or forcing the entry of one or the other parent into the workplace.

Along with the single-parent family form, also quite common today is the parallel situation we call the dual-career family, in which both the mother *and* father work. Even in such families, the mother is generally the parent viewed as responsible for child care, although this responsibility is typically undertaken with baby-sitting help, formal day care, or the assistance of relatives, friends, and siblings. Raspberry (1980), in discussing particularly the situations of children from dual-career families, calls attention to what may be the most important point for all working parents: to make their children feel "that they are a vital part of a general family enterprise and not just impediments to their parents' careers. It seems obvious to me that if children don't see themselves as valuable to others, they are unlikely to feel that they are valuable to themselves" (p. 15).

The "Reconstituted" Family

The majority of individuals with children, who obtain a divorce, or whose spouse dies while they have growing children, eventually remarry. This has created a large population of stepchildren and stepparents, so much so that many greeting card companies now offer birthday cards for one's stepson, stepmom, stepdad, etc.

Whether or not a remarriage and second family will function successfully, and whether the newly formed family will be adjusted as a unit depends on many different factors. "The impact of remarriage on a family, regardless of how high the expectations, is second only to the crisis of divorce" (Francke & Reese, 1980, p. 66). There are many variables that affect its future. "The most important predictor of a remarriage's success," according to Weiss (1975, p. 304), "appears to be its acceptability to other individuals in the lives of the prospective spouses. A remarriage that not only has the approval of the two spouses' children, but also the support of their kin and friends, appears especially likely to be successful." This, as we will see below, has been borne out by further research which emphasizes the importance of a number of external social factors as predictors of success or failure in second marriages.

In her landmark study of the reconstituted family, sociologist Lucile Duberman, herself a member of a reconstituted family, investigated in depth remarried couples and their children, focusing on the stepchild-stepparent-stepsibling interactions. This is a fascinating book, well worth reading; we will summarize only a few of the key points from her research in this section.

1. For most remarried people, the greatest single problem they faced (and the most arguments they had with their spouse) concerned childrearing. The second most troubling problem was outsiders' (exspouses, in-laws, kin, etc.) influences on the new family. Middle-class remarried husbands viewed money as the second most bothersome problem that caused marital discord.
2. The younger the remarried couple the greater the "integration" of their reconstituted family. Integration increased if (1) the previous marriage had dissolved because of death of a spouse; and (2) there was a child from the present marriage.

3. Husband-wife relationships were rated excellent in fifty-four percent of the sample and "poor to good" in forty-six percent, with about seventy percent of the couples perceiving their relationship as "improving." The chief causes of quarreling were childrearing and money.

4. The better the relationship between husband and wife, the higher the integration of the family.

5. Stepfathers (especially those who had never been married before) generally had better relationships with their stepchildren than did stepmothers, regardless of the sex of the stepchild.

6. Stepsibling relationships varied. "When both sets of children lived in the same house, the relations between them were more likely to be 'excellent' than if they lived in different houses. Furthermore, when the remarried couple had a child together, their children were likely to have more harmonious relations" (p. 75).

7. Though most remarried people are fairly indifferent to their ex-spouses, there was a higher incidence of ex-spousal conflicts and anger for men than for women. This was probably because the men were responsible for alimony, and sometimes quarreled with their ex-wives about money.

When we consider the implications of these findings, it becomes evident that a reconstituted family can only work as well as the remarried spouses are able to get along with one another. Specifically, according to these findings, when there is harmony between the parents, when their marriage meets the criteria of overall psychological and social adjustment, there is more likelihood of harmony among the children.

Having now examined the predominant family forms in contemporary America, let us consider some of the widely accepted criteria for healthy family functioning, norms which transcend the family structure and become the basis for individual and family adjustment.

Criteria of Healthy Family Functioning

The family is so much a part of our life that we do not typically stop and stand back to ask objectively what is its purpose, both in our own development and in the functioning of society as a whole. But psychologists, anthropologists, and sociologists have long been fascinated by this question. It is generally agreed that the family serves three basic purposes: to protect the children and provide for their safety needs; to teach the children how to function appropriately in society (socialization); and to help the children as they mature to establish a sense of individual identity with which they will develop a new family (procreation).

In the early years of a person's life the family provides the child with the basic physical needs as well as furnishing the emotional warmth and nurture necessary for full psychological development. The socialization function of the family makes it possible for a culture to transcend the idiosyncrasies of its individual members, in order to maintain a continuity from one generation to another. Through socialization we learn how to perceive ourselves and others in the social hierarchy, we learn what kinds of behaviors are expected from us and by us, and we are given an opportunity to practice these behaviors (Reiss & Hoffman, 1979). Socialization is also a road to individual growth and development, especially as it pertains to the family. "Clearly," Cole (1979) points out, "the family is the most important agent for socialization of young children. As children grow older and attend school and make friends," he continues, "the peer group and schools become important agents of socialization" (p. 102). In this regard, it can be said that one important function of socialization is providing the child, who is initially totally dependent upon and influenced by his or her nuclear family, an opportunity to become an individual, socially-functioning person.

From the point of view of the individual in the nuclear family of orientation, perhaps the most important function of socialization is the formation, development, maintenance, and transformation of *identity*. Who you are, and what you see yourself becoming in your projected future, emerges to a large extent from the crucible of experience we call socialization. It is through our interaction with others, their responses to us, and our interpretation of their reactions that we come to see ourselves in a certain way that each of us defines as our "ME." Consequently, identity formation is another, and from the individual's perspective, probably *the* important, function of the socialization process.

The Healthy Family

With these comments on the purposes of family in mind, we can now ask, "What makes a family healthy and health-engendering for the children?" or expressed another way, "What are some of the generally recognized criteria of healthy family functioning?" Although there are no universally accepted answers to these questions, there are some general criteria and expectations for the fully-functioning family in our culture. These criteria are the result of thousands of professional interactions among psychologists, clinicians, and family members; and the key quality appearing in all of them is that the healthy family provides to its members diverse opportunities for growth.

Ebert (1978) has identified several criteria of a healthy, fully-functioning family, that is, norms and traits about which most psychologists and psychotherapists, even those of different theoretical orientations, would agree. These include the following characteristics:

Sharing feelings . . . each member can communicate freely to the others about both positive and negative feelings. An open form exists for the expression of such feelings and the presentation comes in a nonaccusatory manner.

Understanding feelings Family members understand and accept the feelings of all members.

Acceptance of individual differences The family structure allows and supports the differences of individual members. It is perfectly understood that each constituent has the right to act in his/her unique, creative and separate manner in the family. . . . There is an overall respect for the differences which fosters a sense of individuality and positive self-concept for each member.

Highly developed sense of caring   There is a strong sense of caring permeating interactions and encounters. While this may not always be expressed verbally, an air of caring exists within the family.

Cooperation   Healthy families share the responsibilities of living and are willing to participate in the daily chores and mundance actions such as cleanup and repairs. . . .

Sense of humor   Family members are able to laugh at themselves and joke about various family events.

Survival and safety needs met   Food, shelter, clothing, and to some degree economic security are adequately provided for so that family energy is not excessively devoted to worrying about them.

Nonadversary problem solving   More often than not, problems are solved jointly without creating excessive friction within the family system.

Overall philosophy   There is some set of values governing the direction of the family. It can come from religion, philosophy, or some other system of evaluation and guidance.

Evidently, to explore in detail each of these would require an analysis far beyond the scope of this book. But there are a few underlying ideas we should take note of. First, we should make clear that though there are major differences among families, and though many of the family members' behaviors are culturally determined, there are criteria, such are those listed above, that are generally accepted as evidence of sound or unsound family functioning, successful or unsuccessful family communication and balance.

In trying to determine what these criteria are and to provide an operational definition of the term "healthy family functioning," Fisher and Sprenkle (1978) surveyed 310 members of the American Association of Marriage and Family Counselors. Using the information provided by these family counselors and therapists, a picture of healthy family functioning emerged. "A healthy family" the survey showed, "is one in which members feel valued, supported, and safe." They go on to paint a picture that is in accord with what we have been saying. Describing members of the fully-functioning family, Fisher and Sprenkle (1978, p. 9) point out:

> They can express themselves openly without fear of judgment, knowing that their opinions will be attended to carefully and empathically. Family members are able to negotiate and change when necessary. These perceptions of the healthy family echo many theoretical and research concepts. . . .

With these criteria in mind as tentative goals, let us begin our examination of family counseling by focusing on some of the major factors that underlie the process itself: the setting, the goals, and the main theories.

Issues in Family Counseling

The Setting

Family counseling may take place in the counselor's office, in a clinic, in the family's home, in an institution, in a hospital, or in some other setting. In any case, the counselor should see that the physical arrangement of the environment reflects the population that is there for treatment. Family members should have opportunities for proximity or for distance; they should be able to face each other or to turn away. Seating choices, as the family initially enters the room, are significant and should be noted by the therapist.

What brings the members to the family counseling setting? One member may have already been in counseling and encouraged the other members to begin. Sometimes in the course of counseling a person realizes that his or her problem is one that is shared by the entire family. Or the entire family may have made the decision to begin treatment based on some recent family crisis. There are important procedural differences between working with a family when the counselor has already been seeing one member for a period of time and working with a family from the beginning of the counseling. In both situations, counselors often find that one family member is specified as the "disturbed" one, the one who really needs the help. Satir (1967) suggests using the term *identified patient* (or, "I.P.") for the family member who carries the symptom. Still, she points out, "when one person in a family (the patient) has pain which shows up in symptoms, all family members are feeling this pain in some way" (p. 1).

In either case, "family therapy [or counseling] begins at the first moment of the therapist's contact with the family" (Prosky, 1974, p. 45). The counselor should, from the beginning, convey the feeling that he or she is there for the family, not to take sides with individual members against other members of the family. By showing himself or herself as a concerned but neutral individual, the counselor establishes the comfortable, open setting in which family counseling can take place.

The Goals

Although the specific goals of counseling differ from family to family, and the broad parameters of goals that influence the counselor depend to a large extent on his or her orientation, we can offer a few general statements about the goals of family counseling as opposed to the goals of individual counseling or treatment. The four basic statements of goals are:

1. The family should be taught to communicate openly with each other. This includes the principle of "constructive emotional honesty" and learning to read verbal and nonverbal cues of other family members.
2. The family should learn constructive new ways of solving their own problems. They should learn to come to grips with their conflicts by observing the way the family counselor helps them to do so.
3. The socioemotional intactness of the family should be preserved wherever possible. Even in cases where physical or legal separation becomes necessary (a family member leaving for prison or the military, a divorce, an illness that confines a family member to a

distant place), there are opportunities to maintain contact and to allow that family member to remain a part of the family.

4. Family members have to be able to "individuate" themselves from the family as a total unit.

In the following pages we will look briefly at each of these goals: improving intra-family communication, increasing problem-solving skills, maintaining intactness, and facilitating individuation.

One of the major difficulties in many family and marriage situations is the inability of members to communicate effectively and directly with each other. Communication has been stifled by years of inactivity and stasis within the family dynamics. Many aspects of family relationships have a tendency to get "stuck" in patterns, and family communication is no exception. As Bell (1975) points out,

Effective Communication

> Many of the ways in which parents learn to communicate in early days during a child's infancy are clung to as the children and the parents mature. So we find later, where we may now be dealing with older children and adolescents, that the family still communicates on the same level. We now see it primarily in the subverbal language—through . . . facial expressions, gestures, postures, movement—rather than through words. This is private communication within the family, derivative of a time when words were not available for communication. These nonverbal modes of speech were functional, and continue to be so as they accumulate added significance by repeated use within the family. (p. 177)

Primitive patterns of communication, where "shorthand" messages have come to replace more discursive and meaning-filled communications, are often to blame for difficulties in marriage. For the husband to say "your *mother*" to the wife in a certain tone and context, may indicate a great amount of animosity, while for the wife to say "your *job*" in a negative tone, may indicate a great amount of angry feelings. In marital arguments, words often belie their true significance.

Besides the shorthand language, which is imprecise, likely to be misunderstood, and full of innuendo that could be expressed more directly and openly, couples and families are prone to *deny* many of their feelings. When their feelings become too dangerous and threatening, they may choose to ignore them as if they didn't exist. This involves a shift in communication from the open and forthright to the defensive and repressive. It is almost as if one family member says to the others, "Don't talk about that because I don't want to know." The other members agree because they too don't want to admit that an unpleasant situation exists.

Effective communication between marital partners is an especially notable example of how communication skills can affect, positively or negatively, family balance and stability. The core of a stable, continuing marital relationship is largely the ability of the pair to be able to change with situations, to adapt their marital roles as their partner's needs change, to adjust and grow as their mutual needs change. It is essential, therefore, that they be able to communicate effectively with each other. Effective communication between partners provides a solidifying bond, a stabilizer, in the marital relationship.

As research in this area has intensified, a number of specific factors have been identified as contributing to and facilitating enriched marital communication. Miller, Corrales, and Wackman (1975) point out, for example, the following concepts which have received strong empirical support: awareness, rules, disclosure and receptivity, skills, esteem building. Let us look at each of these briefly in order to understand some of the foundations of effective communication in marriage.

Awareness   The term is used in its general meaning, but is also broken down into component parts, which Miller, Corrales, and Wackman (1975) call *topical* awareness, *self* awareness, awareness of *partner,* and *relationship* awareness.

Topical awareness means that we take cognizance of things not in the immediate environment, of things which are going on in the world. Topical awareness means we are not living in a shell limited by our own experiences. Self-awareness refers to our ability to understand our emotions, sensations, and thoughts. The clarity with which one can understand him or herself often affects how well one deals with others.

Awareness about one's partner "involves knowing accurately what it is your partner is experiencing in terms of his own self-awareness" (p. 145). It is the ability to be sensitive to your partner, to experience empathy and see the world and the relationship as it is experienced by the partner. It is much like the condition of empathy we discussed in the development of intimacy.

Finally, we have awareness of the *relationship,* which focuses on the *interaction* of the couple rather than the behavior of each alone. This type of awareness helps each spouse to understand clearly the relationship in its full perspective. It helps them understand how they express their feelings to each other, the co-equality of their rights and responsibilities, and how balanced or equable their footing in the relationship is. In short, it touches the inner "pattern" of the relationship, and helps reveal the structural rules by which the relationship is governed.

Rules   Every marriage relationship has certain rules. These can be expressed in terms of "who can do what, where, when, and how, for what length of time" (p. 147). Marital rules may be complex, changing from situation to situation. But because they are rules, they can always be understood in their complexity by both partners, who are able to make adjustments to the rules, or to change them by mutual agreement. It is through these rules, moreover, that roles evolve and change.

A partner can conceivably be aware of much that is happening in the relationship, but unwilling to express it. Levels of disclosure and receptivity refer to the ability and willingness of a partner to disclose his or her feelings to the spouse and the corresponding ability and willingness of the spouse to be receptive to those feelings. This is integral to "helping a couple look at their typical patterns of interaction, sometimes for the purpose of creating change in the way they relate" (p. 148).

Disclosure and Receptivity

There are specific behaviors and skills that facilitate communication in a relationship. These include such general communication skills as "speaking for self and owning one's own statements (usually done by using personal pronouns which refer to oneself), giving specific examples (documenting interpretations with specific sensory data), making feeling statements (verbally expressing what it is one is feeling at that moment), and so forth" (p. 148). These communication skills will be explored in greater detail below, when we consider feedback.

Relationship Communication Skills

Interpersonal communication generally functions on two levels: one, a level of content, and the other a level of intent. Intent, which can be viewed as the underlying feeling or intention behind a message, is emotionally more important than the content of what is said. Also, if there is a discrepancy between content and intent, this leads to "incongruity," to a double message, which produces confusion in the relationship and may lead to discord.

Esteem Building

Esteem building is often a part of the intent level of messages couples routinely send to each other. "Messages," Miller et al. (p. 149) point out, "tend to either value or devalue self and partner." The intentions behind many of our messages can be explicitly stated only if we are aware and receptive, and then we can see whether it is esteem building or degrading to our partner.

These communication factors—awareness, rules, disclosure and receptivity, and building of self-esteen—help us in our efforts to understand how partners negotiate and then communicate marital roles to each other. To the degree that they are successful in these areas, there is greater likelihood of their being able to establish mutually agreeable and satisfying marital roles; that is, to enjoy successful adjustment in their marriage.

What this means is that we view the family as a unit, and anything which preserves that unity, either on a social or emotional level, is a sign of socio-emotional intactness, and therefore productive. Anything which tears the family apart is viewed as counterproductive. Earlier, in our definition, we referred to the "family systems conception of psychopathology." This means that psychopathology is viewed as a sign of the breaking-up of the family intactness, either through direct physical separation or through emotional distancing.

Socio-emotional Intactness

To appreciate the importance of this, we should recognize that at the present rate, within this decade the majority of American families will fail to survive as nuclear family units before all their children come of age. This no doubt indicates that the family is in trouble, or at least facing some difficult transitions. Skolnick (1980) points out that although the contemporary family may be in trouble, it is still a "cherished value," of our culture, which we are striving to maintain. Most of us "share an intuitive sense of what the 'ideal' family should be—reflected in the precepts of religion, the conventions of etiquette, and the assumptions of law" (pp. 8–9). With this in mind, we can see how working toward socioemotional intactness is a central part of the family counselor's role.

Problem-Solving in the Family

One of the key goals of all family counseling efforts is teaching the family how to go about solving their problems. In fact, quite often the family conflict can be defined as an inability to find direct means to solve fairly simple problems. This has been emphasized time and again in different contexts. "In relation to diagnosis," Haley (1972) points out, "a sharp difference between the beginner and the experienced therapist is in the concern with using a diagnosis that defines a solvable problem" (p. 162). He goes on to point out how experienced family counselors use diagnosis as a way of helping the family learn to state the problems that they must solve.

It is not enough that the counselor attempt to solve the family's immediate problems with them, for this will do little good in the long run. Rather, the counselor *should determine what is blocking the family from solving its own problems.* Families often find, as they explore what is preventing them from solving a specific problem, a general pattern of underlying resistance which, when resolved, can open up many new avenues for solving other problems. As Bell (1975) points out,

> Sometimes parents will ask the therapist how to solve their problems. When they ask me, I say, in a simple way, "I could answer this question (assuming I could), but this is not my job. My job is not to provide information or give advice; my job is to help you arrive at your own answers for your own family. . . ." The therapist's action is that which will help the family itself work out the problem. It may be through helping a child to express his anger, his desires, his needs, and his resistance to the dominance of a parent; or through helping the parent to expose the reasons for his point of view. . . . The course of problem solving is not always even. Digressions are common. Some problems outside the family may be introduced because they are pressing on the family and seem to have urgency. (p. 142)

It is the primary job of the therapist then not to solve the family's problems for them, but to help them find appropriate ways of problem solving. This enables them to solve not only the immediate problem, but long-range problems as well.

The Forester family came to Dr. Singer for counseling after a year and a half of continual fighting between the parents and the children, and between the children themselves. Richard, age 14, and Donna, age 12, couldn't get along together, and teamed up only when they became involved in loud, nasty fights with their parents. Between themselves they fought about property and personal space. They shared a room, and there was constant bickering about who could use which drawer, about whose phonograph record was whose, about who could bring a friend to the room at a certain time. With the parents, they fought about rights and privileges. They found that they had to stick together because they both felt strongly that the parents were too strict with them. Richard complained that he was not being allowed more liberties than Donna, who was two years his junior; Donna complained that she was not treated as an adult, as her friends were. The parents told Dr. Singer that Richard and Donna were "difficult children," and they expressed the feeling that there was little they—or Dr. Singer—would be able to do about it.

Dr. Singer was especially interested in finding the answers to two questions: (1) What was the relationship between the siblings' inability to get along with each other, and their allied fights with the parents? and (2) Were the parents really being overly strict or did their children unfairly perceive them that way? Simply asking the questions directly, of course, would only provoke another argument between them, and it was not the counselor's place to try to answer the questions on her own. She had to find a way for the family to answer the questions on *their* own.

After much work, in which channels of communication were opened, innuendos brought into the forefront, and some underlying conflicts clarified, three important points that the whole family could agree on emerged:

1. Richard and Donna had an *inflexible* attitude when it came to dealing with their parents: they expected the worst and they got it. When they approached the parents with a request, they did it in almost a challenging and brazen way, which they knew would encourage the parents to refuse their request.
2. Richard always gave Donna the feeling that *their* room was *his* room; a feeling she always resented. The parents subtly supported this, since during the first two years of his life they had actually called it "Richard's room."
3. Mr. and Mrs. Forester had some very firm beliefs about what their children could and could not do. Some of these beliefs did not tally with the beliefs of other parents of the area, and Richard and Donna were treated somewhat more harshly and firmly than most of the other children they were friends with.

As each of these points came to light, steps were taken to solve the problems. For example, it was soon discovered (in the 14th session) that Richard and Donna had deeply buried fears and anxieties about sharing a room, and that neither had ever discussed it openly with each other or with their parents. This was one of the underlying causes of their fighting. It also came out (in the 9th session) that Mrs. Forester had had a miscarriage when Donna was three, and that she had been told she could not have any more children. Perhaps she was trying to keep

Richard and Donna as children and not letting them grow up? This point was explored, but not fully resolved. Mr. Forester's passive attitude in family conflicts did not make him a neutral party; rather, it contributed to the family's inability to resolve problems.

By examining forthrightly the ways in which they communicated, or did not communicate, this family learned ways to solve their own problems. The therapist did not act as a mediator and judge, but instead taught the family members to express, concretize, clarify, probe—and, in short, to use among themselves those counseling techniques that can help individuals understand each other. The family learns how to counsel themselves in this manner.

Individuation
Each family member develops his or her individual identity within the context of the family unit. This individual identity is not a rejection of one's place in the family, but a concomitant identity: one that refines and enriches the family identity. To be able to say, "I exist individually as a person—with my own ideas, feelings, needs, insights—with a life of my own" is a cogent sign of emotional health and sound interpersonal functioning. The ability to individuate is a direct consequence of the relationship with the mother during the early years of life. Individuation may be seen as the socialized end product of the lengthy process of separating from the mother and forming one's own identity. Fried (1970) relates this early phase of individuation to later, more sophisticated developmental signs:

> In the child, individuation . . . is assumed to start at the end of the second year of life. As the encompassing dependence on the mother that is the core of the symbiotic phase wanes, as the child begins to acquire the rudiments of body autonomy, as new ego skills are acquired, the now semiliberated child wants more often to do than to be done for. . . .
>
> In higher measure than we usually acknowledge, the striving for individuation—for forming convictions that are truly self-made and for relying on inner strength to cope with perils and pleasures—continues throughout any vital life. Never is there an end to the process of achieving self-determination and self-expression. (p. 452)

In the family counseling setting, many of the difficulties arise from individual family members' struggles to individuate. Karpel (1975) has proposed a model for understanding the marital and family problems of adult couples based on the struggle of each person to individuate. His model suggests that the individual has to make a transition from *fusion,* in which the "I" does not exist as a distinct and separate entity, to *dialogue* in which there is an "I-Thou" relationship. He identifies different stages in the clinical setting in which couples can be encouraged to form this dialogical relationship.

Along the same lines, Robinson (1975) correctly points out that "family therapists have ample experience indicating that dysfunctional families are established by parents who have achieved low levels of separation from their own

Table 12.1
Family Counseling Approaches

Approach	Leading Theoretician(s)	Main Contribution
Strategic	Jay Haley Paul Watzlawick Don Jackson	Views the family as a system with several subsystems. Emphasizes aspects of communication among members, focusing on feedback, communication problems, and the mutual misinterpretation of messages.
Structural	Salvador Minuchin	Overlaps with strategic theory, although emphasizing structural aspects of the family's organization, power, alliances, and boundaries. Conflict and adjustment are conceptualized in terms of adaptation of family members to internal and external stresses.
Behavioral	Gerald R. Patterson John Gottman	Relies on most behavioral concepts, and uses family members (or spouses) as reinforcing agents. Relies on much empirical research and continual measurement of outcomes. Offers several paradigms for training family members to function better.
Psychodynamic	Nathan Ackerman Robin Skinner	Built on psychoanalysis, with special emphasis on the infant's ego development (object relations) within the family context. The family is viewed by most theorists as an integral part of the child's passage through developmental stages.
Multigenerational	Ivan Boszormenyi-Nagy Murray Bowen	Views family problems in a multi-generational context, connected in various ways through successive generations. These connections involve needs, emotional communications, and learned behaviors.

parents, and are poorly prepared to construct an independent marital relationship" (p. 1047). This is an example of how the failure to individuate becomes a multi-generational problem, handed down from parents to children. When individuation has not been successfully completed early in life, it is the job of the family counselor to see that it takes place in the counseling setting.

Theories and Approaches to Family Counseling

The number of different approaches to family treatment today is truly staggering. Each year, new innovations, new theoreticians, and schisms in professional organizations and training institutes bring forth a slew of theories, techniques, and metatheories that build upon one another with a labyrinthine perplexity. New technical terms are introduced regularly and the proliferation of seemingly unnecessary nomenclature is matched only by enough obscure controversies to easily dull Occam's razor. Table 12.1 sorts out some of the more established originators and their theories.

Despite this theoretical and linguistic quagmire, considerable evidence indicates that collectively the family approaches work, and work well. None of the theories, in fact, exists independently of the others and all depend on the credibility of direct observations for their theoretical validity. Each theory, and each theoretician, has "implicit assumptions, premises, presuppositions, and rules for understanding and knowing things about the world . . . as exemplified by how one extracts, orders, and analyzes observed data" (Benjamin, 1982, p. 38). We will survey briefly some of the main theories, but keep in mind that often what makes a family counseling process work has little to do with the theory underlining it.

Nathan Ackerman and the Beginnings of Family Counseling

Nathan W. Ackerman, an American psychiatrist, is generally recognized as the father of family counseling. Ackerman realized early in his career when working with children that many of the personal and emotional difficulties his clients were experiencing were related to the family setting in which they lived. He began an intensive observational and clinical study of families, and in the early 1960s founded the Ackerman Family Institute to train family counselors and offer low-cost treatment to families who could not afford private practitioners.

Ackerman combined many of the insights and practices from psychoanalysis (in which he was trained) with his growing awareness of the impact of social roles and socioeconomic forces on the family. He believed that psychoanalysis offered only a partial explanation; that a more complete understanding of the patient and his world would be found only after investigating the family pattern and especially the patient's functioning within the family. He pointed out in his early work how his approach to family counseling derived from the weaknesses inherent in the individual approach.

Ackerman's family approach emphasizes that conflicts are part of the organic structure of all families but that learning to resolve these family conflicts leads to the successful development of each individual family member. When the family is treated as a unit, the emotional growth of the individual members becomes a concomitant of the healthy functioning of the family as a whole.

Within the family, according to Ackerman, each individual learns to enact certain roles. These roles are related to one's sense of self, and in effect one's self is expressed in the family setting through the roles one plays. His study of the psychodynamics of family life indicated that treatment should help clarify and change some of the assigned family roles as well as alter the self-perceptions of the individual family members. Family stability (and individual adaptation) come about when the roles assigned to family members lead to resolving rather than causing conflict. This is called family homeostasis (or balance) and is viewed by Ackerman as the single most important criterion for healthy family functioning.

Structural Theory

Perhaps the most widely cited of all the family theories, the structural theory was largely developed by Salvador Minuchin, a psychiatrist whose work with disturbed children led to unique insights about family functioning. Minuchin recognized that family members act and interact in a context with each other, and that most families are constantly in the process of structuring or restructuring themselves, almost in the way that organic creatures regenerate parts of the whole when necessary. Within the family system are several subsystems, such as the spousal or sibling subsystem, that interact with the larger system.

Of the many concepts contributed by Minuchin, one of the most cited is the idea of family *boundaries*. These boundaries are established and maintained through the multiple contexts of intrafamilial communications and behaviors. While, on the one hand, they assure some privacy and autonomy, on the other hand, they are intricately connected with intimacy and nurturing. Part of the health of a family is the ability of its members to recognize each other's boundaries and the boundaries of the subsystems within the family. Boundaries can be clear, rigid, underdefined, overdefined, or conflicting. Family dysfunctioning or an individual family member's symptoms often arise because of what are really boundary disputes.

Jay Haley, the founder of strategic therapy, comes from a different background than most of the other important figures in the field. He was originally not a therapist but a theoretician in communications, with special interest in human communication and a focus on family communication. His research on the common factors that underlie all forms of therapy, combined with his work with Minuchin, led to the development of his strategic approach. It is strategic in the sense that it tries to directly attack the problem head-on.

According to Haley, intergenerational communication as well as communication among coeval family members is central to understanding the family pathology as well as its strengths. Instead of viewing family communication in a linear way, Haley utilizes a dynamic feedback system in which erroneous inference breeds new erroneous communications. Along with the work of Paul Watzlawick and Don Jackson, the strategic viewpoint suggests two realities—a "first order reality" and a "second order reality." The former refers to a factual situation, while the latter refers to one's premises and perceptions about the situation. "These two levels of reality may or may not be congruent," Benjamin (1982, p. 60) points out. "The family's premises about the facts may be regarded as 'more real' than reality, with inappropriate responses to the facts." Thus, the nature of many conflicts is in the perceptual differences of family members.

The Milan group has contributed a family therapy approach that has made an important impact on therapy in the United States. The approach was developed at the Milan Center for Family Studies where Mara Selvini-Palazzolia, introducing the use of family techniques in working with anorectics and their parents, and three other psychotherapists (Luigi Boscolo, Gianfranco Cecchin, and Givliana Prata) have evolved a body of techniques that have proven effective in many family situations, extending well beyond the original work with anorectics.

Strategic Therapy

The Milan Group

The Milan group is especially notable in integrating many of the predominant theories in family therapy. While they cannot exactly be called eclectic, their work combines communications theory, system theory, linguistics, and other important family therapy modalities. While the bulk of their theoretical rational and practical procedures is consistent with the other approaches (particularly Haley and Watzlawick), their unique contribution appears to be the use of paradox as a particular communication strategy.

The concept of paradox relates to the patterns of communication among family members. Communication between two people may be consonant or dissonant. In consonant communication, the message of the exchange and its emotional impact are the same. In dissonant communication, the objective message differs from its emotional implications.

While theoretically the Milan group subscribes to the theories of family communication and balance articulated by most of the other approaches, it has developed a number of its own useful intervention strategies. One of the most important techniques is known as *positive connotation.* Hansen and L'Abate (1982) describe the technique:

> This is done by construing the symptom and the other's reaction to it (and therefore the maintenance of it) as positive, because it serves the purpose of holding the family together. By reframing the symptom positively, it involves the whole family, not just the patient, in the problem . . . the therapist aligns himself or herself with the homeostatic function of the system (thus gaining access to the system itself instead of meeting with resistance). Thus, it paves the way for the second technique it uses: prescription of the symptom. . . . The prescription is usually given at the end of the first session. This method involves a defined concept: for example, "During the week to come, the parents were to write down, with great detail and care, each in his own notebook, all the utterances made by the child." (Hansen and L'Abate, 1982, p. 154)

Techniques of Family Counseling

Many of the techniques we have mentioned earlier (in Part 3) are appropriate to the family treatment setting, but there are a number of specialized applications of some of the basic techniques. We will look at these in this section.

A Structural Approach

Because the family members may have different goals for or expectations about treatment, it is necessary at the outset that there be a clearly delineated *plan* of treatment and a clearly formulated, albeit tentative, set of rules and guidelines. This not only prevents counterproductive misunderstandings later on, but also allows each member of the family to express what he or she feels is his or her primary goal and rationale for participating in the treatment. Aponte (1974) suggests that the general direction of treatment has to be organized around the family's structure and the problems they bring with them into treatment. He views the therapeutic process as including three critical stages: the family's *agreement on the problem; identification of the participants involved in the problem;* and the family's *pledge to cooperate* in solving the problem. He emphasizes the need for this structural scheme, since several people have to work together to solve the problem that may involve all of them.

Closely related to the structural approach is the use of contracts. These establish, either orally or in writing, the rules, regulations, guidelines, and goals of the treatment. The behavioral contract is the most commonly used. This type of contract sets out acceptable and unacceptable behaviors, and the parties to the contract agree to abide by it. Its purpose is to increase the frequency of desirable behaviors and decrease, or eliminate, the frequency of undesirable behaviors. Firestone and Moschetta (1975) see behavioral contracts as a major tool in breaking down family members' resistances to change and in encouraging flexibility and the experimentation with new behaviors. "The family therapist," they point out, "adopting the role of behavior modifier, serves as a catalyst enabling family members to risk flexibility" (p. 27).

Contracting

The use of contracts has become so popular that a number of counseling approaches have developed around them. Although originally the contract was only a means to an end, these strategies have helped make the contract a valuable therapeutic tool. Weathers and Liberman (1975) have discussed an innovative use of the *family contracting exercise,* a therapeutic learning experience in which family members learn to negotiate with each other. The exercise consists of five steps: (1) identifying the family members' needs and desires; (2) setting priorities on self rewards; (3) empathizing with each other; (4) setting costs for providing gains to others; and (5) bargaining and compromising. The purpose of the exercise is to help the family members learn to negotiate with each other so that they eventually provide for each others' needs. They suggest four guidelines for generating successful contracts, which are central to the entire procedure:

1. The negotiation of a contract must be open and honest, free from explicit or subtle coercion.
2. The terms of a contract should be expressed in simple, explicit, clearly understood words.
3. For a contract to be effective it has to provide an opportunity for each participant to optimize his reinforcement or minimize his costs and losses in the area of his life covered by the contract. The contract must provide advantages to each party over the status quo.
4. The behaviors contracted for must be in the repertoire of the person agreeing to do them. It is very easy to make the mistake of asking too much from a person. (p. 209)

Timing of Interventions   As in individual counseling, the timing of an intervention is of critical importance in the family context. Whether an intervention is effective or not is determined mostly by its timing. The same comment or interpretation or suggestion may be entirely *in*appropriate one session and entirely appropriate the next session. Foley and Dyer (1974) offer eight occasions when counseling interventions should be made. We will discuss each one briefly.

1. When labeling takes place, and family members are classified according to the label—such as "the good child" or "the dull child" or the "nice parent," and so forth—the counselor may intervene to point out the inaccuracy of this; to show that people are too complex to be labeled.
2. When one family member speaks for another, the counselor may intervene to help the other member speak for himself or herself. "The therapist must constantly intervene and point out that each person is an individual with his own feelings and thoughts" (p. 376).
3. When the family denies that the problems stem from within, and suggests instead, "If it weren't for them," indicating that forces outside are causing all or most of their problems, the counselor will step in to show how the family is not meeting the challenge of dealing with these forces from outside. "Obviously a family has to unload," Foley and Dyer point out, "has a need to ventilate. But when it has been given time to do this, the counselor must intervene and face it with the responsibility that change is within its power and no one else's" (p. 376).
4. Likewise, sometimes a single member of the family becomes the scapegoat for the family's problems. "If it weren't for you," they say, "we wouldn't have these difficulties." Again, it is the job of the family counselor to show how the total interaction between all the family members, rather than the actions of one member, are responsible for the problems the family is experiencing.
5. "Families believe that certain laws operate in their lives. . . . An intervention ought to be made whenever such an immutable law is articulated" (p. 378). Deeply rooted family myths, which are taken as truths—such as the "smart child/dull child" or "good child/bad child" stereotypes—may prevent the family from coming to grips with their real problems.
6. The counselor should intervene when the family adopts what the authors call the mañana (tomorrow) position, insisting that things will get better by themselves. "This hope," they point out, "is not one which flows from change in the interaction, but from hope based on fantasy rather than reality. The therapist must cut through the wish for improvement and insist that change will result from realistic steps which are accompanied by action" (pp. 378–379).

7. The counselor may help the family members learn the meaning of their nonverbal cues.

8. The counselor may intervene when "discrepancies of feelings, words, or actions are noted." This relates back to the balance theory, and the need for congruence between the perceptions and feelings of family members.

These eight criteria for intervention, while not exhaustive, are quite comprehensive and helpful to the family counselor. Each of them is a practical tool since the family counselor is likely to come into touch with a situation representative of each one. Moreover, when the appropriate intervention is used in each case, it is likely to facilitate the family's growth and cohesiveness.

Behavioral Techniques

Although we covered the behavioral techniques quite thoroughly in chapter 11, there are some specific applications in the family setting that should be mentioned at this point. Rosen and Schnapp (1974) use the technique of *thought-stopping* in counseling couples. In dealing with a husband who was obsessed by his wife's brief affair, the counselor encouraged the husband to use thought-stopping. They describe the use of this technique:

> The patient begins by imagining and verbalizing the obsessional train of thought. The therapist suddenly shouts "stop." The patient discovers that his train of thought has in fact momentarily ceased. The procedure is repeated until the patient is able to covertly shout "stop" whenever the obsession presents a problem. (p. 263)

Systematic desensitization has also been used in the family counseling setting. Operant conditioning procedures are used widely in training parents to be behavior counselors for their own children. Research has constantly supported the view that as family behavior is modified, improved functioning results. In treating of sexual dysfunctions, the employment of behavioral methods has been recognized as the most widely used and probably the most effective set of techniques.

Family Counseling Applications

When we think of severe disorganization and dissolution in the family, the kinds of things that bring family members into counseling, we tend to think in terms of intolerable fighting between the parents, day after day, year after year, until finally there comes separation or divorce, and then the child custody battles, and fighting over visiting rights. These do exist, to be sure, and are indeed the most visible signs of widespread family troubles in our society. But these symptoms are usually the end products of many different social and psychological factors which have evolved over a period of years, like a cancer eating its way through the underlying family structure.

Families break up for many reasons: because of violence; because of the forced absence of a family member (such as if the father or mother is sent to prison, or into war); because of the death of a family member; or because of other factors. As we attempt to understand the qualities of a healthy functioning family, we must also come to grips with the myriad causes of family dissolution. This will help present a realistic three-dimensional picture for the family counselor. In this section, we will examine several of the prevalent patterns of family disorganization that lead to marital separation, divorce, and family dissolution. We will begin with the more common applications of marriage counseling and then look at severe examples of post-divorce adjustment and family violence.

Marriage Counseling

In essence, maintaining a functional marriage involves the ability of two people to adapt to compatible role situations. This is the principal process of resolving marital conflicts. As a team, the partners have to cooperate in order to play out and reinforce each other's roles. There may be points of intersection, however, in which each partner feels some behavior is within his or her role, and a conflict may arise.

Typically, a young couple entering into marriage do not explicitly state what their respective roles will be, although this may be understood implicitly. As the relationship changes over time, the implicit role expectations may come to the fore. Of course, nowadays, there are such profound changes in what is expected of men and women that there is no longer a universally accepted husband role and wife role. Options are now available, and they are being explored. "Many couples are searching for a different formula. A few are experimenting, tearing down the old barriers, reversing roles, living separate social lives. Getting away from the stifling, conventional idea of togetherness is of crucial importance" (Russell, 1973).

What enables a modern marriage relationship to endure—and to remain stable—in the midst of these rapid social changes in husband-wife role designation is good *communication* about marital roles: when one partner can openly and uninhibitedly tell the other what is expected of him or her, and the other partner can respond. When there is a sharing of ideas through communication, roles can more flexibly evolve, decisions can be made with less inherent conflict. Good communication allows a couple to make explicit to each other the role expectations that may have been implicit, leading to the development of *mutually acceptable* marital roles. These, in turn, allow the couple to make critical marital choices *together*, in a way that will be satisfactory and beneficial to each of them individually, and to the relationship as a totality.

What are some of the most common choices couples have to make during the course of a marriage? A few of the more difficult decisions that challenge at one point or another almost every relationship are:

Should we have children—how many and when?

Should we buy a house or co-op or condo? When? How much? Where? How do we finance it?

Should we spend or save? What percentage of our income?

How often should we be making "required" family visits to relatives we really don't want to see?

How do we make choices about which friends we associate with and what activities we engage in during our leisure time?

Should we have a sexually exclusive relationship, or are extra-marital relations allowed? To what degree are we allowed to flirt with others?

Each of these challenges requires effective communication between the spouses as a prerequisite to making positive choices and for the ultimate prevention or resolution of inter-spousal conflict.

We can state then as our general principle that the specific challenges of marriage usually revolve around the task of finding mutually acceptable marital roles and communicating this effectively to one's partner. When this is successfully done, the couple's chance of adjustment is greatly enhanced.

Marital conflicts may occur over virtually anything. Couples fight about who takes out the garbage, in-law problems, and career vs. marriage. Some areas which can lead to severe difficulties are jealousy, money, childrearing, and sex. However, despite the specific issue over which a battle is fought, the basic source of most difficulty is that marriage is an intimate interpersonal relationship between two separate individuals who are not only themselves constantly changing, and not always jointly in the same direction or at the same rate, but who also live in a complex and shifting social environment which is often beyond their control (e.g. war, inflation, recession, illness, a car accident). While the courtship and mate selection process often reduces, it does not eliminate, personal and social background differences. These other surface issues—who takes out the garbage, etc.—become concrete manifestations of the difficulties of intimate pair living: they are important in their own right, but they must also be seen in the proper context.

For example, when jealousy becomes firmly entrenched in a relationship it can be a vicious enemy, eroding the very foundations of trust and love that hold the two partners together. As a married couple come into conflict, when one or both partners are jealous, there is sometimes slight opportunity to resolve the problem, since any explanation is rejected as untrue, and the jealousy becomes even stronger.

What does jealousy really mean? How does it survive in a relationship? What part does it play? In our society by far the single greatest reason for jealousy is the standard of sexual exclusivity in monogamous relationships. Most jealousy centers on the belief that the other partner is sexually interested in or involved with another person. It may be a specific other person, or just the general belief that the other person is carrying on. In most jealousy situations one partner acts as the ACCUSED and the other as the ACCUSER. Sometimes each partner

Sources of Marital Conflict

may alternately play a role, but typically it is one or the other who plays the same role. As this continues over a period of time, the couple may become accustomed to playing this type of role.

Or jealousy may sometimes be of a nonsexual quality. The ACCUSER may feel that a person is overstepping his or her role, is providing for the needs of the ACCUSED that should be provided for within the relationship. Generally, when anything threatens to weaken the relationship bond, this can become a possible cause for jealousy (Clanton & Smith, 1977).

Another of the main areas over which marriages seem to come to heated conflict is in quarreling over money. There may be disagreement about how to spend the money available, a dispute about priorities, or simply angry exchanges about the fact that there is insufficient money to meet the couple's needs.

Evidently, it does not matter significantly how much money is objectively available; rich people fight about money just as much as poor people. Although poverty may place a stress on a relationship, and although most people feel there would be less fighting about money if only they had more money, what is actually more important than the *amount* of money involved is whether or not the couple's expectations and assignment of roles about who makes spending decisions has been implicitly and explicitly determined, such as how decisions are made and what takes priority.

The actual process of earning the income is also of importance. It has been shown that the relationship between satisfaction in the workplace and satisfaction in marriage is causally related. For example, in one recent study, Bahr and Bahr (1981) found that the way men perceive their job, specifically whether or not they see it as meaningful and deserving of their abilities and talents, is directly relevant to their level of marital satisfaction. The reverse is also true: men who tend to be satisfied in their marriage have a higher level of job satisfaction. In both cases, the husbands' perceptions of their work are more significant than their objective incomes, in correlating with marital satisfaction. This implies that for men at least it is not the objective income that affects marital happiness, but rather whether or not the man feels satisfied with his work. His feelings about his work are brought home with him and affect the way he interacts with his wife. These results support the notion that "it is *perception* of economic well-being rather than objective income that supports marital satisfaction" (p. 55).

A number of cultural factors come into play here too. Traditionally, in our culture, the man has been the chief "breadwinner," the one who "brings home the bacon." In recent years this has been changing dramatically (as we pointed out earlier); increasingly more women have been entering the work force as at least secondary breadwinners. But this does not mean that these two-paycheck couples have worked out more satisfactory ways of dealing with the sharing of financial responsibilities or the division of their moneys. In fact, sometimes when both partners are out there earning a living, there are more intense conflicts at home about how it should be spent. Caroline Bird (1979), in her book, *The Two-Paycheck Marriage,* points out that the working wife's new status has changed the entire family configuration, including the delegation of power, sex roles, childrearing responsibilities, and more. This can actually encourage quarreling over money for a number of reasons.

Another potential source of conflict in a marital relationship is wrangling about the children. The conflicts may begin even before the child is conceived, at the point when a couple cannot agree whether or not to have children at this time. And then there may be areas of conflict about how large a family to have. Questions regarding discipline, education, and expectations of what the child should do are other areas parents sometimes find themselves in disagreement about, and which become potential sources of conflict. Abramowitz (1977) has pointed out that many of the parents' anxieties arise because they cannot see how trends in economic development and large-scale social conditions are affecting their childrearing attitudes, and this can lead to misunderstandings between them regarding their roles as parents. This is especially true if the parents are pressured by the media and by their peers into behaviors which are not consistent with their own upbringing.

The arrival of a new child, especially the first child, invariably places a strain on the couple. As they learn their new parenting roles there is an increasing likelihood that something has to be eliminated from what they formerly put into their relationships with each other. They may be giving less attention to each other now, less time; and there may be significant changes in their sexual functioning. There are also significant changes in the life-style to which they have become accustomed. As Nass and Weidhorn (1978) point out, "one may discover, as more and more couples are doing nowadays, that although one likes children, one does not like them enough to put up with a cramped lifestyle" (p. 95).

Another area of childrearing that tends to lead to conflict occurs as children reach adolescence. Because they are now at a period where some rebellion against their parents is inevitable, this can lead to an invisible but persistent tension in the home; this, in turn, can precipitate fighting between the parents, and make it even more difficult to help the child adjust to his or her situation.

Finally, fighting about sex is central to many marital conflicts. Sex is such an integral part of the marital relationship that inevitably it becomes a source of heated conflict, either directly or symbolically. Sex is sometimes used as a weapon, to be withheld as punishment or offered to force compliance of the partner. It is also a source of many arguments. When the partners are dissatisfied sexually, they may take it out on each other, and this in turn makes even less likely the hope of sexual reconciliation. It is a vicious cycle. Edwards and Edwards (1977) studied 110 married couples over a three-month period. They found that there was a functional relationship between arguments and sex; that "couples who engaged in sexual intercourse at a higher rate than they argued described their marriage as 'happy.' Marriages with rates of argument higher than rates of intercourse described their relationship as 'definitely unhappy' " (p. 187). This should not be interpreted as implying that marital satisfaction or dissatisfaction rests primarily on how well or how poorly the couple is functioning sexually.

Rather, the conclusion of the study may be that a successful, enjoyable, satisfying sexual relationship involves a series of intimate communications between spouses, requiring great subtlety, warm feeling, and considerable cooperation between the two partners; in fact, those same interpersonal characteristics that are also required for general marital satisfaction. In effect the sexual relationship may be considered, in part, as a barometer of the overall marital relationship.

One of the most difficult and painful types of family problems often seen in the treatment setting are sexual disturbances. The treatment of such disturbances has become a major counseling field in itself, and should be covered briefly in this section.

Ellis (1975) points out, quite correctly, that "a marriage counselor almost invariably has to be something of a sex therapist; and, in fact a goodly number of the cases he or she sees, especially these days, will be called upon to do what might be primarily called sex therapy" (p. 111). Although Ellis uses the rational-emotive approach, the bulk of empirical studies use behavioral approaches. Lobitz and LoPiccolo (1972) have found positive outcomes in using the behavioral treatment for sexual dysfunction. Sayner and Durrell (1975) suggest a combination of behavioral techniques, including desensitization, biofeedback, general relaxation training, and extinction.

According to Kaplan (1974), the six specific sexual disturbances that have proven most responsive to counseling are: (1) male impotence, inability to produce or maintain an erection; (2) premature ejaculation, inability to control orgasm; (3) retarded ejaculation, inability to trigger orgasm; (4) general female dysfunction, lack of erotic response to sexual stimulation, commonly called frigidity; (5) female orgasmic dysfunction, difficulty in reaching orgasm; (6) vaginismus, spasm of the muscles at the entrance of the vagina, preventing penetration. There have been numerous reports on the successful treatment of each of these, using behavioral techniques or other approaches.

Separation and Divorce Counseling

Divorce confers a special social status on the individual, on the children, and on the family as a whole (Levinger, 1976). Therefore, it demands special kinds of recognition and sensitivity. Beyond general trends, it is difficult to predict what specific factors lead to a high-risk divorce probability. We know statistically that ninety-six percent of the adults in the United States marry, thirty-eight percent of whom divorce. We also know that seventy-nine percent of those who divorce then remarry, and that forty-four percent of these marriages end in divorce again (Blumberg & Schwarz, 1984). We also know that a number of social factors have been associated with the incidence of divorce. For example, second marriages have a higher divorce rate than first marriages. People who marry in their teens have the highest divorce rate. Divorce rate is lower for college-educated people than for less educated and higher for the poor than for the upper-middle class. Blacks, we know, have a significantly higher divorce rate than whites of comparable income level. And, blacks who do divorce have more children, so that in

1988 approximately half the black children under 18 years were living with only one of their natural parents. Also, even among educated blacks there is a considerably higher divorce rate than among educated whites. Several reasons for this have been suggested, ranging from the increased pressures brought upon blacks as minority groups to the residual effects of historical racism and slavery. But at the present time it is still not clear why this is so.

Although the incidence of divorce has been shown to fluctuate with certain social variables such as race, socioeconomic level, educational attainment, etc., more important in understanding marital failure in terms of the dynamics of family adjustment are the factors within the marriage that increase the risk of divorce. Research has identified a number of concrete factors, aside from general marital instability and dissatisfaction, that affect the likelihood of divorce.

Factors Affecting Divorce

There now exists, for example, a considerable body of evidence indicating a causal association between premarital pregnancy and subsequent marital dissolution. Couples who marry when the woman is pregnant are more likely to culminate in divorce. Several reasons have been suggested for this phenomenon, most emphasizing either or both partners' lack of preparation for their respective marital roles. This is sometimes known as *accelerated role transition,* meaning that a person has to assume a new role before he or she is capable of fully understanding or fulfilling it.

The changing role of women in the American family may also play a part in the divorce rate. "Perhaps the most significant of the hallmarks that distinguished the modern family that emerged in the early nineteenth century from its predecessors," Schmidt (1980) argues, "were the sharply differing roles assigned by social custom to wife and husband. Women, who were idealized as the 'angels of the house,' were said to be the moral guardians of the family, responsible for the ethical and spiritual character of the home, as well as for its comfort and tranquility" (p. 17). This of course had the insidious effect of depriving them of the same rights, opportunities, and expectations men enjoyed. Schmidt goes on to point out the problem with this:

> A major problem for society emerges, however, as this basic understanding increasingly becomes subject to new expectations and pressures. If the principal function of the family is to rear children and to provide a "haven in a heartless world," what happens if women now perceive the principal purpose of their work not that of supporting and advancing the family, but rather as the primary means for realizing themselves as individuals? Is there not, in fact, a fundamental tension, if not conflict, between the individualistic interests of women and those of the family? (p. 23)

Clearly, the American family is going to have to come to grips with this question if the rights of women and the stability of the family are to coexist productively. It is easy to say "If women remained in the home where they belong, we wouldn't be having these family problems today." And, such a view is just as accurate as saying, "If we still had slavery, we wouldn't be having problems with the economy now."

Post-Divorce
Counseling
Regardless of the specific circumstances, divorce is always a traumatic, emotionally-difficult experience. It affects all areas of one's functioning and poses serious challenges to our psychological and social adjustment. Goetting (1981) points out that there is abundant evidence of "poorer health, higher mortality and more accidents among the divorced than among the married"; and this is supported by other research which indicates too that marital status is a key predictor of physical and mental health.

Following the period of separation and the legalities of the divorce itself, family members have to adjust to a variety of new circumstances that can easily tax their adaptability. A new residence has to be established, financial arrangements which may have been working well for years have to be revised, the wife may have to return to work if she has been home raising the children, and the husband may find his spending capacity severely impaired, because his income is divided into supporting two separate households. Socially, both ex-spouses have to learn to be single again, an especially difficult adjustment if a person has been away from the dating scene for too long. "The return to the dating game is invariably a chaotic time for both parent and child. Both men and women feel compelled to join a social whirl to re-establish their attractiveness, leading to a temporary neglect of the children" (Francke et al., 1980, p. 62).

One of the most critical determinants of how divorced men and women reestablish themselves is the presence or absence of children:

> The greater the probability that if there are young children they will be with the mother means that: (1) more women than men will be heads of households; (2) fewer will live alone; (3) fewer will live in families as nonhead; and (4) fewer will live in households of unrelated individuals, usually not hospitable to children. (Bernard, 1975, pp. 586–587)

We noted above how the emerging institution of the "reconstituted family" has become an important form of American family life today.

The Post-Divorce
Reaction
There is a tendency to develop a set of attitudes and behaviors that have sometimes been referred to as the post-divorce reaction. Taibbi (1979) points out that the period following divorce or loss of a significant relationship is a time of crisis, change, and, for some, growth. Many individuals pass through what some have termed a "second adolescence"; like the growing adolescent, the individual adjusting to divorce must struggle with changing roles. It is a period of redefinition, of relabeling. Especially for a person who has either felt "trapped" in an

unhappy marriage, or who has felt terribly burdened by the arduous and emotionally trying process of trying to work out complex marital problems, there may be a mixed feeling of simultaneous elation and depression following the divorce. Elation is based on being free of the burden, that it is finally over with; the depression is a residual feeling of having failed at something that, at one time, was viewed as important.

At the same time the individual is experiencing this ambivalent feeling and complex role transformation, an adjustment to a new social status, that of divorced person, is required. Suddenly, and without any preparation, the formerly-married person is perceived differently by others, and this becomes evident to him or her. This is true too for the children who experience, along with their divorced parents, a post-divorce reaction. The entire process is complicated all the more by confusion in parent-child interaction patterns, which had probably been well established in the original family. Ex-spouses and their children are caught in a quandary. "Divorcing with children requires in adults the capacity to maintain entirely separate social and sexual roles while they continue to co-operate as parents," point out Wallerstein and Kelly (1980, p. 76), who analyzed a large body of data about the psychological health and social functioning of children of divorce in California in the mid to late 1970s. Their key finding helps us understand how the general criteria of psychological adjustment play a central role in the post-divorce adjustment process:

> What made the biggest difference for the children [of divorce] was not the divorce itself, but the factors that make for good adjustment and satisfaction in intact families; psychologically healthy parents and children who are involved with one another in appropriate ways. Yet providing these optimal conditions is difficult for the postdivorce family, with its characteristic climate of anger, rejection, and attempt to exclude the absent parent. (p. 67)

Figure 12.1 shows the types of situations in which these children found themselves five years after the breakup.

About sixty percent of the couples obtaining a divorce have children at home, most of these below high school age. For the children, the adjustments following parental divorce are even more complicated and difficult. They are made so by a number of factors: their likely dependency on both parents; their dual loyalties and mixed feelings; the divided time they spend with each parent; and the reactions of their peers.

While "on the surface, the children of divorce don't seem any different from kids whose families are intact, they are different" Francke et al (1980) point out, "for divorce, though no longer a stigma, is nonetheless a wrenching series of crises that sets these children apart" (p. 58). The authors go on to point out some findings by psychologists of what determines how well or poorly the child is likely to

Children of Divorce

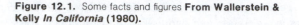

Figure 12.1. Some facts and figures **From Wallerstein & Kelly In California (1980).**

Five Years After The Breakup

| | 10 | 20 | 30 | 40 | 50 | 60 | 70 | 80 |

Child happy and thriving

Child doing reasonably well

Child depressed

Child living with mother

Child living with father

Child shuttled back and forth, not in joint custody arrangement

Adolescents living on own

Divorced father had remarried

Divorced mother had remarried

Father paid child support regularly

Father paid support irregularly

Father was delinquent in support payments

survive the divorce period; namely, the age of the child at the time of divorce, the sex of the child, the compatability of the parents, and the institutional supports are all applicable. Although there are no easy formulas, the large majority of children cannot emerge unscathed from the trauma. A detailed report by the Ketering Foundation and the National Association of Elementary School Principals, for example, points out that "by all indicators, children from one-parent families fare more poorly in school than their two-parent counterparts" (American Federation of Teachers, 1980).

Even the most conscientious of parents will have difficulty helping the child through the post-divorce trauma. The parent is, after all, not only emotionally involved in the situation and working out his or her own adjustment, but may well be viewed by the child as the one responsible for the divorce, or at least half-responsible. Inasmuch as many of these children are of school age, the school is taking an increasing role in providing group and individual counseling support for children of divorce in much the same way as adult post-divorce adjustment groups are springing up for the ex-spouses (Green, 1978). In a way, what this indicates to us is that divorce is becoming recognized as a fact of life in the United States, and social institutions are changing to accommodate to it.

For example, in years past, unless the mother could be shown beyond a reasonable doubt to be unfit to care for a child, the custody of the child of divorce was routinely awarded to the mother. This was done for two reasons. First, women were viewed as being more fit as parents, with "natural instincts" for taking care of their children. And, second, the role of the ex-husband following divorce was to earn enough money to support his ex-wife and child in the style to which they had become accustomed.

In recent years, however, this practice has begun to give way to a more equal treatment of the parents as custodians of their children. As women began to enter the workplace en masse, many divorcing couples were living on two incomes, not one, with the mother's earnings just as important as the father's. Thus, the argument about the father having to work lost ground. At the same time, psychologists began to point out how important the father was in the development of the child. Men, it was learned, are just as capable of rearing children as are women. With these changing attitudes and circumstances, a new concept, called "joint custody," came into prominence.

The awarding of joint custody has required some serious rethinking by parents and by the counseling profession on the entire issue of custody (Cleveland & Irvin, 1982). Mothers and fathers have to ask themselves both if they are fit for the task and if it will ultimately be beneficial to the child. "There is no single reason for choosing joint custody," Dullea (1980), who has interviewed a number of parents and children involved in joint custody arrangements, points out. "To some, it offers the best of the married and single world: each parent enjoys a block of time with and without the children. For others, it represents a compromise to spare the children a court confrontation. And for a smaller number of others, joint custody spares the wife the stigma society still places on a mother who 'abandons' her children—even to a loving father" (Dullea, 1980, p. 35). It has also influenced much of the divorce process. Where once mothers took for granted that they would be awarded custody, they now find that they may have to fight for it, and so custody becomes a part of the total divorce battle. The child, of course, is a pawn in this battle, and gets caught in the middle. In recent years this has led to an increase in children's problems, especially as they are caught in the middle of a division of loyalties between their battling parents (Musetto, 1978).

As long as there have been families, violence has been exerting a disruptive force on the family structure (Steinmetz, 1978a). But it is only during the past decade that it has received so much attention from the mass media and from social agencies which, with federal and state funding, have begun to support wide-scale research and intervention efforts aimed at understanding and preventing family violence.

Family Violence Counseling

Family violence can be defined as the physical abuse of one family member by another. It can (and does!) occur between any combination of family members. Grandparents may be abused (or killed) by their children or grandchildren, just as grandchildren have been abused and killed by their grandparents. Siblings may do violence to each other, and there are many cases of children inflicting violence on their parents (Steinmetz, 1978b). Forced incest and rape can occur between brother and sister, or between parent and child. By far the most serious problems are violence by one spouse against the other, or violence (including sexual abuse) by a parent against the child. The former is called *spouse abuse* or *wife abuse,* because it is typically the husband inflicting harm on the wife. The latter is called *child abuse*. Both are serious, often life-endangering, social problems that lead to family disorganization and ultimately, to family dissolution.

Both spouse abuse and child abuse have two central points in common. First, they are part of a pattern that Renvoize (1978) has called the "web of violence," to indicate that family violence spreads from member to member, from generation to generation, and that it invariably "traps every newborn member of long-ensnared families." The web of family violence, like a spider's web, traps its victim without killing him right away, and no matter how hard the victim tries to escape, he or she may remain scarred for life.

Second, spouse abuse and child abuse are complex social problems which afflict individuals with certain psychological predispositions. They are classic examples of how some types of personalities under certain types of social conditions and pressures will react in detrimental ways, while other personality types under the same social conditions will react quite differently. Although it was once believed that these problems were predominantly limited to lower-class, uneducated families, more comprehensive and convincing data show that they are spread across all social classes and all educational levels (Steinmetz, 1978a).

There are many specific factors that precipitate spouse abuse, none of which explains its deeper causes. Heavy drinking is probably the foremost reason. A person under the influence of alcohol tends to be more violent than normal; and if a man is angered at his wife, he may suddenly do what he would not do if he were sober. Some abusing husbands suffer from severe psychological problems, and even when sober cannot control their violent impulses. They take out their frustrations and failures brought on by their jobs or by their interpersonal relationships on their wives, who are less powerful physically. Gelles (1977) has also remarked that wife abuse often precedes forced sexual compliance, and that there are many more instances of marital rape than have generally been acknowledged.

Women who are continually abused by their husbands tend to come from families where either or both parents physically abused them, or where the father demonstrated frequent violence against the mother (Carroll, 1977). Most of the men come from families where warmth and a sense of familial love were missing. A relatively large number of the husbands and wives come from step-parent families, where they were mistreated or neglected. Although spouse abuse occurs at all social and economic levels, it is more common among the lower classes, and among the less educated (Wolfgang, 1976). In short, the social and psychological family backgrounds of spouse abusers and spouse abuse victims have contributed, directly and indirectly, to socializing them for their present situation (Higgins, 1978).

As with spouse abuse, only in recent years (although about ten years before spouse abuse was so recognized) has the widespread problem of child abuse been recognized for what it is: a serious social issue which produces psychological disturbances in the perpetrators and victims alike. Recognition of the extent of the problem has led to a large body of research seeking to understand the causes of child abuse.

Child Abuse

There is no clear-cut, universally accepted definition of child abuse. Generally, however, those who have concentrated on this issue are careful to distinguish between the physically abused, or "battered" child, and the child who is psychologically or physically "neglected," but not physically assaulted by the parents. A number of operational definitions have been proposed for research purposes. Child abuse may be defined narrowly to include only physical assault (Lauer, Ten Broeck & Grossman, 1974), or more broadly to include severe neglect as well as assault (Burland, Andrews & Headsten, 1973). Although this poses a certain problem, inasmuch as the evidence against the abusive parent usually emphasizes the violent physical assault in which the parent loses control as a result of experiencing rage, a broader definition is probably more helpful, since it includes more children who are at risk.

Who is the child-abusing parent? This question has been researched by psychologists for almost 30 years; and a great deal is now known about parents who abuse their children. In many ways, they are not much different than spouse abusers. Child-abusing parents are usually highly disturbed individuals who themselves were severely abused in childhood. *Child abuse is viewed as a self-perpetuating disorder in which the abused child grows up to be an abusing parent.* Moreover, the abusing parent is usually insecure, violent, and unable to control anger, and has a tendency to project his or her own inadequacies on the child (Kinard, 1982).

Whatever the specific causes, it is widely agreed that the abusing parent is a product of social and psychological strains that lead to such behavior. Kalmar (1977), in her book of definitive papers on child abuse, highlights the role of society in the problems of child abuse. She points out:

While the parents of abused children may be held directly responsible for their acts, society too must bear part of the blame for child abuse. This is so in part because ours is a society which is prone to violence and exploiting the powerless and because ours is a society which does not adequately meet the needs of minorities, the unemployed, the emotionally ill or the mentally re-tarded. The continued manifestations of child abuse is also related to our Constitutional structure which mandates greater emphasis on parental rights than on children's rights. In reality there appears to be an inherent conflict between parental rights and the best interests of the child. (p. iv)

No matter how empathic we may be about the parent's background, it is uni-versally agreed that the abusing parent is in need of help. Quite often the parent knows this, but for fear of legal and social retaliation is unable to seek the help needed. But when the child is finally referred to the appropriate authorities, and this may be through the school, or through the hospital facility which was re-sponsible for the intake, then the possibility of obtaining help becomes more likely, since the *cycle of abuse* is broken, and the *cycle of prevention* is simultaneously initiated. The Queensboro Society for the Prevention of Cruelty to Children (1976) presents a chart which dramatically illustrates the cyclical nature of abuse and prevention, and points out their interaction (see Figure 12.2).

Prevention and Treatment

What kind of help is available to the abused child and to the parents? This varies from state to state, from county to county, and within states from one school district to another. In recent years, most of the states have enacted specific laws for the reporting of child abuse, and many schools and social agencies (in-cluding hospitals) have issued guidelines for teachers and administrators who observe instances of or suspect the existence of child abuse. It is generally agreed today that the mistreatment and abuse of children is a result of many different interacting influences, and that any attempts at treatment or prevention have to be broadly based, taking into account a matrix of social, ecological, develop-mental, and psychological factors (Chibucos, 1980). Thus, most of the successful efforts have brought together specialists from different disciplines or practi-tioners from different settings.

One problem is to detect abuse before a child is hospitalized and to intervene before the problem has reached the critical point of no return. This can take place in the social agency setting, in the school, in the private practitioner's office, or through some combined effort, usually involving the participation of parents, ed-ucational personnel and medical staff (Fairorth, 1980). Reis and Herzberger (1980) suggest that social service screening activities combined with parent ed-ucation efforts, run jointly by the school and social agency, are useful in pre-venting conditions that lead to abuse as well as to detecting already existing cases of abuse.

The American Humane Association conducted a national survey to evaluate the scope of the problem and the services available. It was found that forty-nine percent of child abuse and neglect cases involve school-age children, the re-mainder being pre-schoolers (Kline, Cole & Fox, 1981). According to the au-thors, because of the high percentage in the school setting, "the school psychologist

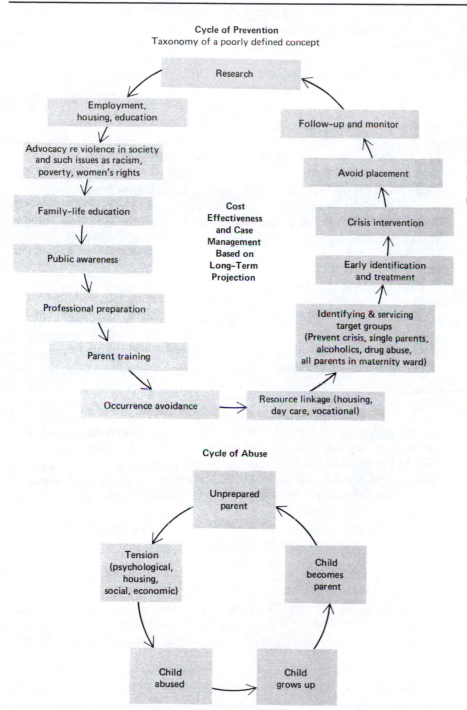

Cycle of Prevention
Taxonomy of a poorly defined concept

Research

Employment, housing, education

Advocacy re violence in society and such issues as racism, poverty, women's rights

Family-life education

Public awareness

Professional preparation

Parent training

Occurrence avoidance

Cost Effectiveness and Case Management Based on Long–Term Projection

Resource linkage (housing, day care, vocational)

Identifying & servicing target groups (Prevent crisis, single parents, alcoholics, drug abuse, all parents in maternity ward)

Early identification and treatment

Crisis intervention

Avoid placement

Follow-up and monitor

Cycle of Abuse

Unprepared parent

Tension (psychological, housing, social, economic)

Child becomes parent

Child abused

Child grows up

Figure 12.2. Cycle of prevention as compared to cycle of abuse. We see in this Queensboro Society chart the causative cycle of child abuse and the complex cycle of prevention in which the counselor can play a key role. **From *Child Abuse.* Published by Queensboro Society for the Prevention of Cruelty to Children, 161–20 89th Avenue, Jamaica, N.Y. 11432. Reprinted by permission.**

is in a particularly advantageous position to assist in the prevention and treatment of child abuse and neglect" (p. 65). Of course, the school psychologist, counselor, teacher, or social worker can be helpful only to the degree that the situation is reported to him or her, and, unfortunately, this is not always the case. As Sanders, Kibby, Creaghan, and Tyrrel (1975) point out, "the biggest barrier to aiding the abused child is the willingness of those who notice the child's distress to report the abuse," and no matter how well-intentioned is the system, this remains a refractory barrier that only a change in attitudes can overcome.

When the child-abusing parent does finally enter treatment, the counselor has a variety of tried and tested approaches available. Tracy and Clark (1974) report on a successful model used in a Philadelphia hospital, where the staff "worked with the parents in their own homes to help them develop greater competence as adults and parents." Using social learning theory, the parents were taught new behavioral skills and shown new ways to respond to their children. Polakow and Peabody (1975) also report on the use of behavioral techniques, including "contracting" in treating child-abusing parents and their abused children.

Peterman (1981) reports a successful project in which a group of urban mothers who sought help in learning about the parenting role, and how to deal with difficulties they were experiencing with their children, were taught self-help skills that could help them better deal with their children. At the same time these skills could lead to reducing the incidence of child abuse caused by frustration and lack of parenting education.

Practical Suggestions

Whenever a counselor plans to intervene with the parents of an abused child, it is essential to keep in mind that not only will the parents most likely be defensive, but they will often become aggressive as well. It is not unusual to find that the parent, called in by a teacher, counselor, physician, or agency psychologist, returns home to take out his or her rage on the child, whose victimization brought the parent there in the first place. This is a very real danger and must be kept constantly in mind.

Goldberg (1975) perceptively discusses some of the difficulties in the initial interview with the parent, which she calls an "emotionally charged situation":

> The parent is upset, whether wracked by guilt for having injured his child, shame for having lost control of himself, or embarrassment over having his "inadequacy" exposed. The parent fears the legal or psychiatric consequences of child abuse, the degradation ceremony through which his social identity is lowered, the right of transition from a normal social position to a deviant role. (p. 274)

Goldberg offers six behaviors that are appropriate during the initial interview. They are positioning; reaching for feelings; waiting; "getting with" feelings; asking information and giving information. We will use these as our model for a constructive interview with the abusing parent. Let us consider them individually.

Positioning refers to the nonverbal behaviors in terms of physical placement and room arrangement that the helper communicates to the client. "Since there is ample evidence to indicate that such nonverbal behavior affects comfort and communicates positive or negative feeling, to break the communication barrier, the worker should position himself in ways likely to increase the parent's comfort and convey positive feeling" (p. 278). The counselor can then use the nonverbal feedback provided by the parent to judge how effectively or ineffectively she or he is positioning himself.

Reaching for feelings involves the counselor's efforts to help the client express his or her feelings in words, or to convert nonverbal behaviors into verbal expressions. While every client has a variety of reasons that prevent him or her from being able to fully express himself or herself, there is usually some degree of willingness—some motivation—to find appropriate ways of expression. "It is particularly important to reach for feelings when (1) the parent does not express any emotion, (2) his expression of emotion is nonverbal, or (3) he expresses feelings not appropriate to such a situation" (p. 277). It should also be mentioned, that if the counselor is not aware of what feelings the client is trying to express, she or he should avoid "reaching" for feelings until she or he can be more certain.

Waiting is the period of comfortable silence in which the parent engages in his or her own internal dialogue. It is a period during which many of the inchoate insights can become relevant to the parent; a period in which questions may arise; in which doubts may be resolved. The counselor tries to avoid communicating tension during the "waiting period." The counselor's role is best accomplished when she or he waits along with the parent, communicating to the parent to take his or her time, to come to grips with feelings, to be open and honest with himself or herself.

"Getting with" feelings involves the counselor's ability to empathize with the way the parents feel and to make statements that are congruent with their feelings. Goldberg (1975) offers an example of how a helper did this with a client:

Mr. H. said angrily that everybody wants and wants and wants. He said, "You might think it's enough I work two different jobs. Yeh! Full time at a department store and part time at a gas station. And what do I get when I finally drag my ass home at night? How tired *she* is. Y'know, I dropped out of college to marry her." There was a short pause during which he rubbed his hands together and looked at the floor. I [the helper] waited. When he looked up again he said, "And the baby yells . . . and she tells me it's my turn because she's had it all day. It's a nightmare." "Wow," I [the helper] said, "You keep giving, but nobody gives you anything." "It's gotta stop," he said. (p. 280)

The final two behaviors, *asking for information* and *giving information,* are self-explanatory. Both open-ended and closed-ended questions can be used in asking the client for information, depending upon the kind of information the helper wishes to receive. Information may be used to help the parent better understand the situation objectively. "Information given to the parent reduces uncertainty and the accompanying discomfort" (p. 281).

Goldberg's suggestions are helpful for the general counselor or the health counselor who plans to intervene with the family. While at the present time, so many cases of child abuse tragically go unreported, we foresee a period in the near future when professionals in hospitals, schools, and social agencies, stirred by a new awareness, will routinely report all cases of child abuse. We have taken the time to go over these practical suggestions in some detail, since we believe that when this new attitude becomes dominant, counselors will have an immense role in ameliorating this difficult situation.

Evaluation of Family Counseling

Over the course of the past two decades, scores of case studies and research studies have supported the efficacy of family counseling. In fact, during the 1970s and 80s, an increasing number of professional journals have devoted themselves exclusively to the topic. Family counseling has been shown, in many instances, to be an effective treatment modality for a wide range of symptoms or disorders, including depression, crisis intervention, alcoholism (Harrell, 1983), child behavior disorders and school-related problems (Coppersmith, 1982), and parent-child and multigenerational problems within the family (Lamb, 1982). In recent years, the application of principles of family counseling to effective parenting has proven valuable in defining parenting as a learnable skill and providing appropriate training (Cohen, Cohler & Weissman, 1984).

Summary

In this chapter, we examined family counseling as a specific modality, including a number of different theories and approaches. We began by offering an operational definition of family counseling, which included a variety of helping efforts in which two or more members of a family are brought together into treatment. Surveying the predominant family forms in the U.S. today (nuclear family, extended family, single-parent family), we pointed out some of the contexts in which family members seek treatment. We noted too some of the accepted criteria for healthy family functioning: sharing and understanding feelings; accepting individual differences; caring, problem-solving, and cooperating; and aspects of good communication.

Next, we discussed some of the main issues in family counseling, including why and how family members enter treatment, how goals are established for the family, effective communication strategies, and other aspects of family improvement and growth. We considered the stages of problem-solving in the family and the counselor's role in this process, which we suggested is not to solve the family's problems for them, but rather to help them find and practice appropriate ways of problem-solving both for the present and the future. We also noted how individuation becomes a central issue not only for the individual family member, but for the entire family's functioning as well.

We examined some of the main approaches to and theories of family counseling practiced in the United States today, outlining each briefly: strategic, structural, behavioral, psychodynamic, multigenerational, and the Milan group approach. We also surveyed some of the techniques and interventions effective in family counseling, including methods of establishing a therapeutic contract, the timing of interventions, and behavioral techniques and goals. Finally, we addressed ways the counselor can help the family member or family unit deal with specific issues such as marital conflicts, pre- and post-divorce counseling, children's reactions to marital dissolution and their post-divorce adjustment, and issues in intrafamily violence.

Chapter Aim

To offer a general overview of group counseling, including its origins, its contemporary relevance, how it differs from individual counseling, and some specific techniques and approaches to group work.

The social group evolved as individuals began to band together for survival; to govern and provide for themselves. Many of the processes of an individual's behavior in a group—including identification, goals, decision-making and why people join groups—have been studied in detail by social psychologists.

Psychology of Groups

We develop the theme that the group leader's status is an *interaction* between his or her personality, the group setting, and the group members. Several aspects of the group counselor's job are defined, and the differences between the roles of humanistic, dynamic, and behavioral group leaders are discussed.

The Group Leader

Not all groups are the same, either in structure or function. We differentiate among the different types of counseling groups and explain the major characteristics of each.

Types of Groups

Some specific considerations of the group approach are enumerated. We look at client needs, the available resources, the setting for the group and some conceptualizations of the group process. We note how in practice these intermix to provide the qualitative reality of the group experience.

Factors in Group Counseling

Counseling groups have been used successfully to treat a wide range of behavioral and emotional-adjustment problems.

Evaluation and Applications

Group Counseling

13

Group counseling can be an effective therapeutic and educational modality in almost every counseling setting. It is widely used in schools, agencies, and private practices, not only because it is effective, but because it often proves more economical than individual counseling, both in terms of the client's and the counselor's time and money. Butcher (1982) points out several reasons groups are so popular. Besides their advantages in time and efficiency, groups are also advantageous, she contends, because they offer a parallel to real-life situations and create a climate of cooperation among members that would not be possible in the individual counseling experience.

If one surveys the wealth of research on group counseling, one is sure to notice a number of direct parallels to the literature on individual, face-to-face counseling. Between these two approaches there is a striking similarity of goals, processes, and rationales. Although this parallel attests to the similar nature of the two endeavors, it belies subtle but significant differences between them. In this chapter, we will explore the basic components of the group counseling experience, beginning with an examination of the psychology of the group.

As long as individuals have needed and relied upon others for survival, companionship, or other areas of social interest, the formation of groups has been inevitable. Groups have existed in different forms over the years. The hunting groups of primitive tribes closely parallel the "herd" instinct in animal societies. The rise of political systems through which people learned to govern themselves is rooted in the phenomenon of "grouping." The rise of religious factionalism illustrates the inherent strength of the human being's inexorable tendency to form group loyalties. Culture itself, which is transmitted from generation to generation through the socialization process, reflects the cumulative ideas and values of chronologically successive groups.

Psychology of Groups

Because the group was formed originally for survival or social benefit, cooperation is integral to effective group functioning. If members of a group fight among themselves, and if factionalism outweighs cooperative participation, then the group is doomed to failure and destruction through the process of *implosion*. On the other hand, if each member of a group is oblivious of other members, if each member functions primarily as an individual rather than as a group member, then the group will not hold together and will be doomed to failure and destruction through *explosion*. To avoid these problems, two important phenomena arose to assure the survival of the group: *group identification* and *shared goals*.

Group identification is the process whereby the individual identifies a part of himself with the larger group. If I say, "I am an American," or "I am a Democrat," or "I am a Red Sox fan," these are all identifications with groups. So too, the fraternity or sorority member who sees himself or herself as a member of a group shows signs of this group identification. The individual identity becomes subsumed in the group identity. This does not imply that the person renounces his own identity; but rather, that a part of his identity becomes merged with the identity of the group.

A group has goals of its own which may harmonize or conflict with individual members' goals. At times, every member of the group feels the same way about the goals, but often there are disagreements. The essence of the democratic system is the idea that if people come together openly and honestly, they can find common meeting points where they share similar or identical goals. While each person has many different goals in life, most of us share several goals with others. We belong to many different groups, and we identify with each to the extent that we share common goals. I may belong to the American Personnel and Guidance Association, the American Psychological Association, the Society for the Prevention of Cruelty to Animals, a church group, a football team, a glee club, and so forth. I share certain of my goals and identify certain parts of myself with each of these groups.

Why People Join Groups

Two questions that have consistently proven of special interest to psychologists studying groups are (1) why does a person choose to join one group over another? and (2) in what ways does the group tend to influence a person's behavior? Many years of research have thrown light on both these questions, and have demonstrated how the group situation can change the individual's normal behaviors and response patterns.

Manifestly, people form groups for many different reasons; and within any given group are usually subgroups. Although a class may function as a group, with the teacher as a leader, within a single class may be several subgroups, each with its own leader or leaders. There may be a group of the "tough" kids, who hang out together after school. There may be a group of students who are interested in science, who know each other from their advanced science class and from their field trips. There may be a group of friends who are all underachievers.

Although they might not admit that this coincidence prompts them to be friends, they are in fact finding solace in each other. When we consider some of the different reasons people join groups we will see why these subgroups within the larger group serve a purpose.

Several key reasons why people join groups have been identified. One reason is in order to attain a common goal or to engage in common activities. People who enjoy movies, concerts, or sports events may form a group to attend these together. Or a number of individuals who want a certain candidate elected may form a group to attain that goal. But there are also some less obvious reasons people join groups.

As a rule, when individuals select a group to join, they seek out others who are similar to themselves in order to obtain information which will enable them to evaluate their own reactions (Singer, 1980). To college students, for example, the opinions of their classmates on sexual behavior or environmental pollution are more informative than the views of their parents. Thus, counseling groups are particularly effective in working with individuals who, because of specialized problems, need the reinforcement and input of their peers to better gain a perspective of their situation with the assistance of positive social consensus and social support (Mardoyan & Weis, 1981).

One theory which explains why people choose which groups to join is explained by the old adage, "misery loves company." In a famous experiment, Schachter (1959) told a group of subjects that they would be receiving, as part of their participation in a psychological experiment, a series of painful electric shocks. They were offered a chance to wait either in the company of others or by themselves for ten minutes before the beginning of the experiment. Sixty-three percent of the subjects chose to wait with others, while among control subjects, who were told that they would receive only very mild, nonpainful shocks, only thirty-three percent chose to wait with others. Other experiments conducted by Schachter and his colleagues also showed that people in a state of anxiety preferred to wait with others in a similar state. These findings indicate that many people join groups because they want to affiliate with other people as miserable as they are.

In short, there are several reasons people join groups, and because of the variety of reasons, there are likely to be subgroups within a larger group to satisfy the needs of the many individual members.

Whenever we are a member of a group, this can, and usually does influence our behavior in a variety of ways. When a group is formed, certain standards of behavior emerge, implicitly and explicitly, and there is strong pressure on individual members to conform to the majority's standards in order to obtain the benefits of group membership. In fact, groups influence their members' behaviors most powerfully through their social norms. A norm is defined as a standard of behavior and thought; it is the expectation the group has about an individual's

How Groups Influence Behavior

behavior. We must conform to the expectations of the group or suffer its disapproval. The longer people interact and the more they interact, the more they tend to adopt common ways of interpreting the world and common standards for the behavior of each group member. That is why in friendships that have lasted for many years, we may find that the friends seem to think alike on just about every subject.

Conformity, the tendency to modify one's behavior in order to correspond with what others in a group are doing, has a powerful influence on an individual's behavior in a group situation. A classic study on conformity was reported by Asch in 1952. Male college students who had volunteered for an experiment in visual judgment were brought into a room where from 6 to 9 other students were waiting to participate. Actually, all the others were confederates, or stooges, who, unbeknown to the subjects, had been coached to behave in a certain manner. Everyone was shown a white card with a black line on it. This was called the standard line, and the subjects were asked to remember it. Then the experimenter removed this card and displayed another card that had three lines of different sizes drawn on it, one of which was the same as the standard. He then asked each subject to report out loud his judgment as to which comparison line matched the standard line. The "stooges" were always called on to report before the experimental subject did. For the first two trials, everyone picked the correct line, but all the confederates had previously been instructed to give incorrect answers on twelve of the remaining sixteen trials. Since they all answered in the same way, they were in effect creating a group norm which was incorrect, thus putting the experimental subject under pressure to conform.

In his first study, Asch found that there was a marked movement toward the majority—about one-third of all judgments given by the subjects were errors in the direction of the distorted estimates of the majority—but most of the estimates (68%) were correct, despite the majority pressure. There was a wide range of individual differences, however. One-fourth of the subjects remained completely independent on all trials, ten percent went along with the majority on every trial, and one-third tended to yield to the majority in at least half the trials. This shows that individuals differ in how much they will conform, and can therefore be identified as high-conformers or low-conformers.

Since rarely is any individual fully committed to any one group, and since even within the group context, identification and conformity is only partial, it is essential that there be some cohering force to hold together the members of the group and to help them achieve the goals they share. That person is the group leader.

The Group Leader

In broad terms, the function of the group leader is the same as that of the counselor in individual, face-to-face counseling. "In actuality," Trotzer (1977) points out, "the leader role is a conglomeration of subroles that emerge on the basis of interaction between the group leader's personality and philosophical orientation and the needs of the group" (p. 92). Likewise, techniques and stratagems are the same for individual and group counseling in many ways.

There are some differences, too. One problem the group counselor faces is getting together enough individuals to form a group. Sometimes a group is formed to accommodate people with a common problem; sometimes it is limited by the client population of the agency. The counselor may not be sure if certain individuals will be able to function well together, or if there will be counterproductive personality conflicts. Is it better to place people with a common problem in a group or are heterogeneous groups more effective? Hyman Spotnitz (1961), a pioneer in modern psychoanalytic group counseling, describes his approach to forming a group:

> In forming a group, I put together persons who will be able to develop intense emotional reactions to each other. The sexes get equal representation. The patients are usually alike in some respects and different in others. Divergence in personality structure blended with reasonably compatible backgrounds . . . usually make it possible for group members to relate well to each other and to function efficiently as a unit. With diverse personalities represented, interchanges go on among the calm, the excitable, those who easily arouse excitement, and others who tend to check it. As they stimulate each other in different ways, group process is mobilized. (p. 120)

A second situation particularly applicable to the group setting is maintaining order and continuity in the face of anxiety and tension. Several individuals functioning as a group can be more untoward and unmanageable than a single individual, no matter what his or her resistances. The group leader must work toward a positive group attitude by demonstrating to the group members the security that is present in the group situation.

Finally, the group leader, like the individual counselor, must be a facilitator. Carl Rogers (1971), an innovator in encounter group practices, described his way of facilitating the group experience:

> I tend to open in an extremely unstructured way, perhaps with no more than a single comment: "I suspect we will know each other a great deal better at the end of these group sessions than we do now. . . ." I listen as carefully and as sensitively as I am able. . . . I wish very much to make the climate psychologically safe for the individual—I have found that it "pays off" to live with the group exactly where it is. Thus I have worked with a group of very inhibited top-notch scientists, mostly in the physical sciences, where feelings were rarely expressed openly, and personal encounter at a deep level was simply not seen. Yet this group became much more free and innovative, and showed many positive results of our meetings. . . . I am willing for a

participant to commit himself to the group. . . . I am willing to accept silence and muteness in the individual, provided I am quite certain it is not unexpressed pain or resistance. . . . I tend to accept statements at their face value. . . . I try to make clear that whatever happens will happen from the choices of the group. . . . When talk is generalized or intellectualizing, I tend to select the self-referent meanings to respond to out of this total context. (pp. 275–278)

We see how Rogers's approach toward group leadership is both a reflection of his personality and of his theoretical orientation. A Gestalt group leader would use vastly different types of techniques, involving preassigned actions and specific behavior by the group members (Mintz, 1971). These Gestalt "games" are designed to facilitate growth within the group, but in a manner that is incompatible with the Rogerian stance.

The orientation of the group leader will profoundly influence the kind of role he or she sees as appropriate. The functional discrepancies in therapeutic techniques and goals that we catalogued in Part 2 are just as applicable in the group setting. Rogers's comment above is indicative of the role of the *humanistic* leader. Other group leaders would conceptualize their roles somewhat differently.

The Psychoanalytic Group Leader

While the psychoanalytic group leader emphasizes the parallels between group and individual counseling, he or she also recognizes the differences. As Kirman (1976) points out,

You proceed with groups much as you do with individuals from the modern psychoanalytic point of view. In individual counseling, you want the client to say whatever comes to mind. But everything can't be said in a group. *An important function of the group is learning what can and cannot be said in group.* (p. 86, italics added)

Generally, the psychoanalytic group leader believes that within the group context each member re-experiences emotionally and repeats behaviorally his early situation within the family structure. Needs that were not met in childhood cry out for satisfaction in the group; but the individual attempts to satisfy these needs in the same ways that repeatedly failed during the early years. One of the important roles of the psychoanalytic group leader, therefore, is to teach the individual *how* to satisfy his or her legitimate needs in an appropriate, effective way.

Counselors using the psychoanalytic method are also sensitive to the phenomenon of *group transference*. This simply means that the group-as-a-whole perceives the leader as a parental, or authority, figure. The group leader, recognizing this, attempts to respond to group communications in the same way a "good" parent would act. This phenomenon, it should be pointed out, works in conjunction with all of the individual transference relationships that also exist simultaneously in the group.

The group serves two significant purposes for the behaviorally oriented group leader. First, it provides rich behavioral resources after which individual group members can *model* themselves (modeling is discussed in chapter 10). The group leader may attempt to point out to the individual members types of new (or different) behaviors that he or she feels will be beneficial to them. The members are then able to learn these new and productive behaviors by watching other members of the group, or by directly observing the group leader.

The second purpose of the behaviorally oriented group is that members of the group can be used to dispense reinforcement (either positive or negative). Peer pressure can be brought to bear on any member to encourage or discourage certain specified behaviors. Although reinforcers can be provided by the group leader, it is far more effective if the behavioral group leader, as a *manager of contingencies,* helps all the group members learn to give or withhold reinforcers effectively. The critical concept here is known as *group contingencies;* these can be defined as making the consequences of an individual's behaviors dependent on the group as well as on the individual. Axelrod (1977, p. 50) gives an example:

> An example of a group contingency is found in the sport of professional baseball. After the World Series has been completed, all members of the winning team receive the same pay, even though their individual performances may have varied greatly. The team has been scored as a unit. Similarly, all members of the losing team receive the same, smaller share, in spite of the fact that the performance of some members of the losing team may have exceeded that of some of the players on the winning team. (p. 50)

The important point, Axelrod emphasizes, is that the reinforcement each student receives "depends not only on his own behavior, but also on the behavior of other members of the group" (p. 50). This has several practical advantages over individually administered behavioral-change programs. It teaches the learner by example the values of group cooperation. It also introduces the element of peer pressure, where desired behaviors are encouraged and supported by one's peer group. And especially in the school setting, it is easier to implement than are a variety of simultaneous individual programs for different students. Thus, the behavioral group leader can serve an important purpose as the manager of group contingencies in the school counseling setting.

In the rational and reality counseling approaches, the group leader mobilizes the group-as-a-whole to point out to individual members the irrationalities or improprieties of individual behaviors, perceptions, and feelings. In this sense, the group becomes an extension of the leader's perceptions which, presumably, are in accord with reality and with emotionally satisfying functioning. It is not uncommon to find pressure brought to bear on group members to change behaviors that are viewed as detrimental or unhealthy. But at the same time, the group provides feedback, both to the leader and to individual members, and this feedback helps the individuals arrive at realistic options and perceptual frameworks from which decisions can be made. As communication in the group increases, the group member's general functioning increases accordingly (Stafford, 1978). In many respects, the rational approach is a hybrid of the behavioral and psychodynamic positions, integrating teaching and learning principles along with the counseling approach.

We should also note that the ramifications of the leader's role, of how the leader conceptualizes his or her functioning in the group, affects profoundly the entire group process. Table 13.1 shows how the group participants and the leader function and react somewhat differently in the three main psychological models: psychoanalysis, behaviorism, and humanism. We observe that in terms of facilitating change and in terms of specific applications, there are significant differences to be considered when selecting a group approach.

The Cognitive Leader

The cognitive perspective suggests that the individual's understanding of reality is *constructed* from his or her interactions with people and with the physical environment, and then perceived through the cognitive interpretation of these interactions. From this perspective a central part of the group experience is the provision for diverse emotional, social, and intellectual opportunities for enriched experiences which, when appropriately guided by the leader, in turn allow for more complex and advanced constructions.

In terms of group processes, cognitive counselors, whether oriented more toward the behavioral or humanistic ends of the spectrum, would argue that the group setting should provide a context in which clients can experience group interactions that increase their ability to use their logical processes in order to arrive at a better understanding of the world and of themselves.

The Gestalt psychologist, representative of this position, considers the individual's perceptions (and this means perceptions of oneself, one's feelings, one's relationships, etc.) in terms of the *figure-ground* dichotomy. In terms of higher-level functioning, the Gestalt psychologist believes that a healthy personality exists when a person's experiences form a meaningful whole, when there is a smooth transition between those sets of experiences which are immediately within the focus of awareness (what they call the *figure*) and those that are in the background (which they call the *ground*). "The basic premise of Gestalt psychology," Perls (1973) writes, "is that human nature is organized into patterns or wholes, that it is experienced by the individual in these terms, and that it can only be understood as a function of the patterns of wholes of which it is made." Proper functioning is dependent upon one's abilities to continually shift the figure-ground relationship. The gestalt group works toward this end by using some members' perceptions of themselves and others as a catalyst for changing other members' cognitions of themselves and others in the group (Kaplan, 1978).

Table 13.1
Four Psychological Models of Group Processes

Category	Psychoanalysis	Behaviorism	Humanism	Cognitive
Actions of Group Participants	Repeat the infantile behaviors of the family setting.	Responses to stimuli from within the group setting.	Inhibited or uninhibited tendencies toward growth and change.	Reflect through their behaviors ways in which they are constructing their individual interpretations of reality.
Methods of Facilitating Change	Pointing out *(interpreting)* the unconscious meanings of behaviors as they are revealed in the group.	Positive and negative reinforcement; modeling.	The leaders' own personal capacity to ''give'' to the group members.	Using objective information relevant to the level of the learner (e.g. simple commands and direct rules at the preoperational level; more complex reasoning at the formal operational level); changing thinking in order to change behavior: correction misperceptions and misinterpretations.
Role of the Leader	To encourage the transferring of feelings; to resolve resistances; to teach the individual to satisfy needs from childhood in a socially appropriate manner.	To reinforce positive behaviors and to provide models whereby the member can learn appropriate behavior patterns.	To accept; to clarify; to teach; to participate. In all, to help the group attain a high level of expressive freedom.	To provide contextual clues which will help members develop their abilities to perceive the world around them, accurately to process this information in their individual constructions of reality.
School Applications	Resolving resistances in the classroom.	Direct behavior change.	In all areas the full inclusive growth of the total person.	Using enriching educational experiences to facilitate intellectual as well as emotional growth; Changing behavior and thought simultaneously.
	Lessening neurotic interference to mastering learning tasks.	Increasing the rate of learning.		
	Meeting maturational needs that arise in a social context.	Resolving school phobias, test anxiety, underachievement, etc. Drug prevention programs.		

Types of Groups

Both the limitations of settings and the varying needs of the participants have given rise to different types of groups, most of which are associated with a wide variety of different settings. Nowadays, it is not uncommon to hear the terms "t" group, "sensitivity" group, "workshop" group, "encounter" group, and so on. The counselor should understand the basic differences among these groups, how the terminology is typically used, and be aware of the setting with which each type of group is normally associated.

Because of overlap, many groups do not clearly fall in one category or another. To determine general group types, however, we can use a classification system developed by Betz, Wilbur and Roberts-Wilbur (1981) which identifies three categories of groups according to a conceptual model of the group processes involved: (1) task-, (2) socio-, and (3) psychological groups. The objectives (and processes) of these three kinds of groups respectively are:

1. extrapersonal—to accomplish a task;
2. interpersonal—to cause examination of attitudes, values, and beliefs and to inform or orient;
3. intrapersonal—to change or modify behavior by focusing that behavior in the group.

Using these three general categories, we can differentiate between four popular types of counseling groups, under whose headings many other types would be included: therapy groups; discussion groups; training groups; and, guidance groups. A therapy group is generally designed to treat a specific problem, usually psychological in nature and manifesting an undesirable symptom. An example might be a group in which college students who are experiencing severely high levels of death anxiety (thanatophobia) receive treatment in a group context to lessen the anxiety level (Peal, Handal & Gilner, 1982).

A discussion group is designed more for prevention and for working out feelings. An example would be a group in which teachers meet with the school counselor to discuss disciplinary problems they are experiencing with their students. These types of groups fall under the heading of what Cerio (1979) calls educational growth groups (EGG). They may be used to deal with any kind of educational problem. Figures 13.1 and 13.2 show the direction of group progress and the goals of a typical EGG, which is probably the most widely used modality in the schools. As we see from the display, this model allows for the provision of information to group members, offers opportunities for clarifying their values, for experiential learning, and for future planning—all of which are integral to solving any educational problem.

A training group is a time-limited group intended for achieving a specific learning goal or goals. An example of this would be a group designed to train elementary-school peer counselors in appropriate counseling skills over a short period. Mastroianni and Dinkmeyer (1980) used this type of group to train 5th graders as peer counselors who then worked as group co-leaders, facilitators, and as tutors for other students at the school who needed assistance.

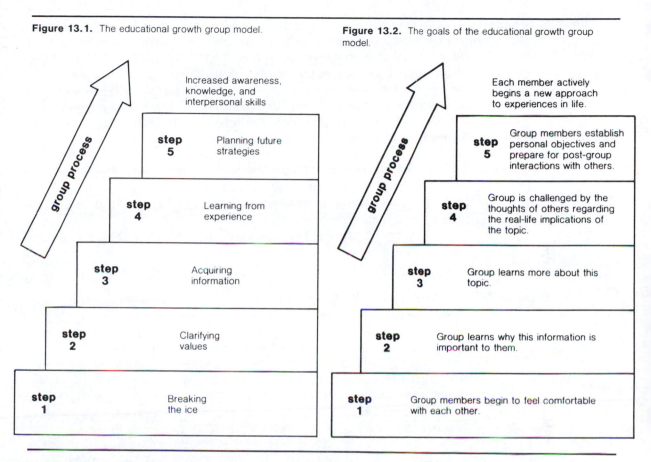

Figure 13.1. The educational growth group model.

Increased awareness, knowledge, and interpersonal skills

group process

step 5	Planning future strategies
step 4	Learning from experience
step 3	Acquiring information
step 2	Clarifying values
step 1	Breaking the ice

Figure 13.2. The goals of the educational growth group model.

Each member actively begins a new approach to experiences in life.

group process

step 5	Group members establish personal objectives and prepare for post-group interactions with others.
step 4	Group is challenged by the thoughts of others regarding the real-life implications of the topic.
step 3	Group learns more about this topic.
step 2	Group learns why this information is important to them.
step 1	Group members begin to feel comfortable with each other.

Note: From "Structured Experiences with the Educational Growth Group Model" by J. E. Cerio, *Personnel and Guidance Journal,* 1979, *57* (8), 400.

A guidance group combines elements of all of the above, but emphasizes *future role-activity improvement* over personality integration. Usually a guidance group brings together the social-, the task- and the psychological dimensions of its members' lives to arrive at procedural (or practical) guidelines for future actions. Such a group might be useful, for example, in helping college student athletes talk about some of the common problems they are experiencing, share these experiences, and work out methods for preventing many of the problems to which student athletes are typically prone (Wittmer, Bostic, Phillips & Waters, 1981). Through the social interaction and the psychological processes, in the group context, specific role-oriented goals are worked through in a guidance group.

We see then, even from this abridged catalogue of the many different types of groups, that there is an almost confusingly wide choice available to the counselor. Some of the factors influencing the decision as to what type of group is appropriate for what type of situation are: (1) the needs of the clients; (2) the resources available; (3) the setting. Let us consider each of these individually.

Factors in Group Counseling

Much has been written on group processes, and there is some consensus in the field about the general (although not the specific) direction in which an effective counseling group progresses over time. Although theorists of different perspectives may classify the progression differently, using their own terminology, it is generally agreed that in an effective group, cohesiveness is the prerequisite for trust and awareness, and these, in turn, become the precipitators of change. Gill and Barry (1982) offer a three-stage framework to explain what happens in the group, in terms of the group leader's actions:

1. *Group formation* Facilitating cooperation toward common goals through development of group identity;
2. *Group awareness* Facilitating a shared understanding of the group's behavior;
3. *Group action* Facilitating a shared understanding of the group's behavior.

Client Needs

There are no specific guidelines about what types of client needs would favor group counseling over individual counseling, but we can make a few statements that, if not absolute, are at least generally agreed upon. First, for specifically symptomatic disorders (e.g. school phobia, behavioral problems, learning disorders, drug abuse, truancy), group counseling has proven especially helpful. Not only is it less expensive than individual counseling to provide and ably reach more clients, but many prospective clients who might not respond to individual counseling for these and related types of problems may respond well within a group context, where the support network is different (Kaufman & Bluestone, 1974). Also, for the client who feels more comfortable speaking in a group than relating to a counselor alone in an individual session, the group approach would also be indicated.

Finally, where the client's diffidence in his or her interpersonal relationships is an integral part of the problem, the group serves as a good medium to facilitate one's confidence in interpersonal relationships. As a more general rule, we can say that groups are effective wherever the acquisition of social skills is a primary consideration. Weissberg and Gesten (1982) discuss the value of classroom groups, for example, in helping children develop "social problem-solving skills," which they describe as "an approach to primary prevention and competence-building designed to promote children's abilities to resolve interpersonal conflicts and consequently, [help] their adjustment." We can state further that group modality is applicable to helping school students refine a whole range of social skills that are more effectively developed in the group context than individually.

Available Resources

In some settings it is not feasible for the counselor to see the large client population on an individual basis. In such situations, the group is a perfect compromise. The history of group treatment, as a unique modality, illustrates how the limitations and constraints of available resources *and* the needs of the clients interact to make the group movement possible. The great pioneers of the group counseling movement, S. R. Slavson, Joseph Walsh, and Joseph Pratt, among others, originally formed groups for these reasons. Walsh and Pratt, both physicians, were working with tuberculosis patients in a hospital setting. Recognizing the need to help these patients emotionally as well as physically, they organized groups where the patients could be given information as well as gain confidence in their prognosis. Patients' feelings about their disease were brought out into the open, and group counseling methods were established that are still used today. Slavson was working with groups of disturbed children, also in an institutional setting, when he realized that the group modality itself rather than the specific therapeutic activities offered was responsible for the improvement (Hadden, 1975).

Thus, the assessment of available resources is not only valuable in determining to use a group, but historically has proven of value in the development of the group movement. In the schools, where resources are always in short supply, this should prove a particularly cogent point in many situations for choosing a group over individual counseling.

Not only are the available resources in part defined by the setting, but client expectations, expectations of superiors and administrative personnel, as well as the delineation of social boundaries are also, to a large extent, determined by the setting. Counseling underachievers in a school, as opposed to second career employees in an organization, or inmates in a prison—each holds different implications precisely because of the differences in setting. **The Setting**

Moreover, the behavior of individual participants is affected by the physical setting. The way the room is laid out, the arrangement of lighting and chairs, the floor, all create their facilitative, neutral, or nonfacilitative mosaic; all these factors make a difference. Just as Marshall McLuhan has pointed out that in communication, the "medium is the message," the group context presents to each participant an emotional and psychosocial message that has a profound influence on their behavior. Maines and Markowitz (1981) use the term "ecology of participation" to describe conceptually an influential aspect of the counseling setting: the relationship between spatial orders in a group, that is, where people sit, as well as their social interaction among one other. The counselor might take note of this and suggest ways of reordering the group to improve communication among members.

Just as different types of group leaders conceptualize their jobs differently, the process of group counseling varies according to the leader's perceived role and the clients' needs. Lacoursiere (1980) offers an essentially eclectic model of the group process, based on extensive research of group practice, which he calls the predictable "life cycle of groups." He differentiates this cycle into five stages: **The Process** orientation, dissatisfaction, resolution, production, and termination. During the first stage, the stage of orientation, members come to understand what the group is all about, what behaviors are expected of them, and they learn something about the other group members. Some dissatisfaction arises during the second stage, that of dissatisfaction, either about the process, the leader, or about other group members. As this is discussed and worked through, it is resolved and progress toward resolving problems begins. During this stage of resolution their commitment to the group grows. The fourth stage, production, is where most of the problem-solving actually takes place. The final stage of termination occurs when the members feel their problems are resolved and are able to function on their own.

Evaluation and Applications

As we have seen from the above sections, group approaches can be valuable in just about any counseling setting. Research on the efficacy of group treatment is extensive, and generally favorable. We will survey briefly a few recent studies which show how group approaches can be (and have been!) used effectively in different settings; the counselor trainee may wish to consult these studies directly to determine specific ways of implementation.

Counseling groups have been used effectively in many creative ways. Blohm (1978), among others, has shown that group methods work well with learning disabled elementary school children; and it is now generally recognized that groups are the primary counseling modality for dealing with most learning disabilities. Amerikaner and Summerlin (1982), for example, found group counseling methods especially effective in working with learning disabled children. Using group approaches, including social skills training and relaxation techniques, they noted significant increases of self-concept and positive classroom behaviors. Huber (1979) used group counseling as a method for helping parents of handicapped children work out many of their feelings about the child, about the handicapping condition, and about the situation in general. "The parent group," he points out (p. 268), "provides a unique opportunity for participants to become more aware of what is happening in their lives through feedback from other parents about their experiences. . . . Parents contribute to each other and develop new ways of coping with their situations."

One specialized form of group counseling which has been substantiated in the research is peer group counseling. Here, the student, along with his or her peers, function as models and often leaders for other students in the group setting. Hoffman (1976) has reviewed applications of this approach and finds it generally effective, especially where teachers and parents are involved, at least peripherally.

Group guidance approaches have been widely used in the school setting. One recent application of group guidance procedures which has found widespread acceptance in the schools is the vocational exploration group (VEG), in which students develop career maturity and job readiness through the group experience (Yates, Johnson & Johnson, 1979). This procedure is particularly valuable and economical where the counselor cannot provide individual career counseling to students.

Groups are widely used in the medical and clinical settings. Many crisis counseling approaches (discussed in greater detail in chapter 15) use the group method to help individuals get through their most difficult moments. This is especially useful where all the group's members are undergoing the same type of crisis. Davis and Jessen (1982), among others, have used group counseling interventions in helping clients cope with bereavement crises; and it is also widely used in rape crisis counseling. Groups of cancer patients on chemotherapy, or in remission, renal dialysis patients, and those with chronic arthritis and heart disease have also become valuable treatment modalities during the past twelve years. Honig (1982) points out how groups can be helpful in working with physically ill adolescents on a medical ward, as they try to overcome both the stigmatizing effects of their illness and many of the practical problems it creates.

Summary

In this chapter, we presented an overview of group counseling, showing its practical benefits and contemporary relevance, pointing out how it differs from individual counseling, and considering some specific approaches to group counseling and guidance in the school setting. The advantages of the group approach are many: it is economical, it is more representative of the social milieu in which the individual must function, it provides the individual with a wider range of emotional responses, and it allows clients to practice dealing with social situations.

We examined the group leader's role and function, pointing out that the role is often an interaction between his or her personality, the group setting, social and professional role expectations, and the behavior of group members. Several aspects of the group counselor's job were defined, and the differences between the roles of humanistic, psychodynamic, and behavioral group leaders discussed.

Some distinct types of groups were then enumerated, with a consideration of client needs and available resources. Counseling groups, we concluded, have been used successfully to treat a wide range of behavioral and emotional-adjustment problems.

Chapter Aim

To provide an overview and focus on the major topics of the developing field of health counseling, including: medical-surgical health counseling, preventive efforts; nutritional counseling; health and stress control; fertility counseling; problem pregnancy counseling; and other applications.

Defining health as "a state of complete, physical, mental, and social well-being," we evolve a concept of health counseling comprising a variety of related efforts to assist people achieve their maximum state of physical and mental health. The historical and philosophical origins of health counseling are found in preventive medicine and public health, as well as in basic counseling ideology.

Background

Preventive counseling brings together individual counseling actions as well as public education and group counseling approaches. Its rationale is that "an ounce of prevention is worth a pound of cure." The holistic emphasis on health as "positive wellness" takes into account all aspects of the person's environmental, physical, and spiritual-interpersonal reality.

Preventive Counseling: The Holistic Perspective

This field is relatively new and still in the process of definition. The type of medical counseling offered depends largely on the setting and on the training of the counselor. Preventive health counseling works on the principle that we can identify for most clients the areas in which they are most likely to experience difficulties, and help them learn to prevent problems in those areas. Medical and surgical counseling prepares patients for surgery and helps them adjust afterward.

Medical and Surgical Counseling

Nutritional counseling involves helping individuals learn to assess their nutritional intake and to apply this information in making health-inducing improvements. The school is viewed as an appropriate setting for many of the goals of nutritional counseling to be implemented.

Nutritional Counseling

Health and Stress Control

Recognizing that stress is a contributory factor in many physical as well as psychological disturbances, we examine some of the variables which govern how stress affects us; its intensity, a person's innate or acquired ability to cope with it, its duration, and the perceived possibility of alleviating it. We then look at psychosomatic components of major illnesses, including heart disease, asthma, GI disturbances, and cancer.

Fertility Counseling

Fertility counseling includes two types of situations: providing counseling and information to couples who want to have children but who have not been successful in their efforts to conceive; and, furnishing guidance and contraceptive information to people who do not wish to have children. It is essential that the counselor have technical knowledge about these matters, as well as a helping attitude, and a sense of empathic understanding.

Planned Pregnancy Counseling

This includes providing information and emotional support to help the prospective parents deal with all the ramifications of pregnancy. Natural childbirth classes would be included in this category.

Problem Pregnancy Counseling

This includes all efforts to help the pregnant woman, who views being pregnant as a problem. This may include presenting the options available, and helping her arrive at a decision she can live with. It also involves providing follow-up services and emotional support.

Alcohol Abuse Counseling

One of the major health problems in the country today is alcohol and drug abuse. There are an estimated 10–12 million alcoholics or serious problem drinkers in the United States. We look at the progressive stages of alcohol abuse, problem drinking, and alcoholism and examine some of its effects on the marital relationship and the family. We also consider some counseling implications.

Health Counseling

14

Health counseling is a relatively new field, one not yet fully established in the counseling profession. There is no basic text in the field, no professional organization dedicated solely to its pursuance, and no clear boundaries and guidelines about its purview. Its origins are diverse, its concepts fluid and adaptive, and its practitioners do not always call their activity "health counseling." Moreover, health counseling overlaps with professional concerns and responsibilities in such diverse fields as psychiatry, nursing, paramedical training, public health, and social work. In this chapter, we will define the basic parameters of this growing movement, articulate a few broad principles of practice and areas of investigation, and outline the still uncharted territory of this new domain. Then, we shall focus in detail on five applied areas of health counseling: medical health counseling; stress reduction approaches; counseling alcoholics and problem-drinking clients; fertility counseling; and pregnancy counseling. Two other major concerns in health counseling, adolescent drug and alcohol abuse and family violence, including child abuse, are covered separately in chapters 11 and 14.

From the beginnings of recorded history, individuals have been deeply concerned about their health. All civilized societies, in fact, have established explicit rules and regulations governing the health of their citizenry. It has long been recognized that health is more than simply a private or personal matter, that it has profound social, economic significance. In the United States, for example, annual health expenditures are now in excess of $200 billion, or more than 10% of our country's GNP. The majority of health researchers and medical personnel now "believe that the financial, as well as the human, costs associated with such currently preventable dysfunctions as lung cancer, cardiovascular disease, drug and alcohol abuse, and vehicle accidents are a needless waste of this country's human and fiscal resources" (Matarazzo, 1982).

Background

403

There have been many attempts, in a variety of disciplines, ranging from religion to biology to psychology, to understand how the individual's health can best be maintained or improved. As we use the term, the study of health involves the interaction of many different disciplines. In defining health, it is generally agreed that it is not enough to be free from disease, but one must also be able to function effectively, to utilize the body resources, and to experience a state of well-being. As Schifferes and Peterson (1972) point out:

It is difficult to define health. Thousands of attempts to define it have been made. Currently the definition given by the World Health Organization is commonly accepted: *"Health is a state of complete physical, mental, and social well-being, and not merely the absence of disease or infirmity."* A person can have a healthy attitude toward life despite pain and physical handicaps. Health and disease are not complete opposites. . . . Even the sickest person retains a number of normal functions and even in the apparently most healthy specimens of mankind a rigorous clinical examination can detect some flaws. (pp. 10–11, italics added)

In its ordinary usage, *health*, as Plato defined it, refers to "a sound mind and a sound body." The study of psychosomatic diseases, for example, has focused attention on ways in which emotional problems—intrapsychic conflicts, as the psychoanalysts call them—precipitate organic problems. Other research has shown that the converse is also true, that physical problems can take their toll mentally, causing anxiety and stress. Studies have also shown that many specific states of being, such as stress or fear or other intense emotions, have both a physical and psychological component. Thus, the interaction between mind and body is two-fold: on the one hand, emotional conditions precipitate bodily reactions; and on the other hand, physical conditions (such as illness) can influence us emotionally.

There are three important points to keep in mind as we explore health counseling. First, a true state of health is more than the absence of illness and disease. One can strive toward maximum health, regardless of his or her physical condition. Second, for each of us there are some definite, often undiagnosed, deficiencies of health; or another way of saying this is that there is always room for improvement. Third, that good health involves psychological well-being as well as good physical care. Together, these three points add up to what will be our central thesis: namely, *health counseling involves assisting people achieve their maximum state of health*.

The origins of health counseling can be found in clinical medicine and in public health, as well as in the underlying premises of many counseling ideologies. Preventive medicine dates back to the Greeks, but it has generally focused only on physical health. Included in preventive medicine approaches have been informal efforts in providing individuals with information, as well as more formal, large-scale efforts in public education. Practitioners in helping professions such as counseling have recently become involved in areas related to medicine. Recognizing the mind-body continuum, they have become interested in helping clients work toward states of physical health through psychological well-being. Allen (1977), for example, sees the role of the counselor heading in this direction:

> Just when many traditional slots for counselors and psychologists are filled or disappearing, the appearance of some exciting new vistas seems providential. One of these exciting new areas is physical well-being, the prevention and remedy of bodily disease. Counseling and psychotherapy have been construed as attempts to help people modify certain troublesome ways of dealing with their experience. Counselors' and psychotherapists' intention is to change their clients' behavior and increase clients' subjective sense of satisfaction. But there is even more at stake in these efforts to reprogram the human computer, the central nervous system. *An increasing amount of evidence suggests that the central nervous system is the most critical single determinant of physical health.* (p. 40, italics added)

Allen goes on to show how counseling interventions, which direct themselves to the improved functioning of the central nervous system, can affect such critical areas as disease control and pain relief. This is not to suggest that the counselor has entered the realm of medicine. Rather, we wish to emphasize that the kinds of changes included under the goals of counseling can—and should!—include physical as well as psychological and behavioral changes.

Since the field is new, and its scope has not yet been fully defined, we will look at a tentative overview of some of the types of situations in which the health counselor will work. The settings for health counseling range from the private clinical setting to the hospital setting to the social work (or other agency) setting. Although the setting may make some impact on the type of counseling that takes place, the specific difficulties being treated are of far greater importance. In other words, the type of counseling, and to some degree the setting, will be determined by the kind of problem the client comes into treatment with. For example, individuals undergoing renal dialysis treatment will probably be seen in group counseling within the hospital setting, while clients who are going through post-abortion trauma may be seen in the private office setting.

The type of counseling will also depend on the training of the counselor. If the counselor has some background in public health, nursing, or medicine, he or she will be more competent to deal with certain types of problems than would a person who does not have such training. Workers in all public health areas can benefit from courses in health counseling, where they can apply their medical and paramedical abilities to help resolve emotional problems that accompany many physical disturbances. In the recent literature, health counseling approaches and relevant insights about the interrelationship between physical and psychological states of well-being have been employed in such health-related areas as working with alcoholics and drug addicts (Brodie & Manning, 1976); treating psychiatric out-patients (Freedman, Kaplan & Sadock, 1975); sexual counseling (Hoch, 1974); bereavement counseling (Crowder, Yamamoto & Simonowitz,

1976); counseling the parents of victims of Sudden Infant Death Syndrome (Nakushian, 1976; Wilkenfeld, 1977); counseling individuals with severe physical problems following surgery (Bird, 1976); counseling renal dialysis patients (Fisher, 1976); and, widely, in rehabilitation counseling (Jaques, 1970). Together, these efforts contribute substantially to the field of health counseling as we define it today.

With this in mind, let us look at some of the ways in which the health counselor might work.

Preventive Counseling: The Holistic Perspective

"An ounce of prevention is worth a pound of cure," is the first rule of healthy functioning. This effort toward prevention may involve reevaluating our diet, honestly assessing our use of drugs, alcohol, and tobacco, or coming to grips with the pluses and minuses of our life-style and behavior in general. Health education, whether offered by a physician, social worker, counselor, teacher, or friend, may be particularly useful in trying to prevent small health problems from becoming major health crises (Thornburg, 1981). Preventive health education, like preventive medicine, works on the principle that we can detect in most individuals the areas in which they are most likely to experience difficulties, and by teaching them appropriate behaviors we can lessen the chance of problems later on.

> Mr. Forcinito began seeing a counselor following a brief hospital stay in which he was treated for an ulcer condition. Surgery was not necessary, but the doctors warned him that if he continued his high stress-poor diet regimen, he would probably require surgery within the year. Dr. Wong, his counselor, consulted with the physician and was told the appropriate diet that Mr. Forcinito should follow. Dr. Wong discussed this with Mr. Forcinito, and considered some of the problems involved in following the diet. "I have to have a drink now and then for business reasons," Mr. Forcinito protested, until it was pointed out that he could sip a Seven Up and conduct his business just as well. "It's hard for me to arrange a leisurely meal," Mr. Forcinito argued, until it was shown that those few minutes he set aside each day would amount to only 15% of the time he would waste if he were confined to a hospital for three days per year! In short, the counselor helped resolve Mr. Forcinito's many resistances to conducting his life in such a way that his health would be improved. These preventive counseling efforts may work to keep Mr. Forcinito out of the hospital.

One approach to preventive counseling brings together a unified matrix of interactive counseling and educational efforts, along with a strong underlying philosophy, that goes far beyond merely helping people avoid illness. This is known as the holistic approach, and it is currently the preeminent perspective in this field.

From the holistic point of view, good health is more than a matter of being free from illness. When we are children we often make the dichotomy between healthy and ill. "If I am not sick then I must be healthy," runs this type of reasoning. But good health actually involves a lot more than just not being sick. Health is a positive state, it is the quality of something, not the absence of something. And that something is a quality Gross (1980) calls "positive wellness." Viewing health in such a way, we come to recognize the full scope of the health counselor's task. As Gross (1980) points out, holistic health focuses on "positive wellness, environmental concerns and self-responsibility and strives toward a full view of health including not only standard medical treatment, but also meditation, nourishment, exercise, vitality and spirituality."

The holistic health counselor attempts to anticipate the problems most likely to affect his or her constituency and to provide education and information that can prevent these problems. Information about fertility and contraception, about basic hygiene, about diet and nutrition, about smoking, alcohol, and drugs—these are but a sampling of some of the areas in which the preventive health counselor works. It is most advantageous to provide information and assistance designed to promote a better, richer, healthier life situation, and not to wait until illness strikes or is imminent before offering health counseling. Pion and Delliquadri (1979) correctly point out that "traditional health education . . . and counseling services are overly passive and disease-oriented. A revised approach is called for that will emphasize the more positive elements of physical, mental and spiritual well-being. . . ."

There are two general types of preventive counseling approaches: *individual* and *public*. The individual approach involves working with a single client, often dealing with problems that are only tangentially related to health. The public approach means working with a group of people, not necessarily the "general public." There are differences in substance and in style between the two. In the individual setting, for example, the counselor attempts to find the areas in which the client needs information. This varies from individual to individual; but always presupposes that the person is willing to learn, but doesn't have the knowledge:

> Susan, aged thirteen, was having sexual relations but not using contraception. She was under the belief that if she confined her sexual relations to the week after her period, she could not become pregnant. Her counselor explained the vicissitudes of fertility and ovulation, and informed Susan about the different kinds of contraception available. The counselor then referred Susan to Planned Parenthood.

In some individual cases, it is not a lack of knowledge, but rather unconscious resistances that prevent the person from acting in a healthy way. John knows that smoking is injurious to his health, but feels that he cannot quit the habit. The counselor discusses these feelings to find out why he feels inadequate in this area.

Large-scale efforts in public health prevention counseling cannot identify specific individual areas of misinformation or lack of information, nor can they deal with individual resistances. Instead, public health counseling attempts to identify the needs of the audience to whom these efforts are directed. For instance, *consumerism* is becoming an increasing area of importance in public health counseling. This involves treating the medical patient as a consumer of services. The health counselor may try to show the public, through advertising, through brochures, through publications in local newspapers, and so on, the health resources that are available. The goals of this type of counseling, according to Carroll, Miller, and Nash (1976) are:

1. Identifying and evaluating sources of medical assistance
2. Developing and implementing a personal program for procuring health information and services
3. Replacing fears and superstitions with scientific facts and objectivity in health-related matters, and
4. Avoiding fraudulent health practices and worthless devices (p. 401)

We can see from these objectives how public health counseling, when it focuses on prevention, makes the client an alert consumer, more competent in dealing with the available resources.

Medical and Surgical Counseling

This form of health counseling is usually done in the hospital setting, or in conjunction with a physician. It involves dealing with the myriad problems that face an individual suffering from some kind of physical illness. The types of illnesses are vast, ranging from relatively minor and temporary conditions (appendectomy) to catastrophic and chronic cases (terminal cancer, a major stroke). What is most important is that the health counselor work along with the rehabilitation counselor, the former concentrating on keeping the individual healthy after surgery or medical treatment, and the latter concentrating on helping the individual adjust back to "normal" functioning.

Chronic kidney disease, which is treated by hemodialysis (a purification of the blood by dialysis), places a massive psychological strain on the patient and on the patient's family. The dialysis machine becomes the patient's "lifeline," and the patient develops complex feelings toward his or her need to be maintained by this technological marvel. Strict regimens contribute to the patient's tendency to develop concomitant psychological problems. Numerous studies have examined the emotional implications of renal dialysis (DeNour & Czakes, 1971), and they generally acknowledge the need for close counseling. Fisher (1976) offers an innovative rational-emotive therapy approach, geared for the specific needs of the renal dialysis client. He breaks down the approach into the following processes:

1. The activating event (disability) occurs. The patient learns of kidney failure or of other physical or imposed restrictions. The renal dialysis treatment, the family's reactions, or other events that happen are perceived.

2. The patients formulate beliefs, thoughts, or attitudes about the disability in general or about kidney failure specifically; they may be influenced by opinion, folklore, superstition, or family medical cures received from the cultural group.
3. Subsequent emotional reactions to these beliefs about the disability might involve guilt, anger, depression, or anxiety.

The RET-oriented health counselor attempts to help the patient discover how his or her false beliefs and misperceptions may be contributing to intransigent depressions, debilitating anxiety conditions, and overpowering feelings of frustration. The counselor does this in two ways: "First, the counselor can serve as a counter propangandist, who directly contradicts and denies the patient's self-defeating, restrictive beliefs and folk myths about the disability. . . . Second, the . . . counselor can employ a wide range of persuasive techniques to persuade clients who have been medically cleared but are fearful of returning to work to engage in gradually increasing levels of physical activity" (pp. 560–561).

These same principles of rational-emotive counseling can be used in counseling many other medical and surgical patients. The important points to keep in mind are that the counselor should be able to help the patient appreciate the "reality" of the situation and should be able to persuade the patient to act in an appropriate way.

Nutritional counseling is a good example of a new health-related field that is beginning to gain recognition and importance in the counseling profession. Like many other areas of health counseling, the subject itself—human nutrition—has long been an issue of public concern and intense laboratory research. But only in the past decade have counselors themselves come to play a significant role in promoting educational and interventional strategies to promote better nutritional intake—efforts we refer to as nutritional counseling.

Why should counselors concern themselves with nutrition? Isn't this more the province of dietitians, health educators, and medical personnel? Responding to this question, Pearson and Long (1982) point out that because "current literature suggests that nutritional deficits, food allergies, hypoglycemia, and salt may adversely alter emotional adjustment . . . counselors should be trained in nutritional counseling." They go on to argue,

If nutrition is a determining factor in mental illness, it is possible that counseling and psychotherapy could be aided by dietary interventions. If dietary deficiences lead to impaired metabolism that influences thought and mood, then counselors may want to learn to recognize and understand the symptoms of inadequate diet or malnutrition in their clients. Equipped with such knowledge, counselors could develop new treatment models that help clients improve the quality of their lives. . . . (p. 389)

Nutritional Counseling

In addition to this, because good nutrition is an integral part of healthy living we can view nutritional counseling as a central part of the health counselor's total efforts at helping clients attain positive wellness.

One factor that has been the subject of much research is the effect that early nutrition (prenatal and early childhood) has on subsequent development, particularly on the development of intelligence. Evidence is abundant at this point that severe nutritional deprivations during the early years of life do retard, either temporarily or permanently, the development of intelligence and the concomitant development of related skills (such as language and perception, social abilities, etc.). Tizard (1974) for instance, has reviewed much of the vast literature, concluding that "both chronic subnutrition and severe clinical malnutrition in childhood are statistically associated with subsequent growth retardation" (p. 173). He points out how nutritional deprivations affect physical development, brain structure, psychological development, and intelligence in general.

Jani and Jani (1975, p. 155) maintain that nutritional deprivation may be one of the major contributing causes of learning disabilities in the United States, and they point out the main causes of inappropriate nutritional intake resulting in damage:

1. lack of knowledge of good food patterns, e.g. skipping breakfast, or other meals;
2. lack of concern about quality of food intake, e.g., the overuse of high calorie, low nutrient density foods;
3. inappropriate food habits;
4. intake of interfering substances, e.g., avidin of raw egg whites;
5. lack of food due to poverty or unavailability of foodstuffs.

They point out that all of these problems can be corrected to some extent by educational efforts, and therefore that teachers and counselors can play important roles in correcting or preventing a health condition which potentially could lead to severe learning problems and physical disabilities later on.

Counseling Implications   Several suggestions have been made about how the teachers and school counselors can be helpful. Chethik (1976) points out that the counselors and teachers can offer information about nutrition and can evaluate the individual learner's nutritional intake to determine if the basis for a nutritional problem is present. If so, it could then be presented to school health personnel who may make specific recommendations. Smith (1975) too urges school personnel to become involved in the child's nutritional problems. She points out that "parents, as well as children, in all socioeconomic classes are in need of instruction about the development of greater concern for food needs," and advocates the teacher's participation in this effort. Raman (1975), considering the educational implications, sees early

nutrition as an essential element in the individual's fulfillment of his or her potentialities. In all, it is generally agreed today that nutrition is a relevant part of
health counseling and that teachers and counselors can prove effective in providing information to ameliorate nutritional problems (Miller, 1980).

Anxiety and stress are inevitable parts of our lives, but their effects on us **Health and Stress**
vary according to how well or how poorly we are able to deal with them. Anxiety **Control**
is a mental state of nervousness, disquietude, worry, and fear. Stress is its physical
counterpart, marked by specific bodily changes (increased blood pressure, secre-
tion of acidity in the digestive tract, etc.). It is not entirely clear which one causes
the other, since psychologists disagree as to whether the physiological or psychological component comes first, and what role thinking plays in mediating between them. The questions that are most relevant to us as counselors are: What
brings on unnecessary stress? How much stress can a person handle at a given
period of life? How capable is the person of discharging the stress? and, What
effect is the stress having on the body and mind of our client? In this section, we
will examine some of the research, paying special attention to how anxiety and
stress affect different areas of our health functioning. We will also consider some
counseling implications.

Although we all know how it feels to be under stress, psychologists have spent What Is Stress?
a lot of time (and words) trying to define stress in a way which is conducive to
study and research. Although there is no single definition, each of the perspectives presents its own view of stress, and thus helps us understand how it affects
us and how we can lessen its impact. Warheit (1979) points out that stress has
been defined in a number of different ways by various researchers, often reflecting their presuppositions and biases. A behavioral psychologist will look at
stress as a learned reaction to a stimulus, while the psychoanalytic viewpoints
see stress in terms of early life conflicts (or present conflicts that revive feelings
from early in life). A social psychologist may emphasize social and cultural factors that precipitate stress. A partisan of the cognitive perspective might say,
"Stress is the result of the way you think about certain things, and if you change
your thinking you won't feel stress."
Recognizing these discrepant viewpoints, Warheit offers a synthetic definition, one that combines elements of all these, and defines stress as "the altered
state of an organism produced by agents in the psychological, social, cultural,
and/or physical environments." He goes on to point out that this altered state
produces negative and very unpleasant effects "on the physical and/or mental
well-being of affected individuals" (Warheit, 1979, p. 502). Moreover, this altered state has noticeable physiological indices, which together constitute what
is often called the stress reaction. This *stress reaction* is an individual's characteristic psychological and physiological way of responding to stress. Some people
may begin sweating profusely, some may cry at the first signs of stress, while

others will become totally prepared for action immediately upon confronting a stressful situation. Some people will eat more under stress, while others will eat less, or stop eating altogether. Likewise, some of us will not be able to sleep in the throes of a stress reaction, while others will not be able to get out of bed.

But stress should not be viewed simply as a problem. It also serves a purpose. Because it is universal and often precedes important, life-saving behaviors, stress plays an important part in our survival (Wilson, 1978). It prepares us to deal with a situation from which we might otherwise retreat and shapes us into a physical condition to do so. Still, in large amounts or over long periods of time, its detrimental effects far outweigh its occasional benefits.

Effects of Stress

Two important questions are: Why do some people experience stress with more difficulty than do others? and Why does the same person react differently to stress at different times? The effects of stress, research has shown, are dependent on several factors. The main factors cited are:

1. the intensity of the stress;
2. the individual's innate and acquired ability to cope with stress;
3. the duration of the stress;
4. the perceived possibility of alleviating the stress.

Each of these factors has been studied in the laboratory and in real life.

Common sense tells us that stress may be strong or weak. In general, the stronger the level of stress the more difficulty an individual experiences in coping with it. But what this does not tell us is why some things are more stressful than others. Certainly, if one sees a wild dog, foaming at the mouth, coming towards him or her, the individual will experience much stress. This is not only normal, but a part of our physiological adaption, since it allows us to escape from truly dangerous situations. But some situations cause stress when they are not really dangerous. One person will experience very high levels of stress before taking an exam while another person will take it in stride. Some people will become tongue-tied and terrified when about to ask a person out for a date, while others can be casual and stress-free about it. The intensity of stress, then, is not some objective factor which we can measure in relation to the event itself. Rather, it is the perceived stress of the individual, based on many different variables, ranging from present perceptions to past experiences.

A second factor, the individual's innate and acquired ability to cope with stress, is also more complex than it appears on the surface. Many psychologists now believe that there is a biological, genetic, innate characteristic of the human organism's ability to deal with stressful situations. Even studies of infants have shown differences in temperament with respect to handling stress. But it is also generally agreed that we learn through the early family situation how to deal with stress. We learn from modeling, from conditioning, from how our parents make us feel emotionally, and from the ways they teach us to think. Some children will be taught to experience stress and dread if their report card is not straight

A. Others will be taught to feel stress and guilt if they think the wrong thing or feel the wrong thing, that certain types of thinking are bad. On the other hand, parents who teach children that they *can* overcome most difficult situations will be instilling in them a confidence necessary for dealing with stressful situations as an adult.

Third, the duration of stress manifestly affects our ability to deal with it. A short period of stress, both for animals and humans, is considerably easier to resolve (or live through) than is a long period. The problem here is that sometimes one brief stressful situation will lead to other stressful situations, and that one piled on the other results in a lengthy period of stress. This principle can be used constructively in reverse, if we take each stressful situation by itself, isolated from the other stresses in our life, and try to solve just one rather than readjusting our entire life, which is much more difficult.

The fourth factor, the perceived possibility of alleviating the stress, is directly related to the other three, along with an added cultural dimension. If one has had experiences in the past where stress has been successfully reduced, then one is more likely to have an optimistic outlook about resolving present stress. There are also cultural factors which play a part. People in positions of power and financial security have more resources to alleviate certain types of stress than poor, powerless individuals. If we have continually suffered from childhood the ravages of poverty and humiliations of failure, we are less likely to see a way out and more likely to succumb, physically and emotionally, to the stress. Race has been shown a factor too. In a study of stress and suicide (IMNS, 1980), it was found that, "one-half of the black women reported moderate to severe levels of stress, and in almost one-third, their distress was comparable to that reported by three-quarters of all mental health patients. In general, blacks have a higher level of stress and a considerably higher level of blood pressure, indicating the physical reaction to this stress.

Many of the illnesses we suffer are to some extent products of a mind-body interaction, the products of protracted periods of stress and anxiety which affect our physical well-being. This includes psychological disturbances instigated by physical problems as well as physical problems instigated by psychological stresses. Sheehan, Sheehan, and Minichiello (1981), for example, point out how excessive levels of physical stress can even precipitate phobia, a condition we are used to thinking of as psychological.

When a physical disorder is brought on largely by emotional or psychological factors, it is called a psychosomatic disorder. The term psychosomatic comes from the Greek words *psyche* ("mind") and *soma* ("body"), indicating the interrelationship between mind and body in the production of such illnesses. One of the key questions about psychosomatic disease is "What are the relative contributions of the psyche—the mind—and the soma—the body—in its cause, its perpetuation, and ultimately, its cure?" This has been debated endlessly over the years. While the traditional definition and approach "has focused on psychological factors playing a predominant causal role in a limited number of disorders"

Psychosomatic Disorders

Block (1978), this is changing to include an increasing number of psychosocial and cultural factors that play a precipitating or influential role in many diseases. Wright (1977), for example, has suggested taking into account all aspects of mind-body disease production, such as the psychological consequences of physical diseases and the role of learning as a part of psychosomatization. In summing up the situation, Block (1978) points out,

> . . . when considered as a whole, the [traditional] concept of psychosomatic disorder is outmoded because it sets up a false dichotomy by suggesting that a few physical disorders are predominantly caused by psychological factors, while current evidence indicates that psychosocial factors may be varyingly important in many disorders. Further, the traditional psychosomatic concept has been focused exclusively on causal aspects of physical illness, while psychological factors have been shown to be important across the entire disease process. Replacing traditional thinking with the notion that physical and psychological factors play complimentary roles across all phases of physical disorders would seem much more in keeping with available research findings. (p. 397)

Thus, as we look at some of the specific disorders, we should keep in mind the multifarious factors that influence them, and the potential role health counseling can play in alleviating at least some of the precipitating problems.

Heart Disease

One of the key areas of medical and psychological research over the past two decades has been to determine if there are specific behaviors or personality types associated with the increasing incidence of heart disease. Some studies have linked personality traits to the probability of succumbing to heart attacks. Friedman and his associates (1970, 1971) have classified two types of behavior patterns: Type A, prone to heart attacks, and Type B, less prone to heart attacks. The Type A behavior pattern is characterized by an "excessive sense of time urgency, drive and competitiveness," a person characterized by ambitiousness and occupational aggressiveness, who has little patience, is very competitive and wants to get things done now, and quickly. Type B, on the other hand, represents a "converse, more relaxed pattern of behavior." The early studies found that individuals exhibiting Type A behavior are more prone to coronary heart disease than are individuals exhibiting Type B behavior. They also suggested that "Type A subjects frequently possess (long before they may actually suffer a heart attack) many of the same biochemical abnormalities which have been observed in the majority of patients with coronary heart disease" (1971, p. 929).

These earlier findings were confirmed in the final follow-up report of the Western collaborative group study of coronary heart disease (Rosenman, Brand, Jenkins, Friedman, Straus & Wurm, 1975). The study of more than three thousand men ranging in age from thirty-nine to fifty-nine at the start of the eight-and-a-half year project found that men with a Type A behavior pattern had heart attacks more than twice as often as those with a Type B pattern. Of one thousand and sixty-seven Type A men, ninety-five suffered heart attacks, while of one thousand one hundred and eighty two Type B men, fifty had heart attacks, a statistically significant difference. Jenkins (1976) among others, in later research efforts, has also shown a definite relationship between at least parts of the Type A behavior pattern and a higher incidence of coronary disease.

There is also evidence that hypertension (high blood pressure), which is a major contributor to heart disease, may have a key psychosomatic component. Even in people not suffering from hypertension, blood pressure is related to suppressed anger and failure to cope with certain feelings, and there is abundant evidence that the greater this anger the more the blood pressure increases (Gentry, Chesney, Gary, Hall & Harburg, 1982). Consensus at this point is that diet and psychological factors interact, within the context of hereditary predispositions, to cause chronic hypertension.

Is asthma psychosomatic? This question generates much heated controversy. Ask the parents of an asthmatic child and they will probably look at you with scorn as if you are *blaming them* for this terribly frustrating affliction their child is suffering from. Yet, although there may well be a constitutional or a genetic predisposition toward asthma, and toward respiratory problems in general, there is considerable evidence of a psychological component, at least insofar as it affects the intensity and frequency of the asthmatic attacks. Under stress, for example, asthmatics are much more likely to suffer an attack than under relaxed conditions. For this reason we can think of asthma as at least partially psychosomatic.

But just what this psychological component is, and if and how it affects adjustment, are still not understood. In one of the more comprehensive papers on the subject, Benjamin (1977) reviewed a great deal of evidence. He points out first of all that there is not strong evidence to associate any particular kind of personality with asthma prevalence, and "that in any case the commonly reported traits may simply reflect the effects of prolonged incapacitating illness" (Benjamin, 1977, p. 468). In other words, the symptoms themselves may be causing the personality problems. Then, using a sample population to which he had access, he found few differences in the incidence of mental illness between asthmatics and non-asthmatics, and found that there was only a slightly greater level of social impairment by asthmatics, causing him to question how reliable were the data which places asthma in the category of a neurotic impairment.

Just about everyone experiences stomach aches and abdominal cramps at times. Just as common is diarrhea and constipation. These gastro-intestinal disturbances, GI problems, as they are called, are part of the normal range of health

Asthma

GI Disturbances

problems. Some people have continuing persistent problems in this area, however, leading to ulcers, inflammation of the colon, hiatus hernias, and chronic stomach acidity. If these degenerative conditions are not treated medically, they may ultimately require surgery and other extreme measures.

Various kinds of gastrointestinal disturbances have been shown to be correlated with stress, neurosis, emotional immaturity, and an inability to discharge aggression appropriately. Some research has indicated that fear, hostility, and inner-directed rage may be a major cause of ulcers (Lewis & Lewis, 1972). Even the common expressions such as "swallow my rage or pride," and "my stomach is tied in knots," reflect the relationship between anger, frustration, and gastrointestinal disturbances. Moreover, we know that most of these GI problems are aggravated by tension and stress.

Still, it would be a mistake to believe that all GI problems are directly the result of immediate life stresses. Such a belief often leads not only to an incorrect analysis of the problem, but a failure to take the proper treatment measures as well. As Owen (1981) points out, although stress is a major factor in causing ulcers, it is not alone to blame. There are also genetic characteristics, a combination of personality traits, and environmental characteristics which are beyond the individual's control. Often, people suffering from ulcers, colonic disturbances, or other GI problems tend to overblame themselves, saying things like, "I know that because I'm so nervous that is why I am suffering like this." Such a rationalization may be missing the point entirely and may even contribute to the pattern of self-blame that prevents the individual from doing whatever is necessary to correct the problem.

Cancer   Can cancer be psychosomatic in origin? The very question conjures up images of faith healers and charlatans, claiming they can cure cancer by willpower. Although no one knows exactly what causes cancer, many researchers argue it is most likely the end result of prolonged exposure to cancer-causing substances, and has little, if anything to do with human psychology. And in fact, there is substantial evidence that environmental factors (smoking, air pollution, ingestion of chemicals and prolonged breathing of substances such as coal dust and asbestos) are directly related to cancer. Yet there is a persistent school of thought, backed by some persuasive research, that at least some forms of cancer may have a psychosomatic component.

Several researchers have asserted that certain family behavior patterns help produce physical ailments, including cancer. Bahnson (1975), for instance, claims that while heart attacks tend to occur in "outer-directed" families, who stress the need for outsiders' approval, cancer tends to appear in families that are "inner-directed." These families often channel their emotional responses to stress internally through the nervous system. According to Bahnson, this upsets the body's hormonal balance and perhaps immunological processes, both of which play a significant role in combatting cancer. In agreement with this basic thesis is that of Kerr (1975), who believes that emotional problems played a part in producing cancer in 25 of 30 cases he treated, and that the complex emotional system of the family is a central factor. In the view of these medically-trained researchers (Bahnson and Kerr), the physical illness is both a symptom of high stress and an attempt to cope with it.

Despite the studies that have appeared in the research over the past decade, it is still unclear which, if any, personality factors, family situations, or strains of living contribute to either the so-called "cancer personality," to an increased risk of developing cancer, or even directly to the onset of the disease. An alternative explanation of much of the supportive research is that the cancer symptoms, and the individual's knowledge that he or she has cancer, may lead to the cancer personality and not the reverse.

Counseling Implications

There are three main implications we can deduce from our discussion of the effects of stress on health and its general relation to psychosomatic disorders. First, in all types of counseling, the counselor's recognition that a variety of life stresses experienced by the client, especially severe stress, may be contributory to what appear on the surface to be purely physical illnesses is essential. Such a recognition can be critical, in a preventive sense, in anticipating problematic physical conditions as well as in being conducive to better understanding the causative relationship after the fact.

Second, those in the helping professions should work toward promoting the acquisition and use of facilitative counseling skills in all the health care settings. Bartnick and O'Brien (1980) point out quite accurately that if persons working in health care settings learn such basic counseling skills as empathic listening, they will be better able to carry out their health care functions. And finally, as we come to recognize the myriad health implications of psychosomatization, we are better able to see how many individuals act out their self-destructive fantasies, little by little eating their bodies away, without the drama of overt action that would make it more obvious to the world.

Fertility Counseling

Fertility counseling includes two basic types of situations: first, when a couple wishes to have children but have not been successful in their efforts to conceive; and second, when information about contraception is needed. We can define fertility counseling as assisting individuals or couples in their efforts to *control* procreation, either by increasing or decreasing the likelihood of conception. Generally, the nonmedical counselor's role in this effort falls into three areas:

1. Providing information
2. Offering follow-up services and emotional support
3. Acting as a consultant with medical, nursing, and paramedical personnel

In order for the health counselor to provide useful and accurate information, it is of course necessary that he or she have a full, accurate, "de-mystified" understanding of human reproduction. In addition to reading about the subject, the counselor might attend classes regularly given by hospitals and nursing schools to their staff, and may avail himself or herself of the services of Planned Parenthood, which provides literature and individual information. Some of the areas with which the counselor should be conversant are the biology of human reproduction; medical complications that interfere with conception; the types of diagnostic tests used to determine if there are fertility problems; the kinds of treatment available; and reputable practitioners in the area.

> The Carpenters, Frank and Marianne, came for counseling because of difficulties they were having in her becoming pregnant. They had been fighting, and their clergyman-confidant felt that many of their difficulties were the result of the infertility. They had seen their family physician, the GP of their small town, but had only been told to "keep on trying." The counselor, Mrs. Ramakrishna, who had been trained in health counseling in India, explained to the Carpenters some of the possible problems involved in infertility, and she suggested they see a fertility specialist in a nearby metropolitan area. She gave them the name and some information about how many visits would be required and what to expect. After a visit with this physician, they were encouraged to have several tests: Mr. Carpenter was referred for a sperm count and Mrs. Carpenter for a Rubens test. They were somewhat apprehensive, but Mrs. Ramakrishna, familiar with the tests, explained just how they worked and reassured them that it would not be painful. At the same time, she consulted with their family counselor, and pointed out how there is often an antagonism between couples when they can't conceive; a tendency to blame each other. She suggested that the couple, in conjunction with the clergyman, explore their unconscious feelings and fears about having children.
>
> When the Carpenters' tests were completed, it was discovered that Frank had a low sperm count. Further testing revealed that a simple operation could alleviate this problem. He was at first terrified, and Mrs. Ramikrishna determined there may be some psychological resistances to having a child in addition to any physical problems. These were worked out and he went for the operation. Within a year, Marianne became pregnant and had a successful delivery.

In this case, we see that the health counselor provided information about possible problems and modes of treatment, offered a direct referral, and gave supportive therapy. These combined efforts resulted in the effective treatment of the problem.

Fertility counseling may also involve providing information about contraception. For couples who do not wish to have children, there is often a need for someone other than the family physician to provide this information. The client may be reluctant to discuss contraception with the physician. The counselor should have a full understanding of the contraceptive methods presently available, their effectiveness and drawbacks. The counselor should also be able to refer the client to the appropriate agency or physician, in order for the client to have a medical examination and, where necessary, be given a prescriptive contraceptive.

Perhaps even more essential than providing information are the follow-up services and emotional support given the client. Many problems in fertility and contraception have dynamic emotional components and to merely deal with the information without venturing into the emotional realm is fruitless. The infertile client may experience marital stress or feelings of inadequacy or failure. The person in need of contraceptive information may be experiencing a variety of sexual fears because of his or her lack of knowledge. Some individuals mistakenly fear that the use of contraceptives will limit their sexual enjoyment. The fears and the conflicts must be dealt with along with the objective role of providing information.

Finally, the health counselor acts as a liaison person with medical personnel. What this means in practice is that the counselor *represents the best emotional interests of the client* to the medical practitioners with whom the client must deal. This involves not only initial referral but ongoing consultation as well. Physicians especially, with their demanding schedules and scientific outlooks, must be trained to work along with counselors in touching the dynamic emotional lives of their patients.

Another important area we call *planned pregnancy* counseling (to differentiate it from *problem-pregnancy* counseling discussed later), covers the periods from conception through the birth of the baby. This type of health counseling involves giving the mother and the father the emotional support necessary for successful and pleasurable childbearing. Planned pregnancy counseling includes such activities as:

Planned Pregnancy Counseling

1. Explaining to the prospective parents about what to expect during pregnancy, including both physical and psychological changes.
2. Informing the prospective parents about the options of different types of delivery: anesthetized, prepared, Lamaze, Leboyer, and so forth.
3. Educational and psychological preparation for parenthood. This includes learning how to physically treat the newborn infant (feeding, bathing, etc.), and decisions that have to be made before birth (Should I breast-feed? Should I have "rooming-in" at the hospital? etc.).
4. Genetic counseling, where necessary.

This last point is particularly important in some instances. Recent developments in medicine have made it possible to determine in advance genetic anomalies of the developing fetus. Some familiarity with the procedures, and some knowledge of their risks and limitations, will enable the counselor to advise the client, where necessary, when genetic investigation is indicated. Again, it is useful for the counselor to keep in mind that physicians are not always willing or able to spend as much time as necessary informing the patients of all the risks and options. The counselor, acting as an "advocate" of the patient's best interests, can serve this role if he or she is knowledgeable about medical procedures and sensitive to clients' subtle emotional communications.

Problem Pregnancy Counseling   The unplanned and unwanted pregnancy may precipitate a crisis situation that should be dealt with by the crisis intervention procedures outlined in chapter 15. We have decided to discuss problem pregnancy counseling in more detail here, however, because it complements the subjects we have just covered, and because we would rather approach it more broadly as a health counseling procedure than as strictly a crisis intervention procedure.

The task of the health counselor in problem pregnancy counseling is threefold:

1. To help the client understand the options available, and to help her arrive at a decision that she can live with
2. To offer the client appropriate referral, where necessary, and to assist the client in making necessary and often painful plans
3. To provide follow-up services and emotional support

Frequently, the woman who finds herself with an unplanned, unwanted pregnancy is not in a position to make a realistic decision about what to do. She is often overcome by powerful emotions, or in a state of crisis in which her decision-making abilities are seriously impaired. And, since time is essential in decisions about whether or not to have an abortion, it is imperative that the counselor help in this decision. Smith (1972) points out:

> Women confronted with this crisis may decide to terminate the pregnancy without considering other alternatives or discussing their feelings about the situation. In panic they may obtain illegal abortions. . . . Tragically, some later regret their decision and suffer guilt and self-recrimination. During the crisis, these women lose their emotional equilibrium because their habitual problem-solving devices are inadequate for the situation. (p. 67)

In addition to helping the crisis-client make an appropriate decision, the health counselor will want to see that the client, if she elects for an abortion, is referred to the best facilities. This requires, of course, that the counselor be familiar with the resources available in the community. Feminist groups have been useful in assembling information about the availability and evaluation of community facilities. Moreover, many of these groups have had extensive experience in abortion counseling, and can understand the trauma the woman experiences as she gropes for her "right" decision.

Recent developments in abortion counseling have been thoroughly covered by Kalmar (1977b), who discusses the emotional implications of abortion from the legal, economic, social, political, and religious contexts in which the critical decisions are inevitably made. She points out that the abortion decision can never be viewed *in vacuo*, but must always be approached within the social context. Despite the wide range of research on the emotional effects of abortion, she points out, "there is a wide discrepancy, from those findings which indicate that abortion yields little or no negative consequences to those which reveal it to be a traumatic and damaging experience" (p. 1). In situations where the client experiences a crisis—where the client's rational decision-making abilities are overcome by the attendant anxiety—the emergency procedures for handling anxiety crises outlined in chapter 15 would be particularly germane.

Abortion counseling, especially in its post-decision phase, also involves providing information about contraception (Gedan, 1974). There is clearly a tendency among women who have an unwanted pregnancy and an abortion to repeat this, and without appropriate information about contraception, the likelihood increases. Often the unwanted pregnancy-abortion syndrome involves the woman's underlying feelings of emptiness that she is unconsciously trying to compensate for with the child; but because she is ambivalent about men, she cannot bear to carry the child into the world.

One other point should be mentioned. Barglow and Weinstein (1973) have taken note of the psychiatric aspects of the abortion decision in adolescent girls. They found that two major factors distinguished the adolescent's decision making from the adult's, and these should be kept in mind when working with the adolescent client:

1. The abortion decision is more "outer-other" directed by parents, peer group, or sexual partner, and is therefore more difficult or hazardous (for the girl).
2. Developmental immaturity contributes to ambivalence about the decision, to a distorted perception of the procedure, and to a variety of pathological reactions.

These observations emphasize the need for follow-up counseling, which will focus not only on contraception, but also on resolving the emotional difficulties precipitated by the abortion.

Alcohol Abuse Counseling

One of the major health problems, if not the major problem, which affects millions in our society is alcoholism and drug abuse. Alcohol abuse, in fact, is the largest single factor cited in the high cost of health care and the leading cause of mental institutionalization in the United States today.

There are an estimated 10 to 12 million alcoholics or serious problem drinkers in the United States today, "approximately one-third [of whom] are women" (Eddy & Ford, 1979). They include all the social classes, all ethnic groups, most religions, and all regions of the country. A large number of these alcoholics are parents, heads of families, financial providers, and primary caretakers of their children. If either parent is an alcoholic, a problem drinker, or is prone to any form of drug dependence or abuse, there is an indication that the family-as-unit is in some kind of serious trouble. If both parents are alcoholics, the family is in even greater difficulty. In this section we will consider briefly some of the effects of alcoholism on the individual and the family. By necessity we must cover a very complex and difficult subject in a brief space. But we do so with the suggestion that the counselor take at least one course in alcohol counseling, since this is such a great problem in our contemporary society.

Defining Terms Let us first define our terms. An *alcoholic* is a person with a physical and psychological dependency on alcohol. Alcoholism is an addictive disorder. The alcoholic is, for all intents and purposes, unable to function normally, and tends to focus vital energy and to fix goals on consuming enough alcohol to feel physically relieved (from the terrible withdrawal symptoms, called DTs, caused by not having sufficient alcohol in the system) and psychologically numb. Although many alcoholics may be able to function reasonably well at least part of the time, emotionally the alcoholic is much like an infant, who, when not fed, cries and cries without the ability to do much about the hunger. Then, like the infant, when the true alcoholic is fed (intoxicated), he or she goes to sleep or "blacks out," only to awaken when the body craves more alcohol. Socially, the alcoholic has withdrawn from most situations, and is unable to interact with others under expected role conditions.

The problem drinker, a more common phenomenon, is one step from alcoholism. This person typically exhibits normal role behaviors most of the time, but needs alcohol as a regular part of his or her routine. While these individuals are not as yet suffering from alcoholism per se, they may experience many of the alcohol effects. Eddy (1979) points out that this type of drinker is one who drinks to escape from an inner anxiety, from which the individual can find no other effective form of escape.

Usually, those people closest to the problem drinker, with the most opportunity to directly observe his or her private behaviors, will be more aware of the problem than those with whom the problem drinker has less consistent contact. This is why many people who may socialize with a problem drinker are not aware of it, because in the social setting drinking is an expected behavior. But in these situations ironically the need to drink becomes especially pronounced. The popular saying, "If you need a drink to be social then you're not a social drinker," best explains the problem drinker's needs in terms of his or her anxiety in interacting with others.

While both the problem drinker and the full-fledged alcoholic exhibit serious signs of maladjustment, the alcoholic is by far the worse. Though the problem drinker may experience a serious loss of functioning, much of the time he or she is able, with varying degrees of productivity, to maintain a normal lifestyle. Unfortunately, problem drinking is usually a step on the road to alcoholism.

The Path to Alcoholism Alcoholism does not appear overnight, but develops over a period of many years, usually in a fairly predictable progression. Of course, to become an alcoholic one first has to be a consumer of alcoholic beverages. But the large majority of drinkers never become alcoholics or problem drinkers. The indications that one is becoming an alcoholic stand out from casual social drinking, and others can see these signs if they are open to them.

Many psychiatrists and mental health researchers have attempted to define clearly the path to alcohol dependency. Jellinek (1971) delineates four stages of alcoholism, which are widely accepted. During the first stage, which is called the *prealcoholic phase,* the person becomes a heavy social drinker and finds that drinking relieves tension and reduces levels of anxiety. This continues to the point where the person can no longer tolerate even the normal tensions of living, and has to use alcohol almost daily.

During the next stage, the *prodromal phase,* the person begins to exhibit many of the behaviors we associate with true alcoholics: sneaking a drink so that others don't "hassle" him or her about drinking too much; thinking about alcohol almost obsessively; always being sure to have a bottle "handy," even going so far as to keep a small flask in the suit pocket or pocketbook; avoiding the company of people who don't drink, and especially those who attempt to tell him or her that he or she has a drinking problem; adamant self-denial about his or her dependency on alcohol. Also during this prodromal phase, there are often amnesiac episodes, in which the person forgets days or hours of his or her life.

The third phase is what Jellinek calls the *crucial phase,* and it is here that the person loses complete control and becomes physically dependent upon alcohol. It is here too that the alcohol itself serves as a triggering mechanism for more alcohol, and the vicious cycle of alcohol dependency becomes painfully evident. It is also at this particular phase that Alcoholics Anonymous's message is most true: ONE DRINK IS TOO MANY AND ALL THE DRINKS IN THE WORLD ARE NOT ENOUGH.

Finally, there is what Jellinek calls the *chronic phase,* in which the individual's life becomes dominated by drinking. It is here that normal interpersonal relations cease, and the quality of life becomes one drunken binge after another. It is also at this point that the family tends to experience the greatest degrees of hopelessness, the greatest stresses.

We observe that these stages of alcoholic deterioration, even if they take years, wear away the layers of healthy functioning and appropriate learned behaviors that took so many years to develop. Gradually, the effects of alcoholic addiction will wreak havoc on family unity and place unbearable strains on a marital relationship. Counseling interventions at different points along the way can mitigate many of the deleterious problems; but the treatment of alcoholism as a specific syndrome is best left to experts, since there are many types of knowledge and skill which are necessary to deal effectively in this area.

Counseling Implications

It is not difficult to imagine the profound effects alcoholism has on the individual, on the family, on a spouse, and on close friends. Within the context of the marital relationship especially, the bottle can replace the marriage partner as the basic source of solace and relief. Who can forget the role played by alcohol in tearing apart a developing relationship in *Lost Weekend* or destroying a marriage in *Days of Wine and Roses?* There, you may recall, the couple both became alcoholics, and when either one would try to reform, the other partner would fight against it. Finally, they sank into despair and hopelessness together. This is what often happens when both partners are alcoholics: each one reinforces the other's behavior, for fear of being isolated if the other goes on the wagon.

Problem drinking is often the superficial symptom of role tension or conflict that troubles a marriage. For example, gender-related role conflicts within the marital relationship may be expressed through drinking. As Kirkpatrick points out, this differs for men and women, showing some consistent patterns:

> Many women's emotional problems and disturbances are all tied up in the male-female relationship. . . . All women in our culture feel a modicum of guilt for not being "perfect," for not fitting into the unrealistic mold that American society has cast for them. For alcoholic women, this guilt is almost unbearable at times. . . . *Women alcoholics have this strong feeling of having failed as a wife, as a mother, as a sister or daughter, or as a woman.* . . .
>
> On the other hand, the male alcoholic feels much remorse for having hurt his family . . . his wife and children. He rarely feels guilt and he never feels the same as women do. There is a vast and distinct difference in this particular area between male and female alcoholics. . . . (Kirkpatrick, 1977, italics added)

There are many problems of adjustment which arise when any one family member is an alcoholic. There may be a social stigma attached to it, whereby all the family members feel "contaminated" by the antisocial behavior of one. Children of alcoholic parents feel ashamed of their parents' behavior. There is also a much higher incidence of family violence in alcoholic families. Financial problems are common, especially when the family breadwinner becomes unable to adequately provide because of the alcohol addiction. Sexual relationships between the spouses invariably suffer, as does the ability to communicate with other family members. In short, one alcoholic family member can short-circuit the entire family network.

It is generally agreed that the successful treatment of alcoholism depends on two factors: the motivation of the alcoholic to change, and the support given that person by friends, colleagues, and family. Because it is usually a lengthy battle with many setbacks, a great deal of external social and interpersonal support is needed in order to provide the degree of encouragement necessary for cure. The prognosis is not always good. Dinsburg, Glick, and Feigenbaum (1977) point out that although traditional counseling and psychotherapy approaches can be helpful in preventing the development of alcoholism to some degree, they are of little proven value once a person is an alcoholic. They recommend that these techniques be used in conjunction with an effective self-help group such as Alcoholics Anonymous.

In recent years there has been a great increase in alcoholic support groups and therapy groups, especially for women alcoholics. While AA (Alcoholics Anonymous) is still widely regarded as the best source of help available, many women believe the program is geared more toward the male alcoholic, and hence female-oriented organizations such as *Women for Sobriety* have been springing up throughout the country, with the special needs of women in mind (Kirkpatrick, 1977).

Summary

We began by defining health as "a state of complete, physical, mental, and social well-being," and then presented a picture of health counseling as a variety of related efforts to assist people to achieve their maximum state of physical and mental health. We next examined an underlying philosophy and several specific areas of health counseling applications.

Preventive health counseling operates on the principle that for most clients we can detect the areas in which they are likely to experience health difficulties, and help them learn to prevent problems in these areas. Medical and surgical counseling prepares patients for surgery and assists them to adjust afterward. Nutritional counseling involves helping individuals learn to assess their nutritional intake and to apply this information in making health-inducing improvements. The school is viewed as an appropriate setting for many of the goals of nutritional counseling to be implemented.

Recognizing that stress is a contributory factor in many physical as well as pyschological disturbances, we examined some of the variables that govern how stress affects us, its intensity, a person's innate or acquired ability to cope with it, its duration, and the perceived possibility of alleviating it. We then looked at psychosomatic components of major illnesses, including heart disease, asthma, GI disturbances, and cancer.

Fertility counseling includes two types of situations: providing counseling and information to couples who want to have children but who have not been successful in their efforts to conceive, and providing guidance and contraceptive information to people who do not wish to have children. It is important that the counselor have technical knowledge about these matters, as well as a helping attitude, and a sense of empathic understanding.

Pregnancy counseling comprises planned and problem-pregnancy situations. The first includes providing information and emotional support to help the prospective parents deal with all the pregnancy. Problem-pregnancy counseling includes all efforts to help the pregnant woman, who views being pregnant as a problem. This may include presenting the options available, and helping her arrive at a decision she can live with. It also comprises providing follow-up services and emotional support.

One of the major health problems in the country today is alcohol and drug abuse. There are an estimated 10–12 million alcoholics or serious problem drinkers in the United States. We examined the progressive stages of alcohol abuse, problem drinking, and alcoholism and considered some of its effects on the marital relationship and on the family. We also discussed some counseling considerations.

Chapter Aim

To delineate crisis intervention counseling as a distinct modality, and to illustrate specific counseling strategies by which the person in crisis can be helped. Several specific categories of crisis situations will be outlined.

15

A crisis is operationally defined by its external manifestations; namely, that it immobilizes the person from effectively dealing with life situations. Some perspectives on the psychological origins of crisis are presented.

What Is a Crisis?

Several models of crisis intervention are presented: the equilibrium model, the cognitive model, and the psychosocial transition model. Eight principles of intervention are enumerated.

Crisis Intervention Theory

Basic suggestions for crisis intervention are outlined. First, be aware that a crisis condition may be contagious and some emotional insulation may be necessary. Second, the counselor should not automatically reassure the client that everything is all right. Third, the counselor should communicate a calming, tranquilizing attitude.

The Counselor and the Crisis

The concept of working through grief, the "grief work" as it is called, is considered as an integral phase of crisis resolution.

Grief Crisis

Like grief crisis, a loveloss crisis requires a person to learn to live in the world without the closeness of one to whom there is deep and pervasive attachment.

Loveloss Crisis

Klein and Lindemann's four stages of planning for crisis intervention are applied to the family crisis situation.

Family Crisis

Anxiety Crisis   The use of object-oriented questions to calm the person in an anxiety crisis is emphasized.

Suicidal Crisis   The counselor has to experience the severe depression of the suicidal client in order to understand and help her or him. Several helpful rules in suicide prevention are outlined.

Rape Crisis   Appropriate interventions may include providing the victim with objective information of what to expect from police and other authorities; seeing that a medical examination takes place; and smoothing the confrontation with other family members, especially the spouse.

Crisis Intervention
Counseling

15

Crisis intervention is to counseling what first aid is to medicine, a temporary but immediate relief for an emergency situation presented by an incapacitated client. Like first-aid procedures, crisis intervention procedures are specific and clear-cut, and the counselor should have more than a superficial acquaintance with them.

In many respects, crisis intervention utilizes basic counseling and psychotherapy strategies, but in other respects, it differs markedly. S. Nass (1977) contrasts crisis counseling therapy to standard psychotherapy practices:

> In contrast to psychotherapy which is almost exclusively focused on the long-term goals associated with personality reorganization, crisis intervention is admirably suited to satisfy both distant and immediate objectives. Depending upon the demands of the presenting situation and the unique qualities of the client, the direction and emphasis of treatment can be tailored to meet these requirements by undergoing continual modification and revision. Crisis intervention therapy is, however, more often addressed to resolving the immediate problem at hand than to rooting out the deep-seated causes of personality dysfunction. (p. iv)

We will note throughout this chapter ways in which crisis intervention is tailored to meet long-range and short-range goals, and we will observe some basic criteria for determining the strategies used.

The first and foremost problem of crisis counseling is the same problem one encounters in first-aid treatment: the sudden and unexpected nature of the situation. *Be prepared!* The Boy Scout's motto is an appropriate slogan for this type of situation. Because the counselor is never entirely ready for a crisis situation, since he or she usually does not expect it to happen, there is an immediate intuitive tendency to want to escape the situation instead of confronting it head on. Obviously, this is not to the client's advantage and should be avoided at all costs. But avoiding this tendency requires the ability to understand how to use crisis intervention techniques and to see their relationship to the basic theory of crisis states and crisis intervention. In this chapter, we shall explore a variety of techniques and insights that the counselor may find helpful in dealing with crisis situations, and we shall examine a segment of a crisis intervention session conducted by a skilled counselor.

What Is a Crisis?

The type of crisis to which we are referring in this chapter is determined by its external symptoms. All of us, at some time in our lives, have witnessed or experienced crisis situations: the loss of a loved one, an anxiety crisis, a general inability to cope with some life situations, a family crisis, an interpersonal crisis with one we love or care about, and so on. When a crisis reaches the stage where it immobilizes the person and prevents one from consciously controlling oneself, then it becomes the kind of crisis for which a person seeks treatment. Brockopp (1973) explores the dynamics of this type of crisis:

> When a person is confronted by a problem situation in which the previously used methods of restructuring his life or environment are either not available to him or not successful in solving his problem, the person is confronted by a critical situation; that is, one in which he is uncertain about the end or resolution of the problem. Since he is unable, through the use of his normal problem-solving techniques, to resolve the difficulty with which he is faced, the critical situation is emotionally hazardous and he may rapidly move toward a state of crisis. . . . *A crisis then is an intolerable situation which must be resolved, for it has the potential to cause the psychosocial deterioration of the person.* (p. 74, italics added)

The critical quality of a crisis, then, is the person's inability to deal with a situation. In this sense, a crisis is a subjective experience. What may be a mildly difficult situation to one person may be a crisis to another. Evaluation of the seriousness of the crisis, as well as diagnostic and prognostic considerations, are not determined by the situation itself but by the individual's response to the situation. Brockopp (1973) is sensitive to this subtle point of differentiation:

> The crisis . . . is not the situation itself, but the person's response to the situation. And the person's response is initially ambivalence and uncertainty, not knowing where he is relative to the problem or what he needs to do or can do to solve the problem and return to a point of equilibrium or homeostasis. (p. 76)

The implication of this statement is that what the person needs is some type of structured orientation suggesting how to go about solving his or her problem. And, indeed, one of the chief difficulties of the crisis situation is the individual's feeling of disorientation—of not being able to "get hold of oneself."

Bloom (1963) has attempted to clarify the contextual definition of what constitutes a crisis by focusing on the client's awareness or lack of awareness, the precipitating event, and the anticipated length of time required for recovery. In true crisis situations, the client is often unable to specify what brought about the crisis, and it may require several months for this fundamental question to be accurately explored.

Caplan (1964), like Brockopp, views the crisis in terms of intrapsychic equilibrium: "The normal consistency of patterns, or equilibrium, is maintained by homeostatic reequilibrating mechanisms, so that temporary deviations from the pattern call into operation opposing forces which automatically bring the pattern back to its previous state" (p. 38). In a crisis situation, the reequilibrating forces are unsuccessful within the usual time range.

Forer (1963) differentiates between three levels of a crisis: a situational crisis brought about by a sudden change in the environment; an intrapsychic conflict crisis between the ego and superego (crisis of values); or a disintegration of the ego. A crisis of grief caused by the loss of a loved one is typical of the first type. A sexual crisis in which one's deepest values are challenged is the second type. An ego-fragmenting drug crisis induced by a hallucinogenic drug is an example of the third type. The three types will be explored more closely later in this chapter.

There may be some positive aspects to crisis as well. Leitner and Stecher (1974), for example, suggest that "crises can lead to self-exploration and this may lead to clearer personal meaning and identity" (p. 29). They go on to suggest that crisis states give the individual a motivation for changing, for growing, for becoming:

> When forces of life push our daily existence to some edge whereupon we find ourselves in the midst of crisis, then we have a chance to emerge as changed beings. Growth implies change and change may imply growth. Emerging from a crisis can be a movement toward a new being-state, one that we may not have been capable of before the crisis. . . . Crises call for risking. People in crisis, under intense pressure, become introspective—they can look at themselves more deeply and honestly than in times of tranquility. (p. 32)

Although the fundamentals of the crisis situation per se are described by these general ideas, there are a number of different types of crises. Lindemann (1944), in an often cited paper, describes the crisis of acute grief. Family crisis situations have been discussed by Klein and Lindemann (1961). Suicide crisis, the most commonly investigated class of crises, has been explored by Lester and Brockopp (1973). Drug crisis, a painfully prevalent problem of our time, has been discussed by Foreman and Zerwekh (1971), among others. Bieber (1972) has presented an interesting analysis of sexual crisis, a topic of increasing significance in crisis counseling. All of these will be considered in the following sections.

Although there is no single theory of crisis intervention, there are a number of underlying principles inherent in all of the different crisis intervention approaches. These principles are usually the result of rich practical experiences, rather than of any theoretical or a priori constructs. Thus, counseling approaches as diverse as psychoanalysis and client-centered counseling use much the same strategies in dealing with crisis situations.

Leitner (1974) discusses three basic crisis models, which would cover a generous variety of specific approaches: the *equilibrium model,* the *cognitive* model, and the *psychosocial transition* model. The equilibrium model views crisis as a state of psychological disequilibrium, in which the usual problem-solving methods fail to work. It is the conceptualization quoted from Caplan (1964) earlier. The cognitive model "defines a crisis as a breakdown of thinking resulting from a physical or psychological overload. This breakdown in thinking is considered to be a dysfunction in handling incompatible information" (p. 19). The psychosocial model "takes the viewpoint of the individual moving through necessary transitions in terms of *psycho-social development.*" This may involve changes in the internal or external life space of the individual.

Within these three models are many specific treatment paradigms for crisis intervention. The theory is to some degree indicative of the *goals* of the treatment; but in most respects the way a crisis situation is handled is totally independent of the underlying crisis theory. Strickler and Bonnefil (1974), writing from the social-work point of view, cite eight similarities between crisis intervention and the traditional psychosocial approach to casework. These illustrate how the diverse theories of crisis merge with traditional psychotherapeutic considerations on the practical level of treatment.

1. Treatment goals are devised to enhance the individual's ability to cope with problems of living in a problem-solving manner.
2. There is a circumscribed focus of treatment around specific and pertinent problem areas involving interpersonal conflicts and role dysfunctioning.
3. Active focusing techniques are utilized to maintain the concentration of the client on the "problem to be solved."
4. Treatment is basically geared to the level of conscious and near-conscious emotional conflicts. These conflicts are dealt with by seeking out their situational references and by maintaining a focus within them.
5. There is recognition of the importance of precipitating events in understanding the dynamics of the problem situation.
6. The goal is not to modify character traits or personality patterns, although such changes do occur at times as a by-product of the treatment.
7. The treatment does not generally or characteristically involve working with the transference to the therapist except in circumstances where such transference manifestations are providing insurmountable

obstacles to the treatment situation. The therapist recognizes transference impulses and moves to replace them with analogous feelings related to the client's current external situation and relationships.

8. The background of information on which treatment is based includes a knowledge of personality development and ego functioning, as well as a special knowledge of cultural-social determinants. (p. 38)

These eight principles are the bridge between crisis theory and intervention practice. They show most clearly how the ideas underlying crisis psychology form the foundation for clinical practice. Let us now focus on the practical dimensions of treatment.

While we generally do not associate the term *contagious* with psychological states, there is considerable evidence that the concept is applicable to particularly turbulent states, such as a state of crisis. No doubt when the counselor first comes into contact with the extremely agitated and perturbed client in a crisis condition, she or he, if not careful, will begin to experience parallel crisis feelings. Just as laughing is infectious (as anyone who has been overcome by a case of the "giddies" knows), so are crisis and grief, in the sense that one can experience another's feelings during difficult times.

The counselor who "catches" the client's turbulent and disorganized feelings will probably be ineffective in helping the client get a grip on herself or himself; and the person in the crisis situation may be unable to function altogether. Direct observations have shown repeatedly that the counselor who "catches" the crisis feelings becomes frightened and defensive. The first manifestation of this is hasty and ill-timed attempts to assure the client that nothing is really the matter, that things will work themselves out. Although such assurance may seem to the counselor to be what the client needs, in fact it is reassurance for the counselor rather than the client.

A good rule for the counselor to remember is this: *do not try to reassure the client that everything is all right;* whenever the counselor does so, unless the client specifically asks for reassurance, the counselor is actually reassuring himself or herself, defending his or her own anxiety, isolating himself or herself from the client's feelings.

What, then, should the counselor do when confronted unexpectedly by a client in a state of crisis? Probably the most significant help the counselor can offer at the outset is to remain calm, poised, and well in control of himself or herself. The client will then be able to begin to relate to the counselor on a constructive level.

The communication of a calming attitude serves two distinct but related purposes. First, it enables the counselor to function effectively, to allow the desperate client full expression of his or her fears and conflicts, to listen to these expressions without severe censorship, to empathize with the client even when the empathic feelings are difficult for the counselor to deal with. If we view crisis as the failure of the psychological balancing (regulating) mechanism, it is easy to understand how the counselor's stability—his or her inflexible certainty, helps the client to re-establish his or her psychic balance.

A second factor also plays a part here. Just as emotionally turbulent feelings are contagious, very calming and relaxed feelings can also be transferred from one person to another. How many times have we come into the presence of a calm, relaxed person and then have begun to feel that calmness and relaxation in ourselves? The counselor's calmness serves as an emotional tranquilizer, subtly helping the client to pull herself or himself together. It communicates to the client, in effect, the emotional message: you see, even though these problems you are discussing are so difficult, we can remain calm while we talk about them. This will help us find a solution; it will enable us to deal with the problems.

To remain calm in the turbulence of the client's stormy emotions, however, is often no easy matter. If the counselor has foreknowledge of the crisis to come (or of the client's visit), he or she can be prepared for the task at hand. But more often than not, the client's visit comes as a complete surprise to the counselor, who may or may not be emotionally ready for it. Even before the client says a word, the counselor unconsciously senses the crisis in the client's expression. Who cannot remember instances in which we have seen a person looking highly distressed, and even before the person says a word, we are ready to ask, "What happened?"

In such a case, when the counselor is not ready for the client and has not had an opportunity to compose himself or herself, the counselor should ask the client to sit down and then excuse herself or himself for a moment. "Have a seat. I'll be with you in a minute," is an excellent therapeutic intervention for both the client who is excited and for the counselor who is expected to help this person. The pause reduces the anxiety and allows the counselor an opportunity to prepare for the highly emotional confrontation that is to ensue.

The next step, and probably the most important, is to encourage the client to enter into a dialogue. In order for the client to receive help at this critical time, it is necessary above all else that he or she be able to communicate feelings and difficulties to the counselor. This will probably require that the client focus on the immediate situation. For, as Kardener (1975) points out, "it is essential in crisis treatment to determine what specifically caused the patient to seek help at the time of the initial presentation." This is always a good place to begin.

While the specifics of the dialogue that follows will depend in large measure on the precipitating trauma, Rapoport (1962) has outlined three patterns of responses that lead to a healthy crisis resolution:

1. Correct cognitive perception of the situation, which is furthered by seeking new knowledge and by keeping the problem in consciousness.
2. Management of affect through awareness of feelings; an appropriate verbalization leading toward tension discharge and mastery.

3. Development of patterns of seeking and using help with actual tasks and feelings by using interpersonal and institutional resources. (p. 216)

Just which of these three will be utilized and in which specific way depends on the client, his or her condition, and the particulars of the crisis-producing situation. Let us consider five types of individual crises that the counselor is likely to encounter and see what we can determine about the course of each one.

Certainly one of the most common of life's tragic situations is the crisis of grief. An individual is unable to manage his or her feelings following the death, either unexpected or after a long illness, of a loved one or someone who is important in his or her life; he or she just cannot cope with this difficult and painful situation. The client may wish to talk about memories of the deceased, possibly about not being as good to the deceased as he thinks he should have been, about how the deceased enjoyed life and deserved to live, or about how unjust the world is, taking away such a good person. The client may recall, with painful clarity, long-past incidents involving interactions with the deceased, and may express feelings about these incidents that have been concealed for some time.

Grief Crisis

While the client is speaking, the counselor listens and tries to experience the client's painful feelings along with him or her. The death may have been recent, or some time ago. "The duration of a grief reaction," Lindemann (1944) points out,

> seems to depend on the success with which a person does the *grief work,* namely, emancipation from the bondage to the deceased, readjustment to the environment in which the deceased is missing, and the formation of new relationships. One of the big obstacles to this work seems to be the fact that many patients try to avoid the intense stress connected with the grief experience and to avoid the expression of emotion necessary for it. (p. 143)

The task of the counselor, in this case, is to help the client get through the "grief work." The counselor must recognize that the client's possible disorientation and confusion is caused by an inability to deal with self and with the world, without the presence of the deceased person. The client is, in Lindemann's words, "in bondage" to the deceased. To free the individual from this bondage, the counselor must be willing to experience along with the client the profound sense of loneliness and isolation that follows the initial mourning, the feelings of guilt and responsibility that plague the survivor. To do this, the counselor, of course, must have his or her own feelings well in control.

The most significant work on grief crisis, and on dealing with death as a reality of life, has been done by Elisabeth Kübler-Ross, whose book *On Death and Dying* (1969) paved the way for much of the subsequent research on this subject. Her work is especially meaningful because it represents the first serious effort to deal with the grief crisis experienced by the dying person *while in the process of dying,* rather than by the survivors. Kübler-Ross (1969) emphasizes the need to keep communication open between the dying person and the family, and suggests that the grief crisis can be worked through before the person dies, not just after. She delineates a five-stage process through which we adjust to the idea of death. The first stage involves denial, when the person refuses to believe he or she is dying. Then there is anger—"Why is this happening to me?"—followed by bargaining, depression, and finally, with appropriate emotional interventions, such as empathic understanding, a stage of acceptance. Dr. Kübler-Ross's book is well worth reading for any counselor involved in this type of counseling.

Factors in Working through Grief There are a number of key factors that play a part in how well or how poorly a grief crisis can be resolved. First, the suddenness of the death is of much practical importance. Even though it is said that we can never fully prepare for a loved one's death, there is a qualitative difference between our loved one suddenly dropping dead and a loved one lingering on for a period of time, wasting away with illness.

Rubin's Model Rubin (1981) has proposed a two-track model of bereavement, similar to Lindemann's, but particularly applicable for understanding our complex adjustment process. The two-track model of bereavement refers to the bereavement response both from the perspective of the bereaved's emotional bond with the deceased and the bereaved's personality change as a result of the grief. The task of the grief response is to reestablish functioning in all areas, even if it does not necessarily reach the preloss levels of functioning.

Rubin outlines three main stages. The first stage requires the bereaved to accept the reality of the loss and to begin the loosening of emotional attachments to the deceased. This stage, known as the *acute grief period,* is typically marked by dramatic changes in behavior and by pronounced personality modifications.

The second stage is known as the *mourning period.* It is characterized by a more subdued process of detachment from the deceased and more subtle changes in personality. During this stage, some personality variables may have stabilized, while others are still influenced by the continuing process of affective detachment from the loved individual. As the detachment proceeds, they too will stabilize or subside.

At the final stage, a resolution has been achieved. The detachment process has reached its conclusion and personality changes have also stabilized. Equilibrium has been achieved. It is at this point that persisting effects of the loss can be identified. Now it is possible to discuss objectively the affective relationship to the deceased and the presence or absence of persisting personality change. At this point, in other words, the bereaved is more rational, even if still deeply scarred.

Weisman (1973) differentiates between three kinds of untimely death: premature, unexpected, and calamitous and suggests that they require different kinds of management. *Premature* refers to the death of a young person, a child. *Unexpected* refers to the sudden death of a normal and healthy person. "The emotional impact upon survivors," he points out, "is gauged and sharpened by how independent, autonomous, and distinctive the deceased happens to be at the time of death" (p. 367). It is not uncommon to hear, "he or she was such a vital, alive person . . . I can't believe he or she is dead." Finally, *calamitous* death "is not only unpredicted, but violent, destructive, demeaning, and even degrading." This last category would include murder and suicide.

The point is that each of these requires different kinds of management. The feelings attendant to each naturally differ; and Weisman correctly points out, "There are no ready-made, cookbook recipes for coping with untimely death." However, he does offer a range of appropriate interventions, which can be summarized as follows:

1. To facilitate the reorientation and adjustment process by "fostering a timely and appropriate bereavement process" and by "transforming the most malignant untimely deaths into more acceptable forms"
2. "To change calamitous deaths into unexpected deaths, unexpected deaths into premature deaths, and premature deaths into appropriate deaths"
3. Breaking bad news in the least devastating way, and providing immediate support for the survivors
4. Helping the survivor find significant and supportive individuals, who can empathically assist in the reorientation process
5. Helping the survivor learn to deal with feelings of guilt
6. Helping the survivor learn to openly express his or her feelings

Together, these six applications of grief-crisis theory can help the bereaved person adjust in the most expeditious way. This does not imply that the adjustment will be quick, facile, or complete, but only that the counselor has a clear idea of the direction in which he or she is assisting the grief-stricken client.

When Children Die

One particularly difficult situation for the counselor to deal with is the death of a child. While many of the standard processes of bereavement are relevant here, there are other attendant difficulties as well. A child's death, whether expected or unexpected, is always premature, and people have difficulty understanding it. Wilkenfeld (1977) points out that "We have been led to believe that all the ills of the world—including death—are conquerable through technology. When a child dies, these misconceptions about the omnipotence of technology are rudely shattered and the event seems all the more tragic, unjust, and incomprehensible" (p. iv). She goes on to suggest that it is more difficult to adjust to this than it is to the death of an older person, even one who was in good health.

Usually, the death of a child requires that other children—friends, class-mates, and siblings—be told about the death—and death itself—and that their feelings be dealt with. This is no easy task, and often parents and teachers are not up to the challenge because they themselves are having so much difficulty dealing with their feelings. "From the time that a child is about two or three," Yudkin (1968) points out, "fantasy joins hands with experience, and death takes on new dimensions of curiosity, anxiety, and fear." Empathic communications allow the child to express the fantasy, to relieve himself or herself of the incumbent anxiety, and to grasp the reality of the situation.

The treatment of the terminally ill child is a related problem. Crisis intervention is often indicated both for the child and the family. Children, perceptive creatures that they are, recognize that they are dying, even if they do not fully understand the meaning of *dying,* of the effect of their illness upon others. Weininger (1975) points out:

> In my experience, the most prominent emotion displayed by children who are dying of various diseases was hostility. The young child of 2 to 3 years of age in the hospital also experienced great separation anxiety lest hospital staff leave him like his parents did and then resultant resentment toward the staff as well as his parents. . . . The child of perhaps 6 or 7 would speak to me about death by expressing his fear in a confused and very angry way, still perceiving death as a punishment for being "bad." By this age, children seemed to think that in some way they had caused their own illness and thus deserved to die. (p. 18)

Special training is necessary in working with the terminally ill; and it is extremely important that the counselor be aware of his or her own feelings. All of us are victims when children are dying: for all of us suffer their pains with them.

Loveloss

One of the most personally painful crises that clients bring to the counseling setting is *loveloss,* the nonreciprocal dissolution of a romantic love relationship. We can define loveloss crisis as one in which rage, guilt, confusion, panic, loneliness, and self-loathing are combined in an overpowering feeling of helplessness that cannot be adequately articulated. In many ways, this crisis emulates a grief crisis, certainly in intensity and intransigence, but there are enough significant differences to warrant a brief separate discussion.

Like grief, resolving loveloss requires learning to live in the same old world in a new way—without the certainty and closeness of the person to whom one is emotionally attached and with whom one has come to associate the things of the world. It also requires accommodating in day-to-day living a deep and frustrating longing for another who is not available. Unlike the grief crisis, however, the person in loveloss usually still hopes to "win back" the other person, to continue the relationship after some change in one individual or the other. Whereas grief, with all its painful complexity, is circumscribed by an unequivocal finality, loveloss is characterized by a more ambivalent complex of contradictory feelings including hopefulness and hopelessness, hurt and love, loss of ego esteem, self-blame, rage toward the other, etc.

The circumstances of the loveloss are often significant in working toward its resolution. It may occur as a sudden event, when one lover is told unexpectedly by the other that the relationship is over. When one partner wants to terminate the relationship and the other doesn't, the one who wants to hold on typically feels not only endangered and confused, but also a complete lack of control over life and destiny and a total loss of security and comfort. "I just didn't know how to feel," one client told me when her boyfriend announced a week before her engagement party that he didn't think he loved her anymore. "I mean, I was in the same kind of shock as if he were killed in a car crash or something. Except that he wasn't killed—no, it was like he was killing me with his words. I didn't know whether to hate him or to still love him. I still don't know." In such instances, the client has to learn to reinterpret his or her feelings and to understand there is no particular way he or she is supposed to feel.

Often, the loveloss crisis is the inevitable consequence of a long process of relationship dissolution. If a painful period of interpersonal struggle results in termination of a relationship, it is likely that the rejected partner will experience loveloss. It is helpful in such instances for the client to see that the loveloss is a mourning for a fantasy relationship that has not existed for a long time.

Before seeking counseling, a person confronted with loveloss will typically have spoken to friends, family, and others, trying to make sense of what has happened. Counseling is often a last resort.

The counselor can help the loveloss client in several ways. First, the client should be able to express all the contradictory feelings without any judgmental feedback from the counselor. The effective counselor will neither encourage nor discourage the client's hopes of resuming the relationship; will neither agree nor disagree with an unrealistically positive or negative evaluation of the former lover. It is better to listen, in order to get an idea of the ambivalence and confusion that is causing the painful mourning, than to try to clarify the situation realistically.

Cognitive and behavioral methods can be used to minimize the pain until readjustment is feasible. For instance, I [this author] have used methods of cognitive desensitization where the client and I travelled vicariously to all the places he or she associated with the former lover. In the confines of my office, we vicariously dined at restaurants where favorite meals had been eaten, went to visit places and friends, and laughed at jokes—all in the context of trying to relive these experiences without the haunting of the former lover's ghost.

Finally, supportive counseling, over a period of four to eight months, can help the client get a new footing in reality and begin the search for a new love partner. During this period of support, the counselor should encourage the client to ex-

Counseling
Interventions

amine the basic issues of self-esteem and self-worth. When one's image of self, which has been shattered by the rejection, begins its lengthy process of reconstruction, the loveloss crisis begins to resolve itself in a healthy way.

Family Crisis   Another type of common crisis situation is the family crisis. Usually a family crisis has been a long time in the making, and it is only when it comes to a head and becomes totally intolerable that the family members (or a single member of the family, in many cases) seek professional help. The counselor should assess the full situation carefully before attempting any intervention because she or he wants to avoid being accused of siding with one member or one faction over others. This requires the skill of a counselor and the tact of a diplomat; and the counselor should be aware when she or he is treading on emotionally dangerous ground. Klein and Lindemann (1961) offer four stages for planning the interventions that are appropriate in family crisis situations:

1. Appraisal of the predicament——Attempts are made to mobilize the ego resources of the client by enlisting him in assessing the problem.
2. Planning the intervention——The extent to which the crisis exists, potential or actual impact on client and others in his social orbit, and the strengths and resources of the people involved must be recognized.
3. Altering the balance of forces——Restoration of reasonably healthy equilibrium in the social orbit, and redefining and clarifying the predicament.
4. Resolving the crisis and anticipatory planning service continues to be available . . . review of progress and resolution, somewhat follow-up. (pp. 287–293)

These four stages are logical, viable steps to helping the client caught in the midst of a family crisis. We note that they are based on the balance of forces theory— that a crisis is a loss of homeostasis, when some force outweighs others and slips out of control. These stages represent organizing layers of bringing the forces back into check.

Anxiety Crisis   The fourth type of common crisis situation is termed the *anxiety crisis*. In this situation, the client is in a state of high anxiety and turmoil, usually uncertain of exactly what it is that has precipitated this feeling. Drugs, particularly hallucinogenic drugs, are a common cause of this type of crisis, although certainly the counselor should not assume that such a crisis is caused by drugs until he or she has adequately explored this possibility with the client. The best rule of thumb in an anxiety crisis is to ask the client *object-oriented* questions. These are questions of fact or circumstance that do not infringe upon the client's ego domain. What time did you leave for school today? and, How old are you? and,

When did these feelings begin to bother you? are object-oriented questions. If a drug is suspected, the counselor should learn from the client what drug was ingested, how much, and when it was taken, in order to determine whether medical attention is needed. The counselor should obtain a thorough drug history to assess patterns of drug use, which will prove important during the therapeutic and rehabilitative stages of the process.

Object-oriented questions have a calming effect upon anxiety-crisis clients because they compel them to reorganize their thinking so that they can respond rationally to stimuli from the external world (the counselor's questions). As the client focuses his or her attention upon these factual questions, he or she begins to reexperience logical awareness of the world. Asking object-oriented questions is one of many ways to help the client reestablish his or her psychic balance (Spotnitz, 1976).

Foreman and Zerwekh (1971) have suggested establishing feelings of rapport to help the victim of a drug crisis. If the client feels she or he is able to speak freely to the counselor, it will better enable her or him to "come down" from a bad trip. Bieber (1972) has discussed some of the methods for handling homosexual crises, resulting from overwhelming ego-dystonic feelings of homosexual panic. Tayal (1972) has examined the level of suggestibility in crisis states and found that the suggestibility of girls who were pregnant out of wedlock was significantly higher than a control group. These girls were more readily compliant than the girls in the control group, more willing to be followers than to seek their individuality.

One of the most difficult types of crisis for the counselor to deal with is the suicidal crisis. In this situation the client expresses to the counselor either a specific or vague intention of committing suicide. Usually such a client is suffering from a feeling of overwhelming helplessness and futility, the belief that nothing can help, nothing can make a difference. He or she feels closed in, confined in an unbearable situation from which there is no escape. The fact that the suicidal client is speaking to someone about these feelings indicates a desire for help, but it is an error to assume that the request for help means that the individual is not serious about suicidal intentions. The case books are filled with tragic examples of successful suicides committed shortly after an interview with a psychiatrist or counselor (Marilyn Monroe or Freddie Prinz are good examples of this).

In dealing with the suicidal client, the counselor must be willing to listen to the client and to recognize the miasma of depression that overcomes him or her. This is indeed a difficult thing to do, especially if the subject of suicide makes the counselor overly anxious. "In order to recognize depression in others," Motto (1978) points out, "counselors must resolve their own anxiety about the issue of suicide sufficiently to elicit pertinent information from clients" (p. 539). Otherwise, the counselor may attempt to deny or minimize the severity of the depression.

Suicidal Crisis

Therapeutically, it is necessary that the counselor experience along with the client feelings of total despair and hopelessness, the sense of futility and isolation, sentiments of abject grief and failure, the client's rage directed at himself or herself and at the world. The very worst thing the counselor can do is to tell the client that things are not as bad as they seem, that things will improve, that he or she has plenty of reasons to go on living. Although realistically all of these statements may be true, they make the client feel that she or he is not understood by the counselor; and this reinforces feelings of isolation from the people around her or him. For the counselor truly to help the client, she or he must fully experience reality from the client's inexorably hopeless perspective. This means, among other things, that the counselor is willing and able to explore in herself or himself those feelings of despair and emptiness that she or he personally tries to avoid confronting for the sake of personal mental health.

Experience and research have developed a number of helpful rules in dealing with the suicidal client. It is generally a good idea to ascertain whether the method of destruction has been arrived at. "How do you intend to kill yourself?" the counselor may ask. The more specific the client's plans, the closer he or she is to carrying out the act. Second, it is not advisable to have the client "look at the bright side" of the situation; if the client could accept a bright picture emotionally, she or he would not be in this predicament in the first place. Third, always take all suicidal threats seriously. Many a counselor has had deep regrets after dismissing a serious suicide threat as an immature bid for attention.

The following section from a transcript of a counseling interview conducted between a skilled counselor (Bob) and a suicidal client illustrates some of the better ways of handling this type of situation.

Counselor (13)   Do you feel you can speak about it?

Client (13)   There's nothing to tell. It's just not worth it, man. Like I believe we have a right to live or die, and that it's my choice. I just can't take it anymore. If I can't have her I don't want to live. There is nothing else to it.

Counselor (14)   You love her very much, don't you?

Client (14)   (*Laughs hysterically, out of control*) Love her! I love her so much I could kill her. I love her more than anything—more than God, more than my family, more than myself. I can't go on, Bob. It's just not worth it. If I'm dead, I won't have to think about it—that's why.

Counselor (15)   How are you going to do it?

Client (15)   With the car. I'll crash it at 70 into a wall. I'm just gonna drive and drive until I have the guts to do it—then whammo! Right into the fucking wall. (*Laughs hysterically*) You call her up, Bob, you tell her. You tell her what she did to me. Let her know.

Counselor (16)   There is no one like her, is there? I mean, is there a chance, even, of finding someone else?

Client (16) (*Laughs hysterically*) No, Bob, no way out. I wish. But there's only her, Bob. You met her, you know. She was *the one*—the one for me and I blew it. Now, what's left—fifty years of pain and suffering—a lifetime of looking back at what could have been? It's not for me. I couldn't take it.

Counselor (17) Can you take it for another two days? Can you stand the pain for that long?

Client (17) Why? You think I'll get over it in a couple of days? You're kidding yourself. If you're trying to tell me she'll come back, Bob, you're not kidding *me*. I know what the score is. She told me.

Counselor (18) No, I don't think any of those things. I see what the situation is, and I don't know what to say. But suicide's a big decision, a final one, and I think we should at least talk about it again before you go ahead. I'm not going to stop you—I'm not going to feed you a line about how things will work out. I just want us both to be sure. I'd like to see you Friday—just to talk about it one more time. If you want to go ahead then . . . I won't stop you. I don't feel I have the right.

Client (18) (*Friday*) That's two more days of this. I don't know if I can hold on till then.

Counselor (19) If you don't think you can, call me; I'll see you before then. I just want to discuss it one more time before you make the big move. Of course, the final decision is up to you—but I'd like to talk with you first.

Client (19) OK. Let's make it Friday. But if I can't hold out till then, I'll call you. Can I call at home?

Counselor (20) Of course. Any time. . . .

The skill of the counselor shines through these brief lines of interaction. Note what he did and did not do. He never tried to convince the client that things weren't that bad, that he would find another girl friend. Certainly if the client were able to understand and appreciate such a realistic assessment, he would not be contemplating suicide in the first place. The counselor did allow the client to freely express his fantasies of self-destruction and inquired as to the means of this act. In this way he was able to assess the client's determination to carry out what he was threatening. The counselor did not ask the client to give up his suicidal plans, but rather to postpone them for a couple of days to give the two of them a chance to discuss them again. "The final decision is up to you," he told the client (Counselor [19]), assuring the client that he would not attempt to dissuade him from his plans. The counselor joined the client in his fantasy and emotionally understood the hopelessness and pain of the client's predicament. Everything he said to the client, everything he communicated both verbally and nonverbally, he actually felt in a manner parallel to the way the client felt it. To treat the suicidal client, it is always necessary for the counselor to feel the full force of the client's depression. Figure 15.1 shows some of the more critical *do's and don'ts* of crisis counseling extracted both from the literature and from the author's personal experiences in this area.

Figure 15.1. Do's and don'ts in crisis intervention counseling
From Belkin Gary S., *Practical Counseling in the*
Schools. **Copyright © 1975, Wm. C. Brown Company**
Publishers, Dubuque, Iowa.

Do's

1 Remain calm and stable. Prepare yourself psychologically for the turbulence of emotion that is soon to flow from the client.
2 Allow the client full opportunity to speak. Attempt to determine the type of crisis, its precipitating forces, and its severity. Interrupt only when it is for the client's benefit, never to relieve yourself of distressing feelings being induced by the client.
3 When indicated, ask object-oriented questions. These should, if asked properly, have a calming effect upon the client. If they fail to have such an effect, the counselor should consider the possibility that he or she is asking ego-oriented questions.
4 Deal with the immediate situation rather than its underlying, unconscious causes that may be left for later. "In the crisis period," Brockopp (1973) points out, "the person is open to change; the sooner we can work with him the more likely we are to minimize the possible deterioration of the personality and to develop an effective solution which will improve the personality functioning of the individual."
5 Have readily available local resources to assist the counselor: community, medical, legal, etc.

Don'ts

1 Don't try to "cheer up" the client, to tell him or her that his or her problems are not as bad as they seem, to reassure him or her *unless* he or she specifically requests these types of interventions (which is, by the way, the exception rather than the rule).
2 Don't ask the suicidal client to abandon his or her plans. Always make such a request a temporary delay.
3 Don't attempt to solve the total personality adjustment difficulty. Some counselors make the error of minimizing the crisis itself and attempting to get the client to speak about more "fundamental" things.

Two other points should be mentioned about suicide-prone individuals. First, they often express their suicidal intentions inversely through homicidal threats. When such murderous rage is expressed very strongly in the clinical setting, it can quickly upset the counselor who feels that the client may lose control. "The murderous impulses of our patients are threatening to our defenses against aggression, and we may react with support and reassurance in order to support and reassure ourselves and not the patient. . . . Rather than helping the patient with his impulse control, this false reassurance may be interpreted as a prohibition against expressing these impulses outwardly and may *encourage* the patient to kill himself" (Rhine & Mayerson, 1973, p. 8). Practitioners then should be especially sensitive to the possibility that the client who is frustrated in his or her homicidal rage may take it out on himself or herself.

Second, counselors must be aware of subtle but extremely important "distinctions among the wish to die, the act of self-injury, and the terminal outcome" (Cutter, 1971, p. 125). Clarification of the client's degree of intent at the beginning can help not only to formulate the correct course of treatment, but can also help assure that the client's vague death wish does not become a suicidal reality.

As the public becomes increasingly sensitive to the plight of the rape victim, counselors and other mental health professionals are finding themselves more involved in efforts to provide supportive counseling services to the victim of rape. Now that the general public, which for so many years did not know how to deal with the victim of rape, has begun to recognize that a rape victim is not like other victims but a special type of victim who has suffered a trauma of a unique nature, there is a growing concern for providing counseling services, either immediately following the rape trauma or in the days, weeks, and months thereafter.

With this increased professional interest has evolved a comprehensive literature on the psychodynamics of rape and the psychological treatment of the rape victim. D. Nass (1977) has edited a volume that examines in depth the kinds of problems encountered by the rape victim, the extent of services available, and practical treatment considerations. She points out,

> The stigma attached to the victim of rape, traceable to cultural sex-role stereotypes and irrational popular judgments of female complicity, discourages the woman in crisis from reaching out for help. Hesitant to divulge her experience for fear of meeting with public ridicule and scorn, the rape victim is isolated from the supports available to victims of other kinds of misfortunes. This sense of isolation is aggravated by her knowledge of the customary treatment accorded rape victims by police authorities, representatives of the court, hospital personnel, social peers, and even close relatives. (p. 3)

Specific counseling interventions depend, to a large extent, on the setting. In the hospital emergency room, where the victim may first be brought, a different kind of approach will be required than in the individual counseling setting some weeks after the traumatic event (Williams & Williams, 1973). Broadly speaking, we can divide post-rape counseling into three periods: the hours immediately following the rape; the weeks thereafter; and long-range considerations.

During the hours immediately following the rape, the victim is likely to be seen either at a police station or in a hospital emergency room. The goals of any counseling endeavors will be influenced in these settings by the need to obtain objective information about the crime, the circumstances, the victim, and about the perpetrator—information that may be helpful to the police and to prosecutors. Since a calm and clear-headed witness is a good witness, the time taken to relax the victim—to reduce her state of distress as much as possible—will be of practical value later on.

It may also be essential at this time to obtain relevant medical information necessary for treatment. Is the woman using contraceptives? Is she pregnant? Does she suffer from any gynecological problems? Is she under medication (a diabetic may forget to take her insulin during this period of distress)? What injuries did she suffer at the hands of her attacker? A thorough medical examination is routinely performed, and the woman should be apprised of this.

Moreover, an assessment of other family members' reactions should be noted by the interviewer. There have been many tragic incidents where an enraged husband, father, or friend has acted impulsively immediately following an attack upon his loved one. This unnecessary violence (and it can be directed at anyone!) could have been prevented by appropriate interventions. But it was not prevented because it was not noticed.

The "rape trauma syndrome," as it is described by Holmstrom and Burgess (1975), comprises an *acute phase* and a *long-term phase*. The acute phase "includes many physical symptoms, especially gastrointestinal irritability, muscular tension, sleep pattern disturbance, genito-urinary discomfort, and a wide range of emotional reactions" (p. 223). These problems are dealt with soon after the attack, and many of them will be directed to the physician. But the counselor plays an especially vital part in helping the rape victim get through the long-term phase, which "includes changes in life-style, such as changing residence, seeking family and social network support, and dealing with repetitive nightmares and phobias."

During the weeks following the rape, counseling should aim to find out the total effect upon the client's life. Has her sex life been upset? Have her relations with men been affected? Has she noted any physical complaints? Have there been any adverse comments in the office? In the community? With whom has she discussed the rape, and what kind of reaction has she found? Because there is always a possibility of a delayed shock response, it may be a good idea to schedule an appointment six to ten months following the rape to see if the immediacy of the trauma has subsided.

Summary

The state of crisis is characterized by a loss of orientation, a disequilibrium of the intrapsychic forces, and profound feelings of confusion, alienation, disruption, and panic. When the crisis client presents himself or herself to the counselor, he or she exhibits an emotional turbulence that may inadvertently be induced in the counselor, in the form of emotional contagion. The counselor must, to be effective at such times, remain calm and poised. The therapeutic processes of treatment depend upon the nature of the specific crisis. But we examined several general guidelines that would be applicable to all kinds of crisis situations.

In a grief or loveloss crisis, the counselor must help the client get through the grief work and deal with separation; in a family crisis, the counselor can help the client(s) understand the underlying dynamics of the family crisis; in an anxiety crisis, the counselor should determine the source of the problem and use object-oriented questions to help the client come to grips with it; in a suicidal crisis, the counselor must allow the client full expression of his or her feelings, determine if a method of destruction has been arrived at, experience the hopelessness along with the client, and request a temporary postponement of his or her plans; in the rape crisis, it is imperative to provide information about available medical and legal services, as well as give the full emotional support that the victim requires.

In all these cases, the counselor must be willing (and emotionally stable enough!) to experience along with the client the fears and frustrations that inevitably accompany a crisis situation. He or she must react empathically and honestly, but with enough self-control and emotional detachment to avoid becoming overwhelmed by the impact of the crisis.

Chapter Aim

To outline the scope of rehabilitation counseling and to illustrate some of the kinds of problems to which it is applied. To delineate community counseling as an integrated modality and present some successful paradigms of community counseling programs.

Rehabilitation counseling consists of all efforts to help the individual adjust psychologically and behaviorally to a variety of life processes in his or her role areas such as work, interpersonal relationships, and the like. The goal of all rehabilitation counseling is to help the person achieve optimal functioning, that is, the most efficient level of functioning he or she is capable of. Vocational rehabilitation is the foundation of almost all other rehabilitation efforts. It consists of much more than job placement; it is helping the person adjust totally to the world of work. Some specific types of individuals who come for rehabilitation are the ex-offender, the drug addict, the mentally retarded, and the physically disabled.

**Rehabilitation
Counseling**

Community counseling includes the provision of general and specific counseling services within the boundaries of the physical neighborhood. It is a distinct form of advisement, having its own theoretical rationale. It is "consumer" oriented, flexible and responsive to the needs of members of the community. A number of theoretical models have been proposed, and many successful programs, especially for working with adolescents or the aging, have been implemented.

**Community
Counseling**

Rehabilitation and Community Counseling

16

These two forms of counseling—rehabilitation and community counseling—have been grouped together for two reasons. First, both are directed toward people who may not ordinarily avail themselves of counseling services, but who, because of certain unanticipated needs, now find themselves in need of such help. This sometimes requires special adaptations. Second, in recent years a great amount of attention has been focused on both, resulting in new attitudes, new methods, and wider availability. We will clarify these points in this chapter.

Rehabilitation counseling has developed as a distinct goal-directed form of counseling over the years in recognition of and in response to the needs of large populations that have demonstrated the need for intensive rehabilitative efforts. This client population includes the physically disabled; ex-offenders who have served time in prison and are now trying to adjust to life outside, and recidivists (chronic repeaters of criminal behavior); drug addicts and alcoholics; the emotionally disturbed; the mentally retarded; the chronically unemployed; and other groups that are having difficulty adjusting to societal demands and expectations. What the individuals in these groups all have in common is that they are functioning well below the level at which they should be functioning, that is, they are not fulfilling their potential for growth and accomplishment in life.

Rehabilitation Counseling

Broadly defined, rehabilitation counseling consists of all efforts to help the individual adjust psychologically and behaviorally to a variety of life processes in role areas such as work, interpersonal relations, travel and other physical activities. Hirschberg, Lewis, and Thomas's (1964) basic definition is still the best: that rehabilitation is the *total* process by which a "person is restored to a state of optimal effectiveness and given an opportunity to enjoy a meaningful life" (p. 6). This is a succinct and precise definition. They go on to point out that in the full sense, rehabilitation is "both preventive and restorative; directed toward improvement of function." A number of factors may be at the root of the problems that require rehabilitation; these include accidents, congenital defects, maladjustments of social origin, or other reasons.

In this section, after we outline some of the basic premises and principles of rehabilitation, we will focus on some basic categories of rehabilitation counseling. Each of these will be directed toward certain types of problems and/or a specific client population.

Basic Premises and Principles

The goal of all types of rehabilitation counseling, as we mentioned in the definition, is to help a person achieve optimal functioning. This comprises three elements. First, that counselors are able to measure with some precision the individual's optimum level, that is, that their goals for the person are realistic. If counselors believe that blind people can never hold any meaningful kind of job, then it is unlikely that they will be able to help them, or accurately perceive the potentialities of the blind client with whom they are working. Likewise, if counselors feel that an outpatient from a mental hospital can never be stable enough to hold responsible employment, they are at a serious strategic disadvantage in their efforts to help this person. To be effective as a rehabilitation counselor, therefore, it is necessary that counselors put aside all of their preconceptions, that they attempt to help each individual on his or her own level of functioning. To this end it is often most effective to allow the client to determine the level of functioning that should be the objective.

After the initial goals are set, the client usually needs some direction about how to achieve these goals. This involves a twofold process: first the counselor should have immediate access to the available resources, to know where to send the client for different kinds of services. The counselor who can direct the blind client to Recordings for the Blind or the emotionally disturbed client, when necessary, to individual counseling, or the physically disabled client to physical rehabilitation agencies is providing a concrete service. The need for information is great in rehabilitation. Hardy and Cull (1974) point out that "a substantial number of clients need considerable advice and information which the counselor has to offer concerning social and rehabilitation services from which they can profit." They suggest, from a practical point of view, that,

> When the counselee needs advice and information, the rehabilitation counselor must be able to recognize this need and provide what is required. There also will be many instances in which the client and counselor must enter into a number of counseling sessions in depth. The counselor must make the judgment concerning what type of help is needed for the client to solve his particular problem. (pp. 89–90)

The other half of the coin, to which Hardy and Cull allude, is that the counselor should provide the emotional and therapeutic dimensions necessary to get the client on his or her feet again. This involves appropriate interventions designed to help the person overcome anxieties and doubts about his or her abilities. Newman (1974), in speaking of drug rehabilitation counseling, however, makes the point that although psychological services should be made available to the client, they should not be imposed, lest the client feel threatened and alienated.

Finally, the committed rehabilitation counselor provides follow-up services. It is not enough simply to see that the client gets a start, but the counselor should also attempt to see that this start is a start of something—that the goals of the process are attained as fully as possible.

All of these processes are most clearly illustrated in vocational rehabilitation, the foundation of almost all other rehabilitation efforts, to which we will now turn our attention.

Vocational rehabilitation is directed specifically at helping individuals develop the skills and attitudes necessary for gainful employment and helping them find jobs appropriate to their needs and abilities. But it is much more than simply job placement. As McLaughlin conceptualizes it, it is "a process which helps the individual become more aware of and evaluate his assets" (p. 265). This awareness is then used as a tool in finding work that can be emotionally fulfilling, socially productive, and financially rewarding. In its total sense then, vocational rehabilitation is an integral part of a broader range of therapeutic efforts at helping the person function at maximum level. As Morgenstern and Smith (1973) point out, the term *vocational rehabilitation* is in some ways misleading since it implies indirectly that the main purpose is job training and job placement. They, instead, consider the job as:

> only one aspect of the functioning of the whole person. It becomes the goal as an expression of the optimum use of the individual's faculties. The basic psychological approach underlying the rehabilitation effort is therapeutic, not vocational. A main result of the therapeutic process is vocational rehabilitation. In this sense we can describe our efforts with the individual as therapeutic rehabilitation. (p. 26)

This is a key point in understanding the psychological dimension of vocational rehabilitation, especially as it contributes to the total growth of the person.

Effective vocational rehabilitation comprises several related processes. Initial assessment, both through standardized instruments and through the counseling interview, establishes the level of client skill, the areas of weakness, and the client's interests and aptitudes. These can be used as guidelines to explore with the client his or her personal goals. Are the goals realistic? Does the client know how to go about finding work? Are further educational efforts necessary? These are a few of the questions the counselor would ask at this stage.

Vocational rehabilitation next requires the counselor to help the client adjust to a job. Many disabled individuals find that the world of work is far greater a task than they had expected, and if they are not given enough support at the beginning, feel a complete sense of failure and regret.

Finally, vocational rehabilitation requires that the counselor provide the client with the emotional support necessary to confront and deal with some very difficult life challenges. Looking at the client as a total person, we see all of the in-

Vocational Rehabilitation

teractive areas of supportive and developmental counseling brought to bear in rehabilitative efforts. With these general principles in mind, let us consider some specific aspects of vocational and other types of rehabilitation. The categories which we shall discuss reflect generally the status of the client, or the client's specific need for rehabilitation.

Ex-Offender
Rehabilitation

The individual who is making the adjustment from the constraints of the penal setting to the relative freedom of the societal setting generally requires intensive rehabilitative efforts. The longer the time spent in prison, the greater is the need for rehabilitation counseling. "Ex-offenders are persons of marginal social status," Krieger (1975) points out:

> They have spent a certain amount of time in prison . . . and this will have had a profound effect on them, most likely a negative one. They probably show resentment toward correctional officials or toward society in general and may be distrustful of anyone who attempts to help them. They will have to face the negative attitudes of others, especially in the area of employment. . . . Ex-offenders who are rehabilitation clients will have many psychological and social needs at the time of release. They will have to reestablish contact with the community; besides needing a residence, a job, and friends, they may have to adjust to a changing society, one from which they were forcibly removed. . . . They will need help altering a life style that has predisposed them to commit one or more crimes. (p. 154)

Krieger accurately summarizes the scope of related efforts which the rehabilitation counselor may have to make in working with the ex-offender.

The main problem in working with ex-offenders is the high rate of recidivism; i.e., those who commit other offenses and are returned to prison. Although there are no precise and reliable figures on recidivism because of confusing methods of data collection and statistical analysis, the rate is generally estimated at around 75 percent or over (Webb, Wakefield, & Drell, 1976). This is alarmingly high. Moreover, those working closely with ex-offenders are generally not able to predict in advance who will revert to criminal behavior. In one diction study, Friedman and Mann (1976) found that "despite contact with the youth during his rehabilitation program, staff members at three correctional institutions were unable to accurately predict violent and nonviolent criminal behavior during the two-year follow-up period for their trainees" (p. 162). This indicates that the rehabilitation counselor working with the ex-offender can never be too certain that his or her judgment about the chances of success are too accurate.

In addition to the problems that face us with any client, there are several additional problems in working with the ex-offender. The challenges of vocational counseling are monumental. The business world is typically reluctant to hire ex-offenders. Dale (1976) has pointed out the large number of restrictions on employment opportunities, including exclusion from many licensed professions, inability to obtain bonding, and the stigma of having spent time in prison. These present a formidable challenge to the rehabilitation counselor whose resourcefulness is put to the test.

Despite these many problems, ex-offender rehabilitation can lead to highly successful outcomes. Bennight (1975) has described what seems like an effective program, which was designed to deliver services to offenders while in prison and until they are placed in training or employment. In what is called the Maryland Comprehensive Offender Model Program, structured groups and reality therapy were used, along with a number of vocational test instruments. Staff training and a high level of administrative competency added to the efficacy of the program. Summarizing the points of the program, Bennight says, "The main ingredients in this program were good client assessment, counseling toward the definite goal of getting a job, and individualized job development" (p. 173). These would seem to be the main ingredients in any such program.

The rehabilitation of the released mental patient has striking similarities with ex-offender rehabilitation. In both cases, the individual has to learn a repertoire of adjustments to society, and in both situations, society is reluctant on a variety of levels to admit the individual back. The problem of persons who have been released from mental hospitals and returned to their communities without adequate aftercare support has become enormous since the discovery of tranquilizers twenty-five years ago. Sheer numbers have made adequate individualized treatment of released mental patients nigh impossible, and large-scale social welfare operations have all but ignored the individual.

Psychiatric Rehabilitation

Moreover, the bureaucratic machinery responsible for overseeing rehabilitation has broken down. Koenig (1978) has drawn a pathetic portrait of some of the estimated 40,000 released patients who live in New York City, showing the filth and squalor in which they live, their victimization by young criminals and a welfare system that isolates them, their chronic dependency on tranquilizing drugs. This area of the rehabilitation of released mental patients has come under harsh criticism for failing to objectively deal with the problem. Anthony (1977), for instance, has argued that the bulk of research "indicates that the field of mental health is not doing an adequate job of rehabilitating psychiatric patients back into the community" (p. 658).

And yet, despite these obstacles, there is evidence that when sufficient time is devoted, when funds are available, when the climate is right, psychiatric rehabilitation can be effective; that it can make a difference. This is especially true when services are made available in the community (as we shall discuss later in this chapter). For example, Black (1976) has argued that a community mental health facility can make a profound impact on helping ambulatory mental patients. He cites four basic areas in which such a program could be helpful: encouraging psychological treatment; monitoring the patients' behavior in the community setting; providing social and legal advocacy; and, offering leisure-time and vocational counseling. These could serve just as well as excellent guidelines for any counselor working with the ambulatory psychiatric patient.

Ex-drug addicts or alcoholics constitute another large class of individuals who require intensive rehabilitative efforts. Phillipson (1972) has identified the major treatment modalities currently used to treat drug abusers in the United States today. These include (1) in-patient treatment in a traditional institutionalized facility; (2) therapeutic communities (which are "live-in treatment environments staffed primarily by ex-addicts where 'total personality restructuring and re-education' is the stated goal"); (3) the psychiatric outpatient model, used for aftercare for abusers released from a more traditional facility; (4) supervision and counseling by a probation-parole officer; (5) behavior modification programs; (6) crisis centers, including hot lines and store-front clinics in the community; (7) halfway houses; (8) methadone maintenance programs. Almost all drug rehabilitation takes place in one or another of these settings.

Each of these has been thoroughly documented in the literature and at this time there is no one method that is clearly preferred over the others. The therapeutic community-halfway house efforts have had a promising history, and would certainly be worth considering. Bookbinder (1975) has shown in detail how a school can be set up at a halfway house to provide the academic and vocational skills necessary for full rehabilitation.

A great deal of work has been done in this area of rehabilitation of the mentally handicapped person. The rehabilitation of a retarded person, depending on the degree of retardation, can range from providing basic living skills to job training and placement, to sex education, to the development of other social skills. With this group of persons, the result of rehabilitation is often striking and immediate, although many of the effects will be far-ranging. Brolin (1972), in a valuable study of retarded males, found that those who had adequate vocational rehabilitation had higher incomes than those who did not have such training.

Rehabilitation of the mentally retarded involves much more than simply teaching job skills. It reflects the full import of our initial definition of rehabilitation, taking in the psychological-emotional dimension of the client, as well as helping develop cognitive skills. Because retarded children "encounter a disproportionately large number of frustrations and difficulties in their attempts to solve their problems," DeBlassie and Cowan (1976) suggest, "it is subsequently more difficult for them to develop realistic and healthy self-concepts." This concern for the psychological-emotion dimension of the client must, therefore, become an integral part of rehabilitative counseling with the mentally retarded. They go on to offer some practical suggestions:

A counseling relationship with educable mentally handicapped children of all ages must always involve mutual understanding and trust. The children are assisted in clarifying their problems, understanding their choices for solutions or modifications, and then selecting solutions that are satisfactory to them.

One major concern of the counselor is an understanding of the mentally handicapped child's self-concept. An autobiography in verbal or possibly written form, test results, anecdotal records, and conferences with those people closely associated with the educable mentally handicapped child are ways to help the counselor better understand the child's self-concept. . . .

Group counseling is one way to work with those educable mentally handicapped children who are overly sensitive about their handicap or their inability to function like other children. These children [through the group] perceive that there are others with problems like themselves and frequently experience a reduced fear or suspicion of the counselor. (pp. 249–251)

Of course, most of the rehabilitative efforts with the mentally handicapped will be in conjunction with a school or agency, and the impact of the helping team's cooperation is especially important in auguring success.

We often take for granted our good health and physical abilities. We accept without gratitude our sensory abilities. But to be able to see, to hear, to smell— to be able to get up and walk around, to withstand the physical stresses of living in this world—to lift, to move, to be able to change our physical position (locomotion)—these are the most fundamental and basic gifts of life. They should never be taken for granted.

Not taking them for granted is the first step in reaching the client with physical or sensory disabilities. When we can appreciate what we have, and how it affects our lives, then we can better understand how physical disabilities impose upon the orderliness of life and the expectations of others. Such an understanding is the essential underlying attitude for helping rehabilitate the physically and sensory disabled.

These kinds of disabilities include, but are not limited to, orthopedic, motor, and neurological impairments; metabolic, gastrointestinal, respiratory and cardiovascular impairments; hearing impairment; and visual impairment. These are broad categories, and include such things as total blindness, epilepsy, quadraplegia, chronic colitis, and less manifest conditions such as asthma, diabetes, and kidney disorders. In this section we can only touch upon a few of these disabilities.

Research has generally supported the position that an individual's "perceptions of disability are a significant and central aspect of the self-concept, relating to both self-esteem and satisfaction with social relationships" (Linkowski & Dunn, 1974, p. 31). The ways that this perception affect the individual's psychological development, interpersonal functioning, and social standing have been studied in depth.

Psychologically, patterns of development differ between the congenitally disabled, the adventitiously disabled, and the early-childhood disabled. The studies in this area are quite complex, and at this time we still cannot clearly attribute

Rehabilitation of the
Physically Disabled

specific psychological anomalies to any specific condition. A few important findings should throw us some clues, however. Hopkins (1971), in a study of the orthopedically disabled, found that their suicide rate was significantly higher than the general population, with amputees committing suicide even more frequently than those who had spinal cord injuries, who were of course paralyzed in different degrees. Lynch and Arndt (1973) found that "at age 6 handicapped children were more likely to minimize or deny the existence of frustration than nonhandicapped children of that age, while at age 10, handicappeds were more likely to use an intropunitive approach than their nonhandicapped counterparts" (p. 135). This means that they tended more to blame themselves. These and other studies show a general depressive tendency (toward self-punishment) among the physically handicapped, and some difficulty in dealing with the intransigent frustrations caused by the disability. This provides us an important clue in counseling the physically disabled.

One interesting question is whether these developmental differences are uniformly advantageous or disadvantageous. One could argue that the challenges the handicapped have to overcome to survive lead to a strength of character and general resourcefulness that may be lacking in individuals who do not have to cope with such problems. In some respects this hypothesis is supported by the remarkable success with which handicapped individuals have coped with a variety of obstacles despite a general lack of social support and encouragement.

In general, "the socialization process of the physically disabled will vary with regard to the time of onset of the disability. When a physical abnormality is identified at birth or shortly thereafter, the parents' initial attention to the baby's bodily appearance and functioning will be greatly intensified" (Smith-Hanen, 1976, p. 135). Just what this intensification leads to depends on the parents' specific attitudes, of course. Research has shown that the disabled person has to learn to accept the disability, and this process of acceptance may take a long time, and may in itself alter socialization patterns. Smith-Hanen (1976) who researched the problem, surveying the literature, found, among other things:

1. In cases of congenital disabilities or those experienced in early childhood, the afflicted individual is obliged to incorporate the disability into the formation of his body image.
2. Adventitious disabilities in older persons require changes in an already-existing body image. . . . However, the existing body image at the time of the acquired disability will have a great effect on the inclusion of the disability into the body image.
3. A clear differentiation of what a disabled person can and cannot do aids a smoother adjustment.
4. Another important aspect in the adjustment to the physical disability are the barriers to free locomotion that the disability manifests. *The less obvious and more compatible with customary situations the adjustments to the handicap are, the less that the handicap adversely affects the socialization of the disabled person.*

5. The family and friends of the disabled person can greatly affect his socialization and adjustment to his handicap.
6. The changes in role created by the disability cause problems. When a disability occurs late in life there is a role discontinuity that results in confusion, stress, and anxiety.
7. Another problem encountered by the disabled is role conflict. The disabled may have two very different expectations of what his role should be. When contradictory role expectations of what his own role should be are held by the same person, role definitions are in conflict. When is he disabled and when is he normal? (pp. 133–137)

It has been suggested that the physically and sensory disabled are especially in need of counseling interventions because of interpersonal adjustment difficulties caused by the disabilities. Specific-task programs are also needed in many areas, particularly in the areas of vocational counseling and sex education (including sexual adjustment). In these two areas, the physically handicapped have traditionally experienced serious problems because of the disability. Genrich (1975), for example, has pointed out how the physical disability can lead to poor vocational aspirations:

> Studies have shown that handicapped young people lack an understanding of their physical, intellectual, and emotional limitations as well as capabilities. These individuals demonstrate more inappropriate job choices than nondisabled youths, due to their narrow exposure to the work world and their limited understanding of the possibilities open to them. (p. 185)

She goes on to suggest that vocational programs include work activities that will allow the physically disabled client to "test out" his or her abilities in the real world of work.

In the areas of sexual functioning, much still needs to be done. Sidman (1977) argues correctly, I believe, that "most health professionals acknowledge the importance of sexual functioning within the total personality of a normal adult [but] when the same concern is raised by or for the physically disabled, may tend to turn away" (p. 81). Most physically disabled are capable of sexual activity, and someone has to teach them what type they are capable of, how to maximally enjoy their bodies, and so on. Differences in erectile potency and orgasmic ability make this especially important for the spinal-cord injured male, and corrective training, including behavior modification and sensitivity training, are becoming a major part of rehabilitation therapy.

In the following section we will turn our attention to community counseling, another area of considerable practical importance.

Community Counseling

During the turbulent period of social change that we associate with the last half of the 1960s and the first half of the 1970s, the counseling profession came to recognize its obligation to step beyond the boundaries to which it had been traditionally limited, and to provide broad-based services within communities, particularly inside the large urban communities where many underprivileged people live.

This increased consciousness, this new sensitivity and heightened awareness, offered the counseling profession a new commitment: to reach out to members of the community and to provide services that might not otherwise be taken advantage of by them. In this section, we will survey briefly the scope of community counseling and examine some of its philosophical foundations and primary concerns.

Baldwin (1975) gives a clear picture of the background from which this movement emerged, and it is in this context that we will discuss the subject:

> During the 1950s there was a growing national disillusionment with the private practice model of therapy and the inadequacy of centralized institutional treatment for mental illness. The Mental Health Studies Act of 1955 created the Joint Commission on Mental Illness and Health, which studied the nation's mental health needs for a period of five years. The inadequacies documented in this evaluation led to the adoption of the Community Mental Health Centers Act of 1963.
>
> This legislation mandated that communities become the base for treatment and support of the mentally ill. Community resources were to be developed and coordinated, and a network of community mental health centers were to be established to provide local care for the mentally ill. Federal funds were made available to subsidize the development and operation of these community centers. . . . Professional help was made available to large segments of the community in a form they could accept and at a cost they could bear. Localizing care and mobilizing community resources was a major effect of this act, which in turn legitimated the approach of alternative services that soon followed suit. (p. 736)

Overview

Counseling in the community includes the provision of general and specific counseling services, usually within the physical neighborhood. It differs from general private practice and counseling in an academic or agency setting in four respects:

1. It is located in a setting that is easy for community members to reach, and that is viewed by the community as being associated with them. This differs from having to take a car, train, or bus to some distant, possibly downtown location, which may be viewed as threatening, alien, or hostile.

2. The community facility is generally geared to specific problems of the community. For example, in a community where there is a high rate of substance abuse, addiction prevention and drug rehabilitation programs may be instituted to deal with the problems of drug abuse. Certain kinds of problems that are common to all communities would, of course, be included in all such facilities.

3. The professional and paraprofessional staff at such centers is trained to relate to the community members. This can take place on many different levels. For instance, in a Spanish-speaking community, you would have staff who not only can speak and understand the Spanish language, but who also understand the cultural uniqueness of the constituency (Blatt, 1976).

4. There is a willingness to experiment with counseling modalities that are less traditional than those the counselor may otherwise employ. Because of special population needs, it is often necessary to design innovative and creative programs to reach large numbers of the population.

There are several other key differences that should be pointed out as well. Because of its location in the community and dependence on community members as clientele, such a center tends to view the client as a *consumer* of services. This attitude encourages a flexibility and responsiveness, especially when it is observed that members' needs are not being adequately met.

Also, whereas many counseling activities are focused on the individual client's needs, community counseling places emphasis on setting up programs that can benefit *the community as a whole,* as well as individual community members. Lewis and Lewis (1977) speak, in this regard, of the human services approach to community counseling, which "defines appropriate action in terms of the needs of individuals and the community, and never in terms of the helping methods with which professionals are already familiar and comfortable" (p. 6). They show how the study of the community often reveals both the cause of the problem and its cure. Prevention and remediation, according to their integrated model, go hand-in-hand; in one key respect this differentiates community counseling from other forms of counseling. Moreover, positive interaction between the client and the community in which he or she lives is the central purpose, and counseling efforts are well directed toward making the community a better place to live:

Community counselors are aware that human beings constantly interact with their surroundings. Because of this, counselors seek to affect the community as a total environment. Their goal is the creation of a community in which all people are allowed—and, in fact, encouraged—to grow and develop in their own unique ways. Extensive environmental programs are meant to help the community as a whole to become responsive to the needs, rights, and values of all community members. (p. 121)

Figure 16.1. Four approaches to community work. **Adapted from "A Formula for Identifying Styles of Community Work" by M. Morris, *Community Development Journal*, 1977, *12*, pp. 24–28. Used with permission.**

	Directive techniques	Nondirective techniques
Conflict theory	Community action Social action Radical social engineering techniques Psychoanalytic techniques	Community development, conflict style Client–directed attitude "Turbulent environment perspective" —sees organizational goals as problematic
Consensus theory	Community organization Traditional social welfare model Traditional bureaucracies Psychoanalytic techniques	Community development, consensus style Human relations approaches Client–centered techniques

Theory and Practice

One of the problems facing the community counselor today is the dearth of theoretical basis for action. Over the past few years, however, a number of highly sophisticated theoretical models have been proposed to help aspiring counselors better evaluate their options and take into account the different possible perspectives. Norris (1977) has developed an insightful four-cell theoretical model that differentiates between directive and nondirective techniques (fused with conflict theories or consensus theories). Conflict theories are those which explain the social order in terms of conflict, while consensus theories explain the social order in terms of agreement. The combination results in four cells, illustrated in figure 16.1. These cells represent management styles, program approaches, as well as counseling attitudes. Her work is particularly valuable in establishing research to measure efficacy, and there are currently several studies underway to determine the more effective approaches in the fieldwork setting.

One of the valuable contributions of the community counseling movement has been the integration of a wide range of helping personnel into the mainstream of counseling. It is now recognized that they have much to offer. See and Mustian (1976) discuss the role of the sociologist in the field of community mental health. As the focus of delivering services touches upon the interacting forces in the community, the significance of the sociologist becomes all the more clear. The sociologist, they suggest, may act as a consultant or participant. "As a consultant his contribution will include his efforts in the comprehensive community mental health center and in the community around such a center serving in a liaison relationship between agencies, and in promoting the importance of interactional processes through the training of mental health professionals and aides as well as the general public" (p. 274).

Many of the community-based programs are geared toward adolescents or older persons as their target populations, both of whom are covered in more detail in chapter 11. In this section, we will focus on programs that specifically highlight a community orientation.

Why do adolescents need community-based services, as opposed to individual counseling or group counseling approaches outside the community? Nuttall, Nuttall, Pallet, and Clark (1977) distributed a questionnaire to determine mental health needs for adolescents as they are perceived by both providers and consumers. Alcohol abuse and unemployment were generally rated their top priority problems, and "traditional one-to-one therapy and mental health consultation were given low priority." The researchers conclude that "mental health services should reduce their reliance on traditional modes of providing services. . . . More outreach and 'off-beat' approaches are needed" (pp. 284–285). Community efforts fit this bill nicely.

Many community-based programs are designed to assist emotionally disturbed adolescents who fare considerably better in their own community rather than in the institutional setting. Linnihan (1977) had described the Adolescent Day Treatment Center of San Francisco, which is "an effective community alternative to hospitalization for the treatment of severely disturbed adolescents" (p. 688). Many other programs deal with troubled, but not necessarily severely disturbed, young people. O'Brien and Lewis (1975) describe just such a program—a community-based adolescent self-help center, in a storefront setting indicated by a sign, "THE CITY . . . PEOPLE GROWING AND BECOMING." The center coordinates counseling, social work, employment placement, fund raising, and other activities, and the adolescents are brought into all phases. They are given responsibilities and are an integral part of the planning that will affect their center. This self-help concept is central:

> The self-help concept denotes members who work on their own behavior, striving to control their futures and change those conditions that affect their lives. Members gain a sense of prestige, self-esteem, and responsibility as positions of leadership and control within their organizations are made available to each of them. Self-help centers narrow the social distance between the care giver and the recipient by empowering members and equipping them with the tools and information necessary to meet their needs. (p. 213)

This is especially helpful in working with adolescents, they point out, since they are "traditionally treated as passive recipients of whatever service is offered," and this tends to weaken their enthusiasm and dull their resourcefulness.

The key to many successful programs is that the services reach the largest number of clients at the lowest cost. This action makes community counseling especially cost-effective. For example, Signell (1976) has described in considerable detail an innovative and economical community program that trains parents to be mental health workers with their own children. Steinberg and Chandler

(1976), in considering the problems of school-community-child coordination, have described community work in Hamden, Connecticut, in which coordination with the public schools enabled the implementation of constructive facilitative strategies. Some of the problems of communication and coordination are considered and the solutions presented, illustrating that where there is a recognition of the importance of such services, these services can be provided.

Community-based approaches have been used effectively with adults. Schlossberg (1975) has suggested community-based guidance services to meet the needs of the adult population that is experiencing some confusion in dealing with its new opportunities for growth and education. She cites a specific advantage of the availability of community counselors:

> The community-based counselors would act as educational brokers between clients and resources, their primary duty being to serve the client, not to maintain the system. Indeed as independent professionals, the counselors would be in a position to push particular institutions in ways—and with a wholeheartedness—that would be impossible if the institution were their employer. (p. 683)

In conclusion, we should point out that there is considerable overlap at times between agency-setting counseling and community counseling, and it is the underlying attitude as well as the scope of services provided that places the emphasis on one or the other.

Summary   In this chapter, we examined rehabilitation counseling and community counseling. We defined rehabilitation counseling as all efforts to help the individual adjust psychologically and behaviorally to role areas in a variety of life processes such as work, interpersonal relationships, locomotion, and other physical activities. We then considered vocational rehabilitation and the rehabilitation of the ex-offender; the released psychiatric patient; the drug addict; the mentally retarded; the physically disabled.

Community counseling was examined as a theoretical concept as well as a practical program approach, and several examples of successful implementation were cited.

Chapter Aim

To survey the scope of the school counselor's role, both in terms of expectation of the population served and the counselor's own perceptions, to examine the professional relationship between the counselor and other helping personnel, and to survey the needs and special characteristics of exceptional learners and consider specialized counseling approaches.

The scope and role of the school counselor's work is discussed from the points of view of the counselor, the teacher, and the student. We derive from these discussions some general principles of positive action that will help the school counselor perform more effectively in the school setting.

Three Perspectives

We note that much of the helping that takes place in the school represents a cooperative effort among counselors, teachers, psychologists, and other helping personnel. The "counseling team," which includes these helpers and the students' parents, is viewed as central for successful counseling outcomes.

The Counseling Team

Beginning with the Education for All Handicapped Children Act (PL 94–142), we survey the range of characteristics, needs, and special requirements of exceptional learners in the school setting. Topics covered include: the individual education program (IEP), the learning disabled, and the hyperactive child.

Counseling the Exceptional Student

Specific counseling approaches are discussed. The use of groups, consultation with parents as an intervention, and treating school problems, including discipline and adjustment problems, are all given attention.

Counseling Approaches

Counseling in the Schools

17

The term *school counselor,* which is preferable to the redundancy *guidance counselor,* poses a few problems of its own. Is the school counselor a counselor who simply works in the school setting, or is she or he a specialized type of counselor—as a psychiatrist is a specialized type of physician? How do school colleagues and clients perceive school counselors? What can they do to make an impact on the quality of school life, and how can they best assure that their services will be utilized and appreciated? How can they most effectively implement the driving force of the counseling stance within the context of the school setting? Before we can answer these questions, let us listen to a typical counselor, teacher, and student discuss some of their feelings and perceptions of the school counselor. Each of these monologues is extracted from a set of recorded interviews conducted at different urban and suburban schools. At the end of the three monologues, I will offer some comments to clarify the issues brought to light.

Three Perspectives

The Counselor Speaks

(I asked the counselor Mr. Davis to describe his duties and responsibilities at the school and to tell me if he thought his preparation and training had been adequate.) "It's really difficult to answer those questions, although when you first asked them, I had stock answers to give you. But you see, the problem is that in this school the principal is shorthanded because of the budget, so I have to fill in a lot of times when people are out, or maybe if there's a vacant staff position. You know, doing administrative types of things, like programming, attendance reports, filing, even . . . things that probably the secretary could do, only he can't afford to hire another secretary. . . . I don't know if this is the usual situation 'cause this is the first school that I've worked in, but frankly, I resent it.

"Sure, some of the time I'm doing what I was trained to do. The other day a fourth-grader came down, crying, and she couldn't stop. Her teacher had tried to find out what was wrong, but the girl refused to tell the teacher, so she sent her down to me. I sat down with her and we spoke for about fifteen minutes, establishing a good rapport, and she finally told me that her mother had gone away for the afternoon and she didn't have her house key to get in after school. She was afraid that the mother would yell at her, and that's why she didn't tell the teacher, either. But I guess she felt she could talk to me. . . . I guess I did the 'right' thing with her. You know, after that short interview, I felt real good . . . like I had accomplished more in half an hour than I sometimes accomplish in a week. I could really enjoy my job if I didn't have to put up with all the trivial paperwork."

(I asked him how he came to be given these minor clerical jobs.) "Well, it happened right from the beginning. The second day of school, the principal came up to my office. . . . I was just sitting and waiting for someone with a problem to come in, and he made a joke about how he wished he were a guidance counselor, living the life of leisure. Then he asked me if I would mind helping him with a little something—that's the words he used—so what could I say? Besides, I had nothing to do at that time, and I thought it would be a nice gesture. That little something involved setting up eight hundred folders for the new files. It took four weeks to finish. . . . Oh, about the teachers. We get along real well. They all seem to like me and we have some good laughs together in the cafeteria. To them, I have an easy job because I don't have to teach and I have my own office. But I don't see it that way. I always find that I'm busy with something, usually doing something for someone else. Also, the teachers don't really treat me as a professional . . . I mean they would never come down and talk about a problem or a teaching situation. They send down some of the kids they can't control, but that's about it. . . . Oh, it also upsets me that the students see coming down to my office as a threat, because they know that that's where they go when they don't behave. But it really shouldn't be like that. I'm not a disciplinarian."

The Teacher Speaks

(I asked this teacher, Mrs. Bruce, to discuss what she thought of the school counselor and if she thought the counselor was doing her job well.) "All the teachers have great respect for the counselor in our school because of something she did the first week of the term—in fact, it was the first day of school, when we had our teachers' meeting. She had just replaced Mr. Davis who is on sabbatical and who never did much of anything during his three years here. But at the beginning of the term, as I said, when we had our meeting, which she didn't even have to attend, she asked us if she could speak with all of us a few minutes after the principal concluded the official meeting. All of us stayed to listen. Then she told us a little of her background and invited us to meet with her once a week after school to discuss how things were going in our classes, what problems we were having, and so forth. At first there was some grumbling because most of the teachers didn't want to stay late, but she made it clear that the meeting was optional and only for those teachers who had things to discuss or wanted to learn from listening to the other teachers discussing their problems. We all thought it was nice, and unusual, that she was willing to stay late to help us. First impressions are important, and they certainly were correct in this case.

"She turned out to be a very dedicated and conscientious counselor. She always gave the feeling that she knew what she was doing, and that she had plans. For example, she offered to speak in our classes, either to assist us if we wished or to supplement some lessons in hygiene and the like. We all thought that was nice. She also organized quite a few after-school activities that the kids seemed to like, and we had a joke about how she would always run around the school doing things—always busy and active. Most of the teachers, especially after they got to know her, began to come to the once-a-week meeting, and you'd be surprised how helpful those meetings were to us. Instead of having to send down our difficult children every time they got out of hand, we knew that we could discuss at the next meeting our problems with these children. I guess you could say that each of us began to act a little like counselors because of those regular meetings with her.

"A few of the teachers, from what I understand, met with her to discuss some personal problems that they were having. I don't know if that's a part of her job, but it sure did a lot to increase our feelings toward her. I guess you could say that we really *appreciate* all the things she has done for us. She gives us the feeling of caring, and even more important, the feeling that she is competent and willing to work to improve things around here. She's always so busy that we try to handle our problems first, before going to her for advice. We're lucky to have her as our counselor, and she's done a lot to change my whole view of what counseling is . . . especially after that Mr. Davis."

(The student, an eighth-grade boy, was asked to offer his opinion about the guidance counselor at his school.) "I never met Mr. S (C3) when I was in seventh grade, but I heard the kids talking about him a lot, and I knew they liked him. I never got in any trouble, so I never *had* to go to see him, but my friend R—— was sent down last year for cutting, and he told me Mr. S is an all-right guy. . . . Near the beginning of this year my father died, you know, and I missed almost a month of school and fell behind in all my work. No one told me to, but I decided to see Mr. S on my own. I don't even know why. I was scared and kept putting it off, but finally I figured I'd go down to talk to him. When I got down to his office, he wasn't there, so I just left and figured I'd come back another time. But later that day he came up to my class and asked Mrs. B if he could speak to me. He said that the office secretary had seen me looking for him, and if I had a few minutes now, we could talk for awhile. I was really surprised that he came to see me—I mean he's probably busy and all. . . .

"Anyway, we talked for—it must have been over an hour. I missed my next class, and he said it's OK, he'd write a note for me. I don't even remember what we talked about—I guess about school, my friends, drugs, about my father's dying. . . . I know that when I left his office, I felt a lot better. He told me that he had a group of a few kids at the school who met once a week just to talk about anything they wanted to, and he asked if maybe I'd like to come to the group just to give it a try. . . . I said I'd think about it, and then decided to go. . . .

"Now I've been going for almost four months, and I think it's really a good thing for my head. We just sit around and talk, about anything we want to, and some of the kids really seem to have problems, even though I don't, but I can relate to them anyway. . . ." (I asked if there were any other guidance services offered in the school.) "Sure, there's a community club where some of the kids do things for the community, like have a 'clean-up drive,' and there's a work program for the ninth graders who want to work in a store part-time helping out, but I didn't get involved in any other things than the group. . . . Mr. S is always telling us about different things he's doing at the school, and some of the kids are interested, but I don't have more time than for just the group. . . .

"It's funny, you know, how in a lot of schools the guidance counselor is someone you get sent down to if you're in trouble, but in our school he's a real nice guy and you feel that you can talk to him about anything you want. . . . I mean, he's not a fink or anything."

Commentary   Clearly, there is some discrepancy between the way our first counselor perceives his job and carries out his duties; the way the teacher describes the counselor at her school; and the way the student presents the counselor at his school. These examples were chosen to illustrate the problems and pitfalls confronting the school counselor, as well as to show the many opportunities available to prove himself or herself of service to the school and to the community. Let us examine each issue, to gain a sense of perspective about the problem.

We note that our counselor Mr. Davis (C1) described on page 469, complains about being given unrelated work to do—things such as filing, administrative tasks, and so on. This is a common complaint of school counselors, perhaps the most common complaint. But it is evident, both from his attitude and from what he says, that the clerical encumbrances placed upon him are indirectly a result of his own doing and not entirely the principal's fault. By failing to communicate to the other school personnel the scope of his job as he saw it, by not having a clearly defined idea of what he was supposed to be doing—and doing it—C1 invited the opportunity he now complains about. It is not uncommon to find that counselors who complain most about the low level of the functions they are asked to perform are the very same counselors who fail to take the initiative in performing the higher level functions that they believe their jobs entail. Likewise, we find that those counselors who, from the beginning of their tenure, assume an active and dynamic approach, who make their presence felt from the first day of school until the end of the semester, suffer less from the misunderstandings and exploitation that plague these others. It is only assertive and confident school counselors, counselors with a sense of certainty about why they are there and what they are expected to do, who are not taken advantage of by others around them, particularly by those in administration.

Returning to the present case, the evidence is clear and indisputable. Compare the behavior of Mr. Davis (C1) with the behavior of the counselor who replaced him (C2), and we can immediately pinpoint the cause of the problem. C1, by his own admission, spent the first day of school sitting in his office, waiting for something to happen. He took no initiative, made no effort to bring his services out to the teachers and the students. C2, on the other hand, did just the opposite. She went out recruiting, actively and enthusiastically presenting herself and her services to the teachers. Unlike C1, she didn't wait for things to happen—she made them happen. When the principal came into C1's office, he noted the lack of activity on the counselor's part and felt comfortable suggesting some busywork for the counselor. C1 invited this to happen, and there is no way around that conclusion. It would be difficult for me to imagine the principal at C2's school asking her to do the same type of chores, since she was so clearly engaged in a definitive, constructive counseling policy which took up her time.

An important first rule, then, is this:

The school counselor should walk in the first day of school with a clearly defined course of action and begin at once to implement this plan and to let it be known to colleagues and to the students.

In this way, she or he not only protects herself or himself from the opportunism and misunderstandings of the other school personnel, but puts forth a professional appearance that will ultimately prove efficacious to implementing her or his plans.

Next let us look at the relationships between the teachers in the school and the counselor. C1 describes the relationship as "lots of laughs," but then goes on to complain that the teachers do not treat him as a professional. But how can they, if he does not establish a professional relationship with them? C2, the opposite of C1, establishes from the very beginning a totally professional and serious relationship with the teachers at her school. She explains what her services are, and she offers her services to the teachers. Consequently, they respond to her as a professional and respect her accordingly. They not only seek her advice but feel free to speak to her about their own personal problems. It would be difficult to imagine the teachers at C2's school asking her to do clerical work, in view of the polished professional appearance she articulates. It should be pointed out, however, that while conducting himself or herself professionally, the counselor must be careful not to become alienated from the teachers by implying either in words or in actions that she or he is more professional, or on a higher level, than the teachers or the other school personnel. This is a difficult balance to maintain—between eliciting respect and still maintaining friendship and cordiality—and it is a successful counselor who is able to hold the tenuous line between the virtues of confidence and certainty and the vice of elitism, without recourse to such artificial facades as coldness, detachment, and snobbishness. The school counselor, like the small-town doctor, is at most times a friend and comforter; but when needed for professional services, he or she must be someone who is held in the highest regard by constituents.

C2 seems to have achieved this balance well, while C1 chose to retreat from the professional stance and immerse himself in the pleasures of friendly badinage, which ultimately served little professional good. Our second rule, therefore, could be stated like this:

The school counselor must at all times maintain a professional attitude, which should not interfere with the ability to conduct harmonious and cordial relationships with other school personnel and with students. He or she must embody professionalism, but avoid elitism.

Finally, let us examine the relationships established between these counselors and the students at their schools. C1, we note, did quite well when given an opportunity to work with a student who was experiencing a distressing problem. But it was pure chance that this student availed herself of C1's services, for C1 made no efforts to reach out to the students. Mr. S (C3), on the other hand, made a conscientious effort to reach out to the students, to tell them about his services and to publicize them in the school. He did not wait for our student to come back down to his office, but rather he went up to the student's classroom to find him and to ask him why he had come earlier. This type of initiative is not only admirable and compassionate, but it is an effective counseling tool as well.

What we have discussed so far does not fully explain the scope of counseling in the school setting, although it does give us some context in which to understand it. In fact, the school counselor's role is not always clearly defined, and he or she may well be perceived differently by each of the people with whom he or she interacts during the typical workday in the school setting. And we should also note that in the school setting there may be some conflict or confusion about what the school as an institution expects and what the counselor sees as the legitimate counseling role.

The counselor's role definition is a crucial phase of his or her professional activity because it influences profoundly everything that is done. The job or role defining can be made somewhat simpler if the counselor can communicate to associates in the school the multifaceted, integrative approach he or she is willing to use. The counselor need not and should not emphasize either the therapeutic, the informational, the appraisal, the consultative, or the administrative functions, but rather should show the other staff members that he or she is integrating all these functions in order to improve the total service program for the student population as well as for the benefit of the professional staff. Such an integration will not only be appreciated by the others, but more than anything the counselor can say, it will help them understand the practical application of counseling and the essential role of the practical counselor.

The Counseling Team

Much of the work of the school counselor is carried out in conjunction with other members of the counseling team, along with parents, community people, and other interested parties who have the benefit of the student population at heart. Counseling is always an interactive activity, not only between the counselor and the counselee but between the counselor and other concerned people as

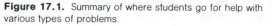

Figure 17.1. Summary of where students go for help with various types of problems.

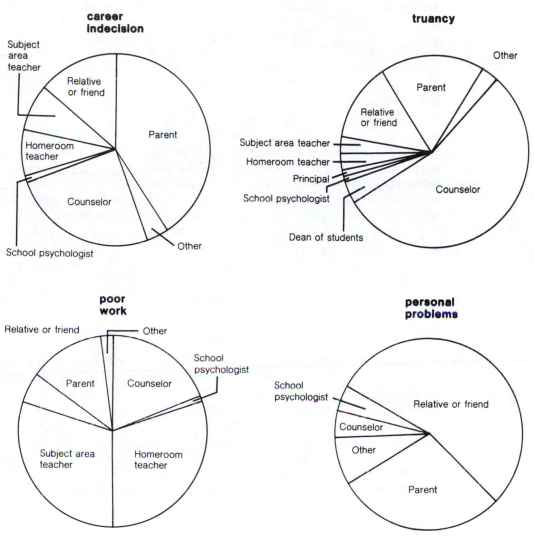

career indecision

Subject area teacher
Relative or friend
Homeroom teacher
Parent
Counselor
School psychologist
Other

truancy

Other
Parent
Relative or friend
Subject area teacher
Homeroom teacher
Principal
School psychologist
Counselor
Dean of students

poor work

Relative or friend
Other
School psychologist
Parent
Counselor
Subject area teacher
Homeroom teacher

personal problems

School psychologist
Relative or friend
Counselor
Other
Parent

Note: From "Consumer Feedback on a Secondary School Guidance Program" by H. S. Leviton, *Personnel and Guidance Journal,* 1977, *55* (5), p. 243. Used by permission.

well. Leviton (1977) found, for example, that in addition to the counselor, other concerned people to whom students go for help when they have problems included relatives, especially parents, friends, and at times, teachers. Most interestingly, as we see in figure 17.1 (from Leviton, 1977), the person sought for help depends much on the type of problem. By and large, parents were most important for resolving career indecisions, while the school counselor was important in

Counseling in the Schools

dealing with truancy problems. Note too that while 54 percent of the students would seek out a relative or friend to discuss a personal problem, only four percent would seek out the counselor. Later in this book, when we examine the role of the school counselor, we will see that this disparity is important, but at this point we should keep in mind that the counselor as a consultant or team member can be much more responsive to a wider range of client problems than could a counselor acting alone. In this section we will consider some approaches to the coordinated counseling function and examine the specific role of the counselor as a consultant.

The counseling team typically consists of the counselor, the teacher, the school psychologist or social worker, the consulting psychiatric specialist, medical and paramedical personnel (physicians, nurses, etc.), community personnel, and other specialists in the mental health and educational professions. We shall examine individually, constructive modes of professional interaction between the counselor and the teacher, between the counselor and the school psychologist, and between the counselor and other members of the team. As we do so, we should keep in mind that the contributions of these other team members are equal to the contributions brought to the team by the counselor. The teacher contributes an intimate knowledge of the client in the classroom setting; the school psychologist brings specialized psychological skills, including diagnostic ability, psychometric information, and the like; other members of the team contribute in their own ways.

The Counselor and the Teacher	Probably the single most important member of the counseling team, in addition to the counselor, is the teacher. Helpern (1964) describes ways in which the counselor can effectively assist teachers in the performance of their duties and in expediting the comprehensive counseling function:

Since he is concerned with on-going developmental processes and with a continuous study of the individual needs of all children as they progress through group situations, his [the teacher's] work must necessarily take the form of frequent communication and consultation with teachers. Teachers . . . frequently need additional help if they are to assess accurately the needs of children and of themselves. They need further information about child growth and development, about how children learn, about what constitutes normal behavior, about the importance of individual methods of response, about the exploded myths of the past (as the over-emphasis on the I.Q.) and about the new experiments currently being conducted. They need this type of continuing cognitive experience but need above all . . . the opportunity to talk about how they feel about what is happening in the classroom, in the school, about their reactions to the children, about their own anxieties and frustrations in their teaching roles, about their own interpersonal relationships and expectations. . . . Such opportunities for discussion may be offered in one-to-one teacher-counselor relationships or may be extended to discussion groups, to child-study workshops or to in-service training courses. (pp. 17–18)

According to their view, *the counselor functions as a facilitator of the teacher's growth and development as well as in a consultative capacity.* The counselor's two-fold function—facilitator and consultant—illustrates the complexity of the balance that must be maintained so delicately as she or he deals with the teacher, most likely to be seen on a day-to-day basis.

Lauver (1974) has developed what he calls a "systematic approach" for consulting with teachers. This approach consists of seven steps:

Step 1 Identify a problem situation in which a need for change may exist.

Step 2 Identify what constitutes a desirable outcome in operational terms—terms that will allow you to know whether or not the outcome has been achieved.

Step 3 Observe the situation for relevant information about relationships among important people, objects, and actions.

Step 4 Identify encouragers for desirable behavior and discouragers for undesirable behavior.

Step 5 Devise a plan for using encouragers and discouragers to achieve the desired outcomes.

Step 6 Try out the plan.

Step 7 Observe the results and compare what has actually happened with what was desired.

In many cases such a structured approach may prove helpful—especially to the beginning counselor who has not yet found an individual style.

Unfortunately, many instances of conflict between the counselor and the school pyschologist have prevented these two related specialties from achieving the harmony and cooperation they so much need in order to work effectively. Sources of conflict between the counselor and the school psychologist usually are a result of failure to adequately define their roles or the relationships between their respective roles, or failure of communication, which invariably leads to misunderstandings. Where the two are able to work together, as is sometimes the case, the consequences are most advantageous to the students.

A number of writers have scrutinized the coordination between the counseling and school psychology functions (Byrne, 1963; Gray & Noble, 1965). Gray and Noble, who have reviewed the literature, point out that "working together always demands some compromises and some giving up of cherished functions," and they argue that both the school psychologist and the school counselor must

The Counselor and the School Psychologist

recognize this in order to work together effectively. Perhaps the simplest solution to the difficulties that divide the professions is for school counselors and school psychologists to engage in mutual consultation, in which each utilizes the expertise of the other for the benefit of the student. The psychologist may be more adept at testing and statistical interpretation, while the counselor may prove to be a more skillful interviewer. By combining their talents and skills, it is inevitable that the student-client will benefit in the long run.

Consulting with Parents
There are three major reasons for conscientiously consulting with parents. First, the counselor is meeting an ethical obligation to parents, who are, after all, citizens and taxpayers responsible for the counselor's salary. Second, and more important, consultation with parents can and should help them become more responsible family members and able to deal more effectively with whatever difficulties in the home are manifesting themselves in the school setting. Third, and most important, parents become active members of the counseling team. By definition, they are working *with* the counselor to improve the life situation *for* the student-client, whom the counselor is directly interested in helping.

Consultation with parents reflects a specialized skill of the counselor. He or she must understand how to communicate effectively with a parent in a manner and style that is open and straightforward, yet not threatening nor accusatory. At all times, unnecessary nomenclature should be avoided; parents respond best to language which they can readily understand. When the counselor begins to flaunt technical vocabulary at the expense of clarity, although it may impress parents, it does little to promote a feeling of trust and rapport between the counselor and parents.

Parents can also serve as resource persons for the counselor. Rothney (1972) discusses this aspect of the counselor-parent interaction:

> Parents can make contributions that no one else can provide to the information needed about a counselee. They can describe patterns of their child's development; reactions to norms and pressures he has met; frustrations and opportunities he has experienced; persons to whom he has showed strong attachment or repulsion; and the models which through imitation and introjection he has adopted. Only parents can provide dependable information about financial matters when expenditure of funds is required to further the counselee's plans. (pp. 90–91)

Approaches to Consultation
Consultation is an art of its own. Simply meeting with a teacher, parents, or a professional colleague is not in itself necessarily consultative. What determines consultation is the approach used by the counselor in meetings with others. Technically, *consultation is meeting of counselor and another person (third party) to*

Table 17.1
Summary of Where Students Go for Help
(All figures are percentages of total responding)

Source	Choosing a College	Changing a Class	Conflict with a Teacher	Problem with a Friend	Financial Aid Question	Graduation Requirements	Career Decision	A Question about Sex	Problem between Students and Parents	Decision on a College Major	Information about Career Opportunities	A Personal Problem	Help in Finding a Job	When Student Is in Serious Trouble	Planning a School Program
Counselor	29	81	40	6	24	80	26	4	12	26	8	4	4	7	51
Dean	1	3	18	2	2	3	1	0	1	1	1	0	0	4	1
Career counselor	27	1	0	1	17	6	29	2	1	29	78	2	52	0	6
Teacher	4	7	8	3	2	6	4	3	4	4	2	1	1	2	5
Principal	0	1	10	1	3	1	0	0	0	0	0	0	0	3	0
Relative or friend	8	2	6	49	7	1	5	32	54	5	5	46	11	32	7
Parents	27	5	17	28	38	2	28	45	16	28	4	35	21	43	26
Other	2	0	1	10	5	0	7	14	12	7	1	11	10	6	4

Note: From "Paperwork, Pressure and Discouragement: Student Attitudes toward Guidance Services and Implications for the Profession" by C. E. Wells and K. Y. Ritter, *Personnel and Guidance Journal*, 1979, *58*(3), p. 171. Copyright 1971 American Personnel and Guidance Association. Reprinted with permission.

discuss a client. There are a number of guidelines the counselor may find useful in consultative endeavors. These guidelines are admittedly general and would at times have to be modified to meet the special needs of particular situations:

1. In a consultative capacity, the counselor must conduct himself or herself in a fully professional manner, recognizing limitations and strengths, aware of ethical and legal responsibilities, and sensitive to philosophical and theoretical axioms which underlie his or her work and support a commitment.
2. As a consultant, the counselor always recognizes that the primary responsibility to the client dictates the substance and spirit of this third-party intervention.
3. In providing advice or information to others, the counselor must always attempt to present it objectively and unbiasedly: to show the other person, when it is appropriate, that there may be more than one

way to look at a situation, that there may be legitimate points of view different from the one the counselor favors. In short, the person with whom the counselor consults always has a right to know and to choose.

4. Consultation implies cooperation. It is the counselor's obligation, more than anyone else's, to work toward this cooperative spirit. At times this may require compromise, at times, retreat. The counselor must be willing to subordinate at times the needs of his or her ego to the demands of the situation.

5. Goals of consultation should be mutually established by the consultant and the consultee. Misunderstandings can often be avoided when there is a mutually acceptable reason for sharing a consultative session.

6. When the person consulting with the counselor is overly impressed by professionals (as parents often are), the counselor must take extra care to impress upon the consultee that the counselor is not infallible and is as likely to make errors as anyone else.

Counseling the Exceptional Student

In the school setting, an important contribution made by the school counselor is in working with the exceptional student. It is estimated that approximately 15 percent of the students enrolled in school today are exceptional. By definition, exceptional students are those who "deviate from the average or normal child (1) in mental characteristics, (2) in sensory abilities, (3) in neuromotor or physical characteristics, (4) in social behavior, (5) in communication abilities, or (6) in multiple handicaps. Such deviation must be of such an extent that the child requires a modification of school practices, or special educational services, to develop to maximum capacity" (Kirk, 1979, p. 3). The school counselor works with such learners in a variety of capacities, ranging from individual program design to group counseling to vocational guidance. In this section we will examine some specific ways the counselor can be helpful in detecting exceptionalities and in providing appropriate services. We will begin by examining the implications of what is probably the most important legislation ever passed affecting exceptional learners in the school: the Education for All Handicapped Children Act of 1975.

Education for All Handicapped Children Act

In 1975 the Congress passed a law known as P.L. (for Public Law) 94–142. This law is called the Education for All Handicapped Children Act, and was designed to specifically mandate guidelines for the education of exceptional learners. Probably the most deep-seated ramifications of this federal law are found in its directive that all handicapped children are entitled to an appropriate free public education. The law goes on, in considerable detail, to explicate the meaning of *appropriate* in terms of what the school is expected to offer the handicapped, or exceptional, child. It also requires that the state provide all necessary special services for the child and evaluate the effectiveness of its program for each child, at least on an annual basis.

Further details of PL 94–142 reveal its philosophy as well as some of the problems of its practical implementation. First, it mandates that a child-study team, consisting of various professionals, evaluate each handicapped child's special needs. Second, it requires that parents be directly involved in the planning of their child's program and placement in special classes, schools, or programs. This includes setting up a conference between the parents and school officials in which the child's individual placement is discussed. Third, it mandates that each child be placed in the *least restrictive environment*. This is not the same as "mainstreaming," the placing of special learners in regular classes, with which it has been confused, but rather says that the child should receive maximum services to help overcome his or her disability, whether this is in a special or a regular class. Finally, it requires that each child have an *individualized education program,* an IEP as it has come to be called, which sets forth in detail that particular child's individual curriculum. This last feature is most important.

One of the most important features of the law, and certainly the one that has the greatest impact on the school personnel, is the individualized education program. In the language of the law itself, "The term 'individualized education program' means a written statement for each handicapped child developed in any meeting by a representative of the local educational agency or an intermediate educational unit who shall be qualified to provide, or supervise the provision of, specially designed instruction to meet the unique needs of handicapped children."

The Individualized Education Program (IEP)

The law goes on to explicitly state that this IEP shall include—

1. a statement of the present levels of educational performance of such child,
2. a statement of annual goals, including short-term instructional objectives,
3. a statement of the specific educational services to be provided to such child, and the extent to which such child will be able to participate in regular educational programs,
4. the projected date for initiation and anticipated duration of such services, and
5. appropriate objective criteria and evaluation procedures and schedules for determining, on at least an annual basis, whether instructional objectives are being achieved.

The counselor can (and should!) be an instrumental part in designing, implementing, and evaluating the IEP. This is helpful both in maintaining contact with the student's progress and in offering professional input from the counseling viewpoint. The state is required to maintain these records and to demonstrate that the programs are actually being implemented and regularly evaluated.

The Role of Parents	Possibly in part stimulated by the civil rights and antiwar movements, parents of handicapped children began to become militant during the 1960s and 1970s. Their demands, which stated in effect that their children deserved a free appropriate education in the least restrictive learning environment, became in substance the very language of the law that was finally passed by Congress in 1975. Moreover, parents were fully included in that law, included in such a way that they became responsible along with the professional team for the education of their children. They have become what is known as program participants.

First, the due process regulations of the IEP law require that parents be informed at the outset of the purpose and scope of the intended evaluation, and that they approve it in writing. Parents must also be informed of the results of the evaluation and told of the decisions made for placement. They have a right to challenge these decisions through appropriate established channels, and they should be informed of this right. In short, parents are participant partners of the team throughout the procedure.

In addition to the legal requirement of involving parents, there is a practical reason for doing so, and this should be kept in mind at IEP conferences or any other conferences. If the parent feels that he or she is a part of the effort there is more likely to be cooperation at home, and the parent will do everything in his or her power to encourage the child to do well in school.

Figure 17.2 shows the sequence of steps from initial referral through the development of the IEP. We see that the procedure is quite specific and well-organized.

The School Counselor	Because the law has been in effect for only a few years, it is still not evident at this point exactly what part the counselor will play in its implementation, although clearly counselors will become "increasingly involved in program planning, mainstreaming efforts, program monitoring, and counseling parents" (Humes, 1978, p. 192). Manifestly, the counselor can be helpful in the initial appraisal phase of the program, since the counselor will be familiar not only with the relevance, validity, and reliability of specific test instruments that are being considered, but also with the ways of communicating these test results to the parents at the IEP conference. Moreover, the counselor can serve throughout the year as a consultant to the teachers who are working with the handicapped learner.

Huckaby and Daly (1979), in looking at the actual activities of the school counselor during the first year of PL94–142's implementation, point out,

> When a teacher sees students who need more than what is being provided for them in the regular classroom, the teacher usually refers them to the school counselor. The counselor is involved in the process from the beginning referral for special education through placement and follow-up. After the referral is made, achievement data must be gathered, psychological testing done, case conferences with the teacher or team teachers held, Individual-

Figure 17.2. Flow chart of service arrangements

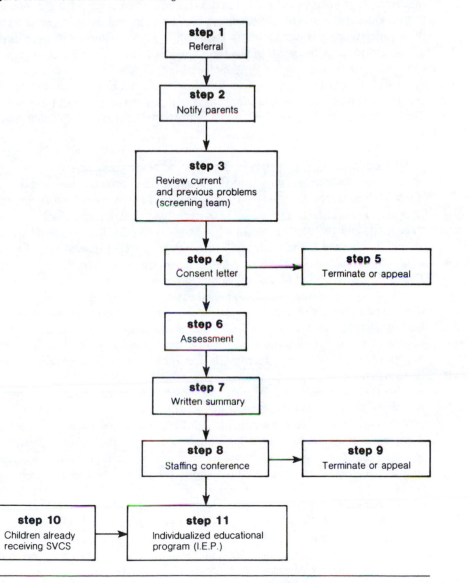

step 1
Referral

step 2
Notify parents

step 3
Review current
and previous problems
(screening team)

step 4
Consent letter

step 5
Terminate or appeal

step 6
Assessment

step 7
Written summary

step 8
Staffing conference

step 9
Terminate or appeal

step 10
Children already
receiving SVCS

step 11
Individualized educational
program (I.E.P.)

Note: From "An Approach to Operationalizing the IEP" by F. G. Hudson and S. Graham, *Learning Disability Quarterly*, 1978, (1), 1.

ized Educational Plans (IEPs) developed, a conference with the parent held, and proper placement made for the student. Throughout this procedure the counselor is involved, not only with coordination, but in interpreting data, in understanding and explaining the student's needs, and in helping develop plans to meet the needs of the total child. (p. 70)

With this in mind, let us briefly look at some major categories of learning exceptionalities, and then consider some of the counseling implications. We will begin with the most common single classification: the learning disabled student.

What Is a Learning Disability?

In answering this seemingly simple question, some gross misconceptions arise; misconceptions that not only lead to incorrect diagnosis, but work against appropriate treatment. Gearheart (1977) states that "in introducing the concept of learning disabilities to groups such as experienced classroom teachers, school principals, and the like I have found in the past that *at least* 30 to 45 minutes should be planned for the definition [and the subsequent discussion] of what is meant by or included in the learning disabilities definition" (p. 8). We see, then, that defining "learning disability" is no easy matter.

The most inclusive and accurate definition of a *learning disability* is that it consists of any condition or set of conditions which prevent a person from functioning at grade level in one or in several areas. This would include such conditions as perceptual disorders, motor disorders, brain damage (mild), or what are generally referred to as learning blocks that affect only one specific area of learning endeavor.

Several conditions may interact to produce a learning disability. A perceptual disability may be compounded by motor problems, with the result that the student cannot learn to write even though he or she is intellectually capable of doing so. Almost all learning disabilities are in areas that interact with other areas, so that the single problem can blossom into a serious symptom, similar to retardation. However, closer analysis shows that the child is not retarded, but simply experiencing difficulty in one or several areas. Six basic categories of problem areas are usually cited (Myers & Hammill, 1976, p. 26): (1) motor activity, (2) emotionality, (3) perception, (4) symbolization, (5) attention, and (6) memory. "These categories," they point out, "are not mutually exclusive groupings; in fact, learning disabled children tend to exhibit behavior associated with several, and occasionally all, categories." It is necessary, therefore, that in order to diagnose a problem as a learning disability, we should be able to assess in which of these categories the specific problem falls."

Table 17.2
Various Diagnoses Ascribed to H–LD Children

Group 1/Organic Terminology	Group 2/Symptomatic Terminology
association deficit pathology	aggressive behavior disorder
cerebral dysfunction	aphasoid syndrome
cerebral dys-synchronization syndrome	attention disorders
choreiform syndrome	character impulse disorder
diffuse brain damage	clumsy child syndrome
minimal brain damage	conceptually handicapped
minimal brain injury	dyslexia
minimal cerebral damage	educationally handicapped
minimal cerebral injury	(California State Legislature AB464)
minimal cerebral palsy	hyperexcitability syndrome
minimal chronic brain syndromes	hyperkinetic behavior syndrome
minor brain damage	hyperkinetic impulse disorder
neurophrenia	hyperkinetic syndrome
organic behavior disorder	hypokinetic syndrome
organic brain damage	interjacent child
organic brain disease	learning disabilities
organic brain dysfunction	perceptual cripple
organic drivenness	perceptually handicapped
	primary reading retardation
	psychoneurological learning disorders
	specific reading disability

Note: From "Hyperkinesis and Learning Disabilities Linked to Artificial Food Flavors and Colors" by B. F. Feingold, *American Journal of Nursing*, 1975, *75*(5), p. 799.

This is not always easy to accomplish. The counselor, teacher, school psychologist, or other helping personnel are confronted at the outset by a quagmire of confusion surrounding not only the acceptable definition of learning disability, but also diagnostic differentiation among the varying disabilities. As Komm (1982) points out,

> The term learning disabilities (LD) has proliferated to such a degree and has been used to cover so many problems that it is now an integral part of practically every teacher's lexicon. It has so permeated the educational literature that it is often used as a "catch-all" rather than a springboard to specific and detailed remediation.

It is clear from this passage, that there is much confusion surrounding the terms. Table 17.2 shows a variety of different diagnoses that are typically ascribed to learning disabled children (Feingold, 1975). But this is only the beginning of the confusion.

Hyperactivity is one of the most prevalent of childhood disorders and a major cause of concern to parents, teachers, and school counselors. It is estimated that 5 percent of the elementary school population exhibit mild to severe symptoms of hyperactivity (Ross and Ross, 1976). In this section, I will briefly outline the major theories and findings about hyperactivity, emphasizing the practical applications for the teacher working with the elementary school-age child.

Diagnosis

It is important for the teacher or clinician to distinguish at the outset between *hyperactivity* and *hyperkinesis*. Although the two terms are used interchangeably, it has been argued (by Zukow, 1975, among others) that they are not the same. Hyperactivity is a descriptive term: it adjectivally pinpoints certain manic types of behavior that are generally inappropriate to the situation. Hyperkinesis, on the other hand, designates a specific disorder: it is characterized by the child's inability to control behavior and actions. A hyperactive child need not necessarily be hyperkinetic. Rather, he or she may be a child with surplus energy, with a great need for physical activity, and with a symptomatic restlessness. The hyperkinetic child, on the other hand, in addition to these characteristics, has a short attention span and other attendant difficulties.

Zukow (1975) points out the difficulties of using the terms interchangeably:

The problem which arises in using the terms *hyperactive* and *hyperkinetic* interchangeably is more than semantic. For instance, frustrated adults reacting to a child who does not meet their standards can easily exaggerate the significance of the child's occasional inattention and label a youngster hyperkinetic.

A January 1971 HEW report on hyperkinesis says "the normal ebullience of childhood . . . should not be confused with the very special problems of the child with hyperkinetic behavior disorders." The report gives the following definitions: "There is no known single cause or simple answer for such problems. The major symptoms are an increase of purposeless physical activity and a significantly impaired span of focused attention. The inability to control physical motion and attention may generate other consequences, such as disturbed moods and behavior within the home, at play with peers, and in the schoolroom." (p. 39)

With these admonitions in mind, we can use the terms *hyperactive* and *hyperkinetic* interchangeably, with the assurance that a vital, active young child will not be misdiagnosed and misclassified.

Since hyperactivity may interfere with all major aspects of the child's life, it is vital for the diagnostician to know how the behavior is affecting the child's home life, social interactions, and school performance. A thorough history of the child can be compiled through the use of interviews, behavioral rating scales, physical and neurological examinations, and specific laboratory studies (Cantwell, 1975).

A personal interview with the child's parents serves a dual function. The skilled interviewer can elicit specific factual information about the child, as well as the feelings and expectations of the parents. It is also important to assess the manner in which the alleged "hyperactivity" of the child affects family dynamics. The following are some questions suggested by Cantwell (1975) for use in a parental interview: Is he or she more active than his or her siblings and peers? Do trivial things unduly upset the child? Is she or he quick-tempered and unpredictable? Is this child able to follow directions? The importance of these questions lies in the possibility that the parents might be encouraged to elaborate on "specific examples . . . and the circumstances which appear to precipitate certain aspects of behavior" (p. 22).

To further assess the degree of hyperactivity, parents and teachers are frequently requested to complete rating-scales. Ross and Ross (1976) recommend the Werry-Weiss-Peter Activity Scale for the parents' use. This questionnaire contains items specifically related to the child's activities in the home and should be completed by each parent. To evaluate school behavior, performance, and academic achievement, the Connors Teacher Questionnaire is available for school use. The behavioral rating scales are useful tools for diagnosis, formulation of a treatment plan, and follow-up evaluation.

The final phase of diagnosis consists of a physical and neurological examination together with a laboratory work-up to determine whether the disorder is due to organic defects, such as brain damage (including small lesions) or nonspecific visual or auditory impairment.

In addition to these procedures, investigation of familial and cultural factors is a valuable element in the diagnosis of hyperactivity. Many children who exhibit hyperactive symptoms may be experiencing severe reactions to their current life situations. Many of the behaviors that appear to a middle-class teacher as excessively active and socially inappropriate may be part of the normal repertoire of the culturally disadvantaged youth. Moreover, in many families, children are encouraged, either directly or indirectly, to behave in a way that most teachers would view as socially inappropriate. For example, the child may learn, either at home or in the peer-group environment, that it is necessary to exhibit continual bodily activity in order to gain any type of attention or recognition. It is not that such children *cannot* control themselves, but rather that they have been conditioned not to. When students such as these are referred to as hyperactive children, it is recommended that they be evaluated in relation to their siblings and peers (Klein & Gittleman-Klein, 1975).

Prognosis

It is generally assumed that hyperactive boys tend to "outgrow" this condition by the time they reach adolescence, although there is some evidence to contradict this assumption. At the present time, there is insufficient empirical evidence from which to generalize. Even if hyperactive youngsters *do* outgrow the condition, however, if appropriate interventions have not been made by adolescence, the damage is already done. The learning deficits that are acquired during the years that the hyperactive child is not able to function properly in the classroom result in a serious deficit later on. For this reason it is imperative that early interventions be undertaken in order to avoid these problems later on.

Borland and Heckman (1976) conducted a twenty-five year follow-up study of hyperactive boys. They examined the patient records at a Pennsylvania guidance clinic for boys between the ages of four to eleven who were treated between 1950 and 1955. From these records, they identified a specific group of what we would now call hyperactive youngsters. From this group of thirty-seven subjects selected, they were able to locate (25 years later) twenty-five men, twenty of whom agreed to participate in the study. Detailed interviews were conducted with eighteen of these men and, wherever possible, with their brothers. The interview focused on information about subsequent education, family relations, emotional problems, drug and alcohol addiction, neurosis (hysteria), and other related matters. Information was also obtained about the children of these subjects, and specifically about any problems they might be having in school. School records for these children were also examined wherever possible.

A perceptive analysis of the data showed some significant findings. By the time of the follow-up, all of the subjects and their brothers were either working full time or were college students. Many of the early symptoms (as obtained from the clinic records) were still present, although the number of the symptoms had been significantly reduced, as noted by the interviewers; but the subjects were functioning appropriately. Compared with their brothers, the subjects of the study worked more hours, many holding part-time jobs in addition to their full-time occupations. They also exhibited greater symptoms of nervousness and restless, hyperactive behavior.

The study was quite thorough and furnishes us some information about what happens to hyperactive boys when they grow up. Although there were a number of useful conclusions drawn, the researchers summarize some of their remarkable observations in this comment:

> Our findings indicate the men who were hyperactive 20 to 25 years ago are not experiencing serious social or psychiatric problems as adults. A large majority had completed high school, a few had gone to college, each man was steadily employed and self-supporting, and most had achieved middle-class status. However, half of the men who had been hyperactive continued to show a number of major symptoms of hyperactivity. Nearly half of the probands [subjects] had problems of a psychiatric nature, and despite normal IQ scores and levels of education, men who were hyperactive had never achieved a socioeconomic status equal to their brothers. . . .
>
> The number and intensity of symptoms of hyperactivity had decreased considerably in men who were hyperactive 20 to 25 years ago. Relative to their brothers, however, these men continued to show an excess of symptoms of hyperactivity and problems associated with the disorder. Restlessness, nervousness, and difficulty with temper were present in half of the probands at

the interview, and a substantial minority of these men continued to be impulsive, easily upset, or often sad, blue, or depressed. These characteristics clearly distinguish at least half of the men who were hyperactive from their brothers. (p. 673)

While much of the literature concerns itself with the diagnosis and etiology of hyperactivity, the bulk of recent writings has directed attention to ways of treating the hyperactive child both in and out of the classroom setting. Wide varieties of treatment approaches, ranging from formal psychoanalysis, to curricular innovations, to the use of amphetamine drugs have been proposed. Many, but not all of these theories, have been tested, with varying degrees of success. Silver (1975) has surveyed the vast literature and identified what he calls the "acceptable" and the "controversial" therapies now being used in the treatment of hyperkinesis. The acceptable therapies include special education, medication with stimulant drugs, medication with tranquilizers and antidepressants and anticonvulsants, and different forms of psychotherapy. These have not all proved successful, by any means, but they are acceptable modes of treatment, simply because of their repeated use. The "controversial" forms of treatment are neurophysiological retraining, orthomolecular medicine, alpha-wave conditioning, and food additives. Within each of these broad categories there are hundreds of different treatment approaches, many of which can be considered to fall into the "acceptable" categories.

Specific counseling approaches for reaching the exceptional student in the school and in the clinical counseling settings are plentiful. Some studies have demonstrated the effectiveness of the school as a setting for improving young people's intellectual, social, and emotional development. There are several major points that have consistently been included in most of the approaches that have been tried out in the school or clinical settings, some particularly relevant for preadolescents, some for adolescents, and some for all exceptional learners:

Counseling Approaches

1. Most students respond best when there is support from (or, at the least, when there is minimum opposition from) their peers. For this reason, the likelihood of a program's success is increased when the program comprises a peer approach (such as peer-group counseling or cooperative school projects).
2. Because of the adolescent's strong social orientation, which favors the norms of conformity and unabashedly ostracizes the very different, an adolescent's exceptional—or atypical condition—is likely to have profound social consequences. For example, a physically disabled adolescent is more likely to feel psychologically alienated and socially stigmatized than is the physically disabled younger child, who is more dependent on the family for emotional support and social recognition.

3. Complementing the peer group, especially for the preadolescent, is the influence of the family. The family should be included then, in most situations. Since many of the difficulties experienced by the preadolescent have either their causes from or their ramifications in the family setting, the most direct approach to effective counseling suggests the active participation of family members.

4. Adolescents (and often preadolescents) typically respond well to informational programs, so long as their emotional needs have been taken into account. Because the adolescent is capable of formal operational thought, the provision of information and the exchange of ideas can be conducted on a relatively high level.

With these general points in mind, we can consider some specific types of programs and counseling intervention.

The Use of Groups   The group setting is probably the most widely used modality in treating the exceptional student. While the general practices and applications of group counseling are discussed in the following chapter, we will point out here some specific group applications for the exceptional learner. In this way we will better understand the practical principles of implementation.

Generally, positive changes occur in the group context because clients are "given an opportunity to release their tensions and to examine their behavior with the help of their peers" (Goodman, 1976, p. 520). This is equally true of almost any type of counseling group, but it can be modified to reflect the specific needs of exceptional learners insofar as it allows them to share their common experiences with each other:

> Mr. Chien, a school counselor, organized a voluntary after-school group of students who were having difficulty making the grades that would help them get into college. They just got together to "rap," without a specific goal in mind. During the course of the semester, Mr. Chien noted that many of the concerns that prevented one student from studying were also preventing another student [from studying]. He realized that worries about dating, about being financially independent from parents, and fears of competitiveness were underlying many of the adolescents' problems. He encouraged them to share their feelings about these, and began to organize this general group into a problem-solving group to focus on these universal problems.

Sometimes the group's initial goals and methods may be less general, more oriented toward a specific problem or challenge. Career counseling groups, for example, have become extremely popular in recent years. Many school counselors run short-term groups to help students arrive at career decisions. This may prove valuable for the troubled adolescent who may not have realistic expectations about his or her place in the world of work. However, as Swails and Herr

(1976) point out on the basis of their research, the efficacy of such approaches is far from proven, "and the one clear finding is that the direct application of group techniques, such as those used in this study, to affect the complex process of career development in an eight-week period is expecting more than can be delivered for most students" (p. 259).

Particularly important in practice is the recurring observation by those who have implemented programs that the group approach with exceptional students works best when it is supported by parents, by the community, and by school personnel. No matter how well organized a group is, it can easily fail if it does not have this kind of support. On the other hand, where there is support, even a weak group can gain strength. Webster (1974), for example, describes a group for troubled adolescents that she organized in a rural mining town. "Faculty interest in dealing with problem students started a chain reaction. Teachers became motivated to select students who can benefit from group counseling and provided referrals for groups led by the two teachers and the [social] worker. The group treatment program is now built into the school's system, and can continue to operate with minimal consultation from the worker" (p. 657). Huber (1979) has described a group counseling approach for helping the parents of handicapped children get in touch with their feelings. At the other end of the spectrum, Miran, Lehrer, Koehler and Miran (1974) describe a behavior modification group designed to treat deviant adolescent boys that "ultimately failed because of social pressure. . . . [There was] a tendency for a suburban, middle-class community to give up on disorders, to declare them deviant and to punish them" (p. 370). They conclude that, in practice, "the behavior modifier must address the social system in which the deviant behavior occurs" (p. 374).

One of the main areas in which exceptional youngsters experience problems is in dealing with their parents. To be sure, parental conflicts are inherent in growing up, and even in the best of families these conflicts may lead to persistent misunderstandings. Where the young person is emotionally troubled, and therefore less capable than others in dealing with problematic situations, this challenge may prove especially stubborn. Moreover, many of the difficulties experienced by exceptional children and adolescents may directly or indirectly be a result of their parents' inability to understand their needs and/or an unwillingness to deal with them on their terms.

Consulting with Parents

The counselor can play a unique role in bridging the communication gap between troubled students and their parents. Kifer, Lewis, Green and Phillips (1974) have described an innovative approach for training predelinquent adolescents and their parents to negotiate conflict situations. The results indicate that with appropriate training, the adolescent and the parents can learn ways to communicate that will avoid conflict. Woods (1974), too, has argued that parents' groups are important contributors to growth in the treatment of their adolescent children.

Specific counseling approaches have also been translated into group and individual applications for dealing with exceptional problems. Underlying most adolescent problems, for example, is a lack of self-esteem, and this should be a goal of change underlying any program. As Lowendahl (1975) describes it,

> An adolescent—from the impression he has received from others and from himself—views himself in a dilemma. He has not the maturity as yet to accept the competence with the incompetence—a real mix—which is normal. His self-image may be entirely negative. He may not even realize it. The feeling of "I cannot" predominates his personality and if the areas of "I can" keep retreating to the point of complete disappearance—most avenues of help and restoration may be ineffectual. (Lowendahl, 1975, p. 170)

Counseling approaches, she points out, should be built on the strengthening of self-esteem. Of course, these may include a variety of approaches, implemented in different settings. Protinsky (1976) suggests, for instance, the suitability of using rational emotive counseling with troubled youngsters. RET helps the individual change his or her irrational thinking, which, presumably, is the source behind much of the trouble, into rational thinking. Hipple and Muto (1974) describe the use of transactional analysis (TA) in the treatment of adolescents and argue that this can be an effective method of treatment. Whichever method is used, it is generally agreed that the participation of parents is a significant advantage in assuring effective counseling interventions and programs.

School Problems

It is an error, I believe, to view the exceptional student's school problems in a vacuum; rather, academic or social problems should always be perceived as part of a complex interaction between different facets of the individual's world of interpersonal functioning. For the adolescent, poor performance in school may be a result of family problems, emotional difficulties, a frustrating or hurtful "love life," or any of the other failures to adjust to the demands of the adolescent period. Likewise, poor school performance may contribute to problems in any of the aforementioned areas. Parents and their children frequently quarrel about schoolwork, and many a student has had her or his immediate wishes and future plans thwarted by academic or behavioral problems.

Consider, for example, the widespread "reading problem," which we hear so much about. Often, when we think of reading disabilities we think of the elementary school; but in fact, many high school students read well below the minimum performance criteria. Shuman (1975) has pointed out the prevalence of the problem and makes the point that "by the time the poor reader or nonreader gets to high school, he is likely to be highly sensitive about his disability" (p. 38). For this reason, poor reading can become an emotional problem as well. A student may become truant, delinquent, or socially awkward because of inability to read. Consequently, an assessment of the adolescent's reading performance should be considered in any type of psychosocial diagnosis.

Many of the behavioral problems in the school may be a consequence of the young person's attempt to try out new styles of behavior. This actually serves a productive purpose. As Konopka (1976) points out, the adolescent has an "intensive need for experimentation," which includes a willingness to take risks that a younger child or an adult might not take. "Only thus," she concludes, "do they learn about themselves and the surrounding reality" (p. 178).

Many of the social adjustments required of all youths are more difficult for the exceptional adolescent, and this can in turn influence school behavior as these examples illustrate:

Joe, who has epilepsy, finds himself increasingly alienated from his peers as they all get their driving permits and he cannot. Throughout elementary school he tried to keep his epilepsy a secret, but when he had a seizure in eighth grade the whole school found out about it. The teachers, sensitive to the situation, educated the students about epilepsy and Joe did not encounter unusual cruelty from his classmates. Now, however, the practical consequences of his condition make him stand out, and he doesn't know how he is going to compete socially.

Pam, an attractive and intelligent senior, performs well below average in school because of a learning disability that was not properly diagnosed until tenth grade. She is placed in the slow classes, even though she is as intelligent as those in the top classes. She finds that she cannot relate to her classmates, and that she is not able to meet the kind of fellow she would like to date. The bright young men she is interested in think she is dull because she is in the slow classes. She also has difficulty in making friends because of this.

Vincent, who is in ninth grade, is hearing impaired, but refuses to wear a hearing aid. His parents have seen that he remains in the regular classes (despite his poor academic performance), fearing that he will be socially stigmatized if placed in a program for the deaf; but they do not make sure that he uses his hearing aid. Consequently, his performance in school is poor and he is shy but impulsive, unable to establish relations with his peers. He has a phobic dread that the other kids will find out about his hearing impairment, and much of his time is spent in trying to devise ways of getting out of situations where this could happen. Thus, he refuses to socialize and freely uses his fists whenever he is involved in what he views as a threatening situation.

We see in each of these situations how an exceptional condition makes the challenges of adjustment even more difficult.

Summary   School counseling was the focus of this chapter. We began by looking at the school setting from three points of view: the counselor's, the teacher's, and the student's. We noted how each perceives the role and function of the counselor, and pointed out possible areas of misunderstanding. We also looked at some literature that helped us understand where students choose to go when they have personal or school and career problems.

We then examined the counseling team: how the counselor works with other school personnel, such as the school psychologist or teacher, to help students. Parents are an integral part of the helping team, and we discussed some of the key issues in consulting with parents. Finally, we considered specific applications, theories, and questions regarding the exceptional student, and surveyed a variety of models to better understand the hyperactive and learning disabled client.

Chapter Aim

To examine the major challenges confronting the contemporary career counselor in today's world of work, and to consider the principal theories and specific applications of career counseling, particularly as it applies to client decision making.

A general survey of how social and economic factors have shaped a world of work which is different from the one which dominated our thinking years ago. A discussion of how these factors affect the way one looks at occupational prospects and some of the decision-making factors involved.

The World of Work Today

We examine career counseling as a synthesis of different counseling skills designed to help the client explore occupational opportunities and make satisfying decisions. The function of career counseling as a specific counseling modality is defined.

What Is Career Counseling?

We consider some practical counseling situations and examine how a counselor can be effective. We begin by considering the basic process of finding the right job and then examine two special situations: second careers and women in the world of work. We also look at how our work life affects all areas of our adjustment, and illustrate some of the points with two short case vignettes. First, we consider the situation of a client we call "Dr. Tom," whose unrealistic thinking prevented appropriate career decisions until a counselor was able to help. Next, we look at Carla who experienced internalized sex-role stereotyping in her career decisions. Finally, we look at applications of school counseling and observe how a "career day" can prove an effective means of reaching a large number of students with appropriate career information.

Practical Applications

The importance of leisure time is discussed in terms of overall work adjustment. A three-stage model of leisure-time counseling is presented: exploration, discussion, and integration. Each stage is then discussed individually.

Leisure-time Counseling

Theories of Career Development

The concept of "career" is discussed, and the major theories of career development are explicated. Super's theory, which links self-concept with occupational choice through a series of specific propositions, is first discussed. Next we examine Holland's theory, which views vocational interests and preferences as an integral part of the individual's personality "type." Roe's theory of needs combines insights from Maslow's self-actualization psychology and Freud's emphasis on early life development. Hoppock's theory, which integrates the strongest elements of all the above positions, is the last major theory elaborated. Brief attention is then given to the work of Ginzberg and to Tiedeman and O'Hara, who have developed a system based in part on the constructs of ego psychology. Finally, the ten "exploratory" propositions developed by Stefflre are enumerated.

Counseling Applications

Career Counseling

18

As a unified approach, career counseling comprises integrated efforts in what have traditionally been termed educational and vocational counseling. Vocational and educational counseling are specialized types of counseling applications, designed to provide informational and psychological assistance which may directly affect the decisions and choices the client is about to make with respect to schooling, immediate employment, and future job directions.

Career counseling directly touches upon the client's "real life" role activities. Moreover, career counseling incorporates in practice all of the different aspects of counseling we have discussed throughout this book: the psychodynamic phase of counseling, the behavioral change model, the group approach, the information-giving services, the phenomenological interaction between counselor and client, evaluation and appraisal functions. For that reason, it may be fairly stated that career counseling typically challenges the counselor to use all available resources and to apply all his or her training and skills in a single problem area.

In this chapter we will examine the value of career counseling in the midst of the rapidly changing occupational realities our contemporary society, paying particular attention to its articulated goals and applied techniques. We will see how theory translates into practice in such specific areas as second-career counseling, counseling women in the world of work, and occupational adjustment. It should be kept in mind that these types of counseling efforts are excellent examples of the integrative, functional, nondynamic counseling approach in its finest form.

The World of Work Today

Over the years, not only have there been pronounced changes in the myriad factors which determine the type of work one does, but cultural perceptions about working have also changed dramatically. While throughout history a person's work was usually a consequence of his birth—I say "his" because women were not considered a part of the world of work—as democratic societies evolved, large numbers of people found themselves with occupational options never before available. Coupled with this social change was an expanding technology that created new jobs considerably faster than old jobs were made obsolete, contrary to the widespread belief that technology displaces people from jobs (Bach, 1977). Whereas work opportunities were once basically divided between agriculture and commerce, in our contemporary society, we have jobs in agriculture, commerce, manufacturing, sales, technological development, and so on. But the single largest category of job is the service occupations, where the product itself is an individual's skill, an idea that would be incongruous in earlier societies.

Because the situation has changed so rapidly, it now requires quite a bit of self-assessment and cognitive adaptability for a client to understand his or her relation to the working world. Many challenging questions arise as one thinks about the future: What skills, qualities, and interests do I possess that would be relevant to the world of work? What kinds of opportunities are available? What do I have to do to avail myself of these opportunities? What will work offer me; what will it contribute to my life? As Tolbert (1978, p. 4) points out,

> Many young people today are uncertain and confused by the conflicting attitudes about work. They hear that the work ethic is disappearing . . . and that in many specialities a flooded market will cause unprecedented unemployment. But they also hear the unemployed asking for a chance to work, that work is the path to equality for minorities, that you have to develop salable skills to meet the demands of a technological society.

There is also the matter of choosing an occupational or educational level. Should I enter a profession, such as law, medicine, or pharmacy, which will require extensive training, or should I attend a two-year college to train for a position like paralegal assistant or medical assistant, which will enable me to earn a living sooner? Should I attend a vocational school to learn a trade? The choice between the so-called "blue-collar" and "white-collar" jobs, which in the past was usually determined by one's father's status, is now, for most adolescents planning ahead, a voluntary decision.

These questions lead to complex levels of decision making and many challenges of adjustment, especially for the adolescent. Many of the decisions made during these years of high school and college lead to career patterns in later life. Thus, appropriate career counseling interventions during the secondary (and even elementary) school years can have positive lifelong implications. In reality, whether one ends up at "just a job" or engaged in a career is often determined by the age of 18. It is desirable, therefore, to understand the functional distinction.

In describing the differences between jobs, careers, and work, Holt (1980) says,

> A job [is] something you do for money, something that someone else tells you to do and pays you for doing, something you would probably not do otherwise but do only to get the money. A career is a kind of ladder of jobs. If

you did your first job reasonably well for a while, your boss might give you a new job, maybe slightly more interesting or at least not so hard-dirty-dangerous. . . .

By "work" I mean something very different, what people used to call a "vocation" or "calling"—something so worth doing for its own sake that you would gladly choose to do it even if you didn't need or get any money from it. I add that to find our work, in this sense, is one of the most important and difficult tasks that we have in life, and that even if we find our work once we may later have to look for it again, since work that is right for us at one stage of our life may not be right for us at the next. (p. 14)

Working at a job one likes or does not like, for money, prestige or experience, the adolescent begins to come to grips with the multifaceted world of work. Different counseling perspectives may characterize this experience in somewhat varied terms. From the psychodynamic point of view, this phase of adolescence represents a breaking free of the family, the beginnings of an economic self-sufficiency which serves as an integral part of the adolescent's quest for individual identity. The humanists would view the adolescent's work as a fundamental component of the self-actualization process, of fulfilling one's potentialities in life. To the cognitive psychologist, the first real work experiences change our entire way of thinking about ourselves and the world. And according to the behavioral psychologist, the meaning of money, as a method of achieving our goals and satisfying our needs, undergoes conditioning during this period.

Although it has generally been believed that work is a useful part of the adolescent's total education and preparation for living, Cole (1980) and others have found in research that many young people who are working are experiencing a number of problems while they are gaining these benefits. While the "findings do confirm that for young people, working is a way to acquire practical knowledge that may help them later on" (p. 46), she points out that for many working adolescents, grade averages decline and the use of alcohol and marijuana increases. Still, she ends on a positive note, pointing out that "young people working at even the simplest jobs had gained a striking amount of practical knowledge. . . . Jobs are an important arena in which to test oneself and one's dreams" (p. 53).

Of course, the opportunities for growth and development through one's work are not limited to the adolescent years. Especially in our times, the world of work has become an important arena of development and adjustment throughout a life span. We will look at some ways in which career counseling can provide effective interventions for young persons and for older persons, who are either making career entry decisions or are thinking about career change in later life.

The terms career counseling and vocational counseling have been used interchangeably, although they have different connotations. Traditionally, vocational counseling, which is an offshoot of the vocational guidance movement,

What Is Career Counseling?

comprised only information-giving and directive job counseling. Specifically, it focused on the goal of providing the appropriate training and information which would enable applicants to learn about the job market and to develop the skills necessary to secure the jobs to which they aspired. But during the years there evolved a number of innovative theories of vocational choice, which, combined with the basic informational aspect, comprise the contemporary vocational counseling approach. We will see, however, that although early efforts centered heavily around the objective-informational approach, and later developments viewed the vocational choice within a dynamic, familial, and interpersonal context, there is a growing inclination today to "return to basics," and again to try to provide clients with the skills and information needed to succeed in a highly competitive job market.

Gelso et al. (1985) found that the quality of counseling intake for career counseling was significantly lower and less professional than for personal counseling, reflecting the lowered status of career counseling in the profession. In another study, Pinkney and Jacobs (1985) also found that career counseling was one of the least preferred titles and least desirable job activities for new counselors entering the profession. Looking at these two studies, Dorn (1986) concludes, "These results imply that career counseling is perceived as a secondary service within the counseling discipline and that this attitude may be having some deleterious effects on the quality of services that are being delivered to clients who seek career counseling" (p. 217). This is only going to change as career counseling comes to enjoy a better status, which can be done both through training and through the professional organizations.

The emphasis in contemporary occupational counseling is on *career counseling* (or, career guidance). Not only is the term different from its predecessor, but the focus of career counseling is more on the total person in the process of choosing a career, rather than on the single choice itself. When we view an individual's career as an integral part of his or her life-style, we can easily understand why appropriate career counseling interventions have ramifications in other areas of functioning. Tolbert (1974) defines career counseling in its contemporary usages:

> Career counseling . . . is really much the same as other types of counseling except that it focuses on planning and making decisions about occupations and education. As in all counseling, the personal relationship is critical. It includes exploration of values and attitudes, but information and factual data . . . are more significant than in personal counseling. Even so, it usually is not possible to help someone with a vocational problem without recognizing such other aspects of his life as needs, conflicts, and relations with others.

Expanding this concept to make it specifically applicable to the school setting, where most career counseling actually takes place, Tolbert (1978, p. 260) defines the scope of career education as covering the entire life span "from preschool years, and includes acquiring values and competencies, and setting goals for both in- and out-of-school experiences." These definitions show us the long way that the vocational guidance movement has come since its earlier days of supplying information. This is not to minimize the role of information in contemporary career counseling, but rather to emphasize the host of other significant factors which also play a vital role.

Contemporary occupational counseling service includes many factors, but it still relies heavily on occupational information. Concisely stated, the informational aspect of vocational counseling provides to the client all of the necessary information he or she will need to make valid, well-thought-out occupational choices. Two publications which will be useful to the counselor are the *Dictionary of Occupational Titles (DOT)* and the *Occupational Outlook Handbook,* both U.S. Government Printing Office publications. The former is a detailed listing and analysis of practically every conceivable job title and function in the United States today. The latter is an updated reference work that discusses more briefly the job function and presents current relevant data to illustrate job opportunities and predicted growth in each specific area.

Underlying all serious efforts in career counseling are a number of highly sophisticated and carefully developed theories of career development. The term *career* has come to replace its alternative terms *occupation* and *vocation* because of its broader, more inclusive emphasis. A career, Super (1969) points out, is "the sequence of occupations, jobs, and positions occupied during the course of a person's working life. Careers actually extend beyond either the end of the working life to include prevocational and postvocational positions such as those of students preparing for work and of retired men playing substitute roles." A recent objection, however, to the use of the term *career* over *vocational* has been lodged by Herr and Cramer (1972):

Theories of Career Development

> While the term "career development" has a more favorable connotation for some persons than the term "vocational development," "career development" does not lend itself to use in summarizing the behavioral development that parallels socialization. The term "vocational development," on the other hand, does. Recent theories view vocational behavior as a continuing, fluid process of growth and learning, and they attach considerable importance to individual self-concept(s), developmental experiences, personal history, and the psycho-social environment of the individual as major determinants of the process. (p. 39)

They go on to suggest that the term *vocationalization* be used to describe this dynamic process that is a "corollary of socialization." One could say, however, that this perennial debate over which term is preferable—*career* or *vocational*—is largely unnecessary and suggests academic carping. What is important, and what does influence all these theories, is the recognition that a theory of career development must account for the fluid, changing process of vocational awareness and feelings.

In this section, we shall examine a number of the major theories of career/vocational development. As we look at these theories we must keep in mind that a "vocational development theory is *not* a general theory of development that could serve as a basis for all counseling and guidance" (Tolbert, 1974). Rather, it is a specific, purposeful theory designed to help the counselor in his or her vocational counseling. Hewer (1963) argues that no single theory of vocational development is sufficient to explicate the many complexities of the individual. In sum, however, the bulk of these theories reflect the growing awareness of the intricate matrix of psychological, social, and educational factors that play a part in vocational choice and career satisfaction.

Super's Theory of Development

Donald E. Super has developed a theory of vocational choice based on the idea that the individual's self-concept influences his or her occupational choice, as well as ultimate satisfaction or dissatisfaction with that choice. The vocational choice, according to Super (1957), is the result of a developmental process that puts the individual's self-concept into practice. He lists ten propositions which characterize his theory:

1. People differ in their abilities, interests, and personalities.
2. They are qualified, by virtue of these circumstances, each for a number of occupations.
3. Each of these occupations requires a characteristic pattern of abilities, interests, and personality traits, with tolerances wide enough, however, to allow both some variety of occupations for each individual and some variety of individuals in each occupation.
4. Vocational preferences and competencies, the situations in which people live and work, and hence their self-concepts, change with time and experience (although self-concepts are generally fairly stable from late adolescence until late maturity), making choice and adjustment a continuous process.
5. This process may be summed up in a series of life stages characterized as those of growth, exploration, establishment, maintenance, and decline, and these stages may in turn be subdivided into (a) the fantasy, tentative, and realistic phases of the exploratory stage, and (b) the trial and stable phases of the establishment stage.
6. The nature of the career pattern (that is, the occupational level attained and the sequence, frequency, and duration of trial and stable jobs) is determined by the individual's parental socio-economic level, mental ability, and personality characteristics, and by the opportunities to which she or he is exposed.
7. Development through the life stages can be guided, partly by facilitating the process of maturation of abilities and interests and partly by aiding in reality testing and in the development of the self-concept.

8. The process of vocational development is essentially that of developing and implementing the self-concept; it is a compromise process in which the self-concept is a product of the interaction of inherited aptitudes, neural and endocrine makeup, opportunity to play various roles, and evaluations of the extent to which the results of role playing meet with the approval of superiors and fellows.

9. The process of compromise between individual and social factors, between self-concept and reality, is one of role playing, whether the role is played in fantasy, in the counseling interview, or in real-life activities such as school classes, clubs, part-time work, and entry jobs.

10. Work satisfactions and life satisfactions depend upon the extent to which the individual finds adequate outlets for his or her abilities, interests, personality traits, and values; they depend upon the establishment in a type of work, a work situation, and a way of life in which he or she can play the kind of role which growth and exploratory experiences have led him or her to consider congenital and appropriate. (pp. 189–190)

Super and his associates have developed these early premises into a comprehensive framework for assessing vocational choice and vocational development. He differentiates between the exploratory stage and the establishment stage of vocational development. The exploratory stage is characterized by fantasy, searching, investigating, experimenting, and testing out hypotheses. It is the period during which vocational images are molded and refined. The establishment stage consists of the period during which the individual actually begins to enact a career role and shape the career model into his or her own unique style. These stages may be considered maturational-psychological stages and may also be divided according to chronological ages.

Holland also looks at vocational interests and preferences as a part of the total personality of the individual. He refers to his theory as a *heuristic* theory because it is intended to stimulate "research and investigation by its suggestive character rather than by its logical or systematic structure" (Holland, 1966). In this sense, his theory is a working hypothesis by which he can investigate the details of vocational psychology. He explains the essence of his theory this way:

Holland's Heuristic Theory

Briefly, the theory consists of several simple ideas and their more complex elaborations. First, we assume that we can characterize people by their resemblance to one or more personality types. The closer a person's resemblance to his particular type, the more likely it is he will exhibit the personal traits and behaviors associated with that type. Second, we assume that the environments in which people live can be characterized by their resemblance to one or more model environments. Finally, we assume that the pairing of persons and environments leads to several outcomes that we can predict and understand from our knowledge of the personality types and the environmental models. These outcomes include vocational choice, vocational stability and achievement, personal stability, creative performance, and susceptibility to influence. (Holland, 1966)

The details, as he suggests, are more complex and form the basis for his empirical investigations. He defines six character types that include most persons: *realistic, intellectual, social, conventional, enterprising, and artistic* (Holland, 1962). The realistic type is "masculine, physically strong, unsociable, aggressive; has good motor coordination and skill; lacks verbal and interpersonal skills; prefers concrete to abstract problems. . . . Laborers, machine operators, aviators, farmers, truck drivers, and carpenters resemble this type." The intellectual type is "task oriented, intraceptive, asocial; prefers to think through rather than act out problems; needs to understand. . . . Physicists, anthropologists, chemists, mathematicians, and biologists resemble this type."

The social type is "sociable, responsible, feminine, humanistic, religious; needs attention; has verbal and interpersonal skills; avoids intellectual problem solving, physical activity, and highly ordered activities; prefers to solve problems through feelings and interpersonal manipulations of others; is orally dependent. Social workers, teachers, interviewers, vocational counselors, and therapists resemble this type."

The conventional type "prefers structured verbal and numerical activities and subordinate roles; is conforming (extraceptive). . . . Bank tellers, secretaries, bookkeepers, and file clerks resemble this type." The enterprising type has "verbal skills for selling, dominating, leading . . . avoids well-defined language or work situations requiring long periods of intellectual effort; is extraceptive; differs from the conventional type in that he prefers ambiguous social tasks and has a greater concern with power, status, and leadership; is orally aggressive. Salesmen, politicians, managers, promoters, and business executives resemble this type." The artistic type "is asocial; avoids problems which are highly structured or require gross physical skills . . . prefers dealing with environmental problems through self-expression in artistic media. Musicians, artists, poets, sculptors, and writers resemble this type."

Holland (1973) has attempted to measure each of these personality types through a Vocational Preference Inventory, which ranks the subject's personal orientations in terms of these six categories. Building upon this idea of six character types, Holland sets forth the following theory: *people search for environments and vocations that will permit them to exercise their skills and abilities, to express their attitudes and values, to take on agreeable problems and rules, and to avoid disagreeable ones* (Holland, 1966). A realistic personality type would function best in a realistic environment, while a social type would function best in a social environment, and so on. The choice and satisfaction of an occupation depends heavily upon the degree of concordance between the individual's type and his environment.

Holland's theory is complex and sophisticated. He discusses such diverse concepts as the relationship between heredity and environment, and the application of psychoanalytic insights to vocational choice. One main difficulty with his formulation is the serious question of whether people can truly be placed in the confines of a single category on the basis of their vocational interests and occupations. To support his theory, its chief points have been extensively tested and supported by Holland and his associates (Holland 1973); this is probably the most thoroughly tested of all the vocational theories. Other findings over the years have not been as clearcut. For example, while Hearn and Moos (1976) found confirmation for many aspects of Holland's typology in a study of choice and decision-making among college students, Mitchell (1981) was unable to confirm its predictive validity with a parallel group of students.

Anne Roe has developed a theory of occupational choice and job satisfaction based upon Maslow's ideas of the personality formed around interacting levels of needs, arranged in a hierarchy of importance. "In order to understand the role of the occupation in the life of the individual," Roe (1956) suggests, "we must first have some understanding of the individual and his needs." As she expounds this conceptual understanding of the individual and his or her needs, she builds a theory of vocational development upon this framework, utilizing both psychoanalytic and empirical methodology for the construction.

Roe's Theory of Needs

One of Roe's more important insights concerns the relationship between the individual's family background, upbringing, and later occupational situation (Roe, 1957). Deficiencies during childhood, she suggests, may be compensated for through the work that one does. If one did not receive sufficient praise and respect from parents, one may attempt to elicit these through one's job and consequently seek jobs where such praise and respect would be forthcoming. Likewise, for all the needs that were unmet at earlier stages of development, one turns to work to find gratification.

"In our society," Roe (1956) argues, "there is no single situation which is potentially so capable of giving some satisfaction at all levels of basic needs as is the occupation." She goes on to suggest that Maslow's hierarchy of basic needs (which she lists as "the psychological needs; the safety needs; the need for belongingness and love; the need for importance, respect, self-esteem, independence; the need for information; the need for understanding; the need for beauty; the need for self-actualization") can be all satisfied within the job situation. The job therefore becomes a primary determinant of one's psychological fulfillment:

In our culture, social and economic status depend more upon the occupation than upon anything else. Sociological as well as psychological studies are practically unanimous on this point, although there are, of course, exceptions. Feelings of personal esteem are also closely linked to the amount of responsibility the job entails. This is reflected in ratings of the prestige of occupations and in studies of job satisfaction. The degrees of freedom and responsibility in an occupation enter into these evaluations more importantly than do the levels of skill and training, or than do salaries.

People whose life situation is especially difficult may find that the status and prestige conferred by the occupation, or received from fellow workers, are the greatest sources of satisfaction for these needs. . . . Occupations as a source of need satisfaction are of extreme importance in our culture. It may be that occupations have become so important in our culture just because so many needs are so well satisfied by them. Whether the relation is casual or not, and if so which is cause and which is effect, does not particularly matter. . . . What is important is that the relationship exists and is an essential aspect of the value of the occupation to the individual. (Roe, 1956, p. 33)

In developing her ideas comprehensively, Roe has attempted to fit her ideas into a matrix-like structure, utilizing groups and levels to explain the occupational phenomena. The eight groups she lists are:

1. Service
2. Business contact
3. Organizations
4. Technology
5. Outdoor
6. Science
7. General culture
8. Arts and entertainment

The levels range from "professional and managerial" to "unskilled." Determinations about the personality of the individual can be made from considerations about the group and the level of his or her occupation and the group and level toward which he or she strives.

In an important paper written by Marvin Siegelman (1964), Roe discusses the influence of early childhood developmental factors on occupational choice. Figure 18.1 shows the relationship between the personality characteristics and the chosen profession (according to groups just listed). The basic core of all the different components—the center of the circle—differentiates between the *warm* and *cold* early home environments. The hypotheses suggested from this model, according to Roe and Siegelman, are:

1. Loving, protecting, and demanding homes would lead to person-orientation in the child and later to person-orientation in occupations.
2. Rejecting, neglecting, and casual homes would lead to non-person orientation in occupations.
3. If extreme protecting and extreme demanding conditions were felt by the child to be restricting, he might, in defense, become non-person oriented.
4. Some individuals from rejecting homes might become person-oriented in search for satisfaction.
5. Loving and casual homes might provide a sufficient amount of relatedness that other factors such as abilities would determine interpersonal directions more than personal needs. (pp. 7–8)

Figure 18.1. Early home climate and its relation to Roe's occupational classification. **From Anne Roe and Marvin Seigelman, *The Origin of Interest*, 1964, p. 6, by the American Personnel and Guidance Association. Reprinted with permission.**

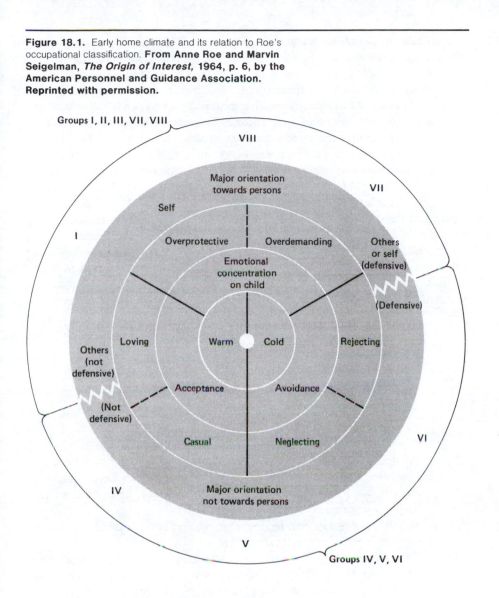

As much influence as Roe has had upon subsequent theories of career development and occupational choice, she has suffered her fair share of criticism as well. Carkhuff, Alexik, and Anderson (1967) give a well-tempered summary of the weaknesses of Roe's position:

Instead of attempting to generalize her findings into a unique and comprehensive system, Roe apparently seeks to "rationalize" her results by drawing from analytic theory and Maslow's postulates to support her findings. She has neither systematically deduced her hypotheses from these systems nor does she work inductively to these systems. . . . Roe neither makes systematic derivations from the theories that she proposes nor is the theory with which she deals a generalization of her findings, serving to organize the available evidence and guide the search for better evidence. Rather, she appears to seek entrance to already existing systems. She does not make sufficient attempt to qualify the existing theories in terms of her findings and, thus, provides no unique theory of her own to encompass her results. In summary, then, according to the schema, Roe makes no justifiable generalizations from her data above the level of what has been defined as laws. (pp. 337–338)

While these laws do have some validity, there are a number of strong points about Roe's system that should also be mentioned. Her system allows an integrative role for the job function and relates occupational choice to the entire structure of the personality. From a counseling point of view, Roe's insights help the counselor better understand the variety of factors that play a part in the individual's decision to pursue or avoid certain types of jobs and help the counselor understand why a job does or does not meet the client's needs. Moreover, her work sets a foundation from which further empirical research may be conducted to supplement the work that Roe and her associates have already undertaken (Roe et al., 1966; Roe & Siegelman, 1964).

Hoppock's Theory

Hoppock (1967) lists the ten major points of his theory as follows:

1. Occupations are chosen to meet needs.
2. The occupation that we choose is the one that we believe will best meet the needs that most concern us.
3. Needs may be intellectually perceived, or they may be only vaguely felt as attractions which draw us in certain directions. In either case, they may influence choices.
4. Vocational development begins when we first become aware that an occupation can help to meet our needs.
5. Vocational development progresses and occupational choice improves as we become better able to anticipate how well a prospective occupation will meet our needs. Our capacity thus to anticipate depends upon our knowledge of ourselves, our knowledge of occupations, and our ability to think clearly.
6. Information about ourselves affects occupational choice by helping us to recognize what we want and by helping us to anticipate whether or not we will be successful in collecting what the contemplated occupation offers to us.
7. Information about occupations affects occupational choice by helping us to discover the occupations that may meet our needs and by helping us to anticipate how well satisfied we may hope to be in one occupation as compared with another.

8. Job satisfaction depends upon the extent to which the job that we hold meets the needs that we feel it should meet. The degree of satisfaction is determined by the ratio between what we have and what we want.

9. Satisfaction can result from a job which meets our needs today or from a job which promises to meet them in the future.

10. Occupational choice is always subject to change when we believe that a change will better meet our needs. (pp. 111–112)

We see how Hoppock's ideas represent a "composite theory," and it is probably for this reason that his writing has enjoyed the wide popularity it has over the years. His ideas are compatible with other theorists, and the concordance between various points of view in vocational counseling attests both to the unity of the discipline and to the integrity of the different systems.

In addition to these theories discussed, there are three other significant theories of career development which, because of limitations of space, will be discussed only briefly. For a more comprehensive discussion of any of these theories, the reader should check the bibliographic information in the relevant references at the end of the book to obtain the particular publication in which it appears.

Other Theories of Career Development

Eli Ginzberg's (1972) "Theory of Occupational Choice," as it has been reformulated over the years, is briefly summarized as follows:

Occupational choice is a process that remains open as long as one makes and expects to make decisions about his work and career. In many instances it is coterminous with his working life.

While the successive decisions that a young person makes during the preparatory period will have a shaping influence on his later career, so will the continuing changes that he undergoes in work and life.

People make decisions about jobs and careers with an aim of optimizing their satisfactions by finding the best possible fit between their priority needs and desires and the opportunities and constraints that they confront in the world of work.

Our reformulated theory is that *occupational choice is a lifelong process of decision-making in which the individual seeks to find the optimal fit between his career preparation and goals and the realities of the world of work.* (p. 172, italics added)

This reformulation differs somewhat from the original theory. Because it is more recent and based on more experimentation, it should be considered the definitive statement, supplanting the original formulation.

Tiedeman and O'Hara have developed a system based in part on the constructs of ego personality. They view vocational development as part of a continuing process of the individual differentiating his or her ego identity. They describe career development as "the process of fashioning a vocational identity through differentiation and integration of the personality as one confronts the problem of work in living" (Tiedeman & O'Hara, 1963). Heavy on theory and conceptual frameworks, the writings of Tiedeman and O'Hara integrate many of the insights developed by Freud, Erikson, Super, Roe, and Ginzberg. They have attempted over the years to integrate a plethora of new research data into their models, with the result that "their theory cannot emerge beyond the status of a collection of lower-level generalizations. Instead of streamlining and simplifying their theorems, they seem to be moving in the opposite direction—toward encompassing as diverse data as possible, hoping that in the future, out of the midst of chaos, order will emerge" (Carkhuff, Alexik & Anderson, 1967).

Stefflre (1966) has developed ten propositions, which he calls "exploratory," that summarize many of the insights developed by some of the other theorists we have considered. These ten propositions are:

1. An occupation permits an expression of the individual's public personality which is a special instance of differentiation of function.
2. The occupational persona represents the individual's choice among those masks he would like to wear and those that society will permit him to wear.
3. An occupational role may represent avoidance reaction as well as, or instead of, approach reaction.
4. The importance of the work aspect of the public personality—the occupational persona—varies from being psychologically peripheral to being central. In Havighurst's phraseology, the occupation may vary from being "ego involving" to being "society maintaining."
5. The societally limiting forces that determine the occupational persona of any individual vary from the accidental to the essential. If we agree that it is a rare individual who can choose his occupational persona with complete freedom, we must see what sort of limitations he may encounter from society.
6. The expression of the public personality through an occupation—the selection of an occupational persona—must be made on incomplete information. . . . We cannot possibly know all about ourselves when we move into an occupation, nor can we know all about a particular occupational role until we experience it.
7. The stability of the choice of an occupation after additional information about the work role becomes available varies directly with the psychological commitment to the occupation on the part of the chooser.
8. As further information about the self comes into light, it is more apt to lead to change within the occupation for those who are psychologically committed to the occupation as opposed to change to a different occupation for others.

9. The occupational persona and the self-concept have a symbiotic relationship that moves them toward congruence.
10. The selection of an occupational persona may express any of four relationships between the self and society. The first relationship might be called "fitting.". . . A second relationship might be called "permitting." In this situation the self-concept is not completely congruent with the self. . . . A third relationship might be called "transforming." In this situation the self-concept is congruent with the self but the individual does not wish to display all of his self-concept in an occupation. . . . A fourth relationship may be thought of as "binding." In this situation the self-concept is congruent with the occupational persona and the occupational persona congruent with the self-concept. However, the occupational persona had been selected on the basis of accurate occupational role expectations.

We see from Stefflre's propositions, as well as from the other theories presented, that contemporary models of career development are highly sophisticated theories which account for the psychological as well as the sociological and educational influences on career choices, career satisfaction, and adjustment to career patterns.

When a client comes for vocational counseling, the total effort usually involves any of the following job functions of the vocational counselor, either independently or in conjunction with each other:

Practical Applications

1. Identifying the client's vocational interests and abilities. This may be accomplished by an interview, or may require the administration of vocational interest and aptitude inventories.
2. Helping the client learn how to increase his or her vocational skills, aiming toward levels of competency necessary for success in the job market.
3. Helping the client deal with his or her feelings about work. This may include persistent feelings of frustration in finding the right job; difficulties at work; feelings of hopelessness that preclude looking for work.

In many cases, these three aspects of career counseling are combined in practice. The theories of career development we discussed above are sometimes useful in carrying out integrated efforts designed to help a person find and adjust to productive work. The theories give us a rationale for what we are doing, and guide us in our actions (in the same way general theories of counseling guide the counselor during the counseling interview). Let us examine some specific situations in our contemporary world of work and two case illustrations that help us understand the application of some of the principles.

We will begin by looking at the basic process of finding a job and all that this includes: working through conflicts that inhibit successful job hunting, learning appropriate behaviors, preparing an effective resumé, making the right impression at the job interview, etc. Then, we will look at two particular situations: second careers and the special plight of women in the contemporary world of work. Finally, we will consider how work affects all different aspects of our psychological adjustment and consider how a counselor can be helpful in occupational-stress counseling.

To illustrate some of these points, we will consider the case vignette of "Dr. Tom," a young man unable to hold on to a job because his self-image and self-assessment of his abilities were unrealistic. The second case, "A Woman's Place," is about a girl who is not able to break away from the sex-role stereotypes she had been taught.

Finding the "Right" Job

The theories discussed above are typically helpful in understanding why we seek certain kinds of jobs, why we are likely to find satisfaction in some job categories more than others, and how our past exerts an influence in our present vocational aspirations. But actually, they tell us little about such practical matters as how to obtain the "right job" when once we find it. And, if our client becomes frustrated in getting a job, all the theories in the world will do little for his or her well-being. Fortunately, psychological research has been helpful in this area, pointing out the factors that weigh for and against a prospective employer hiring you.

Once a person has decided the kind of job he or she wants, the next step is to find the job and to try to obtain it. This is the core of the competitive process in the world of work; and many of us will, unfortunately, associate much of our feeling of self worth with how well or poorly we fare in securing a job we feel right about (Super & Hall, 1978). In reality, job-seeking, interviewing for a job, and making career changes are stressful periods of life, accompanied often by anxiety, self-doubt, and a possible loss of self-esteem.

It is essential, therefore, to help the client learn to remain as objective as possible, not confusing rejection of one's job application with personal rejection. Employers can sense when an applicant feels secure; and such an applicant is more likely to get the job since he or she is communicating a sense of self-worth to the interviewer.

Preparing a Resumé

Typically, one's resumé precedes an applicant to the job. In fact, it is from the mass of resumés submitted that potential employers make decisions about whom to interview, and for which positions. The effective career counselor should be familiar with the basic principles of effective resumé preparation and should possess the capacities needed to help the client with his or her specific resumé problems.

One's resumé should reflect accurately (and favorably) what the applicant has to offer. Much empirical research has been conducted on preparing an effective resumé, and for a good reason. Field and Holley (1976) correctly point out that an effective resumé is one of the best assurances of obtaining an initial interview. Moreover, the process of preparing a resumé can help a person determine where he or she is heading, where he or she stands objectively in relation to what the individual wants to do occupationally.

Stephens, Watt, and Hobbs (1979) conducted an objective survey to learn what factors dispose employers favorably when they look at resumés. In surveying personnel managers who read resumés regularly, and who actually do the hiring in many cases, they found that,

> . . . a succinct clear, well-organized resumé that is high in information content and conservative in style, will likely obtain the most favorable response, independent of other format variations. . . . (p. 33)

Specifically, the following factors were found to be most important in effective resumé preparation:

Resumé Content	*Resumé Format*
Education	Proper English
Work Experience	Clean Corrections
Professional References	Neatness
Affiliations	Correct Spelling
Awards and Achievements	
Personal Data	

Figure 18.2 shows a resumé that accurately and favorably reflects the work experience and professional potential of a person applying for a position as computer programmer.

The Employment Interview

If the resumé functions in arousing the interest of the prospective employer, the next step is the employment interview. This is the opportunity for applicant and employer to "take stock" of each other on a more personal level. The applicant should freely ask questions to determine whether the position is right for him or her, and should try to communicate, in the limited time available, a picture which is representative of what the employer should expect if the applicant is selected.

Most of the qualities evaluated in the employment interview do not differ from job to job, although certain kinds of positions may require special abilities in any of these areas. In general, however, these are the eight key factors evaluated by interviewers:

Grooming This varies from job to job, but for every job category there are acceptable and unacceptable styles of dress. Cleanliness and personal orderliness are always important, since a disheveled and dirty person will make a negative impression on any interviewer.

Figure 18.2.

Victor K. Ratliff
568 Edgewater Road
Fairview, NJ 07022
(201) 931-1279

GENERAL OVERVIEW:

During my 5 years as a special education teacher, I have worked consistently to broaden the life possibilities, the skills development, and the vocational opportunities for my educable mentally retarded students. In addition to emphasizing survival skills, I have attempted to instill in each student a sense of initiative and purpose-- of his or her self-worth-- and to foster and nurture each student's creative possibilities to their fullest. Moreover, my diverse responsibilites at the Quentin Compson School have demanded a mix of teaching, administrative, testing, and interpersonal skills. During my internship as a Learning Consultant, I administered diagnostic tests, worked with the Child Study Teams, and wrote Individualized Educational Plans, working with a group of professionals and academic supervisors. I am now seeking a position where I can bring to bear the fruits of my experience in a challenging new role, with expanded opportunities for enjoying the rewards of what I can offer.

EDUCATION:

1978	Certification, LDT/C	Bloomfield State College
1974	M.A.	Drake University
1969	B.S.E.	Memphis State University

NEW JERSEY STATE CERTIFICATIONS:

Learning Disabilities Teacher -- Consultant, Regular
Principal, Regular
Supervisor, Regular
Teacher of the Handicapped, Regular

PROFESSIONAL EXPERIENCE:

1969 to   Teacher, Quentin Compson School
                 Qeuntin Compson School is a public, non-graded school
present   for students ranging in age from 13 to 21 years who have
                 been classified as educable mentally retarded.

REFERENCES:

    Attached

Presentation of Self   Invariably, one's personality will break through, even in a ten or fifteen minute interview. Be yourself, but you don't necessarily show every aspect of yourself. Normal etiquette is better than being overly flattering or obsequious.

Confidence   This should not be confused with conceit or self-preoccupation, but rather should represent a fair picture of one's realistic abilities.

Expression of Ideas   For many, this is a big problem. Sometimes because we are nervous, we cannot express our ideas fluently, and we stumble, become embarrassed, and do not show the interviewer how clearly we really are capable of thinking. If you are someone who becomes tongue-tied at interviews, it might be a good idea to have a rehearsal with a friend, or to write down and organize some of the ideas you think you will be speaking about at the interview.

Alertness   The interviewer will probably test the applicant's alertness by asking questions and observing whether the applicant is able to respond appropriately, whether he or she is paying attention.

Motivation/Attitude   For almost every job, motivation is a prime requisite for success. The interviewer will probably ask questions designed to ascertain whether the job means more to the person than just a way of earning money.

Educational Background   This should be accurately described on the resumé, and elaborated upon during the interview.

Prior Experience   The interviewer may want to know, in addition to descriptions of past jobs, just how well or poorly the applicant got along with coworkers, supervisors, etc. The applicant should point out wherever past experience is directly relevant to the position sought.

He came to Dr. Winder's office with the enthusiasm and spirit of a person who had just landed the best of jobs. In fact, he was unemployed. He dressed as a successful man of no small means would, conservatively but expensively. In fact, his wife gave him just enough money for carfare and for the office visit. He spoke to Dr. Winder as one professional to another, conveying the feeling that it was difficult today for professional people like them to find the right position. In fact, although he had graduated from an excellent community college, he had not done well enough in the competitive atmosphere to get into a four-year college. He discussed his personal life openly, giving the clear and unequivocal impression that his wife deeply respected him and had "married up" when she married him, since she herself never went to college. In truth, she was ready to divorce him, so disgusted had she become with his bloated posturing and his never working. Thus began Dr. Winder's case, which came to be known as "Dr. Tom."

During the first few sessions, a number of key points were brought out. Tom felt himself eminently capable of functioning in the role of a psychotherapist, and belittled the need for legitimate professional training. He recognized, how-

"Dr. Tom": A Case Example

ever, that from a practical point of view it was necessary. But he couldn't quite accommodate the fact that no college would accept him. He had been working while attending community college, and attributed his poor grades to the enervating effect of the job. He vowed, therefore, not to work anymore at anything except what he really wanted to do—to be a professional. Since this was completely unrealistic, he was at the present time neither working nor going to school. Instead, he spent his days at home, happily dispensing "psychological advice" to the women on the block. They talked to him about their children, about their problems, about their nephews and nieces. It was these women, believing that Tom was enrolled in a psychology doctoral program, who dubbed him "Dr. Tom."

Tom liked Dr. Winder, and this was used advantageously in the treatment. When Dr. Winder determined what type of counseling would be best, he used his "professional colleague" approach to communicate with Tom, whom he knew would deeply resent being treated as a client. He decided to discuss with Tom the possibility of taking some vocational interest tests and some aptitude tests to see if perhaps there could be some intersection between what Tom could do and what he wanted to do.

Tom agreed and took the tests. They showed he was slightly above average in intelligence, and interested in a job where he would work with people in a helping capacity. Almost all of the jobs required advanced degrees, and Dr. Winder felt that he could earn such a degree if he applied himself. But Dr. Winder also recognized that Tom's problems in schools were an indirect result of his poor writing skills. Since many of his courses required term papers, Tom had received low grades in these courses despite receiving "B's" on the finals. Thus, in Dr. Winder's opinion Tom would have to enroll in a remedial writing course.

Because this was presented to Tom as a means to an end, he agreed to it. Since he seemed to be agreeable, Dr. Winder discussed with him the possibility of getting a part-time job. Tom was at first reluctant, but he did acknowledge that his marriage was not going to work out if Gina went to work each day and he did not. The next question was, What kind of job could Tom get and would he be able to hold on to it? Dr. Winder got the distinct impression that Tom had alienated his bosses by making them feel stupid; that if they didn't have an advanced college degree, he had no respect for them. Thus, even if he did manage to get a job, there would be problems ahead. Dr. Winder explored this with Tom, and we offer a brief section of the transcript.

DW Tom, even if you do get a job, what do you think is going to happen?

TM Are you worried that I'll botch it up again? You don't understand what it's like to have to work with some of those idiots I have to work with. They're so uneducated, and what really ticks me off is that they are the bosses and I am only looked at as a measly worker . . . an employee.

DW You may feel that way, and that's fine. But why do you have to let *them* know it? Why can't you feel that way without expressing it?

TM   (*Thinks for a minute*) Because if I don't tell them, then how are they going to know? If I don't let them see where I'm heading, then they're naturally going to think that I am nothing but what I appear on the job. And that's just not true.

DW   So you are telling them in order that they'll think a certain way about you.

TM   You could say that. Yes.

DW   And how would it be if they didn't feel that way about you? If you had to work with a bunch of people who didn't respect you?

TM   It would be awful. I wouldn't know what to think . . . I mean, what the truth was.

What is important here is that the counselor worked through a conflict that was interfering with the client's job performance. Further discussion revealed that Tom acted self-destructively at work to the degree that he felt inadequate inside. As long as he was making some progress in his life, he could act appropriately. If he continued in his writing skills course, if he pursued college programs that would consider his admission, if he managed to earn some money while attending school—in short, if he was doing constructive things with his life that he could feel confident about, then he lost the need to act out at work. But the minute his plans went astray, his feelings of inadequacy began to overcome him and once again he would attempt to compensate by making his bosses feel inferior. Over the years, this had become a vicious cycle.

Dr. Winder helped Tom by combining in practice some of the most important vocational counseling functions. He assessed Tom's abilities through the use of vocational tests, and helped Tom formulate realistic plans. These plans represented a compromise between the unrealistic plans that Tom held on to and his real abilities and interests, as determined by the tests and the interviews. While he did not cure the poor self-image that was underlying many of Tom's problems, he did help Tom control himself to the degree that he was no longer impelled to act out at his job. In short, Dr. Winder offered guidance and counseling—he offered objective information and advice, as well as dynamic psychological interventions to help the "total person" approach to the complex task of finding the right job.

Second Career Counseling

There is also a new social phenomenon today that is having a profound effect not only on many individuals' lives, but on the working world (and economy) in general. It is called the second career. Because of a variety of social and economic factors, many people, typically in their late forties or early to mid-fifties, have completed one career cycle and are now in the process of planning or training for a second career. As the adult's life expectancy has increased, and with it the promise of healthy physical functioning well into the later years, the vocational options available to the adult have changed dramatically (Rebelsky, 1975). This new population includes women who have been in the home raising their children and are now looking to make a new life for themselves outside the home, as well as civil service employees and others who have reached the optional retirement age, collect their pensions, and seek some values in life through work.

What most second career clients need to know, for a realistic assessment of their future plans, are some of the problems they will face, including age-discrimination and the challenges of adjusting socially to working closely at a job with much younger people who may have many different values and interests. But what they will also find are many rewards in work that they may have never expected to find: rewards that can come to each of us through our work, and are especially appreciated by a person in a second careeer (Landau, 1978).

Women and Work

Although the woman's place in the world of work has not traditionally extended much beyond the minimal levels of occupational status, obviously this is in the process of changing, although many feel not rapidly enough. Nowadays, many young women consider their career plans before they consider marriage and family. Many older women, having raised their children, are eager to get into—or get back into—the job market (Robinson, Rotter & Wilson, 1982). There was a significant increase in the percentage of women over 16 years of age in the labor force, from the beginning of the century through the 1980s. Still, despite this enormous increase "even today when childbearing and family responsibilities are less significant components of women's lives, it is true and probably will continue to be true that many women will withdraw from participation in the occupational structure for periods due to family responsibilities" (Richardson, 1979, p. 35). This can cause many frustrations when a woman finds there is no place for her talents in the job market, that she has no contacts, that her skills are no longer needed. She may resent the younger women who are working, or she may mobilize her resources and try to develop the skills and contacts necessary for job survival.

There are differences between the young women entering the world of work and the older woman reentering or hoping to join the ranks of working people. Often, for the woman who is past the childbearing and childrearing years, the path to occupational success is education. This is one reason that more and more middle age and older women today are enrolling in college to continue (or to begin) their education during or after raising their children. Educational opportunities for older women have generally been well-received. Laden and Crooks (1976) studied a group of representative mature women who went back to school to determine what influenced their decision. They found that these women were seeking self-fulfillment and personal growth and that the college experience was, on the whole, a boost to their self-esteem. Others associated with them, such as their children and spouses, reacted positively to their choice, although many husbands' initial enthusiasm during the spouse's first year began to lessen during the second year—"perhaps," Laden and Cross suggest, "as a consequence of the woman's increasingly liberalized perception of her roles and the likely loss [to the husband] in traditional services. . . ." (p. 34)

For the younger woman entering the work world, there is often a conflict between the prospects of having a family and striving toward career success. Many women choose both. And as more and more women with preschool and school-age children enter the labor force the issue has become a national priority, with serious attention directed toward day care and its economic importance. Langway et al. (1980) point out too that women in this situation are often caught in what they call the "superwoman squeeze, the constant pressure to juggle home, family and job" (p. 72). This is compounded for many by the problems women face which are not familiar to men. Bardwick and Douban (1976), for example, point out that women have to deal with such practical and psychological difficulties as social stereotyping, coming to grips with their own competence, and learning to feel comfortable with what were formerly male-oriented behaviors.

There are a number of excellent resources available to help women adjust to their new and expanding career roles, and the career counselor should be familiar with them. These include many helpful books on the subject, a proliferation of women's groups in which the exchange of ideas helps participants develop healthy perspectives, and new social perceptions reflected in the media where images of working women are becoming more typical.

McGraw (1982) suggests that counseling is of vital importance to the reentry woman. In reviewing the literature, she points out three specific ways in which counseling can be helpful.

1. Because the reentry woman is a part of a family system, counseling should focus on the needs of the entire system rather than the individual concerns of the reentry women.
2. Counseling should help the reentry woman recognize which problems she encounters are a function of her environment and which are a part of her feelings about herself. "Counselors should help women accept their personal strengths and teach them to attribute conflicts to the characteristics of the situation rather than to personal inadequacy." (p. 471)
3. External supports should be identified that enhance skill development outside of the counseling setting. . . . Women need assistance [both] in overcoming the psychological blocks impeding the acquisition of new roles and in learning to make critical decisions that can affect future career plans and successes.

Loring and Otto (1976) have organized a helpful book, *New Life Options: The Working Woman's Resource Book* (New York: McGraw-Hill, 1976), designed to familiarize women with the changing role of women and the new options they are offered. They point out how this change in the career situation affects the woman's freedom to choose:

Many women have joined in common objectives—to know themselves as they are and as they could be and then to be free to do as they decide. To be sure, freedom is an endless, and rather vague, quest. To be free enough to choose between possible options is perhaps a clearer statement of intent. To choose between an ever-widening assortment of real options is even closer to the mark. (p. 21)

Realistically, it should also be pointed out that the types of jobs women hold differ from the kinds generally made available to men. Although there are more women in executive positions, this is the exception and not the norm. Sandmeyer (1980) has demonstrated how counseling workshops for reentry women can help them gain an accurate picture of the job market, learn job-seeking skills for the 1980s, and learn to anticipate those problems that are likely to occur before they happen.

The implications of these changes would be viewed differently by the four basic counseling perspectives. Social learning (behavioral) counselors would point out how women are learning, especially through the processes of *role modeling,* to pursue avenues of work they would have thought unavailable or inappropriate before. Moreover, they are *reinforced* by the changing ideas propounded by the mass media of communication to look in new directions for their work. The psychoanalytic partisan would more likely focus on how women are learning to *sublimate* their unconscious impulses in ways that before were only open to men. Both cognitive and humanistic counselors would point out how women's thinking about themselves in relation to the world of work is profoundly changing not only their overt behaviors, but their inner view of self, their feelings about their role in the world, and their esteem and self-valuing.

A Woman's Place

Carla entered the world of work with the confidence of a woman who had been an overachiever through much of her life. The only girl in a family of four boys (two older and two younger), where a successful father strongly encouraged all his children to be successful themselves, Carla identified more with her powerful father than with her docile mother, whom she viewed as a "nice" woman but not too dynamic and not too bright. Throughout her school career, Carla was treated by her father with the same respect and the same expectations that he had for the boys in the family; in short, she was expected to be the best at whatever she did.

She completed her undergraduate and graduate degrees in political science, specializing in polling and market research. She was a straight "A" student and had many extracurricular activities which were not only impressive on her resumé but also provided her with practical experiences in dealing with people. She was attractive, spoke clearly, and generally got along well with others. Despite her mother's subtle injunctions that "a woman's place is in the home . . . why don't you find a nice husband and have children," Carla was determined that for her, a woman's place was in the job market right along with men, side by side, each person competing on his or her own merits.

After a month of looking for jobs, however, Carla's feelings of optimism began to turn to anger . . . and then to despair. It was not that she couldn't find a job; many had been offered to her. It was just that each job that was offered was clearly below her proven abilities. She saw herself becoming nothing more than a glorified secretary if she accepted any of these offers, and decided she would rather not work at all if she couldn't get a job that was totally challenging. It was at this point that she decided to see Dr. Block, with whom she discussed her vocational problem.

It became clear right away that Carla was an extremely bright woman, and that the jobs she was being offered were indeed somewhat below her abilities. What Dr. Block explored, however, was whether these jobs were standard entry level positions that led to greater opportunities in a relatively short period of time or whether they were dead-end positions where women of competence were routinely placed while men obtained better jobs. She suggested that when Carla was offered a job, she should speak to other people at the firm to find out the opportunities available and the promotion policies. In this way, she could distinguish between "live" and "dead" jobs.

This advice led to a discussion of Carla's feelings about work and her feelings, in general, about competing and about success. Here is a section of the transcript.

DR How do you think having to compete in the work world will be different from having to compete in your house when you were growing up?

CA Well, at least at home I had my father (*laughs*). I am kidding, you know.

DR How are you kidding?

CA I mean my father always treated me like anyone else. And that's all I'm asking now. I just want to be treated like anyone else applying for a job. I don't want any special treatment because I am a woman.

DR But you haven't found out if everyone else is treated like you or not. You don't know how other applicants are treated?

CA Well, you are right there, I don't know.

DR Could it be that there are two forces working in your mind? The force of your father and the force of your mother?

CA You mean that that little message my mother has been implanting in my brain all these years hasn't been entirely ignored? That could be. I'd never thought about it. Maybe I'm expecting one of these people who interview me to say, "A woman's place, little Carla, is in the home." Maybe I do expect that, at least on one level.

Here again, we see how the vocational counselor helped reach a feeling that was interfering with the client's ability to find work. Getting in touch with this feeling enabled the client to objectively approach the situation and determine to what extent her feelings were preventing her from finding a job in which she could grow and prosper. A few weeks later, Carla was able to find an entry-level position that, although not glorious, had enormous opportunities for advancement in a relatively brief period of time.

Work and	It is certainly true on the surface that people who are happy at work tend to
Adjustment	feel better about themselves and to perform better. This common observation has

also been borne out by the research. One's feelings of self-esteem, one's interpersonal relationships, and one's physical health all prosper from a satisfying
work environment (Frankenhaeuser, 1977). For many, in fact, work is one of the
more satisfying aspects of life, offering innumerable rewards, far beyond exclusively monetary remuneration.

The opposite is also true. People who don't like their work tend to suffer
because of it, as does their work performance. In fact, occupational stress and
job related problems are one of the leading public health problems in contemporary technological society (Gardell, 1977). The important question for us to
answer is, What factors make a job satisfying for some people?

In general, we know that there is a matrix of factors which contribute to
successful adjustment in the world of work. It is generally agreed that some of
the principal factors which auger success include: need-satisfaction through one's
work; mutual appreciation between employer and employee; respect by co-
workers on the job and by family outside. On the whole, job satisfaction may be
seen as the single most significant variable in job adjustment.

Several factors have been identified as relevant to job satisfaction. Oldham
(1976) cites five characteristics that have been consistently related to job satisfaction:

Task Significance The extent to which the job has a substantial and
    perceivable impact upon others in the immediate organization or external
    environment.

Task Identity The extent to which the job requires completion of a "whole"
    and identifiable piece of work: doing a job from beginning to end, with a
    visible outcome.

Skill Variety The extent to which the job requires the worker to perform
    different activities calling for a variety of skills and abilities.

Autonomy The extent to which the job gives the worker freedom,
    independence, and discretion in scheduling work and determining
    procedures.

Feedback The extent to which the worker, in carrying out the activities
    required by the job, receives information about the effectiveness of his
    efforts.

In the professional literature these factors have been found, over and again, to
be key determinants of job satisfaction and of high-level job performance.

One other factor which is highly significant is job challenge. People who find
their jobs boring, repetitive, and uninteresting, rate their jobs far less positively
and perform less well. Seybolt (1976) has pointed out that work satisfaction is
often determined by the "fit" between educational level and the demands of the
work environment. People with little education derive more satisfaction from jobs
with low variety and little challenge than do individuals with higher educational

backgrounds. Those who have more education than a job demands require greater inducement (more money, more prestige or titles, etc.) to find the job satisfactory than do those with lower levels of education (who find the job intrinsically challenging).

Factors which cause stress on the job include various types of job dissatisfaction, including the failure to meet any or all of the criteria discussed above. Some of the more common complaints people express when discussing their work dissatisfaction are:

I Find the Job Too Frustrating   This can mean that one is either frustrated in efforts to do what is expected or that one's successful efforts are not recognized, appreciated, or rewarded.

My Work Is Too Boring   This usually reflects a situation where an individual has a job which demands less than he or she is able to offer.

I'm Not Getting What I Deserve for What I Do   This involves frustration, but even more, it states that the superiors or bosses are not perceiving the job with the same degree of interest or respect as the individual who is complaining. It is often expressed as dissatisfaction with pay, but usually represents much more.

It should also be pointed out that certain kinds of occupations are invariably prone to certain kinds of stresses. These are called job-related stresses. Air traffic controllers, who work under extreme pressure, are one example of this. So too are emergency room personnel at busy hospitals. Research has identified specific stresses related to such diverse professions as pharmacy (Curtiss, 1978), police work (Hageman, 1977), and teaching (Kirman, 1977); and it would be desirable for the new employee entering such a job field to be aware of the attendant stresses. This would help the individual develop coping strategies to minimize the effects of job-related stress on other areas of functioning.

Recognizing all these principles, the effective career counselor, working either with the individual client or with the family, can make appropriate interventions to help the client lessen the stresses of the job, find greater satisfaction in the work setting, or take constructive steps to find a new field—one which will offer greater personal satisfaction and less stress.

There is a particular group of people in the world of work to whom career counselors should pay special attention: those individuals who are ostensibly satisfied with their jobs and are performing well (or even superlatively), but who, at the same time, are exhibiting in other areas signs of poor adjustment. I am speaking of those vocationally-successful persons who may well be compensating in the workplace for their deep feelings of inadequacy and low self-esteem. These individuals are called *workaholics;* in them we can clearly observe how the principles of effective living, when carried to extremes, become patterns of a self-destructive, unsatisfying, ineffective, lifestyle.

We all know people whom we would describe as all tied up with their work, whether it is school work, professional work, or some other kind of job. While no one could argue that conscientiousness and the work ethic are not good, healthy qualities, there is a degree of emotional involvement with one's work which goes beyond effectiveness and becomes a sign of disturbance. The typical workaholic is actually running away from himself, and avoiding his relationships with others, especially family. As an ex-workaholic describes himself,

> I was addicted to business and making money so I could impress others. My life became more and more wrapped up in my work. It became my god and was the first priority in my life. All other aspects of my life including my wife and children were subordinated to my work and the opinion of some nebulous "others." To watch me, you would have thought the whole world depended on the way I worked. (Lair, 1975, p. 116)

Although the compulsive overworker, the workaholic, would probably argue that he or she is just trying to do the best job possible, in fact, the workaholic often creates unnecessary work to fill time. Moreover, the superficially reasonable motives prompting the compulsive overworker often conceal deeper psychological reasons. Dr. E. James McCranie, a Professor of Psychiatry at the Medical College of Georgia, points out that "[A] person may work to the point of exhaustion because of his overeagerness to help others, his obsession with achieving perfection, or his insistence on doing everything himself" (McCranie, 1980, p. 19). He suggests that such compulsive overworking has several functions, including defensiveness:

> . . . by keeping others pleased and happy, the defensive aim is to avoid their rejection and mistreatment. By working hard and doing things exactly right, the aim is to avoid criticism. Keeping busy and being independent are also ways of avoiding involvement from being hurt. . . . [Another] goal is to make up for feelings of worthlessness and helplessness. By doing for others, performing and achieving, and being independent, worth and adequacy are demonstrated. . . . (McCranie, 1980, p. 20)

We see then in the example of the workaholic how what is actually poor adjustment may appear to others as successful coping (at least to coworkers and boss who admire the workaholic's energy and spirit). Truly effective counseling probes deeper levels than the behavioral: levels of deep psychological functioning and personal satisfaction that only the individual client can know about him- or herself. At these levels, feelings about work are often interwoven with other feelings, such as our feelings about play and joy. In fact, counselors are beginning to realize now that the effective use of leisure time, play time, can make our working time more pleasant and productive and can contribute in a number of ways to our overall adjustment. We will examine this idea in a later section.

During the 1970s, the corporate world began to recognize the benefits of offering employees and executives a range of relevant counseling and personal assistance services. The compass of these services is broad. A middle-level executive at a steel company receives alcohol rehabilitation treatment at a private clinic, paid for totally by the company. A secretary for a chemical company brings her three-year-old son to work each day, where he is cared for in a day-care center on the company premises. A vice president of a publishing company is told of his firing in the presence of a counselor from an outplacement firm, whose fee (about 15 percent of annual compensation) is being paid fully by the publishing company. An airline executive being relocated to a distant city is given information about differences between the region he comes from and the one where he is going, and is helped to find a new home, adjust to the new city and find schools for his children. This relocation service is paid for by the company. What has brought about this willingness by American corporations to offer such services is a new attitude toward employees that reflects the changing view of how businesses function best.

In some cases, this humanistic recognition was fueled by a desire to increase productivity. For example, it is estimated that alcoholism and drug abuse cost American businesses over $20 billion a year, and that the relatively small cost of providing alcohol treatment programs could offset this debit substantially. In other cases, the recognition was prompted by legal concerns. For instance, many companies realize that when layoffs are required by economic necessities, outplacement counseling for employees will diminish the number of lawsuits that typically accompany such layoffs. In other instances, corporations were motivated by studies which demonstrated that healthy functioning employees offer more to the organization than unhealthy ones. And finally, pressures by unions and employee groups impelled corporate decision-makers to recognize that providing counseling services is as essential to a sound benefits program as medical or life insurance.

Whatever the reason, counseling and human development programs are rapidly emerging as the employer's response to the alcohol, drug, and emotional problems of today's work force (Pelletier, 1984). Such problems destroy lives, stunt industrial production, and disrupt the integrity and working spirit of the organization. Experts claim that 20 percent of America's work force suffer from serious personal or emotional problems during their careers. It is estimated that U.S. industry today is sustaining a staggering loss of over $30 billion a year as a result of such problems. In addition, practical family responsibilities, such as caring for young children or elderly dependent adults, have their own disruptive effects on American businesses. Corporations are increasingly addressing this problem by providing a range of in-house or vendor-provided assistance services, from day care to the treatment of drug abuse to eldercare. We will outline below the scope of these services and place them in their current context. Counseling and business departments in universities throughout the country are beginning to offer coursework in these areas. At this time, an ever-increasing number of graduate level programs and courses train business students, psychology majors, social workers, and counselors for the complexities of counseling in the corporate world.

Presently, the main areas of corporate counseling in America are employee assistance programs, outplacement counseling, alcohol and substance abuse counseling, child care assistance, eldercare, relocation and reentry counseling, career exploration and change, health care assistance, and retirement counseling.

Employee Assistance Programs

It is estimated that 60 to 70 percent of all employers with 3,000 or more employees offer some form of employee assistance programs (EAPs). Some EAPs are provided by outside vendors at field sites, while others are run and staffed by company personnel at the company headquarters plant. Although the origins of EAPs are in alcohol treatment programs offered by and within the company, by the mid-1980s, "they have expanded much beyond the alcohol-only focus and have been able to grow because of a somewhat more humane attitude shift on the part of management about the real value of employees. EAPs have moved out of the business and industrial work sites and are being provided by government units, agencies, hospitals, schools, and colleges" (Forrest, 1983, p. 106). Moreover, alcohol and drug problems are only a part of their focus nowadays, as their ever-broadening scope includes marriage and family problems, interpersonal situations, depressions and anxiety, and anything else that may interfere with work performance and effective interpersonal functioning.

Outplacement Counseling

With the increasing number of corporate mergers and across-the-board cost cutting marathons, American corporations are terminating a larger number of mid- to high-level executives than ever before. For such fired executives, traumatized and stricken by their unexpected separation, outplacement assistance has become the saving balm. Outplacement counseling comprises a comprehensive range of services designed to help the terminated employee cope with the stresses of termination and conduct an effective job search. Outplacement counseling, which usually begins at the separation interview, consists of four main steps: (1) defining appropriate career objectives; (2) preparing the job campaign; (3) conducting the campaign; and (4) planning for the new position and working one's way into it.

Alcohol and Substance Abuse Counseling

According to a 1987 federally sponsored study on alcohol and drug abuse in business, the U.S. economy lost $26.9 billion as a result of absenteeism, slowdowns, mistakes, and sick leave among alcoholic and drug-abusing workers. Corporations, both large and small, are becoming aware of the insidious effects of this problem on their day-to-day and long-range operations. While alcohol problems may be handled by the corporate EAP, many companies are addressing this problem with specific alcohol treatment programs made available to all employees.

Child care is now provided by more than two thousand corporations in the U.S. This increase follows a series of studies indicating that time taken off for child care is a major disruptive force in American businesses, especially as the number of families with both parents working has increased (Adolf & Rose, 1985). A real concern among human resources personnel is the problem of tardiness, absenteeism, and loss of productivity when an employee bears part or all the responsibility for caring for minor children. These problems are addressed by corporations that provide facilities, either on-site or nearby, to help working parents in both their parenting and work roles. Counselors help in the development of such centers and in the implementation, staffing, and provision of services beyond basic day care and education.

Corporate Child Care Assistance

American corporations, such as Pepsico, Pitney Bowes, and Ciba-Geigy, have begun providing services to the elderly parents and grandparents of employees by implementing eldercare assistance programs. Recognizing that many of the problems faced by employees charged with the care of elderly parents are similar to those faced by working parents with young children, a growing number of corporations are examining the productivity and morale benefits realized by their day-care programs to determine the potential usefulness of eldercare implementation. Eldercare assistance programs provide a myriad of services, including education, health assistance, adult day-care centers, government benefits information, and personal counseling, as well as seminars to educate employees about aging issues.

Eldercare in the Corporate Environment

These expanding new areas of corporate counseling involve a multifaceted approach for assisting personnel who are relocating to new geographic areas or reentering the country from foreign lands. Relocation counseling "helps ease the family's acclimation to a new environment by diffusing what initially may seem to be a traumatic change" (HBAC, 1987). The relocation counselor offers a range of practical services, from helping the employee and family find the most appropriate housing to assisting the children in enrolling at the best schools. Reentry counseling primarily helps reentering personnel adjust to the stresses of inter-cultural reassignment. In addition to working with the returning employee in such practical matters as finding new living quarters and filling out government-required forms, the counselor helps the client deal with language, culture shock, personal relationships, and family adjustment issues (Grove & Torbiorn, 1985).

Relocation and Reentry Counseling

A recent study indicated that more than 70 percent of all corporate managers and executives go through the processes of career exploration and change at least once in their careers. Formal assistance in this area is provided by private counselors, by career counseling firms (which also provide placement services),

Career Exploration and Change

and by many corporations who hope to exploit the full potential of their employees by encouraging occupational growth and skills development (London & Mone, 1987). The primary modalities of career counseling, discussed earlier in this chapter, can be applied to people making career changes.

Health Care Assistance

Health care assistance is a broadly used term that comprises a variety of health-promotion and illness-prevention campaigns, health counseling, medical programs, substance abuse prevention and treatment, and psychiatric/psychological assistance for employees and their families. Defining health in a broad manner to include sound physical and mental functioning, it is clear that management decisions and corporate policy can have a profound impact on employees' lives. Counselors, working with medical personnel, have become active in health issues ranging from alcoholism to AIDS.

Retirement Counseling

According to most sources, approximately 90 percent of workers, managers, and executives retiring from the work force are fully capable both physically and mentally of continuing their present jobs or developing skills to hold another job of equal importance. While some employees at age 65 or 70 do wish to retire from the work force and enjoy their remaining years without the burdens and challenges of work, many do not. Those planning strictly for retirement may need financial planning assistance and leisure-time counseling. Many of those who hope for a second career lack the understanding or know-how to find the right job, get the proper training, write a resumé, or make use of networking. Even when they do, they find that competition is stiff in the job market, with many younger employees vying for the same few positions (McGoldrick & Copper, 1987). Retirement counseling is the process of assisting a person prepare for retirement or for a second career. This assistance may deal with the psychological ramifications of retirement, financial planning, family matters, or second-career training. An increasing number of American businesses are providing (or co-supporting) retirement counseling services for their employees, especially in situations where early retirement is encouraged.

Career Counseling in Schools

In the school setting, career counseling involves both educational efforts and intensive applications of psychological counseling paradigms. At the educational end we have such services as the establishment of a career resource bank, individual and group resumé preparation assistance, and a school "career day" which provides students important opportunities to assess realistically their career options. Combining the student-directed insights from all areas of the counseling profession, a career day is a generalized counseling effort designed to reach the greatest number of students in a school. In the following section, we will see how a career day can be successfully implemented.

A career day is a day set aside for the single purpose of helping students learn about career opportunities. If it is presented near the beginning of the school year, it can provide a point of reference and feedback throughout the year. This eight step program will show exactly how such a program can be implemented.

Career Day: A Case Example

By Robert Cuccioli

1. *Organize a Career Questionnaire* The counselor begins by distributing a form to students, asking them to list five choices of professions which they would like to have represented at the school. This allows the counselor a realistic sample of student interests. Questionnaires can be distributed during the home room period. It is usually necessary to ask the homeroom teachers to remind the students to return the questionnaires, if they are taking them home rather than filling them out at school.

2. *Collect and Tabulate* The questionnaires are collected by the homeroom teachers and returned to the counselor. Usually with some assistance, the counselor lists each occupation cited by the students. Wherever there is duplication (as in many instances there will be), a tally is kept to determine which professions have scored the highest interest. No choice should be omitted, but weight should certainly be given to those choices cited most often. Differences between schools will reflect differences between school populations. There may also be sex-related differences. Here is a typical result of the five top choices at three very different types of schools:

	School A	School B	School C (science-oriented)
1	Policeman	Prof. Athlete	Engineer
2	Construc. Wrkr.	Retail Sales	Scientist
3	Prof. Athlete	Firefighter	Physician
4	Nurse	Teacher	Lawyer
5	Firefighter	Plumber/Electrc.	Teacher

The counselor should also keep in mind, when tabulating the results, that students may be unaware of an occupational category that could be of interest to them. For example, in *School A,* students may find some interest in the profession of teaching, in the growing paralegal or paramedical professions, in the crafts (plumbing, etc.), and in other areas they did not explicitly list. The counselor should try to supplement the list using his or her own judgment.

3. *Consulting with Faculty and Staff* This step is specifically designed to supplement the list, as mentioned above. The tabulated results can be distributed to faculty, asking for additional suggestions. This also serves the essential purpose of getting teachers involved, and of encouraging them to support the project enthusiastically.

4. *Recruiting Speakers* In order to find individuals who represent the chosen occupations, the counselor should be resourceful. Teachers can be asked for recommendations of individuals they know who would be willing to participate. Professional organizations (such as unions, societies, etc.) often have a speaker available. The uniformed services of a city are also generally eager to

participate in such activities. Large business organizations, including banks, insurance companies, entertainment conglomerates, publishing houses, etc. have all been helpful either in directly providing career day speakers or in referring the counselor to the appropriate source. Before the event the speaker should be given an idea of the type of audience he or she will be addressing, and what types of information will prove most helpful to them.

5. *Determining Student Preferences*   After the final determination of speakers has been made, a roster (of speakers and their occupations) should be distributed in the classes through the same channels used for the original questionnaire. Students will be asked to make five choices from the list, in order of preference.

6. *Scheduling and Confirmation*   Using the tabulation of student preferences from above, together with the list of speaker availability, a schedule is constructed. Each student is assigned, whenever possible, the first three of the five stated preferences. Seniors are usually given preference in assignment, since they will be the first students to graduate. While the scheduling is taking place, speaker confirmation is undertaken. Each speaker who has agreed to participate is sent a letter, stating the time and date, together with instructions how to get to the school. A return postcard is enclosed for the speaker to confirm his or her plans to attend. Careful record keeping will assure a smooth operation on career day.

7. *The Day Is Here*   On the day of the conference, the counselor arranges for speakers to be met at the entrance of the school by students who are assigned to escort the speakers to the special area where they will be greeted. This comfortable room, in which all the speakers are assembled, should provide a welcoming atmosphere. Coffee and cake may be served. Each speaker will have an opportunity to meet the counseling staff and the faculty in this informal friendly ambiance. Written room assignments can be handed out here, and a student will be assigned to each speaker to make sure he or she finds the room and is introduced to the group to whom he or she will be speaking. During the day, the counselor should visit as many rooms as possible to be sure things are going smoothly. If a lunch period is arranged, it may be a good idea for the school counselor or principal to speak to the group of visitors. This makes them feel welcome and provides a basis for continuity and follow-up.

8. *Follow-up*   For a career day to be a most productive experience, there should be an organized follow-up. This can include student and faculty evaluations of the experience, along with group and individual conferences to determine whether the opportunity has been helpful to the students in deciding upon their future course of study or their tentative career choice. There may also be follow-up with the speakers who can, in the future, become a valuable occupational resource to the counselor.

In addition to career day, there are of course many other useful applications of career counseling in the schools. One of the most important of these is the establishment of a career resource center.

The school counselor's office can serve as a career resource center. This means that in addition to providing vocational information and individual or group career counseling, the office provides specific *skills* training that is necessary for successful vocational planning. This would include resumé preparation, job interview training and practice, and even such basic but necessary functions as how to read the want ads in the newspapers. Communication skills, especially speaking skills, are essential in all areas of job attainment and job functioning. They should be an integral part of the services offered by an effective career resource center.

Heitzmann, Schmidt, and Hurley (1986) have developed a career encounter program in which students use on-site career exploration, linked to a professional in the field, to learn more about a career in which they express an interest. By speaking to a knowledgeable person, visiting the site, and getting feedback in the school career counseling office, they gain an objective view of the suitability of the career to their needs.

1. The student works individually with a career counselor and uses career resources, such as books, filmstrips, and computer programs, before arranging a career encounter.
2. The student completes a short application and agrees to spend a day or part of a day with a sponsor.
3. After an interview with the program coordinator, who outlines the kind of experience desired, the student is encouraged to become as familiar as possible with the career through reading and research in the career library.
4. A sponsor working in the desired occupation is contacted.
5. The student is provided with the sponsor's name and work telephone number and is then responsible for making the final plans—setting a specific date and time and arranging to meet the sponsor on the selected day.
6. When the visit has been completed, the student reviews the visit with the program coordinator and career counselor to evaluate the visit and consider appropriate follow-up in the form of additional reading, counseling sessions, or other career encounters. (p. 209)

Although much of what we have been speaking about is applicable to the secondary school level, it is imperative to recognize that career education must begin on the elementary school level if it is to be effective. "Elementary schools that fail to give attention to vocational education and careers," Georgiady (1976, p. 122) points out, "are failing to deal with the realities of our world." He continues,

Ours is a highly complex society, one in which change is occurring at a bewilderingly increasing rate. Ours is also a society in which technology is playing an ever increasing role. To expect that pupils will somehow magically find an appropriate place in such a complex society without any preparation, or with inadequate preparation, is unrealistic and does violence to an acceptable concept of the true role of education. . . .

The elementary-school teacher is the key person in the development of elementary-school programs. Efforts to change programs must begin with the teachers in the elementary school. . . . To have any impact on the education of children, changes must be made in the teachers' attitudes, understandings, and skills regarding vocational education. . . . What is now needed is a large-scale effort to reach a greater number of teachers. (p. 122)

Moreover, we should recognize that substantial research has consistently shown that some of a person's later-life vocational interests and values begin as early as the third grade, and that career-role identification exercises and early career exploration should begin around Grade 4 (Parks, 1976). Thus, the elementary school counselor has an important place in career guidance.

Leisure-Time Counseling

Because one's leisure time is directly related to one's work on many levels, functional and psychological, we include leisure-time counseling in this chapter. The definitions of leisure vary, from those which view leisure simply as the time not spent working or fulfilling some obligation, to those definitions which emphasize the positive aspects of leisure or focus on the kinds of activity engaged in. But, despite specific variants, it is generally agreed that leisure consists of "varied patterns of activity which people engage in during the social time freed from work and other obligations" (Boserman & Butler, 1976, p. 28).

Although common sense might suggest that people always look forward to their leisure time, this is not always the case. In fact, for many, such as the workaholic, leisure time, with its lack of structure and its many opportunities for new activities, may prove a special time of stress. Many of these attitudes and behaviors result from our feelings about work, productivity, and earning money. Because the process of earning money is considered to be inherently productive, we tend to attribute to our work possibly more than it is actually worth. Consequently, there may be some difficulty coming to grips with leisure-time activities. As Overs (1976, p. 22) points out,

Most individuals in our culture believe that earning money justifies everything else. The widespread attitude is that bringing home a paycheck relieves one from questioning whether the job one is paid to do is useful or meaningful. In pursuing an avocational activity with no paycheck to hide behind, the question of whether the activity is useful or meaningful to the individual should be answered immediately. If it is not, there is no reason to continue it. (p. 22)

It is agreed by most in the counseling profession that if leisure time is to be used advantageously, in terms of an individual's adjustment and life satisfaction, there will have to be efforts to educate the public about how to derive the most from leisure time. It is also generally agreed that leisure counseling can contribute a great deal to these efforts. McDowell (1977) defines leisure counseling as an integrated counseling process that facilitates affective and behavioral changes in the use of leisure time; changes leading toward the individual's well-being. McDowell goes on to point out,

> Some people need to develop coping means for leisure-related behavior problems; others need to explore leisure within a holistic lifestyle perspective. . . . Leisure counseling orientations can be suggested to relate to some theoretical notions of human behavior and so do not exist as counseling practice (in isolation). . . . (p. 54)

While much of the literature on leisure has been strongly influenced by theory, there is a variety of practical applications that emerge from this rich theoretical base. But there is also an attendant conflict.

The controversy surrounds the purview of leisure-time counseling. This is an important issue, insofar as its function is to a large extent derived from its sources and commitments. Neulinger (1977) points out correctly that there is presently much controversy over whether leisure counseling rightly belongs to education, counseling, or psychotherapy. He believes that the answer depends upon the nature of the particular problem and the goal to be achieved. He points out that "there is a need for the development of each of these approaches, either as separate programs or, ideally, under one umbrella, so that the clients could choose or be advised to take the one that would serve their needs best" (p. 27).

And yet there is a substantial resistance to doing this, opposition which can be expressed in the idea, Why should we have to spend money and effort to help people enjoy themselves in their time off? But there is a reason. As much research has indicated, most people do not have healthy attitudes toward leisure time and need education to learn how to derive more from it. Thus, Mobley, Light, and Neulinger (1976) point out, after surveying 400 college students, that "as a group, students are quite work oriented, more so, as a matter of fact, than an earlier sample of full-time working adults," and that this shows "the need for an extensive program of leisure education" (p. 22). But even without such a program, each of us should sit down and ask whether we are using our leisure time in such a way that it reduces the general stresses of our life and provides us with enriching experiences that may help us in other areas of endeavor. And, once answering that, we should confront our clients with the same question.

How does the counselor go about helping the client develop a healthy attitude toward leisure-time activities? If we conceptualize leisure as Iso-Ahola (1976) does as "a person's own perception and inference of quantity and quality

Practical Considerations

of [nonwork] activities," and realize that "leisure becomes a subjective perception of an actual and imagined activity a person participates in at a given time," then we are compelled to acknowledge the subjective world of the individual as a critical factor in all leisure-time counseling. With this view, we can examine leisure-time counseling as a three-stage process, involving *exploration, discussion, and integration.* Let us consider each of these individually.

Exploration   During the course of the typical counseling interview, particularly if it is a vocationally-oriented counseling interview, the counselor attempts to find out how much leisure time the client presently has available and how he or she spends that time. The counselor should not be satisfied with ready-made or superficial answers. He or she must keep in mind that many clients do not know how they spend their leisure time. They have no concept of what leisure time means, and therefore they do not conceptualize ways of spending leisure time. They merely view some segments of time as periods without specific obligations, and they may not be consciously aware of how they are spending this time. Some specific questions the counselor may ask to elicit a full analysis of leisure time are: "What hobbies do you have?" "How much time do you spend at this hobby?" "Do you watch much television?" "Do you read?" "Do you have many friends?" "Are you active in sports?" "Do you travel much?"

These types of questions, placed in juxtaposition and examined by the skilled counselor, can reveal to the counselor what types of activities occupy the bulk of the client's free time. Ideally, there should be an interest in and an involvement in free-time activities to the extent that these contribute productively to the client's life.

It should be pointed out too that there is an initial difference in attitude between the client who comes for voluntary leisure-time counseling, and the involuntary client who might be found in the institutional and rehabilitative settings. Edwards (1977) points out that the involuntary client is often initially hostile, but that "the initial hostility usually lessens when you tell [them] that the object of leisure counseling is to help them enjoy life more. You can see their eyes suddenly start to focus on you. Then it's up to you to capitalize on this lessening of tension and increase in attention" (p. 17).

Discussion   The dialogue that ensues between the counselor and the client has a twofold purpose. First, it is to help the client identify the use of his or her leisure time and to understand ways in which he or she may be able to appropriate more time productively; to get more use out of the leisure time. Second, it is to explore with the client the extent to which he or she is seriously engaged in meaningful projects during leisure time. Is the client happy to have leisure time or does she or he suffer from boredom and inactivity? Is the client a so-called workaholic? Is there an integration between leisure-time activities and his or her need to learn to explore fully different kinds of activities? It is essential to consider client attitudes and values during this phase; especially as they relate to the ability or inability to use leisure time productively (Williams, 1977, pp. 9–11). The discussion phase of the interview is designed to bring out all these things into the open and to enable the client to grasp them and to deal with them.

During this phase, the counselor actively sets out to help the client readjust his or her leisure-time activities in ways determined through the discussion phase of the interview. Consider, for example, a situation (which is rather typical) in which a male adult client finds himself bored during his leisure time, suffering from feelings of "not having anything to do." This type of boredom may lead to depression or anxiety, to drug and alcohol abuse, juvenile delinquency, and family conflicts. The counselor, having by this time determined what the client's interests are, may suggest certain types of activities that will help him fill his time constructively. A creative counselor may use after-work or after-school activities to interest a large number of clients in constructive leisure-time activity.

Integration

This phase of the interview is called integration because it serves to combine the leisure-time activity with the counselee's total life-style. Leisure-time activity should be an integral, harmonious, constructive phase of the client's existence, not something apart from it. The client should learn and grow during his or her leisure time just as during other moments of his or her life.

In this chapter, we attempted to examine the major challenges confronting the contemporary career counselor in today's ever changing world of work. We began with a general survey of how social and economic factors have shaped today's world of work and pointed out how this matrix of interacting factors affects the way one looks at occupational prospects and some of the decision-making involved.

Summary

We defined career counseling as a synthesis of different counseling skills directed toward helping clients explore occupational opportunities and make satisfying decisions. The function of career counseling as a specific counseling modality was defined, and the major theories of career development were explicated.

Next, we considered some practical counseling situations. We began by looking at the basic process of finding the right job and at two special situations: second careers and women in the world of work. We also considered how our work life affects all areas of our adjustment, and illustrated some of the points with two short case vignettes. We then considered school counseling applications and saw how a "career day" can prove an effective method of reaching a large number of students. Finally, the importance of leisure time was discussed in terms of work adjustment. A three-stage model of leisure-time counseling was presented.

Chapter Aim

To provide an overview of some of the major problems and obstacles involved in the effective counseling of minorities. To consider possible areas of change.

Many professionals have commented on the failure to find effective ways to deal with minority group clients. Some of the important research in this area is cited and discussed.

The Unfulfilled Promise of Counseling for Minorities

Some criticisms of the traditional counseling role are discussed. First, the intra-psychic model, which assumes that clients' problems are the result of personal disorganization rather than social dysfunctioning, does a disservice to the minority client. Second, it has been pointed out that the contemporary counseling approaches widely used and taught were developed by and for a white, middle-class constituency. Third, a large number of cultural barriers resulting from cultural differences which impede the counseling interaction, have been cited.

Criticism of the Traditional Counseling Role

Specific barriers are discussed. These can involve minority counselors, whether they are counseling minority clients or clients from the majority group.

Barriers to Minority Counselor— Minority or Majority Client Counseling

We point out that cross-cultural counseling can not only be effective for resolving client difficulties but can also serve as a forum for a unique learning experience. It appears that the primary barrier to effective cross-cultural counseling is the traditional counseling role itself, which is not applicable to many cross-cultural interactions.

Potential Benefits in Cross-Cultural Counseling

Cross-Cultural
Counseling

19

Until the mid 1960s, the counseling profession demonstrated little interest in or concern for the status of racial, ethnic, or other minority groups. Counseling and Guidance, with its traditional focus on the needs of the "average" student, tended to overlook the special needs of students who, by virtue of their skin color, physical characteristics, socioeconomic status, etc., found themselves disadvantaged in a world designed for white, middle-class, physically able, "normal" or "average" people. Psychotherapy, with its development and practice limited primarily to middle- and upper-class individuals, also overlooked the needs of minority populations. By the late 1960s, however, "The winds of the American Revolution [second] . . . (were) . . . howling to be heard" (Lewis, Lewis & Dworkin, 1971, p. 689). And as Aubrey (1977) points out, the view that counseling and guidance dealt with the normal developmental concerns of individuals to the exclusion of special groups' concerns could no longer be accepted.

Events in the 1960s, however, would blur this simple dichotomy by suddenly expanding potential guidance and counseling audiences to include minority groups, dissenters to the war in Viet Nam, alienated hippie and youth movements, experimenters and advocates of the drug culture, disenchanted students in high schools and universities, victims of urban and rural poverty and disenfranchised women. (p. 293)

The forces that led to this voluminous, and often emotional, outcry in the professional counseling literature go far beyond the condition of social unrest existing in the United States in the late 1960s and early 1970s. The note of dissatisfaction was struck when the guidance movement first began and accepted, intentionally or unintentionally, the practically unfulfilled, idealistic promises of the Declaration of Independence as a guideline (Byrne, 1977). As Shertzer and Stone (1974) state, "The pervasive concept of individualism, the lack of rigid class lines, the incentive to exercise one's talents to the best of one's ability may have provided a philosophical base" (p. 22) for the dramatic shift in emphasis the profession took almost sixty years after its inception. Fuel for the fire was added when the Civil Rights movement of the 1950s provided convincing evidence that the educational establishment had failed to make provision for equal educational opportunity to all and that the time had come to correct existing discrepancies. The fire of discontent was fanned into a bright flame as the political activism associated with the Viet Nam war touched almost all phases of American life.

Yet the promise of counseling and guidance for minority individuals remains unfulfilled. Nor has counseling to date been able to bring much clarity to issues raised in the minority group literature. Central to all other considerations is the role of the profession itself vis à vis minorities. Should counselors work in the domain of "special" minority needs and experiences or should they continue to aim at serving the "middle American" population? While to some extent the question appears moot, one need only examine the curricula of major counselor training programs to determine that the profession continues to train counselors for working with white, middle-class, straight, mainstream clientele. Indeed, this has been a serious bone of contention for many minority professionals.

The Unfulfilled Promise of Counseling for Minorities

Minority group authors, particularly those representing racial/ethnic minority groups, have been vociferous and unequivocal in their denunciations of the counseling profession since the mid 1960s. In a comprehensive review of counseling literature related to racial/ethnic minority groups, Pine (1972) found the following view of counseling to be representative of that held by most minority individuals:

> . . . that it is a waste of time; that counselors are deliberately shunting minority students into dead-end non-academic programs regardless of student potential, preferences, or ambitions; that counselors discourage students from applying to college; that counselors are insensitive to the needs of students and the community; that counselors do not give the same amount of energy and time in working with minority as they do with white middle-class students; that counselors do not accept, respect, and understand cultural differences; that counselors are arrogant and contemptuous; and that counselors don't know themselves how to deal with their own hangups. (p. 35)

Although Pine's article deals primarily with racial/ethnic minorities, similar views of counseling have been expressed by feminist, gay, pacifist, and other activist minority groups ("Counseling and the Social Revolution," 1971).

To some extent minority group unhappiness with counseling reflects disillusionment with all the organized social sciences because of their poor performance as instruments for correcting social ills (Sanford, 1969). Psychology in particular has been criticized for its role as the "handmaiden of the status quo" (Halleck, 1971, p. 30). Frequently minorities see psychology functioning to maintain and promote the status and power of the Establishment (Sue & Sue, 1972).

To a large degree, minority group dissatisfaction with the counseling profession can be explained as disenchantment with unfulfilled promises. As stated earlier, counseling has at least in theory accepted such ideal rights as "equal access to opportunity," "pursuit of happiness," "fulfillment of personal destiny," and "freedom" as omnipresent, inherent goals in the counseling process (Adams, 1973; Belkin, 1975; Byrne, 1977). Although these lofty ideals may seem highly commendable and extremely appropriate goals for the counseling profession to promote, in reality they have often been translated in such a way as to justify support for the status quo (Adams, 1973).

Although the validity of minority criticisms can and will be argued by professional counselors, there is little doubt that, for whatever reasons, counseling has failed to serve the needs of minorities, and in some cases, has proven counterproductive. The fact that various minority groups are underrepresented in conventional counseling programs (Sue, 1973) suggests these groups see counseling as irrelevant to their needs. There is also substantial evidence that Asian Americans, blacks, Chicanos, and native Americans terminate counseling after an initial counseling session, at a much higher rate than do Anglos (Sue, Allen & Conaway, 1986; Sue & McKinney, 1975; Sue, McKinney, Allen & Hall 1974). Clearly, minorities see the counseling process, as currently implemented, contrary to their own life experiences and inappropriate or insufficient for their felt needs.

Perhaps the most insidious commentary on the failure of counseling for minorities is the evidence that minorities are diagnosed differently and receive "less preferred" forms of treatment than do majority clients. In the area of diagnosis, Lee and Temerlin (1968) found that psychiatric residents were more likely to arrive at a diagnosis of mental illness when the individual's history suggested lower-class origin than when a high socioeconomic class was indicated. Haase (1956) demonstrated that clinical psychologists given identical sets of Rorschach test records made more negative prognostic statements and judgments of greater maladjustment when the records were identified as the products of lower-class individuals than when associated with middle-class persons. Broverman, Broverman, Clarkson, Rosenkrantz, and Vogel (1970) found sex also to be a factor in diagnosis, with less favorable judgments by clinical psychologists with respect to female clients than for male clients. In a related study, Thomas and Stewart (1971) presented counselors with taped interviews of a high school girl in counseling and found the girl's career choice rated more appropriate when identified as traditional than when identified as deviant (traditionally male attitude). Similar results have been cited by Schlossberg and Pietrofesa (1973).

In the area of treatment, Garfield, Weiss, and Pollack (1973) gave two groups of counselors identical printed descriptions (except for social class) of a nine-year-old boy who engaged in maladaptive classroom behavior. The counselors indicated a greater willingness to become ego-involved when the child was identified as having upper-class status than when assigned lower-class status. Habermann and Thiry (1970) found that doctoral degree candidates in Counseling and Guidance more frequently programmed students from low-socioeconomic backgrounds into a non-college-bound track than a college preparation track. Research documentation of the inferior quality of mental health services provided to racial/ethnic minorities is commonplace (Clark, 1965; Cowen, Gardner & Zox, 1967; Guerney, 1969; Lerner, 1972; Thomas & Sillen, 1972; Torion, 1973; Yamamoto, James, Bloombaum & Hattem, 1967; Yamamoto, James & Palley, 1968).

Criticism of the Traditional Counseling Role

Due in part to the unfulfilled promise of counseling for minorities, a great deal of criticism has been directed at the traditional counseling role in which an office-bound counselor engages the client in verbal interaction with the intention of resolving the client's psychological problems. For the most part, this criticism can be summarized as three interrelated concerns: criticism of the intrapsychic counseling model, criticism of how counseling approaches have developed, and criticism related to counseling process variables.

Criticism of Intrapsychic Counseling Model

Perhaps the strongest, most cogent indictment of the traditional counseling role has been criticism of the intrapsychic view of client problems inherent to some degree in all current counseling approaches. The intrapsychic model assumes client problems are the result of personal disorganization rather than institutional or societal dysfunctioning (Bryson & Bardo, 1975). Counselors, these critics argue, should view minority clients as victims of a repressive society and rather than intervene with the victim, counselors should attempt to change the offending portion of the client's environment (Banks, 1972; Williams & Kirkland, 1971).

The issue of whether one focuses on the *person* or *system* is an important one. Counseling in this country has grown out of a philosophy of "rugged individualism" in which people are assumed to be responsible for their own lot in life. Success in society is attributed to outstanding abilities or great effort. Likewise, failures or problems encountered by the person may be attributed to some inner deficiency (lack of effort, poor abilities, etc.). For the minority individual who is the victim of oppression, the person-blame approach tends to deny the existence of external injustices (racism, sexism, age, bias, etc.).

Pedersen (1976) has suggested that the counselor can help the minority client either adopt or adapt to the dominant culture. Vexliard (1968) has coined the terms *autoplastic* and *alloplastic* to define two levels of adaption; the first, ". . . involves accommodating oneself to the givens of a social setting and structure and the latter involves shaping the external reality to suit one's needs" (Draguns, 1976, p. 6). Thus, critics of the traditional counseling role see cultural adoption and the autoplastic model of adaption as repressive but predictable outcomes of the intrapsychic counseling model. The counseling roles they advocate can be viewed as directed toward the alloplastic end of the auto-alloplastic adaption continuum. . . .

Minority intellectuals have criticized contemporary counseling approaches which they contend have been developed by and for the white, middle-class person (Bell, 1971; Gunnings, 1971; Mitchell, 1971). Little or no attention has been directed to the need to develop counseling procedures which are compatible with minority cultural values. Unimodal counseling approaches are perpetuated by graduate programs in counseling that give inadequate treatment to the mental health issues of minorities. Cultural influences affecting personality, identity formation, and behavior manifestations frequently are not a part of training programs. When minority group experiences are discussed, they are generally seen and analyzed from the "white, middle-class perspective." As a result, counselors who deal with the mental health problems of minorities often lack understanding and knowledge about cultural differences and their consequent interaction with an oppressive society.

Criticism of How Counseling Approaches Have Developed

Majority counselors who have not had firsthand experience with the minority client's specific cultural milieu may overlook the fact that the client's behavior patterns have different interpretations in the two cultures represented. Behavior that is diagnosed as pathological in one culture may be viewed as adaptive in another (Wilson & Calhoun, 1974). Grier & Cobbs (1968) in their depiction of black cultural paranoia as a "healthy" development make reference to the potential for inappropriate diagnoses. Thus, the determination of normality or abnormality tends to be intimately associated with a white, middle-class standard.

Furthermore, counseling techniques which are a product of the white middle-class culture are frequently applied indiscriminately to the minority population (Bell, 1971). In addition, counselors themselves are often culturally encapsulated (Wrenn, 1962), measuring reality against their own set of monocultural assumptions and values, and demonstrating insensitivity to cultural variations in clients (Pedersen, 1976). New counseling techniques and approaches are needed, it is argued, that take into account the minority experience (Gunnings, 1971).

The issue is perhaps best represented semantically by the emic-etic dichotomy, which was first presented by the linguist, Pike (1954). Draguns (1976) offers the following definition of these two terms:

Emic refers to the viewing of data in terms indigenous or unique to the culture in question, and etic, to viewing them in light of categories and concepts external to the culture but universal in their applicability. (p. 2)

The criticisms relevant to the current discussion, then, focus on what can be called the "pseudoetic" approach to cross-cultural counseling (Triandis, Malpass & Davidson, 1973); culturally encapsulated counselors assume that their own approach and associated techniques can be culturally generalized and are adequate to cope with cultural variations. In reality, minority critics argue, we have developed emic approaches to counseling that are designed by and for white, middle-class individuals.

Criticisms Related to Counseling Process Variables

Much of the criticism related to minority group counseling focuses upon the interactions that occur between counselor and client. Counseling is seen as a process of interpersonal interaction and communication which requires accurate sending and receiving of both verbal and nonverbal messages. When the counselor and client come from different cultural backgrounds, barriers to communication are likely to develop, leading to misunderstandings that destroy rapport and render counseling ineffective. Thus, process manifestations of cultural barriers pose a serious problem in minority group/cross-cultural counseling.

Most of the writing on barriers to minority group/cross-cultural counseling has focused on racial/ethnic minorities as clientele with a major portion of these studies examining the white counselor-black client relationship. It is evident, however, that many of the concepts developed by these authors have relevance to any counseling situation involving an individual from a minority (i.e., oppressed) group. It is equally clear that although presented from a majority counselor-minority client perspective, many of the same barriers may exist between a counselor and client who represent two different minority groups (i.e., two different cultures).

In the present discussion, we make a distinction between cultural barriers that are unique to a minority group/cross-cultural counseling situation (e.g., language differences) and those that are process barriers present in every counseling relationship but are particularly awkward and more likely to occur in a cross-cultural situation (e.g., transference).

Barriers Indigenous to Cultural Differences

In discussing barriers and hazards in the counseling process, Johnson and Vestermark (1970) define barriers as, ". . . real obstacles of varying degrees of seriousness" (p. 5). They go on to describe cultural encapsulation as one of the most serious barriers that can affect the counseling relationship. Padilla, Ruiz, and Alvarez (1975) have identified three major impediments to counseling that a non-Latino counselor may encounter when working with a Latino client. Sue and Sue (1977) have generalized these barriers as relevant to all Third World people. We expand the concept further and attempt to relate the three barriers to all minority group/cross-cultural counseling situations. The three barriers are (a) language differences; (b) class-bound values; and (c) culture-bound values. These three categories are used to facilitate the present discussion; it should be pointed out, however, that all three categories are recognized as functions of culture broadly defined.

Much of the criticism related to the traditional counseling role has focused on the central importance of verbal interaction and rapport in the counseling relationship. This heavy reliance by counselors on verbal interaction to build rapport presupposes that the participants in a counseling dialogue are capable of understanding each other. Yet many counselors fail to understand the client's language and its nuances sufficiently so as to make rapport building possible (Vontress, 1973). Furthermore, educationally and economically disadvantaged clients may lack the prerequisite verbal skills required to benefit from "talk therapy" (Calia, 1966; Tyler, 1964), especially when confronted by a counselor who relies on complex cognitive and conative concepts to generate client insight.

Sue and Sue (1977) have pointed out that the use of standard English with a lower-class or bilingual client may result in misperceptions of the client's strengths and weaknesses. Certainly the counselor who is unfamiliar with a client's dialect or language system will be unlikely to succeed in establishing rapport (Wilson & Calhoun, 1974). Furthermore, Vontress (1973) suggests that counselors need to be familiar with minority group body language lest they misinterpret the meaning of postures, gestures, and inflections. For example, differences in nonverbal behavior are frequently seen in the comparison of blacks and whites. When speaking to another person, Anglos tend to look away from the person (avoid eye contact) more often than do black individuals. When listening to another person speak, however, blacks tend to avoid eye contact while Anglos make eye contact. This may account for statements from teachers who feel that black pupils are inattentive (they make less eye contact when spoken to) or feel that blacks are more angry (intense stare) when speaking.

Similar observations can be made regarding cross-cultural counseling with other, non-racially-identified minority groups. For instance, prison inmates have developed a language system that tends to change over a period of time. The naive counselor who enters the prison environment for the first time may find that his or her use of standard English may elicit smiles or even guffaws from clients, to say nothing of what this does to the counselor's credibility. Gays, too, have developed a vocabulary that may be entirely foreign to a "straight" counselor. Anyone who doubts this statement need only visit a gay bar in San Francisco or elsewhere and listen to the public dialogue. Any counselor unfamiliar with gay vocabulary is likely to be perceived by a gay client as too straight to be of any help. Gays, like other minority groups, rely heavily upon their own vernacular to convey emotions and, understandably, they prefer a counselor who can grasp these emotions without further translation into standard English.

Unique language patterns can also be associated with poor Appalachian whites, drug users, the handicapped, and to some extent, almost any category which qualifies as a minority group. . . . Often with political activism, minority groups will develop expressive language that is not common to, or has a different connotation than, standard English. Inability to communicate effectively in the client's language may contribute significantly to the poor acceptance which counseling has received from minorities.

Class-bound Values   Differences in values between counselor and client that are basically due to class differences are relevant to minority group/cross-cultural counseling since, almost by definition, many minority group members are also of a lower socioeconomic class. Furthermore, . . . differences in attitudes, behaviors, beliefs, and values among the various socioeconomic groups constitute cultural differences. The interaction of social class and behavior has been well documented by Hollingshead (1949). The importance of social class for school counseling has been discussed by Bernard (1963). Combining the results of several studies, Havighurst and Neugarten (1962) concluded that at least 50 percent of the American population falls into either the upper lower or lower lower socioeconomic classes, suggesting that a large portion of the counselor's potential clientele may be from these socioeconomic classes. The impact of social class differences on counseling in general acquires added significance if one accepts the statement presented earlier in this chapter, that existing counseling techniques are middle- and upper-class based.

One of the first and most obvious value differences encountered by the middle-class counselor and the lower-class client involves the willingness to make and keep counseling appointments. As Sue and Sue (1977) point out, ". . . lower-class clients who are concerned with 'survival' or making it through on a day-to-day basis expect advice and suggestions from the counselor . . . (and) . . . appointments made weeks in advance with short weekly fifty-minute contacts are not consistent with the need to seek immediate solutions" (p. 424). Vontress (1973) states that Appalachian whites refuse to be enslaved by the clock and not only do they refuse to adhere to values of promptness, planning, and protocol, but they suspect people who do adhere to these values.

Differences in attitudes toward sexual behavior often enter the counseling relationship between a counselor and client representing different socioeconomic classes. For the most part, open acceptance of sexual promiscuity differs from one socioeconomic level to another, although other factors (e.g., religious beliefs) play heavy roles. Middle-class counselors, whether consciously or unconsciously, often attempt to impose middle-class sexual mores on lower- and upper-class clients.

The fact that the clients' socioeconomic status affects the kind of therapeutic treatment clients receive has been well documented. Ryan and Gaier (1968), for instance, found that students from upper socioeconomic backgrounds have more exploratory interviews with counselors than do students representing other social classes. Middle-class patients in a Veterans Administration clinic tend to remain in treatment longer than do lower-class patients. And Hollingshead and Redlich (1958) found that the level of therapeutic intensiveness varies directly with socioeconomic background.

Culture-bound Values   Culture, as broadly defined for the purposes of this book, consists of behavior patterns shared and transmitted by a group of individuals. In addition to language and class-bound values already discussed, culture-bound values obviously involve such elements as attitudes, beliefs, customs, and institutions identified as integral parts of a group's social structure.

Unintentionally and through ignorance, counselors frequently impose their own cultural values upon minority clients, reflecting an insensitivity to the clients' values. Referring to clients from racial/ethnic minorities as "culturally deprived" is an example of this attribution. "Straight" male counselors sometimes make sexual remarks about females in front of a male client that may be repugnant to the client if he is gay (to say nothing about how it would affect females who overheard it). Nor is the experience reported by Granberg (1967) in which he found himself incorrectly assuming his homosexual client wanted to become "straight" an unusual example of the counselor's cultural values interfering with the counseling relationship. Drug and prison "counselors" often fulfill roles of instilling the values of the larger society upon their clientele without full awareness of their impact.

For some time the role of the counselor's values in the counseling relationship has been a difficult professional issue. The issue becomes even more poignant when a majority counselor and minority client are involved. In this case, ". . . the values inherent in (the) two different sub-cultures may be realistically as diverse as those of two countries" (Wilson & Calhoun, 1974). While the major concern with this issue, in the broader context, centers on the counselor's influence upon the client, class- and culture-bound value differences can impede further rapport building.

For example, one of the most highly valued aspects of counseling entails self-disclosure, a client's willingness to let the counselor know what he or she thinks or feels. Many professionals argue that self-disclosure is a necessary condition for effective counseling. Jourard (1964) concludes that people are more likely to disclose themselves to others who will react as they do, implying that cultural similarity is an important factor in self-disclosure. Furthermore, self-disclosure may be contrary to basic cultural values for some minorities. Sue and Sue (1972) have pointed out that Chinese American clients, who are taught at an early age to restrain from emotional expression, find the direct and subtle demands by the counselor to self-disclosure very threatening. Similar conflicts have been reported for Chicano (Cross & Maldonado, 1971) and native American (Trimble, 1976) clients. Poor clients, of whatever racial or ethnic background, frequently resist attempts by the counselor to encourage client self-exploration and prefer to ascribe their problems, often justifiably, to forces beyond their control (Calia, 1966). In addition, many racial minorities have learned to distrust whites in general and may "shine on" a majority counselor, since this has proven to be adaptive behavior with whites in the past. Sue and Sue (1977) suggest that self-disclosure is itself a cultural value and counselors who "value verbal, emotional, and behavioral expressiveness as goals in counseling are transmitting their own cultural values" (p. 425).

Related to this last point is the lack of structure frequently provided by the counselor in the counseling relationship. Often, in order to encourage self-disclosure, the counseling situation is intentionally designed to be an ambiguous one, one in which the counselor listens empathically and responds only to encourage the client to continue talking (Sue & Sue, 1972). Minority clients frequently find the lack of structure confusing, frustrating, and even threatening

(Haettenschwiller, 1971). Atkinson, Maruyama, and Matsui (1978) found that Asian Americans prefer a directive counseling style to a non-directive one, suggesting the directive approach is more compatible with their cultural values. Black students also were found to prefer a more active counseling role over a passive one (Peoples & Dell, 1975).

Process Manifestations of Cultural Differences

Many of the problems encountered in minority group/cross-cultural counseling which have been identified as cultural barriers might better be conceived of as process manifestations of cultural differences, since they may be present to some extent in any counseling relationship but are aggravated by cultural differences. We will briefly discuss five of them: stereotyping, resistance, transference, countertransference, and client expectations.

Stereotyping

Stereotyping is a major problem for all forms of counseling. It may broadly be defined as rigid preconceptions that are applied to all members of a group or to an individual over a period of time, regardless of individual variations. The key word in this definition is *rigidity,* an inflexibility to change. Thus, a counselor who believes that blacks are "lazy," "musical," "rhythmic," and "unintelligent"; that Asians are "sneaky," "sly," "good with numbers," and "poor with words"; or that Jews are "stingy," "shrewd," and "intellectual" will behave toward representatives of these groups as if they possessed these traits. The detrimental effects of stereotyping have been well documented in professional literature (Rosenthal & Jacobsen, 1968; Smith, 1977; Sue, 1973). First, counselors who have preconceived notions about minority group members may unwittingly act upon these beliefs. If black students are seen as possessing limited intellectual potential, they may be counseled into terminal vocational trade schools. Likewise, if Asian Americans are perceived as being only good in the physical sciences but poor in verbal-people professions, counselors may direct them toward a predominance of science courses. The second and even more damaging effect is that many minorities may eventually come to believe these stereotypes about themselves. Thus, since the majority of stereotypes about minorities are negative, an inferior sense of self-esteem may develop.

Due to stereotyping or attempts to avoid stereotyping by the counselor, majority counselors frequently have difficulty adjusting to a relationship with a minority client. The most obvious problem in this area occurs when the counselor fails to recognize the client as an individual and assigns to the client culturally stereotypic characteristics that are totally invalid for this individual (Smith, 1977). In an effort to treat the client as just another client, on the other hand, the counselor may demonstrate "color or culture blindness" (Wilson & Calhoun, 1974). In this case the counselor may avoid altogether discussing the differences between the two participants, thus implying that the client's attitudes and behaviors will be assessed against majority norms. The content of the counseling dialogue may also be restricted by the preoccupation of the majority counselor with fear that the client will detect conscious or unconscious stereotyping on the part of the counselor (Gardner, 1971).

Resistance is usually defined as client opposition to the goals of counseling and may manifest itself as self-devaluation, intellectualization, and overt hostility (Vontress, 1976). While it is a potential difficulty in any counseling encounter, the problem becomes particularly acute when the counselor and client are culturally different, since the counselor may misinterpret the resistance as a dynamic of the client's culture.

Resistance

Transference occurs when the client responds to the counselor in a manner similar to the way he or she responded to someone else in the past (Greenson, 1964, pp. 151–152), and this may manifest itself as either a liking or disliking of the counselor. Clients may or may not be aware of the transference effect themselves. This phenomenon is particularly problematic in the majority counselor-minority client dyad, ". . . because minority group members bring to the relationship intense emotions derived from experiences with and feelings toward the majority group" (Vontress, 1976, p. 49). Minority clients for instance, due to their experiences with an oppressive, majority-controlled society, are likely to anticipate authoritarian behavior from the counselor.

Transference

Countertransference occurs when the counselor responds to a client as he or she responded to someone in the past (Wilson & Calhoun, 1974, p. 318). Countertransference is particularly difficult for the counselor to recognize and accept since counselors typically view themselves as objective, although empathic, participants in the counseling relationship. It seems highly unlikely, however, that majority counselors in this society are entirely free of the stereotypic attitudes toward minority peoples (Jackson, 1973). An argument can be made that counselors, like everyone else, carry with them conscious and unconscious attitudes, feelings, and beliefs about culturally different people, and that these will manifest themselves as countertransference (Vontress, 1976).

Countertransference

Closely related to transference, client expectations for success in the counseling relationship can directly affect counseling outcome. When the minority client finds him/herself assigned to a majority counselor, the client's prognostic expectations may be reduced (Wilson & Calhoun, 1974). Prior to the initial counseling session the client may experience feelings of distrust, futility, and anger which generate an expectation that counseling will not succeed. Such an expectation usually dooms the counseling relationship to failure.

Client Expectations

As used in the counseling literature, minority group counseling frequently implies that the counselor is a member of the dominant culture and the client a minority group member, suggesting that this combination is of greatest threat to effective counseling. A few authors have referred to the problems encountered in counseling when the client and counselor are from the same minority group.

Barriers to Minority Counselor-Minority or Majority Client Counseling

Virtually none have discussed the difficulties experienced when the counselor is from a different minority group than the client. Lest the impression be given that culturally related barriers only exist for the majority counselor-minority client dyad, we now turn briefly to difficulties experienced by minority counselors and their clients.

Intra-Minority Group Counseling

Several authors have identified problems that the minority counselor may encounter when working with a client from a cultural background similar to that of the counselor. Jackson (1973) points out that the minority client may respond with anger when confronted by a minority counselor. The anger may result from finding a minority person associated with a majority controlled institution. Some clients may express anger, on the other hand, because they feel a majority counselor would be more competent, thus enhancing the probability of problem resolution. Or the client's anger may reflect jealousy that the counselor has succeeded through personal efforts in breaking out of a repressive environment. In the case of a third-world counselor, the counselor may also be seen as:

> too white in orientation to be interested in helping, as less competent than his colleagues, as too far removed from problems that face the patient, or as intolerant and impatient with the patient's lack of success in dealing with problems. (Jackson, 1973, p. 277)

The minority counselor may respond to minority client anger by becoming defensive (Jackson, 1973), thus impeding the counseling process. Minority counselors may also either deny identification with or over-identify with the client (Gardner, 1971). Sattler (1970) has suggested that minority counselors may have less tolerance and understanding of minority clients and view the contact as low status work compared to counseling a majority client.

Calnek (1970) points out the danger that third-world counselors too often adopt stereotypes which whites have developed, concerning how minority clients think, feel, and act. The counselor may deny that the client is also a minority person, for fear the common identification will result in a loss of professional image for the counselor. Over-identification, on the other hand, may cause the counseling experience to degenerate into a gripe session. Calnek also refers to the danger of the counselor projecting his/her own self-image onto the client because they are culturally similar.

While the foregoing comments are, for the most part, directed at the black counselor-black client dyad, it is easy to see that the problem could be generalized to include other intra-minority group situations.

Counselors representing one minority group who find themselves working with a client representing a different minority group often face the problems associated with both the majority counselor-minority client and the intra-minority group counseling situations. Although the camaraderie of third-world peoples which results from awareness of shared oppression helps to bridge cultural differences on college and university campuses, in the non-academic world these differences are often as intense or more intense than those between the dominant and minority cultures. One need only observe Chicano students and parents in East Los Angeles or black students and parents in Bedford-Stuyvesant to gain an appreciation of ethnocentrism and the difficulty which culturally different-minority counselors can perceive in these situations. Furthermore, the counselor representing a different minority than the client may be suspect to the client, for the same reasons counselors of similar minority backgrounds would be suspect.

Almost no attention has been given in the counseling literature to identifying the benefits of cross-cultural counseling. In reference to the minority counselor-majority client dyad, Jackson (1973) believes that the client may find it easier to, ". . . share information that is looked on as socially unacceptable without censor from the therapist" (p. 275), suggesting self-disclosure, at least of some materials, may be enhanced. Students who are rebelling against the Establishment, for instance, may prefer a minority counselor, feeling that the counselor's experience with oppression qualifies him/her to acquire empathy with the client (Gardner, 1971). Gardner (1971) also suggests majority clients may prefer minority counselors if they are dealing with material that would be embarrassing to share with a majority counselor. Jackson (1973) points out that there is a tendency in this situation to perceive the counselor more as another person than as a superhuman, notwithstanding those cases where the counselor is perceived as a "super-minority." In the latter case, the client may view the minority counselor as more capable than his or her majority counterpart, owing to the obstacles the counselor had to overcome. The net effect in this case may be a positive expectation. The possibility that minority counselors are less likely to let secrets filter back into the client's community is also cited by Gardner (1971) as a positive variable in cross-cultural counseling.

Several authors (Draguns, 1975, 1976; Trimble, 1976), while referring in part to national cultures, have suggested that cross-cultural counseling is a learning experience to be valued in and of itself. The counseling process, with its intentional provision for self-disclosure of attitudes, values, and intense emotional feelings, can help the counselor and client gain a perspective on each other's culture, frequently in a way never experienced outside of counseling.

Again it seems apparent that much of the foregoing can be generalized to apply to non-racially or ethnically identified minorities. It also seems evident that further research and discussion are needed regarding both the barriers and benefits of cross-cultural counseling. Those discussed above, along with several proposed by the current authors, are outlined in figure 19.1. In addition to citing

Inter–Cultural Counseling

Barriers	*Benefits*
—client resistance	—client's willingness to self-disclose some material
—client transference	
—client cultural restraints on self–disclosure	—client less likely to view counselor as omniscient
—client expectations	
—counselor countertransference	—client expectation for success may be enhanced
—counselor maladjustment to the relationship	—potential for considerable cultural learning by both client and counselor
—counselor misdirected diagnosis	
—counselor patronization of client's culture	—increased need for counselor and client to focus on their own processing
—counselor denial of culturally dissonant component of client problem	—potential for dealing with culturally dissonant component of client problem
—counselor "missionary zeal"	
—language differences	
—value conflicts	

Intra–Cultural Counseling

Barriers	*Benefits*
—unjustified assumption of shared feelings	—shared experience may enhance rapport
—client transference	—client willingness to self-disclose some materials
—counselor countertransference	
	—common mode of communication may enhance process

positive and negative aspects of cross-cultural situations, we have attempted, as shown in figure 19.1, to identify their counterparts when counselor and client are culturally similar.

We agree that cross-cultural counseling can be effective not only for resolving client difficulties, but can also serve as a forum for a unique learning experience. That barriers to cross-cultural counseling exist is not at issue here. Obviously, cultural differences between counselor and client can result in barriers that are, in some instances, insurmountable. As noted earlier, however, cross-cultural counseling can involve benefits to both client and counselor that may not be possible in intra-cultural counseling.

Furthermore, it is our contention that the primary barrier to effective counseling and one which underlies many other barriers is the traditional counseling role itself. No one has yet offered conclusive evidence that differences in status variables (e.g., race, ethnicity, sex, sexual orientation) alone create barriers to counseling. The fact that one person in a counseling dyad is born black and one white, for instance, should not negate the possibility of their working together effectively. From our perspective, it is how we perceive and experience our and our client's blackness and whiteness which creates barriers to constructive communication. For the most part, our perceptions and experiences are shaped by a socialization process that begins at birth. We feel that the traditional counseling role (nonequalitarian, intrapsychic model, office bound, etc.) often helps to perpetuate the very socialization process which creates a barrier between culturally different individuals.

Some critics will argue that differences in experiences are paramount, that a counselor who experiences being black will understand the black client's perspective better than any white counselor ever can. We agree up to a point. There is simply no conclusive evidence, however, that a counselor must experience everything his/her client does. Carried to the extreme, the similarity of experience argument suggests that all counseling is doomed to failure since no two individuals can ever fully share the same life experiences. Furthermore, while cultural differences result in unique experiences for both the client and the counselor, our experiences as human beings are remarkably similar. This view—that we are more alike than different—is perhaps best expressed by the sociobiologist De Vore (1977):

> Anthropologists always talk about crosscultural diversity, but that's icing on the cake. The cake itself is remarkably panhuman. Different cultures turn out only minor variations on the theme of the species—human courtship, our mating systems, child care, fatherhood, the treatment of the sexes, love, jealousy, sharing. Almost everything that's importantly human—including behavior flexibility—is universal, and developed in the context of our shared genetic background. (p. 88)

Summary

In this chapter, we surveyed a range of research that helps clarify the implications of cross-cultural differences on effective counseling. We began by pointing out the "unfulfilled promise of counseling for minorities," the general feeling of dissatisfaction and lack of progress that characterized minority and nonwhite counseling through the 1970s. Some limitations of traditional counseling models and approaches were indicated, along with an explication of the barriers that come between clients and their counselors to interfere with the counseling process. These include language differences, class-bound values, culture-bound values, stereotyping, resistance, transference, and countertransference. We also noted some of the more typical barriers that exist when a minority counselor counsels either a minority client or a majority client. Finally, we closed on a positive note, examining some of the potential benefits in cross-cultural counseling.

Glossary

AACD American Association for Counseling and Development, representing psychological and non-psychological counselors in all types of private, agency, and school settings.

alienation A feeling of loss of significance in the world; of apathy and diminished consciousness.

anal stage The second of Freud's psychosexual stages, named for the part of the body (the anus) that is the primary erogenous zone during that period and through the actions of which the child expresses many of his or her feelings to the world.

analytical psychology The system of dynamic psychology and psychotherapy developed by Carl Gustav Jung.

antidepressant A drug that inhibits severe organic depression by altering certain chemicals in the brain that are believed to be associated with depression.

anti-illness movement The tendency to reject the medical model as an explanation of psychological problems.

anxiety A state of tension, typically characterized by rapid heartbeat, shortness of breath, and other similar manifestations of arousal of the autonomic nervous system.

APA American Psychological Association, the chief representative professional organization of psychologists in the United States.

archetype According to Jung, a universal idea that is present in the collective unconscious. Examples include the old wise man, demons, and the concept of mother.

autism A disorder, of unknown cause, in which a child seems to be completely withdrawn from the outside world.

aversion therapy A general term used to describe any type of behavior therapy in which strong avoidance stimulus is presented when the individual is making an undesired response.

axiology The branch of philosophy, underlying many counseling approaches, that deals with values.

back region In sociological theory, the counselor's private self not specifically related to his or her counseling role.

balance theory In family counseling, a cognitive theory that states that whenever an imbalance exists between cognitive perceptions, thoughts, and attitudes, there is an inner tendency that compels us to resolve the discrepancy.

behaviorism The system of psychology founded by the American, John B. Watson, which defines psychology as the study of observable behavior and limits the scope of research to that which can be observed, measured, and replicated.

biofeedback A set of procedures in which some aspect or aspects of an individual's biological functioning, such as heart rate, skin temperature, or muscle tension, is "fed back" to the subject via a measuring instrument. The purpose of this feeding back is to learn to consciously control such a biological function.

castration anxiety According to Freud, a psychosexual stage characterized by a young boy's fear of losing his penis.

chemotherapy The treatment of psychological disorders through the use of drugs.

classical conditioning A form of learning in which a neutral stimulus is paired with an unconditioned stimulus. As a result of the association, the response associated with the latter (unconditioned response) becomes associated also with the former (conditioned response).

client-centered therapy A nondirective method of therapy developed by Carl R. Rogers, which stresses the inherent worth of the client and the natural capacity for growth and health.

cognitive flexibility A characteristic of an effective counselor, in which there is a demonstrated willingness to be intellectually open to different beliefs and perceptions.

collective unconscious According to Jung, the level of the unconscious that contains memories and behavior patterns inherited from our collective, ancestral past; also called the transpersonal unconscious.

community counseling The area of counseling practice dealing with the effects of particular environmental settings on community problems; emphasizes the prevention rather than strictly the treatment of mental illness.

compensation According to Adler, the attempt by a person who falls short of his or her goal, or who is deficient in one area, to excel in a different but related activity. An example would be a ninety-eight-pound weakling who becomes a weight lifter.

conditioned response In behavior modification, the learned response to a conditioned stimulus; for example, learning to salivate to the sound of a bell.

conditioned stimulus An initially neutral stimulus that, as a result of its pairing with the unconditioned stimulus, comes to elicit the conditioned (learned) response.

congruence According to client-centered therapy, the necessary quality of a therapist of being in touch with reality and with others' perception of oneself.

contracting The establishment of the rules, regulations, guidelines, and goals of treatment.

conversion reaction A neurotic disturbance (hysteria) in which a physical symptom without an organic cause is the product of an underlying unresolved conflict.

counseling psychology The field of psychology that deals with people's educational, vocational, social, and family problems.

crisis A highly emotional temporary state in which an individual, overcome by feelings of anxiety, grief, confusion, or pain, is unable to act in a realistic healthy manner.

crisis intervention A "first-aid" counseling approach for helping an individual who is in a crisis situation return to normal.

death instinct (*mortido* **or** *thanatos*) According to Freud, the innate drive to aggression and destruction.

defense mechanisms According to Freud, unconscious mental processes designed to protect the ego from thoughts or feelings that might cause anxiety, lowered self-esteem, or total mental collapse.

deindividuation A loss of individual identity as a separate person; sometimes, the feeling of being submerged in a group.

denial The defense mechanism by which a person refuses to see things as they are because such traits are threatening to the ego.

determinism   The belief that all human behavior has a specifiable cause.

diagnosis   The attribution of a name and cause, implying illness, to specific psychological states or behavioral patterns.

diagonal relationship   A description of a counseling relationship in which the counselor's and the client's statuses are defined through their interaction.

disclosure   A characteristic of an effective counselor that allows her or him to open up his or her own feelings when appropriate. Also, the quality of a client that makes possible the disclosure of personal feelings.

displaced aggression   A defense mechanism in which anger is redirected toward a person or object other than the one who provoked the anger.

displacement   According to psychoanalysis, a defense mechanism through which an individual replaces the original object of a drive with a more acceptable substitute.

EC-ER world view   A minority client's view that one's current plight is the result of an oppressive social system, and that one is powerless to do anything about it.

eclectic counseling   The selective application of a variety of counseling methods using counselors' knowledge of effectiveness as a basis for their organization.

educational counseling   The providing of educational information with a view toward future career goals.

ego   According to Freud, the executive of the personality; the ego bridges the instincts (id) with the real world. The ego helps the person channel psychic energy into socially-approved activities.

empathy   The ability to experience another's emotions from the point of view of that person.

encounter group   A therapy group in which the resistances are broken down quickly in order for the members to get in touch with their feelings and experience positive growth.

epistemology   The branch of philosophy that deals with knowledge; an underlying rationale for many counseling interventions.

erogenous zones   According to Freud, the areas of the body most receptive to sexual stimulation.

existential counseling   The philosophically oriented approach to counseling which views the individual's failure to confront choices as the cause of mental disorders and stresses understanding the individual's subjective views of reality by focusing on the "here and now" of existence.

external-control (EC)   The psychological orientation (locus of control) that reinforcements are not entirely contingent on one's own actions. *See also* internal-control.

extraversion   According to Jung, the tendency to be outgoing and sociable, concerned more with the external world than with one's inner experiences.

family counseling   A general term for a variety of counseling approaches in which family members are brought together to cooperatively solve their collective problems.

figure and ground   In Gestalt psychology (and counseling), the idea that in perception we see a figure standing out against the background; the figure appears to have shape, while the ground appears formless. Figure and ground shift back and forth in dominance.

free association   In classical psychoanalysis, the "fundamental rule," in which the patient is encouraged to say whatever comes to mind, freely, without regard to social propriety and without censorship.

free-floating anxiety   According to Freud, the residual anxiety from the Oedipal conflict, which develops later in life into a neurosis characterized by general apprehension and fear.

front region   According to Erving Goffman, the aspect of role presented to others within a defined social establishment.

genital stage According to Freud, the final psychosexual stage of development, associated with puberty and marked by heterosexual interests.

genuineness According to Carl Rogers, the important quality of a therapist of being honest and willing to give of oneself.

Gestalt counseling A humanistic counseling approach based on the principle that a healthy individual can overcome fragmentation of feeling and can organize his or her emotional experiences into a meaningful whole.

group counseling A counseling approach in which three or more clients meet with a counselor and through their interactions with each other and with the counselor work toward growth.

health counseling A variety of integrated counseling approaches designed to maximize the full physical functioning of the individual.

horizontal relationship A description of a counseling relationship in which the counselor's and the client's statuses are defined through their interaction.

humanistic counseling Referred to as the "third force" in psychology and counseling, this approach emphasizes the study of the individual as a whole person who is motivated to fulfill his or her potential by becoming self-actualizing.

hysteria According to psychoanalysis, a general group of neurotic disturbances caused by an unresolved Oedipal conflict and characterized by some form of anxiety.

IC-ER world view The world view that subscribes to the belief in one's ability to achieve personal goals if given a chance. *See also* locus of control; external-control; internal-control.

IC-IR world view The world view in which individuals believe they are the masters of their fate and responsible for what happens to them. *See also* locus of control; external-control; internal-control.

identification In psychoanalysis, the unconscious incorporation of the qualities of another person or object into one's own personality.

implosive therapy A form of behavior therapy in which the client is told to vividly imagine scenes that are very frightening to him or her.

incongruence According to Carl Rogers, the condition in which there is a discrepancy between one's perception of oneself and the way in which one is perceived by others.

individual psychology The system of psychoanalysis with a social orientation, developed by Alfred Adler.

inferiority complex According to Alfred Adler, feelings of inadequacy and worthlessness that result from our inability to successfully strive for superiority.

insight As used in counseling and psychotherapy, the understanding of one's deeper motives (in psychoanalysis they are called unconscious) and their origins.

instrumental self The concept that the counselor uses his or her own personality to facilitate client growth.

internal-control (IC) The psychological orientation (locus of control) that reinforcements are contingent on one's own actions. *See also* external-control.

introjection The process in psychoanalytic theory by which a child incorporates parental values and authority into his or her personality; as a defense mechanism, taking on the qualities or partial identity of another person.

introversion According to Jung, the tendency to withdraw into one's own inner world to avoid contact with other people.

latency The fourth of Freud's psychosexual stages, and the period during which, he believed, the sexual impulses lie dormant and the child concentrates his or her energies on socialization skills.

latent dream content   According to Freud, the underlying meaning of a dream.

law of effect   The learning principle, formulated by E. L. Thorndike and important in behavioral counseling, which states that responses that are rewarded are strengthened and are likely to be repeated, and responses that are punished are less likely to recur.

libido   According to Freud, the energy of the sexual instincts, which motivates behavior.

life instincts   According to Freud, one of the two classes of instincts (the other being the death instinct, or aggression), of which the sexual is the more important.

life script   According to transactional analysis, the analysis that reveals how a person became what he or she is and where he or she is heading.

locus of control   The belief that individual events and circumstances in life are either internally controlled or externally controlled; *see also* internal-control and external-control.

manic-depressive psychosis   A severe mental disorder characterized by radical mood swings between elation and depression.

manifest dream content   The remembered content of a dream, reported by the dreamer, which must be interpreted in order to understand its latent (hidden) meaning.

marathon group   A counseling group that, in a twelve-to-seventy-two hour session, is designed to encourage the expression of inner feelings through exhausting normal defenses.

meaninglessness   The feeling, which can impede effective counseling, of being without meaning and commitment in life.

medical model   The model of psychological and behavioral disturbances, based on medical practice, which sees symptoms as superficial signs of a deeper, underlying cause.

modeling   A social learning process in which a person, observing the behavior of another, will learn that behavior; also called "observational learning." In counseling, modeling is used to help clients learn healthier, less neurotic responses to anxiety-evoking situations.

negative reinforcer   A stimulus (such as an electric shock) that is removed when the subject responds in a desired way, increasing the likelihood of that desired response.

neurosis   A behavior disorder characterized by anxiety and a symptom. According to Freud, a neurosis is the result of unresolved unconscious conflicts.

neurotic anxiety   According to psychoanalysis, tension resulting from an unconscious fear that the instincts will take over and cause the person to behave in ways that will be punished.

nondirective counseling   Originated by Carl Rogers, a counseling approach in which the client acts as the initiator of change and determines the direction of change.

nondominance   According to research, a characteristic of an effective counselor in which the counselor is able to sit back and allow the client to direct the course of the counseling interview.

nonjudgmental attitude   According to research, a characteristic of an effective counselor in which the counselor refrains from presenting value judgments to the client.

Oedipus complex   According to psychoanalytic theory, the sexual attachment of the son for his mother (or daughter for her father), which is usually accompanied by feelings of rivalry and hostility for the other—"rival"—parent. The girl's complex is sometimes called the Electra complex.

ontology   The branch of philosophy dealing with existence and reality.

operant conditioning   A conditioning (learning) model in which a response is strengthened by being positively reinforced when it occurs, or weakened by being ignored or punished.

oral stage   According to psychoanalytic theory, the first stage of psychosexual development, named for the part of the body that is the principal source of pleasure during that period—the mouth.

paradoxical intention   A logotherapy technique, used by Viktor Frankl, in which the individual is told to wish for something, attempt to do something, or think intensely about something when that something represents his or her worst fears.

parapraxis   A mistake such as a slip of the tongue, pen, or the forgetting of a phone number, that represents a compromise between the conscious wishes of the individual and repressed wishes that cry out for expression; more commonly known as a "Freudian slip."

penis envy   According to Freud, the girl's feeling of castration or loss because she lacks the male genitals.

personal unconscious   According to Jung, the level of the unconscious that contains experiences of the individual that were once conscious but are now repressed.

phallic stage   According to psychoanalytic theory, the third psychosexual stage, named for the genital organs, which are the dominant source of bodily pleasure during that period.

phenomenal field   According to Carl Rogers (and other existential-humanists), the totality of an individual's perceptual-affective experience, which includes everything potentially available to awareness that is going on within or nearby the organism at any given moment.

phobia   An irrational, intense, hysterical fear of an object or situation. Also called phobic reaction.

positive regard   According to Carl Rogers, accepting the client as he or she is, and for what he or she is, without imposing judgments or stipulations.

primal therapy   A form of dynamic therapy, developed by Arthur Janov, that requires the individual to relive primal pain (needs that were denied as an infant) in order to release the energy that is causing tensions.

psychic energy   In psychoanalytic theory, the energy that emanates from the id (instincts), which is converted by the ego or superego into actions.

psychoanalysis   The view of personality and accompanying system of psychotherapy developed by Sigmund Freud. Psychoanalysis emphasizes the psychosexual stages of development, and the role of unconscious processes in the formation of symptoms and in treatment.

psychopathology   The elucidation of abnormal behavior patterns as "diseases" of the mind.

psychosexual stages   According to psychoanalytic theory, the five developmental stages of personality, each of which is named for the bodily area that serves as the principal source of pleasure and gratification.

psychosis   Severe mental disorder characterized by loss of touch with reality, impaired self-control, delusional or grossly unrealistic behavior, and social dysfunctioning.

psychosomatic illness   A physical disorder that involves a psychological or emotional component.

psychotherapy   The application of psychological principles to the treatment of behavior or emotional disorders.

punishment   In behavior modification, the presentation of an aversive stimulus or event, or the removal of a positive event after a response. In both cases, punishment is designed to lessen the likelihood of a certain response occurring.

rationalization   The defense mechanism in which one supplies a reasonable explanation for unreasonable behavior, or attributes different motives to his or her actions, in order to see himself or herself in a more favorable light.

reaction formation   The defense mechanism in which the individual acts in a way that is directly opposite to the way he or she unconsciously feels.

reality therapy   A cognitive-dynamic therapy approach developed by William Glasser that concentrates on individual responsibility, objective values, and a reality in which the person has two basic needs: to be loved and to feel worthwhile.

reciprocal inhibition   The behavioral principle that a person cannot make two incompatible responses at the same time. In the behavioral approach, called "systematic desensitization."

regression   According to psychoanalysis, the defense mechanism in which a person "returns" to an earlier level of behavior.

rehabilitation counseling   A series of counseling approaches designed to help an individual who has experienced some disability achieve full functioning.

reinforcement   In classical conditioning, the repeated pairing of the conditioned stimulus and unconditioned stimulus, which strengthens the connection between the two. In operant conditioning, the presentation of an event or stimulus following an operation on the environment by the subject.

reinforcer   In classical conditioning, the unconditioned stimulus; in operant conditioning, any stimulus that increases the probability of the occurrence of a response.

repression   According to psychoanalysis, the defense mechanism by which the individual pushes back into the unconscious unacceptable ideas or impulses.

role   The enactment of certain behaviors associated with a specific social designation (such as the role of counselor versus the role of client).

schizophrenia   A psychotic disorder characterized by a breakdown of personality integration, which manifests itself in cognitive, emotional, and social dysfunctioning.

self-actualization   In humanistic psychology, the process by which one fully uses one's talents and capacities in order to fulfill one's potential for creativity, dignity, and self-worth.

shaping   In social learning theory or behavior modification, teaching a desired complex response by reinforcing a series of successive responses as they become increasingly more similar to the desired final response.

Skinner box   A laboratory apparatus designed by B. F. Skinner to be used for operant conditioning of small animals, such as rats and pigeons.

social learning theory   The theory, underlying behavioral counseling, that much important social learning takes place through the observation and imitation of others' behaviors and by modeling one's behaviors after those whom we observe.

socioemotional intactness   In family counseling, the view that the family is a unit and anything that preserves that unity is a sign of its intactness.

style of life   According to Alfred Adler, the principle by which the individual's personality functions; integrated mode of actions and behaviors.

sublimation   According to psychoanalysis, the "healthy defense" through which instinctual drives are channeled into higher, socially acceptable forms of behavior.

superego   In psychoanalytic theory, the aspect of personality that acts as the conscience as well as the ego ideal. It develops during the Oedipal stage, as the child internalizes many of the parents' values.

systematic desensitization   A behavior therapy approach developed by Joseph Wolpe, in which a patient is put into a relaxed state and instructed to think about anxiety-producing stimuli in order of increasing intensity.

third force The term used by Abraham Maslow to describe the humanistic approach to psychology. The first and second forces are Freudianism and behaviorism.

transactional analysis A form of counseling or therapy in which the individual's ego states are analyzed in terms of a three-part model, comprising Parent, Adult, and Child.

transference In psychoanalysis, the phenomenon whereby the patient transfers on to the analyst all of the feelings he or she previously held in childhood toward emotionally important figures such as parents, brothers, or sisters.

unconditional positive regard *See* positive regard.

unconditioned response A natural, unlearned response originally elicited by an unconditioned stimulus (for example, jumping at an electric shock).

unconditioned stimulus A stimulus that consistently elicits an unlearned response.

vertical relationship A description of a counseling relationship in which the counselor and client's statuses are defined through their interaction.

vocational counseling A counseling approach designed to help the individual discover satisfying work and to function well at the job.

References

Abramowitz, R. Parenthood in America. *Journal of Clinical Child Psychology,* 1977, 5 (3), 43–46.

Abrams, J. C. Minimal brain dysfunction and dyslexia. *Reading World,* 1975, 14 (3), 219–227.

Abramson, E. E. Behavioral approaches to weight control: An updated review. *Behavior Research and Therapy,* 1977, 15 (4), 353–363.

Ackerman, N. W. *The psychodynamics of family life.* New York: Basic Books, 1958.

Adams, H. J. The progressive heritage of guidance: A view from the left. *Personnel and Guidance Journal,* 1973, 51, 531–538.

Adams, J. F. (Ed.). *Understanding adolescence: Current developments in adolescent psychology.* 3rd Ed. Boston: Allyn and Bacon, 1976.

Adler, A. *What life should mean to you.* New York: Capricorn, 1958.

Adolf, B., and Rose, K. *Employer's guide to child care: Developing programs for working parents.* New York: Praeger, 1985.

Ajzen, R. Human values and counseling. *Personnel and Guidance Journal,* 1973, 52, 77–81.

Allen, M. Education through music—an innovative program for hearing impaired children. *The Volta Review,* 1975, 77, 381–383.

Allen, T. W. Physical health: An expanding horizon for counselors. *Personnel and Guidance Journal,* 1977, 56 (1), 40–43.

American Federation of Teachers (AFT). *American Educator,* 1980, 4 (4), 14–15.

American Personnel and Guidance Association. *Ethical standards.* Falls Church, VA: APGA, 1981.

American Psychological Association. *Ethical standards for psychologists.* Washington, D.C.: APA, 1977.

Amerikaner, M., and Summerlin, M. L. Group counseling with learning disabled children: Effects of social skills and relaxation training on self-concept and classroom behavior. *Journal of Learning Disabilities,* 1982, 15 (6), 340–343.

Anderson, C. A.; Lepper, M. R.; and Ross, L. Perseverance of social theories: The role of explanation in the persistence of discredited information. *Journal of Personality and Social Psychology,* 1980, 39, 1037–1049.

Anderson, W. P., and Heppner, P. P. Counselor applications of research findings to practice: Learning to stay current. *Journal of Counseling and Development,* 1986, 65, 152–154.

Anthony, W. A. Psychological rehabilitation: A concept in need of a method. *American Psychologist,* 1977, 32 (8), 658–662.

Aponte, H. J. Organizing treatment around the family's problem and their structural bases. *Psychiatric Quarterly,* 1974, 48 (2), 209–222.

Arbuckle, D. S. Existentialism in counseling: The humanist view. *Personnel and Guidance Journal,* 1965, 44, 558–567.

Archer, J., Jr., and Lopata, A. Marijuana revisited. *Personnel and Guidance Journal,* 1979, 57 (5), 244–251.

Asbury, F. R., and Winston, R. B. Reinforcing self-exploration and problem-solving. *The school counselor,* 1974, 21, 204–209.

Asch, S. *Social Psychology.* New York: Prentice-Hall, 1952.

Atkinson, D. R.; Maruyama, M.; and Matsui, S. The effects of counselor race and counseling approach on Asian Americans' perceptions of counselor credibility and utility. *Journal of Counseling Psychology,* 1978, 25 (1), 76–83.

Aubrey, R. F. Misapplication of therapy models to school counseling. *Personnel and Guidance Journal,* 1967, 48, 273–278.

Aubrey, R. F. *Experimenting with living: Pros and cons.* Columbus: Charles E. Merrill, 1975.

Aubrey, R. F. Historical development of guidance and counseling and implications for the future. *Personnel and Guidance Journal,* 1977, 55, 288–295.

Avis, J. P., and Stewart, L. H. College counseling: Intentions and change. *Counseling Psychologist,* 1976, 6, 74–77.

Axelrod, S. *Behavior modification for the classroom teacher.* New York: McGraw-Hill, 1977.

Axline, V. M. *Dibs in search of self.* New York: Ballantine Books, 1967.

Bach, G. L. *Economics.* 9th Ed. Englewood Cliffs: Prentice-Hall, 1977.

Bahnson, C. B. Quoted in "Family Sickness." *Time,* November 24, 1975, 73.

Bahr, S. J., and Bahr, H. M. Work, friends, and marital satisfaction. *Family Perspective,* 1981, 15 (2), 55–62.

Baldwin, B. A. Alternative services, professional practice and community mental health. *American Journal of Orthopsychiatry,* 1975, 45 (5), 734–743.

Ball, J. D., and Henning, L. H. Rational suggestions for pre-marital counseling. *Journal of Marital and Family Therapy,* 1981, 7 (1), 69–73.

Bandura, A. Interview with Albert Bandura. In R. I. Evans (Ed.), *The making of psychology.* New York: Knopf, 1976.

————. *Principles of behavior modification.* New York: Holt, Rinehart and Winston, 1969.

————. Self-efficacy mechanism in human agency. *American Psychologist,* 1982, 37 (2), 122–147.

Banks, W. The black client and the helping professionals. In R. I. Jones (Ed.), *Black psychology.* New York: Harper and Row, 1972.

Bardwick, J. M., and Douban, E. When women work. In R. Loring and H. A. Otto (Eds.), *New life options: The working woman's resource book.* New York: McGraw-Hill, 1976, pp. 32–45.

Barglow, P., and Weinstein, S. Therapeutic abortion during youth and adolescence: Psychiatric observations. *Journal of Youth and Adolescence,* 1973, 2 (4), 331–342.

Barkhaim, M., and Shapiro, D. A. Counselor verbal response modes and experienced empathy. *Journal of Counseling Psychology,* 1986, 33 (1), 3–10.

Barry, R., and Wolf, B. *Modern issues in guidance-personnel work.* New York: Bureau of Publications, Teacher College, 1963.

Bart, P. B. Ideologies and utopias of psychotherapy. In P. M. Roman and H. M. Trice (Eds.), *The sociology of psychotherapy.* New York: Jason Aronson, 1974.

Bartnick, R. W., and O'Brien, C. R. Health care and counseling skills. *Personnel and Guidance Journal,* 1980, 58 (10), 666–667.

Basker, E.; Beran, B.; and Kleinhauz, M. A social science perspective on the negotiation of a psychiatric diagnosis. *Social Psychiatry,* 1982, 17 (1), 53–58.

Bassin, A.; Bratter, T. E.; and Rachin, R. L. (Eds.). *The reality therapy reader: a survey of the work of William Glasser.* New York: Harper and Row, 1976.

Battle, E., and Rotter, J. Children's feelings of personal control as related to social class and ethnic group. *Journal of Personality,* 1963, 31, 482–490.

Beane, J. "I'd rather be dead than gay": Counseling gay men who are coming out. *Personnel and Guidance Journal,* 1981, 60 (4), 222–226.

Beck, A. T. *Cognitive therapy and emotional disorders.* New York: International Universities Press, 1976.

———. Cognitive therapy, behavior therapy, psychoanalysis and pharmacotherapy: A cognitive continuum. In M. Mahoney and A. Freeman (Eds.), *Cognition and Psychotherapy*. New York: Plenum, 1985.

Beck, A. T.; Rush, A. J.; Shaw, B. F.; and Emery, G. *Cognitive therapy of depression*. New York: Guilford Press, 1979.

Beers, C. W. *A mind that found itself,* 5th Ed. Garden City: Doubleday, 1956.

Belkin, G. S. *Practical counseling in the schools*. Dubuque, IA: Wm. C. Brown Publishers, 1975.

Bell, J. E. *Family therapy*. New York: Jason Aronson, 1975.

Bell, R. L. The culturally deprived psychologist. *Counseling Psychologist,* 1971, 2, 104–107.

Benjamin, A. *The helping interview*. Boston: Houghton Mifflin, 1969.

———. *The helping interview,* 3rd. Ed. Boston: Houghton Mifflin, 1974.

Benjamin, S. Is asthma a psychosomatic illness?: A retrospective study of mental illness and social adjustment. *Journal of Psychosomatic Research,* 1977, 21, 463–469.

Bennight, K. C. A model program for counseling and placement of offenders. *Journal of Employment Counseling,* 1975, 12 (4), 168–173.

Benoit, R. B., and Mayer, G. R. Extinction and timeout: Guidelines for their selection and use. In G. S. Belkin (Ed.), *Counseling: Directions in theory and practice*. Dubuque, IA: Kendall/Hunt, 1976.

———. Extinction: Guidelines for its selection and use. *Personnel and Guidance Journal,* 1974, 52, 290–295.

Berelson, B., and Steiner, G. A. *Human behavior: An inventory of scientific findings*. New York: Harcourt, Brace, Jovanovich, 1969.

Berg, D. H. Sexual subculture and contemporary heterosexual interaction patterns among adolescents. *Adolescence,* 1975, 10 (40), 543–547.

Berger, M., and Wright, L. 1978. Divided allegiance: Men, work and family life. *The Counseling Psychologist,* 7 (4), 50–52.

Bernard, H. S.; Roach, A. M.; and Resnick, H. Training bartenders as helpers on a college campus. *Personnel and Guidance Journal,* 1981, 60 (2), 119–121.

Bernard, J. Note on changing family life styles, 1970–1974. *Journal of Marriage and the Family,* 1975, 37, (3), 582–593.

Bernard, J. Societal values and parenting. *The Counseling Psychologist,* 1981, 9 (4), 5–12.

Bernard, M. E. Private thoughts in rational emotive psychotherapy. *Cognitive Therapy and Research,* 1981, 5 (2), 125–142.

Berne, E. Intuition vs. ego image. *Psychiatric Quarterly,* 1957, 31, 611–627.

———. *Transactional analysis in psychotherapy*. New York: Grove Press, 1961.

————. *The structure and dynamics of organizations and groups.* Philadelphia: J. B. Lippincott, 1963.

————. *What do you say after you say hello?* New York: Grove Press, 1972.

————. *Games people play.* New York: Grove Press, 1964.

Betz, R. L.; Wilbur, M. P.; and Roberts-Wilbur, J. A structural blueprint for group facilitators: Three group modalities. *Personnel and Guidance Journal,* 1981, 60 (1), 31–37.

Bieber, I. Homosexual dynamics in psychiatric crises. *American Journal of Psychiatry,* 1972, 128, 1268–1272.

Biestek, F. P. The non-judgmental attitude. *Journal of Social Casework,* 1953, 34, 235–240.

Bird, B. *Talking with patients,* 2nd Ed. Philadelphia: J. B. Lippincott, 1976, 171–184.

Bird, C. *The two-paycheck marriage.* New York: Rawson Wade, 1979.

Black, B. J. Rehabilitative and community support for mental patients. *Rehabilitation Literature,* 1976, 37 (2), 34–40.

Blatt, I. Counseling the Puerto Rican client. In G. S. Belkin, Ed. *Counseling: Directions in theory and practice.* Dubuque, IA: Kendall/Hunt, 1976.

Bloch, D. *So the witch won't eat me.* Boston: Houghton Mifflin, 1978.

Blocher, D. H. *Developmental counseling.* New York: Ronald Press, 1966.

Block, J. Psychosomatic phenomena. *American Psychologist,* 1978, 33 (4), 396–397.

Blohm, A. A. Group counseling with moderately mentally retarded and learning disabled elementary school children. *Dissertation Abstracts International,* 1978 (Oct.), 39 (6–A), 3362.

Bloom, B. L. Definitional aspects of the crisis concept. *Journal of Consulting Psychology,* 1963, 27, 498–502.

Blumberg, S., and Schwarz, P. *American couples: Money, work, and sex.* New York: Harper and Row, 1984.

Bondroff, B. L. Effecting changes in parents through their involvement in learning behavior modification techniques in client-centered discussion groups. *Dissertation Abstracts International,* 1981, 42 (4–A), 1542.

Bonds-White, F. The special it: Treatment of the passive-aggressive personality. *Transactional Analysis Journal,* 1984, 14 (3), 180–190.

Bookbinder, S. M. Educational goals and schooling in a therapeutic community. *Harvard Educational Review,* 1975, 45 (1), 71–89.

Borland, B. L., and Heckman, H. K. Hyperactive boys and their brothers. *Archives of General Psychiatry,* 1976, 33 (6), 669–675.

Bosco, J. Behavior modification drugs and the schools: The case of Ritalin. *Phi Delta Kappan,* 1975, 56, 489–492.

Bosserman, P., and Butler, N. The leisure revolution: It's about time. *Journal of Physical Education and Recreation,* 1976, 47 (8), 27–29.

Bottoms, G. The mission of career guidance: Definitions and leadership. *American Vocational Journal,* 1976, 50, 50–52.

Boudin, H. M. et al. Contingency contracting with drug abusers in the natural environment. *International Journal of the Addictions,* 1977, 12 (1), 1–16.

Boy, A. V. Motivating elementary school pupils to seek counseling. *Elementary School Guidance and Counseling,* 1974, 8, 166–172.

Bradley, M. K. Counseling past and present: Is there a future? *Personnel and Guidance Journal,* 1978, 57, 42–45.

Breggin, P. Underlying a method: Is psychosurgery an acceptable treatment for "hyperactivity" in children? *Mental Hygiene,* 1974, 58 (1), 19–21.

Briddell, D.W., and Leiblum, S. R. "Multimodal treatment of spastic colitis and incapacitating anxiety: A case study." In A. Lazarus (Ed.), *Multimodal behavior therapy.* New York: Springer, 1976, pp. 160–169.

Brockopp, G. W. Crisis intervention: Theory, process and practice. In D. Lester and G. W. Brockopp (Eds.), *Crisis intervention and counseling by telephone.* Springfield, IL: Charles C Thomas, 1973.

Brodie, T. A., and Manning, W. D. In the Wayzata schools they do more than just talk about alcohol and drug problems: The chemical dependency program and how it helps teenagers. *The American School Board Journal,* 1976, 163, 46–48.

Brolin, D. Value of rehabilitation services and correlates of vocational success with mentally retarded. *American Journal of Mental Deficiency,* 1972, 76 (6), 644–651.

Brooks, D. B. Contingency contracts with truants. *Personnel and Guidance Journal,* 1974, 52, 316–320.

Broverman, I. K.; Broverman, D. M.; Clarkson, F. E.; Rosenkrantz, P. S.; and Vogel, S. R. Sex-role stereotypes and clinical judgments of mental health. *Journal of Consulting and Clinical Psychology,* 1970, 34, 1–7.

Brownmiller, S. *Against our will.* New York: Random House, 1975.

Bruch, H. Teaching and learning of psychotherapy. *Canadian Journal of Psychiatry,* 1981, 26 (2), 86–92.

Bryde, J. F. *Indian students and guidance.* Boston: Houghton Mifflin, 1971.

Bryson, S., and Bardo, H. Race and the counseling process: An overview. *Journal of Non-White Concerns in Personnel and Guidance,* 1975, 4, 5–15.

Buchan, G. L., and Hale, J. B. Growing a community team. *School Psychology International,* 1981, 1 (6), 16–19.

Bugg, C. A. Systematic desensitization: A technique worth trying. *Personnel and Guidance Journal,* 1972, 50, 823–828.

Burland, J. A.; Andrews, R. G.; and Headsten, S. J. Child abuse: One tree in the forest. *Child Welfare,* 1973, 52 (9), 585–592.

Butcher, E. Changing by choice: A process model for group career counseling. *Vocational Guidance Quarterly,* 1982, 30 (3), 200–209.

Butcher, P. Existential-behaviour therapy: A possible paradigm? *British Journal of Medical Psychology*, 1984, 57 (3), 265–274.

Byrne, R. *The school counselor*. Boston: Houghton Mifflin, 1963.

Byrne, R. H. *Guidance: A behavioral approach*. Englewood Cliffs, NJ: Prentice-Hall, 1977.

Calia, V. F. The culturally deprived client: A re-formulation of the counselor's role. *Journal of Counseling Psychology*, 1966, 13, 100–105.

Calnek, M. Racial factors in the counter-transference: The black therapist and the black client. *American Journal of Orthopsychiatry*, 1970, 40, 39–46.

Calvin, A. D.; Clifford, L. T.; Clifford, B.; Bolden, L.; and Harvey, J. Experimental validation of conditioned inhibition. *Psychological Reports*, 1956, 2, 21–56.

Cameron, S. Violence and truancy on the increase. *The Times Educational Supplement*, April 4, 1975, 3123:3.

Cantor, M. B. Karen Horney on psychoanalytic technique: Mobilizing constructive forces. *American Journal of Psychoanalysis*, 1967, 27, 188–199.

Cantwell, D. P. *The hyperactive child: Diagnosis, management, current research*. New York: Spectrum, 1975.

Caplan, G. *Principles of preventive psychiatry*. New York: Basic Books, 1964.

Caplan, N. The new ghetto man: A review of recent empirical studies. *Journal of Social Issues*, 1970, 26, 59–73.

Caplan, N., and Nelson, D. S. On being useful—the nature and consequences of psychological research on social problems. *American Psychologist*, 1973, 28, 199–211.

Caplan, N. S., and Paige, J. M. A study of ghetto rioters. *Scientific American*, 1968, 219, 15–21.

Carkhuff, R. R. An integration of practice and training. In B. G. Berenson and R. R. Carkhuff (Eds.), *Sources of gain in counseling and psychotherapy*. New York: Holt, Rinehart and Winston, 1967. Originally published in R. R. Carkhuff, *The counselor's contribution to facilitative processes*. Urbana, IL: R. W. Parkinson, 1966.

————. *The development of human resources*. New York: Holt, Rinehart and Winston, 1971.

Carkhuff, R. R.; Alexik, M.; and Anderson, S. Do we have a theory of vocational choice? *Personnel and Guidance Journal*, 1967, 46, 335–345.

Carkhuff, R. R., and Berenson, B. G. *Beyond counseling and therapy*. New York: Holt, Rinehart and Winston, 1967.

————. The nature, structure and function of counselor commitment to client. *Journal of Rehabilitation*, 1969, 35, 13–14.

Carkhuff, R. R., and Pierce, R. M. *Trainer's guide: The art of helping*. Amherst, Mass.: Human Resources Development Press, 1975.

Carkhuff, R. R.; Pierce, R. M.; and Cannon, J. R. *The art of helping III.* Amherst, Mass.: Human Resources Development Press, 1977.

Carmer, J. C., and Rouzer, D. L. Healthy functioning from the gestalt perspective. *Counseling Psychologist,* 1974, 4 (4), 20–23.

Carroll, C.; Miller, D.; and Nash, J. C. *Health: The science of human adaptation.* Dubuque, IA: Wm. C. Brown Publishers, 1976.

Carroll, J. C. The intergenerational transmission of family violence: The long-term effects of aggressive behavior. *Aggressive Behavior,* 1977, 3 (3), 289–299.

Carter, R. D., and Stuart, R. B. Behavior modification theory and practice: A reply. *Social Work,* 1970, 15, 37–50.

Cash, T. F.; Begley, P. P.; McCowen, D. A.; and Weise, B. C. When counselors are heard but not seen: Initial impact of physical attractiveness. *Journal of Counseling Psychology,* 1975, 22 (4), 273–279.

Celotta, B., and Telasi-Golubcow, H. A problem taxonomy for classifying clients' problems. *Personnel and Guidance Journal,* 1982, 61 (2), 73–76.

Cerio, J. E. Structured experiences with the educational growth group. *Personnel and Guidance Journal,* 1979, 57 (8), 398–401.

Chethik, B. Turning kids on to good nutrition. *Teacher,* 1976, 93, 44–46.

Chibucos, T. R. A perspective on the mistreatment of children. *Infant Mental Health Journal,* 1980, 1 (4), 212–223.

Claiborn, C. D. Interpretation and change in counseling. *Journal of Counseling Psychology,* 1982, 29 (5), 439–453.

Clanton, G., and Smith, L. G. (Eds.). *Jealousy.* Englewood Cliffs, NJ: Prentice-Hall, 1977.

Clark, K. B. *Dark ghetto: Dilemmas of social power.* New York: Harper and Row, 1965.

Clark, R., and Spengler, J. *Population aging in the 21st century.* U.S. Dept. of Health, Education and Welfare, 1978, 8, 279–280.

Clarke, K. M. The differential effects of the Gestalt two-chair experiment and cognitive problem-solving on career decision-making. *Dissertation Abstracts International,* 1981, 42 (3–B), 1164.

Clarke, K.M., and Greenberg, L.S. Differential effects of Gestalt two-chair intervention and problem solving in resolving decisional conflict. *Journal of Counseling Psychology,* 1986, 33 (1), 11–15.

Cleveland, M. Sex in marriage: At 40 and beyond. *The Family Coordinator,* 1976, 25, 237–240.

Cleveland, M., and Irvin, K. Custody resolution counseling: An alternative intervention. *Journal of Marital and Family Therapy,* 1982, 8, 105–111.

Cohen, B., and Sordo, I. Using reality therapy with adult offenders. *Journal of Offender Counseling, Services and Rehabilitation,* 1984, 8 (3), 25–39.

Cohen, C. I., and Corwin, J. An application of balance theory to family treatment. *Family Process,* 1975, 469–479.

Cohn, H.W. An existential approach to psychotherapy. *British Journal of Medical Psychology*, 1984, 57 (4), 311–318.

Cole, S. Send our children to work? *Psychology Today,* 1980, 14 (2), 44–67.

Cole, S. *The sociological orientation,* 2nd Ed. Chicago: Rand McNally, 1979.

Cole, S. O. Hyperkinetic children: The use of stimulant drugs evaluated. *American Journal of Orthopsychiatry,* 1975, 45, 28–35.

Combs, A. W. Self-actualization and the teaching function of counselors. In G. S. Belkin (Ed.), *Counseling: Directions in theory and practice.* Dubuque, IA: Kendall/Hunt, 1976, pp. 43–53.

Combs, A. W., and Snygg, D. *Individual behavior: A perceptual approach to behavior.* New York: Harper and Bros., 1959.

Combs, A. W. et al. *Florida studies in the helping professions.* Gainesville: University of Florida Press, 1969.

Cormier, L. S., and Bernard, J. M. Ethical and legal responsibilities of clinical supervisors. *Personnel and Guidance Journal,* 1982, 60 (8), 486–491.

Cormier, W. H., and Cormier, L. S. *Interview strategies for helpers.* Monterey, CA: Brooks/Cole, 1979.

———. *Interview strategies for helpers: A guide to assessment, treatment, and evaluation.* Monterey, CA: Brooks/Cole, 1979.

Cowen, E. L.; Gardner, E. A.; and Zox, M. (Eds.) *Emergent approaches to mental health problems.* New York: Appleton-Century-Crofts, 1967.

Cox, A.; Rutter, M.; and Holbrook, D. Psychiatric interviewing techniques vs. experimental study: Eliciting factual information. *British Journal of Psychiatry,* 1981, 139, 29–37.

Crandell, V.; Katkovsky, W.; and Crandell, V. Children's beliefs in their own control of reinforcements in intellectual achievement situations. *Child Development,* 1965, 36, 91–109.

Cremin, L. A. The progressive heritage of the guidance movement. In E. Landy and P. A. Perry (Eds.), *Guidance in American education* (Vol. I). Cambridge, MA.: Harvard University Press, 1964.

Cross, W. C., and Maldonado, B. The counselor, the Mexican American, and the stereotype. *Elementary School Guidance and Counseling,* 1971, 6, 27–31.

Crowder, J. E.; Yamamoto, J.; and Simonowitz, J. Training registered nurses as bereavement counselors in an occupational health service. *Hospital and Community Psychiatry,* Dec. 1976, 27 (12), 851–852.

Csikszentmihalyi, M., and Graef, R. Feeling free. *Psychology Today,* 1979, 13 (7), 84–90 & 98–99.

Curran, C. A. *Counseling and psychotherapy.* New York: Sheed and Ward, 1968.

Curtis, G. et al. Flooding in vivo as a research tool and treatment method for phobias: a preliminary report. *Comprehensive Psychiatry,* 1976, 17 (1), 153–160.

Curtiss, F. R. A study of role stress and psychological strain among young practicing pharmacists. *Dissertation Abstracts International,* 1978, 38: 10–B, 4741.

Cutter, F. Suicide: The wish, the act, and the outcome. *Life-Threatening Behavior,* 1971, 1 (2), 125–137.

Dale, M. W. Barriers to rehabilitation of ex-offenders. *Crime and Delinquency,* 1976, 22 (3), 322–337.

Darley, J. G. In A. H. Brayfield (Ed.), *Readings in modern methods of counseling.* New York: Appleton-Century-Crofts, 1950.

Davis, G., and Jessen, A. A clinical report on group intervention in bereavement. *Journal of Psychiatric Treatment and Evaluation,* 1982, 4 (1), 81–88.

Davis, S. M., and Harris, M. B. Sexual knowledge, sexual interests and sources of sexual information of rural and urban adolescents from three cultures. *Adolescence,* 1982, 17 (66), 229–237.

Davison, G. C., and Stuart, R. B. Behavior therapy and civil liberties. *American Psychologist,* 1975, 30 (7), 755–763.

DeBlassie, R. R., and Cowan, M. A. Counseling with the mentally handicapped children. *Elementary School Guidance and Counseling,* 1976, 10, 246–251.

DeNour, A. K., and Czakes, J. W. Professional team opinion and personal bias in a study of chronic hemodialysis unit team. *Journal of Chronic Diseases,* 1971, 24, 533–451.

DeVore, I. The new science of genetic self-interest. *Psychology Today,* 1977, 10 (9), 42–51, 84–88.

Deffenbacher, J. L., and Hahnloser, R. M. Cognitive relaxation coping skills in stress innoculation. *Cognitive Therapy and Research,* 1981, 5 (2), 211–215.

Diaz-Guerrero, R. A Mexican psychology. *American Psychologist,* 1977, 32, 934–944.

Dienalt, K. The quest for meaning among today's youth. *International Forum for Logotherapy,* 1984, 7 (2), 89–95.

Dilly, J.; Lee, J. L.; and Verrill, E. L. Is empathy ear-to-ear or face-to-face? *Personnel and Guidance Journal,* 1971, 50, 188–191.

Dimick, K. M., and Huff, V. E. *Child counseling.* Dubuque, IA: Wm. C. Brown Publishers, 1970, 68–74.

Dinsburg, D.; Glick, I.; and Feigenbaum, M. Marital therapy of women alcoholics. *Journal of Studies on Alcohol,* 1977, 38 (7), 1247–1257.

Dollard, J., and Miller, N. E. *Personality and psychotherapy.* New York: McGraw-Hill, 1950.

Dorn, F.J. Needed: Competent, confident, and committed career counselors. *Journal of Counseling and Development*, 1986, 65, 216–217.

Dowd, E. T., and Boroto, D. R. Differential effects of counselor self-disclosure, self-involving statements, and interpretation. *Journal of Counseling Psychology, 1982,* 29 (1), 8–13.

Draguns, J. G. Counseling across cultures: Common themes and distinct approaches. In P. B. Pedersen, W. J. Lonner, and J. G. Draguns (Eds.), *Counseling across cultures.* Honolulu: University of Hawaii Press, 1976.

Dreger, R.M. Does anyone really believe that alcoholism is a disease? *American Psychologist*, 1986, 41, 322.

Dreyfus, E. A. An existential approach to counseling. In C. Beck (Ed.), *Philosophical guidelines for counseling.* Dubuque, IA: Wm. C. Brown Publishers, 1971.

Dulchin, J., and Segal, A. J. The ambiguity of confidentiality in a psychoanalytic institute. *Psychiatry,* 1982, 45 (1), 13–25.

Dullea, G. Is joint custody good for children? *The New York Times Magazine,* 1980, Feb. 3, 32–46.

Ebert, B. The healthy family. *Family Therapy,* 1978, 5 (3), 227–232.

Eddy, C. The effects of alcohol on anxiety in problem and nonproblem drinkers. In C. Eddy and J. Ford (Eds.), *Women and alcohol.* Dubuque, IA: Kendall/Hunt Publishing Co., 1979.

Edwards, D. D., and Edwards, J. S. Marriage: Direct and continuous measurement. *Bulletin of Psychonomic Society,* 1977, 10 (3), 187–188.

Edwards, H. P.; Boulet, D. B.; Mahrer, A. R.; Chagnon, G. J.; and Mook, B. Carl Rogers during initial interviews: A moderate and consistent therapist. *Journal of Counseling Psychology,* 1982, 29 (1), 14–18.

Egan, G. The skilled helper. Monterey, CA: Brooks/Cole, 1974.

Ehrenwald, J. (Ed.) *The history of psychotherapy: From healing magic to encounters.* New York: Jason Aronson, 1976.

Eisenberg, S., and Delaney, D. J. *The Counseling Process,* 2nd Ed. Chicago: Rand McNally, 1977.

Ellis, A. Rational psychotherapy. *The Journal of General Psychology,* 1958, 59, 35–49.

———. *Reason and emotion in psychotherapy.* New York: Lyle Stuart, 1962.

———. *The art and science of love.* New York: Lyle Stuart, 1969.

———. *Growth through reason.* Palo Alto, CA: Science and Behavior Books, 1971.

———. The no cop-out therapy. *Psychology Today,* 1973, 7, 56–62.

———. Rational-emotive therapy. In R. Corsini (Ed.), *Current psychotherapies.* Itasca, IL: F. E. Peacock, 1973b.

————. Does rational-emotive therapy seem deep enough? *Rational Living,* 1975a, 10 (2), 11–14.

————. The treatment of sexual disturbance. *Marriage and Family Counseling,* 1975b, 2, 111–119.

————. Answering a critique of rational-emotive therapy. *Canadian Counsellor,* 1976a, 10 (2), 56–59.

————. Personality hypotheses of RET (Rational Emotive Therapy) and other modes of cognitive-behavior therapy. *The Counseling Psychologist,* 1977, 7 (1), 2–42.

————. Rational-emotive therapy and cognitive behavior therapy: Similarities and differences. *Cognitive Therapy and Research,* 1980, 4 (4), 325–340.

————.82 Entry in *Who's who in America,* 1982 edition, p. 1276.

Ellis, A., and Grieger, R. *Rational-emotive therapy: A handbook of theory and practice.* New York: Springer, 1977.

Ellis, A., and Harper, R. A. *A guide to rational living.* Englewood Cliffs, NJ: Prentice-Hall, 1961.

————. *A new guide to rational living.* Englewood Cliffs, NJ: Prentice-Hall, 1975.

Erikson, E. H. *Childhood and society,* 2nd Ed. New York: Norton, 1963.

Evans, D. B. Reality therapy: A model for physicians managing alcoholic patients. *Journal of Reality Therapy,* 1984, 3 (2), 20–26.

Ewing, D. B. Twenty approaches to individual change. *Personnel and Guidance Journal,* 1977, 55 (6), 331–338.

Eysenck, H. J., and Rachman, S. *The causes and cures of neurosis.* London: Routledge and Kegan Paul, 1965.

Ezell, B., and Patience, T. G. The contract as a counseling technique. *Personnel and Guidance Journal,* 1972, 51, 27–31.

Fagan, J. The tasks of the therapist. In J. Fagan and I. L. Shepherd (Eds.), *Gestalt therapy now.* Palo Alto, CA: Science and Behavior Books, 1970.

Fairchild, T. N., and Zins, J. E. Accountability practices of school counselors: A national survey. *Journal of Counseling and Development,* 1986, 65, 196–199.

Fairorth, J. W. Child abuse and the school. *Dissertation Abstracts International,* 1980, (Oct.) Vol 41 (4–A), 1553.

Falck, V. T., and Kilcoyne, M. E. Occupational stress in special education: A challenge for school health professionals. *Journal of School Health,* 1985, 55, 258–261.

Falkowski, W.; Ben-Tovim, D. I.; and Bland, J. M. The assessment of ego states. *British Journal of Psychiatry,* 1980, 137, 572–573.

Farson, R. Carl Rogers, quiet revolutionary. *Education,* 1974, 95 (2), 197–203.

Feingold, B. F. Hyperkinesis and learning disabilities linked to artificial food flavors and colors. *Journal of Nursing,* 1975 (May), 75 (5), 797–803.

Feinstein, B., and Brown, E. *The new partnership: Human services, business, and industry.* Cambridge: Schenkman, 1982.

Feldman, L. B. Goals of family therapy. *Journal of Marriage and Family,* 1976, 2, 103–115.

Felker, S. How to feel comfortable when you don't know what you are doing. *Personnel and Guidance Journal,* 1972, 50, 683–685.

Ferber, A.; Mendelsohn, M.; and Napier, A. (Eds.) *The book of family therapy.* New York: Jason Aronson, 1972.

Ferenczi, S. Further contributions to the theory and practice of psychoanalysis. London: Hogarth, 1950.

Ferrari, M. Can differences in diagnostic criteria be stopped? *Journal of Autism and Developmental Disorders,* 1982, 12 (1), 85–88.

Field, H. S., and Holley, W. H. Resume preparation: An empirical study of personnel managers' perceptions. *Vocational Guidance Quarterly,* 1976, 24, 229–237.

Fimian, M. J. Teacher stress: An expert appraisal, *Psychology in the Schools,* 1987, 24:5–14.

Fimian, M. J., et al. Occupational stress reported by teachers of learning disabled and nonlearning disabled handicapped students [use of teacher stress inventory]. *Journal of Learning Disabilities,* 1986, 19, 154–158.

Fine, R. *The meaning of love in human experience.* New York: Wiley-Interscience, 1985.

Fine, R. M. The application of social reinforcement procedures to improve the school attendance of truant Chicano junior high school students. *Dissertation Abstracts International,* 1974 (Sept.), 35 (3A), 1442–1443.

Firestone, E., and Moschetta, P. Behavioral contracting in family therapy. *Family Counseling,* 1975, 3, 27–31.

Fisher, B. L., and Sprenkle, D. H. Therapists' perception of healthy family functioning. *International Journal of Family Counseling,* 1978, 6 (2), 9–18.

Fisher, S. The renal dialysis client: A rational counseling approach. *Rehabilitation Counseling Bulletin,* 1976 June, 19 (4), 556–562.

Fitzgerald, L.F., and Osipow, S.H. An occupational analysis of counseling psychology. *American Psychologist,* 1986, 41 (5), 535–544.

Foley, V. D., and Dyer, W. W. "Timing" in family therapy: The "when," "how," and "why" of intervention. *The Family Coordinator,* 1974, 23 (4), 373–382.

Ford, E. E. Case examples of the application of reality therapy of family therapy. *Journal of Reality Therapy,* 1983, 2 (2), 14–20.

Foreman, N. J., and Zerwekh, J. V. Drug crisis intervention. *American Journal of Nursing,* 1971, 71, 1736–1739.

Forer, B. R. The therapeutic value of crisis. *Psychological Reports,* 1963, 13, 275–281.

Forrest, D. V. Employee assistance programs in the 1980s: Expanding career options for counselors. *Personnel and Guidance Journal,* October 1983, 105–108.

Forster, J. R. Counselor credentialing revised. *Personnel and Guidance Journal,* 1978, 56, 593–598.

Forster, J. R. What shall we do about credentialing? *Personnel and Guidance Journal,* 1977, 55, 573–576.

Forward, J. R., and Williams, J. R. Internal-external control and black militancy. *Journal of Social Issues,* 1970, 26, 75–92.

Francke, L. B., and Reese, M. After remarriage. *Newsweek,* February 11, 1980, 95 (6), 66.

Francke, L. B.; Sherman, D.; Simons, P. E.; Abramson, P.; Zabarsky, M.; Huck, J.; and Whitman, L. The children of divorce. *Newsweek,* February 11, 1980, 95 (6), 58–63.

Frankel, M. J., and Merbaum, M. Effects of therapist contact and a self-control manual on nailbiting reduction. *Behavior Therapy,* 1982, 13, 125–129.

Frankenhaeuser, M. Quality of life: Criteria for behavioral adjustment. *International Journal of Psychology,* 1977, 12 (2), 99–110.

Frankl, V. *Man's search for meaning: An introduction to logotherapy.* (Preface by G. W. Allport). Boston: Beacon Press, 1962.

———. *Psychotherapy and existentialism: Selected papers on logotherapy.* New York: Simon and Schuster (Clarion Books), 1967.

Freedman, A. M.; Kaplan, H. I.; and Sadock, B. J. *Comprehensive textbook of psychiatry.* 2nd ed. Philadelphia: Williams and Wilkins, 1975.

Freeman, L. *The story of Anna O.* New York: Walker, 1972.

Freeman, R. D. Minimal brain dysfunction, hyperactivity, and learning disorders: Epidemic or episode? *School Review,* 1976, 85 (1), 5–30.

Fremont, S., and Anderson, W. What client behaviors make counselors angry? An exploratory study. *Journal of Counseling and Development,* 1986, 65, 67–70.

Freire, P. *Cultural action for freedom.* Cambridge: Harvard Educational Review Press, 1970.

Fretz, B. R., and Mills, D. H. *Licensing and certification of psychologists and counselors.* San Francisco: Jossey-Bass, 1980.

Freud, A. *The ego and the mechanisms of defense.* New York: International Universities Press, 1966. (Originally published 1935.)

———. *The psychoanalytic treatment of children.* New York: Schocken Books, 1964.

Freud, S. The interpretation of dreams. In J. Strachy (Ed.), *The standard edition of the complete psychological works of Sigmund Freud* (Vol 12). London: Hogarth Press, 1957a. (Originally published 1900.)

———. "Analysis of a phobia of a five-year-old-boy." In J. Strachy (Ed.), *The standard edition of the complete psychological works of Sigmund Freud* (Vol 10). London: Hogarth Press, 1957b. (Originally published 1900).

———. Recommendations to physicians practicing psychoanalysis, 1912. In J. Strachey (Ed.), *The standard edition of the complete psychological works of Sigmund Freud.* London: Hogarth, 1953–1970, Vol. 12 (1958), 111–120.

———. *A general introduction to psychoanalysis, 1924.* (Lecture 19).

———. *The psychopathology of everyday life.* New York: Signet, 1961. (Originally published 1901.)

Frey, D. H. Conceptualizing counseling theories: A content analysis of process and goal statements. *Counselor Education and Supervision,* 1972, 11, 243–250.

Fried, E. Individuation through group psychotherapy. *International Journal of Applied Psychotherapy,* 1970, 20 (4), 450–459.

Friedman, J. C., and Mann, F. Recidivism: The fallacy of prediction. *International Journal of Offender Therapy and Comparative Criminology,* 1976, 20 (2), 153–163.

Friedman, M.; Beyers, S. O.; Rosenman, R. H.; Newman, R.; et al. Coronary-prone individuals (type-A behavior patterns: growth hormone responses). *Journal of the American Medical Association,* 1971, 217, 929–932.

Friedman, M.; Beyers, S. O.; Rosenman, R. H.; et al. Coronary-prone individuals (type-A behavior pattern). *Journal of the American Medical Association,* 1970, 212, 1030–1037.

Fromm, E. *The sane society.* New York: Fawcett, 1967. (Originally published: New York: Holt, Rinehart and Winston, 1955.)

Furstenberg, F. J., Jr., and Spanier, G. B. *Recycling the family: Remarriage after divorce.* Beverly Hills, CA: Sage, 1984.

Furstenberg, F. J., Jr.; Winquist, N.; Peterson, J. L.; and Zill, N. The life course of children of divorce. *American Sociological Review,* 1983, 48 (5), 656–667.

Gadlin, H. Private lives and public order: A critical view of the history of intimate relations in the United States. In G. Levinger and H. L. Raush (Eds.). *Close relationships: Perspectives on the meaning of intimacy.* Amherst: University of Massachusetts Press, 1982.

Gaddis, W. *Carpenter's gothic.* New York: Viking, 1985.

————. *The recognitions.* New York: Viking, 1953.

Garcia, C., and Levenson, H. Differences between blacks' and whites' expectations of control by change and powerful others. *Psychological Reports,* 1975, 37, 563–566.

Gardell, B. Psychological and social problems of industrial work in affluent societies. *International Journal of Psychology,* 1977, 12 (2), 125–134.

Gardner, L. H. The therapeutic relationship under varying conditions of race. *Psychotherapy: Theory, Research and Practice,* 1971, 8 (1), 78–87.

Garfield, J. C.; Weiss, S. I.; and Pollack, E. A. Effects of the child's social class on school counselor's decision-making. *Journal of Counseling Psychology,* 1973, 20, 166–168.

Garfield, S. I. Effectiveness of psychotherapy: The perennial controversy. *Professional Psychology: Research and Practice*, 1983, 32, 35–43.

Garvey, W. P., and Hegrenes, J. R. Desensitization techniques in the treatment of school phobia. *American Journal of Orthopsychiatry,* 1966, 36, 147–152.

Gazda, G. M. Licensure/certification for counseling psychologists and counselors. *Personnel and Guidance Journal,* 1977, 55, 570.

————. Theories and methods of group counseling in the schools. Springfield, IL: Charles C Thomas, 1972.

Gearheart, B. R. Learning disabilities: Educational strategies, 2nd Ed. St. Louis: C. V. Mosby, 1977.

Gedan, S. Abortion counseling with adolescents. *American Journal of Nursing,* 1974, 74 (10), 1856–1858.

Gellen, M. I. Finger blood volume responses of counselor, counselor trainees, and non-counselors to stimuli from an empathy test. *Counselor Education and Supervision,* 1970, 10, 64–73.

Gelles, R. J. Power, sex and violence: The case of marital rape. *The Family Coordinator,* 1977, 26 (4), 339–347.

Gendlin, E. Personal communication to author, October 23, 1982.

Gendlin, E. *Focusing.* New York: Bantam Books, 1981.

Gendlin, E. T. Experiencing: A variable in the process of therapeutic change. *American Journal of Psychotherapy,* 1961, 16, 233–245.

Genrich, S. The need for pre-vocational exploration to include work experience for the physically disabled. *Journal of Applied Rehabilitation Counseling,* 1975, 6, 183–187.

Gentry, W. D.; Chesney, A. P.; Gary, H. E., Jr.; Hall, R. P.; and Harburg, E. Habitual anger-coping styles: I. Effect on mean blood pressure and risk for essential hypertension. *Psychosomatic Medicine,* 1982, 44 (2), 195–198.

Georgiady, N. P. Blue-collar careers? Why not? *Elementary School Journal,* 1976, 77, 116–124.

Geronilla, L., and Walker, D. Speak easy: A positive alternative group for single adults using reality therapy. *Journal of Reality Therapy,* 1986, 5 (2), 11–14.

Gibb, J. R. The counselor as a role free person. In C. A. Parker (Ed.), *Counseling theories and counselor education.* Boston: Houghton Mifflin, 1968.

Gill, S. J., and Barry, R. A. Group-focused counseling: Classifying the essential skills. *Personnel and Guidance Journal,* 1982, 60 (5), 302–305.

Ginzberg, E. Toward a theory of vocational choice. *Vocational Guidance Quarterly,* 1972, 20, 169–175.

Giuffra, M. J. Demystifying adolescent behavior. *American Journal of Nursing,* 1975 (10), 1725–1727.

Gladstein, G. A. Empathy and counseling outcome: An empirical and conceptual review. *Counseling Psychology,* 1977, 6 (4), 70–78.

———. Is empathy important in counseling? *Personnel and Guidance Journal,* 1970, 48, 823–826.

Glaser, W. *The identity society.* New York: Harper and Row, 1972.

Glasser, W., and Zunin, Z. M. Reality therapy. In R. Corsini (Ed.), *Current psychotherapies.* Itasca, IL: F. E. Peacock, 1973.

Glasser, W. Interview by D. B. Evans, What are you doing? An interview with William Glasser. *Personnel and Guidance Journal,* 1982, 61, 460–462.

Glasser, W. *Mental health or mental illness?* New York: Harper and Row, 1961.

Glasser, W. *Reality therapy: A new approach to psychiatry.* New York: Harper and Row, 1965.

Glasser, W. *Schools without failure.* New York: Harper and Row, 1969.

Glasser, W. Reality therapy and counseling. In C. Beck (Ed.) *Philosophical guidelines in counseling,* 2nd Ed. Dubuque, IA: Wm. C. Brown Publishers, 1971.

Gledich, N. M. Field study in a bilingual school. *Language Arts,* 1976, 53 (4), 407–408.

Glenn, A. A.; Pollard, J. W.; Denovcheck, J. A.; and Smith, A. F. Eating disorders on campus: A procedure for community intervention. *Journal of Counseling and Development,* 1986, 65, 163–165.

Globetti, G. Problem and non-problem drinking among high school students in abstinence communities. *International Journal of Addictions,* 1972, 7 (3), 511–523.

Goble, F. *The third force*. New York: Grossman, 1970.

Goddard, R. C. Increase in assertiveness and actualization as a function of didactic training. *Dissertation Abstracts International,* 1981, 41 (12–B, Pt. 1), 4663.

Godenne, G. D. Sex and today's youth. *Adolescence,* 1974, 9 (33), 67–72.

Goetting, A. Divorce outcome research: Issues and perspectives. *Journal of Family Issues,* 1981, 2 (3), 350–378.

Goffman, E. *The presentation of self in everyday life*. Garden City: Doubleday (Anchor), 1959.

Goldberg, G. Breaking the communication barrier: The initial interview with an abusing parent. *Child Welfare,* 1975, 54 (4), 274–281.

Goldhaber, G. M., and Goldhaber, M. B. (Eds.). *Transactional analysis: Principles and applications*. Boston: Allyn and Bacon, 1976.

Goldman, L. Behavior therapy faces middle age. *The Counseling Psychologist,* 1978, 7 (3), 25–28.

Goodman, J. Group counseling with seventh graders. *Personnel and Guidance Journal,* 1976, 54 (6), 519–520.

Gorden, R. L. *Interviewing: Strategy, techniques, and tactic*. Homewood, IL: Dorsey, 1975.

Gould, S. J. *The mismeasure of man*. New York: Norton, 1981.

Grala, C., and McCauley, C. Counseling truants back to school: Motivation combined with a program for action. *Journal of Counseling Psychology,* 1976, 23, 166–169.

Granberg, L. I. What I've learned in counseling. *Christianity Today,* 1967, 2, 891–894.

Gray, S. W., and Noble, F. C. The school counselor and the school psychologist. In J. F. Adams (Ed.), *Counseling and guidance: A summary view*. New York: Macmillan, 1965.

Green, B. J. Helping children of divorce: A multimodal approach. *Elementary School Guidance and Counseling,* 1978, 13 (1), 31–45.

Greenson, R. R. *The technique and practice of psychoanalysis,* Vol. 1. New York: International Universities Press, 1964.

Greer, R. D., and Dorow, L. G. *Specializing education behaviorally*. Dubuque, IA: Kendall/Hunt, 1976.

Grier, W. H., and Cobbs, P. M. *Black rage*. New York: Bantam, 1968.

Grinspoon, L., and Singer, S. B. Amphetamines in the treatment of hyperactive children. *Harvard Educational Review,* 1973, 43 (4), 515–555.

Gross, S. J. The holistic health movement. *Personnel and Guidance Journal,* 1980, 59 (2), 96–100.

Grotgen, J. F. Administration and assessment of a systematic nonverbal skill training program for beginning counselors. *Dissertation Abstracts International,* 1981, 42 (3–A), 1008.

Grove, C. L., and Torbior, I. A new conceptualization of intercultural adjustment and the goals of training. *International Journal of Intercultural Relations,* 1985, 9, 205–233.

Guerney, B. G. (Ed.). *Psychotherapeutic agents: New roles for nonprofessionals, parents, and teachers.* New York: Holt, Rinehart and Winston, 1969.

Gunnings, T. S. Preparing the new counselor. *The Counseling Psychologist,* 1971, 2 (4), 100–101.

Gurin, P.; Gurin, G.; Lao, R.; and Beattie, M. Internal-external control in the motivational dynamics of Negro youth. *Journal of Social Issues,* 1969, 25, 29–54.

Gurry, J. Career communication in the secondary school. *Communication Education,* 1976, 25, 307–316.

Haase, W. *Rorschach diagnosis, socio-economic class and examiner bias.* Unpublished doctoral dissertation, New York University, 1956.

Hackney, H. The evolution of empathy. *Personnel and Guidance Journal,* 1978, 57, 35–38.

Hadden, S. B. A glimpse of pioneers in group psychotherapy. *International Journal of Group Psychotherapy,* 1975, 25 (4), 371–378.

Haettenschwiller, D. L. Counseling black college students in special programs. *Personnel and Guidance Journal,* 1971, 50, 29–35.

Hageman, M. J. Occupational stress of law enforcement officers and marital and familial relationships. *Dissertation Abstracts International,* 1977, 38, 3–A, 1674.

Haldane, D., and McClusky, U. Existentialism and family therapy: A neglected perspective. *Journal of Family Therapy,* 1982, 4 (2),117–132.

Haley, J. Marriage therapy. In H. Greenwald (Ed.), *Active psychotherapy.* Chicago: Aldine, 1967, 189–223. (Originally published 1963.)

―――. Beginning and experienced family therapists. In A. Ferber, M. Mendelsohn, and A. Napier (Eds.), *The book of family therapy.* New York: Aronson, 1972, pp. 155–167.

Hall, W. S.; Cross, W. E.; and Freedle, R. Stages in the development of black awareness: An exploratory investigation. In R. L. Jones (Ed.), *Black psychology.* New York: Harper and Row, 1972.

Hamburg, B. A. Early adolescence: A specific and stressful stage of the life cycle. In G. V. Coelho, D. A. Hamburg, and J. E. Adams (Eds.), *Coping and adaptation.* New York: Basic Books, 1974, 101–124.

Hansen, J. C.; Stevic, R. R.; and Warner, R. W., Jr. *Counseling: Theory and practice,* 2nd Ed. Boston: Allyn and Bacon, 1977.

Hardy, R. E., and Cull, J. G. *Educational and psychosocial aspects of deafness*. Springfield, IL: Charles C Thomas, 1974.

Harman, R. L. Techniques of Gestalt therapy. *Professional Psychology*, 1974, 5 (3), 257–263.

Harman, R. L., and Franklin, R. W. Gestalt interactional groups. *Personnel and Guidance Journal*, 1975, 54 (1), 49–50.

Harris, T. A. *I'm OK—You're OK*. New York: Harper and Row, 1969. (Edition quoted is Avon paperback, 1973).

Hatcher, C., and Himmelstein, P. (Eds.) *Handbook of Gestalt Therapy*. New York: Jason Aronsom, 1983.

Havighurst, R. J., and Neugarten, B. L. Society and education, 2nd Ed. Boston: Allyn and Bacon, 1962.

Hawes, L. C. The effects of interview style on patterns of dyadic communication. *Speech Monographs*, 1972, 39 (2), 114–123.

HBAC (Home Buyers Assistance Corporation). *Fact sheet (1987) on relocation counseling services*. HBAC, 251 Riverside Avenue, Westport CT 06880, 1987.

Hearn, J. C., and Moos, R. H. Social climate and major choice: A test of Holland's theory in university student living groups. *Journal of Vocational Behavior*, 1976, 8, 293–305.

Heilburn, A. B., Jr. Cognitive factors in early counseling termination: Social insight and level of defensiveness. *Journal of Counseling Psychology*, 1982, 29 (1), 29–38.

Heitzmann, D.; Schmidt, A. K.; and Hurley, F. W. Career encounters: Career decision making through on-site visits. *Journal of Counseling and Development*, 1986, 65, 209–210.

Helpern, J. M. G. The role of the guidance consultant at the elementary school. *Journal of Education*, 1964, 146, 16–34.

Herlihy, B., and Sheely, V. L. Privileged communication provisions in statutes and regulations of selected helping professions. *Journal of Counseling and Development*, 1987, 65, 479–483.

Herr, E. L., and Cramer, S. H. *Vocational guidance and career development in the schools: Toward a systems approach*. Boston: Houghton Mifflin, 1972.

Herrnstein, R. J. The evolution of behaviorism. *American Psychologist*, 1977, 32 (8), 593–603.

Hersch, P., and Scheibe, K. Reliability and validity of internal-external control as a personality dimension. *Journal of Consulting Psychology*, 1967, 31, 609–613.

Hewer, V. H. What do theories of vocational choice mean to a counselor? *Journal of Counseling Psychology*, 1963, 10, 118–125.

Hipple, J. L., and Muto, L. The TA group for adolescents. *Personnel and Guidance Journal,* 1974, 52 (10), 675–681.

Hirschberg, G. G.; Lewis, L.; and Thomas, D. *Rehabilitation: A manual for the care of the disabled and elderly.* Philadelphia: J. B. Lippincott, 1964.

Hoch, Z. Sexual counseling and therapy. *Journal of Family Counseling,* 1974, 4 (1), 7–13.

Hoehn-Sarie, R. Emotions and psychotherapies. *American Journal of Psychotherapy,* 1977, 31 (1), 83–96.

Hoffman, L. R. Peers as group counseling models. *Elementary School Guidance and Counseling,* 1976, 11 (1), 37–44.

Holdstock, T. L., and Rogers, C. R. Person-centered theory. In R. J. Corsini (Ed.), *Current personality theories.* Itasca, IL: F. E. Peacock, 1977, 125–152.

Holland, J. *Making vocational choices: A theory of careers.* Englewood Cliffs, NJ: Prentice-Hall, 1973.

————. *The psychology of vocational choice.* Waltham, MA: Blaisdall, 1966.

————. *Some explorations of theory of vocational choice.* Washington, DC: Monographs of American Psychological Association, 1962.

Hollingshead, A. B. *Elmtown's youth: The impact of social classes on adolescents.* New York: John Wiley and Sons, 1949.

Hollingshead, A. B., and Redlich, F. C. *Social class and mental health.* John Wiley and Sons, 1958.

Holmstrom, L. L., and Burgess, A. W. Assessing trauma in the rape victim. *American Journal of Nursing,* 1975, 75 (8), 214–231.

Holt, J. Growing up engaged. *Psychology Today,* 1980, 14 (2), 14–23.

Holt, J. Quackery. *New York Review of Books,* August 13, 1970.

Honig, R. G. Group meetings on an adolescent medical ward. *Adolescence,* 1982, 17 (65), 99–106.

Hopkins, J. R. Sexual behavior in adolescence. *Journal of Social Issues,* 1977, 33 (2), 67–85.

Hopkins, M. T. Patterns of self-destruction among the orthopedically disabled. *Rehabilitation Research and Practice Review,* 1971, 3, 5–16.

Hoppock, R. *Occupational information,* 3rd Ed. New York: McGraw-Hill, 1967.

Horner, M. S. Toward an understanding of achievement-related conflicts in women. *Journal of Social Issues,* 1972, 28, 157–175.

Horney, K. *The neurotic personality of our time.* New York: Norton, 1937.

————. *New ways in psychoanalysis.* New York: Norton, 1939.

————. *Neurosis and human growth.* New York: Norton, 1950.

Horowitz, M. B. A comment on "An empirical investigation of the construct validity of empathic understanding ratings." *Counselor Education and Supervision,* 1977, 16 (4), 292–295.

Houser, B. B., and Berkman, S. L. Aging parent/mature child relationships. *Journal of Marriage and the Family*, 1984, 46 (2), 295–300.

Hsieh, T.; Shybut, J.; and Lotsof, E. Internal vs. external control and ethnic group membership: A cross cultural comparison. *Journal of Consulting and Clinical Psychology,* 1969, 33, 122–124.

Huber, C. H. Parents of the handicapped child: Facilitating acceptance through group counseling. *Personnel and Guidance Journal,* 1979, 57 (5), 267–269.

Huckaby, H., and Daly, J. Got those PL94–142 blues. *Personnel and Guidance Journal,* 1979, 58 (1), 70–72.

Humes, C. W. II. School counselors and PL94–142. *School Counselor,* 1978, 25, 192–195.

Hunt, M. *The universe within.* New York: Simon and Schuster, 1982.

Ivey, A. Toward a definition of the culturally effective counselor. *Personnel and Guidance Journal,* 1977, 55, 296–302.

Jackson, A. M. Psychotherapy: Factors associated with the race of the therapist. *Psychotherapy: Theory, Research and Practice,* 1973, 10 (3), 273–277.

Jackson, B. Black identity development. *Journal of Educational Diversity,* 1975, 2, 19–25.

James, J. Grandparents and family script parade. *Transactional Analysis Journal,* 1984, 14 (1), 18–28.

Jani, S., and Jani, L. Nutritional deprivation and learning disabilities—an appraisal. *Academic Therapy,* 1975, 10, 151–158.

Jaques, M. E. *Rehabilitation counseling: Scope and services.* Boston: Houghton Mifflin, 1970.

Jeffrey, T. B. The effects of operant conditioning and electromyographic biofeedback on the relaxed behaviors of hyperkinetic children. *Dissertation Abstracts International,* 1976 (Nov.), 37 (5–B), 2510.

Jellinek, E. M. Phases of alcohol addiction. In G. D. Shean (Ed.), *Studies in abnormal behavior.* Chicago: Rand McNally, 1971.

Jenkins, C. D. Recent evidence supporting psychologic and social risk factors for coronary disease. *New England Journal of Medicine,* 1976, 294, 987–994.

Jennings, J.L. Husserl revisited: The forgotten distinction between psychology and phenomenology. *American Psychologist*, 1986, 41 (11), 1231–1240.

Jensen, S. M.; Baker, M. S.; and Kopp, A. H. TA in brief psychotherapy with college students. *Adolescence,* 1980, 15 (59), 683–689.

References

Jessee, E., and L'Abate, L. Enrichment role-playing as a step in the training of family therapists. *Journal of Marital and Family Therapy,* 1981, 7 (4), 507–514.

Jessee, R. E., and Guerney, B. G. A comparison of Gestalt and relationship enhancement treatments with married couples. *American Journal of Family Therapy,* 1981, 9 (3), 31–41.

Jevne, R. Counsellor competencies and selected issues in Canadian counsellor education. *Canadian Counsellor,* 1981, 15 (2), 57–63.

Johnson, D. E., and Vestermark, M. J. *Barriers and hazards in counseling.* Boston: Houghton Mifflin, 1970.

Johnson, R. E. *In quest of a new psychology: Toward a redefinition of humanism.* New York: Human Sciences Press, 1975.

Jones, J. M. *Prejudice and racism.* Reading, MA: Addison-Wesley, 1972.

Josselyn, I. M. *Psychosocial development of children.* New York: Family Services Association of America, 1948.

Jourard, S. M. *The transparent self.* Princeton: D. Van Nostrand, 1964.

Jung, C. G. The development of personality (1954) Vol. I. In *The collected works of Carl Gustav Jung.* Princeton, NJ: Princeton University Press, 1964.

Kadushin, A. *The social work interview.* New York: Columbia University Press, 1972.

Kagan, N. Presidential address: Division 17. *The Counseling Psychologist,* 1977, 7 (2), 4–8.

Kahn, M. The mythical oligarchy of clinical psychologists in Florida. *Clinical Psychologist,* 1981, 34 (2), 18–19.

Kalis, B. L.; Harris, R. M.; Prestwood, R. A.; and Freeman, E. H. Precipitating stress as a focus in psychotherapy. *Archives of General Psychiatry,* 1961, 5, 219–228.

Kalmar, R. (Ed.). *Child abuse.* Dubuque, IA: Kendall/Hunt, 1977a.

———. *Abortion: the emotional implications.* Dubuque, IA: Kendall/Hunt, 1977b.

Kaplan, H. B. A guide for explaining social interest to laypersons. *Journal of Individual Psychology,* 1986.

Kaplan, H. S. No-nonsense therapy for six sexual malfunctions. *Psychology Today,* 1974, 8 (5), 77–86.

Kaplan, M. L. Uses of the group in Gestalt therapy groups. *Psychotherapy: Theory, Research and Practice,* 1978, 15 (1), 80–89.

Kardener, S. H. A methodological approach to crisis therapy. *American Journal of Psychotherapy,* 1975, 29, 4–13.

Karpel, M. Individuation: From fusion to dialogue. *Family Process,* 1975, 65–82.

Kastner, M., and Neumann, M. A model combining two psychotherapeutic approaches in group psychotherapy. *Psychotherapy,* 1986, 23 (4), 593–97.

Kaufman, M., and Bluestone, H. Patient-therapist: Are we free to choose therapy? *Groups: A Journal of Dynamics and Psychotherapy,* 1974, 6 (1), 1–13.

Kaufman, Y. Analytical Psychotherapy. In R. J. Corsini (Ed.), *Current Psychotherapies.* Itasca, IL: F.E. Peacock, 108–141, 1984.

Kazdin, A. E. Current developments and research issues in cognitive-behavioral interventions: A commentary. *School Psychology Review,* 1982, 11 (1), 75–82.

Kemp, C. G. Existential counseling. *The Counseling Psychologist,* 1971, 2, 2–30.

Kendler, K. S., and Tsuang, M. T. Nosology of paranoid schizophrenia and other paranoid psychoses. *Schizophrenia Bulletin,* 1981, 7 (4), 594–610.

Kerr, M. Quoted in "Family Sickness." *Time,* November 24, 1975, 73.

Kifer, R.; Lewis, M.; Green, D.; and Phillips, E. Training predelinquent youths and their parents to negotiate conflict situations. *Journal of Applied Behavioral Analysis,* 1974, 7 (3), 357–364.

Kimmel, D. C. Adult development: Challenges for counseling. *Personnel and Guidance Journal,* 1976, 55, 103–105.

Kinard, E. M. Experiencing child abuse: Effects on emotional adjustment. *American Journal of Orthopsychiatry,* 1982, 52 (1), 82–91.

King, K.; Blaswick, J. O.; and Robinson, I. E. The continuing premarital sexual revolution among college females. *Journal of Marriage and the Family,* 1977, 39 (3), 455–459.

Kirk, S. A., and Gallagher, J. J. *Educating exceptional children,* 3rd Ed. Boston: Houghton Mifflin, 1979.

Kirkpatrick, J. *Turnabout: Help for a new life.* New York: Doubleday, 1977.

Kirman, W. J. *Modern psychoanalysis in the schools.* Dubuque, IA: Kendall/Hunt, 1977.

Kirman, W. J. Emotional education in the classroom: A modern psychoanalytic approach. In G. S. Belkin (Ed.), *Counseling: Directions in theory and practice.* Dubuque, IA: Kendall/Hunt, 1976.

Klein, D. C., and Lindemann, E. Preventive intervention in individual and family crisis situations. In G. Caplan (Ed.), *Prevention of mental disorders in children.* New York: Basic Books, 1961.

Klein, D. F., and Gittleman-Klein, R. Problems in the diagnosis of minimal brain dysfunction and the hyperkinetic syndrome. In R. Gittleman-Klein (Ed.), *Recent advances in child psychopharmacology.* New York, Human Sciences Press, 1975.

Kline, D. F.; Cole, P.; and Fox, P. Child abuse and neglect: The school psychologist's role. *School Psychology Review,* 1981, 10 (1), 65–71.

Knapp, T. J. Ralph Franklin Hefferline: The Gestalt therapist among the Skinnerians or the Skinnerians among the Gestalt therapists? *Journal of the History of the Behavioral Sciences,* 1986, 22 (1), 49–60.

Koenig, P. The problem that can't be tranquilized. *New York Times Magazine,* May 21, 1978, pp. 14–17, 44–46.

Kohler, W. G. Personality correlates of client directiveness preference. *Dissertation Abstracts International,* 1981, 41 (9–B), 3577.

Komm, R. A. He's "LD"—I mean he's "ADD." *Academic Therapy,* 1982, 17 (4), 431–435.

Konopka, G. The needs, rights and responsibilities of youth. *Child Welfare,* 1976, 55 (3), 173–182.

Krathwohl, D. R.; Bloom, B. S.; and Masia, B. B. *Taxonomy of educational objectives: The classification of educational goals—handbook II: Affective domain.* New York: David McKay, 1964.

Krieger, G. W. Rehabilitation counseling and the ex-offender. *Journal of Employment Counseling,* 1975, 12 (4), 154–158.

Krumboltz, J. D. Behavioral counseling: Rationale and research. *Personnel and Guidance Journal,* 1965, 44, 383–387.

————. Behavioral goals for counseling. *Journal of Counseling Psychology,* 1966a, 13 (2), 153–159.

————. (Ed.) *Revolution in counseling: Implications of behavioral science.* Boston: Houghton Mifflin, 1966b.

Krumboltz, J. D., and Thoresen, C. E. *Behavioral counseling: Cases and techniques.* New York: Holt, Rinehart, and Winston, 1969.

Kubler-Ross, E. *On death and dying.* New York: Bantam, 1973. (Originally published 1969.)

Kurtz, R. R., and Grummon, D. L. Different approaches to the measurement of therapist empathy and their relationship to therapy outcomes. *Journal of Consulting and Clinical Psychology,* 1972, 39, 106–115.

Lacoursiere, R. *The life cycle of groups.* New York: Human Sciences Press, 1980.

Laden, C. J., and Crooks, M. Some factors influencing the decision of mature women to enroll for continuing education. *Canadian Counsellor,* 1976, 10, 29–36.

Laing, R. D. *The politics of experience.* New York: Ballantine Books, 1967.

————. *Self and others.* New York: Pantheon, 1969.

Lair, J. *'I ain't well—but I sure am better': Mutual need therapy.* Greenwich, CT: Fawcett, 1975.

Landau, S. A study of successful career changes among middle-age adults: Implications for adult education. *Dissertation Abstracts International,* 1978, 39 (3–A), 1264.

Langs, R. On the properties of interpretation. *Contemporary Psychoanalysis,* 1980, 16 (4), 460–468.

Langway, L. et al. The superwoman squeeze. *Newsweek,* May 19, 1980, p. 72–79.

Lauer, B.; Ten Broek, E.; and Grossman, M. Battered-child syndrome review of 130 patients with controls. *Pediatrics,* 1974, 54 (1), 67–70.

Lauver, P. J. Consulting with teachers: A systematic approach. *Personnel and Guidance Journal,* 1974, 52, 535–540.

Lawe, C. F., and Smith, E. W. Gestalt processes and family therapy. Individual Psychology: Journal of Adlerian Theory, Research and Practice, 1986, 42 (4), 537–44.

Lazarus, A. A. Multimodal behavior therapy: Treating the basic id. *Journal of Nervous and Mental Diseases,* 1973, 156, 404–411.

———. Multimodal therapy. *Psychology Today*, 1974, 7 (10), 59–63.

———. Multimodal assessment. In A. Lazarus (Ed.), *Multimodal behavior therapy.* New York: Springer, 1976a, 25–47.

———. Some theoretical and clinical foundations: Introduction and overview. In A. Lazarus (Ed.), *Multimodal behavior therapy.* New York: Springer, 1976b, 1–8.

———. Has behavior therapy outlived its usefulness? *American Psychologist,* 1977, 32 (7), 550–554.

Ledwidge, B. Cognitive behavior modification: A step in the wrong direction? *Psychological Bulletin,* 1978, 85 (2), 353–375.

Lee, S. D. *Social class bias in the diagnosis of mental illness.* (Doctoral dissertation, University of Oklahoma, 1968). Ann Arbor, MI: University Microfilms, No. 68–6959.

Lefcourt, H. Internal versus external control of reinforcement: A review. *Psychological Bulletin,* 1966, 65, 206–220.

Leibin, V. M. Adler's concept of man. *Journal of Individual Psychology,* 1981, 37 (1), 3–5.

Liebowitz, M. R. *The chemistry of love.* Boston: Little, Brown, and Co., 1983.

Leitner, L. A. Crisis counseling may save a life. *Journal of Rehabilitation,* 1974, 40, 19–20.

Leitner, L. A., and Stecher, T. Crisis intervention for growth: Philosophical dimensions and strategies. *Psychology,* 1974, 11, 29–32.

Lerner, B. *Therapy in the ghetto: Political impotence and personal disintegration.* Baltimore: Johns Hopkins University Press, 1972.

Lester, D., and Brockopp. G. W. (Eds.). *Crisis intervention and counseling by telephone.* Springfield, IL: Charles C Thomas, 1973.

Levenson, H. Activism and powerful others. *Journal of Personality Assessment,* 1974, 38, 377–383.

Levin, L. S., and Shepherd, I.L. The role of the therapist in gestalt theory. *The Counseling Psychologist,* 1974, 4 (4), 27–30.

Levinger, G. A social psychological perspective on marital dissolution. *Journal of Social Issues,* 1976, 32 (1), 21–43.

Levinger, G., and Huesmann, L. R. An "incremental exchange" perspective on the pair relationship: Interpersonal reward and level of involvement. In K. J. Gergen, M. S. Greenberg, and R. H. Willis (Eds.), *Social exchange: Advances in theory and research.* New York: Holt, Rinehart, and Winston, 1980, 165–196.

Levinson, D. J. *The seasons of a man's life.* New York: Random House, 1978.

————. A conception of adult development. *American Psychologist,* 1986, 41 (1), 3–13.

Levinson, D. J.; Darrow, D. N.; Klein, E. B.; Levinson, M. H.; and McKee, B. Periods in the adult development of men: Ages 18 to 45. In N. K. Schlossberg and A. D. Entine (Eds.), *Counseling adults.* Monterey, CA: Brooks/Cole, 1977, 47–59.

Levis, D. J. Behavioral therapy: The fourth therapeutic revolution? In D. J. Levis (Ed.), *Learning approaches to therapeutic behavior change.* Chicago: Aldine, 1970.

Leviton, H. S. Consumer feedback on a secondary school guidance program. *Personnel and Guidance Journal,* 1977, 55 (5), 242–244.

Lewis, E. C. *The psychology of counseling.* New York: Holt, Rinehart, and Winston, 1970.

Lewis, H. R., and Lewis, M. E. *Psychosomatics—how your emotions can damage your health.* New York: Viking, 1972.

Lewis, J. A., and Lewis, M. D. *Community counseling: A human services approach.* New York: John Wiley and Sons, 1977.

Lewis, M. D.; Lewis, J. A.; and Dworkin, E. P. Editorial: Counseling and the social revolution. *Personnel and Guidance Journal,* 1971, 49, 689.

Lindemann, E. Symptomatology and management of acute grief. *American Journal of Psychiatry,* 1944, 101, 141–148.

Lindsley, O. R. Theoretical basis for behavior modification. In C. E. Pitts (Ed.), *Operant conditioning in the classroom.* New York: Thomas Y. Crowell, 1971, 54–60.

Linkowski, D. C., and Dunn, M. A. Self-concept and acceptance of disability. *Rehabilitation Counseling Bulletin,* 1974, 31 (2), 28–32.

Linnihan, P. C. Adolescent day treatment: A community alternative to institutionalization of the emotionally disturbed adolescent. *American Journal of Orthopsychiatry,* 1977, 47 (4), 679–688.

Linton, R. *The study of man.* New York: Appleton-Century-Crofts, 1936.

Lipsett, S. M. Introduction: The mood of American youth. Reston, VA: National Education Association, 1974.

Liston, E.; Yager, J.; and Strauss, G. D. Assessment of psychotherapy skills: The problem of interrater agreement. *American Journal of Psychiatry,* 1981, 138 (8), 1069–1074.

Lobitz, W. C., and LoPiccolo, J. New methods in the behavioral treatment of sexual dysfunctions. *Journal of Behavioral Therapy and Experimental Psychiatry,* 1972, 3, 265–271.

Loesch, L. C., Crane, B. B., and Rucker, B. B. Counselor trainee effectiveness: More puzzle pieces. *Counselor Education and Supervision,* 1978, 17, 195–204.

London, M., and Mone, E. M. *Career management and survival in the workplace: Helping employees make tough career decisions, stay motivated, and reduce career strees.* San Francisco: Jossey-Bass 1987.

Loring, R. K., and Otto, H. A. *New life options: The working woman's resource book.* New York: McGraw-Hill, 1976.

Love, J. M., and Parker-Robinson, C. Children's imitation of grammatical and ungrammatical sentences. *Child Development,* 1972, 14, 311–318.

Love, S. Treating the resistive family. In H. Strean (Ed.), *New approaches in child guidance.* Metuchen, NJ: Scarecrow Press, 1972.

Lowendahl, E. Therapeutic approaches to adolescence. *American Corrective Therapy Journal,* 1975, 29 (5), 169–172.

Lutwak, N., and Hennessy, J. J. Conceptual systems functioning as a mediating factor in the development of counseling skills. *Journal of Counseling Psychology,* 1982, 29 (3), 256–260.

Lynch, D. J., and Arndt, C. Developmental changes in response to frustration among physically handicapped children. *Journal of Personality Assessment,* 1973, 37 (2), 130–135.

Mahoney, M. J., and Kazdin, A. E. Cognitive behavior modification: Misconceptions and premature evacuation. *Psychological Bulletin,* 1979, 86 (5), 1044–1049.

Mahoney, M. J. Reflections on the cognitive-learning trend in psychotherapy. *American Psychologist,* 1977, 32 (1), 5–13.

Mahoney, S. C. *The art of helping people effectively.* New York: Association Press, 1967.

Maines, D. R., and Markowitz, M. A. Status symbolism and the ecology of participation in group counseling sessions. *Psychological Record,* 1981, 31 (4), 543–551.

Marcus, I. M. Countertransference and the psychoanalytic process in children and adolescents. *Psychoanalytic study of the child,* 1980, 35, 285–298.

Mardoyan, J. L., and Weis, D. M. The efficacy of group counseling with older adults. *Personnel and Guidance Journal,* 1981, 60 (3), 161–163.

Margulies, A., and Havens, L. L. The initial encounter: What to do first? *American Journal of Psychiatry,* 1981, 138 (4), 421–428.

Marks, M. J. Conscious/unconscious selection of the psychotherapist's theoretical orientation. *Psychotherapy: Theory, Research, and Practice,* 1978, 15 (4), 354–358.

Martin, J. External versus self-reinforcement: A review of methodological and theoretical issues. *Canadian Journal of Behavioral Science,* 1980, 12 (2), 121–125.

Marx, M. H. Sticking with fundamentals in theory construction: Diversity does not require new rules. *Academic Psychology Bulletin,* 1981, 3 (3), 437–449.

Maslow, A. H. *Toward a psychology of being.* New York: Van Nostrand Reinhold, 1954.

Massong, S. R.; Dickson, A. L.; Ritzler, B. A.; and Layne, C. C. Assertion and defense mechanism preference. *Journal of Counseling Psychology,* 1982, 29 (6), 591–596.

Mastroianni, M., and Dinkmeyer, D. Developing an interest in others through peer facilitation. *Elementary School Guidance and Counseling,* 1980, 14 (3), 214–221.

Matarazzo, J. D. Behavioral health's challenge to academic, scientific and professional psychology. *American Psychologist,* 1982, 37 (1), 1–14.

Mattingly, M. A. (Ed.). New perspectives on job stress and burnout; A symposium. *Child Care Quarterly,* 1986, 15, 80–109.

May, R. *Psychology and the human dilemma.* New York: Van Nostrand, 1967a.

May, R. *The art of counseling.* Nashville: Abingdon Press, 1967b.

McCary, J. L. *Human sexuality.* New York: Van Nostrand Reinhold, 1967. 2nd Ed., 1973.

McCranie, E. J. Neurasthenic neurosis: Psychogenic weakness and fatigue. *Psychosomatics,* 1980, 21 (1), 19–24.

McDowell, C. F., Jr. Integrating theory and practice in leisure counseling. *Journal of Physical Education and Recreation,* 1977, 48 (4), 51–54.

McGoldrick, A., and Copper, C. *The experience of early retirement.* London: Gower, 1987.

McGraw, L. K. A selective review of programs and counseling interventions for the reentry woman. *Personnel and Guidance Journal,* 1982, 61, 469–472.

McLaughlin, B. *Learning and social behavior.* New York: Free Press, 1971.

Medora, N., and Woodward, J. C. Premarital sexual opinions of undergraduate students at a midwestern university. *Adolescence,* 1982, 17 (65), 183–189.

Meichenbaum, D. *Cognitive-behavior modification.* New York: Plenum, 1977.

Meichenbaum, D. Cognitive-behavioral therapies. In S.J. Lynn and J. P. Garske (Eds.), *Contemporary psychotherapies: Models and methods.* Columbus, OH: Charles E. Merrill, 1985, 261–286.

Mellecker, J. Transactional analysis for non-TA counselors. In G. S. Belkin (Ed.), *Counseling: Directions in theory and practice.* Dubuque, IA: Kendall/Hunt, 1976.

Messer, S. B., and Boals, G. F. Psychotherapy outcome in a university-based psychology training clinic. *Professional Psychology,* 1981, 12 (6), 785–793.

Mezzich, J. E.; Coffman, G. A.; and Goodpastor, S. M. A format for DSM-III diagnostic formulation: Experience with 1,111 consecutive patients. *American Journal of Psychiatry,* 1982, 139 (5), 591–596.

Michael, J., and Meyerson, L. A. A behavioral approach to guidance and counseling. *Harvard Educational Review,* 1962, 32, 382–401.

Midura, B. J. Psychodynamic, existential, and religious views pertaining to psychological healing: A comparative analysis. *Dissertation Abstracts International,* 1981, 42 (3–B), 1153.

Miller, C. M. An experimental study of the effects of Gestalt two-chair experiment with conflicted adolescent offenders. *Dissertation Abstracts International,* 1981, 41 (10–A), 4291.

Miller, D.; Belkin, G. S.; and Gray, J. *Educational psychology,* 2nd Ed. Dubuque, IA: Wm. C. Brown Publishers, 1982.

Miller, M. J. Cantaloupes, carrots, and counseling: Implications of dietary interventions for counselors. *Personnel and Guidance Journal,* 1980, 58, 421–424.

Miller, S.; Corrales, R.; and Wackman, D. B. Recent progress in understanding and facilitating marital communication. *The Family Coordinator,* 1975, 24 (2), 143–152.

Milliken, R., and Kirchner, R., Jr. Counselor's understanding of student's communications as a function of the counselor's perceptual defense. *Journal of Counseling Psychology,* 1971, 18, 14–18.

Mintz, E. E. *Marathon groups: Reality and symbol.* New York: Appleton-Century-Crofts, 1971.

Miran, M.; Lehrer, P.; Koehler, R.; and Miran, E. What happens when deviant behavior begins to change? The relevance of a social systems approach for behavioral programs with adolescents. *Journal of Community Psychology,* 1974, 2 (4), 370–375.

Mirels, H. Dimensions of internal versus external control. *Journal of Consulting and Clinical Psychology,* 1970, 34, 226–228.

Mitchell, A. E. Conceptual systems and Holland's theory of vocational choice. *Dissertation Abstracts International,* 1981, 42, (4–A), 1565.

Mitchell, H. Counseling black students: A model in response to the need for relevant counselor training programs. *The Counseling Psychologist,* 1971, 2 (4), 117–122.

Mobley, T. A.; Light, S. S.; and Neulinger, J. Leisure attitudes and program participation. *Parks and Recreation,* 1976, 11 (12), 20–22.

Molyneaux, D., and Lane, V. W. *Effective interviewing: Techniques and analysis.* Boston: Allyn and Bacon, 1982.

Moreland, J., and Schwabel, A. I. A gender role transcendent perspective on fathering. *The Counseling Psychologist,* 1981, 9 (4), 45–54.

Morgenstern, M., and Smith, H. *Psychology in the vocational rehabilitation of the mentally retarded.* Springfield, IL: Charles C Thomas, 1973.

Motto, J. A. Recognition, evaluation and management of persons at risk for suicide. *Personnel and Guidance Journal,* 1978, 56, 537–543.

Mowrer, O. H., and Mowrer, W. M. Enuresis—a method for its study and treatment. *Journal of Orthopsychiatry,* 1938, 8, 436–459.

Mozdzierz, G.J.; Murphy, T.J.; and Greenblatt, R.L. Private logic and the strategy of psychotherapy. *Journal of Individual Psychology,* 1986.

Murphy, M. Esalen—where it's at. *Psychology Today,* 1967, 1, 34–39.

Musetto, A. P. Evaluating families with custody or visitation problems. *Journal of Marriage and Family Counseling,* 1978, 4 (4), 59–65.

Myers, P. I., and Hammill, D. D. *Methods for learning disorders,* 2nd Ed. New York: Wiley, 1976.

Nakushian, J. M. Restoring parents' equilibrium after sudden infant death. *American Journal of Nursing,* 1976, 76 (10), 1600–1604.

Naranjo, C. Present-centeredness: Technique, prescription, and ideal. In J. Fagan and I. L. Sheperd (Eds.), *Gestalt therapy now.* Palo Alto, CA: Science and Behavior Books, 1970.

Nash, R. J., and Griffin, R. S. Review of Carl Rogers on Personal Power. *Teachers College Record,* 1977, 79, 279.

Nass, D. R., and Nass, S. Counseling the fatherless child. In G. S. Belkin (Ed.), *Counseling: Directions in theory and practice.* Dubuque, IA: Kendall/Hunt, 1976.

Nass, D. R. (Ed.). *The rape victim.* Dubuque, IA: Kendall/Hunt, 1977.

Nass, S., and Weidhorn, M. *Turn your life around.* Englewood Cliffs, NJ: Prentice-Hall, 1978.

Nass, S. (Ed.). *Crisis intervention.* Dubuque, IA: Kendall/Hunt, 1977.

Necessary, C. Teen alcoholics: More than 3 million counted, and the number is rising. *Guidepost,* July 12, 1979, 6.

Neilans, T. H., and Israel, A. C. Towards maintenance and generalization of behavior change: Teaching children self-regulation and self-instructional skills. *Cognitive Therapy and Research,* 1981, 5 (2), 189–195.

Nelson, B. Efforts widen to curb sexual abuse in therapy. *New York Times,* November 23, 1982, C1, C3.

Nelson, M. C.; Nelson, B.; Sherman, M. H.; and Strean, H. S. Roles and paradigms in psychotherapy. New York: Grune and Stratton, 1968.

Neugarten, B. L. Adaptation and the life cycle. In N. K. Schlossberg and A. D. Entine (Eds.), *Counseling adults.* Monterey, CA: Brooks/Cole, 1977, 34–46.

Neulinger, J. Leisure counseling: A plea for complexity. *Journal of Physical Education and Recreation,* 1977, 48 (4), 27–28.

Newman, R. G. The role of ancillary services in methadone maintenance treatment. *American Journal of Drug and Alcohol Abuse,* 1974, 1 (2), 207–212.

Newton, F. B., and Caple, R. B. Client and counselor preferences for counselor behavior in the interview. *Journal of College Student Personnel,* 1974, 15 (3), 220–224.

Norris, M. A formula for identifying styles of community work. *Community Development Journal,* 1977, 12 (1), 22–29.

Nuttall, E.V.; Nuttall, R. L.; Palit, D.; and Clark, K. Assessing adolescent mental health needs: The views of consumers, providers, and others. *Adolescence,* 1977, 12 (46), 277–285.

Nystul, M. The impact of birth order and family size on self-actualization. *Journal of Individual Psychology,* 1981, 37 (1), 107–112.

O'Brien, B. A., and Lewis, M. A community adolescent self-help center. *Personnel and Guidance Journal,* 1975, 54, 213–216.

Obstfeld, L. S., and Meyers, A. W. Adolescent sex education: A preventive mental health measure. *Journal of School Health*, 1984, 54 (2), 68–73.

Oetting, E.R., and Beauvais, F. Peer cluster theory: Drugs and the adolescent. *Journal of Counseling and Development*, 1986, 65, 17–22.

Oldham, G. R. Job characteristics and internal motivation: The moderating effect of interpersonal and individual variables. *Human Relations,* 1976, 29 (6), 559–569.

Ostrand, J., and Creaser, J. Development of counselor candidate dominance in three learning conditions. *The Journal of Psychology,* 1978, 99, 199–202.

Overs, R. P. Avocational evaluation and work adjustment: A deterrent to dependency. *Journal of Rehabilitation,* 1976, 42 (6), 21–24.

Owen, L. On ulcers in your future? *America's Health,* 1981, 3 (2), 14–16.

Parks, B. J. Career development—How early? *Elementary School Journal,* 1976, 76, 468–474.

Patterson, C. H. *Theories of counseling and psychotherapy,* 2nd Ed. New York: Harper and Row, 1973.

Patterson, G. R.; Cobb, J. A.; and Ray, R. S. A social engineering technology for retraining the families of aggressive boys. In H. E. Adams and I. P. Unikel (Ed.), *Issues and trends in behavior therapy.* Springfield, IL: Charles C Thomas, 1973, 139–207.

Pattison, E. M. The patient after psychotherapy. *American Journal of Psychotherapy,* 1970, 24, 194–213.

Payne, B., and Whittington, F. Older women: An examination of popular stereotypes and research evidence. *Social Problems,* 1976, 23 (4), 488–504.

Peabody, S. A., and Gelso, C. J. Countertransference and empathy: The complex relationship between two divergent concepts in counseling. *Journal of Counseling Psychology,* 1982, 29 (3), 240–245.

Peal, R. L.; Handal, P. J.; and Gilner, F. H. A group desensitization procedure for the reduction of death anxiety. *Omega: Journal of Death and Dying,* 1982, 12 (1), 61–70.

Pearson, J. E., and Long, T. J. Counselors, nutrition and mental health. *Personnel and Guidance Journal,* 1982, 60 (7), 389–392.

Pedersen, P.; Holwill, C. F.; and Shapiro, J. A cross-cultural training procedure for classes in counselor education. *Counselor Education and Supervision,* 1978, 17, 233–236.

Pedersen, P. B. The field of intercultural counseling. In P. B. Pedersen, W. J. Lonner and J. G. Draguns (Eds.), *Counseling across cultures.* Honolulu: University of Hawaii Press, 1976.

Pelletier, K. *Healthy people in unhealthy places.* New York: Delacorte, 1984.

Peele, S. The "cure" for adolescent drug abuse: Worse than the problem. *Journal of Counseling and Development,* 1986, 65, 23–24.

Peoples, V. Y., and Dell, D. M. Black and white students' preference for counselor roles. *Journal of Counseling Psychology,* 1975, 22, 529–534.

Perez, J. J. *The initial counseling contact.* Boston: Houghton Mifflin, 1968.

Perls, F. S. Theory and technique of personality integration. *American Journal of Psychotherapy,* 1948, 2, 563ff.

Perls, F. S. *Ego, hunger and aggression.* New York: Random House, 1969. (Originally published London: Allen and Unwin, 1947.)

———. *Gestalt therapy verbatim.* Lafayette, CA: Real People Press, 1969.

———. Four lectures (1966). In J. Fagan and I. L. Sheperd (Eds.), *Gestalt therapy now.* Palo Alto, CA: Science and Behavior Books, 1970.

———. The gestalt approach and eye witness to therapy. Palo Alto, CA: Science and Behavior Books, 1973.

Perls, F. S.; Hefferline, R. F.; and Goodman, P. *Gestalt therapy: excitement and growth in the human personality.* New York: Dell, 1969.

Perry, W. G., Jr., et al. On the relation of psychotherapy to counseling. *Annals of the New York Academy of Science,* 1955, 63, 396–407.

Peterman, P. J. Parenting and environmental considerations. *American Journal of Orthopsychiatry,* 1981, 51 (2), 351–355.

Peterson, J. A. *Counseling and values.* Scranton, PA: International Textbook, 1970.

Peterson, L., and Melcher, R. To change, be yourself: An illustration of paradox in Gestalt therapy. *Personnel and Guidance Journal,* 1981, 60 (2), 101–103.

Philliber, S. G., and Tatum, M. L. Sex education and the double standard in high school. *Adolescence,* 1982, 17 (66), 281–283.

Phillipson, R. Drug abuse treatment. *Journal of School Health,* 1972, 42, 625–627.

Phipps, H. The dynamics of the psychotherapeutic relationship. *Psychiatry,* 1959, 22, 17–39.

Pike, K. L. *Language in relation to a unified theory of the structure of human behavior.* Summer Institute of Linguistics, 1954.

Pine, G. J. Counseling minority groups: A review of the literature. *Counseling and Values,* 1972, 17, 35–44.

Pine, G. J. The existential school counselor. Clearing House, 1969, 43, 351–354.

Pion, R. J., and Delliquadri, L. Alive and well. *Elementary School Guidance and Counseling,* 1979, 14 (2), 98–102.

Polakow, R. L., and Peabody, D. L. Behavioral treatment of child abuse. *International Journal of Offender Therapy and Comparative Criminology,* 1975, 19 (1), 100–103.

Ponzo, Z. Integrating techniques from five counseling theories. *Personnel and Guidance Journal,* 1976, 54 (8), 415–419.

Pope, K. S. (Ed.). *On love and loving.* San Francisco: Jossey-Bass, 1980.

Prosky, P. O. Family therapy: An orientation. *Clinical Social Work,* 1974, 2 (1), 45–56.

Protinsky, H. Rational counseling with adolescents. *The School Counselor,* 1976, 23 (4), 240–246.

Queensboro Society for the Prevention of Cruelty to Children. *Child abuse.* Jamaica, NY: QSPCC, 1976.

Rachin, R. L. Reality therapy: Helping people help themselves. *Crime and Delinquency,* 1974, 20 (1), 45–53.

Rachman, S. Behavior therapy. In B. Berenson and R. R. Carkhuff (Eds.), *Sources of gain in counseling and psychotherapy.* New York: Holt, Rinehart, and Winston, 1967a.

Rachman, S. Systematic desensitization. *Psychological Bulletin,* 1967b, 67, 93–103.

Raman, S. Role of nutrition in the actualization of the potentialities of the child. *Young Teacher,* 1975, 31, 24–32.

Raming, H. E., and Frey, D. H. A taxonomic approach to the gestalt theory of Perls. *Journal of Counseling Psychology,* 1974, 21 (3), 179–184.

Rand, C., and Hall, J. A. Sex differences in the accuracy of self-perceived attractiveness. *Social Psychology Quarterly,* 1983, 46 (4), 359–363.

Rank, O. *Will therapy.* New York: Knopf, 1945.

Rapoport, L. The state of crisis: Some theoretical considerations. *Social Science Review,* 1962, 36, 211–217.

Raspberry, W. Kids and responsibility. *American Educator,* 1980, 4 (4), 14–15.

Rebelsky, F. (Ed.). *Life: The continuous process.* New York: Knopf, 1975.

Reich, W.P., and Filsted, W.J. The cultural context of psychological approaches to alcoholism: Should we contest or collaborate? *American Psychologist,* 1986 (March), 322.

Reichelt, P. A., and Werley, H. H. Contraception, abortion, and venereal disease: Teenagers' knowledge and the effect of education. *Family Planning Perspectives,* 1975, 7 (2), 83–88.

Reik, T. *Listening with the third ear.* New York: Farrar, Strauss, 1948.

Reis, J., and Herzberger, S. Problem and program linkage: The early and periodic screening, diagnosis and treatment program as a means of preventing and detecting child abuse. *Infant Mental Health Journal,* 1980, 1 (4), 262–269.

Reiss, D., and Hoffman, H. A. (Eds.). *The American family: Dying or developing.* New York: Plenum Press, 1979, 246.

Renvoize, J. *Web of violence: A study of family violence.* London: Routledge and Kegan Paul, 1978.

Rhine M. W., and Mayerson, P. A serious suicidal syndrome masked by homicidal threats. *Life-Threatening Behavior,* 1973, 3 (1), 3–9.

Rhoades, V. Personal correspondence to author, April 1987 (from Psychology Dept., Brewton-Parker College, Mount Vernon, GA).

Richardson, M. S. 1979. Toward an expanded view of careers. *The Counseling Psychologist,* 8 (1), 34–35.

Ritchie, M.H. Counseling the involuntary client. *Journal of Counseling and Development,* 1986, 64, 516–518.

Roazen, P. *Freud and his followers.* New York: Knopf, 1975.

Robertshaw, P., and Curtin, C. A. Legal definition of the family: An historical and sociological explanation. *The Sociological Review,* 1977, 25 (2), 280–308.

Robinson, L. R. Basic concepts in family therapy: A differential comparison with individual treatment. *American Journal of Psychiatry,* 1975, 132 (10), 1045–1048.

Robinson, S. L.; Rotter, M. F.; and Wilson, J. Mothers' contemporary career decisions: Impact on the family. *Personnel and Guidance Journal,* 1982, 61, 535–539.

Roe, A. *The psychology of occupations.* New York: John Wiley, 1956.

———. Early determinants of vocational choice. *Journal of Counseling Psychology,* 1957, 4, 212–217.

Roe, A.; Hubbard, W. D.; Hutchinson, T.; and Batemen, T. Studies of occupational history. Part I: Job changes and the classification of occupations. *Journal of Counseling Psychology,* 1966, 13, 387–393.

Roe, A., and Siegleman, M. *The origin of interests.* Washington, D.C.: American Personnel and Guidance Association, 1964.

Rogers, C. R. *The clinical treatment of the problem child.* Boston: Houghton Mifflin, 1939.

———. *Counseling and psychotherapy.* Boston: Houghton Mifflin, 1942.

———. *Client-centered therapy.* Boston: Houghton Mifflin, 1951.

Rogers, C. R., and Dymond, R. F. (Eds.). *Psychotherapy and personality change.* Chicago: University of Chicago Press, 1954.

———. A note on "the nature of man." *Journal of Counseling Psychology,* 1957a, 4, 199–203.

———. The necessary and sufficient conditions of therapeutic change. *Journal of Consulting Psychology,* 1957b, 21, 95–103.

———. A process conception of psychotherapy. *American Psychologist,* 1958, 13, 142–149.

———. A theory of therapy, personality, and interpersonal relationships as developed in the client-centered framework. In S. Koch (Ed.), *Psychology: A study of a science (Volume III, Formulations of the person and the social context).* New York: McGraw-Hill, 1959a.

———. Significant learning: In therapy and in education. *Educational Leadership,* 1959b, 16 (4), 232–242.

———. *On becoming a person.* Boston: Houghton Mifflin, 1961.

———. The interpersonal relationship: The core of guidance. *Harvard Educational Review,* 1962, 32, 416–429.

———. Some questions and challenges facing a humanistic psychology. *Journal of Humanistic Psychology,* 1965, 5, 1–5.

———. The condition of change from a client-centered viewpoint. In B. G. Berenson and R. R. Carkhuff (Eds.), *Sources of gain in counseling and psychotherapy.* New York: Holt, Rinehart, and Winston, 1967a. (Originally published as 1957a, see above.)

———. (Ed.). *The therapeutic relationship and its impact.* Madison: University of Wisconsin Press, 1967b.

———. *Freedom to learn.* Columbus, OH: Charles E. Merrill, 1969.

———. *Carl Rogers on encounter groups.* New York: Harper and Row, 1970.

———. Facilitating encounter groups. *American Journal of Nursing,* 1971, 71, 275–279.

———. Some social issues which concern me. *Journal of Humanistic Psychology,* 1972, 12, 45–59.

———. My philosophy of interpersonal relationships and how it grew. *Journal of Humanistic Psychology,* 1973, 13, 3–15.

———. In retrospect: Forty-six years. *American Psychologist,* 1974, 29, 118–122.

———. Empathic: An unappreciated way of being. *Counseling Psychologist,* 1975, 5 (2), 2–10.

———. *Carl Rogers on personal power.* New York Delacorte Press, 1977.

———. *A Way of Being.* Boston: Houghton Mifflin, 1981.

Roman, P. M., and Trice, H. M. (Eds.). *The sociology of psychotherapy.* New York: Jason Aronson, 1974.

Rose, J. D. *Introduction to sociology,* 3rd Ed. Chicago: Rand McNally, 1976.

Rosen, R. C., and Schnapp, B. J. The use of a specific behavioral technique (thought-stopping) in the context of conjoint couples therapy: A case report. *Behavior Therapy,* 1974, 5, 261–264.

Rosen, S. Recent experiences with gestalt, encounter, and hypnotic techniques. *American Journal of Psychoanalysis,* 1972, 32, 90–102.

Rosenham, D. L. On being sane in insane places. *Science,* 1973, 179, 250–258.

Rosenman, R. H.; Brand, R. J.; Jenkins, C. D.; Friedman, M.; Straus, R.; and Wurm, M. Coronary heart disease in the Western collaborative group study: Final follow-up of 8 years. *Journal of the American Medical Association,* 1975, 233 (8), 872–877.

Rosenthal, R., and Jacobson, L. Pygmalion in the classroom: Teacher expectation and pupils' intellectual development. New York: Holt, Rinehart, and Winston, 1968.

Ross, D. M., and Ross, S. A. *Hyperactivity: Research, theory and action.* New York: Wiley, 1976.

Rothney, J. W. M. *Adaptive counseling in schools.* Englewood Cliffs, NJ: Prentice-Hall, 1972.

Rotter, J. B. *Social learning and clinical psychology.* Englewood Cliffs, NJ: Prentice-Hall, 1954.

———. Generalized expectancies for internal versus external control of reinforcement. *Psychological Monographs,* 1966, 80, (1, Whole No. 609).

———. Some problems and misconceptions related to the construct of internal versus external control of reinforcement. *Journal of Consulting and Clinical Psychology,* 1975, 43, 56–67.

Rowe, W.; Murphy, H. B.; and DeCsipkes, R. A. The relationship of counseling characteristics and counseling effectiveness. *Review of Educational Research,* 1975, 45, 231–246.

Rubenstein, C., and Shaver, P. *In search of intimacy.* New York: Delacorte Press, 1982.

Rubenstein, J. S., Watson, F. G. and Rubenstein, H. S. An analysis of sex education books for adolescents by means of adolescents' sexual interests. *Adolescence,* 1977, 12, 47, Fall, 293–311.

Rubin, S. A two-track model of bereavement: Theory and application in research. *American Journal of Orthopsychiatry,* 1981, 51 (1), 101–109.

Rush, A. J., and Giles, D. E. Cognitive therapy: Theory and research. In A. J. Rush (Ed.), *Short-term psychotherapies for depression.* New York: Guilford Press, 1982.

Rumney, A., and Steckel, T. Growing up and getting dependency needs met as an adult: Reparenting in anorexia nervosa. *Transactional Analysis Journal,* 1985, 15 (1), 55–61.

Russell, B. How do you share the responsibilities? *House and Garden,* July, 1973, 49, 106–107.

Ryan, D. W., and Gaier, E. L. Student socio-economic status and counselor contact in junior high school. *Personnel and Guidance Journal,* 1968, 46, 466–472.

Rychlak, J. F. Personality theory: Its nature, past, present and future. *Personality and Social Psychology Bulletin,* 1976, 2 (3), 209–224.

Rycroft, C. *A critical dictionary of psychoanalysis.* New York: Basic Books, 1969.

Ryle, A. Defining goals and assessing change in brief psychotherapy: A pilot study using target ratings and the dyad grid. *British Journal of Medical Psychology,* 1979, 52 (3), 223–233.

Saltzberg, L. The E in RET stands for emotive. *Psychology: A Quarterly Journal of Human Behavior,* 1979, 16 (2), 51–54.

Sanders, L.; Kibby, R. W.; Creaghan, S.; and Tyrell, E. Child abuse, detection and prevention. *Young Children,* 1975, 30 (5), 332–337.

Sandmeyer, L. E. Choices and changes: A workshop for women. *Vocational Guidance Quarterly,* 1980, 28, 352–359.

Sanford, N. Research with students as action and education. *American Psychologist,* 1969, 24, 544–546.

Sanger, S. P., and Alker, H. A. Dimensions of internal-external locus of control and the women's liberation movement. *Journal of Social Issues,* 1972, 28, 115–129.

Satir, V. *Conjoint family therapy.* Revised edition, Palo Alto, CA: Science and Behavior Books, 1967.

Sattler, J. M. Racial "experimenter effects" in experimentation, testing, interviewing and psychotherapy. *Psychological Bulletin,* 1970, 73, 137–160.

Schachter, S. *The psychology of affiliation.* Stanford, CA: Stanford University Press, 1959.

Schifferes, J. J., and Peterson, L. J. *Essentials of healthier living,* 4th Ed. New York: John Wiley, 1972.

Schlossberg, N. K. Programs for adults. *Personnel and Guidance Journal,* 1975, 53, 681–685.

Schlossberg, N. K., and Pietrofesa, J. J. Perspectives on counseling bias: Implications for counseling education. *The Counseling Psychologist,* 1973, 4, 44–54.

Schmidt, J. A. Cognitive restructuring: The art of talking to yourself. *Personnel and Guidance Journal,* 1976, 55 (2), 71–74.

Schmidt, S. The changing role of women in the family. *American Educator,* 1980, 4 (4), 16–23.

Schmolling, P. Schizophrenia and the deletion of certainty: An existential case study. *Psychological Reports,* 1984, 54 (1), 139–148.

Schneider, L. J., and Reuterfors, D. L. The impact of birth order and sex on social interest. *Journal of Individual Psychology,* 1981, 37 (1), 102–106.

Schover, L. R. et al. Multiaxial problem-oriented system for sexual dysfunctions: An alternative to DSM-III. *Archives of General Psychiatry,* 1982, 39 (5), 614–619.

Schubert, M. *Interviewing in social work practice: An introduction.* New York: Council on Social Work Education (345 East 46th Street, New York 10017), 1971.

Shulman, B. H., and Mosak, H. H. Birth order and ordinal position. *Journal of Individual Psychology,* 1977, 33, 114–121.

See, J. J., and Mustian, R. D. The emerging role of sociological consultation in the field of community mental health. *Community Mental Health Journal,* 1976, 12 (3), 267–274.

Seligman, M. E. P. *Helplessness: On depression, development and death.* San Francisco: W. H. Freeman, 1975.

Senour, M. N. How counselors influence clients. *Personnel and Guidance Journal,* 1982, 60 (6), 345–349.

Seybolt, J. W. Work satisfaction as a function of the person-environment interaction. *Organizational Behavior and Human Performance,* 1976, 17, 66–75.

Sheehan, D. V.; Sheehan, D. E.; and Minichiello, W. E. Age of onset of phobic disorders: A reevaluation. *Comprehensive Psychiatry,* 1981, 22 (6), 544–553.

Shertzer, B., and Stone, S. C. *Fundamentals of counseling,* 2nd Ed. Boston: Houghton Mifflin, 1974.

Shoben, E. J. The counseling experience as personal development. *Personnel and Guidance Journal,* 1965, 44, 224–230.

Shuman, R. B. Of course he can read—he's in high school. *Journal of Reading,* 1975, 4, 36–42.

Sicinski, A. The concepts of "need" and "value" in light of the systems approach. *Social Science Information,* 1978, 17 (1), 71–91.

Sidman, J. M. Sexual functioning and the physically disabled adult. *American Journal of Occupational Therapy,* 1977, 31 (2), 81–85.

Signell, K. A. On a shoestring: A consumer-based source of person power for mental health educators. *Community Mental Health Journal,* 1976, 12 (4), 342–354.

Silver, L. B. Acceptable and controversial approaches to treating the child with learning disabilities. *Pediatrics,* 1975, 55 (3), 406–415.

Silverberg, R. A. Reality therapy with men: An action approach. *Journal of Reality Therapy,* 1984, 3 (2), 27–31. "[RT is] the preferred mode of operation for decision making and problem solving for men."

Singer, J. E. Social comparison: The process of self-evaluation. In L. Festinger (Ed.), *Retrospections on social psychology.* New York: Oxford University Press, 1980, 158–179.

Sinick, D. Guest editor's introduction to "counseling over the life span." *Personnel and Guidance Journal,* 1976, 55, 100–101.

Skinner, B. F. *About behaviorism.* New York: Vintage, 1974.

――――. The steep and thorny way to a science of behavior. *American Psychologist,* 1975, 30 (1), 42–49.

――――. Interview with B. F. Skinner. In R. I. Evans (Ed.), *The making of psychology.* New York: Knopf, 1976a, 83–94.

――――. *About behaviorism.* New York: Vintage, 1976b. (Originally published 1974.)

――――. *Particulars of my life.* New York: Knopf, 1976c.

Skolnick, A. The American family: The paradox of perfection. *American Educator,* 1980, 4 (4), 8–11.

Smith, E. J. Counseling black individuals: Some stereotypes. *Personnel and Guidance Journal,* 1977, 55, 390–396.

Smith, E. M. Counseling for women who seek abortion. *Social Work,* 1972, 17 (2), 62–68.

Smith, M.; Glass, G.; and Miller, T. *The benefits of psychotherapy.* Baltimore: Johns Hopkins University Press, 1980.

Smith, N. Child nutrition in a changing world. *Childhood Education,* 1975, 51, 142–145.

Smith-Hanen, S. S. Socialization of the physically handicapped. *Journal of Applied Rehabilitation Counseling,* 1976, 7 (3), 131–141.

Snyder, M. The many me's of the self-monitor. *Psychology Today,* 1980, 13 (10), 32–40, 92–93.

Sorenson, R. *Adolescent sexuality in contemporary America.* Cleveland, OH: World Publishing Company, 1973.

Spiel, W. Some critical comments on a systematic approach to diagnosis: Contribution to a documentation and classification system in child neuropsychiatry. *Acta Paedopsychiatrica,* 1981, 47 (5), 269–278.

Spotnitz, H. *The couch and the circle.* New York: Knopf, 1961.

———. The toxoid response. *The Psychoanalytic Review,* 1963, 50 (4), 81–94.

———. *Modern psychoanalysis and the schizophrenic patient.* New York: Grune and Stratton, 1968.

———. *Psychotherapy of preoedipal conditions.* New York: Jason Aronson, 1976.

Sprinthall, N. *Guidance for human growth.* New York: Van Nostrand Reinhold, 1971.

Sroufe, A. L., and Stewart, M. A. Treating problem children with stimulant drugs. *New England Journal of Medicine,* 1973, 289 (8), 407–413.

Stadlen, F. Truancy—a sign of distress. *The Times Educational Supplement,* January 16, 1976, 3163:8.

Stafford, R. R. Attitude and behavior change in couples as a function of communication training. *Dissertation Abstracts International,* 1978 (Nov.), Vol. 39, (5–B), 2526.

Stephan, C. W., and Langlois, J. H. Baby beautiful: Adult attributions of infant competence as a function of infant attractiveness. *Child Development,* 1984, 55 (2), 576–585.

Stephens, C., and Tully, J.C. The influence of physical attractiveness of a plaintiff on the decision of simulated jurors. *Journal of Science Research,* 1977, 101(1), 149–150.

Stefflre, B. Vocational development: Ten propositions in search of a theory. *Personnel and Guidance Journal,* 1966, 44, 611–616.

Stein, P. J. The lifestyles and life chances of the never-married. *Marriage and Family Review,* 1978, 1 (4), 10ff.

Steinberg, M. A., and Chandler, G. E. Developing coordination of services between a mental health center and a public school system. *Journal of School Psychology,* 1976, 14 (4), 355–361.

Steiner, C. Emotional literacy. *Transactional Analysis Journal,* 1984, 14 (3), 162–173.

Steinmetz, S. K. Violence between family members. *Marriage and Family Review,* 1978a, 1 (3), 1–16.

Steinmetz, S. K. Battered parents. *Society,* 1978b, 15 (5), 54–55.

Stephens, D. B.; Watt, J. T.; and Hobbs, W. S. Getting through the resumé preparation maze: Some empirically based guidelines for resumé format. *The Vocational Guidance Quarterly,* 1979, 28 (1), 25–34.

Stewart, E. C.; Danielian, J.; and Festes, R. J. *Stimulating intercultural communication through role playing* (HRRO Tech. Rep. 69–67) Alexandria, VA: Human Resources Research Organization, May 1969.

Stewart, M. A. Is hyperactivity abnormal?—and other unanswered questions. *School Review,* 1976, 85 (1), 31–42.

Stolz, S. B.; Wienckowski, L. A.; and Brown, B. S. Behavior modification: A perspective on critical issues. *American Psychologist,* 1975, 30 (11), 1027–1048.

Stone, G. L., and Morden, C. J. Effect of distance on verbal productivity. *Journal of Counseling Psychology,* 1976, 23 (5), 486–488.

Stonequist, E. The problem of the marginal man. *American Journal of Sociology,* 1935, 41, 1–12.

Strean, H. S. Choice of paradigms in the treatment of parent and child. In M. C. Nelson et al. (Eds.), *Roles and paradigms in psychotherapy.* New York: Grune and Stratton, 1968.

Strean, H. S. *The social worker as psychotherapist.* Metuchen, NJ: Scarecrow Press, 1974.

Strickland, B. Aspiration responses among Negro and white adolescents. *Journal of Personality and Social Psychology,* 1971, 19, 315–320.

Strickland, B. Delay of gratification and internal locus of control in children. *Journal of Consulting and Clinical Psychology,* 1973, 40, 338.

Strickland, B. A rationale and model for changing values in helping relationships. In J. C. Hansen (Ed.), *Counseling process and procedures.* New York: Macmillan, 1978, 427–435.

Strickler, M., and Bonnefil, M. Crisis intervention and social casework: Similarities and differences in problem solving. *Clinical Social Work Journal,* 1974, 2 (1), 36–44.

Stuart, R. B. *Trick or treatment.* Champaign, IL: Research Press, 1970. (3rd Printing, 1973.)

Stulac, J. T., and Stanwyck, D. J. The revolution in counseling: A sociological perspective. *Personnel and Guidance Journal,* 1980, 58 (7), 491–495.

Stum, D. L. Direct: A consultation skills training model. *Personnel and Guidance Journal,* 1982, 60 (5), 296–302.

Sue, D. W. Ethnic identity: The impact of two cultures on the psychological development of Asians in America. In S. Sue and R. Wagner (Eds.), *Asian Americans: Psychological perspectives.* Ben Lomand, CA: Science and Behavior Books, 1973, pp. 40–149.

———. Asian Americans: Social-psychological forces affecting their life styles. In S. Picon and R. Campbell (Eds.), *Career behavior of special groups*. Columbus, OH: Charles E. Merrill, 1975.

———. Do clients know what they need? *Personnel and Guidance Journal*, 1977, 55 (5), 220–221.

———. Personal communication to Gary S. Belkin, March 30, 1979.

———. *Cross-cultural counseling: Theory and practice*. New York: John Wiley and Sons, 1986.

Sue, D. W., and Sue, D. Barriers to effective cross-cultural counseling. *Journal of Counseling Psychology*, 1977, 24, 420–429.

Sue, D. W., and Sue, S. Counseling Chinese-Americans. *Personnel and Guidance Journal*, 1972, 50, 637–644.

Sue, S., and McKinney, H. Asian Americans in the community mental health care system. *American Journal of Orthopsychiatry*, 1975, 45, 111–118.

Sue, S.; McKinney, H.; Allen, D.; and Hall, J. Delivery of community health care system. *American Journal of Orthopsychiatry*, 1975, 45, 111–118.

Sue, S., and Zane, N. W. Academic achievement and socioemotional adjustment among Chinese university students. *Journal of Counseling Psychology*, 1985, 32 (4), 570–579.

Super, D. E. *The psychology of careers*. New York: Harper and Row, 1957.

Super, D. E.; and Hall, D. T. Career development: Exploration and planning. *Annual Review of Psychology*, 1978, 29, 333–372.

Super, D. F. Vocational development theory: Person, position, and process. *Counseling Psychologist*, 1969, 1, 2–9.

Swails, R., and Herr, E. Vocational development groups for ninth-grade students. *Vocational Guidance Quarterly*, 1976, 24 (1), 256–260.

Szasz, T. The myth of mental illness. *American Psychologist*, 1960, 15, 113–118.

———. *The myth of mental illness*. New York: Paul B. Hoeber, 1961.

Taibbi, R. Transitional relationships after divorce. *Journal of Divorce*, 1979, 2, 269–279.

Tarrier, R. B. et al. *Career counseling: Prediction or exploration*. Paper presented at APGA Convention, Atlantic City, New Jersey, April, 1971. (ERIC Document Reproduction Service, No. Ed 051 510.)

Tayal, S. *Suggestibility in a state of crisis*. Unpublished doctoral dissertation, University of Maryland, 1972. Ann Arbor, MI: University Microfilms.

Thomas, A., and Sillen, S. *Racism and psychotherapy*. New York: Brunner Mazel, 1972.

Thomas, A. H., and Stewart, N. R. Counselor response to female clients with deviate and conforming career goals. *Journal of Counseling Psychology*, 1971, 18, 352–357.

Thompson, A.P. Changes in counseling skills during graduate and undergraduate study. *Journal of Counseling Psychology*, 1986, 33 (1), 65–72.

Thomson, R. The Pelican history of psychology. Baltimore: Pelican Books, 1968.

Thoresen, C. E. Constructs don't speak for themselves. *Counselor Education and Supervision,* 1977, 16 (4), 296–303.

Thoresen, C. E. Behavioral humanism. In *The Seventy-Second Yearbook of the National Society for the Study of Education (NSSE).* Chicago: University of Chicago Press, 1973, 385–421.

Thornburg, E. A conceptual basis for health education in the secondary schools. *High School Journal,* 1981, 64 (6), 239–242.

Thorndike, E. L. *From a connectionist's psychology.* New York: Appleton-Century-Crofts, 1949.

Thorson, J. Attitudes toward the aged as a function of race and social class. *The Gerontologist,* 1975, 15, 343–344.

Thorson, J.; Hancock, K.; and Whatley, L. Attitudes toward the aged as a function of age and education. *The Gerontologist,* 1974, 14, 316–318.

Tiedman, D. V., and O'Hara, R. P. Career development: Choice and adjustment. New York: College Entrance Examination Board, 1963.

Tizard, J. Early malnutrition, growth and mental development in man. *British Medical Bulletin,* 1974, 30, 169–174.

Tolbert, E. L. *An introduction to guidance.* Boston: Little, Brown, and Co., 1978.

Tolbert, E. L. *Counseling for career development.* Boston: Houghton Mifflin, 1974.

Torion, R. P. Socioeconomic status and traditional treatment approaches reconsidered. *Psychological Bulletin,* 1973, 79, 263–270.

Torrey, E. F. *The mind game.* New York: Emerson-Hall, 1972.

———. *The death of psychiatry.* Radnor, PA: Chilton, 1974.

Tracy, J. J., and Clark, E. H. Treatment for child abusers. *Social Work,* 1974, 19 (3), 338–342.

Treece, C. DSM-III as a research tool. *American Journal of Psychiatry,* 1982, 139 (5), 577–583.

Triandis, H. C.; Malpass, R. S.; and Davidson, A. R. Psychology and culture. *Annual Review of Psychology,* 1973, 24, 355–378.

Trimble, J. E. Value differences among American Indians: Concerns for the concerned counselor. In P. Pedersen, W. J. Lonner, and J. G. Draguns (Eds.), *Counseling across cultures.* Honolulu: East-West Center Press, 1976, 65–81.

Trotzer, J. P. *The counselor and the group: Integrating theory, training and practice.* Monterey, CA: Brooks/Cole, 1977.

Truax, C. B., and Carkhuff, R. R. *Toward effective counseling and psychotherapy.* Chicago: Aldine, 1967.

Truax, C. B., and Lister, J. L. Effectiveness of counselors and counselor aides. *Journal of Counseling Psychology,* 1970, 17, 331–334.

Tulkin, S. Race, class, family, and school achievement. *Journal of Personality and Social Psychology,* 1968, 9, 31–37.

Turner, C. B., and Wilson, W. J. Dimension of racial ideology: A study of urban black attitudes. *Journal of Social Issues,* 1976, 32, 143–152.

Tyler, L. The methods and processes of appraisal and counseling. In A. S. Thompson and D. E. Super (Eds.), *The professional preparation of counseling psychologist.* New York: Teachers College, 1964.

Tyler, L. E. *The work of the counselor,* 3rd Ed. New York: Appleton-Century Crofts, 1969.

Tyson, G. M., and Range, L. M. Gestalt dialougues as a treatment for mild depression: Time works just as well. *Journal for Clinical Psychology.* 1987, 43 (2), 227–31. Time heals as well as gestalt therapy.

Udry, J. R., and Cliquet, R. L. A cross-cultural examination of the relationship between ages at menarche, marriage, and first birth. *Demography,* 1982, 19 (1), 53–63.

Ullman, L. P., and Krasner, L. Research in behavior modification. New York: Holt, Rinehart, and Winston, 1965.

Unikel, I. P. Issues in behavior therapy. In H. E. Adams and I. P. Unikel (Eds.), *Issues and trends in behavior therapy.* Springfield, IL: Charles C Thomas, 1973, 43–56.

Usdan, T. D. F. Effects of counseling skill training programs for older adults on selected variables. *Dissertation Abstracts International,* 1981, 41 (10–A), 4296–4297.

Uzoka, A. F. The myth of the nuclear family: Historical background and clinical implications. *American Psychologist,* 1979, 34 (11), 1095–1106.

Vexliard, A. Temperament et modalities d'adaptation. *Bulletin de Psychologie,* 1968, 21, 1–15.

Vogt, S. Reality therapy in a convalescent home. *Activities, Adaptation and Aging* 1985, 6 (3), 55–59.

Vontress, C. E. Cultural barriers in the counseling relationship. *Personnel and Guidance Journal,* 1969, 47, 11–17.

———. Counseling the racial and ethnic minorities. *Focus on Guidance,* 1973a, 5 (6), 1–10.

———. Counseling the racial and ethnic minorities. *Focus on Guidance,* 1973b, 5 (6), 1–10.

———. Racial and ethnic barriers in counseling. In P. B. Pedersen, W. J. Lonner, and J. G. Draguns (Eds.), *Counseling across cultures.* Honolulu: University of Hawaii Press, 1976.

Wallen, R. Gestalt therapy and gestalt psychology (1957). In J. Fagan and I. L. Shepherd (Eds.), *Gestalt therapy now.* Palo Alto, CA: Science and Behavior Books, 1970.

Wallerstein, J. S., and Kelly, J. B. California's children of divorce. *Psychology Today,* 1980, 13 (8), 66–76.

Warheit, G. J. Life events, coping, stress, and depressive symptomatology. *American Journal of Psychiatry,* 1979, 136 (4), 502–507.

Warnath, C. F. Licensing: Learning the game of politics and compromise. *Personnel and Guidance Journal,* 1978, 57, 50–53.

Watson, J. B. Psychology as the behaviorist views it. *Psychological Review,* 1913, 20, 159–170.

————. *Behaviorism.* New York: W. W. Norton, 1930.

Watson, J. B., and Rayner, R. Conditioned emotional reactions. *Journal of Experimental Psychology,* 1920, 3, 1–14.

Watson, R. I. *The great psychologists,* 3rd Ed. Philadelphia: J. B. Lippincott, 1971.

Weathers, L., and Liberman, R. R. The family contracting exercise. *Journal of Behavior Therapy and Experimental Psychiatry,* 1975, 6 (3), 208–214.

Webb, V. J.; Dennis, E. H.; Wakefield, W. O.; and Snell, J. Recidivism: In search of a more comprehensive definition. *International Journal of Offender Therapy and Comparative Criminology,* 1976, 20 (2), 144–146.

Webster, C. Group therapy for behavior problem children in a rural high school. *Child Welfare,* 1974, 53 (10), 653–657.

Weininger, O. The disabled and dying children: Does it have to hurt so much? *Ontario Psychologist,* 1975, 7 (3), 123–134. Reprinted in L. Wilkenfeld (Ed.), *When children die.* Dubuque, IA: Kendall/Hunt, 1976.

Weisman, A. D. Coping with untimely death. *Psychiatry,* 1973, 36, 366–378.

Weiss, R. S. *Marital separation.* New York: Basic Books, 1975.

Weissberg, R. P., and Gesten, E. L. Considerations for developing effective school-based social problem-solving (SPS) training programs. *School Psychology Review,* 1982, 11 (1), 56–63.

White, R. W. The concept of a healthy personality: What do we really mean? *The Counseling Psychologist,* 1973, 4 (2), 3–12.

Whitely, J.M.; Kagan, N.; Harmon, L.W.; Fretz, B.R.; and Tanney, D. (Eds.). *The coming decade in counseling psychology.* Schenectady, NY: Character Research Press, 1984.

Whitmont, E. C., and Kaufman, Y. Analytical psychotherapy. In R. Corsini (Ed.), *Current psychotherapies.* Itasca, IL: F.E. Peacock, 1973.

Whittington, E. R. Critical incidents: Traditional and individual education responses. *Journal of Individual Psychology,* 1981, 37 (2), 247–251.

Widseth, J. C. Reported dependent behaviors towards mothers and use of alcohol in delinquent girls. *Dissertation Abstracts International,* October 1972, 33 (4–B), No. 1833.

Wiggins, J. D. Counselors and the life space of students. *The School Counselor,* 1972, 19, 364–365.

Wikler, D. Ethics: As theory and practice. *Aggressive Behavior,* 1981, 7 (4), 377–381.

Wilkenfield, L. (Ed.). *When children die.* Dubuque, IA: Kendall/Hunt, 1977.

Williams, C. C., and Williams, R. A. Rape: A plea for help in the emergency room. *Nursing Forum,* 1973, 12, 388–401.

Williams, E. W. Reality therapy in a correctional institution. *Corrective and Social Psychiatry and Journal of Behavior Technology, Methods and Therapy,* 1976, 22 (1), 6–11.

Williams, G. H., and Wood, M. M. *Developmental art therapy.* Baltimore: University Park Press, 1977.

Williams, R. L., and Kirkland, J. The white counselor and the black client. *Counseling Psychologist,* 1971, 2, 114–117.

Willis, J. and Giles, D. *Great experiments in behavior modification.* Indianapolis: Hackett, 1976.

Wilson, E. O. *On human nature.* Cambridge, MA: Harvard University Press, 1978.

Wilson, W., and Calhoun, J. F. Behavior therapy and the minority client. *Psychotherapy: Theory, Research and Practice,* 1974, 11 (4), 317–325.

Wittmer, J.; Bostic, D.; Phillips, T. D.; and Waters, W. The personal, academic, and career problems of college student athletes: Some possible answers. *Personnel and Guidance Journal,* 1981, 60 (1), 52–55.

Wolfe, F. *Taking the quantum leap.* New York: NAL, 1981.

Wolfgang, A. Cross-cultural comparison of locus of control, optimism towards the future, and time horizon among Italian, Italo-Canadian, and new Canadian youth. *Proceedings of the 81st annual convention of the American Psychological Association,* 1973, 8, 229–300.

Wolfgang, M. E. Family violence and criminal behavior. *Bulletin of American Academy of Psychiatry and Law,* 1976, 4 (4), 316–327.

Wolpe, J. The systematic desensitization treatment of neuroses. *Journal of Nervous and Mental Diseases,* 1961, 132, 189–203.

Wolpe, J. *Psychotherapy by reciprocal inhibition.* Stanford, CA: Stanford University Press, 1958.

Woods, T. A group method of engaging parents at a child psychiatric clinic. *Child Welfare,* 1974, 53 (6), 394–401.

Wrenn, C. G. The culturally encapsulated counselor. *Harvard Educational Review,* 1962, 32 (4), 444–449.

Wright, L. Conceptualizing and defining psychosomatic disorders. *American Psychologist,* 1977, 32, 625–628.

Wright, L. J. *The use of counselor selection instruments and measures of creativity in the construction of prediction equations for counselor trainee selection.* Unpublished doctoral dissertation, The College of William and Mary, Virginia, 1976.

Yamamoto, J.; James, Q. C.; and Palley, N. Cultural problems in psychiatric therapy. *Archives of General Psychiatry,* 1968, 19, 45–49.

Yamamoto, J.; James, Q. C.; Bloombaum, M.; and Hatten, J. Racial factors in patient selection. *American Journal of Psychiatry,* 1967, 630–636.

Yates, C.; Johnson, N.; and Johnson, J. Effects of the use of the vocational exploration group on career maturity. *Journal of Counseling Psychology,* 1979, 26 (4), 368–370.

Yoder, J. D. The existential mode and client anxiety: Or she chose to hold a porcupine. *Personnel and Guidance Journal,* 1981, 59 (5), 279–283.

Young, J. E., and Beck, A. T. Cognitive therapy: Clinical applications. In A. J. Rush (Ed.), *Short-term psychotherapies for depression.* New York: Guilford Press, 1982.

Yudkin, S. Death and the young. In A. Toynbee (Ed.), *Man's concern with death.* New York: McGraw-Hill,1968.

Zukaw, G. *The dancing wu-li masters.* New York: Bantam, 1982.

Zukow, A. H. Helping the hyperkinetic child. *Today's Education,* 1975, 64 (4), 39–41.

Name Index

Wrenn, C. G., 545
Wright, L., 332, 414
Wundt, W., 10–11
Wurm, M., 414

Y
Yamamoto, J., 405, 544
Yates, C., 399
Young, J. E., 248–50
Yudkin, S., 438

Z
Zabarsky, M., 370–71
Zelnik, R., 320–21
Zerwekh, J. V., 431, 441
Zill, N., 320
Zox, M., 544
Zukaw, G., 110
Zukow, A. H., 486
Zunin, Z. M., 255

Subject Index

in existential counseling, 205–6
expectations of, 139–44
  minority clients, 551
expectations of, motivational factors, 140
four life positions of, 261–63
hyperactive, 486–89
IEPs for, 481–84
involuntary, 140–41
language of as influence in counseling process, 547
learning disabled, 484–93
leisure time activities and counseling, 534–37
life space of and counseling relationships, 105
loveloss and, 438–40
marital conflicts and, 365–68
medical model perception of, 35–37
minority. See Cross-cultural counseling
normal vs. abnormal designation, 37–38
physically disabled, 457–59
pregnant, 417–21
with psychosomatic disorders, 413–17
questions of, 147–150
readiness of, 141
in rehabilitation, 451–59. See also Rehabilitation counseling
relationships with counselors. See Counseling relationship
responsibilities for growth, 101
retarded, 456–57
retiring, 530
Rogerian view of, 211–13
role of behavioral, 279–91
in school setting, 469–94. See also School counseling
sexual contact with, 51
social and personal effects of attractiveness, 315–16
style of life and, 186–87
suicidal, 441–44
taxonomy of problems, 143–44
unconscious of, 33
values of as influence in counseling process, 547–50
women's special issues in career counseling, 520–24
workaholics, 525–26
Clinical psychologist, definition of, 43
Clinical Treatment of the Problem Child (Rogers), 210
Cognitions, social interest and, 186
Cognitive behavior modification (CBM), 293–95
Cognitive counseling, 34, 237–68
  cognitive behavior modification (CBM), 293–95
  cognitive restructuring in, 145–46
  cognitive therapy, 247–53. See also Cognitive therapy
  group approaches, 391–93. See also Group counseling
  rational-emotive therapy, 237–47. See also Rational-emotive therapy
  reality therapy, 254–59. See also Reality therapy
  renal dialysis client, 408–9
  transactional analysis, 259–67. See also Transactional analysis.

Cognitive restructuring, 145–46, 293–94
Cognitive therapy. *See also* Rational-emotive therapy; Reality therapy
  background, 247–48
  cognitive triad, 249
  collaboration in, 249–50
  contrasted with affective therapies, 250
  evaluation of, 253
  process of, 250
  role of the counselor, 249–50
  techniques, 251–53
  view of the person, 248–49
Cognitive triad, 249
Cognitive values, definition of, 79
Collaboration, used in cognitive approach, 249–50
Collective unconscious, 173
Columbia University, 15, 18
Commission on Counselor Licensure (AACD), 52
Commitment,
  in counseling relationship, 106–7
  existential view of, 204
Committee on Rehabilitation, 53
Commonsense bias, 59
Communication skills,
  counselor training and, 47
  effective communication in family, 351–52
  as effective counselor quality, 74–75
  in family counseling, 353
  in marriage counseling, 364–66
  Milan group and, 359–60
  semantics and, 74
  strategic family therapy and, 359
Community counseling, 460–64
  definition of, 460–61
  programs, 463–64
  theories of, 462
Community Mental Health Centers Act of 1963, 460
Compensation, Adler's view of, 187–88
Computerized counseling, 99–100
Conceptual systems functioning, 46
Conditioned response, 276–78
  definition of, 276
Conditioned stimulus, definition of, 276
Conditioning,
  definition of, 276
  instrumental, 276–79, 282–86. See also Instrumental conditioning
  development of, 275–76
  operant. See Conditioning, instrumental; Instrumental conditioning
  respondent, 276–78, 281–82. See also Respondent conditioning
  systematic desensitization, 286–87
Confidentiality, 49–50
Conflict resolution, 155–57
  approach-approach conflict, 155
  approach-avoidance conflict, 156
  avoidance-avoidance conflict, 155
  double approach-avoidance conflict, 156–57
  Horney's theory of, 174
  problem-solving strategies in family counseling, 354–57
  types of conflicts, 155–56
  unconscious and, 173

Conflicts. *See* Conflict resolution
Conformity, in groups, 388
Confrontation, 126–27
Connectionist psychology, 274–75
Consciousness, introspectionism and, 11
Consultation,
  counselor training and, 47
  definition of, 478–79
  IEPs and, 481–84
  with parents of exceptional students, 491–92
  role of parents in school counseling, 478–80
Consumerism, in counseling, 51–52
Contracting, 361
Control ideology, definition of, 83
"Copenhagen interpretation," 109–13
  background of, 110–12
  counseling implications, 112–14
  statement of, 112
Cornell University, 15
Corporate counseling, 527–34
  alcohol abuse counseling, 528
  background, 527
  career exploration and change, 529–30
  child care assistance, 529
  eldercare assistance, 529
  Employee assistance programs (EAPs), 528
  health care assistance, 530
  outplacement counseling, 528
  reentry counseling, 529
  relocation counseling, 529
  retirement counseling, 530
Counseling,
  abortion and, 420–21
  activities in time percentage, 20
  Adlerian, 184–90
  adolescent clients, 313–25. See also Adolescent counseling.
  adult population, *See* Adult counseling
  adults, 519–23
  alcohol abuse, 528
  alcohol abusing clients, 421–25
  anti-illness movement in, 34–39
  behavioral, 273–96. See also Behavioral counseling
  career, 499–534. See also Career counseling
  career development theories, 503–13
  carpenter's gothic and, 80–81
  child clients. See Child counseling
  client-centered, 34
  client expectations and, 139–44
  cognitive, 34
  cognitive restructuring in, 145–46
  commitment of counselor and, 106–7
  in community, 460–64. See also Community counseling
  computerized, 99–100
  confidentiality and, 49–50
  conflict resolution and, 155–57
  constructive expression of feelings in, 100–102
  consumer issues in, 51–52
  "Copenhagen interpretation" and, 109–13

in family counseling, 360–63
interpretation, 127–28
investigating alternatives, 129–30
minority criticisms of, 544–46
paradigms, 193–94
probing, 127, 160
rational-emotive, 242–43
reflection, 126, 215
self-disclosure, 129
silence, 127
"spitting in the soup," 188
thought-stopping, 363
timing of interventions, 362–63
types of, 125–34
used in cognitive approach, 251–53
Counseling theories 39–42
anarchistic vs. formal, 40
Counselor Education and Supervision, 47
Counselor effectiveness. *See* Counselors,
effective of
Counselors,
activities of in time percentage, 20
admission to graduate training programs,
44
alcohol abusing clients and, 421–25
angry feelings of, 150–51
answering clients' questions, 147–50
attitudes of, with client, 33
attitudes of, with minority clients, 544–55
behavioral, 273–96. *See also* Behavioral
counseling
role of, 279–91
burnout problem, 77
carpenter's gothic and, 80–81
client expectations and, 139–44
cognitive approach, 249–53
commitment of, 106–7
commitment to freedom, 146–47
in community. *See* Community
counseling
compared with other mental health
professionals, 43
conceptual systems functioning and, 46
confidentiality and, 49–50
constructive expression of feelings,
100–102
countertransference feelings of, 191–93
crisis situations. *See* Crisis intervention
counseling
defenses and. *See* Defense mechanisms
definition of, 43
effectiveness of, 58–75
alienation and, 76–77
communication skills, 74–75
counselor's personal problems and, 75–
78
courage and, 66
empathy and, 68–70
factors in, 60–75
genuineness and, 70–72
inexperienced counselors, 61
language problems in assessing, 58–60
listening skills, 73
loss of freedom, 77–78
meaninglessness and, 76

nondominance, 72–73
nonjudgmental attitude, 67
open-mindedness, 66
openness and, 67–68
positive regard, 73–74
Rogerian qualities, 63–64
security and, 65
self-knowledge and, 64–65
self-monitoring, 72
sensitivity and, 68
training and, 46–47
trust and, 65–66
employment settings of, 20–21
ethical issues, 48–52
in Gestalt counseling, 224–28
in group counseling, 388–93
helpful attitude communicated to client,
101
impression management and, 72
involuntary clients and, 140–41
language problems in measuring
effectiveness, 58–60
licensure and credentialing in profession,
52–53
locus of control and effectiveness, 81–89
locus of responsibility and effectiveness,
84–89
many roles of, 71–72
minority clients and. *See* Cross-cultural
counseling
need to be liked, 101
nonjudgmental attitude of, 101
personal problems of, 75–78
persona of, 98
phenomenological approach of, 39
philosophical questions of, 32–34
problems of, stereotyping clients, 550
professional attitude of, 474
professionalism of, 98–99
psychodynamic. *See* Psychodynamic
counseling
qualities of effective, 99–100
rational-emotive, 240–43
rational-emotive approach and, 240–45
in Reality therapy, 256–59
reality therapy approaches, 256–58
relationships with clients. *See* Counseling
relationships
relationships with school personnel,
469–75
responding to clients, 144–51
role expectations of, 97–99
role identity of, 19–22
role of, 3
criticisms of traditional role, 544–45
in school setting, 469–94. *See also* School
counseling
as semanticist, 74
sexual contact and, 51
stereotyping and, 550
substance abuse problems and, 321–25
See also Substance abuse counseling
team approach with client, 105
theory applied to practice, 40–42
training of, 44–47
admission to training programs, 44
training models, 46–47

types of, 42–44
values of, 78–89
cultural values, 81–89
types of, 79–80
world views and cultural values, 81–89
valuing processes of, 146–47
world view and client interaction, 81–89
world views of, 85–89
EC-ER world view, 86–89
EC-IR world view, 85–89
IC-ER world view, 87–89
IC-IR world view, 85–89
Countertransference, 191–93, 551
Courage to counsel, 66
Crisis. *See also* Crisis intervention
counseling
definition of, 430–31
Crisis intervention counseling, 429–47
anxiety crisis, 440–41
child's death, 437–38
counselor's role in, 433–35
crisis defined, 430–31
definition of, 429
family crisis, 440
grief crisis, 435–38
loveloss, 438–40
rape crisis, 445–46
suicidal crisis, 441–44
theories of, 432–33
cognitive model, 432
equilibrium model, 432
psychosocial transition model, 432
Cross-cultural counseling, 541–55
autoplastic vs. alloplastic adaptation and,
544–45
background of movement, 541–42
benefits of, 553–55
career development theories, 503–13
Civil Rights movement and, 542–43
countertransference in, 551
criticisms of counseling approaches,
544–46
criticisms of intrapsychic model, 544–45
criticisms of traditional counselor role,
544–45
cultural barriers and differences, 546–50
class-bound values, 548
culture-bound values, 548–50
language differences, 547
group approaches, 552–53
minority attitudes toward profession,
542–44
resistance in, 551
stereotyping and, 550
transference in, 551
Cultural barriers. *See* Cross-cultural
counseling
Cultural differences. *See* Cross-cultural
counseling
Cultural values, 81–89
Culture. *See* Cross-cultural counseling
values and, 548–50
Cycle of abuse, 376–77
Cycle of prevention, 376–77

D

Daily record of dysfunctional thoughts, used in cognitive approach, 251–52
Days of Wine and Roses, 423
Decision-making, 153–57
  conflict resolution and, 155–57
  needs and, 153–55
  values and, 153
Defense mechanisms, 179–84
  denial, 181, 184
  displacement, 182–83
  identification, 182–83
  intellectualization, 181
  introjection, 182–83
  isolation, 181
  projection, 180, 184
  rationalization, 181–82, 184
  reaction formation, 180–81, 184
  regression, 182, 184
  repression, 180, 183
Denial, 181, 184
Depression, 105–5. *See also* Crisis intervention counseling; Suicidal crisis
  cognitive view of, 249
Despair, versus ego integrity, 329
Determinism, 33, 201–2
Diagnosis, 35–37
  of hyperactivity, 486–87
  of learning disabilities, 484–88
  multiaxial approach, 36–37
Diagonal counseling relationship, 107
Dialogue,
  rational-emotive view of, 240
  Rogerian view of, 214
Dialysis, 408–9
Dibs in Search of Self (Axline), 309
Dictionary of Occupational Titles, 503
"Difference of degree" argument, 23–24
Directive counseling, vs. nondirective, 33
Disabilities, rehabilitation counseling with physically disabled, 457–59
Disclosure, in family counseling, 353
Displacement, 182–83
Divorce. *See* Divorce counseling
Divorce counseling, 368–73. *See also* Family counseling
  children of divorce, 371–73
  factors affecting divorce and separation, 369–70
  post-divorce and separation counseling, 370–71
Double approach-avoidance conflict, 156–57
Dreams, early discovery of meaning, 173
Drug abuse. *See* Substance abuse counseling
Drug rehabilitation. *See* Rehabilitation counseling
Dynamic self-understanding, 152

E

EC. *See* External-control people
EC-ER world view, 86–89
EC-IR world view, 85–89
Educational growth groups, 394–95

Education for All Handicapped Children Act, 480–84
Effective counseling,
  definition of, 58–60
  factors in, 60–75
Ego, Hunger, and Aggression (Perls), 222
Ego integrity, versus despair, 329
Ego states, 260–62
Eight ages of man, 306–7
Eldercare assistance, 529
Electrocution, 18
Emotional literacy, definition of, 263
Emotional problems, early treatment of, 12–16
Emotion, rational-emotive view of, 238–43
Empathic response, 128–29. *See also* Empathy
Empathy, 63–64, 97, 145, 214
  counselor's anger and, 151
  counselor training and, 44–47
  as effective counselor quality, 68–70
Employee assistance programs (EAPs), 528
Employment interview preparation, 515–17
"Empty nest syndrome," 336
Enuresis, behavioral treatment of, 281–82
Environment, Rogerian view of, 212
Epistemology, definition of, 32
ER. *See* External-locus-of-responsibility people
Esalen Institute, 221
Essence, existential view of, 203–5
Esteem building, in family counseling, 353
Ethical guidelines,
  American Association for Counseling and Development, 52
  American Psychological Association, 52
Ethical issues,
  confidentiality, 49–50
  in counseling, 48–52
Ethnicity, locus of control and, 82–89
Examining evidence, used in cognitive approach, 252
Exceptional students,
  counseling of, 480–93
  Education for All Handicapped Children Act and, 480–84
  P.L.94–142, 480–84
Existence, existential view of, 204–5
Existential counseling, 109, 203–8
  background, 201, 203
  evaluation of, 230
  focusing exercise, 207–8
  goals, 206–8
  logotherapy, 203
  role of the counselor, 205–6
  techniques 206–8
  view of the person, 204–5
Existentialism, counselor's problems and, 76–78
Ex-offender rehabilitation, 454–55 *See also* Rehabilitation counseling
Experiencing, in counseling process, 134
Experimental method, 31
Experimental psychology, origins of, 10–12
Extended famiy, definition of, 344
External-control people, 81–89
Externality. *See* External-control people

External-locus-of-responsibility people, 84–89
External-reinforcement program. *See* Behavioral self-control programs
Extinction, 284–86
Extroversion, 173

F

Facilitative relationship,
  constructive expression of feelings in, 100–102
  definition of, 97–99. *See also* Counseling relationship
  stages of, 52
Facilitative responses, definition of, 97
Family counseling, 341–81
  awareness as goal, 352
  behavioral approaches, 363
  communication skills in, 353
  contemporary family forms and, 343–47
  contracting with family members, 361
  crisis and. *See* Crisis intervention counseling
  definition of, 341–42
  disclosure in, 353
  divorce counseling applications, 368–73
  effective communication in family, 351–52
  "empty nest syndrome," 336
  esteem building in, 353
  evaluation of, 380
  extended family and, 344
  goals of, 350–51
  healthy family functioning, 347–49
  individuation and, 356–57
  marital conflict, 365–68
  marriage counseling applications, 364–68
  nuclear family and, 343–44
  problem-solving strategies in, 354–57
  "reconstituted" family, 346–47
  rule learning in, 352
  setting of, 350
  single-parent family, 345–46
  socio-emotional intactness and, 353–54
  structural theory applied, 360–61
  techniques used in, 360–63
  theories of, 357–60
    behavioral, 357
    Milan group, 359
    multigenerational, 357
    psychodynamic, 357–58
    strategic therapy, 357, 359
    structural theory, 357, 358–59
  timing of interventions, 362–63
  violence in family and, 373–80
    child abuse, 375–80
    cycles of abuse and prevention, 376
    definition of, 374
    spouse abuse, 374–75
    "web of violence," 374
  women's special issues in career counseling, 520–24
Family crisis, 440
Family therapy, counselor training and, 47
Family violence. *See* Family counseling, violence in family and

Individual psychology. *See* Adlerian counseling
Individual system blame dimension, 84
Individuation, in family counseling, 356–57
Inductive questioning, used in cognitive approach, 251, 253
Industrialization, vocational guidance movement formed, 17–19
Industry, versus inferiority, 307
Inferiority, versus industry, 307
Inferiority complex, 187
Inferiority feelings (complex), 173
Information, with child abuse clients, 379–80
Initial interview, 120–23
  with child abuse clients, 378–79
Initiative, versus guilt, 307
Insanity, approaches to treatment of, 10, 12–15
Instinct. *See also* Psychosexual stages
  Freudian view of, 175
Institute for Advanced Study in Rational Psychotherapy, 238
Institute for Rational Living, 238
Instrumental conditioning, 276–79, 282–86
  definition of, 278
  development of, 275–76
  extinction and, 284–86
  negative reinforcement and, 284
  positive reinforcement and, 283–84
  punishment and, 284
  reinforcement programs, 282–86
Instrumental self, definition of, 109
Insurance reimbursement, 52–53
Integration, 142
Integrative understanding, 152
Intellectualization, 181
Intelligence tests. *See* IQ tests
Intelligent Woman's Guide to Dating and Mating (Ellis), 238
Internal-control people, 81–89
Internality. *See* Internal-control people
Internal-locus-of-responsibility people, 84–89
Interpretation, 127–28, 191–93
Interpretation of Dreams (Freud), 209
Interventions. *See* Counseling techniques
Interviewing, counselor training and, 47
Intimate relationships, development of, 314–17
Introjection, 182–83
Introspectionism, behaviorists' criticisms of, 274
Introspectionist method, 11
Introversion, 173
Involuntary clients, 140–41
IQ tests, 15–16
IR. *See* Internal-locus-of-responsibility people
Isolation, 181

J

Jealousy, psychology of, 365–66
Job, definition of, versus career, 500–501
Job counseling. *See* Career counseling
Job dissatisfaction, 525

Job satisfaction, 524–25
Johns Hopkins University, 15
Joint Commission on Mental Illness and Health, 460
Journal of College Student Personnel, 47
Journal of Counseling and Development, 47
Journal of Employment Counseling, 48
Journal of Humanistic Education and Development, 48
Journal of Multicultural Counseling and Development, 48
Jungian psychology, 173

K

Kidney disease, 408–9
Knowledge, as epistemological question, 32

L

Laboratory psychology, origins of, 10–12
Language, as cultural difference, 547
Latency, 177
Law of effect, 274–75
Learning. *See* Conditioning; Instrumental conditionng; Respondent conditioning
Learning disabilities,
  definition of, 484–85
  nutrition and, 410
Learning disabled students. *See* Exceptional students
Leisure time counseling, 330, 534–37
  definition of, 535
  exploration on, 536
  integration and, 537
Licensed counselors, privileged communication laws, 50
Licensed professional counselors, licensure of, 52–53
Licensure, for mental health professionals, 52–53
Life course, definition of, 305–6
Life cycle,
  definition of, 305–6
  of groups, 397–98
Life span, definition of, 305–6
Lifespan counseling. *See* Adolescent counseling; Adult counseling; Child counseling
Life-style, 186–87
Listening,
  counselor's skill in, 100–101
  as effective counselor quality, 73
"Listening with third ear," 192
Locus of control, 81–89
Locus of responsibility, 84–89
Logotherapy, 203, 206
Loneliness, counselor's problems and, 76
Loss of freedom, and counseling effectiveness, 77–78
Lost Weekend, 423
Love, in adolescence, 316–18
Loveloss, 438–40
Low self-monitoring individuals, 72

M

Maladaptive assumptions, used in cognitive approach, 253
Manhattan Center for Advanced Psychoanalytic Studies (MCAPS), 174
Man's Search for Meaning (Frankl), 76
Marital conflict. *See also* Family counseling
  sources of, 365–68
Marriage, current trends in, 327–28
Marriage and family therapists,
  licensure of, 53
  privileged communication laws, 50
Marriage counseling, 364–68. *See also* Family counseling
MAT (Miller Analogy Test), 44
Maturational needs, 191–93
Meaninglessness, of counselor, 76
Measurement and Evaluation in Counseling and Development, 48
MECA (Military Educators and Counselors Association), 48
Mechanisms of defense. *See* Defense mechanisms
Medical model, 35, 38
Medical/surgical counseling, 408–9
Mental health professionals,
  licensure and credentialing in profession, 52–53
  privileged communication laws, 49–50
  types of, 42–44. *See also* Counselors
Mental Health Studies Act of 1955, 460
Mental hygiene movement, 13–15
Mental illness,
  approaches to treatment of, 10, 12–15
  modern approaches to understanding, 36–38
Mentally retarded clients, 456–57
Metaneeds, definition of, 154
Middle age, 334–35
Middletown (Conn), vocational guidance movement in, 18
Milan group, 359
Military Educators and Counselors Association (MECA), 48
Miller Analogy Test (MAT), 44
Minority clients. *See* Cross-cultural counseling
  locus of control and, 82–89
Modeling, 292
Modern psychoanalysis, 174, 190–93
  background of, 174
  contrasted to classical view, 190
  paradigms in, 193–94
  techniques of, 191–92
Modified extended family, definition of, 344
Money, quarreling over, 366
Moral values, definition of, 79
Motivation,
  of clients, 140–41
  reality therapy view of, 255
Multiaxial diagnosis, 36–37
Multigenerational family counseling, 357
Multimodal behavior therapy, 288–89
Myth of Mental Illness (Szasz), 37

N

"Name game," in Gestalt counseling, 226
Narcissism, modern psychoanalysis and, 174
Narcissistic identification, 183
National Association of Certified Clinical Mental Health Counselors, 53
National Board of the Certification of Counselors, 53
National Career Development Association (NCDA), 48
National Employment Counselors Association (NECA), 48
National Psychological Association for Psychoanalysis (NPAP), 174
National Vocational Guidance Association (NVGA), 47
NCDA (National Career Development Association), 48
NECA (National Employment Counselors Association), 48
Needs,
  decision-making and, 153–55
  metaneeds, 154
  positive regard, 153
  reality therapy view of, 255–56
  self-regard, 153
Negative reinforcement, 284
Negroes. See Cross-cultural counseling
Neurosis,
  behaviorists' view of, 274, 278
  Gestalt layers of, 223–24
  Horney's theory of, 174
New Life Options: The Working Woman's Resource Book (Loring & Otto), 521
New York Psychoanalytic Institute, 260
Nondirective counseling. See also Client-centered counseling
  development of, 210
  vs. directive, 33
Nondirective Counseling and Psychotherapy (Rogers), 210
Nondominance, as effective counselor quality, 72–73
Nonjudgmental attitude, 101
  as effective counselor quality, 67
  counselor's anger and, 151
Nonverbal communication, counselor training and, 47
Normal, vs. abnormal, 37–38
Nuclear family, definition of, 343–44
Nuclear family of orientation, 343
Nuclear family or procreation, 343
Nutritional counseling, 409–11
NVGA (National Vocational Guidance Association), 18, 47

O

Objectivity, as effective counselor quality, 70
Occupational counseling. See Career counseling
Occupational Outlook Handbook, 503
Oedipal conflict, 177

Old age, 335–36. See also Adult counseling
  current trends in, 327–28
  residence choices and, 331–32
On Death and Dying (Kubler-Ross), 435
Ontology, definition of, 32
Open-mindedness, as effective counselor quality, 66
Openness, as effective counselor quality, 67–68
Operant conditioning. See Conditioning, instrumental; Instrumental conditioning
Oral stage, 175–76
Ordinal position, 186–88
Outplacement counseling, 528
Overcoming Procrastination (Ellis), 238

P

Paradigms, 193–94
  definition of, 193
Paradoxical intention, 206
Parent ego state, 261
Parents,
  consultation with counselor, 491–92
  role of, in school counseling, 478–80
Particulars of My Life (Skinner), 276
Pavlovian conditioning. See Respondent conditioning
Pavlov's dog, 277
Peer cluster theory, 323–24
Peer counseling, 394
Perception,
  Gestalt psychology and, 222
  language and, 547
Perceptiveness, as effective counselor quality, 66
Persona, 98
  definition of, 71
Personal control, definition of, 83
Personality,
  A-B-C theory of, 246
  Erikson's view of child's development, 306–7
  Freudian view of, 175–78
  humanistic study of, 202
Phallic stage, 176–77
Phenomenological approach, 39, 204
  development of, 210
Phenomenology, 41
Philosophy, influences on counseling, 32–33
Phobia,
  behaviorists' view of, 274, 278
  logotherapy treatment of, 206
  systematic desensitization of, 287
Physical attractiveness, 315–6
Physics, counseling parallels through "Copenhagen interpretation," 109–13
P.L. 94–142, 480–84. See also Exceptional students
Play therapy, 308–13
POCA (Public Offender Counselor Association), 48
Positioning, with child abuse clients, 379
Positive Addiction (Glasser), 255
Positive connotation, definition of, 360

Positive regard, 153, 214–15
  as effective counselor quality, 73–74
Positive reinforcement, 283–84
Positive wellness, definition of, 407
Post-divorce counseling. See Divorce counseling
Practitioners. See Helpers
Preference values, definition of, 79
Pregnancy counseling, 417–21
Premarital sexual behavior, 319–21
Preventive counseling. See Health counseling
"Private logic," 189
Privileged communication, 49–50
Probability theory, "Copenhagen interpretation" and, 111–12
Probing, 127, 160
Problem solving, in family counseling, 354–57
Progressive education, influences on counseling movement, 24
Projection, 180, 184
Provocation, in Gestalt counseling, 226
Psychiatric rehabilitation, 455. See also Rehabilitation counseling
Psychiatrist, definition of, 43
Psychoanalysis,
  deterministic criticisms of, 201–2
  effectiveness of, 62–63
  historical origins of, 171–74
  impact on counseling movement, 14
  influences on counseling movement, 24. See also Psychodynamic counseling
Psychoanalyst, definition of, 43
Psychodynamic counseling, 171–97
  Adlerian, 184–90
  background of, 171–75
  cross-cultural counseling and, 551
  evaluation of, 196–97
  family approaches, 357–58
  free association and, 172–73
  goals of, 193–94
  group approaches, 390, 393. See also Group counseling
  modern psychoanalysis, 174, 190–93
  psychopathology and, 178
  psychosexual stages and, 175–77
  role of counselor, 178–84
  setting goals in, 142
  techniques of, 193–94
  transference in, 178–79
  view of person, 175–78
Psychological problems,
  approaches to treatment of, 10, 12–15
  diagnosis of, 35–37
Psychologists,
  definition of, 43
  licensure of, 52
  privileged communication laws, 50
Psychology,
  behaviorists' view of, 274
  experimental laboratory psychology, 10–12
Psychopathology, Freudian view of, 178
Psychopathology of Everyday Life (Freud), 178, 181

Psychosexual stages, 173, 175–77
  anal stage, 176
  latency, 177
  Oedipal conflict, 177
  oral stage, 175–76
  phallic stage, 176–77
Psychosomatic disorders, 413–17
  asthma, 415
  cancer, 416–17
  definition of, 413–14
  gastrointestinal disturbances, 415–16
  heart disease, 414–15
Psychotherapist. *See also* Counselor
  role identity of, vs. counselor, 19–25
Psychotherapy. *See also* Counseling
  counseling differentiated from, 21–25
  counseling vs., 9–10
  definition of, 21–25
  identity as profession, 21–25
Puberty,
  challenges of, 314
  definition of, 313
Public Offender Counselor Association
    (POCA), 48
Punishment, 275, 284

Q

Questions,
  answering client's questions, 131–33,
      147–50
  modern psychoanalytic view of, 192–93
  types of, 147–50

R

Race, stress and, 413
Rape crisis, 445–46
Rational-emotive counseling, 34
  group approaches, 391–92. *See also*
      Group counseling
  renal dialysis client, 408–9
Rational-emotive therapy,
  A-B-C hypothesis, 246
  background, 237–38
  contrasted to Rogerian, 241
  evaluation of, 247
  goals of, 242–43
  role of the counselor, 240–42
  session transcript, 243–46
  techniques, 242–43
  view of the person, 238–40
*Rational-Emotive Therapy: A Handbook of
    Theory and Practice* (Ellis), 238
Rationalization, 181–82, 184
Reaction formation, 180–81, 184
Reality,
  cognitive construction of, 248
  "Copenhagen interpretation" and,
      110–13
  paradox of, 112
Reality therapy, 254–59
  background, 254–55
  evaluation of, 259
  goals, 258–59
  group approaches, 391–93. *See also*
      Group counseling

role of the counselor, 256–57
stages of, 258–59
techniques, 257–59
view of the person, 255–56
*Reality Therapy: A New Approach to
    Psychiatry* (Glasser), 255
Reason and Emotion in Psychotherapy
    (Ellis), 238, 241
Reasoning, rational-emotive view of, 238–43
Receiving behavior, 144
Reciprocal inhibition, definition of, 286
"Reconstituted" family, 346–47
Reentry counseling, 529
Reflection, 126, 215
Regression, 182, 184
Rehabilitation counseling, 451–59
  basic premises of, 452–53
  definition of, 451
  drug addict rehabilitation, 456
  ex-offender rehabilitation, 454–55
  with physically disabled, 457–59
  psychiatric rehabilitation, 455
  with retarded clients, 456–57
  vocational rehabilitation, 453–54
Rehabilitation Counseling Bulletin, 48
Reinforcement, definition of, 278
Reinforcement programs, 282–86
  development of, 275–76
  extinction, 284–86
  negative reinforcement, 284
  positive reinforcement, 283–84
  punishment, 284
Reinforcing stimulus, definition of, 278
Relocation counseling, 529
Remarriage, family counseling, and, 346–47
Renal dialysis, 408–9
Repression, 180, 183
Reproductive counseling, 417–21
Resistance, 178–84, 191–93, 551
  counselor's anger and, 151
Respondent conditioning, 276–78, 281–82
  systematic desensitization, 286–87
  techniques of, 281–82
Responding,
  to clients, 144–52
  modern psychoanalytic view of, 192–93
Responding behavior, 144
  satisfaction in, 145
Resume preparation, 514–16
Retirement counseling, 530
Roe's theory of career development, 507–10
Rogerian counseling. *See* Client-centered
    counseling
Role,
  counselor's conformity to, 98–99
  definition of, 98
Role-playing,
  counselor training and, 47
  used in cognitive approach, 251
Roles, in counseling, 71–72
Rules, in family counseling, 352

S

Salpetriere Asylum, 13
San Francisco, vocational guidance
    movement in, 18

Schizophrenia, modern psychoanalysis and,
    174
Schizophrenics, counselor effectiveness
    qualities and, 64
School counseling, 469–94. *See also* Career
    counseling
  counseling team, 474–80
  guidance counselor's relations with
      teachers, 476–77
  guidance with exceptional students,
      480–83, 485–93
  with hyperactive students, 486–89
  learning disabilities and, 484–93
  role of guidance counselor, 469–74
  role of parents in school counseling,
      478–80
  school psychologist and, 477–78
School Counselor, 48
School counselors,
  licensure of, 53
  privileged communication laws, 50
School phobia, systematic desensitization of,
    287
School psychologist, role of, 477–78
Schools Without Failure (Glasser), 255
Scripts, in transactional analysis, 266
Seasons of a Man's Life (Levinson), 334
Second career counseling, 519–23
Security, as effective counselor quality, 65
Selective perception, 41
Self,
  reality therapy view of, 255–56
  Rogerian view of, 212
  vs. role expectations, 98–99
Self-actualization, 142
Self-control programs, 289–91
Self-disclosure, 129
Self-knowledge, 64–65
Self-monitoring, high vs. low, 72
Self-regard, 153
Self-reinforcement program. *See* Behavioral
    self-control programs
Self-understanding, in counseling process,
    152
Self-values, definition of, 79
Selves, revealed in social interactions, 71–72
Semantics, definition of, 74
Sensitivity, as effective counselor quality, 68
Separation counseling. *See* Divorce
    counseling
Setting goals, in counseling, 142–44
Sex and the Liberated Man (Ellis), 238
Sexual behavior,
  during adolescence, 318–21
  adult counseling and, 330–31
  studies of, 319–21
Sexual conflicts, Freudian view of, 173
Sexual contact, between counselor and
    client, 51
Shame, versus autonomy, 307
Shaping, 292
Siblings, influences on development, 188
Silence, 127
Single-parent family, 345–46
Sing Sing Prison, 18
Skinner box, 278
Social class, values and, 548

Social establishment,
definition of, 98
"front" vs. "back" region, 98–99
Social interest, 185–86, 187–88
Social worker, definition of, 43
Social workers,
licensure of, 53
privileged communication laws, 50
Socio-emotional intactness, in family
counseling, 353–54
Solvay Congress (fifth), 112
"Spitting in the soup," 188
Spouse abuse. See Family counseling,
violence in family and
S-R psychology. See Behavioral Counseling;
Conditioning
Stagnation, versus generativity, 329
Stanford University, 15
Stefflre's propositions of career
development, 512–13
Stereotyping, 550
Stoicism, 247
Strategic therapy, 357, 359
Stress. See also Psychosomatic disorders;
Stress control counseling
definition of, 411
effects of, 412–13
Stress control counseling, 411–17
type A/B behavior and, 414–15
Stress reaction, definition of, 411–12
Striving for superiority, 173, 187
Strokes, in transactional analysis, 266
Structuralism, 11
Structural theory, in family counseling,
357–59, 360–61
*Structure and Dynamics of Organizations
and Groups* (Berne), 260
Students. See School counseling
Style of life, 186–87
Sublimation, definition of, 175
Substance abuse counseling, 321–25,
421–25
with adolescents, 321–25
counselor's role in treatment, 324–25
in corporate world, 528
definitions of "abuse," 322
theories of drug abuse, 323–24
Suicidal crisis, 441–44
Suicide, stress and, 413
Superiority, striving for, 173, 187
Super's theory of career development,
503–5
Systematic desensitization, 286–87

T

"Talking cure," 172
Task groups, 394
Tasks, in Adlerian counseling, 188
Teachers, nutritional counseling and,
409–10
Team cooperation, in counseling, 71

Techniques. See also Counseling techniques
definition of, 119–20
types of, 125–34
Termination, 123–25
Testing movement, 15–16
The Identity Society (Glasser), 255
Theory,
as used by counselor, characteristics of,
40
as used by counselors, 39–42
Therapeutic Relationship and its Impact
(Rogers), 210
Therapist. See Psychotherapist
Thinking, rational-emotive view of, 238–43
Thought-stopping, definition of, 363
Tiedeman and O'Hara's theory of career
development, 511–12
Time-out, 292–93
Timing of interventions. See Counseling
techniques
Toxoid response, 190–91
Training, of counselors, 44–47
Transaction,
definition of, 260–61
types of, 263–66
Transactional analysis, 259–67
background, 259–60
counseling process, 263–66
evaluation of, 267
four life positions, 261–63
goals, 266–67
techniques of, 266
types of transactions, 263–66
view of the person, 260–63
Transactional Analysis in Psychotherapy
(Berne), 260
Transference, 178–79, 551
definition of, 178
Transpersonal unconscious, 173
Trust,
as effective counselor quality, 65–66
confidentiality and, 49–50
versus mistrust, 306
Two-Paycheck Marriage (Bird), 366
Type A behavior, 414–15
Type B behavior, 414–15

U

Ulcers, 416
Uncertainty principle, definition of, 111
Unconditional positive regard, 63–64,
214–25. See also Positive regard
Unconditioned response, 276–78
definition of, 276
Unconditioned stimulus, 276–78
definition of, 276
Unconscious,
collective vs. personal, 173
early discovery of, 173
Freud's view of, 177–78

United States,
mental hygiene movement in, 13–15
vocational guidance movement formed,
17–19
University of Chicago, 15
Urbanization, vocational guidance
movement formed, 17–19

V

Values,
as axiological question, 32
in counseling, 78–89
definition of, 78–79
types of, 79–80
as cultural difference, 547–50
decision-making and, 153
Rogerian view of, 212
Valuing, 144
commitment to freedom and, 146–47
Veterans Administration Hospital (San
Francisco), 260
View-toward-death, 205
Violence. See Family counseling, violence in
family and
Vocational counseling. See Career
counseling
Vocational development. See Career
counseling; Career development
Vocational guidance, early efforts in, 18
Vocational guidance movement, 17–19
Vocational Guidance Quarterly, 47
Vocational rehabilitation, 453–54. See also
Rehabilitation counseling

W

Walden Two (Skinner), 276
Warmth, as effective counselor quality, 74
Wellness. See Health counseling
What Do You Say After You Say Hello?
(Berne), 260
Women. See also Adult counseling; Old age
as alcoholics, 424
career counseling and special problems,
520–24
counseling older women, 333, 335–36
rape crisis and, 445–46
vocational guidance movement formed,
17–19
Women for Sobriety, 425
Work. See also Career counseling
and adjustment, 524–27
definition of versus career, 500–501
Workaholic, 525–26
Work world, status today, 499–501
World views, of counselor, four types of,
85–89

Y

Yale University, 15
"Yes–No game," in Gestalt counseling, 226